# INTRODUCTION TO
# Managerial Accounting
## Canadian Edition

*Ray H. Garrison*
Professor Emeritus, Brigham Young University

*Eric W. Noreen*
University of Washington and INSEAD

*Suresh S. Kalagnanam*
University of Saskatchewan

*Ganesh Vaidyanathan*
University of Saskatchewan

**McGraw-Hill**
**Ryerson**

Toronto Montréal Boston Burr Ridge, IL Dubuque, IA Madison, WI New York San Francisco St. Louis Bangkok
Bogotá Caracas Kuala Lumpur Lisbon London Madrid Mexico City Milan New Delhi Santiago Seoul Singapore
Sydney Taipei

McGraw-Hill
Ryerson

**Introduction to Managerial Accounting**
**First Canadian Edition**

ISBN: 0-07-091617-9

1 2 3 4 5 6 7 8 9 10 TCP 0 9 8 7 6 5

Printed and bound in Canada

Statistics Canada information is used with the permission of the Minister of Industry, as Minister responsible
for Statistics Canada. Information on the availability of the wide range of data from Statistics Canada can be
obtained from Statistics Canada's Regional Offices, its World Wide Web site at <http://www.statcan.ca>, and
its toll-free access number 1-800-263-1136.

Care has been taken to trace ownership of copyright material contained in this text; however, the publisher
will welcome any information that enables them to rectify any reference or credit for subsequent editions.

Vice President, Editorial and Media Technology: Patrick Ferrier
Executive Sponsoring Editor: Nicole Lukach
Sponsoring Editor: Tom Gale
Developmental Editor: Brook Nymark
Director of Marketing: Jeff MacLean
Supervising Editor: Jaime Smith
Copy Editor: Rohini Herbert
Senior Production Coordinator: Jennifer Wilkie
Composition: SR Nova Pvt Ltd., Bangalore, India
Cover Design: Dianna Little
Cover Image: © Layne Kennedy/CORBIS
Printer: Transcontinental Printing Group

Library and Archives Canada Cataloguing in Publication

Introduction to managerial accounting/Ray H. Garrison ... [et al.]. — Canadian ed.

Includes index.
ISBN 0-07-091617-9

1. Managerial accounting — Textbooks. I. Garrison, Ray H.

HF5657.4.I696 2004        658.15'11        C2004-904853-8

# What makes **Garrison/Noreen/Kalagnanam/Vaidyanathan**

*Introduction to Managerial Accounting* is full of pedagogy designed to make studying productive and hassle-free. On the following pages, you will see the kind of engaging, helpful pedagogical features that make Garrison/Noreen/Kalagnanam/Vaidyanathan a favourite among both instructors and students.

## Chapter Opener

Each chapter opens with a two-page Chapter Opener featuring a real-world company.

**A Look Back, A Look at This Chapter,** and **A Look Ahead** features helping students to establish bridges between chapters, link concepts and understand how the chapters fit together.

The **Chapter Outline** provides students with a list of the topics to be covered in the chapter.

The **Decision Feature** sets the stage with a short vignette that gives the student a real-world example of how and why an organization applies the concepts and tools found in the chapter.

**Learning Objectives** tied directly to the summaries at the end of the chapter help students preview and review key concepts.

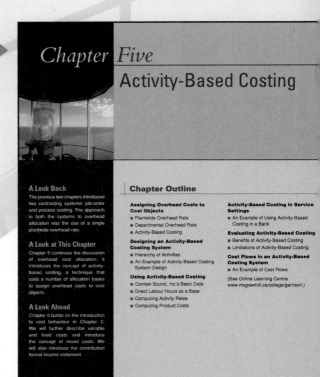

### Chapter *Five*
### Activity-Based Costing

**A Look Back**

The previous two chapters introduced two contrasting systems: job-order and process costing. The approach in both the systems to overhead allocation was the use of a single plantwide overhead rate.

**A Look at This Chapter**

Chapter 5 continues the discussion of overhead cost allocation; it introduces the concept of activity-based costing, a technique that uses a number of allocation bases to assign overhead costs to cost objects.

**A Look Ahead**

Chapter 6 builds on the introduction to cost behaviour in Chapter 2. We will further describe variable and fixed costs and introduce the concept of mixed costs. We will also introduce the contribution format income statement.

**Chapter Outline**

**Assigning Overhead Costs to Cost Objects**
- Plantwide Overhead Rate
- Departmental Overhead Rate
- Activity-Based Costing

**Designing an Activity-Based Costing System**
- Hierarchy of Activities
- An Example of Activity-Based Costing System Design

**Using Activity-Based Costing**
- Comtek Sound, Inc.'s Basic Data
- Direct Labour Hours as a Base
- Computing Activity Rates
- Computing Product Costs

**Activity-Based Costing in Service Settings**
- An Example of Using Activity-Based Costing in a Bank

**Evaluating Activity-Based Costing**
- Benefits of Activity-Based Costing
- Limitations of Activity-Based Costing

**Cost Flows in an Activity-Based Costing System**
- An Example of Cost Flows

(See Online Learning Centre www.mcgrawhill.ca/college/garrison.)

## Managerial Accounting in Action

These highly praised vignettes depict cross-functional teams working together in real-life settings on products and services that students recognize from their own lives. Students are shown step-by-step how accounting concepts are implemented in organizations and how these concepts are applied to solve everyday business problems. First, "The Issue" is introduced through a dialogue. The student then walks through the implementation process. Finally the "Wrap-Up" summarizes the big picture.

Comtek Sound, Inc. makes two products, a radio with a built-in tape player (called a *tape unit*) and a radio with a built-in compact disc player (called a *CD unit*). Both these products are sold to automobile manufacturers for installation in new vehicles. The president of the company, Sarah Kastler, recently returned from a management conference at which activity-based costing was discussed. Following the conference, she called a meeting of the top managers in the company to discuss what she had learned. Attending the meeting were the production manager, Frank Hines; the marketing manager, Nicole Sermone; and the accounting manager, Tom Frazier.

*Sarah:* I learned some things at the conference I just attended that may help resolve some long-standing puzzles here at Comtek Sound.
*Nicole:* Did they tell you why we've been losing all those bids lately on our bread-and-butter tape units and winning every bid on our specialty CD units?
*Sarah:* Nicole, you probably weren't expecting this answer, but yes, there may be a simple explanation. We may have been shooting ourselves in the foot.
*Nicole:* How so? I don't know about anyone else, but we have been hustling like crazy to get more business for the company.
*Sarah:* Nicole, when you talk with our customers, what reasons do they give for taking their tape unit business to our competitors? Is it a problem with quality or on-time delivery?

**MANAGE... ACCOUNT... IN ACT...**

The

com... SOUND,

ment, thereby resulting in greater efficiency and lower costs. Indeed, this is the most widely cited benefit of activity-based costing by managers.[2] When used in this manner, it is often called *activity-based management*. Essentially, **activity-based management (ABM)** involves focusing on activities to eliminate waste. In other words, ABM is a tool that can supplement management practices, such as total quality management and process re-engineering described in Chapter 1.

### ABM in the Service Industry

*in business today*

Reducing the costs to serve clients is a prime objective when using ABM. Mutual Life of Canada decided to use ABM to improve its understanding of the costs of its shared services which provide valuable service to internal customers (departments), such as finance, corporate affairs, strategic development, and human resources. Prior to the implementation, the shared services function for the retail insurance company accounted for one-third of total non-sales-related costs. In addition, many of the internal customers questioned the cost-benefit of the shared services. Mutual Life went through an activity identification process and then mapped those activities to products provided; for example, mapping payroll activity to the payroll product. But more detail was required. ABM revealed where activities could be combined, eliminated, or outsourced. As a result of the ABM effort, service-level agreements were set up with internal customers, along with monthly invoices to bill back to business units for services provided.

Source: Leahy, Tad. "Beyond Traditional Product Costing," 2003. *Business Finance Magazine* Website: http://www.businessfinancemag.com/archives. Reprinted with permission from *Controller Magazine*.

The first step in any improvement program is to decide what to improve. The theory of constraints (TOC) approach discussed in Chapter 1 is a powerful tool for targeting the area in an organization whose improvement will yield the greatest benefit. An ABC sys-... ...on. For example, Comtek's managers may wonder ...ess a purchase order (see Exhibit 5–4). Such a ques-... ...e on **benchmarking** their costs against the costs of ... outstanding performance. Once the activity is tar-... ...an use the ABM approach to study the activity in ... to eliminate the wasteful consumption of resources. ...ot add any value are targeted for elimination. How-... ...sure that eliminating a certain activity does not neg-

## In Business Today

These helpful boxed features offer a glimpse into how real companies use the managerial accounting concepts discussed within the chapter. Every chapter contains two to nine of these current examples.

## Service $\boxed{\text{S}}$

Owing to the growing number of service-based companies in business today, the Canadian edition uses a helpful icon to distinguish service-related examples.

**5**

### DECISION FEATURE e-Cycling to Profitability

MAXUS Technology Inc. offers a one-stop-shop asset recovery and e-waste recycling solution for end-of-life electronic equipment, with special expertise in telecommunications.

Increased technology use and new laws governing disposal are realities that all citizens and companies will soon face. E-waste disposal has the potential to bring financial liability to a company if not handled properly and can seriously damage carefully cultivated reputations, market shares, and sales.

This is because e-waste is the fastest growing waste stream in North America, and obviously, these products do not biodegrade—a problem in and of itself. In addition, e-waste can also contain hazardous goods. A computer monitor, for example, contains up to eight pounds of lead. Increasing product obsolescence only aggravates the situation.

Shelley Whatmore of Calgary founded MAXUS in 1994, which has been in operation ever since. Initially an asset recovery company (buying and selling old assets), MAXUS has, in recent years, moved into total technology solutions in response to a growing problem—what to do with equipment that cannot be resold. MAXUS has found that clients using its services can generate new revenue through selling their old equipment in markets around the world and thus obtain peace of mind through recycling. Essentially, MAXUS will squeeze as much value as possible from client equipment while ensuring the rest is recycled properly.

Needless to say, e-cycling poses its own environmental challenges which MAXUS has decided to face head on. It designed a unique recycling system that ensures that no harmful components from anything it processes are landfills and no harmful waste is shipped overseas for disposal. From the beginning, MAXUS has followed leading-edge environmental practices and is moving toward ISO 14001 certification.

Clayton Miller, MAXUS's Communications Coordinator, says that finding a way to make e-waste recycling profitable is a trial-and-error process that involves many sleepless nights. For one, the equipment required does not come cheap, and most of it must be designed from the ground up. Second, transportation of e-waste is prohibitive because weights are often high. Other issues include the wide range of possible products—literally every electronic device under the sun—and differing expectations and needs of clients. Activity-based costing is the only way MAXUS runs a successful business.

The time to perform every business activity, from dismantling to packing to preparing proposals, has been measured to figure out the true cost. This allows MAXUS to adjust its rates on a client-by-client basis in order to ensure break-even pricing. Without careful attention to overhead, MAXUS could find itself in a situation where growth in market share actually costs money.

### Learning Objectives
*After studying Chapter 5, you should be able to:*

**LO1** Understand the basic approach to activity-based costing and how it differs from traditional costing.

**LO2** Compute product costs using activity-based costing and compare them with costs under a traditional costing system.

**LO3** Describe the use of activity-based costing in service settings.

**LO4** Understand the benefits and limitations of activity-based costing systems.

**LO5** Record the flow of costs in an activity-based costing system.

...nal reports. If the product costs are to be used by ...e modifications should be made. For example, for ...ction between manufacturing costs on the one hand ...e expenses on the other hand is unimportant. Man-... ...uct causes, and it does not matter whether the costs ... ...general administrative expenses. Consequently, for ...ing and general administrative expenses should be assigned to products. Moreover, as mentioned above, facility-level costs should be removed from product costs when making decisions. Nevertheless, the techniques covered in this chapter provide a good basis for understanding the mechanics of activity-based costing. For a more complete coverage of the use of activity-based costing in decisions, see more advanced texts.

### City Controller

*decision maker*

You are the controller of your city office. The managers responsible for utilities and property taxes have complained to you regarding the charges from support services departments, such as information systems and maintenance. The city recently decided to "charge" the internal users of support services an "appropriate" amount to reflect the cost of these services. After meeting with the cost analyst for the city, you discover that the city uses a single "citywide" rate to allocate overhead costs. You are puzzled because you know that the support services departments are quite different from one another and that it does not make sense to combine the overhead costs into one single pool. How do you proceed to resolve the issue?

### Cost Flows in an Activity-Based Costing System

In Chapter 3, we discussed the flow of costs in a job-order costing system. The flow of costs through Raw Materials, Work in Process, and other accounts is the same under activity-based costing. The only difference in activity-based costing is that more than one predetermined overhead rate is used to apply overhead costs to products. Our purpose in this section is to provide a detailed example of cost flows in an activity-based costing system.

**Learning Objective 5**
Record the flow of costs in an activity-based costing system.

## The **Decision Maker**

feature fosters critical thinking and decision-making skills by providing real-world business scenarios that require the resolution of a business issue. The suggested solution is located at the end of the chapter.

# What makes **Garrison/Noreen/Kalagnanam/Vaidyanathan**

## Ethics assignments

serve as a reminder that good conduct is essential in business. Group projects can be assigned either as homework or as in-class discussion projects.

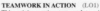

**COMMUNICATING IN PRACTICE** (LO1, LO2)

You often provide advice to Maria Graham, a client who is interested in diversifying her company. Maria is considering the purchase of a small manufacturing concern that assembles and packages its many products by hand. She plans to automate the factory and her projections indicate that the company will once again be profitable within two to three years. During her review of the company's records, she discovered that the company currently uses direct labour-hours to allocate overhead to its products. Because of its simplicity, Maria hopes that this approach can continue to be used.

*Required:*

Write a memorandum to Maria that addresses whether or not direct labour should continue to be used as an allocation base for overhead.

**ETHICS CHALLENGE** (LO1, LO3)

You and your friends go to a restaurant as a group. At the end of the meal, the issue arises of how the bill for the group should be shared. One alternative is to figure out the cost of what each individual consumed and divide up the bill accordingly. Another alternative is to split the bill equally among the individuals.

*Required:*

Which system for dividing the bill is more equitable? Which system is easier to use? How does this issue relate to the material covered in this chapter?

**TEAMWORK IN ACTION** (LO1)

This activity requires teamwork to reinforce the understanding of the hierarchy of activities commonly found in activity-based costing systems in manufacturing companies.

*Required:*

1. The team should discuss and then write up a brief description of how the activity-based costing allocates overhead to products. All team members should agree with and understand the description.

ing dishes, depend on the number of diners served.
Data concerning these activities are displayed belo

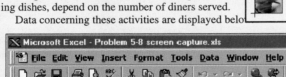

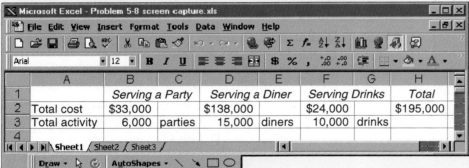

|  | A | B | C | D | E | F | G | H |
|---|---|---|---|---|---|---|---|---|
| 1 |  | Serving a Party | | Serving a Diner | | Serving Drinks | | Total |
| 2 | Total cost | $33,000 | | $138,000 | | $24,000 | | $195,000 |
| 3 | Total activity | 6,000 | parties | 15,000 | diners | 10,000 | drinks | |
| 4 |  |  |  |  |  |  |  |  |

## Spreadsheets

have become an increasingly common tool for managerial accountants; therefore, selected exhibits and data appear as Microsoft Excel® screen captures.

This author team has always been known for its quality and quantity of assignment material. *Introduction to Managerial Accounting* has a wide variety of end-of-chapter materials to assist students, including:

**Questions** that students can use to ensure that they have mastered concepts.

**Brief Exercises** that cover a single learning objective each, and **Exercises** that cover multiple learning objectives.

**Problems** that challenge students to apply themselves.

a **Building Your Skills** section containing problem material that helps students develop communication, teamwork, Internet, and analytical skills.

### Questions

5–1  What are the three common approaches for assigning overhead costs to products?
5–2  Why is activity-based costing growing in popularity?
5–3  Why do departmental overhead rates sometimes result in inaccurate product costs?
5–4  What are the four hierarchical levels of activity discussed in the chapter?
5–5  Why is activity-based costing described as a "two-stage" costing method?
5–6  Why do overhead costs often shift from high-volume products to low-volume products when a company switches from a traditional costing method to activity-based costing?

### Brief Exercises

**BRIEF EXERCISE 5–1  ABC Cost Hierarchy** (LO1)

The following activities occur at Greenwich Corporation, a company that manufactures a variety of products.
a. Receive raw materials from suppliers.
b. Manage parts inventories.
c. Do rough milling work on products.
d. Interview and process new employees in the human resources department.
e. Design new products.

### Exercises

**EXERCISE 5–1  ABC Cost Hierarchy** (LO1)

The following activities are carried out in Greenberry Company, a manufacturer of consumer goods.
a. Direct labour workers assemble a product.
b. Engineers design a new product.
c. A machine is set up to process a batch.
d. Numerically controlled machines cut and shape materials.
e. The HR department trains new employees concerning company policies.
f. Raw materials are moved from the receiving dock to the production line.

### Problems

**PROBLEM 5–1  ABC Cost Hierarchy** (LO1)

Juneau Company manufactures a variety of products in a single facility. Consultants hired by the company to do an activity-based costing analysis have identified the following activities carried out in the company on a routine basis:
a. Machines are set up between batches of different products.
b. The company's grounds crew maintains planted areas surrounding the factory.
c. A percentage of all completed goods are inspected on a random basis.
d. Milling machines are used to make components for products.

### Building Your Skills

CHECK FIGURE
(2) Standard model unit product cost: $29.98 per unit

**ANALYTICAL THINKING\*** (LO2)

"A dollar of gross margin per briefcase? That's ridiculous!" roared Art Dejans, president of CarryAll, Inc. "Why do we go on producing those standard briefcases when we're able to make over $15 per unit on our specialty items? Maybe it's time to get out of the standard line and focus the whole plant on specialty work."

Mr. Dejans is referring to a summary of unit costs and revenues that he had just received from the company's Accounting Department:

|  | Standard Briefcases | Specialty Briefcases |
|---|---|---|
| Selling price per unit | $36 | $40 |
| Unit product cost | 35 | 25 |
| Gross margin per unit | $ 1 | $15 |

# Canadian edition, such a powerful learning tool?

## *Technology solutions to meet your every need*

Create a custom course Website with **PageOut**, free with every McGraw-Hill Ryerson textbook.

To learn more, contact your McGraw-Hill Ryerson publisher's representative or visit www.mhhe.com/solutions

### In North America Alone, over 200,000

postsecondary educators use the Internet in their respective courses. Some are just getting started, while others are eager to embrace the very latest advances in educational content delivery and course management.

That is why McGraw-Hill Ryerson supports instructors and students alike with the most complete range of digital solutions. Your students can use our complete **Online Learning Centre (OLC)** or work with the assessment solutions found in **GradeSummit**.

In addition to an Instructor's CD-ROM, faculty have access to nearly every supplement online. These assets range from the Instructor's Resource Guide and Microsoft® PowerPoint® slides to a range of course-management systems, including **PageOut**, McGraw-Hill's proprietary system.

McGraw-Hill has always set the standard as a leader in bringing helpful technology into the classroom. With **Garrison/Noreen/Kalagnanam/Vaidyanathan**, your class gets all the benefits of the digital age without any setup issues or confusion.

www.blackboard.com

## *Superior Service*

Service takes on a whole new meaning with McGraw-Hill Ryerson and *Introduction to Managerial Accounting*. More than just bringing you the textbook, we have consistently raised the bar in terms of innovation and educational research—both in accounting and in education in general. These investments in learning and the education community have helped us understand the needs of students and educators across the country and allowed us to foster the growth of truly innovative, integrated learning.

## *Integrated Learning*

Your Integrated Learning Sales Specialist is a McGraw-Hill Ryerson representative who has the experience, product knowledge, training, and support to help you assess and integrate any of our products, technology, and services into your course for optimum teaching and learning performance. Whether it is using our test bank software, helping your students improve their grades, or putting your entire course online, your *i*-Learning Sales Specialist is there to help you do it. Contact your local *i*-Learning Sales Specialist today to learn how to maximize all of McGraw-Hill Ryerson's resources!

## *i-Learning Service Program*

McGraw-Hill Ryerson offers a unique *i*Services package designed for Canadian faculty. Our mission is to equip providers of higher education with superior tools and resources required for excellence in teaching. For additional information, visit www.mcgrawhill.ca/highereducation/eservices.

## *Teaching, Technology & Learning Conference Series*

The educational environment has changed tremendously in recent years, and McGraw-Hill Ryerson continues to be committed to helping you acquire the skills you need to succeed in this new milieu. Our innovative Teaching, Technology & Learning Conference Series bring faculty together from across Canada with 3M Teaching Excellence award winners to share teaching and learning best practices in a collaborative and stimulating environment. Pre-conference workshops on general topics, such as teaching large classes and technology integration, will also be offered.

We will also work with you at your own institution to customize workshops that best suit the needs of your faculty. These include our Teaching Excellence and Accounting Innovation symposium series.

## *Research Reports into Mobile Learning and Student Success*

These landmark reports, undertaken in conjunction with academic and private-sector advisory boards, are the result of research studies into the challenges professors face in helping students succeed and the opportunities that new technology presents to impact teaching and learning.

# What's the best way for my students to **brush up on** *their Accounting skills?*

## ONLINE LEARNING CENTRE (OLC)

More and more students are studying online. That is why we offer an Online Learning Centre (OLC) that follows *Introduction to Managerial Accounting* chapter by chapter. It does not require any building or maintenance on your part. It is ready to go the moment you and your students type in the URL: www.mcgrawhill.ca/college/garrison.

As your students study, they can access to the OLC for such benefits as:

- Self-grading quizzes
- Internet exercises
- Alternate problems
- Chapter outlines
- Practice exams
- Excel spreadsheets
- Links to URLs referenced in the text

A secured Instructor Resource Centre stores your essential course materials to save you prep time before class. The Instructor's Manual, Solutions, and Microsoft PowerPoint® presentations are now just a couple of clicks away.

The OLC also serves as a doorway to other technology solutions such as PageOut, which is free to textbook adopters.

*GradeSummit* tells your students what they need to know in order to study effectively. And it provides you, the instructor, with valuable insight into which of your students are struggling and which course topics give them the most trouble.

GradeSummit provides a series of practice tests that can be taken in various formats according to student preference: practice mode, for instance, displays the correct answer immediately, while exam mode simulates a real classroom exam and displays results at the end. There is even a smart testing engine, SummitExpress, that automatically scales the difficulty level of the questions according to the student's responses.

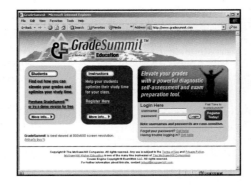

Once a student has taken a particular test, GradeSummit returns a detailed results page showing exactly where the student did well and where he or she needs to improve. Students can compare their results with those of their other classmates or even with those of every other student using the text nationwide. With that information, students can plan their studying to focus exclusively on their weak areas, without wasting effort on material they have already mastered. And they can come back to take a retest on those subjects later, comparing their new score with their previous efforts.

As an instructor, you will know which students are falling behind, simply by consulting GradeSummit's test logs, where results for every student in your course are available for review. Because GradeSummit's results are so detailed, you will know exactly what topics are causing difficulties —an invaluable aid when it comes to planning lectures and homework.

# Supplements

## INSTRUCTOR SUPPLEMENTS

### Instructor CD-ROM

Allowing instructors to create a customized multimedia presentation, this all-in-one resource incorporates the Test Bank, PowerPoint® Slides, Instructor's Resource Guide, Solutions Manual, Teaching Transparency Masters, links to PageOut, and the Spreadsheet Application Template Software (SPATS). Selected supplements are available for download from the text's Online Learning Centre at www.mcgrawhill.ca/college/garrison.

### Check Figures

These provide key answers for selected problems and cases. They are available on the text's website.

### Solutions Manual

This supplement contains completely worked-out solutions to all assignment material and a general discussion of the use of group exercises. In addition, the manual contains suggested course outlines and a listing of exercises, problems, and cases scaled according to difficulty.

### Teaching Transparencies

Contains a comprehensive set of over 260 teaching transparencies covering every chapter that can be used for classroom lectures and discussion.

### PowerPoint® Slides

These slides offer a great visual complement for your lectures. A complete set of slides covers each chapter. They are only available on the Instructor CD-ROM and the text's website.

### Test Bank

Nearly 2,000 questions are organized by chapter and include true/false, multiple-choice, and essay questions and computational problems.

### Diploma Computerized Test Bank

This test bank is delivered in the Diploma Shell, new from Brownstone. Use it to make different versions of the same test, change the answer order, edit and add questions, and conduct online testing. Technical support for this software is available.

### Excel Templates

Prepared by Jack Terry of ComSource Associates, Inc., these Excel templates offer solutions to the Student SPATS version. They are available on the Instructor CD and the text's website.

## STUDENT SUPPLEMENTS

### Excel Templates

This spreadsheet-based software uses Excel to solve selected problems and cases in the text. These selected problems and cases are identified in the margin of the text with an appropriate icon. The Excel templates are available on the text's website at www.mcgrawhill.ca/college/garrison, along with the OLC resources described on page **viii**.

### Workbook/Study Guide

This study aid provides suggestions for studying chapter material, summarizes essential points in each chapter, and tests students' knowledge using self-test questions and exercises.

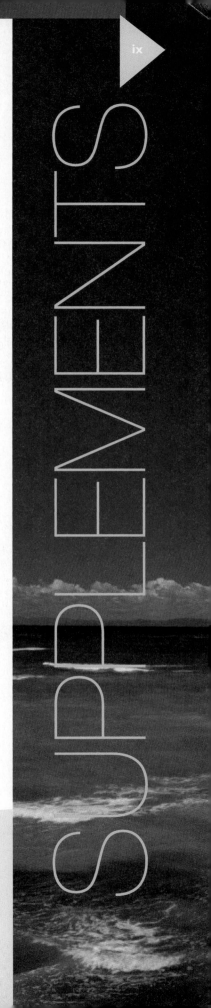

# Reviewers

The efforts of many people are needed to develop and improve a text. Among these people are the reviewers and consultants who point out areas of concern, cite areas of strength, and make recommendations for change. In this regard, the following professors provided feedback that was enormously helpful in preparing the Canadian edition of *Introduction to Managerial Accounting*:

Karen Baker, *Loyalist College*

Bryan Bessner, *Ryerson University*

Donald Brown, *Brock University*

Andrew Dykstra, *Georgian College*

Graham Fane, *Capilano College*

Terry Fegarty, *Seneca College*

Terry Goldthorpe, *Centennial College*

Jane Kaake-Nemeth, *Durham College*

Barb Katz, *Kwantlen University College*

Peter Lubka, *University of Waterloo*

Gail Lynn Cook, *Brock University*

Ann MacGillivary, *Mount St. Vincent University*

Winston Marcellin, *George Brown College*

Claudia Parker, *Northern Alberta Institute of Technology (NAIT)*

Pina Salvaggio, *Dawson College*

Ken Smith, *College of the North Atlantic*

Bob Sproule, *University of Waterloo*

Nancy Tait, *Sir Sanford Fleming College*

# Table of Contents

## Chapter Eight
## Budgeting    278

## Chapter Nine
## Standard Costs    330

# Chapter One

# An Introduction to Managerial Accounting

## A Look at This Chapter

After describing the three major activities of managers and the need for managerial accounting information, this chapter compares and contrasts financial and managerial accounting information. It then exposes you to the changes taking place in the business environment. The design of an appropriate managerial accounting system is critical for managers to be able to make solid decisions.

## A Look Ahead

Chapter 2 focuses on the basics of a managerial accounting system by defining and explaining many terms that are used to classify costs in business. Because these terms will be used throughout the text, you should ensure that you are familiar with each of them.

## Chapter Outline

**The Work of Management and the Need for Managerial Accounting Information**
- Planning
- Directing and Motivating
- Controlling
- The End Results of Managers' Activities
- The Planning and Control Cycle

**Comparison of Financial and Managerial Accounting**
- Emphasis on the Future
- Relevance and Flexibility of Data
- Less Emphasis on Precision
- Segments of an Organization
- Generally Accepted Accounting Principles (GAAP)
- Managerial Accounting—Not Mandatory

**Increased Relevance of Managerial Accounting**

**Globalization**

**Lean Business Model**

**Just-in-Time (JIT)**
- The JIT Approach
- Zero Defects and JIT
- Benefits of a JIT System

**Total Quality Management (TQM)**
- The Plan-Do-Check-Act Cycle
- An Example of TQM in Practice

**Process Re-engineering**
- The Problem of Employee Morale

**The Theory of Constraints (TOC)**
- An Example of TOC
- TOC and Continuous Improvement

**Ethical Responsibility**
- Professional Ethics

**Implications of the New Business Environment on Managerial Accounting**

**Organization of the Book**

## DECISION FEATURE Why Change Matters at Bombardier

Today's competitive environment has forced companies to improve their organizational functions in order to gain a competitive advantage. In response, many companies, such as Bombardier Inc., have implemented the enterprise resource planning (ERP) software to ensure the availability of timely information to guide their decision-making process. However, implementing such a major system is not easy, especially when it can affect over 10,000 employees across all functions, such as finance, management, procurement, human resources, marketing, engineering, and aircraft maintenance. Bombardier feels that a long-term "multidisciplinary" approach to change management is necessary to successfully implement ERP. The framework surrounding ERP change management is designed to focus on the following four areas:

*Change Leadership*
- This area is intended to support the program vision throughout the organization. The entire organization must facilitate the building of a compelling case for change, in order to enable Bombardier to support all levels of change with an active and visible leadership network, and assessing and measuring the readiness of the organization. Managing the involvement, communications, and commitment of key leaders is also important.

*Program Positioning and Communications*
- Using proven marketing approaches and techniques will raise the organization's awareness of the program. It is targeted at creating an identity around what the project stands for as well as encouraging stakeholders to buy into and support the deployment of ERP.

*Organizational Alignment*
- Organizational alignment enables the organization and its employees to optimize and leverage the ERP system and its supporting processes. The change management team obtains thorough knowledge of the business processes in order to support the change that will create real value for the company.

*Deployment Readiness*
- This area integrates all disciplines involved in the change process into a useful set of tools. It also involves measuring the readiness of the facility prior to actually using ERP as well as the "business ramp-up and stabilization after the implementation."

## Learning Objectives

*After studying Chapter 1, you should be able to:*

**LO1** Describe the work of management and the need for managerial accounting information.

**LO2** Describe the key differences between financial and managerial accounting.

**LO3** Describe the impact of globalization on business.

**LO4** Explain the lean business model and its corresponding management practices.

**LO5** Describe the importance of ethical responsibility and explain the need for ethical codes of conduct.

Source: Gowigati, B. and B. Grenier, "The Winds of Change," *CMA Management*, November 2001, pp. 34–38. Reprinted with permission from CMA Canada.

**R**unning a company like Bombardier is by no means an easy task. Senior managers must constantly study the business environment within which the company is operating: the economy, competition, technological developments, and government regulations. Public companies must also report their activities to investors (shareholders). Reporting to investors requires that companies record accounting transactions and prepare a balance sheet, an income statement, and a cash flow statement. Most of you are already familiar with this aspect of accounting, known as **financial accounting.**

A manager's duties do not end with reporting to investors. Managers must also ensure that the business is properly managed so that its objectives are achieved (this may include earning a certain level of profitability or maintaining a certain level of market share). In order to do this, managers must *plan* for the future, *direct* and *motivate* their employees, and *control* the operations—tasks that must be carried out *within* the organization. For this purpose, managers need information that focuses on internal activities. **Managerial Accounting** provides managers with the essential information that they can use to run organizations.

This chapter begins with an introduction to the main functions of management and then explains the need for managerial accounting information. Finally, it examines the changes taking place in the business environment and their impact on the design of managerial accounting systems.

# The Work of Management and the Need for Managerial Accounting Information

**Learning Objective 1**
Describe the work of management and the need for managerial accounting information.

Every organization—large or small—has managers. Someone must be responsible for making plans, organizing resources, directing personnel, and controlling operations. This is true of the Royal Bank of Canada, the Peace Corps, the Simon Fraser University, the Catholic Church, and the Potash Corporation of Saskatchewan, as well as the local 7-Eleven convenience store. In general, there are three types of business organizations: service, merchandising, and manufacturing. Service firms include such organizations as a doctor's clinic, an advertising agency, and a financial institution. Such firms do not sell any products but generate revenues by offering one or more types of services (e.g., legal counselling). Merchandising firms largely refer to retail and wholesale outlets that buy goods from suppliers and resell them to customers. Manufacturing firms engage in the production and sale of different types of products ranging from small consumer goods to large ships and aircrafts. Merchandising and manufacturing firms generate revenue by selling products (e.g., hockey sticks). More will be said later in this chapter about the treatment of costs incurred by these different types of businesses. We will use a particular organization—Good Vibrations, Inc.—to illustrate the work of management. What we have to say about the management of Good Vibrations, Inc., however, is very general and can be applied to virtually any organization.

Good Vibrations runs a chain of retail outlets that sell a full range of music CDs. The chain's stores are concentrated in Pacific Rim cities, such as Sydney, Singapore, Hong Kong, Beijing, Tokyo, and Vancouver, British Columbia. The company has found that the best way to generate sales, and profits, is to create an exciting shopping environment. Consequently, the company puts a great deal of effort into planning the layout and decor of its stores—which are often quite large and extend over several floors in key downtown locations. Management knows that different types of clientele are attracted to different kinds of music. The international rock section is generally decorated with bold, brightly coloured graphics, and the aisles are purposely narrow to create a crowded feeling much like one would experience at a popular nightclub on Friday night. In contrast, the classical music section is wood-panelled and fully sound insulated, with the rich, spacious feeling of a country club meeting room. Managers at Good Vibrations, like managers everywhere, carry out three major activities—**planning, directing and motivating,** and **controlling.**

## Planning

Planning involves selecting a course of action and specifying how the action will be implemented. The first step in planning is to identify alternatives and then to select from among the alternatives the one that does the best job of furthering the organization's objectives. The basic objective of Good Vibrations is to earn profits for the owners of the company by providing superior service at competitive prices in as many markets as possible. To further this objective, every year, top management carefully considers a number of alternatives for expanding into new geographic markets. This year, management is considering opening new stores in Shanghai, Los Angeles, and Auckland.

When making this and other choices, management must balance the opportunities against the demands made on the company's resources. Management knows from bitter experience that opening a store in a major new market is a big step that cannot be taken lightly. It requires enormous amounts of time and energy from the company's most experienced, talented, and busy professionals. When the company attempted to open stores in both Beijing and Vancouver in the same year, resources were stretched too thinly. The result was that neither store opened on schedule, and operations in the rest of the company suffered. Therefore, entering new markets is planned very, very carefully.

Among other data, top management looks at the sales volumes, profit margins, and costs of the company's established stores in similar markets. These data, supplied by the management accountant, are combined with projected sales volume data at the proposed new locations to estimate the profits that would be generated by the new stores. In general, virtually all important alternatives considered by management in the planning process have some effect on revenues or costs, and management accounting data are essential in estimating those effects.

After considering all of the alternatives, Good Vibrations, Inc.'s top management decided to open a store in the burgeoning Shanghai market in the third quarter of the year but to defer opening any other new stores to another year. As soon as this decision was made, detailed plans were drawn up for all parts of the company that would be involved in the Shanghai opening. For example, the Human Resources (HR) Department's travel budget was increased, since it would be providing extensive on-the-site training to the new personnel hired in Shanghai.

As in the HR Department example, the plans of management are often expressed formally in **budgets,** which are prepared annually and represent management's plans in specific, quantitative (often financial) terms, and the term *budgeting* is used to generally describe this part of the planning process. Budgets are usually prepared under the direction of the controller, who is the manager in charge of the Accounting Department. In addition to a travel budget, the HR Department will be given goals in terms of new hires, courses taught, and detailed breakdowns of expected expenses. Similarly, the manager of each store will be given a target for sales volume, profit, expenses, pilferage losses, and employee training. These data will be collected, analyzed, and summarized for management use in the form of budgets prepared by management accountants.

## Directing and Motivating

In addition to planning for the future, managers must oversee day-to-day activities to keep the organization functioning smoothly; this involves directing and motivating people. Managers assign tasks to employees, arbitrate disputes, answer questions, solve on-the-spot problems, and make many small decisions that affect customers and employees (which, in turn, will likely influence future financial performance). In effect, directing is that part of managers' work that deals with the routine and the here and now. Managerial accounting data, such as daily sales reports, are often used in this type of day-to-day decision making.

## Controlling

In carrying out the **control** function, managers seek to ensure that the plan is being followed. **Feedback,** represented by the dashed lines in Exhibit 1–1, signals whether operations are on track and is key to effective control. In sophisticated organizations, this feedback is provided by detailed reports of various types. One of these reports, which compares budgeted with actual results, is called a **performance report.** Performance reports suggest where operations are not proceeding as planned and where some parts of the organization may require additional attention. For example, before the opening of the new Shanghai store in the third quarter of the year, the store's manager will be given sales volume, profit, and expense targets for the fourth quarter of the year. As the fourth quarter progresses, periodic reports will be prepared in which the actual sales volume, profit, and expenses are compared with the targets. If the actual results fall below the targets, top management is alerted that the Shanghai store requires more attention. Experienced personnel can be flown in to help the new manager, or top management may come to the conclusion that plans will have to be revised. As we shall see in the following chapters, providing this kind of feedback to managers is one of the central purposes of managerial accounting.

## The End Results of Managers' Activities

As a customer enters one of the Good Vibrations stores, the results of management's planning, directing and motivating, and control activities will be evident in the many details that make the difference between a pleasant and an irritating shopping experience. The store will be clean, fashionably decorated, and logically laid out. Featured artists' videos will be played on TV monitors throughout the store, and the background rock music will be loud enough to send older patrons scurrying to the classical music section. Popular CDs will be in stock, and the latest hits will be available for private listening on earphones. Specific titles will be easy to find. Regional music, such as CantoPop in Hong Kong, will be prominently featured. Checkout clerks will be alert, friendly, and efficient. In short, what the customer experiences does not simply happen; it is the result of the efforts of managers who must visualize and fit together the processes that are needed to get the job done.

## The Planning and Control Cycle

The work of management can be summarized in a model such as the one shown in Exhibit 1–1. The model, which depicts the **planning and control cycle,** illustrates the

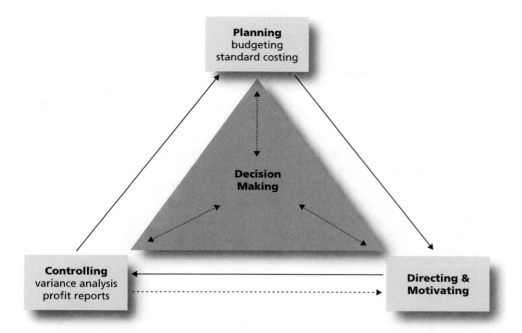

**Exhibit 1–1**
The Planning and Control Cycle

smooth flow of management activities from planning through directing and motivating, controlling, and then back to planning again. All of these activities involve decision making, and so it is depicted as the hub around which the other activities revolve.

## Planning without Direction

*in business today*

Joe works for a large technology company. Unfortunately, the company's sales, profits, and stock price leave much to be desired. Simon, one of the company's vice-presidents, had convinced the company's chairman that a new corporate culture would do the trick. Joe accepted a job to lead the cultural change project, even though all that he could ascertain was that the project was big. He was enticed by the offer of money and his curiosity.

During his first day on the job, Joe attended a project team meeting. None of the ideas put on the table by the team came close to what was envisioned by the vice-president. After the meeting, the team members informed him that this was their fourth attempt at trying to figure out what Simon was thinking. Joe was able to get the team to develop an outline for the project that simply made sense without worrying about whether or not it was what Simon had in mind.

Source: Joe Kay, "My Year at a Big High Tech Company," *Forbes ASAP*, May 29, 2000, pp. 195–198. *(As noted in the article, because Joe does not want to lose his job, his name as well as the name of the company and certain details have been changed.)*

## Comparison of Financial and Managerial Accounting

Financial accounting reports are prepared for the use of external parties, such as shareholders and creditors, whereas managerial accounting reports are prepared for managers inside the organization. This contrast in basic orientation results in a number of major differences between financial and managerial accounting, even though both financial and managerial accounting rely on the same underlying financial data. These differences are summarized in Exhibit 1–2.

**Learning Objective 2**
Describe the key differences between financial and managerial accounting.

**Exhibit 1–2**
Comparison of Financial and
Managerial Accounting

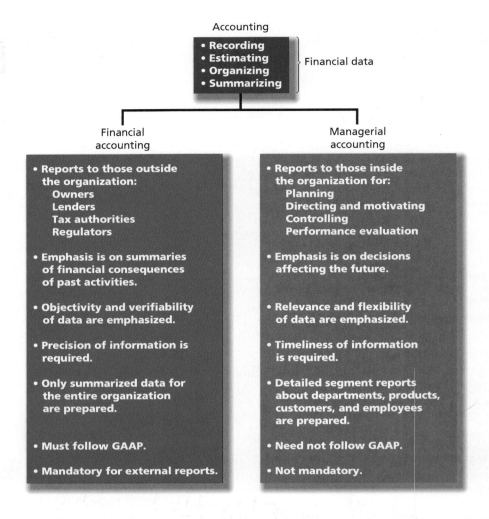

As shown in Exhibit 1–2, in addition to the difference in who the reports are prepared for, financial and managerial accounting also differ in their emphases between the past and the future, in the type of data provided to users, and in several other ways. These differences are discussed in the following paragraphs.

## Emphasis on the Future

Since *planning* is such an important part of the manager's job, managerial accounting has a strong future orientation. In contrast, financial accounting primarily provides summaries of past financial transactions. These summaries may be useful in planning, but only to a point. The difficulty with summaries of the past is that the future is not simply a reflection of what has happened in the past. Changes are constantly taking place in economic conditions, customer needs and desires, competitive conditions, and so on. All of these changes demand that the manager's planning be based, in large part, on estimates of what will happen, rather than on summaries of what has already happened.

## Relevance and Flexibility of Data

Financial accounting data are expected to be objective and verifiable. However, for internal uses, the manager wants information that is relevant even if it is not completely objective or verifiable. By relevant, we mean *appropriate for the decision at hand*. For example, it is difficult to verify estimated sales volumes for a proposed new Good Vibrations store, but this is exactly the type of information that is most useful to managers in their decision making. In addition to monetary information, managers often need non-monetary information to aid the decision-making process (e.g., impact on customer satisfaction). The managerial accounting information system should be flexible enough to provide whatever data are relevant for a particular decision.

## Less Emphasis on Precision

Timeliness is often more important than precision to managers. If a decision must be made, a manager would much rather have a good estimate now than wait a week for a more precise answer. A decision involving tens of millions of dollars does not have to be based on estimates that are precise down to the penny, or even to the dollar. Estimates that are accurate to the nearest million dollars may be precise enough to make a good decision. Since precision is costly in terms of both time and resources, managerial accounting places less emphasis on precision than does financial accounting (the latter reports past activities for which precise data are usually available).

## Segments of an Organization

Financial accounting is primarily concerned with reporting for the organization as a whole. By contrast, managerial accounting focuses much more on the parts, or **segments,** of an organization. These segments may be product lines, sales territories, divisions, departments, branch offices, or any other categorization of the company's activities that management finds useful. Financial accounting does require some breakdowns of revenues and costs by major segments in external reports, but this is a secondary emphasis. In managerial accounting, segment reporting is the primary emphasis.

### Recordkeeping for the Future

*in business | today*

Taking into account the ongoing nature of litigation, executives in the tobacco industry might consider company records to be a liability. However, properly maintained corporate records have significant future benefit and, as such, should be considered an essential asset. Reviews of recordkeeping policies should be performed periodically to ensure that important information, needed for reference in the future, is documented and can be retrieved. Most of the problems uncovered in such reviews tend to relate to how the records are organized, rather than how much information is being documented. There is little value in information that cannot be retrieved when it is needed for decision making.

Source: J. Edwin Dietal, "Improving Corporate Performance," reprinted with permission from the *Information Management Journal*, April 2000, pp. 18–26 © 2000 ARMA International.

## Generally Accepted Accounting Principles (GAAP)

Financial accounting statements prepared for external users must be prepared in accordance with generally accepted accounting principles (GAAP). External users must have some assurance that the reports have been prepared in accordance with a common set of ground rules. These common ground rules enhance comparability and help reduce fraud and misrepresentation, but they do not necessarily lead to the type of reports that would be most useful for internal decision making. For example, GAAP require that land value be stated at its historical cost on financial reports. However, if management is considering moving a store to a new location and then selling the land the store currently sits on, management would like to know the current market value of the land—a vital piece of information that is ignored under GAAP.

Managerial accounting is not bound by GAAP. Managers set their own ground rules concerning the content and form of internal reports. The only constraint is that the expected benefits from using the information should outweigh the costs of collecting, analyzing, and summarizing the data. Nevertheless, as we shall see in subsequent chapters, it is undeniably true that financial reporting requirements have heavily influenced management accounting practice.

## Managerial Accounting—Not Mandatory

Financial accounting is mandatory; that is, it must be done. Various outside parties, such as the Ontario Securities Commission (OSC) and the tax authorities, require periodic financial statements. Managerial accounting, on the other hand, is not mandatory. A company is completely free to do as much or as little as it wishes. There are no regulatory bodies or other outside agencies that specify what is to be done or, for that matter, whether anything is to be done at all. Since managerial accounting is completely optional, the important question is always, "Is the information useful?" rather than, "Is the information required?"

As explained above, the work of management focuses on (1) planning, which includes setting objectives and outlining how to attain these objectives; and (2) control, which includes the steps to take to ensure that objectives are realized. To carry out these planning and control responsibilities, managers need *information* about the organization. From an accounting point of view, this information often relates to the *costs* of the organization. In managerial accounting, the term cost is used in many different ways, as explained in Chapter 2.

# Increased Relevance of Managerial Accounting

Although managerial accounting information has always been useful to managers, its relevance and importance have greatly increased in the past two decades. This is because the last quarter century has been a period of tremendous change in the business environment. *First*, competitive boundaries have expanded due to globalization, and this has been good for consumers because the increased competition has led to lower prices, higher quality, and more choices. However, this means that organizations must find new ways of doing business, which is the *second* aspect of change. The *third* issue is one of ethical responsibility among businesses and other organizations. More and more allegations are being made of management misconduct in many businesses and also in government and not-for-profit and charitable organizations. And, to add even more dynamism, the Internet has been changing the face of business in several industries.

These changes are having a profound effect on managerial accounting practices, as we will see throughout this text. Managers require timely information not only on costs and profits but also on key drivers of these outcomes. We now elaborate upon the changes in the business environment.

# Globalization

**Learning Objective 3**
Describe the impact of globalization on business.

Over the last three decades, several factors have led to an increase in worldwide competition in many industries. These include reductions in tariffs, quotas, and other barriers to free trade; improvements in global transportation systems; and increasing sophistication in international trade markets. These factors work together to reduce the costs of conducting international trade and make it possible for foreign companies to compete on a more equal footing with domestic firms. These changes have been most dramatic within the European Union (EU) and the North American Free Trade Association (NAFTA) free trade zones.

Very few firms can now afford to be complacent. An organization that is very successful in its local market can suddenly face competition from halfway around the globe. It is likely that this threat will become even more potent as business migrates more and more to the Internet. On the bright side, however, this means that businesses have greater opportunities (e.g., networking possibilities with new business partners and access to new markets). Similarly, more choices are available to customers: greater variety of goods and services, higher quality, and lower price.

What are the implications of globalization? One major implication is that organizations must find new ways of conducting business: new strategies, new management practices, more sophisticated management accounting systems. Another implication is that organizations must conduct their affairs in a responsible manner. We will now discuss each of these implications in greater detail.

# The Lean Business Model

International competition has forced companies to find new ways of doing business in order to offer better products/services and to deliver them faster and at a cheaper price. Since the early 1980s, companies adopted different kinds of improvement programs; these fall under the umbrella of what experts now call the **lean business model.** The main idea underlying this model is the elimination of waste. Consider a grocery store which sells fresh produce (fruits and vegetables) and bakery products among other things. The fresh produce damaged in transit as well as the quantity ordered in excess that sits on the shelves too long (and rots) are examples of waste. They cost the grocery store money; this cost cannot be recovered because the damaged and rotten produce cannot be sold to customers. As another example, consider a beautician who decides to hire one additional employee just so that customers never have to wait. The idle time of this additional employee is also an example of waste (especially if the beautician cannot charge higher prices compared with the competition). Similarly, manufacturing companies that produce more than the required quantities in order to spread the cost of resources (equipment and labour) over a larger quantity of production also tend to create waste in the system in the form of excess inventory (or stock) which may remain unsold for a long time and become obsolete in the process. We now have a situation where the money has already been spent but there is a certain amount of uncertainty about whether the goods produced can be sold.

> **Learning Objective 4**
> Explain the lean business model and its corresponding management practices.

In order to eliminate waste, companies must adopt and implement one or more management practices that individually focus on different aspects of the lean business model. Examples of these management practices include *just-in-time*, *total quality management*, *process re-engineering*, and *theory of constraints*. These management practices, or programs of continuous improvement, if properly implemented, can enhance quality, increase efficiencies, eliminate delays, and reduce costs, thereby adding to the profits. Unfortunately, they have not always been properly implemented; as a result, considerable controversy exists about their ultimate economic value. Although each of the above-mentioned programs is worthy of extended study, we will discuss them only briefly, leaving the details to operations management courses.

In addition to adopting these management practices, companies have also refined their management accounting systems. For example, many companies now use the concepts of activity-based costing (ABC) and the balanced scorecard (BSC)—these concepts are discussed in later chapters.

# Just-in-Time (JIT)

In a traditional manufacturing company, work is *pushed* through the system. Enough materials are released to workstations to keep everyone busy, and when a workstation completes its tasks, the partially completed goods are "pushed" forward to the next workstation, regardless of whether that workstation is ready to receive them. The result is that partially completed goods stack up, waiting for the next workstation to become available. They may not be completed for days, weeks, or even months. Additionally, when the units are finally completed, customers may or may not want them. If finished goods are produced faster than the market will absorb, the result is bloated finished goods inventories.

Companies typically maintained large amounts of inventory to shield themselves from any unanticipated disruptions, such as late shipments from suppliers, machine breakdowns, and unexpectedly large orders from customers.

While these inventories provide some insurance against unforeseen events, they have a cost. According to experts, in addition to tying up money, maintaining inventories encourages inefficient and sloppy work, results in too many defects, and dramatically increases the amount of time required to complete a product. For example, when partially completed products are stored for long periods of time before being processed by the next workstation, defects introduced by the preceding workstation go unnoticed. If a machine is out of calibration or incorrect procedures are being followed, many defective units will be produced before the problem is discovered. And when the defects are finally discovered, it may be very difficult to track down the source of the problem. In addition, units may be obsolete or out of fashion by the time they are finally completed.

Large inventories of partially completed goods create many other operating problems that are best discussed in more advanced courses. These problems are not obvious—if they were, companies would have long ago reduced their inventories. Managers at Toyota are credited with the insight that large inventories often create many more problems than they solve, and Toyota pioneered the *JIT approach*.

## *in business* | *today*  **Lean Business Model in Practice**

Cover-All Building Systems, a Saskatoon-based company, is a leading manufacturer of steel-framed, fabric-covered buildings with a North America–wide Dealer network that is dedicated to being a customer-driven, principle-governed enterprise. From a Tommy Hilfiger retail outlet in Las Vegas to Spruce Meadows riding arenas in Calgary, Cover-All is providing innovative building solutions for an ever-expanding number of applications.

In the spirit of continuous improvement, the company decided in 1999 to adopt the lean business model. According to Nathan Stobbe, President, Cover-All has already experienced dramatic results that have led to a significant reduction in costs and increase in revenues. The measurement system put in place at the end of year 1 showed these cumulative results in the following two years: sales went up 30%, but manufacturing inventory went down 24%, and time from order to delivery on standard buildings went down 66%.

Since its inception, Cover-All Building Systems has been recognized locally and nationally for its achievements. Among the most recent honours garnered by the company are the provincial Achievement of Business Excellence (ABEX) in export and Business of the Year awards and recognition as one of the 50 Best-Managed Private Companies in Canada for three consecutive years.

Source: http://www.coverall.ca/about_frame.html and personal interview. Permission granted by Nathan Stobbe, President.

## The JIT Approach

In contrast to the traditional approach, companies that use the **just-in-time (JIT)** approach purchase materials and produce units only as needed to meet actual customer demand. The theory is that simply producing goods does not do the company any good unless someone buys them. Moreover, excess inventories create a multitude of operating problems. In a JIT system, inventories are reduced to an absolute minimum. Under ideal conditions, a company operating a just-in-time system would purchase only enough materials each day to meet that day's needs. Moreover, the company would have no goods still in process at the end of the day, and all goods completed during the day would have been shipped immediately to customers. As this sequence suggests, "just-in-time" means that raw materials are received just in time to go into production, manufactured parts are completed just in time to be assembled into products, and products are completed just in time to be shipped to customers. Although a manufacturing example is used here, the JIT approach can easily be extended to nonmanufacturing settings (e.g., the grocery store example).

Although few companies have been able to reach this ideal, many companies have been able to reduce inventories to only a fraction of their previous levels. The results have been a substantial reduction in ordering and warehousing costs and much more effective operations.

The change from a traditional to a JIT approach is more profound than it may appear to be. Among other things, producing only in response to a customer order means that workers will be idle whenever demand falls below the company's production capacity. This can be an extremely difficult cultural change for an organization to make. It challenges the core beliefs of many managers and raises anxiety among workers who have become accustomed to being kept busy all of the time. It also requires fundamental changes in managerial accounting practices, as we will see in later chapters.

## Zero Defects and JIT

Given that JIT requires smooth operations, the existence of quality problems can create havoc. If a completed order contains a defective unit, the company must ship the order with less than the promised quantity or it must restart the whole production process to make just one unit. At a minimum, this creates a delay in shipping the order and may generate a ripple effect that delays other orders. For this and other reasons, defects cannot be tolerated in a JIT system. Companies that are deeply involved in JIT tend to become zealously committed to a goal of *zero defects*. Even though it may be next to impossible to attain the zero defect goal, companies have found that they can come very close. For example, Motorola, Allied Signal, and many other companies now measure defects in terms of the number of defects per *million* units of product.

In a traditional company, parts and materials are inspected for defects when they are received from suppliers, and quality inspectors inspect units as they progress along the production line. In a JIT system, the company's suppliers are responsible for the quality of incoming parts and materials. And instead of using quality inspectors, the company's production workers are directly responsible for spotting defective units. A worker who discovers a defect is supposed to punch an alarm button that stops the production flow line and sets off flashing lights. Supervisors and other workers go immediately to the workstation to determine the cause of the defect and correct it before any further defective units are produced. This procedure ensures that problems are quickly identified and corrected, but it does require that defects are rare—otherwise there would be constant disruptions to the production process.

## Benefits of a JIT System

The main benefits of JIT are:

1. Funds that have been tied up in inventories can be used elsewhere.
2. Areas previously used to store inventories are made available for other, more productive uses.
3. The time required to fill an order is reduced, resulting in quicker response to customers and consequentially greater potential sales.
4. Defect rates are reduced, resulting in less waste and greater customer satisfaction.

As a result of benefits such as those cited above, more companies are embracing JIT each year. However, the JIT approach is just one aspect of the lean business model.

# Total Quality Management (TQM)

Another management practice that has become popular is known as *total quality management*. There are two major characteristics of **total quality management (TQM):** (1) a focus on serving customers, and (2) systematic problem solving using teams made up of front-line workers. A variety of specific tools is available to aid teams in their problem solving. One of these tools, **benchmarking,** involves studying organizations that are among the best in the world at performing a particular task. For example, when Xerox wanted to improve its procedures for filling customer orders, it studied how the mail-order company L. L. Bean processed its customer orders.

## The Plan-Do-Check-Act Cycle

Perhaps the most important and pervasive TQM problem-solving tool is the *plan-do-check-act (PDCA) cycle*, which is also referred to as the Deming Wheel.[1] The **plan-do-check-act cycle** is a systematic, fact-based approach to continuous improvement. The basic elements of the PDCA cycle are illustrated in Exhibit 1–3. The PDCA cycle applies a scientific method to problem solving. In the Plan phase, the problem-solving team analyzes data to identify possible causes for the problem and then proposes a solution. In the Do phase, an experiment is conducted. In the Check phase, the results of the experiment are analyzed. And in the Act phase, if the results of the experiment are favourable, the plan is implemented. If the results of the experiment are not favourable, the team goes back to the original data and starts all over again.

**Exhibit 1–3**
The Plan-Do-Check-Act Cycle

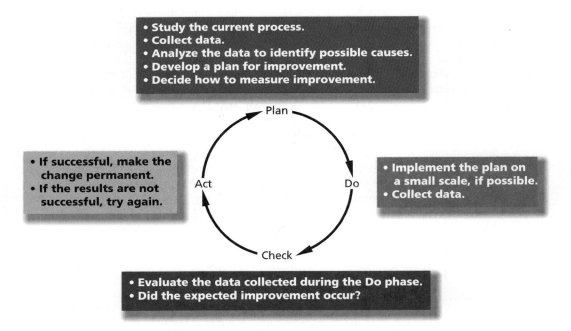

[1]Dr. W. Edwards Deming, a pioneer in TQM, introduced many of the elements of TQM to Japanese industry after World War II. TQM was further refined and developed at Japanese companies, such as Toyota.

## An Example of TQM in Practice

Victor Manufacturing Plant (hereafter, VMP), a branch plant of Victor Corporation (which is the disguised name of a real company), provides a good example of TQM in practice.[2] VMP, based in southern Ontario, is a supplier to the large auto manufacturers (Daimler-Chrysler, Ford, General Motors, Toyota). With quality becoming a very important consideration for the survival of all auto suppliers, VMP initiated a program of continuous improvement, called Excellence in Manufacturing (EIM), by focusing on JIT and TQM programs. Very soon, quality pervaded everyone's thinking within the plant. Management at VMP soon realized the importance of establishing teams to identify and solve quality problems; these teams were known as EIM groups.

In identifying and solving the problem of high scrap on a particular production line, the team used the PDCA cycle. The EIM group proceeded as follows to identify the first-level source of the problem (as recorded in the minutes of the meeting):

> We decided to start at the trunnion grinders as our first objective at reducing scrap. As we investigated the problem, we found that over a period of one year, 4,000 pieces were scrapped out at the grinders. We have 10 grinders, so when you break it down daily, it is less than two pieces a day per grinder. Then we looked at the Kingsbury drill scrap. It was 2,600 pieces for the year and we have only two machines.... Less than half our production goes through this operation, so we are double the percentage scrap off the Kingsbury drill. We will now work on reducing scrap at the Kingsbury.

After identifying the first-level source of the problem, the group ran experiments and collected more data to identify the potential causes of scrap at the Kingsbury drill, prepared pareto charts documenting the causes, identified alternatives, implemented the chosen one, and ran more tests to ensure that scrap was eliminated. They then moved on to attack the next major problem causing scrap. Note how VMP followed the PDCA cycle to problem solving as a group.

In sum, TQM provides tools and techniques for continuous improvement based on facts and analysis, and if properly implemented, it avoids counterproductive organizational infighting.

## Quality Management is Widely Used                    *in business today*

Many Canadian organizations have successfully implemented quality management principles and have received recognition from the National Quality Institute (NQI) whose mission is to inspire excellence in Canada. Recent recipients of the Canada Awards for Excellence include such organizations as AMEX Canada Inc., British Columbia Transplant Society, Canada Post-(Saskatoon Operations), Cardiac Care Network of Ontario, Celestica International Inc., Dana Canada Inc., Delta Hotels, Flemington Public School, Gleneagles Elementary School, Homewood Health Centre, Honeywell Consumer Products Group, IBM Canada Ltd., Mullen Trucking, SKF Canada, and Telus Mobility Inc.

Source: http://www.nqi.ca/english/CAE_recipients.htm

## Process Re-engineering

*Process re-engineering* is a radical approach to improvement that managers can use to remove waste from business processes. **Process re-engineering** diagrams a

---

[2]Source: Lindsay, R. M. and S. S. Kalagnanam, *The Adoption of Just-In-Time Production Systems in Canada and Their Association with Management Control Practices*, Hamilton: The Society of Management Accountants of Canada, 1993, pp. 69–78. Reprinted with permission from CMA Canada.

*business process* in detail, questions it, and then completely redesigns it in order to eliminate unnecessary steps, reduce opportunities for errors, and reduce costs. This is in direct contrast to approaches where an existing process is continuously tweaked to generate small incremental improvements. A **business process** is any series of steps that are followed in order to carry out a task in a business. For example, the steps followed to make a large pineapple and Canadian bacon pizza at Godfather's Pizza are a business process. The steps followed by your bank when you deposit a cheque are a business process.

Process re-engineering focuses on *simplification* and *elimination of wasted effort*. A central idea of process re-engineering is that *all activities that do not add value to a product or service should be eliminated.* Activities that do not add value to a product or service that customers are willing to pay for are known as **non–value-added activities.** For example, moving large batches of partially completed goods from one workstation to another is a non–value-added activity that can be eliminated by redesigning the factory layout to bring the workstations closer together.[3]

*in business* | *today*   **Process Re-engineering Works**

Processing travel claims can often be a nightmare. Necho Systems Corp., supplier of travel and entertainment (T&E) software, allowed various companies to process more efficiently travel claims for business trips. This particular software lets employees enter expenses quickly and easily using their "personal digital assistants (PDAs)," such as Palm Pilots without having to go to the office and manually filling out claims. Most importantly, the forms can be filled during their free time (e.g., while waiting at a hotel or airport), since access is readily available. As for the employers, processing claims becomes straightforward because they are all in one place, which avoids the need for sorting through each claim manually, thereby reducing the amount of handling. An additional benefit is that security is enhanced when employers automate claims processing. It normally costs about $25 to $35 to manually process the claim, but the new software would reduce the cost by more than 50%, asserts Necho. As well, firms can better control their travel spending by ensuring greater compliance with travel policies and striking better deals with travel vendors.

Source: Tausz, A. "Easing Expenses," *CMA Management*, November 2001, pp. 48–49. Reprinted with permission from CMA Canada.

## The Problem of Employee Morale

Employee resistance is a recurrent problem in process re-engineering. The cause of much of this resistance is the fear that employees may lose their jobs. Employees reason that if process re-engineering succeeds in eliminating non–value-added activities, there will be less work to do and management may be tempted to reduce the payroll. Process re-engineering, if carried out insensitively and without regard to such fears, can undermine morale and will ultimately fail to improve the bottom line (i.e., profits). As with other improvement projects, employees must be convinced that the end result of the improvement will be more secure, rather than less secure, jobs. Real improvement can have this effect if management uses the improvement to generate more business, rather than to cut the workforce. If by improving processes the company is able to produce a better product at lower cost, the company will have the competitive strength to prosper. And a prosperous company is a much more secure employer than a company that is in trouble.

---

[3]Activity-based costing and activity-based management, both of which are discussed in a later chapter, can be helpful in identifying areas in the company that could benefit from process re-engineering.

# The Theory of Constraints (TOC)

A **constraint** is some kind of a hurdle (or obstacle) that prevents people from getting more of what they want. For example, each day has only 24 hours, which appears to be a constraint for all of us (students, parents, working adults). We have to juggle our activities such that we are able to complete them (or not complete all of them) within the available time. Every individual and every organization face at least one constraint. For example, Petro Canada has a limited number of pumps at each of its gas stations, which means customers have to wait for their turn or else go to a competitor.

The **theory of constraints (TOC)** framework focuses on effectively managing constraints as the key to success. For example, Petro Canada could consider one of several options: (1) install additional pumps (but this may be prohibitively expensive), (2) increase pumping speed, or (3) introduce fast checkout. All of these can help in reducing customer waiting time and potentially increase revenues.

## An Example of TOC

ProSport Equipment, Inc. manufactures aluminium tennis racquets using the production process illustrated in Exhibit 1–4. The capacity of each workstation is stated in terms of the maximum number of racquets that can be processed in a week. For example, the aluminium extruding workstation can extrude enough aluminium each week to build as many as 2,500 tennis racquets. Referring to Exhibit 1–4, what is the maximum rate of output of tennis racquets that can be sustained in a week? The rate of output of the entire system is limited by the rate of output of the slowest workstation, which is frame assembly with a rate of output of only 1,800 racquets per week. Even though the other workstations can process more than 1,800 racquets per week, the entire production line can process only 1,800 racquets per week. The frame assembly workstation is the *bottleneck*. In addition, if demand exceeds 1,800 racquets per week, the frame assembly workstation is the constraint.

Several important observations can be made using this simple example. First, if managers try to keep each workstation busy all of the time, the result will be frustration and an ever-increasing pile of uncompleted units waiting to be processed through the frame assembly workstation. Shaping can process 2,200 units per week, whereas frame assembly can process only 1,800 units per week. If both workstations are kept busy all of the time processing units, the inevitable result will be 400 units being added each week to the pile of uncompleted units waiting to be processed through the frame assembly workstation.

Second, if demand exceeds 1,800 units per week, the only way the company can satisfy demand (and thereby increase profits) is to increase the capacity of the constraint, which is frame assembly. There are several ways the capacity of the constraint can be increased. These will be discussed in detail in a later chapter, but one way to increase capacity is to focus the TQM and process re-engineering efforts on the constraint.

Consider what would happen if process re-engineering were used to improve one of the workstations that is not a constraint. Suppose, for example, that the handgrip fabrication process is re-engineered so that it requires only half as much time to wrap a handgrip. Will this increase profits? The answer is "Probably not." Handgrip fabrication already has plenty of excess capacity; it is capable of processing 3,200 racquets per week, which is far more than the bottleneck can handle. Speeding up this process will simply create more excess capacity. Unless resources can now be shifted from handgrip fabrication to the constraint area (frame assembly) or unless spending can be cut in the handgrip fabrication work centre, there will be no increase in profits. In contrast, if the processing time were cut in half in frame assembly, which is the constraint, the company could produce and sell more tennis racquets, and this should have a direct and immediate positive impact on profits.

**Exhibit 1–4**
A Flowchart of an Aluminium
Tennis Racquet Production Line

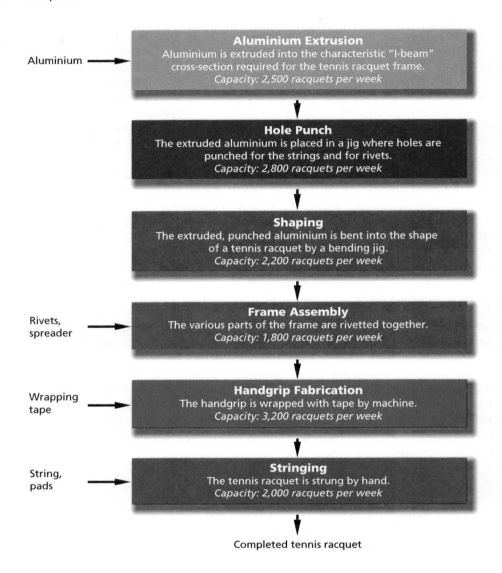

## TOC and Continuous Improvement

In TOC, an analogy is often drawn between a business process—such as the tennis racquet production line—and a chain. What is the most effective way to increase the strength of a chain? Should you concentrate your efforts on strengthening the strongest link, the largest link, all the links, or the weakest link? Clearly, focusing effort on the weakest link will bring the biggest benefit.

Continuing with this analogy, the procedure to follow in strengthening the chain is straightforward. First, identify the weakest link, which is the constraint. Second, do not place a greater strain on the system than the weakest link can handle. Third, concentrate the improvement efforts on strengthening the weakest link. Fourth, if the improvement efforts are successful, eventually the weakest link will improve to the point where it is no longer the weakest link. At this point, the new weakest link (i.e., the new constraint) must be identified, and the improvement efforts must be shifted over to that link. This simple sequential process provides a powerful strategy for continuous improvement. The TOC approach is a perfect complement to TQM and process re-engineering—it focuses improvement efforts where they are likely to be most effective.

# Ethical Responsibility

**Learning Objective 5**
Describe the importance of ethical responsibility and explain the need for ethical codes of conduct.

As mentioned in the opening paragraph of this chapter, the conduct of organizations is an extremely important issue all over the world. As businesses interact more and more with organizations in different parts of the world, they must be cautious that the companies they deal with are worth dealing with. Unfortunately, we find that many businesses, governments, and not-for-profit and charitable organizations have engaged in questionable practices which have affected their own reputations as well as those of other stakeholders (such as employees and investors). When government departments engage in such practices, it affects the tax payer. Although these allegations and scandals have received considerable attention, it is important to remember that there are many other businesses and other organizations that conduct their affairs in a responsible manner. Nonetheless, no organization can claim to be 100% free from the possibility of such events taking place in the future.

Often, unethical behaviour is the result of managers and other top executives focusing exclusively on achieving short-term profits "at any cost." This can be very dangerous as it can drive employees to act unethically in order to meet the expectations of their superiors. "Those who engage in unethical behavior often justify their actions with one or more of the following reasons: (1) the organization expects unethical behavior, (2) everyone else is unethical, and/or (3) behaving unethically is the only way to get ahead."[4]

To counter the first justification for unethical behaviour, many organizations have implemented formal ethical codes of conduct. For example, Manitoba Hydro's purchasing department expects all of its buyers to abide by the Purchasing Management Association of Canada's Code of Ethics. These codes are generally broad-based statements of an organization's responsibilities to its employees, customers, suppliers, and the communities in which it operates. Codes rarely spell out specific do's and don'ts or suggest proper behaviour in specific situations. Instead, they provide broad guidelines.

## Whistle-Blowing Policies

*in business today*

Recent media attention to scandals in businesses and other organizations has increased the importance of ethical policies and procedures and codes of conduct. But employees in many organizations know when they are not followed. Should they "blow the whistle?" According to a 2003 survey conducted in the United States, 65% of the respondents reported that they will likely report misconduct (this number is up from 48% in 1994). Many large corporations, such as the Royal Bank of Canada and Shell Canada, have implemented whistle-blowing policies to protect individuals who speak up. Other organizations, such as Ottawa-based Democracy Watch, continue to press for whistle-blowing provisions in both government and business.

Source: McLearn, Matthew. "A Snitch in Time," *Canadian Business*, Dec.–Jan. 2004, pp. 61–70. Reprinted with permission from Canadian Business.

## Professional Ethics

Accountants are generally considered the "guardians" of an organization's money. But, what if accountants themselves behave in an irresponsible manner? To counter such behaviour, professional accounting bodies in most parts of the world have developed codes of conduct to guide appropriate behaviour of accounting professions. For example, each of the provincial offices of CMA Canada (one of the three professional accounting bodies in Canada) has developed ethical guidelines for practising CMAs (certified

---

[4]Michael K. McCuddy, Karl E. Reichardt, and David Schroder, "Ethical Pressures: Fact or Fiction?" *Management Accounting*, April 1993, pp. 57–61.

management accountants).[5] Essentially, the Code of Ethics focuses on several key factors pertaining to an accountant's role; these include competence, responsibility, independence of thought and action, integrity, fairness, loyalty, confidentiality, and trust. Similarly, the *Guideline on Ethics for Professional Accountants*, issued in July 1990 by the International Federation of Accountants (IFAC), governs the activities of *all* professional accountants throughout the world, regardless of whether they are in public practice or employed in government service or private industry.

In addition to outlining ethical requirements in matters dealing with competence, objectivity, independence, and confidentiality, the IFAC's code also outlines the accountant's responsibilities in matters relating to taxes, fees and commissions, advertising and solicitation, the handling of monies, and cross-border activities. Where cross-border activities are involved, the IFAC ethical requirements must be followed if these requirements are stricter than the ethical requirements of the country in which the work is being performed. Canadian companies dealing with foreign governments are bound by the *Corruption of Foreign Public Officials Act* which prohibits company executives from offering gifts, payments, or other benefits to foreign government officials in order to receive favourable business treatment.

The ethical standards provide sound, practical advice for management accountants and managers. Most of the rules in the ethical standards are motivated by a very practical consideration—if these rules were not generally followed in business, then the economy would come to a screeching halt. Consider the following specific examples of the consequences of not abiding by the standards:

- Suppose employees could not be trusted with confidential information. Then top managers would be reluctant to distribute confidential information within the company. As a result, decisions would be based on incomplete information, and operations would deteriorate.
- Suppose employees accepted bribes from suppliers. Then contracts would tend to go to suppliers who pay the highest bribes, rather than to the most competent suppliers. Would you like to fly in an aircraft that had wings made by a subcontractor who was willing to pay the highest bribe to a purchasing agent? What would happen to the airline industry if its safety record deteriorated due to shoddy workmanship on contracted parts and assemblies?
- Suppose the presidents of companies routinely lied in their annual reports to shareholders and grossly distorted financial statements. If the basic integrity of a company's financial statements could not be relied on, investors and creditors would have little basis for making informed decisions. Suspecting the worst, rational investors would pay less for securities issued by companies. As a consequence, fewer funds would be available for productive investments and many firms might be unable to raise any funds at all. Ultimately, this would lead to slower economic growth, fewer goods and services, and higher prices.

As these examples suggest, if ethical standards were not generally adhered to, there would be undesirable consequences for everyone. Essentially, abandoning ethical standards would lead to a lower standard of living with lower-quality goods and services, less to choose from, and higher prices. In short, following ethical guidelines is not just a matter of being "nice"; it is absolutely essential for the smooth functioning of an advanced economy.

# Implications of the New Business Environment on Managerial Accounting

What are the implications of changes in the business environment described above? Organizations cannot use systems designed in the early 1900s to implement their

[5]For the code of ethics developed by the Certified Management Accountants of Ontario, see Appendix 1A.

strategies and achieve their objectives. To compete in a global world, it is necessary to have well-designed management accounting systems to guide managers. Organizations must question the usefulness of their existing managerial accounting tool kit and replace obsolete tools/techniques with more relevant ones. For example, Chapter 5 explains a new cost management method known as activity-based costing/management (ABC/ABM). In a nutshell, managers must employ methods that take into consideration the factors that drive costs, revenues, and profits. An excellent management accounting system will not by itself guarantee success, but a poorly designed system will certainly lead to failure.

# Organization of the Book

This book is designed to give you a basic idea of the types of management (*or internal*) accounting information useful to managers in their role to ensure that the main purpose of their organization is achieved. In doing so, the book begins by introducing cost terminology that will be used throughout the text. It then proceeds to describe different systems that are used to determine the cost per unit of providing a service or manufacturing a product. The book then focuses on the information required for planning, decision making, and control. In explaining each topic (conceptually and procedurally), the book briefly examines the impact of the lean business model. Although each individual chapter may focus on one or more specific topics, you are encouraged to integrate topics in an attempt to understand the inter-relationships among them.

# Summary

**LO1   Describe the work of management and the need for managerial accounting information.**
Managers carry out three major activities: planning, directing and motivating, and controlling. Managerial accounting information provided in such documents as budgets and profit reports provide valuable information to managers in order to carry out these activities effectively.

**LO2   Describe the key differences between financial and managerial accounting.**
Financial accounting reports are prepared for the use of external parties, such as shareholders and creditors, whereas managerial accounting reports are prepared for managers inside the organization.

**LO3   Describe the impact of globalization on business.**
Many factors have led to an increase in worldwide competition over the past three decades. Although this has resulted in a number of benefits for the customers, this also means that businesses must find new ways of competing.

**LO4   Explain the lean business model and its corresponding management practices.**
In an effort to remain competitive in the global marketplace, many businesses have adopted the lean business model. This consists of implementing management practices, such as just-in-time and total quality management, which can result in improvements in quality and costs.

**LO5   Describe the importance of ethical responsibility and explain the need for ethical codes of conduct.**
Unethical behaviour is often the result of top executives focusing exclusively on short-term profits at any cost. As businesses interact more and more, being ethically responsible is extremely important. Many organizations have implemented ethical codes of conduct to guide behaviour within organizations.

# Glossary

At the end of each chapter, a list of key terms for review is given, along with the definition of each term. (These terms are printed in boldface where they are defined in the chapter.) Carefully study each term to be sure you understand its meaning since the terms are used repeatedly in the chapters that follow. The list for Chapter 1 follows.

**Benchmarking** A study of organizations that are among the best in the world at performing a particular task. (p. 14)

**Budget** A detailed plan for the future, usually expressed in formal quantitative terms. (p. 5)

**Business process** A series of steps that are followed in order to carry out a task in a business. (p. 16)

**Constraint** A hurdle (or obstacle) that prevents people from getting more of what they want. (p. 17)

**Control** The process of instituting procedures and then obtaining feedback to ensure that all parts of the organization are functioning effectively and moving toward overall company goals. (p. 6)

**Controlling** Ensuring that the plan is actually carried out. (p. 5)

**Directing and motivating** Mobilizing people to carry out plans and run routine operations. (p. 5)

**Feedback** Accounting and other reports that help managers monitor performance and focus on problems and/or opportunities that might otherwise go unnoticed. (p. 6)

**Financial accounting** The discipline of accounting concerned with providing information to shareholders, creditors, and others outside the organization. (p. 4)

**Just-in-time (JIT)** A production and inventory control system in which materials are purchased and units are produced only as needed to meet actual customer demand. (p. 12)

**Lean business model** A business model that focuses on continuous improvement by eliminating waste in an organization. (p. 11)

**Managerial accounting** The discipline of accounting concerned with providing information to managers for use in planning, directing and motivating, and controlling within the organization. (p. 4)

**Non–value-added activity** An activity that consumes resources or takes time but that does not add value for which customers are willing to pay. (p. 16)

**Performance report** A detailed report comparing budgeted data with actual data. (p. 6)

**Plan-do-check-act (PDCA) cycle** A systematic approach to continuous improvement that applies the scientific method to problem solving. (p. 14)

**Planning** Selecting a course of action and specifying how the action will be implemented. (p. 5)

**Planning and control cycle** The flow of management activities through planning, directing and motivating, and controlling, and then back again to planning. (p. 6)

**Process Re-engineering** An approach to improvement that involves completely redesigning business processes in order to eliminate unnecessary steps, reduce errors, and reduce costs. (p. 15)

**Segment** Any part of an organization that can be evaluated independently of other parts and about which the manager seeks financial data. Examples include a line of service, a sales territory, a division, or a department. (p. 9)

**Theory of constraints (TOC)** A management approach that emphasizes the importance of managing constraints. (p. 17)

**Total quality management (TQM)** An approach to continuous improvement that focuses on customers and using teams of front-line workers to systematically identify and solve problems. (p. 14)

# Questions

1–1 What is the basic difference in orientation between financial and managerial accounting?
1–2 What are the three major activities of a manager?
1–3 Describe the steps in the planning and control cycle.
1–4 What are the major differences between financial and managerial accounting?
1–5 Describe the lean business model and its corresponding management practices.

# Appendix 1A: Code of Ethics—Certified Management Accountants of Ontario

As professionals and pre-eminent specialists in the field of management accounting, CMAs are bound by the Society's Code of Professional Ethics. This code stipulates and binds them to the highest level of care, duty and responsibility to their clients, the public, and their fellow professionals.

**Code of Professional Ethics**

All Members will adhere to the following:

(a) A Member will act at all times with:
  (i) responsibility for and fidelity to public needs;
  (ii) fairness and loyalty to such Member's associates, clients, and employers; and
  (iii) competence through devotion to high ideals of personal honour and professional integrity.

(b) A Member will:
  (i) maintain at all times independence of thought and action;
  (ii) not express an opinion on financial reports or statements without first assessing her or his relationship with her or his client to determine whether such Member might expect her or his opinion to be considered independent, objective, and unbiased by one who has knowledge of all the facts; and
  (iii) when preparing financial reports or statements or expressing an opinion on financial reports or statements disclose all material facts known to such Member in order not to make such financial reports or statements misleading, acquire sufficient information to warrant an expression of opinion, and report all material misstatements or departures from generally accepted accounting principles.

(c) A Member will:
  (i) not disclose or use any confidential information concerning the affairs of such Member's employer or client unless acting in the course of his or her duties or except when such information is required to be disclosed in the course of any defence of himself or herself or any associate or employee in any lawsuit or other legal proceeding or against alleged professional misconduct by order of lawful authority of the Board or any committee of the Society in the proper exercise of their duties but only to the extent necessary for such purpose;
  (ii) inform his or her employer or client of any business connections or interests of which such Member's employer or client would reasonably expect to be informed;
  (iii) not, in the course of exercising his or her duties on behalf of such Member's employer or client, hold, receive, bargain for, or acquire any fee, remuneration, or benefit without such employer's or client's knowledge and consent; and
  (iv) take all reasonable steps, in arranging any engagement as a consultant, to establish a clear understanding of the scope and objectives of the work before it is commenced and will furnish the client with an estimate of cost, preferably before the engagement is commenced, but in any event as soon as possible thereafter.

(d) A Member will:
  (i) conduct himself or herself toward other Members with courtesy and good faith;
  (ii) not commit an act discreditable to the profession;
  (iii) not engage in or counsel any business or occupation which, in the opinion of the Society, is incompatible with the professional ethics of a management accountant;
  (iv) not accept any engagement to review the work of another Member for the same employer except with the knowledge of that Member, or except where the connection of that Member with the work has been terminated, unless the Member reviews the work of others as a normal part of his or her responsibilities;
  (v) not attempt to gain an advantage over other Members by paying or accepting a commission in securing management accounting work;
  (vi) uphold the principle of adequate compensation for management accounting work; and
  (vii) not act maliciously or in any other way which may adversely reflect on the public or professional reputation or business of another Member.

(e) A Member will:
  (i) at all times maintain the standards of competence expressed by the Board from time to time;
  (ii) disseminate the knowledge upon which the profession of management accounting is based to others within the profession and generally promote the advancement of the profession;
  (iii) undertake only such work as he or she is competent to perform by virtue of his or her training and experience and will, where it would be in the best interests of an employer or client, engage, or advise the employer or client to engage, other specialists;
  (iv) expose before the proper tribunals of the Society any incompetent, unethical, illegal, or unfair conduct or practice of a Member which involves the reputation, dignity, or honour of the Society; and
  (v) endeavour to ensure that a professional partnership or company, with which such Member is associated as a partner, principal, director or officer, abides by the Code of Professional Ethics and the rules of professional conduct established by the Society.

Source: http://www.cma-canada.org/ontario/00_index_60.asp.

# Chapter Two

# Cost Concepts

## A Look Back

In the previous chapter, we introduced the three main activities of a manager and the need for managerial accounting information. We then compared financial and managerial accounting information. We also addressed some of the challenges faced by management and described the lean business model.

## A Look at This Chapter

We define many of the terms that managers use to classify costs in business. Because these terms are used throughout the text, you should ensure that you are familiar with each of them.

## A Look Ahead

Chapters 3, 4, and 5 describe costing systems that are used to compute product/service costs. Chapters 3 and 4 describe two contrasting costing systems: job-order costing and product costing, and Chapter 5 describes activity-based costing, a new approach to cost allocation and cost management.

## Chapter Outline

**Cost Classification by Behaviour**
- Variable Cost
- Fixed Cost

**Cost Classification by Traceability**
- Direct Cost
- Indirect Cost

**Cost Classification by Relevance**
- Differential Cost and Revenue
- Opportunity Cost
- Sunk Cost

**Cost Classification by Function**
- Manufacturing Costs
- Nonmanufacturing Costs

**Product Costs versus Period Costs**
- Product Costs
- Period Costs

**Cost Classifications on Financial Statements**
- The Balance Sheet
- The Income Statement
- Schedule of Cost of Goods Manufactured

**Product Costs—A Closer Look**
- An Example of Cost Flows

**Cost Classification Summary**

## DECISION FEATURE Understanding Costs Important to TELUS

TELUS Corporation, headquartered in Vancouver, is the largest telecommunications company in Western Canada and the second largest in the country, offering a wide range of communication services. In 2002, TELUS's total assets exceeded $18 billion and its revenue $7 billion. Needless to say, the company's costs also run into the billions. Ongoing cost control is important to ensure continued financial success.

In recognition of the importance of cost control, TELUS embarked upon a major operational and capital efficiency program which includes some elements of the lean business model described in Chapter 1. Although TELUS incurred one-time costs, management expected that these costs will be more than offset by the recurring annual expected savings in operating expenses of about $550 million, as well as a reduction in capital expenditures. As at the end of the first quarter of 2003, the program generated savings of $245 and $1,100 million, respectively, in operating expenses and capital expenditures.

Large telecommunication companies, such as TELUS, usually have a high proportion of fixed costs due to the infrastructure required to provide services to customers. Automating processes performed by humans usually means a reduction in recurring salary expenses but a corresponding increase in amortization (depreciation) expenses and maintenance costs. Understanding the nature of costs and the implications of alternative cost reduction programs is very important in order to decide which program to implement.

Sources: http://about.telus.com/investors/annualreport2002/english/downloads/annualreport2002.pdf, and http://about.telus.com/investors/operation_efficiency.html.

## Learning Objectives

*After studying Chapter 2, you should be able to:*

**LO1** Define and give examples of variable and fixed costs.

**LO2** Define and give examples of direct and indirect costs.

**LO3** Define and give examples of cost classifications used in making decisions: differential costs, opportunity costs, and sunk costs.

**LO4** Identify and give examples of each of the three basic manufacturing cost categories.

**LO5** Distinguish between product costs and period costs and give examples of each.

**LO6** Prepare an income statement including calculation of the cost of goods sold.

**LO7** Prepare a schedule of cost of goods manufactured.

osts are incurred by all kinds of organizations: government (e.g., City of Victoria), hospitals (e.g., Ontario General Hospital), educational institutions (e.g., Brandon University), and merchandising, service and manufacturing companies (e.g., Canadian Tire, Myers Norris Penny, and Toyota Canada). The costs incurred may be one-time or recurring and may differ depending on the need. Managers find it useful to classify costs in different ways in order to facilitate their analysis. In general, costs can be classified using four broad categories: behaviour, traceability, relevance, and function. In this chapter, we will discuss each of the cost classification categories.

# Cost Classification by Behaviour

**Learning Objective 1**
Define and give examples of variable and fixed costs.

Managers often need to understand how costs will behave in response to a certain activity; such an understanding is useful for cost estimation, planning, and cost/profitability analysis. For instance, a manager at Air Canada may want to estimate the impact of a 10% increase in passengers on its catering costs. It seems reasonable to assume that an increase in the number of passengers will result in a proportionate increase in catering costs. The airline will have to acquire 10% more food and drinks. Therefore, we will say that catering costs *vary* with respect to the number of passengers. On the other hand, a 10% increase in the number of passengers will not require additional fuel or even additional flight attendants; this means that fuel and flight attendant costs do not vary, or are *fixed*, with respect to the number of passengers.

**Cost behaviour** is the way a cost will respond to changes in the level of business activity (such as the number of passengers flying Air Canada). As the level of activity rises or falls, a particular cost may rise or fall, respectively, or may remain constant. For planning purposes, a manager must be able to estimate how different costs will behave with respect to changes in business activity. Classifying costs as variable or fixed helps a manager make such predictions.

## Variable Cost

A **variable cost** is a cost that varies, in total, in direct proportion to changes in the level of activity. The activity can be expressed in many ways, such as output (units produced, units sold), miles driven, beds occupied, lines of print, hours worked, and so forth. As an example, consider the KIA car. Each auto requires one battery. As the output of autos increases and decreases, the number of batteries used will increase and decrease proportionately. If auto production goes up 10%, then the number of batteries used will also go up 10%. This means the total cost of batteries will also go up by 10%.

It is important to note that when we speak of a cost as being variable, we mean the *total* cost rises and falls as the activity level rises and falls. This idea is presented below, assuming that a KIA's battery costs $24:

| Number of Autos Produced | | Cost per Battery | Total Variable Cost— Batteries |
|---|---|---|---|
| 1 | .......... | $24 | $ 24 |
| 500 | .......... | 24 | 12,000 |
| 1,000 | .......... | 24 | 24,000 |

One interesting aspect of variable cost behaviour is that a variable cost is constant if expressed on a *per-unit* basis. Observe from the tabulation above that the per-unit cost of

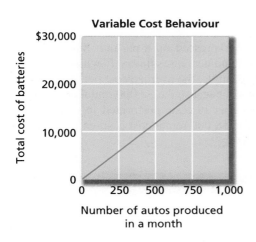

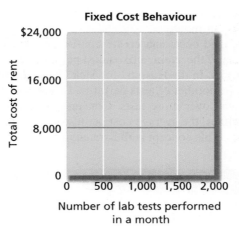

**Exhibit 2–1**
Variable and Fixed Cost Behaviour

batteries remains constant at $24, even though the total amount of cost involved increases and decreases with activity. The concept of a variable cost is shown in graphical form in Exhibit 2–1.

There are many examples of costs that are variable with respect to the products and services provided by a company. In a merchandising company, variable costs include such items as cost of goods sold, commissions to salespersons, and billing costs. In a hospital, the variable costs of providing health care services to patients would include the costs of the supplies, drugs, meals, and perhaps nursing services. In a manufacturing company, variable costs include such items as materials used in the product, wages of operators, lubricants, supplies, shipping costs, and sales commissions.

The activity causing changes in a variable cost need not be how much output is produced or sold. For example, the wages paid to employees at a Blockbuster Video outlet will depend on the number of hours the store is open and not strictly on the number of videos rented. In this case, we would say that wage costs are variable with respect to the hours of operation. Nevertheless, when we say that a cost is variable, we ordinarily mean it is variable with respect to the volume of revenue-generating output—in other words, how many videos are rented, how many patients are treated, and so on.

## Fixed Cost

A **fixed cost** is a cost that remains constant, in total, regardless of changes in the level of activity. Unlike variable costs, fixed costs are not affected by changes in activity. Consequently, as the activity level rises and falls, the fixed costs remain constant in total amount unless influenced by some outside force, such as a price change or a substantial increase in demand leading to an increase in the resource requirement. Rent is a good example of a fixed cost. Suppose the Hospital for Sick Children in Toronto rents for $8,000 per month a machine that tests blood samples for the presence of leukemia cells. The $8,000 monthly rental cost will be incurred regardless of the number of tests that may be performed during the month. The concept of a fixed cost is shown in graphic form in Exhibit 2–1.

Very few costs are completely fixed. Most will change if there is a large enough change in activity. For example, suppose that the capacity of the leukemia diagnostic machine at the hospital is 2,000 tests per month. If the hospital wishes to perform more than 2,000 tests in a month, it would be necessary to rent an additional machine, which would cause a jump in the fixed costs. When we say a cost is fixed, we mean it is fixed within some *relevant range*. The **relevant range** is the range of activity within which the assumptions about variable and fixed costs are valid. For example, the assumption that the rent for diagnostic machines is $8,000 per month is valid within the relevant range of 0 to 2,000 tests per month.

Fixed costs can create confusion if they are expressed on a per-unit basis. This is because the average fixed cost per unit increases and decreases *inversely* with changes in activity. In the Hospital for Sick Children, for example, the average cost per test will fall as the number of tests performed increases. This is because the $8,000 rental cost will be spread over more tests. Conversely, as the number of tests performed in the hospital declines, the average cost per test will rise, as the $8,000 rental cost is spread over fewer tests. This concept is illustrated in the table below:

| Monthly Rental Cost | Number of Tests Performed | Average Cost per Test |
|---|---|---|
| $8,000 | 10 | $800 |
| 8,000 | 500 | 16 |
| 8,000 | 2,000 | 4 |

Note that if the hospital performs only 10 tests each month, the rental cost of the equipment will average $800 per test. But if 2,000 tests are performed each month, the average cost will drop to only $4 per test. More will be said later about the problems created for both the accountant and the manager by this variation in unit costs.

Examples of fixed costs include straight-line depreciation, insurance, property taxes, rent, supervisory salaries, administrative salaries, and advertising.[1]

A summary of both variable and fixed cost behaviour is presented in Exhibit 2–2.

**Exhibit 2–2**
Summary of Variable and Fixed Cost Behaviour

| Cost | Behaviour of the Cost (within the relevant range) | |
|---|---|---|
| | In Total | Per Unit |
| Variable cost | Total variable cost increases and decreases in proportion to changes in the activity level. | Variable cost remains constant per unit. |
| Fixed cost | Total fixed cost is not affected by changes in the activity level within the relevant range. | Fixed cost per unit decreases as the activity level rises and increases as the activity level falls. |

*decision* | *maker*    **Financial Analyst**

You are a financial analyst for several clients who are interested in making investments in stable companies. You become aware of a privately owned airline that has been in business for 20 years and needs to raise $75 million in new capital. When you call one of your clients, she replies that she avoids investing in airlines because of the high proportion of fixed costs in this industry. How would you respond to this statement?

---

[1] *The Canadian Institute of Chartered Accountants (CICA) Handbook* uses the term amortization; however, Section 3061.29 states that the term "depreciation" can also be used.

# Cost Classification by Traceability

In addition to understanding costs by behaviour, managers also need to know whether or not costs can be traced to specific cost objects; this helps managers in accurately assigning costs. A **cost object** is anything for which cost data are desired—department, division, product, product line, customer, geographical territory. Costs that can be traced to specific cost objects are called *direct* costs; those that cannot be traced are called *indirect* costs.

## Direct Cost

A **direct cost** is a cost that pertains to a certain cost object and can be easily and economically traced to that cost object. As an example, the salary of the secretary of the University of Saskatchewan's Accounting Department is directly traceable to the department (the desired cost object).

## Indirect Cost

An **indirect cost** is a cost that cannot be easily and conveniently traced to the particular cost object under consideration. For example, a Campbell Soup factory may produce dozens of varieties of canned soups. The factory manager's salary would be an indirect cost of a particular variety, such as chicken noodle soup. The reason is that the factory manager's salary is not caused by any one variety of soup but, rather, is incurred as a consequence of running the entire factory. *To be traced to a cost object, such as a particular product, the cost must be caused by the cost object.* The factory manager's salary is called a *common cost* of producing the various products of the factory. A **common cost** is a cost that is incurred to support a number of cost objects but that cannot be traced to them individually. A common cost is a particular type of indirect cost.

A particular cost may be direct or indirect, depending on the cost object. While the Campbell Soup factory manager's salary is an *indirect* cost of manufacturing chicken noodle soup, it is a *direct* cost of the manufacturing division. In the first case, the cost object is the chicken noodle soup product. In the second case, the cost object is the entire manufacturing division.

# Cost Classification by Relevance

Given the importance of cost information for decision making, managers must be able to identify costs that are relevant for individual decisions. Cost classification by relevance helps in decision making. Only costs that are relevant to individual decisions must be used in the analysis preceding decision making. In general, *differential* and *opportunity* costs are relevant for most decisions, whereas *sunk* costs are irrelevant for any decision.

## Differential Cost and Revenue

Decisions involve choosing between alternatives. In business decisions, each alternative will have certain costs and benefits that must be compared with the costs and benefits of the other available alternatives. A difference in costs between any two alternatives is known as a **differential cost.** A difference in revenues between any two alternatives is known as **differential revenue.**

A differential cost is also known as an **incremental cost,** although technically an incremental cost should refer only to an increase in cost from one alternative to another; decreases in cost should be referred to as *decremental costs.* Differential cost is a broader term, encompassing both cost increases (incremental costs) and cost decreases (decremental costs) between alternatives.

The accountant's differential cost concept can be compared to the economist's marginal cost concept. In speaking of changes in cost and revenue, the economist employs the terms *marginal cost* and *marginal revenue*. The revenue that can be obtained from selling one more unit of product is called marginal revenue, and the cost involved in producing one more unit of product is called marginal cost. The economist's marginal concept is basically the same as the accountant's differential concept applied to a single unit of output.

Differential costs can be either fixed or variable. To illustrate, assume that Nature Way Cosmetics, Inc. is considering changing its marketing method from distribution through retailers to distribution by door-to-door direct sale. Present costs and revenues are compared with projected costs and revenues in the following table:

|  | Retailer Distribution (current) | Direct Sale Distribution (proposed) | Differential Costs and Revenues |
|---|---|---|---|
| Revenues (V) ................ | $700,000 | $800,000 | $100,000 |
| Cost of goods sold (V) ......... | 350,000 | 400,000 | 50,000 |
| Advertising (F) .............. | 80,000 | 45,000 | (35,000) |
| Commissions (V) ............. | –0– | 40,000 | 40,000 |
| Warehouse depreciation (F) ..... | 50,000 | 80,000 | 30,000 |
| Other expenses (F) ............ | 60,000 | 60,000 | –0– |
| Total ...................... | 540,000 | 625,000 | 85,000 |
| Net income ................. | $160,000 | $175,000 | $ 15,000 |

V = Variable; F = Fixed.

According to the above analysis, the differential revenue is $100,000, and the differential costs total $85,000, leaving a positive differential net income of $15,000 under the proposed marketing plan. The financial analysis suggests that Nature Way Cosmetics should implement the proposed plan. However, before making any changes, management must also consider nonfinancial factors, such as the effect of the new distribution policy on brand image.

In general, only the differences between alternatives are relevant in decisions. Those items that are the same under all alternatives are not affected by the decision and can be ignored. For example, in the Nature Way Cosmetics example above, the "Other expenses" category, which is $60,000 under both alternatives, can be ignored, since it is not affected by the decision. If it were removed from the calculations, the door-to-door direct selling method would still be preferred by $15,000. This is an extremely important principle in management accounting that we will return to in later chapters.

## *in business* *today*  Free Flights for Patients

Many corporate jets fly with only one or two executives on board. Priscilla Blum wondered why some of the empty seats could not be used to fly cancer patients who need specialized treatment outside their home area. Flying on a regular commercial airline can be an expensive and gruelling experience for cancer patients. Taking the initiative, she helped found the Corporate Angel Network. Currently, the organization arranges free flights on some 1,500 jets from over 500 companies. Since the jets fly anyway, filling a seat with a cancer patient does not involve any significant incremental cost for the companies that donate the service. Since its founding in 1981, the Corporate Angel Network has arranged over 11,000 free flights.

Source: Scott McCormack, "Waste Not, Want Not," *Forbes*, July 26, 1999, p. 118.

## Opportunity Cost

**Opportunity cost** is the potential benefit that is given up when one alternative is selected over another. To illustrate this important concept, consider the following examples:

**EXAMPLE 1**
Vicki has a part-time job that pays her $200 per week while attending college. She would like to spend a week at the beach during spring break, and her employer has agreed to give her the time off, but without pay. The $200 in lost wages would be an opportunity cost of taking the week off to be at the beach.

**EXAMPLE 2**
Suppose that Walmart Canada is considering investing a large sum of money in land that may be a site for a future store. Rather than invest the funds in land, the company could invest the funds in high-grade securities. If the land is acquired, the opportunity cost will be the investment income that could have been realized if the securities had been purchased instead.

**EXAMPLE 3**
Steve is employed with a company that pays him a salary of $30,000 per year. He is thinking about leaving the company and returning to school. Since returning to school would require that he give up his $30,000 salary, the forgone salary would be an opportunity cost of seeking further education.

Opportunity cost is not usually recorded in the accounts of an organization, but it is a cost that must be explicitly considered in every decision a manager makes. Virtually every alternative has some opportunity cost attached to it. In example 3 above, for instance, if Steve decides to stay at his job, there still is an opportunity cost involved: it is the greater income that could be realized in future years as a result of returning to school.

## Your Decision to Attend Class

*you decide*

When you make the decision to attend class, what are the opportunity costs that are inherent in that decision?

## Sunk Cost

A **sunk cost** is a cost *that has already been incurred* and that cannot be changed by any decision made now or in the future. Since sunk costs cannot be changed by any decision, they are not differential costs. Therefore, they can and should be ignored when making a decision; in other words, sunk costs are irrelevant.

To illustrate a sunk cost, assume that a company paid $50,000 several years ago for a special-purpose machine. The machine was used to make a product that is now obsolete and is no longer being sold. Even though in hindsight the purchase of the machine may have been unwise, no amount of regret can undo that decision. And it would be foolish to continue making the obsolete product in a misguided attempt to "recover" the original cost of the machine. In short, the $50,000 originally paid for the machine has already been incurred and cannot be a differential cost in any future decision. For this reason, such costs are said to be sunk and should be ignored in decisions.

## Cost Classification by Function

Another cost classification is based on function. Before discussing this further, it might be useful to understand that every organization carries out a sequence of activities to fulfill

**Exhibit 2–3**
Acadian Seaplants' Value Chain

its mission.[2] Such a sequence of activities is known as the **value chain** of that organization. Acadian Seaplants, located in Dartmouth, Nova Scotia, is a diversified, technology-based manufacturer of natural, specialty fertilizers, crop biostimulants, feed, food, food ingredients, and brewery supplies derived from select species of marine plants. Acadian is a fully integrated company involved in activities ranging from marine plant cultivation and the hand harvesting of pure seaweeds to product and application development, manufacturing, and technical customer support. Acadian's value chain is considerably broad (see Exhibit 2–3). In contrast, some competitors of Acadian may be less integrated—involved only in product and application development and in manufacturing. Such competitors must depend on other organizations for the cultivation and harvesting of seaweeds (front end of the value chain) and customer support (back end of the value chain); their value chains would be narrow.

Cost classification by function consists of associating costs with the type of activity for which that cost is incurred (e.g., manufacturing, marketing, or administration). For a retailer, such as Zellers, costs pertaining to the procurement and stacking of the goods to be sold would be classified as merchandising costs, whereas advertising costs and the costs of the accountants and legal personnel may be classified under selling and administrative costs. Such a distinction is more pronounced for manufacturing companies; we can distinguish between manufacturing and nonmanufacturing costs.

## Manufacturing Costs

**Learning Objective 4**
Identify and give examples of each of the three basic manufacturing cost categories.

Similar to merchandising companies that must procure the goods they sell, manufacturing companies must produce the goods they sell; we use the term **manufacturing costs** to identify the costs associated with production activity. Typically, there are three types of manufacturing costs; we discuss each of these below as they might pertain to Ambutech, a division of Winnipeg-based Melet Plastics, Inc., which produces a variety of canes for the disabled and visually impaired.

**DIRECT MATERIALS**    The materials that go into the final product are called **raw materials.** At the least, the raw materials required for one line of Ambutech's canes would include aluminium for the body of the cane and plastic or wood for the handle.

The term "raw materials" is somewhat misleading because it seems to imply unprocessed natural resources. Actually, raw materials refer to any materials that are used in the final (finished) product of a company. Note, however, that the finished product of one company can be the raw material for another company. For example, Ambutech might be purchasing "ready to assemble" cane handles from a supplier, rather than producing them in-house. Whether to make the cane handles or buy them from outside can be an important

---

[2] The term activity was introduced in the section on cost behaviour and was used to denote a cost driver (i.e., something that causes costs to go up or down). However, activity in this section pertains to a series of tasks or steps that are carried out by an organization to fulfill its mission.

United Colors of Benetton, an Italian apparel company headquartered in Ponzano, is unusual in that it is involved in all activities in the "value chain" from clothing design through manufacturing, distribution, and ultimate sale to customers in Benetton retail outlets. Most companies are involved in only one or two of these activities. Looking at this company allows us to see how costs are distributed across the entire value chain. A recent income statement from the company contained the following data:

|  | Millions of Euro | Percent of Net Sales |
|---|---|---|
| Net sales | 1,461 | 100.0% |
| Cost of sales | 814 | 55.7 |
| Selling and general and administrative expenses: |  |  |
| Payroll and related cost | 107 | 7.3 |
| Distribution and transport | 23 | 1.6 |
| Sales commissions | 69 | 4.7 |
| Advertising and promotion | 82 | 5.6 |
| Depreciation and amortization | 74 | 5.1 |
| Other expenses | 109 | 7.5 |
| Total selling and general and administrative expenses | 464 | 31.8% |

Even though this company spends large sums on advertising and runs its own shops, the cost of sales is still quite high in relation to the net sales—56% of net sales. And despite the company's lavish advertising campaigns, advertising and promotion costs amounted to only a little over 5% of net sales. (Note: One Euro was worth about Canadian $1.545 at the time of this financial report.)

decision which would influence Ambutech's costs; we will examine such decisions in Chapter 12.

The aluminium sheets and plastic handles can also be called **direct materials,** since they become an integral part of the cane. As you can see, the quantity of direct materials required varies proportionately with the number of units produced. Therefore, "direct materials" is a variable cost with respect to production activity.

In addition to the direct materials, Ambutech would also be using other **indirect materials** in the manufacturing process (e.g., screws, glue, solder, and other supplies) that are not integral parts of the cane. Indirect materials are relatively insignificant in value, and their costs are either not traceable to, or not worth tracing directly to, the finished product. The cost of indirect materials is included as part of manufacturing overhead, which is discussed later in this section.

**DIRECT LABOUR**  The term **direct labour** is reserved for those labour costs that can be easily (i.e., physically and conveniently) traced to individual units of product. Direct labour is sometimes called *touch labour*, since direct labour workers typically touch the product while it is being made. In the case of Ambutech, this would include the wages and benefits of the individuals directly involved in rolling the aluminium sheets to form the body of the canes and those involved in assembling the canes. As you can see, direct labour costs are variable in nature, although this trend is changing.

Labour costs that cannot be physically traced to the creation of products, or that can be traced only at great cost and inconvenience, are termed **indirect labour** and treated as part of manufacturing overhead, along with indirect materials. Indirect labour includes the labour costs of janitors, supervisors, materials handlers, and night security guards. Although the efforts of these workers are essential to production, it would be either impractical or impossible to accurately trace their costs to specific units of product.

In some industries, major shifts are taking place in the structure of labour costs. Sophisticated automated equipment, run and maintained by skilled indirect workers, is increasingly replacing direct labour. In a few companies, direct labour has become such a minor element of cost that it has disappeared altogether as a separate cost category. More is said in later chapters about this trend and about the impact it is having on cost systems. However, the vast majority of manufacturing and service companies throughout the world continue to recognize direct labour as a separate cost category. In service companies, labour can often be a significant portion of the total cost of providing a service.

**MANUFACTURING OVERHEAD**   In addition to direct materials and direct labour, Ambutech would also be incurring other costs related to manufacturing. These might include indirect materials and indirect labour (discussed earlier), factory maintenance, utilities, property taxes, and depreciation on equipment and factory building. Such costs are included in a separate category called **manufacturing overhead.** It is important to remember that Ambutech will incur utility, maintenance, and depreciation expenses associated with its selling and administrative functions; however, these costs are *not* recorded as part of manufacturing overhead. Only costs that are associated with the manufacturing function (i.e., operating the factory) are included in the manufacturing overhead category.

Various names are used for manufacturing overhead, such as *indirect manufacturing cost*, *factory overhead*, and *factory burden*. All of these terms are synonymous with *manufacturing overhead*.

Manufacturing overhead combined with direct labour is called **conversion cost.** This term stems from the fact that direct labour costs and overhead costs are incurred to convert raw materials into finished products. Direct labour combined with direct materials is called **prime cost.**

## Nonmanufacturing Costs

Generally, nonmanufacturing costs are subclassified into two categories:

1. Marketing or selling costs.
2. Administrative costs.

**Marketing or selling costs** include all costs necessary to secure customer orders and get the finished product or service into the hands of the customer. These costs are often called *order-getting and order-filling costs.* Examples of marketing costs include advertising, shipping, sales travel, sales commissions, sales salaries, and costs of finished goods warehouses.

**Administrative costs** include all executive, organizational, and clerical costs associated with the *general management* of an organization, rather than with manufacturing, marketing, or selling. Examples of administrative costs include executive compensation, general accounting, secretarial, public relations, and similar costs involved in the overall, general administration of the organization *as a whole.*

# Product Costs versus Period Costs

Another classification by function that is often used synonymously with manufacturing versus nonmanufacturing costs is that of *product* versus *period* costs. To understand the distinction between product and period costs, we must first refresh our understanding of the matching principle from financial accounting.

The *matching principle* is based on the accrual concept and states that *costs incurred to generate a particular revenue should be recognized as expenses in the same period that the revenue is recognized.* This means that if a cost is incurred to acquire or make something that will eventually be sold, then the cost should be recognized as an expense only when the sale takes place—that is, when the benefit occurs. Such costs are called *product costs.*

**Learning Objective 5**
Distinguish between product costs and period costs and give examples of each.

## Product Costs

For financial accounting purposes, **product costs** include all of the costs that are involved in acquiring or making a product. In the case of a merchandising firm, such as Hudson's Bay Company (HBC), product costs would include the costs associated with procuring (or acquiring) the merchandise HBC sells, whereas for a manufacturing company, product costs include direct materials and labour and manufacturing overhead. Product costs are "attached" to goods when they are acquired or produced and are carried forward to an inventory account which appears on the balance sheet. Consequently, product costs are also known as **inventoriable costs.** HBC's 2002 annual report showed a merchandise inventory balance of about $1.49 billion (20% of revenue).

As and when the goods are sold, the amounts attached to the quantities sold are "expensed" (i.e., matched against sales revenue) and carried forward to the "cost of goods sold" account which appears on the income statement. It is important to note that product costs may not be "expensed" in the period in which they are incurred; instead, the period when the goods are sold is critical for determining when to expense the product costs.

## Period Costs

**Period costs** are all the costs that are not included in product costs. These costs are expensed on the income statement in the period in which they are incurred, using the usual rules of accrual accounting you have already learned in financial accounting. Period costs are not included as part of the cost of either purchased or manufactured goods. Sales commissions and office rent are good examples of the kind of costs we are talking about. Neither commission nor office rent is included as part of the cost of purchased or manufactured goods. Rather, both items are treated as expenses on the income statement in the period in which they are incurred. Thus, they are said to be period costs.

As suggested above, *all selling and administrative expenses are considered to be period costs.* Therefore, advertising, executive salaries, sales commissions, public relations, and other nonmanufacturing costs discussed earlier would all be period costs. They will appear on the income statement as expenses in the period in which they are incurred.

Exhibit 2–4 contains a summary of cost classifications by function.

## Cost Classifications on Financial Statements

In your prior accounting training, you learned that firms prepare periodic financial reports for creditors, shareholders, and others to show the financial condition of the firm and the firm's earnings performance over some specified interval.

The financial statements prepared by a *manufacturing* company are more complex than the statements prepared by, say, a merchandising company. Manufacturing companies are more complex organizations than merchandising companies because the manufacturing company must produce its goods as well as market them. The production process gives

**Exhibit 2–4**
Summary of Cost
Classifications by Function

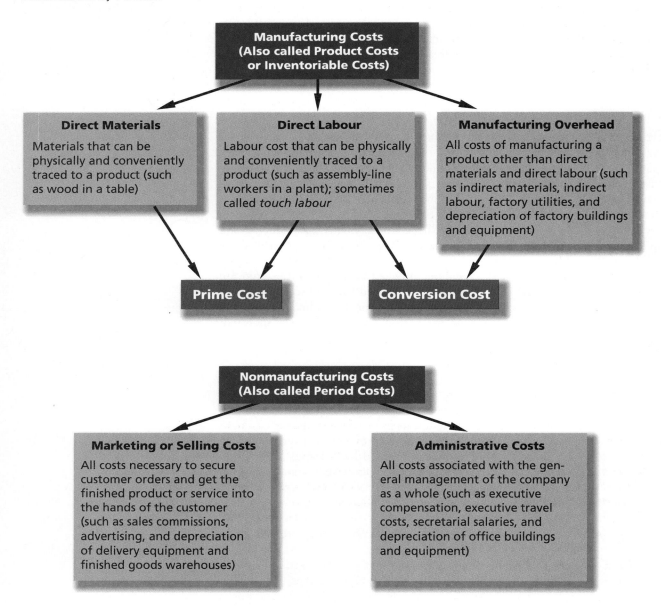

rise to many costs that do not exist in a merchandising company, and somehow these costs must be accounted for on the manufacturing company's financial statements. In this section, we focus our attention on how this accounting is carried out on the balance sheet and in the income statement.

## The Balance Sheet

The balance sheet, or statement of financial position, of a manufacturing company is similar to that of a merchandising company. However, the inventory accounts differ between the two types of companies. A merchandising company has only one class of inventory—

goods purchased from suppliers that are awaiting resale to customers. In contrast, manufacturing companies have three classes of inventories—*raw materials*, *work in process*, and *finished goods*. Raw materials, as we have noted, are the materials that are used to make a product. **Work in process** consists of units of product that are only partially complete and will require further work before they are ready for sale to a customer. **Finished goods** consist of units of product that have been completed but have not yet been sold to customers. The overall inventory figure is usually broken down into these three classes of inventories in a footnote to the financial statements.

We will use two companies—Halifax Manufacturing and Brandon Bookstore—to illustrate the concepts discussed in this section. Halifax Manufacturing makes precision brass fittings for yachts, and Brandon Bookstore specializes in books about Canadian history.

The footnotes to Halifax Manufacturing's Annual Report reveal the following information concerning its inventories:

### HALIFAX MANUFACTURING CORPORATION
#### Inventory Accounts

|  | Beginning Balance | Ending Balance |
|---|---|---|
| Raw materials | $ 60,000 | $ 50,000 |
| Work in process | 90,000 | 60,000 |
| Finished goods | 125,000 | 175,000 |
| Total inventory accounts | $275,000 | $285,000 |

Halifax Manufacturing's raw materials inventory would consist largely of brass rods and brass blocks. The work in process inventory would consist of partially completed brass fittings, and the finished goods inventory would consist of brass fittings that are ready to be sold to customers.

In contrast, the inventory account at Brandon Bookstore would consist entirely of the costs of books the company has purchased from publishers for resale to the public. In merchandising companies like Brandon, these inventories may be called *merchandise inventory.* The beginning and ending balances in this account appear as follows:

### BRANDON BOOKSTORE
#### Inventory Accounts

|  | Beginning Balance | Ending Balance |
|---|---|---|
| Merchandise inventory | $100,000 | $150,000 |

## The Income Statement

Exhibit 2–5 compares the income statements of Brandon Bookstore and Halifax Manufacturing. For purposes of illustration, these statements contain more detail about cost of goods sold than you will generally find in published financial statements.

At first glance, the income statements of merchandising and manufacturing firms like Brandon Bookstore and Halifax Manufacturing are very similar. The only apparent difference is in the labels of some of the entries in the computation of the cost of goods sold.

**Learning Objective 6**
Prepare an income statement including calculation of the cost of goods sold.

## Exhibit 2–5

Comparative Income Statements: Merchandising and Manufacturing Companies

### MERCHANDISING COMPANY
#### Brandon Bookstore

| | | | |
|---|---|---:|---:|
| Sales ..................................... | | | $1,000,000 |
| Cost of goods sold: | | | |
|   Beginning merchandise inventory ............. | | $100,000 | |
|   Add: Purchases ......................... | | 650,000 | |
|   Goods available for sale ................... | | 750,000 | |
|   Deduct: Ending merchandise inventory ........ | | 150,000 | 600,000 |
| Gross margin ............................... | | | 400,000 |
| Less operating expenses: | | | |
|   Selling expense ......................... | | 100,000 | |
|   Administrative expense .................... | | 200,000 | 300,000 |
| Net income ................................ | | | $ 100,000 |

The cost of merchandise inventory purchased from outside suppliers during the period.

### MANUFACTURING COMPANY
#### Halifax Manufacturing

| | | | |
|---|---|---:|---:|
| Sales ..................................... | | | $1,500,000 |
| Cost of goods sold: | | | |
|   Beginning finished goods inventory ........... | | $125,000 | |
|   Add: Cost of goods manufactured ............ | | 850,000 | |
|   Goods available for sale ................... | | 975,000 | |
|   Deduct: Ending finished goods inventory ....... | | 175,000 | 800,000 |
| Gross margin ............................... | | | 700,000 |
| Less operating expenses: | | | |
|   Selling expense ......................... | | 250,000 | |
|   Administrative expense .................... | | 300,000 | 550,000 |
| Net income ................................ | | | $ 150,000 |

The manufacturing costs associated with the goods that were finished during the period. (See Exhibits 2–7 and 2–8 for details.)

In the exhibit, the computation of cost of goods sold relies on the following basic equation for inventory accounts:

BASIC EQUATION FOR INVENTORY ACCOUNTS

$$\text{Beginning balance} + \text{Additions to inventory} = \text{Withdrawals from inventory} + \text{Ending balance}$$

The logic underlying this equation, which applies to any inventory account, is illustrated in Exhibit 2–6A. During a period, additions to the inventory account come through purchases or other means. The sum of the additions to the account and the beginning balance represents the total amount of inventory that is available for use during the period. At the end of the period, some or all of the inventory may have been withdrawn from the inventory account.

These concepts are applied to determine the cost of goods sold for a merchandising company like Brandon Bookstore as follows:

**Exhibit 2–6A**
Inventory Flows

COST OF GOODS SOLD IN A MERCHANDISING COMPANY

$$\text{Beginning merchandise inventory} + \text{Purchases} = \text{Cost of goods sold} + \text{Ending merchandise inventory}$$

or

$$\text{Cost of goods sold} = \text{Beginning merchandise inventory} + \text{Purchases} - \text{Ending merchandise inventory}$$

The cost of goods sold for a manufacturing company like Halifax Manufacturing is determined as follows:

COST OF GOODS SOLD IN A MANUFACTURING COMPANY

$$\text{Beginning finished goods inventory} + \text{Cost of goods manufactured} = \text{Cost of goods sold} + \text{Ending finished goods inventory}$$

or

$$\text{Cost of goods sold} = \text{Beginning finished goods inventory} + \text{Cost of goods manufactured} - \text{Ending finished goods inventory}$$

To determine the cost of goods sold in a merchandising company like Brandon Bookstore, we only need to know the beginning and ending balances in the Merchandise Inventory account, and the purchases (see Exhibit 2–6B). Total purchases can be easily determined in a merchandising company by simply adding together all purchases from suppliers.

To determine the cost of goods sold in a manufacturing company like Halifax Manufacturing, we need to know the *cost of goods manufactured* and the beginning and ending balances in the Finished Goods inventory account (see Exhibit 2–6B). The **cost of goods manufactured** consists of the manufacturing costs associated with goods that were *finished* during the period. The cost of goods manufactured figure for Halifax Manufacturing is derived in Exhibit 2–7, which contains a *schedule of cost of goods manufactured.*

## Exhibit 2–6B
Inventory Flows and Cost of Goods Sold

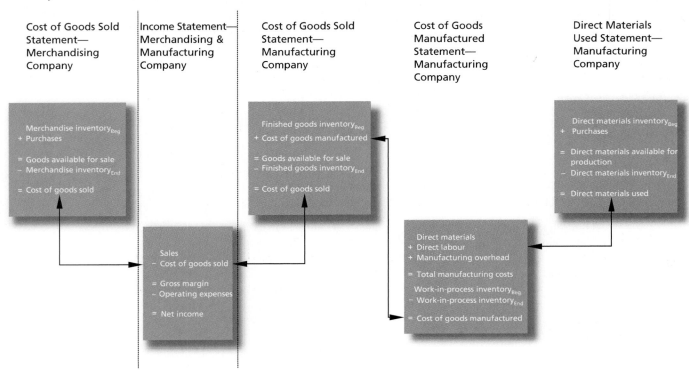

## Exhibit 2–7
Schedule of Cost of Goods Manufactured

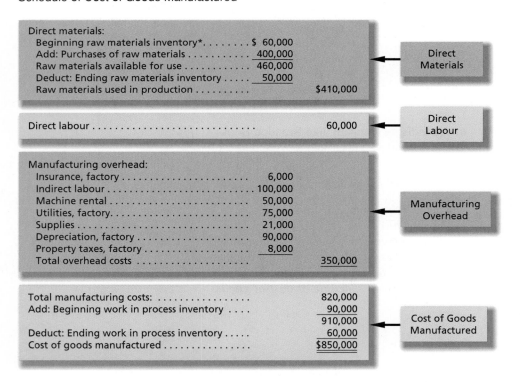

| Direct materials: | | |
|---|---|---|
| Beginning raw materials inventory*. . . . . . . . | $ 60,000 | |
| Add: Purchases of raw materials . . . . . . . . . . . | 400,000 | |
| Raw materials available for use . . . . . . . . . . . | 460,000 | |
| Deduct: Ending raw materials inventory . . . . . | 50,000 | |
| Raw materials used in production . . . . . . . . . | | $410,000 |
| Direct labour . . . . . . . . . . . . . . . . . . . . . . . . . . | | 60,000 |
| Manufacturing overhead: | | |
| Insurance, factory . . . . . . . . . . . . . . . . . . . . . | 6,000 | |
| Indirect labour . . . . . . . . . . . . . . . . . . . . . . . . | 100,000 | |
| Machine rental . . . . . . . . . . . . . . . . . . . . . . . | 50,000 | |
| Utilities, factory. . . . . . . . . . . . . . . . . . . . . . . | 75,000 | |
| Supplies . . . . . . . . . . . . . . . . . . . . . . . . . . . . . | 21,000 | |
| Depreciation, factory . . . . . . . . . . . . . . . . . . | 90,000 | |
| Property taxes, factory . . . . . . . . . . . . . . . . . | 8,000 | |
| Total overhead costs . . . . . . . . . . . . . . . . . . . | | 350,000 |
| Total manufacturing costs: . . . . . . . . . . . . . . . . | | 820,000 |
| Add: Beginning work in process inventory . . . . | | 90,000 |
| | | 910,000 |
| Deduct: Ending work in process inventory . . . . . | | 60,000 |
| Cost of goods manufactured . . . . . . . . . . . . . . . | | $850,000 |

Direct Materials

Direct Labour

Manufacturing Overhead

Cost of Goods Manufactured

*We assume in this example that the Raw Materials inventory account contains only direct materials and that indirect materials are carried in a separate Supplies account. Using a Supplies account for indirect materials is a common practice among companies. In Chapter 3, we discuss the procedure to be followed if *both* direct and indirect materials are carried in a single account.

## Schedule of Cost of Goods Manufactured

At first glance, the **schedule of cost of goods manufactured** in Exhibit 2–7 appears complex and perhaps even intimidating. However, it is all quite logical. Note that the schedule of cost of goods manufactured contains the three elements of product costs that we discussed earlier—direct materials, direct labour, and manufacturing overhead. The total of these three cost elements is *not* the cost of goods manufactured, however. The reason is that some of the materials, labour, and overhead costs incurred during the period relate to goods that are not yet completed. The costs that relate to goods that are not yet completed are shown in the work in process inventory figures at the bottom of the schedule. Note that the beginning work in process inventory must be added to the manufacturing costs of the period, and the ending work in process inventory must be deducted, to arrive at the cost of goods manufactured.

The logic underlying the schedule of cost of goods manufactured and the computation of cost of goods sold is laid out in a different format in Exhibit 2–8. To compute the cost of goods sold, go to the top of the exhibit and work your way down using the following steps:

1. Compute the raw materials used in production in the top section of the exhibit.
2. Insert the total raw materials used in production ($410,000) into the second section of the exhibit and compute the total manufacturing cost.
3. Insert the total manufacturing cost ($820,000) into the third section of the exhibit and compute the cost of goods manufactured.
4. Insert the cost of goods manufactured ($850,000) into the bottom section of the exhibit and compute the cost of goods sold.

**Learning Objective 7**
Prepare a schedule of cost of goods manufactured.

**Exhibit 2–8**
An Alternative Approach to Computation of Cost of Goods Sold

| **Computation of Raw Materials Used in Production** | |
| --- | --- |
| Beginning raw materials inventory | $ 60,000 |
| + Purchases of raw materials | 400,000 |
| − Ending raw materials inventory | 50,000 |
| = Raw materials used in production | $410,000 |
| **Computation of Total Manufacturing Cost** | |
| Raw materials used in production | $410,000 |
| + Direct labour | 60,000 |
| + Total manufacturing overhead costs | 350,000 |
| = Total manufacturing cost | $820,000 |
| **Computation of Cost of Goods Manufactured** | |
| Beginning work in process inventory | $ 90,000 |
| + Total manufacturing cost | 820,000 |
| − Ending work in process inventory | 60,000 |
| = Cost of goods manufactured | $850,000 |
| **Computation of Cost of Goods Sold** | |
| Beginning finished goods inventory | $125,000 |
| + Cost of goods manufactured | 850,000 |
| − Ending finished goods inventory | 175,000 |
| = Cost of goods sold | $800,000 |

# Product Costs—A Closer Look

Earlier in the chapter, we defined product costs as consisting of those costs that are involved in either the purchase or the manufacture of goods. For manufactured goods, we stated that these costs consist of direct materials, direct labour, and manufacturing overhead. To understand product costs more fully, it will be helpful at this point to look briefly at the flow of costs in a manufacturing company. By doing so, we will be able to see how product costs move through the various accounts and affect the balance sheet and the income statement in the course of producing and selling products.

Exhibit 2–9 illustrates the flow of costs in a manufacturing company. Raw materials purchases are recorded in the Raw Materials inventory account. When raw materials are used in production, their costs are transferred to the Work in Process inventory account as direct materials. Note that direct labour cost and manufacturing overhead cost are added directly to Work in Process. Work in Process can be viewed most simply as an assembly line where workers are stationed and where products slowly take shape as they move from one end of the assembly line to the other. The direct materials, direct labour, and manufacturing overhead costs added to Work in Process in Exhibit 2–9 are the costs needed to complete these products as they move along this assembly line.

Note from the exhibit that as goods are completed, their cost is transferred from Work in Process to Finished Goods. Here the goods await sale to a customer. As goods are sold, their cost is then transferred from Finished Goods to Cost of Goods Sold. At this point, the various material, labour, and overhead costs that are required to make the product are finally treated as expenses.

As stated earlier, product costs are often called inventoriable costs. The reason is that these costs go directly into inventory accounts as they are incurred (first into Work in Process and then into Finished Goods), rather than going into expense accounts. *This is a key concept, since such costs can end up on the balance sheet as assets if goods are only partially completed or are unsold at the end of a period.*

**Exhibit 2–9**
Cost Flows and Classifications in a Manufacturing Company

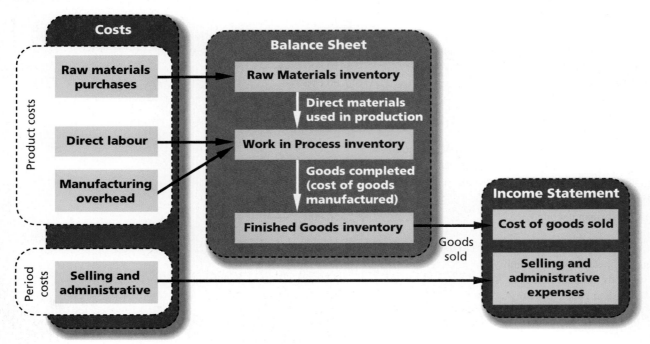

Selling and administrative expenses are not involved in the manufacture of a product. For this reason, they are not treated as product costs but, rather, as period costs that go directly into expense accounts as they are incurred as shown in Exhibit 2–9.

## An Example of Cost Flows

To provide a numerical example of cost flows in a manufacturing company, assume that a company's annual insurance cost is $2,000. Three-fourths of this amount ($1,500) applies to factory operations, and one-fourth ($500) applies to selling and administrative activities. Therefore, $1,500 of the $2,000 insurance cost would be a product (inventoriable) cost and would be added to the cost of the goods produced during the year. This portion of the year's insurance cost will not become an expense until the goods that are produced during the year are sold—which may not happen until the following year or even later. Until the goods are sold, the $1,500 will remain as part of inventory (either as part of Work in Process or as part of Finished Goods), along with the other costs of producing the goods.

By contrast, the $500 of insurance cost that applies to the company's selling and administrative activities will go into an expense account immediately as a charge against the period's revenue.

*Counsellor:* If you might face reprisals for using the hot line, perhaps you should evaluate whether or not you really want to work for a company whose ethical climate is one you are uncomfortable in.

*Caller:* I have already asked ... for a transfer back to the corporate office.

Source: Curtis C. Verschoor, "Using a Hot Line Isn't Whistle-Blowing," *Strategic Finance*, April 1999, pp. 27–28. Used with permission from *Strategic Finance* and the Institute of Management Accountants.

# Cost Classification Summary

As explained earlier in the chapter, costs can be classified in various ways to meet the information needs of managers; Exhibit 2–10 provides a summary of these different classifications. Indeed, the same cost item may be classified in more than one way. For example, the salary of Holiday Inn's catering department manager is a fixed cost with respect to the number of guests staying the hotel. It is directly traceable to the catering department but not to the sales department. It is a period cost because the individual's services cannot be "banked." Finally, it is a relevant cost when deciding whether to eliminate the department and outsource catering. When to use which classification depends on the purpose of the classification. The purposes and corresponding cost classifications are summarized in Exhibit 2–11. You will find it useful to understand the notion of "different costs for different purposes" as you progress through the book.

**Exhibit 2–10**
Cost Classification Summary

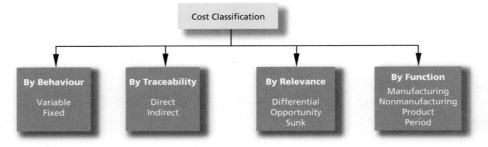

| | | By Behaviour | By Traceability | By Relevance | By Function |
|---|---|---|---|---|---|

**Exhibit 2–11**
Cost Classifications for Different Purposes

| Purpose of Cost Classification | Cost Classifications |
|---|---|
| Preparing external financial statements | • Product costs (inventoriable)<br> • Direct materials<br> • Direct labour<br> • Manufacturing overhead<br>• Period costs (expensed)<br> • Nonmanufacturing costs<br>  • Marketing or selling costs<br>  • Administrative costs |
| Predicting cost behaviour in response to changes in activity | • Variable cost (proportional to activity)<br>• Fixed cost (constant in total) |
| Assigning costs to cost objects, such as departments or products | • Direct cost (can be easily traced)<br>• Indirect cost (cannot be easily traced; must be allocated) |
| Making decisions | • Differential cost (differs between alternatives)<br>• Sunk cost (past cost not affecting a decision)<br>• Opportunity cost (forgone benefit) |

# Summary

**LO1    Define and give examples of variable costs and fixed costs.**

For purposes of predicting cost behaviour—how costs will react to changes in activity—costs are commonly categorized as variable or fixed. Variable costs, in total, are strictly proportional to activity. Thus, the variable cost per unit of activity is constant. Fixed costs, in total, remain at the same level for changes in activity within the relevant range. Thus, the average fixed cost per unit of activity decreases as the volume of activity increases.

**LO2    Define and give examples of direct and indirect costs.**

A direct cost is a cost that can be easily and conveniently traced to a cost object. Direct materials is a direct cost of making a product. An indirect cost is a cost that cannot be easily and conveniently traced to a cost object. The salary of the administrator of a hospital is an indirect cost of serving a particular patient.

**LO3    Define and give examples of cost classifications used in making decisions: differential costs, opportunity costs, and sunk costs.**

The concepts of differential costs and revenue, opportunity cost, and sunk cost are vitally important for purposes of making decisions. Differential costs and revenues are the cost and revenue items that differ between alternatives. Opportunity cost is the benefit that is forgone when one alternative is selected over another. Sunk cost is a cost that occurred in the past and cannot be altered. Differential costs and opportunity costs should be carefully considered in decisions. Sunk costs are always irrelevant in decisions and should be ignored.

**LO4    Identify and give examples of each of the three basic manufacturing cost categories.**

Manufacturing costs consist of two categories of costs that can be conveniently and directly traced to units of product—direct materials and direct labour—and one category that cannot be conveniently traced to units of product—manufacturing overhead.

**LO5    Distinguish between product costs and period costs and give examples of each.**

For purposes of valuing inventories and determining expenses for the balance sheet and income statement, costs are classified as either product costs or period costs. Product costs are assigned to inventories and are considered assets until the products are sold, at which time they are expensed. In contrast, period costs are taken directly to the income statement as expenses in the period in which they are incurred.

In a merchandising company, product cost is whatever the company paid for acquiring its merchandise. For external financial reports in a manufacturing company, product costs consist of all manufacturing costs. In both kinds of companies, selling and administrative costs are considered to be period costs and are expensed as incurred.

**LO6    Prepare an income statement including calculation of the cost of goods sold.**

See Exhibit 2–5 for examples of income statements for both a merchandising and a manufacturing company. In general, net income is computed by deducting the cost of goods sold and operating expenses from sales. Cost of goods sold is calculated by adding purchases to the beginning merchandise or finished goods inventory and then deducting the ending merchandise or finished goods inventory.

**LO7    Prepare a schedule of cost of goods manufactured.**

See Exhibit 2–7 for an example of a schedule of cost of goods manufactured. In general, the cost of goods manufactured is the sum of direct materials, direct labour, and manufacturing overhead incurred during the period.

# Guidance Answers to Decision Maker and You Decide

**FINANCIAL ANALYST** (p. 28)

*Fixed* and *variable* are terms used to describe cost behaviour or how a given cost will react or respond to changes in the level of business activity. A fixed cost is a cost that remains constant, in total, regardless of changes in the level of activity. However, on a per-unit basis, a fixed cost varies inversely with changes in activity. The cost structures of a number of industries lean toward fixed costs because of the nature of their operations. Obviously, the cost of airplanes would be fixed, and within some relevant range, such costs would not change if the number of passengers flown changed. This would also be true in other industries, such as trucking and rail transportation. You might suggest that it would be worthwhile to research the prospects for growth in this industry and for this company. If a downturn in business is not anticipated, a cost structure weighted toward fixed costs should not be used as the primary reason for turning down the investment opportunity. On the other hand, if a period of decline is anticipated, your client's initial impression might be on target.

### YOUR DECISION TO ATTEND CLASS (p. 31)

Every alternative has some opportunity cost attached to it. If you brainstormed a bit, you probably came up with a few opportunity costs that accompany your choice to attend class. If you had trouble answering the question, think about what you could be doing instead of attending class.

- You could have been working at a part-time job; you could quantify that cost by multiplying your pay rate by the time you spend in class.
- You could have spent the time studying for another class; the opportunity cost could be measured by the improvement in the grade that would result from spending more time on that class.
- You could have slept in or taken a nap; depending on your level of sleep deprivation, this opportunity cost might be priceless.

### COST MANAGER (p. 43)

At a conceptual level, the physical flow of goods remains the same, regardless of the inventory levels maintained by a company (see Exhibit 2–6A). Until such time that the company continues to carry some inventory, it becomes necessary to maintain an inventory account. In a company with "near zero" inventory levels, additions to the inventory account are equal to the withdrawals from the account during a given period. In reality, although the goal of a just-in-time program is zero inventories, companies take a long time before that goal is achieved. Once the company can sustain a "near zero" inventory level, the company may consider eliminating the inventory account. In such a situation, all costs will be treated like period costs and expensed during the period in which they are incurred.

# Review Problem 1: Cost Terms

You have been introduced to many new cost terms. It will take you some time to learn what each term means and how to properly classify costs in an organization. Consider the following example: Porter Company manufactures furniture, including tables. Selected costs are given below:
1. The tables are made of wood that costs $100 per table.
2. The tables are assembled by workers, at a wage cost of $40 per table.
3. Workers assembling the tables are supervised by a factory supervisor who is paid $25,000 per year.
4. Electrical costs are $2 per machine-hour. Four machine-hours are required to produce a table.
5. The straight-line depreciation cost of the machines used to make the tables totals $10,000 per year.
6. The salary of the president of Porter Company is $100,000 per year.
7. Porter Company spends $250,000 per year to advertise its products.
8. Salespersons are paid a commission of $30 for each table sold.
9. Instead of producing the tables, Porter Company could rent its factory space out at a rental income of $50,000 per year.

*Required:*
Classify these costs according to various cost terms used in the chapter. *Carefully study the classification of each cost.* If you do not understand why a particular cost is classified the way it is, reread the section of the chapter discussing the particular cost term. The terms *variable cost* and *fixed cost* refer to how costs behave with respect to the number of tables produced in a year.

*SOLUTION TO REVIEW PROBLEM 1*

| | To Units of Product Sold | | Period (selling and adminis- trative) Cost | Product Cost | | | To Units of Product Sold | | Sunk Cost | Oppor- tunity Cost |
|---|---|---|---|---|---|---|---|---|---|---|
| | Variable Cost | Fixed Cost | | Direct Materials | Direct Labour | Manufacturing Overhead | Direct | Indirect | | |
| 1. Wood used in a table ($100 per table) ........... | X | | | X | | | X | | | |
| 2. Labour cost to assemble a table ($40 per table) .... | X | | | | X | | X | | | |
| 3. Salary of the factory supervisor ($25,000 per year) ........... | | X | | | | X | | X | | |
| 4. Cost of electricity to produce tables ($2 per machine- hour) ........... | X | | | | | X | | X | | |
| 5. Depreciation of machines used to produce tables ($10,000 per year) ........... | | X | | | | X | | X | X* | |
| 6. Salary of the company president ($100,000 per year) ........... | | X | X | | | | | X | | |
| 7. Advertising expense ($250,000 per year) ........... | | X | X | | | | | X | | |
| 8. Commissions paid to salespersons ($30 per table sold) ........... | X | | X | | | | X | | | |
| 9. Rental income forgone on factory space ($50,000 per year) ........... | | | | | | | | | | X† |

*This is a sunk cost, since the equipment has already been purchased.
†This is an opportunity cost, since it represents the potential benefit that is lost or sacrificed as a result of using the factory space to produce tables. Opportunity cost is a special category of cost that is not ordinarily recorded in an organization's accounting books. To avoid possible confusion with other costs, we will not attempt to classify this cost in any other way except as an opportunity cost.

# Review Problem 2: Schedule of Cost of Goods Manufactured and Income Statement

The following information has been taken from the accounting records of Klear-Seal Company for last year:

| | |
|---|---|
| Selling expenses .................................... | $ 140,000 |
| Raw materials inventory, January 1 ................... | 90,000 |
| Raw materials inventory, December 31 ............... | 60,000 |
| Utilities, factory ................................... | 36,000 |
| Direct labour cost ................................. | 150,000 |

| Depreciation, factory | 162,000 |
| Purchases of raw materials | 750,000 |
| Sales | 2,500,000 |
| Insurance, factory | 40,000 |
| Supplies, factory | 15,000 |
| Administrative expenses | 270,000 |
| Indirect labour | 300,000 |
| Maintenance, factory | 87,000 |
| Work in process inventory, January 1 | 180,000 |
| Work in process inventory, December 31 | 100,000 |
| Finished goods inventory, January 1 | 260,000 |
| Finished goods inventory, December 31 | 210,000 |

Management wants these data organized in a better format so that financial statements can be prepared for the year.

**Required:**
1. Prepare a schedule of cost of goods manufactured as in Exhibit 2–7.
2. Compute the cost of goods sold.
3. Using data as needed from (1) and (2) above, prepare an income statement.

**SOLUTION TO REVIEW PROBLEM 2**

1.

**KLEAR-SEAL COMPANY**
**Schedule of Cost of Goods Manufactured**
**For the Year Ended December 31**

| | | |
|---|---|---|
| Direct materials: | | |
| Raw materials inventory, January 1 | $ 90,000 | |
| Add: Purchases of raw materials | 750,000 | |
| Raw materials available for use | 840,000 | |
| Deduct: Raw materials inventory, December 31 | 60,000 | |
| Raw materials used in production | | $ 780,000 |
| Direct labour | | 150,000 |
| Manufacturing overhead: | | |
| Utilities, factory | 36,000 | |
| Depreciation, factory | 162,000 | |
| Insurance, factory | 40,000 | |
| Supplies, factory | 15,000 | |
| Indirect labour | 300,000 | |
| Maintenance, factory | 87,000 | |
| Total overhead costs | | 640,000 |
| Total manufacturing costs | | 1,570,000 |
| Add: Work in process inventory, January 1 | | 180,000 |
| | | 1,750,000 |
| Deduct: Work in process inventory, December 31 | | 100,000 |
| Cost of goods manufactured | | $1,650,000 |

2.

The cost of goods sold would be computed as follows:

| | |
|---|---|
| Finished goods inventory, January 1 | $ 260,000 |
| Add: Cost of goods manufactured | 1,650,000 |
| Goods available for sale | 1,910,000 |
| Deduct: Finished goods inventory, December 31 | 210,000 |
| Cost of goods sold | $1,700,000 |

3.

| KLEAR-SEAL COMPANY Income Statement For the Year Ended December 31 | | |
|---|---|---|
| Sales .......................................... | | $2,500,000 |
| Less cost of goods sold (above) ...................... | | 1,700,000 |
| Gross margin ..................................... | | 800,000 |
| Less selling and administrative expenses: | | |
| Selling expenses ................................ | $140,000 | |
| Administrative expenses .......................... | 270,000 | |
| Total expenses ................................... | | 410,000 |
| Net income ...................................... | | $ 390,000 |

# Glossary

**Administrative costs** All executive, organizational, and clerical costs associated with the general management of an organization, rather than with manufacturing, marketing, or selling. (p. 34)

**Common costs** A cost that is incurred to support a number of cost objects but cannot be traced to them individually. For example, the salary and benefit package of the receptionist in a bank is common to all the different services provided by that bank. (p. 29)

**Conversion cost** Direct labour cost plus manufacturing overhead cost. (p. 34)

**Cost behaviour** The way in which a cost reacts or responds to changes in the level of business activity. (p. 26)

**Cost object** Anything for which cost data are desired. Examples of possible cost objects are services, product lines, customers, jobs, and organizational subunits, such as departments or divisions of a company. (p. 29)

**Cost of goods manufactured** The manufacturing costs associated with the goods that were finished during the period. (p. 39)

**Differential cost** A difference in cost between any two alternatives. Also see *Incremental cost.* (p. 29)

**Differential revenue** The difference in revenue between any two alternatives. (p. 29)

**Direct cost** A cost that can be easily and conveniently traced to a particular cost object. (p. 29)

**Direct labour** Those factory labour costs that can be easily traced to individual units of product. Also called *touch labour.* (p. 33)

**Direct materials** Those materials that become an integral part of a finished product and can be conveniently traced to it. (p. 33)

**Finished goods** Units of product that have been completed but have not yet been sold to customers. (p. 37)

**Fixed cost** A cost that remains constant, in total, regardless of changes in the level of activity within a relevant range. If a fixed cost is expressed on a per-unit basis, it varies inversely with the level of activity. (p. 27)

**Incremental cost** An increase in cost between two alternatives. Also see *Differential cost.* (p. 29)

**Indirect cost** A cost that cannot be easily and conveniently traced to a particular cost object. (p. 29)

**Indirect labour** The labour costs of janitors, supervisors, materials handlers, and other factory workers that cannot be traced directly to particular products. (p. 34)

**Indirect materials** Small items of material, such as glue and nails. These items may become an integral part of a finished product but are traceable to the product only at great cost or inconvenience. (p. 33)

**Inventoriable costs** Costs that can be carried forward to inventory. Synonym for *product costs.* (p. 35)

**Manufacturing costs** Costs incurred in production during a certain period. Includes direct materials, direct labour, and manufacturing overhead. (p. 32)

**Manufacturing overhead** All costs associated with manufacturing, except direct materials and direct labour. (p. 34)

**Marketing or selling costs** All costs necessary to secure customer orders and get the finished product or service into the hands of the customer. (p. 34)

**Opportunity cost** The potential benefit that is given up when one alternative is selected over another. (p. 31)

**Period costs** Those costs that are taken directly to the income statement as expenses in the period in which they are incurred or accrued; such costs consist of selling (marketing) and administrative expenses. (p. 35)

**Prime cost** Direct materials cost plus direct labour cost. (p. 34)

**Product costs** All costs that are involved in the purchase or manufacture of goods. In the case of manufactured goods, these costs consist of direct materials, direct labour, and manufacturing overhead. Also see *Inventoriable costs.* (p. 35)

**Raw materials** Materials that are used to make a product. (p. 32)

**Relevant range** The range of activity within which assumptions about variable and fixed cost behaviour are valid. (p. 27)

**Schedule of cost of goods manufactured** A schedule showing the direct materials, direct labour, and manufacturing overhead costs incurred for a period and assigned to Work in Process and finished goods. (p. 41)

**Sunk cost** Any cost that has already been incurred and that cannot be changed by any decision made now or in the future. (p. 31)

**Value chain** A sequence of major activities undertaken by an organization to fulfill its mission. (p. 32)

**Variable cost** A cost that varies, in total, in direct proportion to changes in the level of activity. (p. 26)

**Work in process** Units of product that are only partially complete and will require further work before they are ready for sale to a customer. (p. 37)

# Questions

**2–1**   What is meant by the term *cost behaviour*?

**2–2**   "A variable cost is a cost that varies per unit of activity, whereas a fixed cost is constant per unit of activity." Do you agree? Explain.

**2–3**   How do fixed costs create difficulties in costing units of product?

**2–4**   Why is manufacturing overhead considered an indirect cost of a unit of product?

**2–5**   Define the following terms: differential cost, opportunity cost, and sunk cost.

**2–6**   Only variable costs can be differential costs. Do you agree? Explain.

**2–7**   What are the three major elements of product costs in a manufacturing company?

**2–8**   Distinguish among the following: (a) direct materials, (b) indirect materials, (c) direct labour, (d) indirect labour, and (e) manufacturing overhead.

**2–9**   Explain the difference between a product cost and a period cost.

**2–10** Describe how the income statement of a manufacturing company differs from the income statement of a merchandising company.

**2–11** Of what value is the schedule of cost of goods manufactured? How does it tie into the income statement?

**2–12** Describe how the inventory accounts of a manufacturing company differ from the inventory account of a merchandising company.

**2–13** Why are product costs sometimes called inventoriable costs? Describe the flow of such costs in a manufacturing company from the point of incurrence until they finally become expenses on the income statement.

**2–14** Is it possible for such costs as salaries or depreciation to end up as assets on the balance sheet? Explain.

# Brief Exercises

**BRIEF EXERCISE 2–1   Identifying Variable and Fixed Costs** (LO1)

Below are a number of costs that are incurred in a variety of organizations.

*Required:*

Classify each cost as being variable or fixed with respect to the number of units of product sold or services provided by the organization.

| Cost Item | Cost Behaviour | |
|---|---|---|
| | Variable | Fixed |

Place an X in the appropriate column for each cost to indicate whether the cost involved would be variable or fixed with respect to the number of units of products sold or services provided by the organization.

1. X-ray film used in the radiology lab at your local Hospital.
2. The costs of advertising a Madonna rock concert in Toronto.
3. Depreciation on the Planet Hollywood restaurant building in Hong Kong.
4. The electrical costs of running a roller coaster at West Edmonton Mall.
5. Property taxes on your local cinema.
6. Commissions paid to salespersons at Wavelength Electronics.
7. Property insurance on a Coca-Cola bottling plant.
8. The costs of synthetic materials used to make Nike running shoes.
9. The costs of shipping Panasonic televisions to retail stores.
10. The cost of leasing an ultra-scan diagnostic machine at the American Hospital in Paris.

**BRIEF EXERCISE 2–2   Identifying Direct and Indirect Costs (LO2)**
University Hospital is a full-service hospital that provides everything from major surgery and emergency room care to outpatient clinics.

*Required:*
For each cost incurred at University Hospital, indicate whether it would most likely be a direct cost or an indirect cost of the specified cost object by placing an X in the appropriate column.

| | Cost | Cost object | Direct Cost | Indirect Cost |
|---|---|---|---|---|
| Ex. | Catered food served to patients | A particular patient | X | |
| 1. | The wages of pediatric nurses | The Pediatrics Department | | |
| 2. | Prescription drugs | A particular patient | | |
| 3. | Heating the hospital | The Pediatrics Department | | |
| 4. | The salary of the head of Pediatrics | The Pediatrics Department | | |
| 5. | The salary of the head of Pediatrics | A particular pediatric patient | | |
| 6. | Hospital chaplain's salary | A particular patient | | |
| 7. | Lab tests by outside contractor | A particular patient | | |
| 8. | Lab tests by outside contractor | A particular department | | |

**BRIEF EXERCISE 2–3   Differential, Opportunity, and Sunk Costs (LO3)**
University Hospital is a full-service hospital that provides everything from major surgery and emergency room care to outpatient clinics. The hospital's Radiology Department is considering replacing an old inefficient X-ray machine with a state-of-the-art digital X-ray machine. The new machine would provide higher quality X-rays in less time and at a lower cost per X-ray. The new machine would require less power consumption and would use a colour laser printer to produce easily readable X-ray images. Instead of investing the funds in the new X-ray machine, the Laboratory Department is lobbying the hospital's management to buy a new DNA analyzer.

*Required:*
For each of the items on the next page, indicate by placing an X in the appropriate column whether it should be considered a differential cost, an opportunity cost, or a sunk cost in the decision to replace the old X-ray machine with a new machine. If none of the categories applies for a particular item, leave all columns blank.

| Item | Differential Cost | Opportunity Cost | Sunk Cost |
|---|---|---|---|
| Ex. Cost of X-ray film used in the old machine | X | | |
| 1. Cost of the old X-ray machine | | | |
| 2. The salary of the head of the Radiology Department | | | |
| 3. The salary of the head of the Pediatrics Department | | | |
| 4. Cost of the new colour laser printer | | | |
| 5. Rent on the space occupied by Radiology | | | |
| 6. The cost of maintaining the old machine | | | |
| 7. Benefits from a new DNA analyzer | | | |
| 8. Cost of electricity to run the X-ray machines | | | |

**BRIEF EXERCISE 2–4    Classifying Manufacturing Costs (LO4)**

Your Computer, Inc. assembles custom computers from components supplied by various manufacturers. The company is very small and its assembly shop and retail sales store are housed in a single facility in North Vancouver. Listed below are some of the costs that are incurred at the company.

*Required:*

For each cost, indicate whether it would most likely be classified as direct labour, direct materials, manufacturing overhead, marketing and selling, or an administrative cost.
1. The cost of a hard drive installed in a computer.
2. The cost of advertising in the *Puget Sound Computer User* newspaper.
3. The wages of employees who assemble computers from components.
4. Sales commissions paid to the company's salespeople.
5. The wages of the assembly shop's supervisor.
6. The wages of the company's accountant.
7. Depreciation on equipment used to test assembled computers before release to customers.
8. Rent on the facility.

**BRIEF EXERCISE 2–5    Identifying Product and Period Costs (LO5)**

A product cost is also known as an inventoriable cost. Classify the following costs as either product (inventoriable) costs or period (noninventoriable) costs in a manufacturing company:
1. Depreciation on salespersons' cars.
2. Rent on equipment used in the factory.
3. Lubricants used for maintenance of machines.
4. Salaries of finished goods warehouse personnel.
5. Soap and paper towels used by factory workers at the end of a shift.
6. Factory supervisors' salaries.
7. Heat, water, and power consumed in the factory.
8. Materials used in boxing units of finished product for shipment overseas. (Units are not normally boxed.)
9. Advertising outlays.
10. Workers' compensation insurance on factory employees.
11. Depreciation on chairs and tables in the factory lunchroom.
12. The salary of the switchboard operator for the company.
13. Depreciation on a Lear Jet used by the company's executives.
14. Rent on rooms at a Florida resort for the annual sales conference.
15. Attractively designed box for packaging breakfast cereal.

**BRIEF EXERCISE 2–6    Constructing an Income Statement (LO6)**

Last month CyberGames, a computer game retailer, had total sales of $1,450,000, selling expenses of $210,000, and administrative expenses of $180,000. The company had beginning merchandise inventory of $240,000, purchased additional merchandise inventory for $950,000, and had ending merchandise inventory of $170,000.

*Required:*

Prepare an income statement for the company for the month in good form.

**BRIEF EXERCISE 2–7    Prepare a Schedule of Cost of Goods Manufactured (LO7)**
Lompac Products manufactures a variety of products in its factory. Data for the most recent month's operations appear below:

| | |
|---|---|
| Beginning raw materials inventory ................ | $ 60,000 |
| Purchases of raw materials ...................... | 690,000 |
| Ending raw materials inventory .................. | 45,000 |
| Direct labour .................................. | 135,000 |
| Manufacturing overhead ........................ | 370,000 |
| Beginning work in process inventory ............. | 120,000 |
| Ending work in process inventory ............... | 130,000 |

*Required:*
Prepare in good form a schedule of cost of goods manufactured for the company for the month.

# Exercises

**EXERCISE 2–1    Cost Identification (LO1, LO3, LO4, LO5)**
Wollogong Group Ltd. of New South Wales, Australia, acquired its factory building about 10 years ago. For several years the company has rented out a small annex attached to the rear of the building. The company has received a rental income of $30,000 per year on this space. The renter's lease will expire soon, and rather than renew the lease, the company has decided to use the space itself to manufacture a new product.

Direct materials cost for the new product will total $80 per unit. To have a place to store finished units of product, the company will rent a small warehouse nearby. The rental cost will be $500 per month. In addition, the company must rent equipment for use in producing the new product; the rental cost will be $4,000 per month. Workers will be hired to manufacture the new product, with direct labour cost amounting to $60 per unit. The space in the annex will continue to be depreciated on a straight-line basis, as in prior years. This depreciation is $8,000 per year.

Advertising costs for the new product will total $50,000 per year. A supervisor will be hired to oversee production; her salary will be $1,500 per month. Electricity for operating machines will be $1.20 per unit. Costs of shipping the new product to customers will be $9 per unit.

To provide funds to purchase materials, meet payrolls, and so forth, the company will have to liquidate some temporary investments. These investments are presently yielding a return of about $3,000 per year.

*Required:*
Prepare an answer sheet with the following column headings:

| Name of the Cost | Variable Cost | Fixed Cost | Product Cost | | | Period (selling and administrative) Cost | Opportunity Cost | Sunk Cost |
|---|---|---|---|---|---|---|---|---|
| | | | Direct Materials | Direct Labour | Manufacturing Overhead | | | |

List the different costs associated with the new product decision down the extreme left column (under Name of the Cost). Then place an *X* under each heading that helps describe the type of cost involved. There may be *X*'s under several column headings for a single cost. (For example, a cost may be a fixed cost, a period cost, and a sunk cost; you would place an *X* under each of these column headings opposite the cost.)

**EXERCISE 2–2    Definitions of Cost Terms (LO1, LO3, LO5)**
Following are a number of cost terms introduced in the chapter:

| | |
|---|---|
| Variable cost | Product cost |
| Fixed cost | Sunk cost |
| Prime cost | Conversion cost |
| Opportunity cost | Period cost |

Choose the term or terms that most appropriately describe the cost identified in each of the following situations. A cost term can be used more than once.

1. Lake Company produces a tote bag that is very popular with college students. The cloth going into the manufacture of the tote bag would be called direct materials and classified as a _____ cost. In terms of cost behaviour, the cloth could also be described as a _____ cost.

2. The direct labour cost required to produce the tote bags, combined with the manufacturing overhead cost involved, would be known as _____ cost.

3. The company could have taken the funds that it has invested in production equipment and invested them in interest-bearing securities instead. The interest forgone on the securities would be called _____ cost.

4. Taken together, the direct materials cost and the direct labour cost required to produce tote bags would be called _____ cost.

5. The company used to produce a smaller tote bag that was not very popular. Some three hundred of these smaller bags are stored in one of the company's warehouses. The amount invested in these bags would be called a _____ cost.

6. The tote bags are sold through agents who are paid a commission on each bag sold. These commissions would be classified by Lake Company as a _____ cost. In terms of cost behaviour, commissions would be classified as a _____ cost.

7. Depreciation on the equipment used to produce tote bags would be classified by Lake Company as a _____ cost. However, depreciation on any equipment used by the company in selling and administrative activities would be classified as a _____ cost. In terms of cost behaviour, depreciation would probably be classified as a _____ cost.

8. A _____ cost is also known as an inventoriable cost, since such costs go into the Work in Process inventory account and then into the Finished Goods inventory account before appearing on the income statement as part of cost of goods sold.

9. The salary of Lake Company's president would be classified as a _____ cost, since the salary will appear on the income statement as an expense in the time period in which it is incurred.

10. Costs can often be classified in several ways. For example, Lake Company pays $5,000 rent each month on its factory building. The rent would be part of manufacturing overhead. In terms of cost behaviour, it would be classified as a _____ cost. The rent can also be classified as a _____ cost and as part of _____ cost.

**EXERCISE 2–3  Classification of Variable, Fixed, Direct, and Indirect Costs** (LO1, LO2)
Various costs are associated with running a communications company dealing with the production of video commercials, as given below:

1. Account manager's salary.
2. Rent on building.
3. Videos used in the production of commercials.
4. Marketing manager's salary.
5. Wages of operators involved in editing.
6. Depreciation of equipment used in editing.
7. Depreciation on television sets used for viewing videos.
8. Insurance on building.

*Required:*
Classify each cost as being either variable or fixed with respect to the number of commercials produced. Also indicate whether each cost would typically be treated as a direct cost or an indirect cost with respect to the number of commercials produced. Prepare your answer sheet as shown below:

| Cost Item | Cost Behaviour | | To Number of Commercials Produced | |
|---|---|---|---|---|
| | Variable | Fixed | Direct | Indirect |

**EXERCISE 2–4  Classification of Variable, Fixed, Period, and Product Costs** (LO1, LO5)
Below are listed various costs that are found in organizations.

1. Hamburger buns in a McDonald's outlet.
2. Advertising by a dental office.
3. Apples processed and canned by Del Monte Corporation.
4. Shipping canned apples from a Del Monte plant to customers.
5. Insurance on a Bausch & Lomb factory producing contact lenses.

6. Insurance on IBM's corporate headquarters.
7. Salary of a supervisor overseeing production of circuit boards at Hewlett-Packard.
8. Commissions paid to Encyclopedia Britannica salespersons.
9. Depreciation of factory lunchroom facilities at a General Electric plant.
10. Steering wheels installed in BMWs.

*Required:*
Classify each cost as being either variable or fixed with respect to the number of units sold. Also classify each cost as either a selling and administrative cost or a product cost. Prepare your answer sheet as shown below.

| | Cost Behaviour | | Selling and Administrative Cost | Product Cost |
| Cost Item | Variable | Fixed | | |
| --- | --- | --- | --- | --- |

Place an X in the appropriate columns to show the proper classification of each cost.

### EXERCISE 2–5  Determining Cost of Goods Sold (LO6, LO7)

The following cost and inventory data are taken from the accounting records of Mason Company for the year just completed:

Costs incurred:

| | |
| --- | --- |
| Direct labour cost | $ 70,000 |
| Purchases of raw materials | 118,000 |
| Indirect labour | 30,000 |
| Maintenance, factory equipment | 6,000 |
| Advertising expense | 90,000 |
| Insurance, factory equipment | 800 |
| Sales salaries | 50,000 |
| Rent, factory facilities | 20,000 |
| Supplies | 4,200 |
| Depreciation, office equipment | 3,000 |
| Depreciation, factory equipment | 19,000 |

| | Beginning of the Year | End of the Year |
| --- | --- | --- |
| Inventories: | | |
| Raw materials | $ 7,000 | $15,000 |
| Work in process | 10,000 | 5,000 |
| Finished goods | 20,000 | 35,000 |

*Required:*
1. Prepare a schedule of cost of goods manufactured in good form.
2. Prepare the cost of goods sold section of Mason Company's income statement for the year.

### EXERCISE 2–6  Cost Flows (LO6)

The Devon Motor Company produces automobiles. During April, the company purchased 8,000 batteries at a cost of $10 per battery. Devon withdrew 7,600 batteries from the storeroom during the month. Of these, 100 were used to replace batteries in autos being used by the company's travelling sales staff. The remaining 7,500 batteries withdrawn from the storeroom were placed in autos being produced by the company. Of the autos in production during April, 90% were completed and transferred from work in process to finished goods. Of the cars completed during the month, 30% were unsold at April 30.

There were no inventories of any type on April 1.

*Required:*

1. Determine the cost of batteries that would appear in each of the following accounts at April 30:
   a. Raw Materials.
   b. Work in Process.
   c. Finished Goods.
   d. Cost of Goods Sold.
   e. Selling Expense.
2. Specify whether each of the above accounts would appear on the balance sheet or on the income statement at April 30.

# Problems

CHECK FIGURE

Clay and glaze: variable, direct materials

## PROBLEM 2–1   Cost Identification (LO1, LO4, LO6)

Staci Valek began dabbling in pottery several years ago as a hobby. Her work is quite creative, and it has been so popular with friends and others that she has decided to quit her job with an aerospace firm and manufacture pottery full time. The salary from Staci's aerospace job is $2,500 per month.

Staci will rent a small building near her home to use as a place for manufacturing the pottery. The rent will be $500 per month. She estimates that the cost of clay and glaze will be $2 for each finished piece of pottery. She will hire workers to produce the pottery at a labour rate of $8 per pot. To sell her pots, Staci feels that she must advertise heavily in the local area. An advertising agency states that it will handle all advertising for a fee of $600 per month. Staci's brother will sell the pots; he will be paid a commission of $4 for each pot sold. Equipment needed to manufacture the pots will be rented at a cost of $300 per month.

Staci has already paid the legal and filing fees associated with incorporating her business in the state. These fees amounted to $500. A small room has been located in a tourist area that Staci will use as a sales office. The rent will be $250 per month. A phone installed in the room for taking orders will cost $40 per month. In addition, a recording device will be attached to the phone for taking after-hours messages.

Staci has some money in savings that is earning interest of $1,200 per year. These savings will be withdrawn and used to get the business going. For the time being, Staci does not intend to draw any salary from the new company.

*Required:*

1. Prepare an answer sheet with the following column headings:

| Name of the Cost | Variable Cost | Fixed Cost | Product Cost | | | Period (selling and administrative) Cost | Opportunity Cost | Sunk Cost |
| --- | --- | --- | --- | --- | --- | --- | --- | --- |
| | | | Direct Materials | Direct Labour | Manufacturing Overhead | | | |

List the different costs associated with the new company down the extreme left column (under Name of the Cost). Then place an *X* under each heading that helps describe the type of cost involved. There may be *X*'s under several column headings for a single cost. (That is, a cost may be a fixed cost, a period cost, and a sunk cost; you would place an *X* under each of these column headings opposite the cost.)

Under the Variable Cost column, list only those costs that would be variable with respect to the number of units of pottery that are produced and sold.

2. All of the costs you have listed above, except one, would be differential costs between the alternatives of Staci producing pottery or staying with the aerospace firm. Which cost is *not* differential? Explain.

CHECK FIGURE

Boxes for packaging: variable, direct

## PROBLEM 2–2   Cost Classification (LO1, LO2, LO4)

Listed below are a number of costs typically found in organizations.

1. Property taxes, factory.
2. Boxes used for packaging detergent.
3. Salespersons' commissions.
4. Supervisor's salary, factory.
5. Depreciation, executive automobiles.
6. Wages of workers assembling computers.
7. Packing supplies for out-of-state shipments.
8. Insurance, finished goods warehouses.
9. Lubricants for machines.
10. Advertising costs.
11. "Chips" used in producing calculators.

12. Shipping costs on merchandise sold.
13. Magazine subscriptions, factory lunchroom.
14. Thread in a garment factory.
15. Billing costs.
16. Executive life insurance.
17. Ink used in textbook production.
18. Fringe benefits, assembly-line workers.
19. Yarn used in sweater production.
20. Wages of receptionist, executive offices.

*Required:*

Prepare an answer sheet with column headings as shown below. For each cost item, indicate whether it would be variable or fixed with respect to the number of units produced and sold; and then whether it would be a selling cost, an administrative cost, or a manufacturing cost. If it is a manufacturing cost, indicate whether it would typically be treated as a direct cost or an indirect cost with respect to units of product. Three sample answers are provided for illustration.

| Cost Item | Variable or Fixed | Selling Cost | Administrative Cost | Manufacturing (product) Cost Direct | Manufacturing (product) Cost Indirect |
|---|---|---|---|---|---|
| Direct labour .......... | V | | | X | |
| Executive salaries ...... | F | | X | | |
| Factory rent .......... | F | | | | X |

**PROBLEM 2–3   Cost Identification and Cost Concepts** (LO1, LO2, LO4)

The Dorilane Company specializes in producing a set of wood patio furniture consisting of a table and four chairs. The set enjoys great popularity, and the company has ample orders to keep production going at its full capacity of 2,000 sets per year. Annual cost data at full capacity follow:

| | |
|---|---|
| Factory labour, direct ......................... | $118,000 |
| Advertising .................................... | 50,000 |
| Factory supervision ............................ | 40,000 |
| Property taxes, factory building ................. | 3,500 |
| Sales commissions ............................. | 80,000 |
| Insurance, factory ............................. | 2,500 |
| Depreciation, office equipment .................. | 4,000 |
| Lease cost, factory equipment ................... | 12,000 |
| Indirect materials, factory ...................... | 6,000 |
| Depreciation, factory building ................... | 10,000 |
| General office supplies (billing) ................. | 3,000 |
| General office salaries ......................... | 60,000 |
| Direct materials used (wood, bolts, etc.) ......... | 94,000 |
| Utilities, factory ............................... | 20,000 |

*Required:*

1. Prepare an answer sheet with the column headings shown below. Enter each cost item on your answer sheet, placing the dollar amount under the appropriate headings. As examples, this has been done already for the first two items in the list above. Note that each cost item is classified in two ways: first, as variable or fixed, with respect to the number of units produced and sold; and second, as a selling

CHECK FIGURE
(1) Total variable cost:
$321,000

and administrative cost or a product cost. (If the item is a product cost, it should also be classified as being either direct or indirect as shown.)

| | Cost Behaviour | | Selling or Administrative Cost | Product Cost | |
|---|---|---|---|---|---|
| Cost Item | Variable | Fixed | | Direct | Indirect* |
| Factory labour, direct ........... | $118,000 | | | $118,000 | |
| Advertising ........ | | $50,000 | $50,000 | | |

*To units of product.

2. Total the dollar amounts in each of the columns in (1) above. Compute the average product cost per patio set.
3. Assume that production drops to only 1,000 sets annually. Would you expect the average product cost per patio set to increase, decrease, or remain unchanged? Explain. No computations are necessary.
4. Refer to the original data. The president's brother-in-law has considered making himself a patio set and has priced the necessary materials at a building supply store. The brother-in-law has asked the president if he could purchase a patio set from the Dorilane Company "at cost," and the president agreed to let him do so.
   a. Would you expect any disagreement between the two men over the price the brother-in-law should pay? Explain. What price does the president probably have in mind? The brother-in-law?
   b. Since the company is operating at full capacity, what cost term used in the chapter might be justification for the president to charge the full, regular price to the brother-in-law and still be selling "at cost"?

### PROBLEM 2–4   Classification of Salary Cost (LO5)

You have just been hired by Ogden Company to fill a new position that was created in response to rapid growth in sales. It is your responsibility to coordinate shipments of finished goods from the factory to distribution warehouses located in various parts of Canada so that goods will be available as orders are received from customers.

The company is unsure how to classify your annual salary in its cost records. The company's cost analyst says that your salary should be classified as a manufacturing (product) cost; the controller says that it should be classified as a selling expense; and the president says that it does not matter which way your salary cost is classified.

*Required:*
1. Which viewpoint is correct? Why?
2. From the point of view of the reported net income for the year, is the president correct in his statement that it does not matter which way your salary cost is classified? Explain.

CHECK FIGURE
Case 1: Goods available
for sale = $19,000

### PROBLEM 2–5   Supplying Missing Data (LO6, LO7)

Supply the missing data in the following cases. Each case is independent of the others.

| | Case | | | |
|---|---|---|---|---|
| | 1 | 2 | 3 | 4 |
| Direct materials ................. | $ 4,500 | $ 6,000 | $ 5,000 | $ 3,000 |
| Direct labour .................... | ? | 3,000 | 7,000 | 4,000 |
| Manufacturing overhead .......... | 5,000 | 4,000 | ? | 9,000 |
| Total manufacturing costs ........ | 18,500 | ? | 20,000 | ? |
| Beginning work in process inventory .................... | 2,500 | ? | 3,000 | ? |
| Ending work in process inventory ... | ? | 1,000 | 4,000 | 3,000 |
| Cost of goods manufactured ....... | 18,000 | 14,000 | ? | ? |
| Sales ........................... | 30,000 | 21,000 | 36,000 | 40,000 |
| Beginning finished goods inventory .................... | 1,000 | 2,500 | ? | 2,000 |

continued

| | | | | |
|---|---|---|---|---|
| Cost of goods manufactured ....... | ? | ? | ? | 17,500 |
| Goods available for sale ........... | ? | ? | ? | ? |
| Ending finished goods inventory .... | ? | 1,500 | 4,000 | 3,500 |
| Cost of goods sold ............... | 17,000 | ? | 18,500 | ? |
| Gross margin ................... | 13,000 | ? | 17,500 | ? |
| Operating expenses ............. | ? | 3,500 | ? | ? |
| Net income ................... | $ 4,000 | ? | $ 5,000 | $ 9,000 |

**PROBLEM 2–6   Preparing Financial Statements for a Manufacturer** (LO6, LO7)

Swift Company was organized on March 1 of the current year. After five months of startup losses, management had expected to earn a profit during August, the most recent month. Management was disappointed, however, when the income statement for August also showed a loss. August's income statement follows:

CHECK FIGURE
(1) COGM: $310,000

**SWIFT COMPANY**
**Income Statement**
**For the Month Ended August 31**

| | | |
|---|---|---|
| Sales ........................................ | | $450,000 |
| Less operating expenses: | | |
| Indirect labour cost ......................... | $ 12,000 | |
| Utilities ................................... | 15,000 | |
| Direct labour cost .......................... | 70,000 | |
| Depreciation, factory equipment ............... | 21,000 | |
| Raw materials purchased ..................... | 165,000 | |
| Depreciation, sales equipment ................. | 18,000 | |
| Insurance ................................. | 4,000 | |
| Rent on facilities .......................... | 50,000 | |
| Selling and administrative salaries ............. | 32,000 | |
| Advertising ............................... | 75,000 | 462,000 |
| Net loss .................................. | | $(12,000) |

After seeing the $12,000 loss for August, Swift's president stated, "I was sure we'd be profitable within six months, but our six months are up and this loss for August is even worse than July's. I think it's time to start looking for someone to buy out the company's assets—if we don't, within a few months there won't be any assets to sell. By the way, I don't see any reason to look for a new controller. We'll just limp along with Sam for the time being."

The company's controller resigned a month ago. Sam, a new assistant in the controller's office, prepared the income statement above. Sam has had little experience in manufacturing operations. Additional information about the company follows:

a.  Some 60% of the utilities cost and 75% of the insurance apply to factory operations. The remaining amounts apply to selling and administrative activities.

b.  Inventory balances at the beginning and end of August were:

| | August 1 | August 31 |
|---|---|---|
| Raw materials ............ | $ 8,000 | $13,000 |
| Work in process ........... | 16,000 | 21,000 |
| Finished goods ............ | 40,000 | 60,000 |

c. Only 80% of the rent on facilities applies to factory operations; the remainder applies to selling and administrative activities.

The president has asked you to check over the income statement and make a recommendation as to whether the company should look for a buyer for its assets.

***Required:***
1. As one step in gathering data for a recommendation to the president, prepare a schedule of cost of goods manufactured in good form for August.
2. As a second step, prepare a new income statement for August.
3. On the basis of your statements prepared in (1) and (2) above, would you recommend that the company look for a buyer?

CHECK FIGURE
(1) COGM: $290,000

**PROBLEM 2–7   Financial Statements; Cost Behaviour** (LO1, LO6, LO7)
Various cost and sales data for Meriwell Company for the just completed year follow:

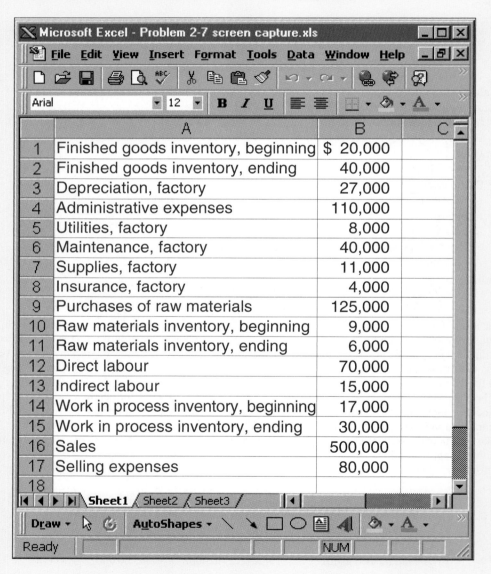

| | A | B |
|---|---|---|
| 1 | Finished goods inventory, beginning | $ 20,000 |
| 2 | Finished goods inventory, ending | 40,000 |
| 3 | Depreciation, factory | 27,000 |
| 4 | Administrative expenses | 110,000 |
| 5 | Utilities, factory | 8,000 |
| 6 | Maintenance, factory | 40,000 |
| 7 | Supplies, factory | 11,000 |
| 8 | Insurance, factory | 4,000 |
| 9 | Purchases of raw materials | 125,000 |
| 10 | Raw materials inventory, beginning | 9,000 |
| 11 | Raw materials inventory, ending | 6,000 |
| 12 | Direct labour | 70,000 |
| 13 | Indirect labour | 15,000 |
| 14 | Work in process inventory, beginning | 17,000 |
| 15 | Work in process inventory, ending | 30,000 |
| 16 | Sales | 500,000 |
| 17 | Selling expenses | 80,000 |
| 18 | | |

***Required:***
1. Prepare a schedule of cost of goods manufactured.
2. Prepare an income statement.

3. Assume that the company produced the equivalent of 10,000 units of product during the year just completed. What was the average cost per unit for direct materials? What was the average cost per unit for factory depreciation?

4. Assume that the company expects to produce 15,000 units of product during the coming year. What average cost per unit and what total cost would you expect the company to incur for direct materials at this level of activity? For factory depreciation? (In preparing your answer, assume that direct materials is a variable cost and that depreciation is a fixed cost; also assume that depreciation is computed on a straight-line basis.)

5. As the manager responsible for production costs, explain to the president any difference in the average cost per unit between (3) and (4) above.

**PROBLEM 2–8   Financial Statements; Cost Behaviour (LO1, LO6, LO7)**

CHECK FIGURE
(1) COGM: $690,000

Selected account balances for the year ended December 31 are provided below for Superior Company:

| Selling and administrative | |
| --- | --- |
| salaries | $110,000 |
| Insurance, factory | 8,000 |
| Utilities, factory | 45,000 |
| Purchases of raw | |
| materials | 290,000 |
| Indirect labour | 60,000 |
| Direct labour | ? |
| Advertising expense | 80,000 |
| Cleaning supplies, factory | 7,000 |
| Sales commissions | 50,000 |
| Rent, factory building | 120,000 |
| Maintenance, factory | 30,000 |

Inventory balances at the beginning and end of the year were as follows:

| | Beginning of the Year | End of the Year |
| --- | --- | --- |
| Raw materials | $40,000 | $10,000 |
| Work in process | ? | 35,000 |
| Finished goods | 50,000 | ? |

The total manufacturing costs for the year were $683,000; the goods available for sale totalled $740,000; and the cost of goods sold totalled $660,000.

*Required:*

1. Prepare a schedule of cost of goods manufactured in good form and the cost of goods sold section of the company's income statement for the year.

2. Assume that the dollar amounts given above are for the equivalent of 40,000 units produced during the year. Compute the average cost per unit for direct materials used and the average cost per unit for rent on the factory building.

3. Assume that in the following year the company expects to produce 50,000 units. What average cost per unit and total cost would you expect to be incurred for direct materials? For rent on the factory building? (In preparing your answer, you may assume that direct materials is a variable cost and that rent is a fixed cost.)

4. As the manager in charge of production costs, explain to the president the reason for any difference in average cost per unit between (2) and (3) above.

# Building Your Skills

CHECK FIGURE
(1) COGM: $870,000

**ANALYTICAL THINKING**   (LO6, LO7)

Visic Company, a manufacturing firm, produces a single product. The following information has been taken from the company's production, sales, and cost records for the just completed year.

| | |
|---|---:|
| Production in units | 29,000 |
| Sales in units | ? |
| Ending finished goods inventory in units | ? |
| Sales in dollars | $1,300,000 |
| Costs: | |
| Advertising | 105,000 |
| Entertainment and travel | 40,000 |
| Direct labour | 90,000 |
| Indirect labour | 85,000 |
| Raw materials purchased | 480,000 |
| Building rent (production uses 80% of the space; administrative and sales offices use the rest) | 40,000 |
| Utilities, factory | 108,000 |
| Royalty paid for use of production patent, $1.50 per unit produced | ? |
| Maintenanc, factory | 9,000 |
| Rent for special production equipment, $7,000 per year plus $0.30 per unit produced | ? |
| Selling and administrative salaries | 210,000 |
| Other factory overhead costs | 6,800 |
| Other selling and administrative expenses | 17,000 |

| | Beginning of the Year | End of the Year |
|---|---:|---:|
| Inventories: | | |
| Raw materials | $20,000 | $30,000 |
| Work in process | 50,000 | 40,000 |
| Finished goods | –0– | ? |

The finished goods inventory is being carried at the average unit production cost for the year. The selling price of the product is $50 per unit.

*Required:*
1. Prepare a schedule of goods manufactured for the year.
2. Compute the following:
   a. The number of units in the finished goods inventory at the end of the year.
   b. The cost of the units in the finished goods inventory at the end of the year.
3. Prepare an income statement for the year.

CHECK FIGURE
(2) COGM: $780,000

**COMMUNICATING IN PRACTICE**   (LO5, LO6, LO7)

"I was sure that when our battery hit the market it would be an instant success," said Roger Strong, founder and president of Solar Technology, Inc. "But just look at the gusher of red ink for the first quarter. It's obvious that we're better scientists than we are businesspeople." The data to which Roger was referring follow:

| SOLAR TECHNOLOGY, INC. Income Statement For the Quarter Ended March 31 | | |
|---|---:|---:|
| Sales (32,000 batteries) | | $960,000 |
| Less operating expenses: | | |
| Selling and administrative salaries | $110,000 | |
| Advertising | 90,000 | |
| Maintenance, production | 43,000 | |
| Indirect labour cost | 120,000 | |
| Cleaning supplies, production | 7,000 | |
| Purchases of raw materials | 360,000 | |
| Rental cost, facilities | 75,000 | |
| Insurance, production | 8,000 | |
| Depreciation, office equipment | 27,000 | |
| Utilities | 80,000 | |
| Depreciation, production equipment | 100,000 | |
| Direct labour cost | 70,000 | |
| Travel, salespersons | 40,000 | |
| Total operating expenses | | 1,130,000 |
| Net loss | | $ (170,000) |

"At this rate we'll be out of business within a year," said Cindy Zhang, the company's accountant. "But I've double-checked these figures, so I know they're right."

Solar Technology was organized at the beginning of the current year to produce and market a revolutionary new solar battery. The company's accounting system was set up by Margie Wallace, an experienced accountant who recently left the company to do independent consulting work. The statement above was prepared by Zhang, her assistant.

"We may not last a year if the insurance company doesn't pay the $226,000 it owes us for the 8,000 batteries lost in the warehouse fire last week," said Roger. "The insurance adjuster says our claim is inflated, but he's just trying to pressure us into a lower figure. We have the data to back up our claim, and it will stand up in any court."

On April 3, just after the end of the first quarter, the company's finished goods storage area was swept by fire and all 8,000 unsold batteries were destroyed. (These batteries were part of the 40,000 units completed during the first quarter.) The company's insurance policy states that the company will be reimbursed for the "cost" of any finished batteries destroyed or stolen. Zhang has determined this cost as follows:

$$\frac{\text{Total costs for the quarter, } \$1,130,000}{\text{Batteries produced during the quarter, } 40,000} = \$28.25 \text{ per battery}$$

$$8,000 \text{ batteries} \times \$28.25 \text{ per battery} = \$226,000$$

The following additional information is available on the company's activities during the quarter ended March 31:

a. Inventories at the beginning and end of the quarter were as follows:

| | Beginning of the Quarter | End of the Quarter |
|---|---|---|
| Raw materials | –0– | $10,000 |
| Work in process | –0– | 50,000 |
| Finished goods | –0– | ? |

b. Eighty percent of the rental cost for facilities and 90% of the utilities cost relate to manufacturing operations. The remaining amounts relate to selling and administrative activities.

*Required:*
1. Write a brief memorandum to the president identifying what conceptual errors, if any, were made in preparing the income statement above.
2. Prepare a schedule of cost of goods manufactured for the first quarter.
3. Prepare a corrected income statement for the first quarter. Your statement should show in detail how the cost of goods sold is computed.
4. Do you agree that the insurance company owes Solar Technology, Inc. $226,000? Explain your answer in another brief memorandum to the president.

**ETHICS CHALLENGE**   (LO5)

M. K. Gallant is president of Kranbrack Corporation, a company whose shares are traded on a national exchange. In a meeting with investment analysts at the beginning of the year, Gallant had predicted that the company's earnings would grow by 20% this year. Unfortunately, sales have been less than expected for the year, and Gallant concluded within two weeks of the end of the fiscal year that it would be impossible to ultimately report an increase in earnings as large as predicted unless some drastic action was taken. Accordingly, Gallant has ordered that wherever possible, expenditures should be postponed to the new year—including cancelling or postponing orders with suppliers, delaying planned maintenance and training, and cutting back on end-of-year advertising and travel. Additionally, Gallant ordered the company's controller to carefully scrutinize all costs that are currently classified as period costs and reclassify as many as possible as product costs. The company is expected to have substantial inventories of work in process and finished goods at the end of the year.

*Required:*
1. Why would reclassifying period costs as product costs increase this period's reported earnings?
2. Do you believe Gallant's actions are ethical? Why, or why not?

**TAKING IT TO THE NET**

As you know, the World Wide Web is a medium that is constantly evolving. To enable periodic update of site addresses, problems have been posted to the textbook website (www.mcgrawhill.ca/college/Garrison). After accessing the site, enter the Student Centre and select the chapter you are working on. Select and complete the "Taking It to the Net" problem.

**TEAMWORK IN ACTION**   (LO3)

Steel production involves a large amount of fixed costs. Since competition is defined primarily in terms of price, steel manufacturers (and many of their manufacturing and service industry counterparts) try to gain a competitive advantage by using economies of scale and investment in technology to increase productivity and drive unit costs lower. Their substantial fixed costs are the result of their size.

*Required:*
1. The team should discuss and then write up descriptions of the definitions of fixed costs and variable costs.
2. Each member of the team should select one of the following types of businesses and perform the following: (a) give examples of fixed costs and variable costs that would be incurred by that type of business, (b) choose a relevant measure of production or service activity for that type of business, and (c) explain the relationship between the production (or service) output and each of the following: total fixed costs, fixed cost per unit, total variable costs, and variable cost per unit.
   a. Steel company
   b. Hospital
   c. University
   d. Auto manufacturer
   Each team member should present his or her notes to the other teammates, who should confirm or correct the presentation. Then, work together as a team to complete steps 3 through 6 below.

3. Using the examples of fixed and variable costs for steel companies from (a) above, explain the relationship between production output at a steel company and each of the following: total fixed costs, fixed cost per unit, total variable costs, variable cost per unit, total costs, and average unit cost.
4. With an *X* axis (horizontal axis) of tonnes produced and a *Y* axis (vertical axis) of total costs, graph total fixed costs, total variable costs, and total costs against tonnes produced.
5. With an *X* axis of tonnes produced and a *Y* axis of unit costs, graph fixed cost per unit, variable cost per unit, and total (or average) cost per unit against tonnes produced.
6. Explain how costs (total and per unit) behave with changes in demand once capacity has been set.

# Chapter Three

# Systems Design: Job-Order Costing

## A Look Back

Chapter 1 described the three major activities of managers and compared and contrasted financial and managerial accounting. In Chapter 2, we defined many of the terms that are used to classify costs in business. We use many of these terms in Chapter 3. Now would be a good time to check your understanding of those terms by referring to the glossary at the end of Chapter 2.

## A Look at This Chapter

Chapter 3 distinguishes between two costing systems, job-order and process costing, and then provides an in-depth look at a job-order costing system. We describe how direct material and direct labour costs are accumulated on jobs. Then, we address manufacturing overhead, an indirect cost that must be allocated (or applied) to jobs. Finally, we take a more detailed look at the flow of costs through a company's accounting system using journal entries.

## A Look Ahead

Chapter 4 continues the discussion of cost determination in the process costing system. We show that many of the issues relating to cost accumulation in a job order costing system also carry over to the process costing system. Nonetheless, there are important differences which are highlighted in that chapter.

## Chapter Outline

**Costing Systems: Issues and Challenges**

**An Overview of Job-Order Costing—The Flow of Documents**
- Measuring Direct Materials Cost
- Job Cost Sheet
- Measuring Direct Labour Cost
- Application of Manufacturing Overhead
- Choice of an Allocation Base for Overhead Cost
- Computation of Unit Costs

**Job-Order Costing—The Flow of Costs**
- The Purchase and Issue of Materials
- Labour Cost
- Manufacturing Overhead Costs

- The Application of Manufacturing Overhead
- Cost of Goods Manufactured
- Cost of Goods Sold
- Summary of Manufacturing Cost Flows

**Problems of Overhead Application**
- Causes of Under-applied and Over-applied Overhead
- Disposition of Under- or Over-applied Overhead Balances
- Multiple Predetermined Overhead Rates
- Nonmanufacturing Costs

# DECISION FEATURE Leveraging Brain Power: System Ecotechnologies

System Ecotechnologies Inc., a Canadian success story, is located in Saskatoon, Saskatchewan. The company founder and owner, Dr. G. Lakshman designs engineering solutions for such clients as the governments of Egypt and El Salvador; public and private for-profit companies, such as Seagram's and EnviroSeed Technologies Inc.; not-for-profit organizations, such as Cities of Estevan, Whitehorse, and Prince George; and SaskPower and Saskatchewan Water Corporation. Dr. Lakshman has developed a reputation for being one of the world's foremost experts in the design of ingenious *customized* solutions to wastewater treatment problems and production of value-added chemicals from forest and agricultural wastes. Consider these two examples. He devised a way for Seagram's to be able to convert "mash"—a by-product of the process of turning grain into 100% ethanol, which has high concentrations of "heavy metals"—into environmentally friendly wastewater. In El Salvador, Dr. Lakshman showed how the "pulp" by-product of coffee production could be treated to extract caffeine and release harmless waste water.

System Ecotechnologies Inc.'s revenues are driven by the stream of contracts and projects—*jobs*—that Dr. Lakshman is able to attract *and* deliver on. Apart from being approached by clients, he also routinely networks with the industrial and research community and bids for government research contracts. He runs a lean operation from a small lab and office in a research park on the grounds of the University of Saskatchewan. Upon obtaining a project, Dr. Lakshman devotes the bulk of his time to designing the engineering and chemical solution and protocol to the client's problem. He conducts only the basic lab analysis on the premises using a lab assistant with general skills. He outsources all of the complex chemical and lab work and bills the client. His approach typically is to model a solution on a scale that can be analyzed and studied in the lab. Following this, a full scale implementation is designed and applied.

Dr. Lakshman's reputation would not be what it is if his own operations and the engineered solutions were not also *cost efficient*. His management system enables him to ride the ups and downs of an uncertain revenue stream. Cost management is a key component in being "lean." His business has many of the classic characteristics of a "job-shop"—a type of production system which is the subject of this chapter. In such systems, the business depends on "artisanship." The skills offered and leveraged relate to thinking creatively and

## Learning Objectives

*After studying Chapter 3, you should be able to:*

**LO1** Distinguish between process costing and job-order costing and identify companies that would use each costing method.

**LO2** Identify the documents used in a job-order costing system.

**LO3** Compute predetermined overhead rates and explain why estimated overhead costs (rather than actual overhead costs) are used in the costing process.

**LO4** Prepare journal entries to record costs in a job-order costing system.

**LO5** Apply overhead cost to Work in Process using a predetermined overhead rate.

**LO6** Prepare T-accounts to show the flow of costs in a job-order costing system and prepare schedules of cost of goods manufactured and cost of goods sold.

**LO7** Compute under- or over-applied overhead cost and prepare the journal entry to close the balance in Manufacturing Overhead to the appropriate accounts.

*crafting* a solution. Quality and timely delivery are key success factors. Each project or job is unique and the price charged comes down specifically to the work done to develop the solution. And, as just mentioned, *cost management* is absolutely critical.

―――――――――

Source: Site visit and personal interviews conducted by the authors and promotional materials furnished by Dr. Lakshman.

**P**roduct costing is the process of assigning costs to products and services provided by a company. An understanding of this process is vital to managers because the cost data provided by the costing systems will help them plan, control, direct, and make decisions.

# Costing Systems: Issues and Challenges

The purpose of costing systems is to accumulate and record the incurrence of costs and to assign the costs to the cost objects—products and activities which lead to their incurrence. Every costing system must accomplish two things: (1) it should tell you which costs are *traceable* to the cost object, and (2) how much has been incurred. These are the cost object's direct costs. And for those costs that cannot be traced directly to a product or activity—such as the costs of using physical facilities, utility and power costs, shop supplies and so on— the costing system or approach must tell you how to *allocate* those costs to the product or activity whose cost you are trying to compute. These are the indirect costs.

Costs are typically incurred when the company makes goods for or provides services to customers. Therefore, the nature of the costing system is intimately tied to the type of production system used by a company. Two types of production systems are common: *job shops* and *flow shops*. Job shops typically make a large variety of products in small quantities called *batches*. Each order or batch is also referred to as a *job*. Flow shops produce a much smaller variety of products in large volumes, using a standardized and fixed sequence of operations. Job shops typically "produce-to-order." These production facilities are capable of making special one-of-a-kind custom order and very often do. Small metal fabrication companies, for example, can make custom components for use in machinery. Golf equipment maker MacGregor Golf, for example, can custom forge its irons by grinding the top-line and the sole of the club in addition to setting the lie angle according to the specification of the customer. Examples of companies that use this type of production system include Bombardier, De Havilland, Hallmark (the greeting card maker), and LSG Sky Chefs (who prepare airline meals).

Flow shops typically "produce-to-stock," and the products that are made by these systems are sold from inventory. Examples include J. G. Schneider Foods in Kitchener, Ontario, that makes processed meats, any soft-drink bottler, the Potash Corporation of Saskatchewan, and Reynolds Aluminium. Television and appliance makers also fall in this category as do flour mills, cement manufacturers, and oil refiners. The difference between an appliance maker and an oil refiner is that oil refining is a *continuous* process, meaning the output is one continuous stream and you cannot distinguish between the first litre and the last litre of oil. Appliance production, however, is a *discrete* process, meaning that it is possible to identify the first unit from the last unit.

The challenge for management accountants in both these settings is not about tracing the use of direct materials or direct labour during production. It is the presence of indirect costs that poses the greatest challenge to managers and complicates the procedure of computing the cost of a product. Whether a product is made in small batches or in large volumes, management would want to know the *cost per unit* of the product. This involves a two-step procedure: (1) the cost of producing the batch must be determined, and (2) the total cost of producing the batch must be divided by the total quantity made to calculate the cost per unit. In a job shop, the overhead costs must be allocated to and included in the batch cost. In a flow shop, because production occurs in large volumes, continuously, over a period of time, the concept of a batch is not very meaningful. Instead, costs of production over a period of time are accumulated first within a process and then divided by the volume of production to compute the unit cost. Since overhead cost need not be incurred uniformly throughout the period, the choices of the period as well as the allocation method become important factors. The time period chosen can also be important to cost determination in a job shop production system because production costs, including overhead, might not stay constant throughout the period.

Lastly, there is one more challenge. To set prices, managers would like to know the cost of the product. This leads to two further issues. First, managers must decide which costs to include. A firm will incur both fixed as well as variable costs when engaged in providing goods and services. If a firm decides that the cost of each unit of product will include a portion of the fixed as well as the variable costs, the unit of product is said to *fully absorb* manufacturing costs. This approach to product costing is called **absorption (or full) costing:** all manufacturing costs are completely assigned to products. In certain circumstances, a different approach called **variable costing** is used. Here, only the variable cost of a product is considered in the analysis of the product's contribution to the firm's profits. The variable costing approach will be discussed later in the book. In this chapter and the next two, we will use the absorption costing approach to determine product costs. The absorption costing approach is common to many businesses, since (1) external financial reporting and tax reporting requirements dictate the use of this approach, and (2) many companies have found this approach useful for management accounting purposes.

The second issue for managers is that the cost of the product is not known until the product is made. Managers may be able to accurately estimate and predict the incurrence of direct costs before they are incurred. But what about manufacturing overhead? Should the manager wait until after the overhead costs are incurred—these are *actual* overhead costs—and then allocate them to the products? Or should managers first *budget* the manufacturing overhead costs and then *apply* these *budgeted* manufacturing overhead costs, using some kind of allocation method, to the products? If managers use *actual* manufacturing overhead costs and allocate them to the product, they are said to be using the **actual costing system.** If managers use *budgeted* manufacturing overhead costs and *apply* these costs to the product using an allocation method, they are said to be using a **normal costing system.** In a normal costing system, actual overhead costs are never assigned to the products, and these costs do not flow through the inventory accounts. Instead of actual costs, applied overhead costs are assigned to products, and only these applied overhead costs will flow through the inventory accounts. Certainly, managers are aware that the amount of the actual manufacturing overhead costs can end up being different (more or less) from the amount budgeted. Such differences are reconciled at the end of the operating cycle. Despite the existence of the difference between budgeted and actual overheads, product costs are never adjusted in a normal costing system. Instead, the adjustment typically occurs to the cost of goods sold as will be shown in detail later. The approach to costing systems taken in this chapter and the next is the absorption costing approach using the normal costing system. Variations to these approaches will be considered in later chapters. One final point that must be kept in mind about manufacturing overhead is that whether actual or budgeted overhead cost is applied, the cost *must be allocated* using an allocation method. The debate about which allocation method to use is separate from the debate regarding the merits of normal versus actual costing systems.

The two costing systems that parallel the job shop and flow types of production systems are called **job-order costing system** and **process costing system,** respectively. This chapter will describe the job-order costing system. Process costing is considered in the next chapter. Our illustration of the job-order costing system will deal with a manufacturing firm, but the same concepts and procedures are used by many service organizations.

*in business today*　**Job-Flow Systems in Canada**

How many Canadian manufacturing companies are designed as job flow systems? According to a survey of manufacturing companies, over 26% were organized as job-flow systems, whereas over 8% were organized as process-flow systems. What about the remaining 66% (two-thirds)? It is important to remember that job-flow and process-flow systems are two pure systems—two ends of a continuum—whereas in practice many companies may adopt some combination of the two. Another interesting point is that over 55% of the companies indicated that they were using just-in-time (JIT) production system, one component of the lean business model.

Source: Murray Lindsay and Suresh Kalagnanam. *The Adoption of Just-in-Time Production Systems in Canada and Their Association with Management Control Practices*. Society of Management Accountants of Canada, 1993. Reprinted with permission from CMA Canada.

# An Overview of Job-Order Costing—The Flow of Documents

**Learning Objective 2**
Identify the documents used in a job-order costing system.

To introduce job-order costing, we will follow a specific job as it progresses through the manufacturing process. Yost Precision Manufacturing has agreed to manufacture two experimental couplings, at cost, for Loops Unlimited, a manufacturer of roller coasters. A coupling connects the cars on the roller coaster and is a critical component in the performance and safety of the ride. Loops Unlimited wants to test a new design and requires only two units. Yost Precision considers the job as an investment; it wants to show Loops that it can make the couplings according to the required specifications and quality. If the tests are successful, Yost will be in a commanding position to win the order to supply couplings for the whole ride.

To get its "foot in the door," so to speak, Yost has agreed to supply the experimental couplings at its cost of goods sold. This means that Yost must carefully document its costs during the manufacturing process. This is the responsibility of Yost's job-order costing system. The cost of manufacturing the couplings will be determined by recording and accumulating the costs of direct materials, direct labour, and manufacturing overhead incurred to complete the job.

## Measuring Direct Materials Cost

The costing system kicks into gear when a production order is issued authorizing production. The production department then prepares a *materials requisition form* for the job. The **materials requisition form** is a detailed source document that (1) specifies the type and quantity of materials to be drawn from the storeroom, and (2) identifies the job to which the costs of materials are to be charged. The form is used to control the flow of materials into production and also for making entries in the accounting records. The information on the materials requisition form about the quantity and type of materials required is typically taken from the product's *bill of materials*. The **bill of materials** is a document that lists the type of and quantity of each item of materials required to complete one unit of product. The bill of materials itself is determined initially from blueprints and engineering specifications and will undergo many revisions as the product goes through its development cycle.

Each coupling will require one M46 housing and two G7 connectors. This means that the order will require four G7 connectors and two M46 housings in total to make two couplings. This information is shown in the materials requisition form in Exhibit 3–1

**Exhibit 3–1**
Materials Requisition Form

| Materials Requisition | | | |
|---|---|---|---|
| Number 14873 | | Date March 2 | |
| Job Number to Be Charged 2847 | | | |
| Department Milling | | | |

| Description | Quantity | Unit Cost | Total Cost |
|---|---|---|---|
| M46 Housing | 2 | $124 | $248 |
| G7 Connector | 4 | 103 | 412 |
| | | | $660 |
| | | | To Job Cost Sheet (Job #2B47) |

Authorized
Signature _Bill White_

prepared by the company's milling department. This completed form is presented to the storeroom clerk, who then issues the necessary raw materials. The storeroom clerk is not allowed to release materials without such a form bearing an authorized signature.

## Job Cost Sheet

After being notified that the production order has been issued, the Accounting Department prepares a *job cost sheet* similar to the one presented in Exhibit 3–2. A **job cost sheet** is a form prepared for each separate job that records the materials, labour, and overhead costs charged to the job.

In addition to serving as a means for charging costs to jobs, the job cost sheet also serves as a key part of a firm's accounting records. The job cost sheets form a subsidiary ledger to the Work in Process account. They are detailed records for the jobs in process that add up to the balance in Work in Process.

## Measuring Direct Labour Cost

Direct labour cost is handled in much the same way as direct materials cost. Direct labour consists of labour charges that are easily traced to a particular job. Labour charges that cannot be easily traced directly to any job are treated as part of manufacturing overhead. As discussed in the previous chapter, this latter category of labour costs is called *indirect labour* and includes such tasks as maintenance, supervision, and cleanup.

Workers use *time tickets* to record the time they spend on each job and task. A completed **time ticket** is an hour-by-hour summary of the employee's activities throughout the day. An example of an employee time ticket is shown in Exhibit 3–3. When working

Concept 3–1

**Exhibit 3–2**
Job Cost Sheet

JOB COST SHEET

Job Number __2847__                    Date Initiated ___March 2___

Date Completed _____

Department __Milling__                  Units Completed _____

Item __Special order coupling__

For Stock _____

| Direct Materials | | Direct Labour | | | Manufacturing Overhead | | |
|---|---|---|---|---|---|---|---|
| Req. No. | Amount | Ticket | Hours | Amount | Hours | Rate | Amount |
| From Materials Requisition Forms | From Materials Requisition Forms | From Time Tickets | From Time Tickets | From Time Tickets | | | |

| Cost Summary | | Units Shipped | | |
|---|---|---|---|---|
| Direct Materials | $ | Date | Number | Balance |
| Direct Labour | $ | | | |
| Manufacturing Overhead | $ | | | |
| Total Cost | $ | | | |
| Unit Cost | $ | | | |
| | | | | |
| | | | | |
| | | | | |

**Exhibit 3–3**
Employee Time Ticket

Time Ticket No. __843__                         Date __March 3__

Employee __Mary Holden__                        Station __4__

| Started | Ended | Time Completed | Rate | Amount | Job Number |
|---|---|---|---|---|---|
| 7:00 | 12:00 | 5.0 | $9 | $45 (To various job cost sheets) | 2847 |
| 12:30 | 2:30 | 2.0 | 9 | 18 | 2B50 |
| 2:30 | 3:30 | 1.0 | 9 | 9 | Maintenance |
| Totals | | 8.0 | | $72 | |

Supervisor __R.W. Pace__

on a specific job, the employee enters the job number on the time ticket and notes the amount of time spent on that job. When not assigned to a particular job, the employee records the nature of the indirect labour task (such as cleanup and maintenance) and the amount of time spent on the task.

At the end of the day, the time tickets are gathered and the Accounting Department enters the direct labour-hours and costs on individual job cost sheets. (See Exhibit 3–2 for an example of how direct labour costs are entered on the job cost sheet.) The daily time tickets are source documents that are used as the basis for labour cost entries into the accounting records.

The system we have just described is a manual method. Many companies now rely on computerized systems. Computers, coupled with such technology as bar codes, can eliminate much of the drudgery involved in routine bookkeeping activities while increasing timeliness and accuracy.

## Application of Manufacturing Overhead

Manufacturing overhead must be included with direct materials and direct labour on the job cost sheet since manufacturing overhead is also a product cost. However, assigning manufacturing overhead to units of product can be a difficult task. There are three reasons for this.

**Learning Objective 3**
Compute predetermined overhead rates and explain why estimated overhead costs (rather than actual overhead costs) are used in the costing process.

1. Manufacturing overhead is an *indirect cost*. This means that it is either impossible or difficult to trace these costs to a particular product or job.
2. Manufacturing overhead consists of many different items ranging from the grease used in machines to the annual salary of the production manager.
3. Even though output may fluctuate due to seasonal or other factors, manufacturing overhead costs tend to remain relatively constant due to the presence of fixed costs.

Given these problems, about the only way to assign overhead costs to products is to use an allocation process. This allocation of overhead costs is accomplished by selecting an **allocation base** that is common to all of the company's products and services. Examples include direct labour hours and machine hours.

The allocation base is used to compute the **predetermined overhead rate** in the following formula:

$$\text{Predetermined overhead rate} = \frac{\text{Estimated total manufacturing overhead cost}}{\text{Estimated total units in the allocation base}}$$

Note that the predetermined overhead rate is based on *estimates*, rather than actual results. This is because the *predetermined* overhead rate is computed *before* the period begins and is used to *apply* overhead cost to jobs throughout the period. The process of assigning overhead cost to jobs is called **overhead application.** The formula for determining the amount of overhead cost to apply to a particular job is:

$$\begin{array}{c}\text{Overhead applied to} \\ \text{a particular job}\end{array} = \begin{array}{c}\text{Predetermined} \\ \text{overhead rate} \\ \text{per unit of allocation base}\end{array} \times \begin{array}{c}\text{Amount of the allocation} \\ \text{base incurred by the job}\end{array}$$

When the allocation base is direct labour-hours (i.e., DLH), the formula becomes:

$$\begin{array}{c}\text{Overhead applied to} \\ \text{a particular job}\end{array} = \begin{array}{c}\text{Predetermined} \\ \text{overhead rate per DLH}\end{array} \times \begin{array}{c}\text{Actual direct labour-hours} \\ \text{charged to the job}\end{array}$$

For example, if the predetermined overhead rate is $8 per direct labour-hour, then $8 of overhead cost is *applied* to a job for each direct labour-hour incurred by the job.

**USING THE PREDETERMINED OVERHEAD RATE**   To illustrate the steps involved in computing and using a predetermined overhead rate, let us return to Yost Precision Machining. The company has estimated its total manufacturing overhead costs to be $320,000 for the year and its total direct labour-hours to be 40,000. Its predetermined overhead rate for the year would be $8 per direct labour-hour, as shown below:

$$\text{Predetermined overhead rate} = \frac{\text{Estimated total manufacturing overhead cost}}{\text{Estimated total units in the allocation base}}$$

$$\frac{\$320{,}000}{40{,}000 \text{ direct labour-hours}} = \$8 \text{ per direct labour-hour}$$

The job cost sheet in Exhibit 3–4 indicates that 27 direct labour-hours were charged to job 2B47. Therefore, a total of $216 of overhead cost would be applied to the job:

$$\begin{array}{c}\text{Overhead applied to} \\ \text{job 2B47}\end{array} = \begin{array}{c}\text{Predetermined} \\ \text{overhead rate}\end{array} \times \begin{array}{c}\text{Actual direct labour-hours} \\ \text{charged to job 2B47}\end{array}$$

$8 per direct labour-hour × 27 direct labour-hours = $216 of overhead applied to job 2B47

**Exhibit 3–4**
A Completed Job Cost Sheet

| JOB COST SHEET | | | | | | |
|---|---|---|---|---|---|---|
| Job Number __2847__ | | | Date Initiated __March 2__ | | | |
| | | | Date Completed __March 8__ | | | |
| Department __Milling__ | | | | | | |
| Item __Special order coupling__ | | | Units Completed __2__ | | | |
| For Stock_____ | | | | | | |

| Direct Materials | | Direct Labour | | | Manufacturing Overhead | | |
|---|---|---|---|---|---|---|---|
| Req. No. | Amount | Ticket | Hours | Amount | Hours | Rate | Amount |
| 14873 | $ 660 | 843 | 5 | $ 45 | 27 | $8/DLH | $216 |
| 14875 | 506 | 846 | 8 | 60 | | | |
| 14912 | 238 | 850 | 4 | 21 | | | |
| | $1,404 | 851 | 10 | 54 | | | |
| | | | 27 | $180 | | | |

| Cost Summary | | Units Shipped | | |
|---|---|---|---|---|
| Direct Materials | $1,404 | Date | Number | Balance |
| Direct Labour | $ 180 | March 8 | — | 2 |
| Manufacturing Overhead | $ 216 | | | |
| Total Cost | $1,800 | | | |
| Unit Cost | $ 900* | | | |
| | | | | |
| | | | | |
| | | | | |

*$1,800 ÷ 2 units = $900 per unit.

This amount of overhead has been entered on the job cost sheet in Exhibit 3–4. Note that this is *not* the actual amount of overhead caused by the job. There is no attempt to trace actual overhead costs to jobs—if that could be done, the costs would be direct costs, not overhead. The overhead assigned to the job is simply a share of the total overhead that was estimated at the beginning of the year. When a company applies overhead cost to jobs as we have done—that is, by multiplying actual activity times the predetermined overhead rate—it is called a *normal costing system.*

The overhead may be applied as direct labour-hours are charged to jobs, or all of the overhead can be applied at once when the job is completed. The choice is up to the company. If a job is not completed at year-end, however, overhead should be applied to value the work in process inventory.

**THE NEED FOR A PREDETERMINED RATE**   Instead of using a predetermined rate, a company could wait until the end of the accounting period to compute an actual overhead rate based on the *actual* total manufacturing costs and the *actual* total units in the allocation base for the period. However, managers cite several reasons for using predetermined overhead rates instead of actual overhead rates:

1. Managers would like to know the accounting system's valuation of completed jobs *before* the end of the accounting period. Suppose, for example, that Yost Precision Machining waits until the end of the year to compute its overhead rate. Then there would be no way for managers to know the cost of goods sold for job 2B47 until the close of the year, even though the job was completed and shipped to the customer in March. The seriousness of this problem can be reduced to some extent by computing the actual overhead more frequently, but that immediately leads to another problem as discussed below.

2. If actual overhead rates are computed frequently, seasonal factors in overhead costs or in the allocation base can produce fluctuations in the overhead rates. Managers generally feel that such fluctuations in overhead rates serve no useful purpose and are misleading.
3. The use of a predetermined overhead rate simplifies record keeping. To determine the overhead cost to apply to a job, the accounting staff at Yost Precision Machining simply multiplies the direct labour-hours recorded for the job by the predetermined overhead rate of $8 per direct labour-hour.

For these reasons, most companies use predetermined overhead rates, rather than actual overhead rates, in their cost accounting systems.

## Choice of an Allocation Base for Overhead Cost

Ideally, the allocation base should be a *cost driver* of the overhead cost. A **cost driver** is a factor, such as machine-hours, beds occupied, computer time, or flight-hours, that causes overhead costs. If a base is used to compute overhead rates that does not "drive" overhead costs, then the result will be inaccurate overhead rates and distorted product costs. For example, if direct labour and overhead costs have been moving in opposite directions in a company because of shift toward automation and the increased use of highly skilled indirect labour, such as engineers, direct labour should not be used as the allocation base. If direct labour is used in this situation, then products with high direct labour hour requirements will be over-costed and products with low direct labour hours requirement will be under-costed. The debate about which allocation base is appropriate has spurred the redesign of costing systems according to the principles of *activity-based costing* (ABC). ABC is a costing technique that is designed to more accurately reflect the demands that products, customers, and other cost objects make on overhead resources. The ABC approach is the topic of Chapter 5.

## The Potential for Inaccurate Product Costs

*in business today*

Labour costs were a large portion of total manufacturing costs as recently as 20 years ago. However, increasing price competition and a strong focus on quality and reliability have forced many manufacturers to automate many of their processes. A 2002–2003 Management Issues survey conducted by Canadian Manufacturers & Exporters suggests that Canadian manufacturers are rapidly adopting computer technology in such areas as design and engineering, fabrication and assembly, materials handling, and control and communication. A direct result of automation is that direct labour is becoming less important and also represents a smaller portion of total manufacturing costs. This raises two issues: (1) whether companies should maintain elaborate systems to track direct labour hours and costs, and (2) whether direct labour is still an appropriate base to allocate manufacturing overhead costs.

Source: http://www.cme-mec.ca/national/documents/management_issues_survey_oct_07_2002.pdf

## Computation of Unit Costs

With the application of Yost Precision Machining's $216 manufacturing overhead to the job cost sheet in Exhibit 3–4, the job cost sheet is almost complete. There are two final steps. First, the totals for direct materials, direct labour, and manufacturing overhead are transferred to the Cost Summary section of the job cost sheet and added together to obtain the total cost for the job. Then the total cost ($1,800) is divided by the number of units (2) to obtain the unit cost ($900). As indicated earlier, *this unit cost is an average cost and should not be interpreted as the cost that would actually be incurred if another unit were produced.* Much of the actual overhead would not change at all if another unit were produced, and so the incremental cost of an additional unit is something less than the average unit cost of $900.

The completed job cost sheet is now ready to be transferred to the Finished Goods inventory account, where it will serve as the basis for valuing unsold units in ending inventory and determining cost of goods sold.

The sequence of events discussed above is summarized in Exhibit 3–5. A careful study of the flow of documents in this exhibit will provide a good overview of the overall operation of a job-order costing system.

---

*decision* *maker*

## Treasurer, Class Reunion Committee

It is hard to believe that 10 years have passed so quickly since your graduation from high school. Take a minute to reflect on what has happened in that time frame. After high school, you attended the local community college, transferred to a university, and graduated on time. You are juggling a successful career, classes in an evening MBA program, and a new family. And now, after reminiscing with one of your high school classmates, you have somehow agreed to handle the financial arrangements for your 10-year reunion. What were you thinking? Well, at least you can fall back on those accounting skills.

You call the restaurant where the reunion will be held and jot down the most important information. The meal cost (including beverages) will be $30 per person plus a 15% gratuity. An additional $200 will be charged for a banquet room with a dance floor. (You do not remember dancing in high school.) A band has been hired for $500. One of the members of the reunion committee informs you that there is just enough money left in the class bank account to cover the printing and mailing costs. He mentions that at least one-half of the class of 400 will attend the reunion and wonders if he should add the 15% gratuity to the $30 per person meal cost when he drafts the invitation, which will indicate that a cheque must be returned with the reply card.

How should you respond? How much will you need to charge to cover the various costs? After making your decision, label your answer with the managerial accounting terms covered in this chapter. Finally, identify any issues that should be investigated further.

---

# Job-Order Costing—The Flow of Costs

**Learning Objective 4**
Prepare journal entries to record costs in a job-order costing system.

We are now ready to look at the *flow of costs* through the company's formal accounting system. To illustrate, we shall consider a single month's activity for Rand Company, a producer of gold and silver commemorative medallions. Rand Company has two jobs in process during April, the first month of its fiscal year. Job A, a special minting of 1,000 gold medallions commemorating the invention of motion pictures, was started during March. By the end of March, $30,000 in manufacturing costs had been recorded for the job. Job B, an order for 10,000 silver medallions commemorating the fall of the Berlin Wall, was started in April.

## The Purchase and Issue of Materials

On April 1, Rand Company had $7,000 in raw materials on hand. During the month, the company purchased an additional $60,000 in raw materials. The purchase is recorded in journal entry (1) below:

(1)

| | | |
|---|---|---|
| Raw Materials   ......................... | 60,000 | |
|      Accounts Payable   ...................... | | 60,000 |

**Exhibit 3–5**

The Flow of Documents in a Job-Order Costing System

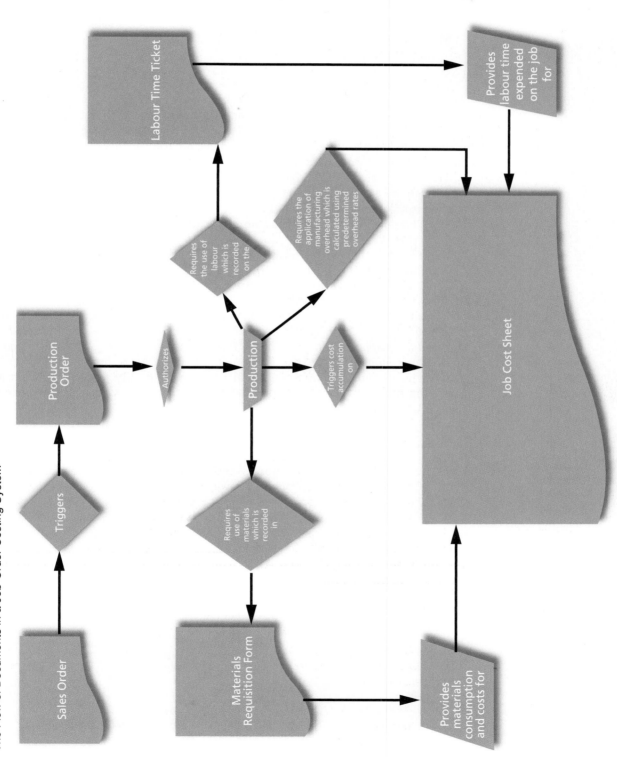

Sales Order

Triggers

Production Order

Authorizes

Production

Requires the use of labour which is recorded on the

Labour Time Ticket

Provides labour time expended on the job for

Requires the application of manufacturing overhead which is calculated using predetermined overhead rates

Triggers cost accumulation on

Requires use of materials which is recorded in

Materials Requisition Form

Provides materials consumption and costs for

Job Cost Sheet

As explained in the previous chapter, Raw Materials is an asset account. Thus, when raw materials are purchased, they are initially recorded as an asset—not as an expense.

**ISSUE OF DIRECT AND INDIRECT MATERIALS**   During April, $52,000 in raw materials were requisitioned from the storeroom for use in production. Entry (2) records the issue of the materials to the production departments.

(2)

| | | |
|---|---|---|
| Work in Process ........................... | 50,000 | |
| Manufacturing Overhead .................... | 2,000 | |
|    Raw Materials ........................... | | 52,000 |

The materials charged to Work in Process represent direct materials for specific jobs. As these materials are entered into the Work in Process account, they are also recorded on the appropriate job cost sheets. This point is illustrated in Exhibit 3–6, where $28,000 of the $50,000 in direct materials is charged to job A's cost sheet and the remaining $22,000 is charged to job B's cost sheet. (In this example, all data are presented in summary form, and the job cost sheet is abbreviated.)

The $2,000 charged to Manufacturing Overhead in entry (2) represents indirect materials used in production during April. Observe that the Manufacturing Overhead account is separate from the Work in Process account. The purpose of the Manufacturing Overhead account is to accumulate all manufacturing overhead costs as they are incurred during a period.

Before leaving Exhibit 3–6, we need to point out one additional thing. Note from the exhibit that the job cost sheet for job A contains a beginning balance of $30,000. We stated earlier that this balance represents the cost of work done during March that has been carried forward to April. Also note that the Work in Process account contains the same $30,000 balance. *The reason the $30,000 appears in both places is that the Work in Process account is a control account and the job cost sheets form a subsidiary ledger. Thus, the Work in Process account contains a summarized total of all costs appearing on the individual job cost sheets for all jobs in process at any given point in time.* Since Rand Company had only job A in process at the beginning of April, job A's $30,000 balance on that date is equal to the balance in the Work in Process account.

**Exhibit 3–6**
Raw Materials Cost Flows

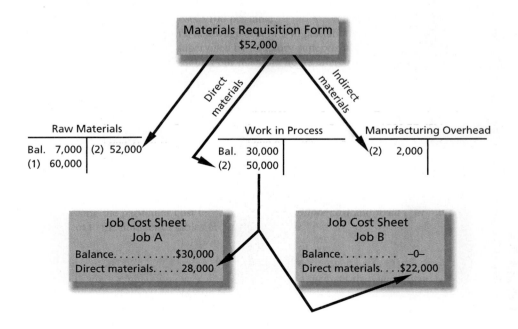

**ISSUE OF DIRECT MATERIALS ONLY**   Sometimes, the materials drawn from the Raw Materials inventory account are all direct materials. In this case, the entry to record the issue of the materials into production would be as follows:

| | | |
|---|---|---|
| Work in Process ........................... | XXX | |
| Raw Materials ........................... | | XXX |

## Labour Cost

As work is performed each day in various departments of Rand Company, employee time tickets are filled out by workers, collected, and forwarded to the Accounting Department. In the Accounting Department, the tickets are costed according to the various employee wage rates, and the resulting costs are classified as either direct or indirect labour. This costing and classification for April resulted in the following summary entry:

(3)

| | | |
|---|---|---|
| Work in Process ........................... | 60,000 | |
| Manufacturing Overhead ................... | 15,000 | |
| Salaries and Wages Payable ................ | | 75,000 |

Only direct labour is added to the Work in Process account. For Rand Company, this amounted to $60,000 for April.

At the same time that direct labour costs are added to Work in Process, they are also added to the individual job cost sheets, as shown in Exhibit 3–7. During April, $40,000 of direct labour cost was charged to job A and the remaining $20,000 was charged to job B.

The labour costs charged to Manufacturing Overhead represent the indirect labour costs of the period, such as supervision, janitorial work, and maintenance.

## Manufacturing Overhead Costs

Recall that all costs of operating the factory other than direct materials and direct labour are classified as manufacturing overhead costs. These costs are entered directly into the

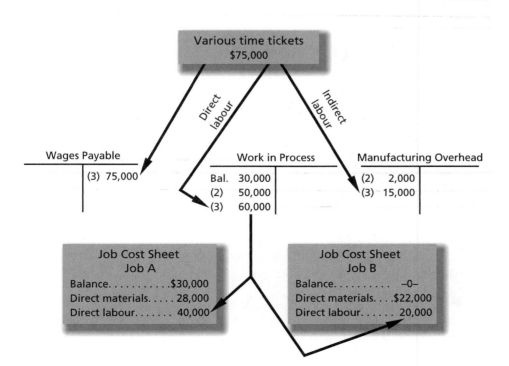

**Exhibit 3–7**
Labour Cost Flows

Manufacturing Overhead account as they are incurred. To illustrate, assume that Rand Company *incurred* the following general factory costs during April:

| | |
|---|---:|
| Utilities (heat, water, and power) ..................... | $21,000 |
| Rent on factory equipment ......................... | 16,000 |
| Miscellaneous factory costs ........................ | 3,000 |
| Total ............................................ | $40,000 |

The following entry records the incurrence of these costs:

(4)

| | | |
|---|---:|---:|
| Manufacturing Overhead .................... | 40,000 | |
|     Accounts Payable ...................... | | 40,000 |

In addition, let us assume that during April, Rand Company recognized $13,000 in accrued property taxes and that $7,000 in prepaid insurance expired on factory buildings and equipment. The following entry records these items:

(5)

| | | |
|---|---:|---:|
| Manufacturing Overhead .................... | 20,000 | |
|     Property Taxes Payable ................... | | 13,000 |
|     Prepaid Insurance ...................... | | 7,000 |

Finally, let us assume that the company recognized $18,000 in depreciation on factory equipment during April. The following entry records the accrual of this depreciation:

(6)

| | | |
|---|---:|---:|
| Manufacturing Overhead .................... | 18,000 | |
|     Accumulated Depreciation ................ | | 18,000 |

In short, *all* manufacturing overhead costs are recorded directly into the Manufacturing Overhead account as they are incurred day by day throughout a period. It is important to understand that Manufacturing Overhead is a control account for many—perhaps thousands—of subsidiary accounts, such as Indirect Materials, Indirect Labour, Factory Utilities, and so on. As the Manufacturing Overhead account is debited for costs during a period, the various subsidiary accounts are also debited. In the example above and also in the assignment material for this chapter, we omit the entries to the subsidiary accounts for the sake of brevity.

## The Application of Manufacturing Overhead

**Learning Objective 5**
Apply overhead cost to Work in Process using a predetermined overhead rate.

Since actual manufacturing costs are charged to the Manufacturing Overhead control account, rather than to Work in Process, how are manufacturing overhead costs assigned to Work in Process? The answer is, by means of the predetermined overhead rate. Recall from our discussion earlier in the chapter that a predetermined overhead rate is established at the beginning of each year. The rate is calculated by dividing the estimated total manufacturing overhead cost for the year by the estimated total units in the allocation base (measured in machine-hours, direct labour-hours, or some other base). The predetermined overhead rate is then used to apply overhead costs to jobs. For example, if direct labour-hours is the allocation base, overhead cost is applied to each job by multiplying the number of direct labour-hours charged to the job by the predetermined overhead rate.

To illustrate, assume that Rand Company has used machine-hours to compute its predetermined overhead rate and that this rate is $6 per machine-hour. Also assume that during April, 10,000 machine-hours were worked on job A and 5,000 machine-hours were worked on job B (a total of 15,000 machine-hours). Thus, $90,000 in overhead cost (15,000 machine-hours × $6 per machine-hour = $90,000) would be applied to Work in

**Exhibit 3–8**
The Flow of Costs in Overhead
Application

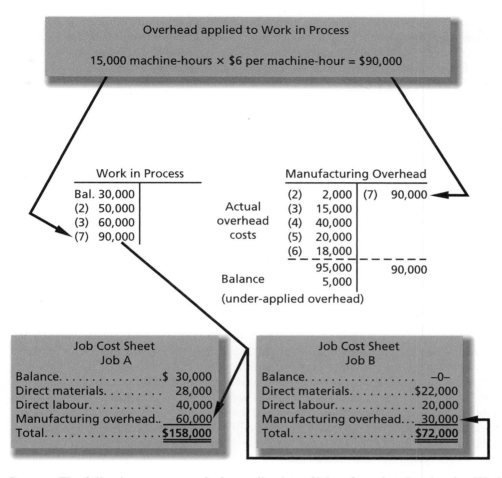

Process. The following entry records the application of Manufacturing Overhead to Work in Process:

(7)

| | | |
|---|---|---|
| Work in Process ........................... | 90,000 | |
|    Manufacturing Overhead .................. | | 90,000 |

The flow of costs through the Manufacturing Overhead account is shown in Exhibit 3–8.

The "actual overhead costs" in the Manufacturing Overhead account in Exhibit 3–8 are the costs that were added to the account in entries (2)–(6). Observe that the incurrence of these actual overhead costs [entries (2)–(6)] and the application of overhead to Work in Process [entry (7)] represent two separate and entirely distinct processes.

**THE CONCEPT OF A CLEARING ACCOUNT**  The Manufacturing Overhead account operates as a clearing account. As we have noted, actual factory overhead costs are debited to the accounts as they are incurred day by day throughout the year. At certain intervals during the year, usually when a job is completed, overhead cost is applied to the Work in Process account by means of the predetermined overhead rate. This sequence of events is illustrated below:

**Manufacturing Overhead**
**(a clearing account)**

| Actual overhead costs are charged to the account as these costs are incurred day by day throughout the period. | Overhead is applied to Work in Process using the predetermined overhead rate. |
|---|---|

As we emphasized earlier, the predetermined overhead rate is based entirely on estimates of what overhead costs are *expected* to be, and it is established before the year begins. As a result, the overhead cost applied during a year will almost certainly turn out to be different from the overhead cost that is actually incurred. For example, note from Exhibit 3–8 that Rand Company's actual overhead costs for the period are $5,000 greater than the overhead cost that has been applied to Work in Process. The resulting $5,000 debit balance in the Manufacturing Overhead account is called "under-applied overhead" because the applied cost ($90,000) is less than the actual cost ($95,000). We will reserve discussion of what to do with this $5,000 balance until the next section, Problems of Overhead Application.

For the moment, we can conclude by noting from Exhibit 3–8 that the cost of a completed job consists of the actual materials cost of the job, the actual labour cost of the job, and the overhead cost *applied* to the job. Pay particular attention to the following subtle but important point: *Actual overhead costs are not charged to jobs; actual overhead costs do not appear on the job cost sheet, nor do they appear in the Work in Process account. Only the applied overhead cost, based on the predetermined overhead rate, appears on the job cost sheet and in the Work in Process account.*

## Cost of Goods Manufactured

When a job has been completed, the finished output is transferred from the production departments to the finished goods warehouse. By this time, the accounting department will have charged the job with direct materials and direct labour cost, and manufacturing overhead will have been applied using the predetermined rate. A transfer of these costs must be made within the costing system that *parallels* the physical transfer of the goods to the finished goods warehouse. The costs of the completed job are transferred out of the Work in Process account and into the Finished Goods account. The sum of all amounts transferred between these two accounts represents the cost of goods manufactured for the period. (This point was illustrated earlier in Exhibit 2–7 in Chapter 2.)

In the case of Rand Company, let us assume that job A was completed during April. The following entry transfers the cost of job A from Work in Process to Finished Goods:

(8)

| | | |
|---|---|---|
| Finished Goods ........................ | 158,000 | |
| Work in Process ........................ | | 158,000 |

The $158,000 represents the completed cost of job A, as shown on the job cost sheet in Exhibit 3–8. Since job A was the only job completed during April, the $158,000 also represents the cost of goods manufactured for the month.

Job B was not completed by month-end, and so its cost will remain in the Work in Process account and carry over to the next month. If a balance sheet is prepared at the end of April, the cost accumulated thus far on job B will appear as "Work in process inventory" in the assets section.

## Cost of Goods Sold

As units in finished goods are shipped to fill customers' orders, the unit cost appearing on the job cost sheets is used as a basis for transferring the cost of the items sold from the Finished Goods account into the Cost of Goods Sold account. If a complete job is shipped, as in the case where a job has been done to a customer's specifications, then it is a simple matter to transfer the entire cost appearing on the job cost sheet into the Cost of Goods Sold account. In most cases, however, only a portion of the units involved in a particular job will be immediately sold. In these situations, the unit cost must be used to determine how much product cost should be removed from Finished Goods and charged to Cost of Goods Sold.

For Rand Company, we will assume 750 of the 1,000 gold medallions in job A were shipped to customers by the end of the month for total sales revenue of $225,000. Since 1,000 units were produced and the total cost of the job from the job cost sheet was $158,000, the unit product cost was $158. The following journal entries would record the sale (all sales are on account):

(9)

| Accounts Receivable | 225,000 | |
| Sales | | 225,000 |

(10)

| Cost of Goods Sold | 118,500 | |
| Finished Goods | | 118,500 |
| ($158 per unit × 750 units = $118,500) | | |

With entry (10), the flow of costs through our job-order costing system is completed.

## Summary of Manufacturing Cost Flows

To pull the entire example together, journal entries (1) through (10) are summarized in Exhibit 3–9. The flow of costs through the accounts is presented in T-account form in Exhibit 3–10. The corresponding model summarizing the cost flows in a job order system appears in Exhibit 3–11. Study Exhibits 3–10 and 3–11 together.[1] A good grasp of the logic of the cost flows will be very helpful in understanding how an income statement for a manufacturing concern is constructed. We have illustrated this process in Exhibit 3–12. This exhibit presents the supporting cost schedules as a series of "waterfalls" which cascade down into the income statement. It is easy to see how the various schedules articulate with each other and where the data in the schedules come from. To illustrate, compare the T-accounts in Exhibit 3–10 to the schedules in Exhibit 3–12. Note that the direct materials used is calculated from the raw materials T-account. Direct materials used then flows into the Work in Process account. The entries in the Work in Process account provide the basis for determining Cost of Goods Manufactured. Then the Cost of Goods Manufactured flows into the finished goods account. The inventory balances in finished goods along with Cost of Goods Manufactured determines Cost of Goods Sold which finally flows into the income statement.

> **Learning Objective 6**
> Prepare T-accounts to show the flow of costs in a job-order costing system and prepare schedules of cost of goods manufactured and cost of goods sold.

## Problems of Overhead Application

You will note from Exhibit 3–10 that the manufacturing overhead account shows a debit balance of $5,000. The cost of goods sold amount of $118,500 does not reflect this $5,000, since it only contains the *applied* manufacturing overhead. Since the *actual* manufacturing overhead costs incurred amount to $95,000 and only $90,000 has been *applied*, the debit balance of $5,000 in manufacturing overhead account represents **under-applied overhead.** The opposite result can also occur in some circumstances. This is where there will be a credit balance in the manufacturing overhead account indicating that *applied* overhead costs are greater than the *actual* manufacturing overhead costs incurred. In this case the credit balance in the manufacturing overhead account is called **over-applied overhead.**

Since the predetermined overhead rate is established before a period begins and is based entirely on estimated data, there generally will be either under-applied or

> **Learning Objective 7**
> Compute under- or over-applied overhead cost and prepare the journal entry to close the balance in Manufacturing Overhead to the appropriate accounts.

---

[1]Note that in Exhibit 3–10, we have shown for completeness some of the entries to the accounts that will have been made prior to start of the manufacturing process. The assignment material in this chapter will not require that such entries be presented and explained.

**Exhibit 3–9**
Summary of Rand Company
Journal Entries

(1)

| | | |
|---|---|---|
| Raw Materials ..................................... | 60,000 | |
|     Accounts Payable ............................ | | 60,000 |

(2)

| | | |
|---|---|---|
| Work in Process ................................. | 50,000 | |
| Manufacturing Overhead ......................... | 2,000 | |
|     Raw Materials ............................... | | 52,000 |

(3)

| | | |
|---|---|---|
| Work in Process ................................. | 60,000 | |
| Manufacturing Overhead ......................... | 15,000 | |
|     Salaries and Wages Payable .................... | | 75,000 |

(4)

| | | |
|---|---|---|
| Manufacturing Overhead ......................... | 40,000 | |
|     Accounts Payable ............................ | | 40,000 |

(5)

| | | |
|---|---|---|
| Manufacturing Overhead ......................... | 20,000 | |
|     Property Taxes Payable ....................... | | 13,000 |
|     Prepaid Insurance ........................... | | 7,000 |

(6)

| | | |
|---|---|---|
| Manufacturing Overhead ......................... | 18,000 | |
|     Accumulated Depreciation .................... | | 18,000 |

(7)

| | | |
|---|---|---|
| Work in Process ................................. | 90,000 | |
|     Manufacturing Overhead ...................... | | 90,000 |

(8)

| | | |
|---|---|---|
| Finished Goods .................................. | 158,000 | |
|     Work in Process ............................. | | 158,000 |

(9)

| | | |
|---|---|---|
| Accounts Receivable ............................. | 225,000 | |
|     Sales ....................................... | | 225,000 |

(10)

| | | |
|---|---|---|
| Cost of Goods Sold ............................. | 118,500 | |
|     Finished Goods .............................. | | 118,500 |

over-applied overhead at the end of the period. To illustrate how this can happen, consider another example. Suppose that two companies—Turbo Crafters and Black and Howell—have prepared the following estimated data for the coming year:

| | Company | |
|---|---|---|
| | **Turbo Crafters** | **Black and Howell** |
| Predetermined overhead rate based on | Machine-hours | Direct materials cost |
| Estimated manufacturing overhead | $300,000 (a) | $120,000 (a) |
| Estimated machine hours | 75,000 (b) | — |
| Estimated direct materials costs | — | $80,000 (b) |
| Predetermined overhead rate, (a) ÷ (b) | $4 per machine-hour | 150% of direct materials cost |

Now assume that *actual* overhead cost and *actual* activity recorded during the year in each company are as follows:

| | Company | |
| --- | --- | --- |
| | **Turbo Crafters** | **Black and Howell** |
| Actual manufacturing overhead costs | $290,000 | $130,000 |
| Actual machine-hours | 68,000 | — |
| Actual direct materials costs | — | $90,000 |

For each company, the actual data for both cost and activity differ from the estimates used in computing the predetermined overhead rate. This leads to under-applied and over-applied overhead as follows:

| | Company | |
| --- | --- | --- |
| | **Turbo Crafters** | **Black and Howell** |
| Actual manufacturing overhead costs | $290,000 | $130,000 |
| Manufacturing overhead costs applied to Work in Process: 68,000 *actual* machine-hours × $4 per machine-hour | $272,000 | — |
| $90,000 *actual* direct materials cost × 150% | | $135,000 |
| Under-applied (over-applied) overhead | $18,000 | $(5,000) |

For Turbo Crafters, the overhead that was applied to Work in Process ($272,000) is less than the actual overhead cost for the year ($290,000). Therefore, overhead is under-applied. The opposite is true for Black and Howell. The applied overhead to Work in Process ($135,000) is greater than the actual overhead cost for the year ($130,000). So, the overhead is over-applied.

It is important for you to note that the impact of the original estimate of the overhead cost is felt only through the predetermined overhead rate that is used. The original estimate is not directly involved in the computation of the under-applied or over-applied overhead.

## Causes of Under- and Over-applied Overheads

What causes under-applied or over-applied overhead? From the example of Turbo Crafters and Black and Howell, it would seem that under-applied overhead or over-applied overhead will exist because the estimates of the manufacturing overhead cost for the year and the quantity of the allocation base made at the beginning of the period will differ from the actual amounts at the end of the year. This can happen if there are unexpected changes in overhead spending and in demand for the companies' products. This way of understanding the cause for under-applied or over-applied overhead suggests that the only problem is with the inputs used and the problem is not with the method itself.

The *method* of applying overhead to jobs using a predetermined rate assumes that actual overhead costs will be *proportional in the amount of the predetermined rate* to the actual amount of the allocation base incurred during the period. At Turbo Crafters, for example, this means that the managers of the company believe (1) that changes in manufacturing overhead are proportional to the change in machine-hours, and (2) that the rate of increase in manufacturing overhead is $4 per machine-hour. Let us consider this carefully. Look at Exhibit 3–13 which summarizes the process of determining the

## Exhibit 3–10
Flow of Costs through T-Accounts: Rand Company

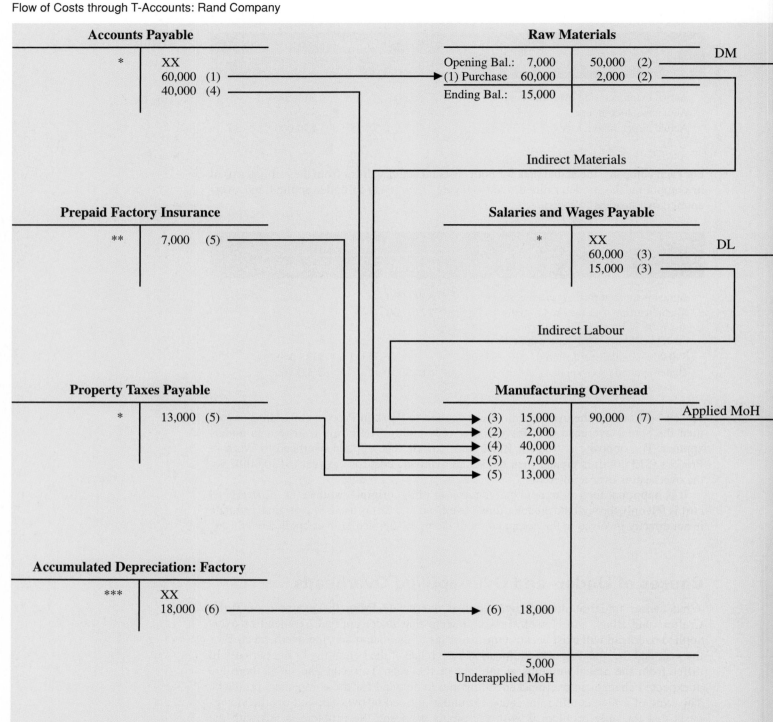

(continued)

| Work-in-Process | | Finished Goods | | | Cost of Goods Sold |
|---|---|---|---|---|---|
| Opening Bal.: 30,000 | | Opening Bal.: 10,000 | 118,500 | (10) → (10) | 118,500 |
| 2)  50,000 | 158,000 (8) → CoGM | (8)  158,000 | | CoGS | |
| | | Ending Bal.:  49,500 | | | |

| | | Sales | | Accounts Receivable | |
|---|---|---|---|---|---|
| | | | 225,000 | (9) → (9) | XX 225,000 |
| 3)  60,000 | | | | | |
| 7)  90,000 | | | | | |
| Ending Bal.:  72,000 | | | | | |

Explanation of Symbols.

\* Debit entry occurs when payment is made. Credit entry will be to cash.

\*\* Debit entry will have been made at start of period when payment was made. Cash will have been credited.

\*\*\* Debit entry will occur on disposal of asset.

XX Normal balance in Account.

**Exhibit 3–11**
A General Model of Cost Flows

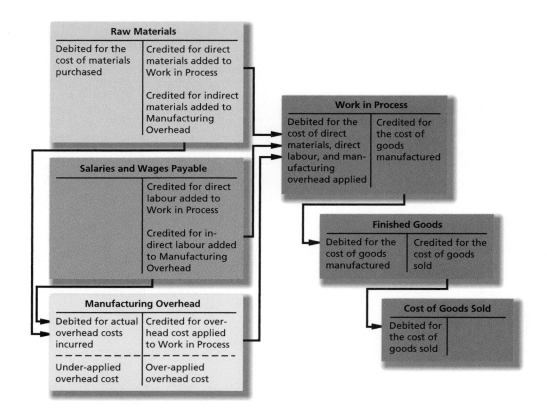

predetermined overhead rate, the allocation of overhead to Work in Process and the computation of the under-applied and over-applied overhead. It can be seen that if the actual total overhead cost is not the same as the amount that was estimated at the start of the period, a discrepancy will result between actual overhead and applied overhead, even if there was no error in estimating the quantity of the allocation base. Manufacturing overhead costs can contain a significant amount of nondiscretionary or unavoidable costs. If this is so, these costs will not be proportional to changes in the allocation base. Therefore, when management estimates the total overhead costs at the start of the period assuming that overhead costs are, in fact, related to the quantity of the allocation base, they are making a mistake in using the method of applying overhead using a predetermined rate. They will discover, at the end of the period, that there will be either under- or over-applied overhead.

Even if management is correct in their belief that actual manufacturing overhead cost is proportional to the actual number of units of the allocation base used during the period, there can be errors in estimating the quantities of the allocation base and total amount of manufacturing cost at the beginning of the period. This was mentioned before. The company can end up actually spending either more or less than what was planned or expected due to circumstances beyond its control (sudden increase in energy costs) or because of poor management (wasteful work practices). Similarly, the company can end up actually using either more or less units of the allocation base than what was planned. Examples of why this is so include unexpected increases in demand, loss of experienced employees, poor maintenance, and so on.

Since at the end of the period, a company is certain to have under- or over-applied overhead, how can management tell if it is because overhead cost is not proportional to the units of the allocation base or because of errors in estimating the data inputs for calculating the predetermined rate? A complete answer is beyond the scope of this book. But we will return to consider this question further in a later chapter.

**Exhibit 3–12**

Flow of Supporting Cost Schedules to the Income Statement

**Direct Materials**

| | | |
|---|---|---|
| Opening balance: | $7,000 | |
| Plus purchases | $60,000 | |
| RM available for use | $67,000 | |
| Less ending balance: | $15,000 | |
| RM used | $52,000 | |
| Less Indirect RM | $2,000 | |
| DM used | $50,000 | >>>>>> |

**COGM**

| | |
|---|---|
| DM | $50,000 |
| DL | $60,000 |
| Applied MOH | $90,000 |
| Total Mfg. Costs | $200,000 |
| Plus beginning WIP | $30,000 |
| Mfg. Cost to account | $230,000 |
| Less ending WIP | $72,000 |
| COGM | $158,000 |

>>>>>>

**COGS**

| | |
|---|---|
| Opening bal. FG | $10,000 |
| COGM | $158,000 |
| Goods avail. for sale | $168,000 |
| Less end. Bal. FG | $49,500 |
| COGS | $118,500 |

>>>>>>

**Income Statement**

| | | |
|---|---|---|
| Sales | | $225,000 |
| COGS | | $118,500 |
| GM | | $106,500 |
| less non – mfg costs | | |
| | Net Income | |

Note:  The schedules shown in this exhibit are *not* in good form. They are presented in the format shown above only to illustrate how the various schedules relate to each other. RM = raw materials; DM = direct materials; DL = direct labour; MOH = manufacturing overhead; WIP = work in process; COGM = cost of goods manufactured; COGS = cost of goods sold; GM = gross margin.

**Exhibit 3–13**
Summary of Overhead Concepts

At the beginning of the period:

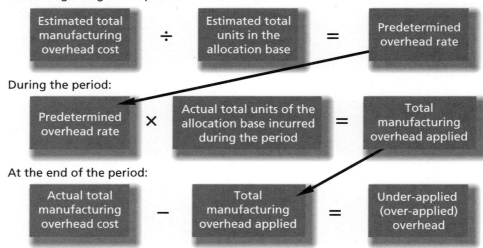

## Disposition of Under- or Over-applied Overhead Balances

Our previous discussion was about why over- or under-applied overhead balances can exist. We have yet to consider what to do with these balances: What disposition of any under- or over-applied balance remaining in the Manufacturing Overhead account should managers make at the end of the period? The simplest method is to close out the balance to Cost of Goods Sold. Other complicated methods exist, but these are beyond the scope of this book. To illustrate the simplest method, recall that Rand Company had under-applied overhead of $5,000. The entry to close this under-applied overhead to Cost of Goods Sold would be:

(11)

| | | |
|---|---|---|
| Cost of Goods Sold | 5,000 | |
|     Manufacturing Overhead | | 5,000 |

Note that since the Manufacturing Overhead account has a debit balance, Manufacturing Overhead must be credited to close out the account. This has the effect of increasing Cost of Goods Sold for April to $123,500:

| | |
|---|---|
| Unadjusted cost of goods sold [from entry (10)] | $118,500 |
| Add under-applied overhead [entry (11) above] | 5,000 |
| Adjusted cost of goods sold | $123,500 |

*you decide*

## Remaining Balance in the Overhead Account

The simplest method for disposing of any balance remaining in the Overhead account is to close it out to Cost of Goods Sold. If there is a debit balance (that is, overhead has been under-applied), the entry to dispose of the balance would include a debit to Cost of Goods Sold. That debit would increase the balance in the Cost of Goods Sold account. On the other hand, if there is a credit balance, the entry to dispose of the balance would include a credit to Cost of Goods Sold. That credit would decrease the balance in the Cost of Goods Sold account. If you were the company's controller, would you want a debit balance, a credit balance, or no balance in the Overhead account at the end of the period?

**Exhibit 3–14**
Schedules of Cost of Goods Manufactured and Cost of Goods Sold

### Cost of Goods Manufactured

Direct materials:

| | | |
|---|---:|---:|
| Raw materials inventory, beginning | $7,000 | |
| Add: Purchases of raw materials | 60,000 | |
| Total raw materials available | 67,000 | |
| Deduct: Raw materials inventory, ending | 15,000 | |
| Raw materials used in production | 52,000 | |
| Less indirect materials included in manufacturing overhead | 2,000 | $ 50,000 |
| Direct labour | | 60,000 |
| Manufacturing overhead applied to work in process | | 90,000 |
| Total manufacturing costs | | 200,000 |
| Add: Beginning work in process inventory | | 30,000 |
| | | 230,000 |
| Deduct: Ending work in process inventory | | 72,000 |
| Cost of goods manufactured | | $158,000 |

### Cost of Goods Sold

| | |
|---|---:|
| Finished goods inventory, beginning | $ 10,000 |
| Add: Cost of goods manufactured | 158,000 |
| Goods available for sale | 168,000 |
| Deduct: Finished goods inventory, ending | 49,500 |
| Unadjusted cost of goods sold | 118,500 |
| Add: Under-applied overhead | 5,000 |
| Adjusted cost of goods sold | $123,500 |

*Note that the under-applied overhead is added to cost of goods sold. If overhead were over-applied, it would be deducted from cost of goods sold.

After this adjustment has been made, Rand Company's Schedule of Cost of Goods Manufactured and Cost of Goods Sold for April will appear as shown in Exhibit 3–14.

## Multiple Predetermined Overhead Rates

Our discussion in this chapter has assumed that there is a single predetermined overhead rate for an entire factory called a **plantwide overhead rate.** This is, in fact, a common practice—particularly in smaller companies. But in larger companies, *multiple predetermined overhead rates* are often used. In a **multiple predetermined overhead rate**

### Enhancing the Accuracy of Overhead Cost Allocation

*in business today*

Only 34% of surveyed manufacturing firms reported that they used a single, plantwide overhead rate. The use of multiple overhead rates to obtain more accurate product costs was reported by 44% of the firms. The remaining 22% use activity-based costing (discussed in Chapter 5)—an even more complex approach to the allocation of overhead costs to products.

Source: Eun-Sup Shim and Joseph M. Larkin, "A Survey of Current Managerial Accounting Practices: Where Do We Stand?" Reprinted with permission from The Ohio Society of CPAs, *Ohio CPA Journal*, February 1994, p. 21 (4 pages).

system, each production department will usually have a different overhead rate. Such a system, while more complex, is considered to be more accurate, since it can reflect differences across departments in how overhead costs are incurred. For example, overhead might be allocated on the basis of direct labour-hours in departments that are relatively labour intensive and machine-hours in departments that are relatively machine intensive. When multiple predetermined overhead rates are used, overhead is applied in each department according to its own overhead rate as a job proceeds through the department.

## Nonmanufacturing Costs

In addition to manufacturing costs, companies also incur marketing and selling costs. As explained in the previous chapter, these costs should be treated as period expenses and charged directly to the income statement. *Nonmanufacturing costs should not go into the Manufacturing Overhead account.* To illustrate the correct treatment of nonmanufacturing costs, assume that Rand Company incurred the following selling and administrative costs during April:

| | |
|---|---:|
| Top-management salaries | $21,000 |
| Other office salaries | 9,000 |
| Total salaries | $30,000 |

The following entry records these salaries:

(12)

| | | |
|---|---:|---:|
| Salaries Expense | 30,000 | |
| Salaries and Wages Payable | | 30,000 |

Assume that depreciation on office equipment during April was $7,000. The entry would be:

(13)

| | | |
|---|---:|---:|
| Depreciation Expense | 7,000 | |
| Accumulated Depreciation | | 7,000 |

Pay particular attention to the difference between this entry and entry (6) where we recorded depreciation on factory equipment. In journal entry (6), depreciation on factory equipment was debited to Manufacturing Overhead and is therefore a product cost. In journal entry (9) above, depreciation on office equipment was debited to Depreciation Expense. Depreciation on office equipment is considered to be a period expense, rather than a product cost.

Finally, assume that advertising was $42,000 and that other selling and administrative expenses in April totalled $8,000. The following entry records these items:

(14)

| | | |
|---|---:|---:|
| Advertising Expense | 42,000 | |
| Other Selling and Administrative Expense | 8,000 | |
| Accounts Payable | | 50,000 |

Since the amounts in entries (12) through (14) all go directly into expense accounts, they will have no effect on the costing of Rand Company's production for April. The same will be true of any other selling and administrative expenses incurred during April, including sales commissions, depreciation on sales equipment, rent on office facilities, insurance on office facilities, and related costs. The income statement showing these costs appears in Exhibit 3–15.

**Exhibit 3–15**
Income Statement Including
Nonmanufacturing Costs

**RAND COMPANY**
**Income Statement**
**For the Month Ending April 30**

| | | |
|---|---:|---:|
| Sales | | $225,000 |
| Less cost of goods sold ($118,500 + $5,000) | | 123,500 |
| Gross margin | | 101,500 |
| Less selling and administrative expenses: | | |
| Salaries expense | $30,000 | |
| Depreciation expense | 7,000 | |
| Advertising expense | 42,000 | |
| Other expense | 8,000 | 87,000 |
| Net Income | | $14,500 |

## A Fair Share of Profits

*in business today*

"Net profit participation" contracts in which writers, actors, and directors share in the net profits of movies are common in Hollywood. For example, Winston Groom, the author of the novel *Forrest Gump*, has a contract with Paramount Pictures Corp. that calls for him to receive 3% of the net profits on the movie. However, Paramount claims that *Forrest Gump* has yet to show any profits, even though it has the third-highest gross receipts of any film in history. How can this be?

Movie studios assess a variety of overhead charges including a charge of about 15% on production costs for production overhead, a charge of about 30% of gross rentals for distribution overhead, and a charge for marketing overhead that amounts to about 10% of advertising costs. After all of these overhead charges and other hotly contested accounting practices, it is a rare film that shows a profit. Fewer than 5% of released films show a profit for net profit participation purposes. Examples of "money-losing" films include *Rain Man*, *Batman*, and *Who Framed Roger Rabbit?* as well as *Forrest Gump*. Disgruntled writers and actors are increasingly suing studios, claiming unreasonable accounting practices that are designed to cheat them of their share of profits.

Source: Ross Engel and Bruce Ikawa, "Where's the Profit?" Reprinted with permission from *Management Accounting*, January 1997, pp. 40–47.

## Summary

**LO1   Distinguish between process costing and job-order costing and identify companies that would use each costing method.**

Job-order costing and process costing are widely used to track costs. Job-order costing is used in situations where the organization offers many different products or services, such as in furniture manufacturing, hospitals, and legal firms. Process costing is used where units of product are homogeneous, such as in flour milling or cement production.

**LO2   Identify the documents used in a job-order costing system.**

In a job-order costing system, each job has its own job cost sheet. Materials requisition forms and labour time tickets are used to record direct materials and direct labour costs. These costs, together with manufacturing overhead, are accumulated on the job cost sheet for a job.

**LO3    Compute predetermined overhead rates and explain why estimated overhead costs (rather than actual overhead costs) are used in the costing process.**

Manufacturing overhead costs are assigned to jobs using a predetermined overhead rate. The rate is determined at the beginning of the period so that jobs can be costed throughout the period, rather than waiting until the end of the period. The predetermined overhead rate is determined by dividing the estimated total manufacturing cost for the period by the estimated total allocation base for the period.

**LO4    Prepare journal entries to record costs in a job-order costing system.**

Direct materials costs are debited to Work in Process when they are released for use in production. Direct labour costs are debited to Work in Process as incurred. Actual manufacturing overhead costs are debited to the Manufacturing Overhead control account as incurred. Manufacturing overhead costs are applied to Work in Process using the predetermined overhead rate. The journal entry that accomplishes this is a debit to Work in Process and a credit to the Manufacturing Overhead control account.

**LO5    Apply overhead cost to Work in Process using a predetermined overhead rate.**

Overhead is applied to jobs by multiplying the predetermined overhead rate by the actual amount of the allocation base used by the job.

**LO6    Prepare T-accounts to show the flow of costs in a job-order costing system and prepare schedules of cost of goods manufactured and cost of goods sold.**

See Exhibit 3–11 for a summary of the cost flows through the T-accounts.

**LO7    Compute under- or over-applied overhead cost and prepare the journal entry to close the balance in Manufacturing Overhead to the appropriate accounts.**

The difference between the actual overhead cost incurred during a period and the amount of overhead cost applied to production is referred to as under- or over-applied overhead. Under- or over-applied overhead is closed out to Cost of Goods Sold. When overhead is under-applied, the balance in the Manufacturing Overhead control account is debited to Cost of Goods Sold. This has the effect of increasing the Cost of Goods Sold and occurs because costs assigned to products have been understated. When overhead is over-applied, the balance in the Manufacturing Overhead control account is credited to Cost of Goods Sold. This has the effect of decreasing the Cost of Goods Sold and occurs because costs assigned to products have been overstated.

# Guidance Answers to Decision Maker and You Decide

**TREASURER, CLASS REUNION COMMITTEE** (p. 76)

You should charge $38 per person to cover the costs calculated as follows:

| | | |
|---|---|---|
| Meal cost . . . . . . . . . . . . . . . . . . . . . . . . . . . . . . . . . . . . . | $30.00 | Direct cost |
| Gratuity ($30 × 0.15) . . . . . . . . . . . . . . . . . . . . . . . . . . . | 4.50 | Direct cost |
| Room charge ($200 ÷ 200 expected attendees) . . . . . | 1.00 | Overhead cost |
| Band cost ($500 ÷ 200 expected attendees) . . . . . . . | 2.50 | Overhead cost |
| Total cost . . . . . . . . . . . . . . . . . . . . . . . . . . . . . . . . . . . . | $38.00 | |

The number of expected attendees (or estimated units in the allocation base) was used to allocate the band cost. Attendees who plan to leave immediately after dinner might object to this allocation. However, this personal choice probably should not override the decision to base the allocation on this very simple base.

If exactly 200 classmates attend the reunion, the $7,600 of receipts (200 @ $38) will cover the expenditures of $7,600 [meal cost of $6,000 (or 200 @ $30) plus gratuity cost of $900 (or $6,000 × 0.15) plus the $200 room charge plus the $500 band cost]. Unfortunately, if less than 200 attend, the Reunion Committee will come up short in an amount equal to the difference between the 200 estimated attendees and the actual number of attendees times $3.50 (the overhead charge per person). As such, you should talk to the members of the Reunion Committee to ensure that (1) the estimate is as reasonable as possible, and (2) there is a plan to deal with the shortage. On the other hand, if more than 200 attend, the Reunion Committee will collect more money than it needs to disburse. The amount would be equal to the difference between the actual number of attendees and the 200 estimated attendees times $3.50. Again, a plan should be in place to deal with this situation. (Perhaps the funds could be used to cover the mailing costs for the next reunion.)

### REMAINING BALANCE IN THE OVERHEAD ACCOUNT (p. 90)

A quick response on your part might have been that you would prefer a credit balance in the Overhead account. The entry to dispose of the balance would decrease the balance in the Cost of Goods Sold account and would cause the company's gross margin and net income to be higher than might have otherwise been expected. However, the impact on decision making during the period should be carefully considered.

Ideally, a controller would want the balance in the Overhead account to be zero. If there is no remaining balance in the Overhead account at the end of the period, that means that the actual overhead costs for the period (which are debited to the Overhead account) exactly equalled the overhead costs that were applied (or allocated to the products made by being added to the Work in Process account) during the period. As a result, the products made during the period would have had the "correct" amount of overhead assigned as they moved from the factory floor to the finished goods area to the customer. Typically, this would not be the case because the predetermined overhead rate (used to apply or allocate overhead to the products made) is developed using two estimates (the total amount of overhead expected and the total units in the allocation base expected during the period). It would be difficult, if not impossible, to accurately predict one or both estimates.

If there is a remaining balance in the Overhead account, then the products manufactured during the period either received too little overhead (if there is a debit or under-applied balance) or too much overhead (if there is a credit or over-applied balance). As such, units carried along with them inaccurate product costs as the costs flowed through system. Decisions that relied on those inaccurate product costs may have been faulty.

# Review Problem: Job-Order Costing

Hogle Company is a manufacturing firm that uses job-order costing. On January 1, the beginning of its fiscal year, the company's inventory balances were as follows:

| | |
|---|---|
| Raw materials | $20,000 |
| Work in process | 15,000 |
| Finished goods | 30,000 |

The company applies overhead cost to jobs on the basis of machine-hours worked. For the current year, the company estimated that it would work 75,000 machine-hours and incur $450,000 in manufacturing overhead cost. The following transactions were recorded for the year:

a. Raw materials were purchased on account, $410,000.

b. Raw materials were requisitioned for use in production, $380,000 ($360,000 direct materials and $20,000 indirect materials).

c. The following costs were incurred for employee services: direct labour, $75,000; indirect labour, $110,000; sales commissions, $90,000; and administrative salaries, $200,000.

d. Sales travel costs were incurred, $17,000.

e. Utility costs were incurred in the factory, $43,000.

f. Advertising costs were incurred, $180,000.

g. Depreciation was recorded for the year, $350,000 (80% relates to factory operations, and 20% relates to selling and administrative activities).

h. Insurance expired during the year, $10,000 (70% relates to factory operations, and the remaining 30% relates to selling and administrative activities).

i. Manufacturing overhead was applied to production. Due to greater than expected demand for its products, the company worked 80,000 machine-hours during the year.

j. Goods costing $900,000 to manufacture according to their job cost sheets were completed during the year.

k. Goods were sold on account to customers during the year at a total selling price of $1,500,000. The goods cost $870,000 to manufacture according to their job cost sheets.

*Required:*

1. Prepare journal entries to record the preceding transactions.
2. Post the entries in (1) above to T-accounts (do not forget to enter the opening balances in the inventory accounts).
3. Is Manufacturing Overhead under-applied or over-applied for the year? Prepare a journal entry to close any balance in the Manufacturing Overhead account to Cost of Goods Sold.
4. Prepare an income statement for the year.

*SOLUTION TO REVIEW PROBLEM*

| | | | |
|---|---|---:|---:|
| 1. | *a.* Raw Materials | 410,000 | |
| |     Accounts Payable | | 410,000 |
| | *b.* Work in Process | 360,000 | |
| |     Manufacturing Overhead | 20,000 | |
| |     Raw Materials | | 380,000 |
| | *c.* Work in Process | 75,000 | |
| |     Manufacturing Overhead | 110,000 | |
| |     Sales Commissions Expense | 90,000 | |
| |     Administrative Salaries Expense | 200,000 | |
| |     Salaries and Wages Payable | | 475,000 |
| | *d.* Sales Travel Expense | 17,000 | |
| |     Accounts Payable | | 17,000 |
| | *e.* Manufacturing Overhead | 43,000 | |
| |     Accounts Payable | | 43,000 |
| | *f.* Advertising Expense | 180,000 | |
| |     Accounts Payable | | 180,000 |
| | *g.* Manufacturing Overhead | 280,000 | |
| |     Depreciation Expense | 70,000 | |
| |     Accumulated Depreciation | | 350,000 |
| | *h.* Manufacturing Overhead | 7,000 | |
| |     Insurance Expense | 3,000 | |
| |     Prepaid Insurance | | 10,000 |

*i.* The predetermined overhead rate for the year would be computed as follows:

$$\frac{\text{Estimated manufacturing overhead, \$450,000}}{\text{Estimated machine-hours, 75,000}} = \$6 \text{ per machine-hour}$$

Based on the 80,000 machine-hours actually worked during the year, the company would have applied $480,000 in overhead cost to production: 80,000 machine-hours × $6 per machine-hour = $480,000. The following entry records this application of overhead cost:

| | | | |
|---|---|---:|---:|
| | Work in Process | 480,000 | |
| |     Manufacturing Overhead | | 480,000 |
| *j.* | Finished Goods | 900,000 | |
| |     Work in Process | | 900,000 |
| *k.* | Accounts Receivable | 1,500,000 | |
| |     Sales | | 1,500,000 |
| | Cost of Goods Sold | 870,000 | |
| |     Finished Goods | | 870,000 |

2.

| Accounts Receivable | | |
|---|---|---|
| (k) | 1,500,000 | |

| Prepaid Insurance | | |
|---|---|---|
| | | (h) 10,000 |

| Raw Materials | | |
|---|---|---|
| Bal. | 20,000 | (b) 380,000 |
| (a) | 410,000 | |
| Bal. | 50,000 | |

| Work in Process | | |
|---|---|---|
| Bal. | 15,000 | (j) 900,000 |
| (b) | 360,000 | |
| (c) | 75,000 | |
| (i) | 480,000 | |
| Bal. | 30,000 | |

| Finished Goods | | |
|---|---|---|
| Bal. | 30,000 | (k) 870,000 |
| (j) | 900,000 | |
| Bal. | 60,000 | |

| Manufacturing Overhead | | |
|---|---|---|
| (b) | 20,000 | (i) 480,000 |
| (c) | 110,000 | |
| (e) | 43,000 | |
| (g) | 280,000 | |
| (h) | 7,000 | |
| | 460,000 | 480,000 |
| | | Bal. 20,000 |

| Accumulated Depreciation | | |
|---|---|---|
| | | (g) 350,000 |

| Accounts Payable | | |
|---|---|---|
| | | (a) 410,000 |
| | | (d) 17,000 |
| | | (e) 43,000 |
| | | (f) 180,000 |

| Salaries and Wages Payable | | |
|---|---|---|
| | | (c) 475,000 |

| Sales | | |
|---|---|---|
| | | (k) 1,500,000 |

| Cost of Goods Sold | | |
|---|---|---|
| (k) | 870,000 | |

| Commissions Expense | | |
|---|---|---|
| (c) | 90,000 | |

| Administrative Salary Expense | | |
|---|---|---|
| (c) | 200,000 | |

| Sales Travel Expense | | |
|---|---|---|
| (d) | 17,000 | |

| Advertising Expense | | |
|---|---|---|
| (f) | 180,000 | |

| Depreciation Expense | | |
|---|---|---|
| (g) | 70,000 | |

| Insurance Expense | | |
|---|---|---|
| (h) | 3,000 | |

3. Manufacturing overhead is over-applied for the year. The entry to close it out to Cost of Goods Sold is as follows:

| | | |
|---|---|---|
| Manufacturing Overhead ........................ | 20,000 | |
|    Cost of Goods Sold ........................... | | 20,000 |

4.

**HOGLE COMPANY**
**Income Statement**
**For the Year Ended December 31**

| | | |
|---|---|---|
| Sales ....................................... | | $1,500,000 |
| Less cost of goods sold ($870,000 − $20,000) ....... | | 850,000 |
| Gross margin ............................... | | 650,000 |
| Less selling and administrative expenses: | | |
|    Commissions expense ....................... | $ 90,000 | |
|    Administrative salaries expense ............... | 200,000 | |
|    Sales travel expense ......................... | 17,000 | |
|    Advertising expense ........................ | 180,000 | |
|    Depreciation expense ........................ | 70,000 | |
|    Insurance expense .......................... | 3,000 | 560,000 |
| Net income .................................. | | $ 90,000 |

# Glossary

**Absorption (or full) costing** A costing method that includes all manufacturing costs—direct materials, direct labour, and both variable and fixed overhead—as part of the cost of a finished unit of product. This term is synonymous with *full costing*. (p. 69)

**Actual costing system** A costing system in which actual overhead costs are applied to jobs by multiplying the actual overhead rate by the actual amount of the allocation base incurred by the job. (p. 69)

**Allocation base** A measure of activity, such as direct labour-hours or machine-hours, that is used to assign costs to cost objects. (p. 73)

**Bill of materials** A document that shows the type and quantity of each major item of materials required to make a product. (p. 70)

**Cost driver** A factor, such as machine-hours, beds occupied, computer time, or flight-hours, that causes overhead costs. (p. 75)

**Full costing** See *Absorption costing*. (p. 69)

**Job cost sheet** A form prepared for each job that records the materials, labour, and overhead costs charged to the job. (p. 71)

**Job-order costing system** A costing system used in situations where many different products, jobs, or services are produced each period. (p. 69)

**Materials requisition form** A detailed source document that specifies the type and quantity of materials that are to be drawn from the storeroom and identifies the job to which the costs of materials are to be charged. (p. 70)

**Multiple predetermined overhead rates** A costing system in which there are multiple overhead cost pools with a different predetermined rate for each cost pool, rather than a single predetermined overhead rate for the entire company. Frequently, each production department is treated as a separate overhead cost pool. (p. 91)

**Normal costing system** A costing system in which overhead costs are applied to jobs by multiplying a predetermined overhead rate by the actual amount of the allocation base incurred by the job. (p. 69)

**Over-applied overhead** A credit balance in the Manufacturing Overhead account that arises when the amount of overhead cost applied to Work in Process is greater than the amount of overhead cost actually incurred during a period. (p. 83)

**Overhead application** The process of charging manufacturing overhead cost to job cost sheets and to the Work in Process account. (p. 73)

**Plantwide overhead rate** A single predetermined overhead rate that is used throughout a plant. (p. 91)

**Predetermined overhead rate** A rate used to charge overhead cost to jobs in production; the rate is established in advance for each period by use of estimates of total manufacturing overhead cost and of the total allocation base for the period. (p. 73)

**Process costing system** A costing system used in those manufacturing situations where a single, homogeneous product (such as cement or flour) is produced for long periods of time. (p. 69)

**Time ticket** A detailed source document that is used to record an employee's hour-by-hour activities during a day. (p. 71)

**Under-applied overhead** A debit balance in the Manufacturing Overhead account that arises when the amount of overhead cost actually incurred is greater than the amount of overhead cost applied to Work in Process during a period. (p. 83)

**Variable costing** A costing method that includes only variable manufacturing costs—direct materials, direct labour, and variable overhead—as part of the finished unit of product. (p. 69)

# Questions

**3–1**  Why aren't actual overhead costs traced to jobs just as direct materials and direct labour costs are traced to jobs?

**3–2**  When would job-order costing be used in preference to process costing?

**3–3**  What is the purpose of the job cost sheet in a job-order costing system?

**3–4**  What is a predetermined overhead rate, and how is it computed?

**3–5**  Explain how a sales order, a production order, a materials requisition form, and a labour time ticket are involved in producing and costing products.

**3–6**  Explain why some production costs must be assigned to products through an allocation process. Name several such costs. Would such costs be classified as *direct* or as *indirect* costs?

**3–7**   Why do firms use predetermined overhead rates, rather than actual manufacturing overhead costs, in applying overhead to jobs?

**3–8**   What factors should be considered in selecting a base to be used in computing the predetermined overhead rate?

**3–9**   If a company fully allocates all of its overhead costs to jobs, does this guarantee that a profit will be earned for the period?

**3–10**   What account is credited when overhead cost is applied to Work in Process? Would you expect the amount applied for a period to equal the actual overhead costs of the period? Why, or why not?

**3–11**   What is under-applied overhead? Over-applied overhead? What disposition is made of these amounts at the end of the period?

**3–12**   Give two reasons why overhead might be under-applied in a given year.

**3–13**   What adjustment is made for under-applied overhead on the schedule of cost of goods sold? What adjustment is made for over-applied overhead?

**3–14**   Sigma Company applies overhead cost to jobs on the basis of direct labour cost. Job A, which was started and completed during the current period, shows charges of $5,000 for direct materials, $8,000 for direct labour, and $6,000 for overhead on its job cost sheet. Job B, which is still in process at year-end, shows charges of $2,500 for direct materials and $4,000 for direct labour. Should any overhead cost be added to job B at year-end? Explain.

**3–15**   A company assigns overhead cost to completed jobs on the basis of 125% of direct labour cost. The job cost sheet for job 313 shows that $10,000 in direct materials has been used on the job and that $12,000 in direct labour cost has been incurred. If 1,000 units were produced in job 313, what is the cost per unit?

**3–16**   What is a plantwide overhead rate? Why are multiple overhead rates, rather than a plantwide rate, used in some companies?

**3–17**   What happens to overhead rates based on direct labour when automated equipment replaces direct labour?

# Brief Exercises

**BRIEF EXERCISE 3–1   Process versus Job-Order Costing (LO1)**
Which method of determining product costs, job-order costing or process costing, would be more appropriate in each of the following situations?
a.  An Elmer's glue factory.
b.  A textbook publisher, such as McGraw-Hill.
c.  A Husky oil refinery.
d.  A facility that makes Minute Maid frozen orange juice.
e.  A Scott paper mill.
f.  A custom home builder.
g.  A shop that customizes vans.
h.  A manufacturer of specialty chemicals.
i.  An auto repair shop.
j.  A Firestone tire manufacturing plant.
k.  An advertising agency.
l.  A law office.

**BRIEF EXERCISE 3–2   Job-Order Costing Documents (LO2)**
Cycle Gear Corporation has incurred the following costs on job number W456, an order for 20 special sprockets to be delivered at the end of next month.

Direct materials:
> On April 10, requisition number 15673 was issued for 20 titanium blanks to be used in the special order. The blanks cost $15 each.
> On April 11, requisition number 15678 was issued for 480 hardened nibs also to be used in the special order. The nibs cost $1.25 each.

Direct labour:
> On April 12, Jamie Unser worked from 11:00 AM until 2:45 PM on Job W456. He is paid $9.60 per hour.
> On April 18, Melissa Chan worked from 8:15 AM until 11:30 AM on Job W456. She is paid $12.20 per hour.

*Required:*
1. On what documents would these costs be recorded?
2. How much cost should have been recorded on each of the documents for Job W456?

**BRIEF EXERCISE 3–3   Compute the Predetermined Overhead Rate (LO3)**
Harris Fabrics computes its predetermined overhead rate annually on the basis of direct labour hours. At the beginning of the year, it estimated that its total manufacturing overhead would be $134,000 and the total direct labour would be 20,000 hours. Its actual total manufacturing overhead for the year was $123,900, and its actual total direct labour was 21,000 hours.

*Required:*
Compute the company's predetermined overhead rate for the year.

**BRIEF EXERCISE 3–4   Prepare Journal Entries (LO4)**
Larned Corporation recorded the following transactions for the just completed month.
a. $80,000 in raw materials were purchased on account.
b. $71,000 in raw materials were requisitioned for use in production. Of this amount, $62,000 was for direct materials and the remainder was for indirect materials.
c. Total labour wages of $112,000 were incurred. Of this amount, $101,000 was for direct labour and the remainder was for indirect labour.
d. Additional manufacturing overhead costs of $175,000 were incurred.

*Required:*
Record the above transactions in journal entries.

**BRIEF EXERCISE 3–5   Apply Overhead (LO5)**
Luthan Company uses a predetermined overhead rate of $23.40 per direct labour-hour. This predetermined rate was based on 11,000 estimated direct labour-hours and $257,400 of estimated total manufacturing overhead.

The company incurred actual total manufacturing overhead costs of $249,000 and 10,800 total direct labour-hours during the period.

*Required:*
Determine the amount of manufacturing overhead that would have been applied to units of product during the period.

**BRIEF EXERCISE 3–6   Prepare T-Accounts (LO6, LO7)**
Jurvin Enterprises recorded the following transactions for the just completed month. The company had no beginning inventories.
a. $94,000 in raw materials were purchased for cash.
b. $89,000 in raw materials were requisitioned for use in production. Of this amount, $78,000 was for direct materials and the remainder was for indirect materials.
c. Total labour wages of $132,000 were incurred and paid. Of this amount, $112,000 was for direct labour and the remainder was for indirect labour.
d. Additional manufacturing overhead costs of $143,000 were incurred and paid.
e. Manufacturing overhead costs of $152,000 were applied to jobs using the company's predetermined overhead rate.
f. All of the jobs in progress at the end of the month were completed and shipped to customers.
g. The under-applied or over-applied overhead for the period was closed out to Cost of Goods Sold.

*Required:*
1. Post the above transactions to T-accounts.
2. Determine the cost of goods sold for the period.

**BRIEF EXERCISE 3–7   Under- and Over-applied Overhead (LO7)**
Osborn Manufacturing uses a predetermined overhead rate of $18.20 per direct labour-hour. This predetermined rate was based on 12,000 estimated direct labour-hours and $218,400 of estimated total manufacturing overhead.

The company incurred actual total manufacturing overhead costs of $215,000 and 11,500 total direct labour-hours during the period.

*Required:*
1. Determine the amount of under-applied or over-applied manufacturing overhead for the period.
2. Assuming that the entire amount of the under-applied or over-applied overhead is closed out to Cost of Goods Sold, what would be the effect of the under-applied or over-applied overhead on the company's gross margin for the period?

**EXERCISE 3–1   Applying Overhead in a Service Firm (LO2, LO3, LO5)**

Leeds Architectural Consultants began operations on January 2. The following activity was recorded in the company's Work in Process account for the first month of operations:

**Work in Process**

| | | | |
|---|---|---|---|
| Costs of subcontracted work | 230,000 | To completed projects | 390,000 |
| Direct staff costs | 75,000 | | |
| Studio overhead | 120,000 | | |

Leeds Architectural Consultants is a service firm, and so the names of the accounts it uses are different from the names used in manufacturing firms. Costs of Subcontracted Work is basically the same thing as Direct Materials; Direct Staff Costs is the same as Direct Labour; Studio Overhead is the same as Manufacturing Overhead; and Completed Projects is the same as Finished Goods. Apart from the difference in terms, the accounting methods used by the company are identical to the methods used by manufacturing companies.

Leeds Architectural Consultants uses a job-order costing system and applies studio overhead to Work in Process on the basis of direct staff costs. At the end of January, only one job was still in process. This job (Lexington Gardens Project) had been charged with $6,500 in direct staff costs.

**Required:**
1. Compute the predetermined overhead rate that was in use during January.
2. Complete the following job cost sheet for the partially completed Lexington Gardens Project.

**Job Cost Sheet—Lexington Gardens Project**
**As of January 31**

| | |
|---|---|
| Costs of subcontracted work . . . . . . . . . . | $? |
| Direct staff costs . . . . . . . . . . . . . . . . . . . . | ? |
| Studio overhead . . . . . . . . . . . . . . . . . . . . . | ? |
| Total cost to January 31 . . . . . . . . . . . . . . . | $? |

**EXERCISE 3–2   Varying Predetermined Overhead Rates (LO3, LO5)**

Kingsport Containers, Ltd. of the Bahamas experiences wide variation in demand for the 200-litre steel drums it fabricates. The leakproof, rustproof steel drums have a variety of uses from storing liquids and bulk materials to serving as makeshift musical instruments. The drums are made to order and are painted according to the customer's specifications—often in bright patterns and designs. The company is well known for the artwork that appears on its drums. Unit costs are computed on a quarterly basis by dividing each quarter's manufacturing costs (materials, labour, and overhead) by the quarter's production in units. The company's estimated costs, by quarter, for the coming year follow:

| | Quarter | | | |
|---|---|---|---|---|
| | **First** | **Second** | **Third** | **Fourth** |
| Direct materials . . . . . . . . . . . . . . . | $240,000 | $120,000 | $ 60,000 | $180,000 |
| Direct labour . . . . . . . . . . . . . . . . . . . | 128,000 | 64,000 | 32,000 | 96,000 |
| Manufacturing overhead . . . . . . . . . . | 300,000 | 220,000 | 180,000 | 260,000 |
| Total manufacturing costs . . . . . . . . | $668,000 | $404,000 | $272,000 | $536,000 |
| Number of units to be produced . . . . | 80,000 | 40,000 | 20,000 | 60,000 |
| Estimated cost per unit . . . . . . . . . . . | $8.35 | $10.10 | $13.60 | $8.93 |

Management finds the variation in unit costs to be confusing and difficult to work with. It has been suggested that the problem lies with manufacturing overhead, since it is the largest element of cost. Accordingly, you have been asked to find a more appropriate way of assigning manufacturing overhead cost to units of product. After some analysis, you have determined that the company's overhead costs are mostly fixed and therefore show little sensitivity to changes in the level of production.

*Required:*
1. The company uses a job-order costing system. How would you recommend that manufacturing overhead cost be assigned to production? Be specific, and show computations.
2. Recompute the company's unit costs in accordance with your recommendations in (1) above.

### EXERCISE 3–3  Journal Entries and T-Accounts (LO4, LO5, LO6)

The Polaris Company uses a job-order costing system. The following data relate to October, the first month of the company's fiscal year.
a. Raw materials purchased on account, $210,000.
b. Raw materials issued to production, $190,000 ($178,000 direct materials and $12,000 indirect materials).
c. Direct labour cost incurred, $90,000; indirect labour cost incurred, $110,000.
d. Depreciation recorded on factory equipment, $40,000.
e. Other manufacturing overhead costs incurred during October, $70,000 (credit Accounts Payable).
f. The company applies manufacturing overhead cost to production on the basis of $8 per machine-hour. There were 30,000 machine-hours recorded for October.
g. Production orders costing $520,000 according to their job cost sheets were completed during October and transferred to Finished Goods.
h. Production orders that had cost $480,000 to complete according to their job cost sheets were shipped to customers during the month. These goods were sold at 25% above cost. The goods were sold on account.

*Required:*
1. Prepare journal entries to record the information given above.
2. Prepare T-accounts for Manufacturing Overhead and Work in Process. Post the relevant information above to each account. Compute the ending balance in each account, assuming that Work in Process has a beginning balance of $42,000.

### EXERCISE 3–4  Applying Overhead; Cost of Goods Manufactured (LO5, LO7)

The following cost data relate to the manufacturing activities of Chang Company during the just completed year:

| | |
|---|---|
| Manufacturing overhead costs incurred: | |
| Indirect materials ............................... | $ 15,000 |
| Indirect labour .................................. | 130,000 |
| Property taxes, factory ......................... | 8,000 |
| Utilities, factory ................................ | 70,000 |
| Depreciation, factory ........................... | 240,000 |
| Insurance, factory .............................. | 10,000 |
| Total actual costs incurred ...................... | $473,000 |
| Other costs incurred: | |
| Purchases of raw materials (both direct and indirect) .. | $400,000 |
| Direct labour cost ............................. | 60,000 |
| Inventories: | |
| Raw materials, beginning ....................... | 20,000 |
| Raw materials, ending .......................... | 30,000 |
| Work in process, beginning ..................... | 40,000 |
| Work in process, ending ........................ | 70,000 |

The company uses a predetermined overhead rate to apply overhead cost to production. The rate for the year was $25 per machine-hour. A total of 19,400 machine-hours was recorded for the year.

*Required:*
1. Compute the amount of under- or over-applied overhead cost for the year.
2. Prepare a schedule of cost of goods manufactured for the year.

**EXERCISE 3–5  Applying Overhead with Differing Bases (LO3, LO5, LO7)**

Estimated cost and operating data for three companies for the upcoming year follow:

| | Company | | |
| --- | --- | --- | --- |
| | X | Y | Z |
| Direct labour-hours ........... | 80,000 | 45,000 | 60,000 |
| Machine-hours ............... | 30,000 | 70,000 | 21,000 |
| Direct materials cost .......... | $400,000 | $290,000 | $300,000 |
| Manufacturing overhead cost ... | 536,000 | 315,000 | 480,000 |

Predetermined overhead rates are computed using the following bases in the three companies:

| Company | Overhead Rate Based on— |
| --- | --- |
| X ................... | Direct labour-hours |
| Y ................... | Machine-hours |
| Z ................... | Direct materials cost |

*Required:*

1. Compute the predetermined overhead rate to be used in each company during the upcoming year.
2. Assume that Company X works on three jobs during the upcoming year. Direct labour-hours recorded by job are: job 418, 12,000 hours; job 419, 36,000 hours; job 420, 30,000 hours. How much overhead cost will the company apply to Work in Process for the year? If actual overhead costs total $530,000 for the year, will overhead be under- or over-applied? By how much?

**EXERCISE 3–6  Journal Entries; Applying Overhead (LO4, LO7)**

The following information is taken from the accounts of Latta Company. The entries in the T-accounts are summaries of the transactions that affected those accounts during the year.

**Manufacturing Overhead**

| | | | |
| --- | --- | --- | --- |
| (a) | 460,000 | (b) | 390,000 |
| Bal. | 70,000 | | |

**Work in Process**

| | | | |
| --- | --- | --- | --- |
| Bal. | 5,000 | (c) | 710,000 |
| | 270,000 | | |
| | 85,000 | | |
| (b) | 390,000 | | |
| Bal. | 40,000 | | |

**Finished Goods**

| | | | |
| --- | --- | --- | --- |
| Bal. | 50,000 | (d) | 640,000 |
| (c) | 710,000 | | |
| Bal. | 120,000 | | |

**Cost of Goods Sold**

| | | | |
| --- | --- | --- | --- |
| (d) | 640,000 | | |

The overhead that had been applied to Work in Process during the year is distributed among the ending balances in the accounts as follows:

| | |
| --- | --- |
| Work in Process, ending .......................... | $ 19,500 |
| Finished Goods, ending .......................... | 58,500 |
| Cost of Goods Sold ............................. | 312,000 |
| Overhead applied ............................. | $390,000 |

For example, of the $40,000 ending balance in Work in Process, $19,500 was overhead that had been applied during the year.

*Required:*
1. Identify reasons for entries (a) through (d).
2. Assume that the company closes any balance in the Manufacturing Overhead account directly to Cost of Goods Sold. Prepare the necessary journal entry.

### EXERCISE 3–7   Applying Overhead; Journal Entries; T-Accounts (LO3, LO4, LO5, LO6)

Dillon Products manufactures various machined parts to customer specifications. The company uses a job-order costing system and applies overhead cost to jobs on the basis of machine-hours. At the beginning of the year, it was estimated that the company would work 240,000 machine-hours and incur $4,800,000 in manufacturing overhead costs.

The company spent the entire month of January working on a large order for 16,000 custom-made machined parts. The company had no work in process at the beginning of January. Cost data relating to January follow:
a. Raw materials purchased on account, $325,000.
b. Raw materials requisitioned for production, $290,000 (80% direct materials and 20% indirect materials).
c. Labour cost incurred in the factory, $180,000 (one-third direct labour and two-thirds indirect labour).
d. Depreciation recorded on factory equipment, $75,000.
e. Other manufacturing overhead costs incurred, $62,000 (credit Accounts Payable).
f. Manufacturing overhead cost was applied to production on the basis of 15,000 machine-hours actually worked during the month.
g. The completed job was moved into the finished goods warehouse on January 31 to await delivery to the customer. (In computing the dollar amount for this entry, remember that the cost of a completed job consists of direct materials, direct labour, and *applied* overhead.)

*Required:*
1. Prepare journal entries to record items (a) through (f) above [ignore item (g) for the moment].
2. Prepare T-accounts for Manufacturing Overhead and Work in Process. Post the relevant items from your journal entries to these T-accounts.
3. Prepare a journal entry for item (g) above.
4. Compute the unit cost that will appear on the job cost sheet.

# Problems

CHECK FIGURE
(2) Overhead applied to job
203: $870

### PROBLEM 3–1   Departmental Overhead Rates (LO2, LO3, LO5)

White Company has two departments, Cutting and Finishing. The company uses a job-order cost system and computes a predetermined overhead rate in each department. The Cutting Department bases its rate on machine-hours, and the Finishing Department bases its rate on direct labour cost. At the beginning of the year, the company made the following estimates:

|  | Department | |
|---|---|---|
|  | **Cutting** | **Finishing** |
| Direct labour-hours ................ | 6,000 | 30,000 |
| Machine-hours .................... | 48,000 | 5,000 |
| Manufacturing overhead cost ......... | $360,000 | $486,000 |
| Direct labour cost ................. | 50,000 | 270,000 |

*Required:*
1. Compute the predetermined overhead rate to be used in each department.
2. Assume that the overhead rates that you computed in (1) above are in effect. The job cost sheet for job 203, which was started and completed during the year, showed the following:

|  | Department | |
|---|---|---|
|  | **Cutting** | **Finishing** |
| Direct labour-hours ................ | 6 | 20 |
| Machine-hours .................... | 80 | 4 |
| Materials requisitioned ............. | $500 | $310 |
| Direct labour cost ................. | 70 | 150 |

Compute the total overhead cost applied to job 203.

3. Would you expect substantially different amounts of overhead cost to be assigned to some jobs if the company used a plantwide overhead rate based on direct labour cost, rather than using departmental rates? Explain. No computations are necessary.

**PROBLEM 3–2   Applying Overhead; T-Accounts; Journal Entries** (LO3, LO4, LO5, LO6, LO7)
Harwood Company is a manufacturing firm that operates a job-order costing system. Overhead costs are applied to jobs on the basis of machine-hours. At the beginning of the year, management estimated that the company would incur $192,000 in manufacturing overhead costs and work 80,000 machine-hours.

CHECK FIGURE
(3) Under-applied by $4,000

*Required:*
1. Compute the company's predetermined overhead rate.
2. Assume that during the year the company works only 75,000 machine-hours and incurs the following costs in the Manufacturing Overhead and Work in Process accounts:

| Manufacturing Overhead | | | | Work in Process | | |
|---|---|---|---|---|---|---|
| (Maintenance) | 21,000 | ? | | (Direct materials) | 710,000 | |
| (Indirect materials) | 8,000 | | | (Direct labour) | 90,000 | |
| (Indirect labour) | 60,000 | | | (Overhead) | ? | |
| (Utilities) | 32,000 | | | | | |
| (Insurance) | 7,000 | | | | | |
| (Depreciation) | 56,000 | | | | | |

Copy the data in the T-accounts above onto your answer sheet. Compute the amount of overhead cost that would be applied to Work in Process for the year and make the entry in your T-accounts.
3. Compute the amount of under- or over-applied overhead for the year and show the balance in your Manufacturing Overhead T-account. Prepare a general journal entry to close out the balance in this account to Cost of Goods Sold.
4. Explain why the manufacturing overhead was under- or over-applied for the year.

**PROBLEM 3–3   Applying Overhead in a Service Firm; Journal Entries** (LO4, LO5, LO7)
Vista Landscaping uses a job-order costing system to track the costs of its landscaping projects. The company provides garden design services as well as actually carrying out the landscaping for the client. The table below provides data concerning the three landscaping projects that were in progress during April. There was no work in process at the beginning of April.

CHECK FIGURE
(3) Balance in WIP: $16,700

| | Project | | |
|---|---|---|---|
| | Harris | Chan | James |
| Designer-hours ............... | 120 | 100 | 90 |
| Direct materials cost ........... | $4,500 | $3,700 | $1,400 |
| Direct labour cost ............. | 9,600 | 8,000 | 7,200 |

Actual overhead costs were $30,000 for April. Overhead costs are applied to projects on the basis of designer-hours since most of the overhead is related to the costs of the garden design studio. The predetermined overhead rate is $90 per designer-hour. The Harris and Chan projects were completed in April; the James project was not completed by the end of the month.

*Required:*
1. Compute the amount of overhead cost that would have been charged to each project during April.
2. Prepare a journal entry showing the completion of the Harris and Chan projects and the transfer of costs to the Completed Projects (i.e., Finished Goods) account.
3. What is the balance in the Work in Process account at the end of the month?
4. What is the balance in the Overhead account at the end of the month? What is this balance called?

CHECK FIGURE
(3) Over-applied by
Rmb7,000
(4) NI: Rmb247,000

**PROBLEM 3–4   Comprehensive Problem** (LO3, LO4, LO5, LO6, LO7)
Gold Nest Company of Guandong, China, is a family-owned enterprise that makes birdcages for the South China market. A popular pastime among older Chinese men is to take their pet birds on daily excursions to teahouses and public parks where they meet with other bird owners to talk and play mahjong. A great deal

of attention is lavished on these birds, and the birdcages are often elabourately constructed from exotic woods and contain porcelain feeding bowls and silver roosts. Gold Nest Company makes a broad range of birdcages that it sells through an extensive network of street vendors who receive commissions on their sales. The Chinese currency is the renminbi, which is denoted by Rmb. All of the company's transactions with customers, employees, and suppliers are conducted in cash; there is no credit.

The company uses a job-order costing system in which overhead is applied to jobs on the basis of direct labour cost. At the beginning of the year, it was estimated that the total direct labour cost for the year would be Rmb200,000 and the total manufacturing overhead cost would be Rmb330,000. At the beginning of the year, the inventory balances were as follows:

| | |
|---|---|
| Raw materials ................................ | Rmb25,000 |
| Work in process ............................... | 10,000 |
| Finished goods .............................. | 40,000 |

During the year, the following transactions were completed:
a. Raw materials purchased for cash, Rmb275,000.
b. Raw materials requisitioned for use in production, Rmb280,000 (materials costing Rmb220,000 were charged directly to jobs; the remaining materials were indirect).
c. Costs for employee services were incurred as follows:

| | |
|---|---|
| Direct labour ................................. | Rmb180,000 |
| Indirect labour ............................... | 72,000 |
| Sales commissions ........................... | 63,000 |
| Administrative salaries ........................ | 90,000 |

d. Rent for the year was Rmb18,000 (Rmb13,000 of this amount related to factory operations, and the remainder related to selling and administrative activities).
e. Utility costs incurred in the factory, Rmb57,000.
f. Advertising costs incurred, Rmb140,000.
g. Depreciation recorded on equipment, Rmb100,000. (Rmb88,000 of this amount was on equipment used in factory operations; the remaining Rmb12,000 was on equipment used in selling and administrative activities.)
h. Manufacturing overhead cost was applied to jobs, Rmb __?__ .
i. Goods that cost Rmb675,000 to manufacture according to their job cost sheets were completed during the year.
j. Sales for the year totalled Rmb1,250,000. The total cost to manufacture these goods according to their job cost sheets was Rmb700,000.

***Required:***
1. Prepare journal entries to record the transactions for the year.
2. Prepare T-accounts for inventories, Manufacturing Overhead, and Cost of Goods Sold. Post relevant data from your journal entries to these T-accounts (do not forget to enter the beginning balances in your inventory accounts). Compute an ending balance in each account.
3. Is Manufacturing Overhead under-applied or over-applied for the year? Prepare a journal entry to close any balance in the Manufacturing Overhead account to Cost of Goods Sold.
4. Prepare an income statement for the year. (Do not prepare a schedule of cost of goods manufactured; all of the information needed for the income statement is available in the journal entries and T-accounts you have prepared.)

CHECK FIGURE
(3) Indirect labour: $30,000
(7) Over-applied: $10,000

**PROBLEM 3–5   T-Account Analysis of Cost Flows (LO3, LO6, LO7)**
Selected ledger accounts of Moore Company are given below for the just completed year:

| Raw Materials | | | | Manufacturing Overhead | | |
|---|---|---|---|---|---|---|
| Bal. 1/1 | 15,000 | Credits | ? | Debits | 230,000 | Credits | ? |
| Debits | 120,000 | | | | | | |
| Bal. 12/31 | 25,000 | | | | | | |

### Work in Process

| Bal. 1/1 | 20,000 | Credits | 470,000 |
|---|---|---|---|
| Direct materials | 90,000 | | |
| Direct labour | 150,000 | | |
| Overhead | 240,000 | | |
| Bal. 12/31 | ? | | |

### Factory Wages Payable

| Debits | 185,000 | Bal. 1/1 | 9,000 |
|---|---|---|---|
| | | Credits | 180,000 |
| | | Bal. 12/31 | 4,000 |

### Finished Goods

| Bal. 1/1 | 40,000 | Credits | ? |
|---|---|---|---|
| Debits | ? | | |
| Bal. 12/31 | 60,000 | | |

### Cost of Goods Sold

| Debits | ? |
|---|---|

*Required:*
1. What was the cost of raw materials put into production during the year?
2. How much of the materials in (1) above consisted of indirect materials?
3. How much of the factory labour cost for the year consisted of indirect labour?
4. What was the cost of goods manufactured for the year?
5. What was the cost of goods sold for the year (before considering under- or over-applied overhead)?
6. If overhead is applied to production on the basis of direct labour cost, what rate was in effect during the year?
7. Was manufacturing overhead under- or over-applied? By how much?
8. Compute the ending balance in the Work in Process inventory account. Assume that this balance consists entirely of goods started during the year. If $8,000 of this balance is direct labour cost, how much of it is direct materials cost? Manufacturing overhead cost?

**PROBLEM 3–6  Overhead Analysis; Schedule of Cost of Goods Manufactured** (LO3, LO5, LO7)
Gitano Products operates a job-order cost system and applies overhead cost to jobs on the basis of direct materials *used in production* (*not* on the basis of raw materials purchased). In computing a predetermined overhead rate at the beginning of the year, the company's estimates were: manufacturing overhead cost, $800,000; and direct materials to be used in production, $500,000. The company's inventory accounts at the beginning and end of the year were:

CHECK FIGURE
(2) COGM: $1,340,000

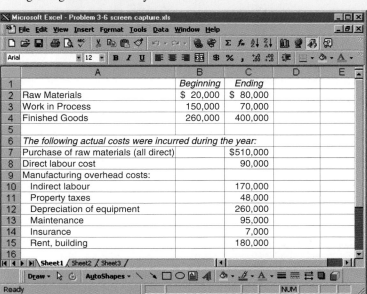

| | Beginning | Ending |
|---|---|---|
| Raw Materials | $ 20,000 | $ 80,000 |
| Work in Process | 150,000 | 70,000 |
| Finished Goods | 260,000 | 400,000 |
| *The following actual costs were incurred during the year:* | | |
| Purchase of raw materials (all direct) | | $510,000 |
| Direct labour cost | | 90,000 |
| Manufacturing overhead costs: | | |
| Indirect labour | | 170,000 |
| Property taxes | | 48,000 |
| Depreciation of equipment | | 260,000 |
| Maintenance | | 95,000 |
| Insurance | | 7,000 |
| Rent, building | | 180,000 |

*Required:*
1. a. Compute the predetermined overhead rate for the year.
   b. Compute the amount of under- or over-applied overhead for the year.
2. Prepare a schedule of cost of goods manufactured for the year.
3. Compute the Cost of Goods Sold for the year. (Do not include any under- or over-applied overhead in your Cost of Goods Sold figure.)

4. Job 215 was started and completed during the year. What price would have been charged to the customer if the job required $8,500 in direct materials and $2,700 in direct labour cost and the company priced its jobs at 25% above cost to manufacture?

5. Direct materials made up $24,000 of the $70,000 ending Work in Process inventory balance. Supply the information missing below:

| | |
|---|---:|
| Direct materials .............................. | $24,000 |
| Direct labour ..................................... | ? |
| Manufacturing overhead .......................... | ? |
| Work in process inventory ....................... | $70,000 |

CHECK FIGURE
(3) $78.16 per unit

**PROBLEM 3–7   Multiple Departments; Applying Overhead** (LO3, LO5, LO7)

High Desert Potteryworks makes a variety of pottery products that it sells to retailers, such as Home Depot. The company uses a job-order costing system in which predetermined overhead rates are used to apply manufacturing overhead cost to jobs. The predetermined overhead rate in the Moulding Department is based on machine-hours, and the rate in the Painting Department is based on direct labour cost. At the beginning of the year, the company's management made the following estimates:

| | Department | |
|---|---:|---:|
| | **Moulding** | **Painting** |
| Direct labour-hours ................... | 12,000 | 60,000 |
| Machine-hours ..................... | 70,000 | 8,000 |
| Direct materials cost ................... | $510,000 | $650,000 |
| Direct labour cost ................... | 130,000 | 420,000 |
| Manufacturing overhead cost ........... | 602,000 | 735,000 |

Job 205 was started on August 1 and completed on August 10. The company's cost records show the following information concerning the job:

| | Department | |
|---|---:|---:|
| | **Moulding** | **Painting** |
| Direct labour-hours ................... | 30 | 85 |
| Machine-hours ..................... | 110 | 20 |
| Materials placed into production ........ | $470 | $332 |
| Direct labour cost ................. | 290 | 680 |

**Required:**

1. Compute the predetermined overhead rate used during the year in the Moulding Department. Compute the rate used in the Painting Department.
2. Compute the total overhead cost applied to job 205.
3. What would be the total cost recorded for job 205? If the job contained 50 units, what would be the cost per unit?
4. At the end of the year, the records of High Desert Potteryworks revealed the following actual cost and operating data for all jobs worked on during the year:

| | Department | |
|---|---:|---:|
| | **Moulding** | **Painting** |
| Direct labour-hours ................... | 10,000 | 62,000 |
| Machine-hours ..................... | 65,000 | 9,000 |
| Direct materials cost ................. | $430,000 | $680,000 |
| Direct labour cost ................... | 108,000 | 436,000 |
| Manufacturing overhead cost ........... | 570,000 | 750,000 |

What was the amount of under- or over-applied overhead in each department at the end of the year?

**PROBLEM 3–8   T-Accounts; Applying Overhead (LO5, LO6, LO7)**

Hudson Company's trial balance as of January 1, the beginning of the fiscal year, is given below:

CHECK FIGURE
(2) WIP balance: $17,300
(4) NI: $18,700

| | | |
|---|---:|---:|
| Cash | $ 7,000 | |
| Accounts Receivable | 18,000 | |
| Raw Materials | 9,000 | |
| Work in Process | 20,000 | |
| Finished Goods | 32,000 | |
| Prepaid Insurance | 4,000 | |
| Plant and Equipment | 210,000 | |
| Accumulated Depreciation | | $ 53,000 |
| Accounts Payable | | 38,000 |
| Capital Shares | | 160,000 |
| Retained Earnings | | 49,000 |
| Total | $300,000 | $300,000 |

Hudson Company is a manufacturing firm and employs a job-order costing system. During the year, the following transactions took place:

a. Raw materials purchased on account, $40,000.
b. Raw materials were requisitioned for use in production, $38,000 (85% direct and 15% indirect).
c. Factory utility costs incurred, $19,100.
d. Depreciation was recorded on plant and equipment, $36,000. Three-fourths of the depreciation related to factory equipment, and the remainder related to selling and administrative equipment.
e. Advertising expense incurred, $48,000.
f. Costs for salaries and wages were incurred as follows:

| | |
|---|---:|
| Direct labour | $45,000 |
| Indirect labour | 10,000 |
| Administrative salaries | 30,000 |

g. Prepaid insurance expired during the year, $3,000 (80% related to factory operations, and 20% related to selling and administrative activities).
h. Miscellaneous selling and administrative expenses incurred, $9,500.
i. Manufacturing overhead was applied to production. The company applies overhead on the basis of $8 per machine-hour; 7,500 machine-hours were recorded for the year.
j. Goods that cost $140,000 to manufacture according to their job cost sheets were transferred to the finished goods warehouse.
k. Sales for the year totalled $250,000 and were all on account. The total cost to manufacture these goods according to their job cost sheets was $130,000.
l. Collections from customers during the year totalled $245,000.
m. Payments to suppliers on account during the year, $150,000; payments to employees for salaries and wages, $84,000.

*Required:*

1. Prepare a T-account for each account in the company's trial balance, and enter the opening balances shown above.
2. Record the transactions above directly into the T-accounts. Prepare new T-accounts as needed. Key your entries to the letters (a) through (m) above. Find the ending balance in each account.
3. Is manufacturing overhead under-applied or over-applied for the year? Make an entry in the T-accounts to close any balance in the Manufacturing Overhead account to Cost of Goods Sold.
4. Prepare an income statement for the year. (Do not prepare a schedule of cost of goods manufactured; all of the information needed for the income statement is available in the T-accounts.)

**PROBLEM 3–9   Journal Entries; T-Accounts; Cost Flows (LO4, LO5, LO6, LO7)**

Almeda Products, Inc. uses a job-order cost system. The company's inventory balances on April 1, the start of its fiscal year, were as follows:

CHECK FIGURE
(3) Under-applied by $4,000
(4) NI: $57,000

| | |
|---|---:|
| Raw materials | $32,000 |
| Work in process | 20,000 |
| Finished goods | 48,000 |

During the year, the following transactions were completed:

a. Raw materials were purchased on account, $170,000.
b. Raw materials were issued from the storeroom for use in production, $180,000 (80% direct and 20% indirect).
c. Employee salaries and wages were accrued as follows: direct labour, $200,000; indirect labour, $82,000; and selling and administrative salaries, $90,000.
d. Utility costs were incurred in the factory, $65,000.
e. Advertising costs were incurred, $100,000.
f. Prepaid insurance expired during the year, $20,000 (90% related to factory operations, and 10% related to selling and administrative activities).
g. Depreciation was recorded, $180,000 (85% related to factory assets, and 15% related to selling and administrative assets).
h. Manufacturing overhead was applied to jobs at the rate of 175% of direct labour cost.
i. Goods that cost $700,000 to manufacture according to their job cost sheets were transferred to the finished goods warehouse.
j. Sales for the year totalled $1,000,000 and were all on account. The total cost to manufacture these goods according to their job cost sheets was $720,000.

### Required:

1. Prepare journal entries to record the transactions for the year.
2. Prepare T-accounts for Raw Materials, Work in Process, Finished Goods, Manufacturing Overhead, and Cost of Goods Sold. Post the appropriate parts of your journal entries to these T-accounts. Compute the ending balance in each account. (Do not forget to enter the beginning balances in the inventory accounts.)
3. Is Manufacturing Overhead under-applied or over-applied for the year? Prepare a journal entry to close this balance to Cost of Goods Sold.
4. Prepare an income statement for the year. (Do not prepare a schedule of cost of goods manufactured; all of the information needed for the income statement is available in the journal entries and T-accounts you have prepared.)

CHECK FIGURE
(3) Over-applied by $9,400
(4) NI: $78,400

**PROBLEM 3–10**     **Cost Flows; T-Accounts; Income Statement** (LO3, LO5, LO6, LO7)

Supreme Videos, Inc. produces short musical videos for sale to retail outlets. The company's balance sheet accounts as of January 1, the beginning of the fiscal year, are given below.

| SUPREME VIDEOS, INC.<br>Balance Sheet<br>January 1 | | |
|---|---:|---:|
| **Assets** | | |
| Current assets: | | |
|   Cash ..................................... | | $ 63,000 |
|   Accounts receivable ...................... | | 102,000 |
|   Inventories: | | |
|     Raw materials (film, costumes) ............... | $ 30,000 | |
|     Videos in process ......................... | 45,000 | |
|     Finished videos awaiting sale ................ | 81,000 | 156,000 |
|   Prepaid insurance ........................... | | 9,000 |
| Total current assets ............................ | | 330,000 |
| Studio and equipment .......................... | 730,000 | |
| Less accumulated depreciation ................... | 210,000 | 520,000 |
| Total assets .................................. | | $850,000 |
| **Liabilities and Shareholders' Equity** | | |
| Accounts payable .............................. | | $160,000 |
| Capital shares ................................ | $420,000 | |
| Retained earnings ............................. | 270,000 | 690,000 |
| Total liabilities and shareholders' equity ............ | | $850,000 |

Since the videos differ in length and in complexity of production, the company uses a job-order costing system to determine the cost of each video produced. Studio (manufacturing) overhead is charged to videos on the basis of camera-hours of activity. At the beginning of the year, the company estimated that it would work 7,000 camera-hours and incur $280,000 in studio overhead cost. The following transactions were recorded for the year:

a. Film, costumes, and similar raw materials purchased on account, $185,000.
b. Film, costumes, and other raw materials issued to production, $200,000 (85% of this material was considered direct to the videos in production, and the other 15% was considered indirect).
c. Utility costs incurred in the production studio, $72,000.
d. Depreciation recorded on the studio, cameras, and other equipment, $84,000. Three-fourths of this depreciation related to actual production of the videos, and the remainder related to equipment used in marketing and administration.
e. Advertising expense incurred, $130,000.
f. Costs for salaries and wages were incurred as follows:

| | |
|---|---:|
| Direct labour (actors and directors) ............ | $ 82,000 |
| Indirect labour (carpenters to build sets, costume designers, and so forth) ............ | 110,000 |
| Administrative salaries ..................... | 95,000 |

g. Prepaid insurance expired during the year, $7,000 (80% related to production of videos, and 20% related to marketing and administrative activities).
h. Miscellaneous marketing and administrative expenses incurred, $8,600.
i. Studio (manufacturing) overhead was applied to videos in production. The company recorded 7,250 camera-hours of activity during the year.
j. Videos that cost $550,000 to produce according to their job cost sheets were transferred to the finished videos warehouse to await sale and shipment.
k. Sales for the year totalled $925,000 and were all on account. The total cost to produce these videos according to their job cost sheets was $600,000.
l. Collections from customers during the year totalled $850,000.
m. Payments to suppliers on account during the year, $500,000; payments to employees for salaries and wages, $285,000.

*Required:*
1. Prepare a T-account for each account on the company's balance sheet, and enter the opening balances.
2. Record the transactions directly into the T-accounts. Prepare new T-accounts as needed. Key your entries to the letters (a) through (m) above. Find the ending balance in each account.
3. Is the Studio (manufacturing) Overhead account under-applied or over-applied for the year? Make an entry in the T-accounts to close any balance in the Studio Overhead account to Cost of Goods Sold.
4. Prepare an income statement for the year. (Do not prepare a schedule of cost of goods manufactured; all of the information needed for the income statement is available in the T-accounts.)

# Building Your Skills

**ANALYTICAL THINKING**   (LO3, LO5)

Kelvin Aerospace, Inc. manufactures parts, such as rudder hinges, for the aerospace industry. The company uses a job-order costing system with a plantwide predetermined overhead rate based on direct labour-hours. On December 16, 2004, the company's controller made a preliminary estimate of the predetermined overhead rate for the year 2005. The new rate was based on the estimated total manufacturing overhead cost of $3,402,000 and the estimated 63,000 total direct labour-hours for 2005:

$$\text{Predetermined overhead rate} = \frac{\$3,402,000}{63,000 \text{ direct labour-hours}}$$
$$= \$54 \text{ per direct labour-hours}$$

This new predetermined overhead rate was communicated to top managers in a meeting on December 19. The rate did not cause any comment because it was within a few pennies of the overhead rate that had been used during 2004. One of the subjects discussed at the meeting was a proposal by the production manager to purchase an automated milling machine built by Sunghi Industries. The president of Kelvin Aerospace, Harry Arcany, agreed to meet with the sales representative from Sunghi Industries to discuss the proposal.

On the day following the meeting, Mr. Arcany met with Jasmine Chang, Sunghi Industries' sales representative. The following discussion took place:

*Arcany:* Wally, our production manager, asked me to meet with you, since he is interested in installing an automated milling machine. Frankly, I'm skeptical. You're going to have to show me this isn't just another expensive toy for Wally's people to play with.

*Chang:* This is a great machine with direct bottom-line benefits. The automated milling machine has three major advantages. First, it is much faster than the manual methods you are using. It can process about twice as many parts per hour as your present milling machines. Second, it is much more flexible. There are some upfront programming costs, but once those have been incurred, almost no setup is required to run a standard operation. You just punch in the code for the standard operation, load the machine's hopper with raw material, and the machine does the rest.

*Arcany:* What about cost? Having twice the capacity in the milling machine area won't do us much good. That centre is idle much of the time anyway.

*Chang:* I was getting there. The third advantage of the automated milling machine is lower cost. Wally and I looked over your present operations, and we estimated that the automated equipment would eliminate the need for about 6,000 direct labour-hours a year. What is your direct labour cost per hour?

*Arcany:* The wage rate in the milling area averages about $32 per hour. Fringe benefits raise that figure to about $41 per hour.

*Chang:* Don't forget your overhead.

*Arcany:* Next year, the overhead rate will be $54 per hour.

*Chang:* So, including fringe benefits and overhead, the cost per direct labour-hour is about $95.

*Arcany:* That's right.

*Chang:* Since you can save 6,000 direct labour-hours per year, the cost savings would amount to about $570,000 a year. And our 60-month lease plan would require payments of only $348,000 per year.

*Arcany:* That sounds like a no-brainer. When could you install the equipment?

Shortly after this meeting, Mr. Arcany informed the company's controller of the decision to lease the new equipment, which would be installed over the Christmas vacation period. The controller realized that this decision would require a recomputation of the predetermined overhead rate for the year 2005, since the decision would affect both the manufacturing overhead and the direct labour-hours for the year. After talking with both the production manager and the sales representative from Sunghi Industries, the controller discovered that in addition to the annual lease cost of $348,000, the new machine would also require a skilled technician/programmer who would have to be hired at a cost of $50,000 per year to maintain and program the equipment. Both of these costs would be included in factory overhead. There would be no other changes in total manufacturing overhead cost, which is almost entirely fixed. The controller assumed that the new machine would result in a reduction of 6,000 direct labour-hours for the year from the levels that had initially been planned.

When the revised predetermined overhead rate for the year 2005 was circulated among the company's top managers, there was considerable dismay.

***Required:***

1. Recompute the predetermined rate assuming that the new machine will be installed. Explain why the new predetermined overhead rate is higher (or lower) than the rate that was originally estimated for the year 2005.
2. What effect (if any) would this new rate have on the cost of jobs that do not use the new automated milling machine?
3. Why would managers be concerned about the new overhead rate?
4. After seeing the new predetermined overhead rate, the production manager admitted that he probably would not be able to eliminate all of the 6,000 direct labour-hours. He had been hoping to accomplish the reduction by not replacing workers who retire or quit, but that had not been possible. As a result, the real labour savings would be only about 2,000 hours—one worker. In the light of this additional information, evaluate the original decision to acquire the automated milling machine from Sunghi Industries.

**COMMUNICATING IN PRACTICE**   (LO1, LO3, LO5)

Look in the Yellow Pages or contact your local chamber of commerce or local chapter of CMA-Canada to find the names of manufacturing companies in your area. Call or make an appointment to meet with the controller or chief financial officer of one of these companies.

*Required:*

Ask the following questions and write a brief memorandum to your instructor that addresses what you found out.

1. What are the company's main products?
2. Does the company use job-order costing, process costing, or some other method of determining product costs?
3. How is overhead assigned to products? What is the overhead rate? What is the basis of allocation? Is more than one overhead rate used?
4. Has the company recently changed its cost system, or is it considering changing its cost system? If so, why? What changes were made, or what changes are being considered?

**ETHICS CHALLENGE**   (LO3, LO5)

Terri Ronsin had recently been transferred to the Home Security Systems Division of National Home Products. Shortly after taking over her new position as divisional controller, she was asked to develop the division's predetermined overhead rate for the upcoming year. The accuracy of the rate is of some importance, since it is used throughout the year and any over-applied or under-applied overhead is closed out to Cost of Goods Sold only at the end of the year. National Home Products uses direct labour-hours in all of its divisions as the allocation base for manufacturing overhead.

To compute the predetermined overhead rate, Terri divided her estimate of the total manufacturing overhead for the coming year by the production manager's estimate of the total direct labour-hours for the coming year. She took her computations to the division's general manager for approval but was quite surprised when he suggested a modification in the base. Her conversation with the general manager of the Home Security Systems Division, Harry Irving, went like this:

*Ronsin:* Here are my calculations for next year's predetermined overhead rate. If you approve, we can enter the rate into the computer on January 1 and be up and running in the job-order costing system right away this year.

*Irving:* Thanks for coming up with the calculations so quickly, and they look just fine. There is, however, one slight modification I would like to see. Your estimate of the total direct labour-hours for the year is 440,000 hours. How about cutting that to about 420,000 hours?

*Ronsin:* I don't know if I can do that. The production manager says she will need about 440,000 direct labour-hours to meet the sales projections for the year. Besides, there are going to be over 430,000 direct labour-hours during the current year, and sales are projected to be higher next year.

*Irving:* Teri, I know all of that. I would still like to reduce the direct labour-hours in the base to something like 420,000 hours. You probably don't know that I had an agreement with your predecessor as divisional controller to shave 5% or so off the estimated direct labour-hours every year. That way, we kept a reserve that usually resulted in a big boost to net income at the end of the fiscal year in December. We called it our Christmas bonus. Corporate headquarters always seemed as pleased as punch that we could pull off such a miracle at the end of the year. This system has worked well for many years, and I don't want to change it now.

*Required:*

1. Explain how shaving 5% off the estimated direct labour-hours in the base for the predetermined overhead rate usually results in a big boost in net income at the end of the fiscal year.
2. Should Terri Ronsin go along with the general manager's request to reduce the direct labour-hours in the predetermined overhead rate computation to 420,000 direct labour-hours?

**TAKING IT TO THE NET**

Do not forget to go to the Net (www.mcgrawhill.ca/college/Garrison).

CHECK FIGURE
(3) WIP inventory: $14,300

**TEAMWORK IN ACTION**    (LO3, LO4, LO5, LO6, LO7)

In an attempt to conceal a theft of funds, Snake N. Grass, controller of Bucolic Products, Inc., placed a bomb in the company's record vault. The ensuing explosion left only fragments of the company's factory ledger, as shown below:

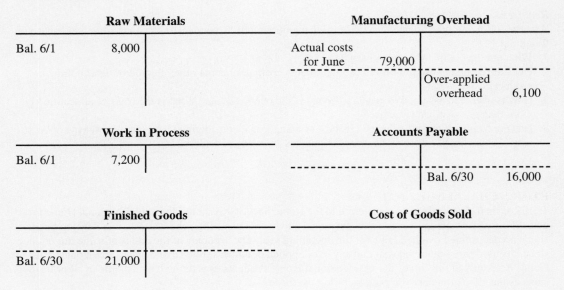

|  | **Raw Materials** |  |  |
|---|---|---|---|
| Bal. 6/1 | 8,000 | | |

|  | **Manufacturing Overhead** |  |  |
|---|---|---|---|
| Actual costs for June | 79,000 | | |
| | | Over-applied overhead | 6,100 |

|  | **Work in Process** |  |  |
|---|---|---|---|
| Bal. 6/1 | 7,200 | | |

|  | **Accounts Payable** |  |  |
|---|---|---|---|
| | | Bal. 6/30 | 16,000 |

|  | **Finished Goods** |  |  |
|---|---|---|---|
| Bal. 6/30 | 21,000 | | |

|  | **Cost of Goods Sold** |  |
|---|---|---|

To bring Mr. Grass to justice, the company must reconstruct its activities for June. Your team has been assigned to perform the task of reconstruction. After interviewing selected employees and sifting through charred fragments, you have determined the following additional information:

a. According to the company's treasurer, the accounts payable are for purchases of raw materials only. The company's balance sheet, dated May 31, shows that Accounts Payable had a $20,000 balance at the beginning of June. The company's bank has provided photocopies of all cheques that cleared the bank during June. These photocopies show that payments to suppliers during June totalled $119,000. (All materials used during the month were direct materials.)

b. The production superintendent states that manufacturing overhead cost is applied to jobs on the basis of direct labour-hours. However, he does not remember the rate currently being used by the company.

c. Cost sheets kept in the production superintendent's office show that only one job was in process on June 30, at the time of the explosion. The job had been charged with $6,600 in materials, and 500 direct labour-hours at $8 per hour had been worked on the job.

d. A log is kept in the finished goods warehouse showing all goods transferred in from the factory. This log shows that the cost of goods transferred into the finished goods warehouse from the factory during June totalled $280,000.

e. The company's May 31 balance sheet indicates that the finished goods inventory totalled $36,000 at the beginning of June.

f. A charred piece of the payroll ledger, found after sifting through piles of smoking debris, indicates that 11,500 direct labour-hours were recorded for June. The company's Human Resources Department has verified that, as a result of a union contract, all factory employees earn the same $8 per hour rate.

g. The production superintendent states that there was no under- or over-applied overhead in the Manufacturing Overhead account at May 31.

*Required:*

1. Each member of the team should determine what types of transactions would be posted to one of the following sets of accounts:
   a. Raw materials and accounts payable.
   b. Work in process and manufacturing overhead.
   c. Finished goods and cost of goods sold.

   Each team member should present a summary of the types of transactions that would be posted to the accounts to the other team members, who should confirm or correct the summary. Then, the team should work together to complete steps 2 through 7.

2. Determine the transaction that should be reflected in the manufacturing overhead account, and then determine the company's predetermined overhead rate.

3. Determine the June 30 balance in the company's work in process account.
4. Determine the transactions that should be reflected in the work in process account. (You will need to back into the amount of direct materials that must have been used during the month to complete the T-account analysis.)
5. Determine the transactions that should be reflected in the finished goods account. (You will need to back into the cost of the finished goods that were sold during the month to complete the T-account analysis.)
6. Determine the transactions that should be reflected in the cost of goods sold account.
7. Determine the transactions that should be reflected in the accounts payable account.
8. Determine the transactions that should be reflected in the raw materials account.
   *(Hint: A good method for determining the transactions that were recorded in a given account is to update the related fragmented T-account by posting whatever entries can be developed from the information provided above.)*

# Chapter *Four*

# Process Costing

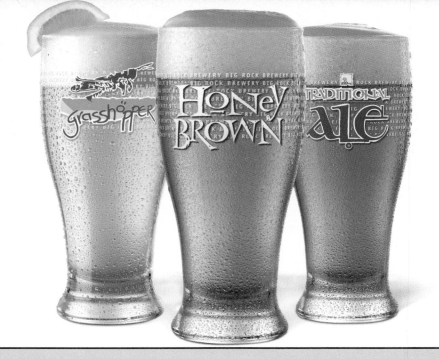

## DECISION FEATURE Quality and Costs Are Important in Beer Making, Too!

Whether you are drinking Grasshopper Wheat Ale, Traditional Ale, or the Black Amber Ale, you care about deriving value for the money you spend. For Big Rock Brewery of Calgary, value means offering distinctive premium quality beers at competitive prices.

So, is there a difference in the way the different beers are made? The process they follow is essentially the same. The raw ingredients are first crushed or milled and then mashed. The wort, resulting from the mashing process is the liquid that will eventually become the beer. This liquid is then boiled to be sterilized. The next step in the process is fermentation, but this requires that the sterilized liquid be cooled before it is sent for fermentation. The fermentation process is important in terms of maintaining the desired consistency and quality of the beer. After the fermentation process, the beer is aged, filtered, packaged (bottled and labelled), and then sent off to distributors.

Like many other industries, the beer industry is also fiercely competitive. However, such companies as Big Rock Brewery have thrived in the marketplace by developing specialty beers, which offer superior quality and taste and by controlling costs. And management's efforts have certainly paid off! In the last five years, sales grew by over 83%, and the net income as a percentage of sales increased from −3.3% in 1999 to over 7.5% in 2003.

Big Rock, however, understands that it cannot afford to be complacent. In an effort to further control costs, the company has invested in a computer system that allows managers to implement more effective cost controls in many areas. The system generates detailed cost information on weekly and monthly bases. This is important, given the number of different processes that add to the costs of brewing a good beer. Knowing the cost added at each stage of the entire process is essential to identify potential avenues for cost management. Managers at Big Rock may also decide to adopt the lean business model to improve quality and efficiency (cost), two important factors in enhancing the value that the company's beers offer to the drinkers.

Source: 2003 Annual Report, obtained at http://www.bigrockbeer.com/pdfs/BRBIncomeTrust.pdf

**A**s explained in Chapter 3, two basic costing systems are in use: job-order costing and process costing. A job-order costing system is used in situations where many different jobs or products are worked on each period. Examples of industries that would typically use job-order costing include furniture manufacture, special-order printing, shipbuilding, and many types of service organizations.

A **process costing** system is used in industries that produce essentially homogeneous (i.e., uniform) products on a continuous basis, such as bricks, corn flakes, or paper. Process costing is used in such companies as Reynolds Aluminum (aluminium ingots), Scott Paper (toilet paper), General Mills (flour), Petro Canada (gasoline and lubricating oils), Coppertone (sunscreens), and Kellogg (breakfast cereals). In addition, process costing is often used in companies with assembly operations, such as Panasonic (video monitors), Compaq (personal computers), General Electric (refrigerators), Toyota (automobiles), Amana (washing machines), and Sony (CD players). As suggested by the length of this list, process costing is in very wide use.

Our purpose in this chapter is to explain how product costing occurs in a process costing system.

# Comparison of Job-Order and Process Costing

## Similarities between Job-Order and Process Costing

The similarities that exist between job-order and process costing can be summarized as follows:

1. The same basic purposes exist in both systems, which are to assign material, labour, and overhead cost to products and to provide a mechanism for computing unit costs.
2. Both systems maintain and use the same basic accounts, including Manufacturing Overhead, Raw Materials, Work in Process, and Finished Goods, and the flow of costs through the accounts is basically the same in both systems.

As can be seen from this comparison, much of the knowledge that we have already acquired about costing is applicable to a process costing system. Our task now is simply to refine and extend this knowledge to process costing.

## Differences between Job-Order and Process Costing

The differences between job-order and process costing arise from two factors. The first is that the flow of units in a process costing system is more or less continuous, and the second is that these units are indistinguishable from one another. Under process costing, it makes no sense to try to identify materials, labour, and overhead costs with a particular order from a customer (as we did with job-order costing), since each order is just one of many that are filled from a continuous flow of virtually identical units from the production line. Under process costing, we accumulate costs *by department*, or process, rather than by order, and assign these costs uniformly to all units that pass through the department during a period.

The job cost sheet is of no use in process costing, since the focal point of this method is on departments. Instead of using job cost sheets, a **production report** is prepared for each department in which work is done on products. The production report serves several functions. It provides a summary of the number of units moving through a department during a period, and it also provides a computation of unit costs. In addition, it shows what costs were charged to the department and what disposition was made of these costs. The department production report is the key document in a process costing system.

**Exhibit 4–1**
Differences between Job-Order
and Process Costing

| Job-Order Costing | Process Costing |
|---|---|
| 1. Many different jobs are worked on during each period, with each job having different production requirements. | 1. A single product is produced either on a continuous basis or for long periods of time. All units of product are identical. |
| 2. Costs are accumulated by individual job. | 2. Costs are accumulated by department or process. |
| 3. The *job cost sheet* is the key document controlling the accumulation of costs by a job. | 3. The *department production report* is the key document showing the accumulation and disposition of costs by a department. |
| 4. Unit costs are computed *by job* on the job cost sheet. | 4. Unit costs are computed *by department* on the department production report. |

The major differences between job-order and process costing are summarized in Exhibit 4–1.

# A Perspective of Process Cost Flows

Before presenting a detailed example of process costing, it will be helpful to see how manufacturing costs flow through a process costing system.

## Processing Departments

A **processing department** is any location in an organization where work is performed on a product and where materials, labour, or overhead costs are added to the product. For example, a potato chip factory might have three processing departments—one for preparing potatoes, one for cooking, and one for inspecting and packaging. A company can have as many or as few processing departments as are needed to complete a product or service. Some products and services may go through several processing departments, while others may go through only one or two. Regardless of the number of departments involved, all processing departments have three essential features. First, the activity performed in the processing department must be performed uniformly on all of the units passing through it. Second, the output of the processing department must be homogeneous. Third, the processing departments involved would probably be organized in a *sequential* pattern. By sequential processing, we mean that units flow in sequence from one department to another as shown in Exhibit 4–2.

**Exhibit 4–2**
Sequential Processing Departments

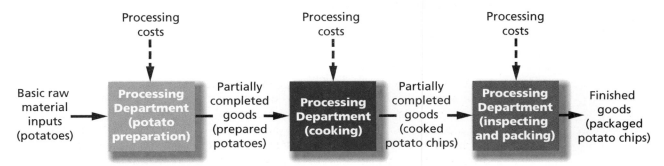

## in business today    A Hybrid Approach

Managers of successful pharmacies understand product costs. Some pharmacies use a hybrid approach to costing drugs. For example, a hospital pharmacy may use process costing to develop the cost of formulating the base solution for parenterals (that is, drugs delivered by injection or through the bloodstream), and then use job-order costing to accumulate the additional costs incurred to create specific parenteral solutions. These additional costs include the ingredients added to the base solution and the time spent by the pharmacist to prepare the specific prescribed drug solution.

Source: "Pharmaceutical Care: Cost Estimation and Cost Management," *Drug Store News*, February 16, 1998, p. CP21 (5 pages).

## The Flow of Materials, Labour, and Overhead Costs

Cost accumulation is simpler in a process costing system than in a job-order costing system. In a process costing system, instead of having to trace costs to hundreds of different jobs, costs are traced to only a few processing departments.

A T-account model of materials, labour, and overhead cost flows in a process costing system is given in Exhibit 4–3. Several key points should be noted from this exhibit. First, note that a separate Work in Process account is maintained for *each processing department.* In contrast, in a job-order costing system, there may be only a single Work in Process account for the entire company. Second, note that the completed production of the first processing department (Department A in the exhibit) is transferred into the Work in Process account of the second processing department (Department B), where it undergoes further work. After this further work, the completed units are then transferred into Finished Goods. (In Exhibit 4–3, we show only two processing departments, but there can be many such departments in a company.)

**Exhibit 4–3**
T-Account Model of Process Costing Flows

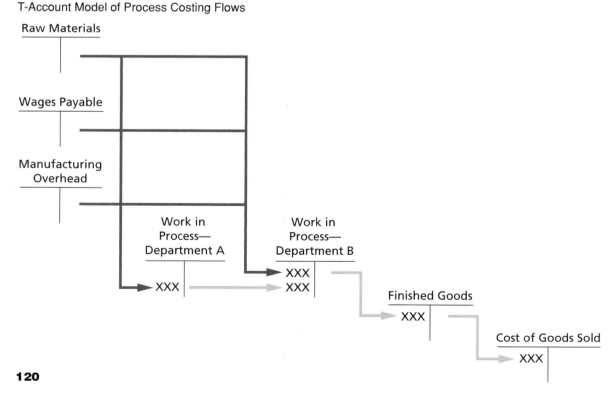

Finally, note that materials, labour, and overhead costs can be added in *any* processing department—not just the first. Costs in Department B's Work in Process account would consist of the materials, labour, and overhead costs incurred in Department B plus the costs attached to partially completed units transferred in from Department A (called **transferred-in costs**).

## Efficiency Boosts Production Levels

*in business* | *today*

Leamington, Ontario, the "Tomato Capital of Canada," is where H.J. Heinz Company of Canada Ltd. has established its operations for ketchup manufacturing. Since its establishment at Leamington, the company has processed close to 300,000 tons of ketchup per year at its 20-acre site that employs 1,000 people. Due to the vast size of the plant, it is important for the company to find ways for maximum efficiency. Line 59 within the facility moves at least 100 containers per minute, thanks to the capital investment of $3.5 million to better fill and package the containers. As well, the Leamington plant's changeover times are faster than in the production facilities in the United States, even though Heinz Canada can take up to five hours, depending on the complexity of the changeover. The company also claims its superiority over the competition in cleaning and sterilizing its machines by utilizing circulating air filters to keep the product edible. In terms of environmental responsibility, the plant produces its own energy from a co-generating system using natural gas. The spare heat goes back into a boiler package to produce free steam used during manufacturing, which increases production levels.

Source: "No Other Kinds," *Canadian Packaging*, December 2001, Volume 54 (12), p. 19. Reprinted with permission from *Canadian Packaging*.

## Product Cost Categories in a Process Costing System

The example described in the *In Business Today* feature illustrates that production environments that use a process costing system for determining product costs are typically highly capital intensive. Labour will usually comprise a small proportion of total manufacturing cost. In such environments, it may not be economical to track three separate product cost categories. Labour costs and manufacturing overhead are commonly combined into a single cost category called **conversion cost.** It is important to realize that this is usually relevant for cost reporting on a production report and illustrates the management accounting philosophy of "different costs for different purposes." The company's cost accounts will record labour and manufacturing overhead cost incurrence separately, and managers will be able to obtain this information, if needed. The manufacturing overhead cost component of conversion cost will still come from assigning it using an overhead allocation rate.

## Materials, Labour, and Overhead Cost Entries

To complete our discussion of cost flows in a process costing system, in the following paragraphs we show journal entries relating to materials, labour, and overhead costs.

**MATERIALS COSTS**   As in job-order costing, materials are drawn from the storeroom using a materials requisition form. As stated earlier, materials can be added in any processing department, although it is not unusual for materials to be added only in the first processing department, with subsequent departments adding only labour and overhead costs as the partially completed units move along toward completion.

Assuming that the first processing department in a company is Department A, the journal entry for placing materials into production is:

Work in Process—Department A . . . . . . . . . . . . . . .    XXX
    Raw Materials   . . . . . . . . . . . . . . . . . . . . . . . .         XXX

> **Learning Objective 1**
> Prepare journal entries to record the flow of materials, labour, and overhead through a process costing system.

If other materials are subsequently added in Department B, the entry is the following:

| | | |
|---|---|---|
| Work in Process—Department B .............. | XXX | |
| Raw Materials  ......................... | | XXX |

**LABOUR COSTS**   In process costing, labour costs do not have to be traced to specific jobs since it is only necessary to keep track of how much labour cost is incurred in each department. The following journal entry will record the labour costs for a period in Department A:

| | | |
|---|---|---|
| Work in Process—Department A .............. | XXX | |
| Salaries and Wages Payable ............... | | XXX |

**OVERHEAD COSTS**   In process costing, predetermined overhead rates are usually used to apply overhead costs to departments (or processes); each department receives a portion of the total overhead based on this rate. Overhead cost is then charged to units of product as the units move through the department using a journal entry, such as the following for Department A:

| | | |
|---|---|---|
| Work in Process—Department A .............. | XXX | |
| Manufacturing Overhead Applied ........... | | XXX |

**COMPLETING THE COST FLOWS**   Once processing has been completed in a department, the units are transferred to the next department for further processing, as illustrated earlier in the T-accounts in Exhibit 4–3. The following journal entry is used to transfer the costs of partially completed units from Department A to Department B:

| | | |
|---|---|---|
| Work in Process—Department B .............. | XXX | |
| Work in Process—Department A ........... | | XXX |

After processing has been completed in Department B, the costs of the completed units are then transferred to the Finished Goods inventory account:

| | | |
|---|---|---|
| Finished Goods  ........................... | XXX | |
| Work in Process—Department B ........... | | XXX |

Finally, when a customer's order is filled and units are sold, the cost of the units is transferred to Cost of Goods Sold:

| | | |
|---|---|---|
| Cost of Goods Sold  ....................... | XXX | |
| Finished Goods  ........................ | | XXX |

To summarize, cost flows between accounts are basically the same in a process costing system as they are in a job-order costing system. The only noticeable difference at this point is that in a process costing system there is a separate Work in Process account for each department.

---

**MANAGERIAL ACCOUNTING IN ACTION**

**The Issue**

Samantha Trivers, president of Double Diamond Skis, was worried about the future of her company. After a rocky start, the company had come out with a completely redesigned ski called The Ultimate, made of exotic materials and featuring flashy graphics. Exhibit 4–4 illustrates how this ski is manufactured. The ski was a runaway bestseller—particularly among younger skiers—and had provided the company with much-needed cash for two years. However, last year, a dismal snowfall in the Canadian Rockies had depressed sales, and Double Diamond was once again short of cash. Samantha was worried that another bad ski season would force Double Diamond into bankruptcy.

**Wood, aluminium, plastic sheets**

| | |
|---|---|
| **Shaping and Milling Department** | Computer-assisted milling machines shape the wood core and aluminium sheets that serve as the backbone of the ski. |
| **Graphics Application Department** | Graphics are applied to the back of the clear plastic top sheets using a heat-transfer process. |
| **Moulding Department** | The wooden core and various layers are stacked in a mould, polyurethane foam is injected into the mould, and then the mould is placed in a press that fuses the parts together. |
| **Grinding and Sanding Department** | The semi-finished skis are tuned by stone grinding and belt sanding. The ski edges are bevelled and polished. |
| **Finishing and Pairing Department** | A skilled technician selects skis to form a pair and adjusts the skis' camber. |

**Finished goods**

**Exhibit 4–4**
The Production Process at Double Diamond Skis*

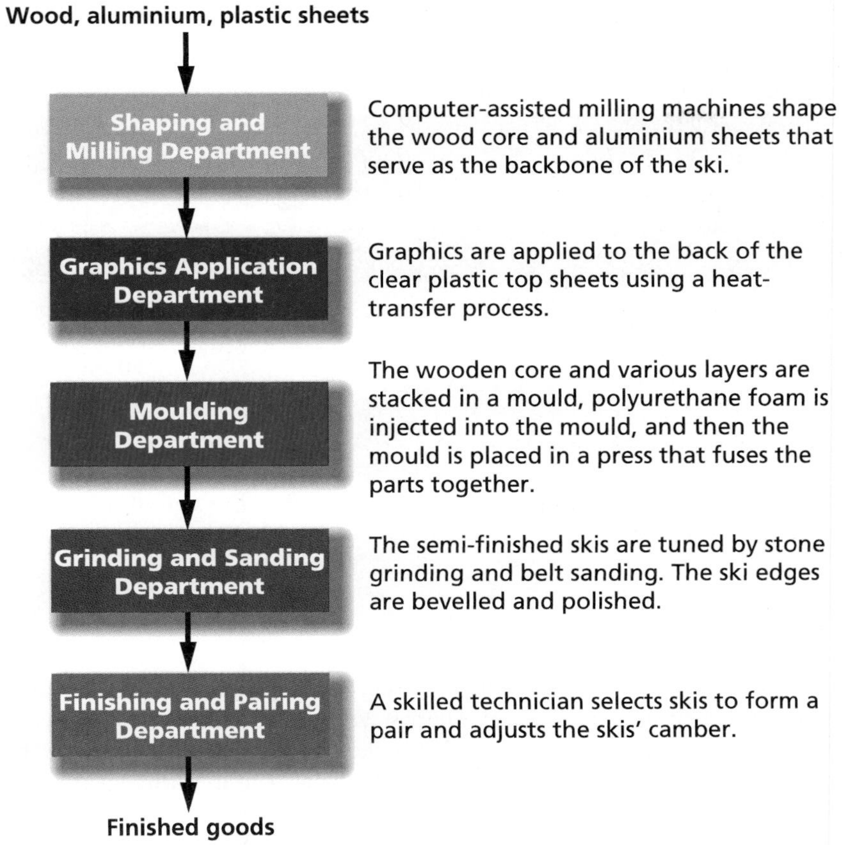

Source: *Adapted from Bill Gout, Jesse James Doquilo, and Studio M D, "Capped Crusaders," *Skiing*, October 1993, pp. 138–144.

Just before starting production of next year's model of The Ultimate, Samantha called Jerry Madison, the company controller, into her office to discuss the reports she would need in the coming year.

*Samantha:* Jerry, I am going to need more frequent cost information this year. I really have to stay on top of things.
*Jerry:* What do you have in mind?
*Samantha:* I'd like reports at least once a month that detail our production costs for each department and for each pair of skis.
*Jerry:* That shouldn't be much of a problem. We already compile almost all of the necessary data for the annual report. The only complication is our work in process inventories. They haven't been a problem in our annual reports, since our fiscal year ends at a time when we have finished producing skis for the last model year and haven't yet started producing for the new model year. Consequently, there aren't any work in process inventories to value for the annual report. But that won't be true for monthly reports.
*Samantha:* I'm not sure why that is a problem, Jerry. But I'm confident you can figure out how to solve it.
*Jerry:* You can count on me.

# The Costing Challenge in a Process Costing Environment

Jerry Diamond, the controller of Double Diamond has the fundamental problem faced by all management accountants in a process costing environment. How can a department's output be determined? Until Samantha asked for more frequent cost reports, Jerry had no

## Exhibit 4–5

Units of Production and Work in Process Inventories

### Business Situation Regarding Work in Process Inventories

| | (1) No WIP | | (2) Zero Beginning WIP and Nonzero Ending WIP | | (3) Nonzero Beginning and Ending WIP | |
|---|---|---|---|---|---|---|
| | DM | Conversion | DM | Conversion | DM | Conversion |
| Costs incurred this period ........ | $100 | $80 | $100 | $80 | $100 | $80 |
| Units in beginning WIP .......... | 0 | 0 | 0 | 0 | 5 | 5 |
| Units started this period ......... | 20 | 20 | 20 | 20 | 20 | 20 |
| Units completed this period ...... | 20 | 20 | 10 | 10 | 10 | 10 |
| Units in ending WIP ............ | 0 | 0 | 10 | 10 | 15 | 15 |
| Cost per unit .................. | $5 ($100 ÷ 20) | $4 ($80 ÷ 20) | ? | ? | ? | ? |

When there are no WIP inventories at both the beginning and at the end of a period, determining the cost per unit is easy (situation 1). But if there are WIP inventories, then determining the cost per unit of product becomes challenging (situations 2 and 3). This is indicated by a "?" in the table.

difficulty. He had been preparing reports annually. During this period, all production initiated in the company was *fully completed*. There never was unfinished, that is, work in process, inventory at the end of the period. This makes it very easy to determine the output of a processing department and the cost per unit of that output. Consider the data shown in Exhibit 4–5 for a fictitious processing department. Situation 1 in this exhibit illustrates a scenario similar to what Jerry Diamond had until now. During a given period, direct material costs of $100 and conversion costs of $80 are incurred to initiate and fully complete 20 units. There are no units in process at the beginning and at the end of the period. This means that all of the work performed and all of the costs incurred must have been to start and complete 20 full units—the output of the department for the period. The material cost per unit will be $5 ($100 ÷ 20), and the conversion cost per unit will be $4 ($80 ÷ 20). The total cost per unit is $9.

But now Samantha has asked for cost reports to be prepared more frequently. This means that at the end of a subperiod (and therefore also at the beginning of the following subperiod) when a cost report is prepared, it is likely that there will be partially completed units in inventory at Double Diamond. This makes the costing problem challenging. How? Consider the data shown in situation 2 in Exhibit 4–5. There are 10 units in ending work in process inventory. These are units yet to be fully completed. Only 10 units of the 20 units started have been fully completed. What costs will you assign to the 20 physical units on which work has been performed—and costs incurred—by this department?

If you decide to treat partially completed units and fully completed units as though they were identical, you would assign, like in situation 1, $5 per unit of direct materials cost and $4 per unit of conversion costs. Or, you can completely ignore the partially completed units and assign all of the incurred costs only to the 10 units fully finished. This would lead to direct materials cost per unit of $10 and conversion cost of $8 per unit. *Both* these approaches are unreasonable and violate a host of fundamental accounting principles. In the first case, the units fully finished are getting a "free ride"; these units have been assigned less than their fair share of the incurred costs because you are treating the partially completed units as if they were fully finished. In the second case, the partially finished units are getting a free ride because none of the costs incurred during the period has been assigned to them even though some of the costs incurred were due to the fact that work was performed on them.

Situation 3 shown in Exhibit 4–5 illustrates what will be typically found in a processing department when a cost report is required. There will be both beginning and ending work in process inventories. The added complication now is that the units in beginning work in process inventory will bring the prior period costs assigned to them into the current period. These costs must be somehow folded into the current period costs incurred to finish these units.

The precise procedure for handling the complications just described which would exist in situations like situation 2 and situation 3 is the subject matter of the remainder of this chapter. We will first learn how to resolve the problem that the partially completed units are not the same as fully completed units. We will then examine the physical flow of units in a processing department to learn about the approaches available to incorporate prior period costs contained in units in beginning work in process inventory, and finally, we will tie it all together by showing you how to prepare a production cost report.

## Degree of Completion and Equivalent Units of Production

From the previous discussion, you know that it is wrong to treat each partially completed unit as if it were one fully completed unit. But every partially completed unit can be thought of as being equivalent to some percentage of a fully completed unit. Using this idea, we can express the units of partially completed product in terms of the number of **equivalent units** fully completed. This is done using the following formula:

Concept 4–1

Equivalent units = Number of partially completed units × Percentage complete

The **percentage completion** of a partially completed unit describes how much work has been done on the product. The figure of 100% describes a fully completed unit, whereas 0% says that no work has been done. There will be percentage completion data *for each cost category*. Before we explain why this must be so, let us show you how to apply the formula. Suppose you know that units in ending work in process are just 60% complete with respect to conversion costs in the sense that only 60% of the work related to conversion has been performed on them. Then, *with respect to conversion costs*, each unit in ending work in process is equivalent to 60% of a fully completed unit. In situation 2 of Exhibit 4–5, there are 10 units in ending work in process. These 10 partially completed units are equivalent to 10 × 0.6 = 6 *fully completed units*. There are already 10 units fully completed. So, adding the 6 equivalent units in ending work in process to the 10 fully finished units gives a total of 16 *equivalent units of production*. Now it is easy to determine *the conversion cost per unit*. Given that $80 of conversion costs were incurred during the period, the conversion cost *per equivalent unit of production* is $80 ÷ 16 = $5.

The above illustration of the concept of equivalent units and its use in calculating cost per unit was in the context of conversion costs. The same process must be applied to the other cost category to calculate the direct materials cost per equivalent unit of production. Consider situation 2 in Exhibit 4–5 once more. Now suppose that the 10 units in ending work in process are 25% complete with respect to the direct materials. This leads us to determine that there are 0.25 × 10 = 2.5 equivalent units in ending work in process with respect to direct materials. Adding the 10 fully completed units to 2.5 equivalent units gives a total of 12.5 equivalent units of production. Given that $100 of direct materials costs were incurred during the period, the direct material cost per equivalent unit of production is $100 ÷ 12.5 = $8. With these calculations in hand, you can say that the total cost per equivalent unit of production is $5 + $8 = $13.

The concept of equivalent units of production is the solution to resolving the problem that partially completed units and fully completed units are not the same. Equivalent units of production are the sum of the number of fully completed units and the number of equivalent units in work in process inventories.

Before proceeding further, note that we *first* calculated the cost per unit *separately for each cost category* and *then* assembled the total unit cost by summing the unit costs from each cost category. Why? The *degree of completion* with respect to direct materials can be different from that for conversion costs. For example, when baking bread, normally all of the ingredients are assembled before mixing and baking. In this case, you can see that all the required direct materials are added right at the beginning of the bread making process. Thus, the degree of completion of partially made bread with respect to the direct materials can be said to be 100%, whereas the degree of completion with respect to conversion costs will not be 100%, it will be some percentage less than 100%. Do not be misled into thinking that direct materials will always be added at the beginning of a production process. The application of materials and conversion to units of product will obviously be determined by the requirements of the production process. Here is an example where the degree of completion for direct materials is less than 100%—a cake making process. When preparing a cake, even though most of the ingredients are introduced at the beginning, the icing is not put on until after the cake has been baked. Some direct materials are added only toward the end, and therefore, in the case of a partially completed cake, the degree of completion with respect to direct materials (as well conversion costs) will not be 100%. In conclusion, each cost category must be considered separately when calculating its equivalent units of production.

## The Flow of Physical Units

Consider situation 3 in Exhibit 4–5. There are 5 units in beginning work in process inventory; 20 units were started from scratch during the period; 10 units were fully completed, and there are 15 units in ending work in process inventory. Note that these data obey the inventory balance relationship for physical units:

$$\begin{array}{ccccccc} \text{\# of units in} \\ \text{beginning work} & + & \text{\# of units} & = & \text{\# of units} & + & \text{\# of units in} \\ \text{in process} & & \text{started} & & \text{finished} & & \text{ending work} \\ & & & & & & \text{in process} \end{array}$$

$$5 \quad + \quad 20 \quad = \quad 10 \quad + \quad 15$$

On the left-hand side, there are 25 units to be accounted for. These are the units on which work *is being* performed. The right-hand side shows what happened to the 25 units on the left-hand side: work was fully completed on 10 of these units, leaving 15 units yet to be fully completed. Therefore, the right-hand side is an accounting of all of the units in the department during the period.

We want to understand how to calculate the equivalent units of production in this situation. The introduction of beginning work in process inventory is an important complication. To illustrate the issues involved, suppose that the units in work in process inventories are partially finished, as follows:

| Situation 3 | Units | Percent Complete | |
| --- | --- | --- | --- |
| | | Materials | Conversion |
| WIP, Beginning ................... | 5 | 80% | 40% |
| Units started ..................... | 20 | n.a.* | n.a.* |
| Units finished .................... | 10 | 100% | 100% |
| WIP, Ending ...................... | 15 | 60% | 40% |
| *Not applicable. | | | |

There are two alternative approaches for calculating equivalent units of production for each cost category: (1) the **weighted average method,** and (2) the **first-in-first-out**

**(FIFO) method.** Each method must tell us how to calculate the equivalent units of production corresponding to the total 25 *physical* units that exist.

**WEIGHTED AVERAGE METHOD**   This method considers only the right-hand side of the balance relationship. There are 10 units fully complete. You can see that these must be 100% complete, and thus, there are 10 equivalent units of production here, regardless of the cost category. There are 15 units in ending work in process. Using the data on degree of completion, the total **equivalent units of production** for each cost category is calculated as before, using the following formula:

> **Learning Objective 2**
> Compute the equivalent units of production using the weighted average method.

**Weighted Average Method Formula**
**(A separate calculation is made for each cost category in each processing department):**

Equivalent units of production  =  # of units fully completed (i.e., transferred to
  the next department or to finished goods)
  + # of equivalent units in ending work in
  process

The formula is illustrated in Exhibit 4–6. The circle on the left represents the units completed in the current period (10 units). These units are complete and therefore, they represent full units. The only partial units in the department are those in ending work in process. These units are shown in the shaded portion of the circle on the right. There are 15 units in this area. These partial units must be expressed in terms of equivalent units of production for each cost category. The computations are shown in Exhibit 4–7. There are 19 equivalent units of production with respect to direct materials and 16 equivalent units of production with respect to conversion costs. Note that the work that was done in the previous period on the units in beginning work in process, and hence, the work that was done in the current period to bring these units to completion is not explicitly accounted for. The weighted average method blends the work done (and the costs incurred) from the previous period with the work done and the costs incurred in the current period.

**Exhibit 4–6**

Flow of Physical Units: The Weighted Average Method View

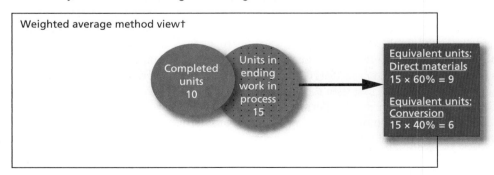

† Units in beginning work in process inventory are ignored in this method and thus not shown
Equivalent units of production: Direct materials 10 + 9 = 19
Equivalent units of production: Conversion 10 + 6 = 16

## Exhibit 4–7
Calculation of Equivalent Units of Production: Weighted Average Method

| Cost Category | (1) Physical Units Processed This Period | (2) Units in Ending WIP Inventory | (3) Degree of Completion | (4) Equivalent Units (2) × (3) | (5) Units Completed This Period | (6) Equivalent Units of Production (4) + (5) |
|---|---|---|---|---|---|---|
| Direct materials | 25 | 15 | 60% | 9 | 10 | 19 |
| Conversion | 25 | 15 | 40% | 6 | 10 | 16 |

**FIFO METHOD**   The FIFO method recognizes that current period's production activity involves three types of work: (1) work to finish off the partially completed units from the previous period, (2) work done on units that were started from scratch and fully completed, and (3) work done on units that were started but were not completed. Costs during the period must have been incurred because these three distinct types of work were performed in the period, and therefore, the FIFO method provides the procedure by which the incurred costs can be allocated among the three types of work. This type of detailed accounting of the costs can be valuable to managers.

The procedure to calculate equivalent units of production consists of three steps. The physical units in beginning work in process are converted to equivalent units using the degree of completion information from the previous period. For example, the data on degree of completion with respect to direct materials tell you that the 5 units in beginning work in process are 80% complete. This is at the start of the period, and thus, these data actually represent work done previously. If 80% of work has already been done, then there must be 20% (100% − 80%) remaining to be done in the current period. Therefore, we can say that the work required and the costs incurred to bring 5 physical units in beginning work in process to completion, with respect to direct materials, is equivalent to work required and costs incurred to make 20% × 5 = 1 fully completed unit. For the case of conversion costs, the number of equivalent units will be (100%−40%) × 5 = 3.

The second step involves finding out how many units were started from scratch and fully completed. This involves answering either of the following questions: (1) How many of the 20 units that were started this period were fully completed? Answer: 20 units were started, there are 15 physical units in ending work in process, and therefore, 20 − 15 = 5 units were started and fully completed in this period. (2) How many of the 10 units that are fully complete and ready to transfer out were started this period (and, therefore, started and finished this period)? Answer: There were 5 units in beginning work in process, and according to the FIFO concept, these 5 physical units must have been completed *first*. Therefore, out of the 10 units that are fully completed, if 5 are the units from beginning work in process, then the remaining 10 − 5 = 5 units must be units that were started and finished during this period.

Note the application of the FIFO principle in answering the questions. With the first question, the principle allows us to infer that the department will not begin to work on new units until the units in beginning work in process have been completed. Therefore, any units in ending work in process cannot be units from beginning work in process still waiting to be completed and consequently must be units that were started during this period. With the second question, looking at the fully finished units, the principle allows us to infer that these must contain the units that were in beginning work in process because these would have been the units completed first. Thus, the balance, as was stated before, must represent the units that were started in the current period. We have now developed the following formula to calculate the number of units that are started from scratch and fully completed in a given period:

$$\text{\# of units started and finished} = \text{\# of units started this period}$$
$$- \text{\# of units in ending}$$
$$\text{work in process inventory}$$

or,

$$\text{\# of units started and finished} = \text{\# of units completed this period}$$
$$- \text{\# of units in beginning}$$
$$\text{work in process inventory}$$

Exhibit 4–8 illustrates this formula. The circle on the left represents the units completed this period (10 units). This circle has two pieces: a piece with horizontal stripes representing the units in beginning work in process (5 units), and a darkly shaded portion shaped like a lens representing the units that were started and fully completed (5 units). The circle on the right represents the units that were started during this period (20 units). This circle has two pieces. A piece with vertical stripes representing ending work in process (15 units) and the lens shaped area representing the units were started and fully finished in the period (5 units). The purpose of the formula is to help you calculate the units in the lens area. This can be found either by taking the units in the left circle and subtracting the units in the area with the horizontal stripes or by taking the units in the right circle and subtracting the units in the area with vertical stripes.

The final step involves calculating the equivalent units in ending work in process. There are 15 units here. These are 60% complete with respect to direct material. Thus, the number of equivalent units in ending work in process is 9 (60% $\times$ 15) with respect to

## Exhibit 4–8
Flow of Physical Units: FIFO View

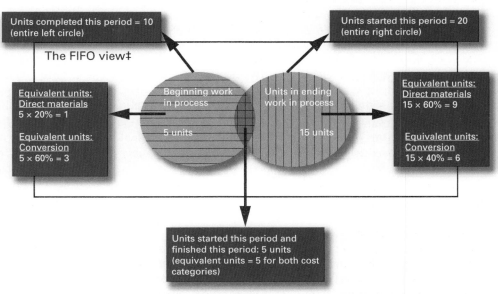

‡ Units in beginning work in process inventory are analyzed for the work done in the current period to complete them, also the costs incurred to complete these units are considered separately from costs incurred in prior periods.

Equivalent units of production: Direct materials 1 + 5 + 9 = 15

Equivalent units of production: Conversion 3 + 5 + 6 = 14

**Exhibit 4–9**
Calculation of Equivalent Units of Production: FIFO Method

| Cost Category | (1) Physical Units Processed This Period | (2) Units in Beginning WIP Inventory | (3) Degree of Completion This Period* | (4) Equivalent Units in Beginning WIP Inventory (2) × (3) | (5) Units in Ending WIP Inventory | (6) Degree of Completion This Period | (7) Equivalent Units in Ending WIP Inventory (5) × (6) | (8) Units Started This Period and Finished This Period† | (9) Equivalent Units of Production (4)+(7)+(8) |
|---|---|---|---|---|---|---|---|---|---|
| Direct materials | 25 | 5 | 20% | 1 | 15 | 60% | 9 | 5 | 15 |
| Conversion | 25 | 5 | 60% | 3 | 15 | 40% | 6 | 5 | 14 |

*Units in work in process inventory at the start of period are already 80% complete with respect to direct materials and 40% complete with respect to conversion cost. This implies the degree of completion for this period will be 20% with respect to direct materials and 60% with respect to conversion.
†Units started this period and finished this period = Units brought into production − Units in ending work in process = 20 − 15 = 5
(Or equivalently: Units finished and transferred out − Units in beginning work in process = 10 − 5 = 5).

direct materials. The 15 units in ending Work in Process inventory are 40% complete with respect to conversion costs. Therefore, there are 6 (40% × 15) equivalent units in ending Work in Process inventory with respect to conversion costs. Combining the results of the three steps, the total equivalent units of production is $1 + 5 + 9 = 15$ for direct materials and $3 + 5 + 6 = 14$. This computation of equivalent units of production under the FIFO method is shown in Exhibit 4–9.

*you decide*

## Writer of Term Papers

Assume that all of your professors have assigned short papers this term. In fact, you have to turn in four separate five-page papers early next month. During the month, you purchased all of the paper that you will need, began and finished two papers, and wrote the first two and one-half pages of the other two papers. You turned in the papers that you had finished to your instructors on the last day of the month.

If instead you had focused all your efforts into starting *and* completing papers this month, how many papers would you have written this month? After answering that question, reconfigure your answer as a computation of equivalent units of production by (1) preparing a quantity schedule, and (2) computing the number of equivalent units for labour.

## Production Report—Weighted Average Method

The production report developed in this section contains the information requested by the president of Double Diamond Skis. The purpose of the production report is to summarize for management all of the activity that takes place in a department's Work in Process account for a period. This activity includes the units and costs that flow through the Work in Process account. As illustrated in Exhibit 4–10, a separate production report is prepared for each department.

Earlier, when we outlined the differences between job-order costing and process costing, we stated that the production report takes the place of a job cost sheet in a process

**Exhibit 4–10**
The Position of the Production Report in the Flow of Costs

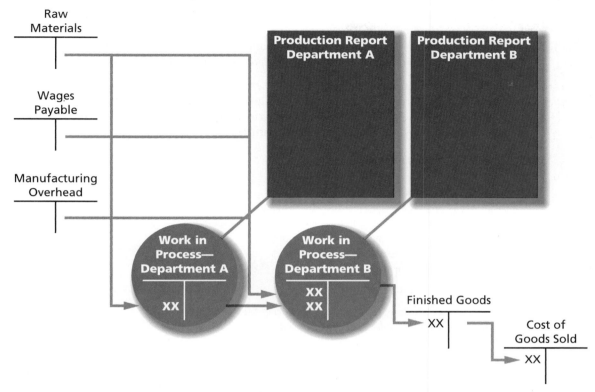

## Home Runs Galore

*in business* today

Remember the summer of 1999? Rawlings, the ball manufacturer, was forced to open its Turrialba facility in Costa Rica to a delegation from Major League Baseball to dispel rumors that Rawlings balls were behind the record numbers of home runs.

The delegation found that the production process is unchanged from earlier years. The red pills (rubber-coated corks purchased from a company in Mississippi) are wound three times with wool yarn and then once with cotton string. The balls are weighed, measured, and inspected after each wind. The covers, cut from sheets of rawhide, are hand-stitched and then machine-rolled. After a trip through a drying room to remove the moisture that kept the leather soft during the sewing process, the balls are stamped with logos. After they are weighed, measured, and inspected once again, the balls are wrapped in tissue and packed in boxes. Balls that don't meet Major League specifications (5–5¼ ounces and 9–9¼ inches in circumference) are sold commercially.

A trip to Mississippi is next on the agenda.

Source: "Behind-the-Seams Look Rawlings Throws Open Baseball Plant Door," *USA Today*, May 24, 2000, pp. 1C–2C. Copyright 2000, *USA TODAY*. Reprinted with permission.

## Cost Analyst

*decision* maker

Assume that you are a cost analyst in the Rawlings plant in Costa Rica that supplies baseballs to Major League Baseball. Your assignment is to identify the production departments in that facility. How many production reports will be needed to summarize the activity in each department?

costing system. The production report is a key management document. The production report has three separate (though highly inter-related) parts:

1. A quantity schedule, which shows the flow of units through the department and a computation of equivalent units.
2. A computation of costs per equivalent unit.
3. A reconciliation of all cost flows into and out of the department during the period.

We will use the data that follow for the May operations of the Shaping and Milling Department of Double Diamond Skis to illustrate the production report. Keep in mind that this report is only one of the five reports that would be prepared for the company, since the company has five processing departments.

| **Shaping and Milling Department** | |
|---|---|
| Work in process, beginning: | |
| Units in process . . . . . . . . . . . . . . . . . . . . . . . . . . . . . . . . | 200 |
| Stage of completion with respect to materials . . . . . . . . . | 50% |
| Stage of completion with respect to conversion . . . . . . . . | 30% |
| Costs in the beginning inventory: | |
| Materials cost . . . . . . . . . . . . . . . . . . . . . . . . . . . . . . . | $ 3,000 |
| Conversion cost . . . . . . . . . . . . . . . . . . . . . . . . . . . . . | 1,000 |
| Total cost in process . . . . . . . . . . . . . . . . . . . . . . . . . . | $ 4,000 |
| Units started into production during May . . . . . . . . . . . . . . | 5,000 |
| Units completed and transferred out . . . . . . . . . . . . . . . . . | 4,800 |
| Costs added to production during May: | |
| Materials cost . . . . . . . . . . . . . . . . . . . . . . . . . . . . . . . | $ 74,000 |
| Conversion cost . . . . . . . . . . . . . . . . . . . . . . . . . . . . . . | 70,000 |
| Total cost added in the department . . . . . . . . . . . . . . . . . | $144,000 |
| Work in process, ending: | |
| Units in process . . . . . . . . . . . . . . . . . . . . . . . . . . . . . . . | 400 |
| Stage of completion with respect to materials . . . . . . . . . . . | 40% |
| Stage of completion with respect to conversion . . . . . . . . . . | 25% |

In this section, we show how a production report is prepared when the weighted average method is used to compute equivalent units and unit costs.

## Step 1: Prepare a Quantity Schedule and Compute the Equivalent Units

The first part of a production report consists of a **quantity schedule,** which shows the flow of units through the department and a computation of equivalent units.

**Learning Objective 4**

Prepare a quantity schedule using the weighted average method.

**Shaping and Milling Department**
**Quantity Schedule and**
**Computation of Equivalent Units**

| | Quantity Schedule |
|---|---|
| Units to be accounted for: | |
| Work in process, May 1 (50% materials; 30% conversion added last month) | 200 |
| Started into production . . . . . . . . . . . | 5,000 |
| Total units . . . . . . . . . . . . . . . . . . . . | 5,200 |

| | | Equivalent Units | |
|---|---|---|---|
| | | Materials | Conversion |
| Units accounted for as follows: | | | |
| Transferred to the next department . . . | 4,800 | 4,800 | 4,800 |
| Work in process, May 31 (40% materials; 25% conversion added this month) | 400 | 160* | 100† |
| Total units and equivalent units of production . . . . . . . . . . . . . . . . | 5,200 | 4,960 | 4,900 |

*40% × 400 units = 160 equivalent units.
†25% × 400 units = 100 equivalent units.

The quantity schedule shows how many units moved through the department during the period as well as the stage of completion of any in-process units. In addition to providing this information, the quantity schedule serves as an essential guide in preparing and tying together the remaining parts of a production report.

## Step 2: Compute Costs per Equivalent Unit

As stated earlier, the weighted average method blends together the work that was accomplished in the prior period with the work that was accomplished in the current period. That is why it is called the weighted average method; it averages together units and costs from both the prior and current periods by adding the cost in the beginning work in process inventory to the current period costs. These computations are shown below for the Shaping and Milling Department for May:

**Learning Objective 5**
Compute the costs per equivalent unit using the weighted average method.

**Shaping and Milling Department**

| | Total Cost | Materials | Conversion | Whole Unit |
|---|---|---|---|---|
| Cost to be accounted for: | | | | |
| Work in process, May 1 . . . . . | $ 4,000 | $ 3,000 | $ 1,000 | |
| Cost added in the Shaping and Milling Department . . . | 144,000 | 74,000 | 70,000 | |
| Total cost (a) . . . . . . . . . . . . . | $148,000 | $77,000 | $71,000 | |
| Equivalent units of production (Step 1 above) (b) . . . . . . . . . . | | 4,960 | 4,900 | |
| Cost per EU, (a) ÷ (b) . . . . . . . . | | $15.524     + | $14.490     = | $30.014 |

The cost per equivalent unit (EU) that we have computed for the Shaping and Milling Department will be used to apply cost to units that are transferred to the next department, graphics application, and will also be used to compute the cost in the ending work in process inventory. For example, each unit transferred out of the Shaping and Milling Department to the Graphics Application Department will carry with it a cost of $30.014. Since the costs are passed on from department to department, the unit cost of the last department, Finishing and Pairing, will represent the final unit cost of a completed unit of product.

## Step 3: Prepare a Cost Reconciliation

The purpose of a **cost reconciliation** is to show how the costs that have been charged to a department during a period are accounted for. Typically, the costs charged to a department will consist of the following:

1. Cost in the beginning work in process inventory.

**Learning Objective 6**
Prepare a cost reconciliation using the weighted average method.

## Exhibit 4–11

Graphic Illustration of the Cost Reconciliation Part of a Production Report

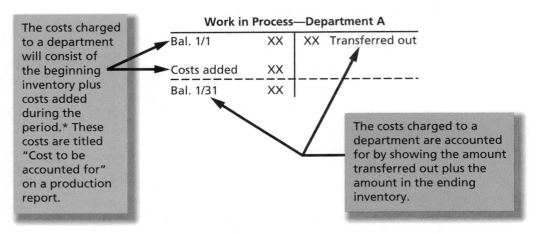

The costs charged to a department will consist of the beginning inventory plus costs added during the period.* These costs are titled "Cost to be accounted for" on a production report.

**Work in Process—Department A**

| | | | |
|---|---|---|---|
| Bal. 1/1 | XX | XX | Transferred out |
| Costs added | XX | | |
| Bal. 1/31 | XX | | |

The costs charged to a department are accounted for by showing the amount transferred out plus the amount in the ending inventory.

\* Departments that follow Department A (Department B and so on) will need to show the amount of cost transferred in from the preceding department.

2. Materials, labour, and overhead costs added during the period.
3. Cost (if any) transferred in from the preceding department.

In a production report, these costs are generally titled "Cost to be accounted for." They are accounted for in a production report by computing the following amounts:

1. Cost transferred out to the next department (or to Finished Goods).
2. Cost remaining in the ending work in process inventory.

In short, when a cost reconciliation is prepared, the "Cost to be accounted for" from step 2 is reconciled with the sum of the cost transferred out during the period plus the cost in the ending work in process inventory. This concept is shown graphically in Exhibit 4–11. Study this exhibit carefully before going on to the cost reconciliation below for the Shaping and Milling Department.

Concept 4–2

**EXAMPLE OF A COST RECONCILIATION**    To prepare a cost reconciliation, follow the quantity schedule line for line and show the cost associated with each group of units. This is done in Exhibit 4–12, where we present a completed production report for the Shaping and Milling Department.

The quantity schedule in the exhibit shows that 200 units were in process on May 1 and that an additional 5,000 units were started into production during the month. Looking at the "Cost to be accounted for" in the middle part of the exhibit, note that the units in process on May 1 had $4,000 in cost attached to them and that the Shaping and Milling Department added another $144,000 in cost to production during the month. Thus, the department has $148,000 ($4,000 + $144,000) in cost to be accounted for.

This cost is accounted for in two ways. As shown on the quantity schedule, 4,800 units were transferred to the Graphics Application Department, the next department in the production process. Another 400 units were still in process in the Shaping and Milling Department at the end of the month. Thus, part of the $148,000 "Cost to be accounted for" goes with the 4,800 units to the Graphics Application Department, and part of it remains with the 400 units in the ending work in process inventory in the Shaping and Milling Department.

Each of the 4,800 units transferred to the Graphics Application Department is assigned $30.014 in cost, for a total $144,067. The 400 units still in process at the end of the month are assigned costs according to their stage of completion. To determine the stage of completion, we refer to the equivalent units computation and bring the equivalent units figures

**Exhibit 4–12**
Production Report—Weighted Average Method

## DOUBLE DIAMOND SKIS
### Shaping and Milling Department Production Report
### (weighted average method)

**Quantity Schedule and Equivalent Units**

| | Quantity Schedule |
|---|---|
| Units to be accounted for: | |
| Work in process, May 1 (50% materials; 30% conversion added last month) ........... | 200 |
| Started into production ....................... | 5,000 |
| Total units ................................ | 5,200 |

| | | Equivalent Units (EU) | |
|---|---|---|---|
| | | Materials | Conversion |
| Units accounted for as follows: | | | |
| Transferred to the next department ............. | 4,800 | 4,800 | 4,800 |
| Work in process, May 31 (40% materials; 25% conversion added this month) ........... | 400 | 160* | 100† |
| Total units and equivalent units of production ........................... | 5,200 | 4,960 | 4,900 |

*40% × 400 units = 160 equivalent units.
†25% × 400 units = 100 equivalent units.

**Costs per Equivalent Unit**

| | Total Cost | Materials | Conversion | Whole Unit |
|---|---|---|---|---|
| Cost to be accounted for: | | | | |
| Work in process, May 1 ........................ | $ 4,000 | $ 3,000 | $ 1,000 | |
| Cost added in the Shaping and Milling Department ............................. | 144,000 | 74,000 | 70,000 | |
| Total cost (a) .............................. | $148,000 | $77,000 | $71,000 | |
| Equivalent units of production (above) (b) ......... | | 4,960 | 4,900 | |
| Cost per EU, (a) ÷ (b) ......................... | | $15.524 + | $14.490 = | $30.014 |

EU = Equivalent unit.

**Cost Reconciliation**

| | Total Cost | Equivalent Units (above) | |
|---|---|---|---|
| | | Materials | Conversion |
| Cost accounted for as follows: | | | |
| Transferred to next department: | | | |
| 4,800 units × $30.014 per unit .............. | $144,067 | 4,800 | 4,800 |
| Work in process, May 31: | | | |
| Materials, at $15.524 per EU ................. | 2,484 | 160 | |
| Conversion, at $14.490 per EU ............... | 1,449 | | 100 |
| Total work in process, May 31 ................. | 3,933 | | |
| Total cost ................................... | $148,000 | | |

down to the cost reconciliation part of the report. We then assign costs to these units, using the cost per equivalent unit figures already computed.

After cost has been assigned to the ending work in process inventory, the total cost that we have accounted for ($148,000) agrees with the amount that we had to account for ($148,000). Thus, the cost reconciliation is complete.

# Production Report—FIFO Method

In this section, we will develop the production cost report for the Shaping and Milling Department at Double Diamond Skis using the FIFO method. The steps we will follow are identical to those shown for the weighted cost approach; only the details of the calculation of the equivalent units of production and the preparation of the cost reconciliation will be slightly different.

## Step 1: Prepare a Quantity Schedule and Compute the Equivalent Units

**Learning Objective 7**
Prepare a Quantity Schedule and Compute the Equivalent Units.

Refer to Exhibit 4–13. The first part of the production report consists of the quantity schedule, which shows the flow of units through the department, and a computation of equivalent units. According to the schedule, 200 units were in process on May 1, and 5,000 units were started into production during the month. Thus, a total of 5,200 units must be accounted for. This is accomplished as follows. In terms of the physical units, applying the FIFO principle, we recognize that the 200 units from work in process on May 1, were fully completed. Since we also know that a total of 4,800 units were fully completed during May, we recognize that 4,600 units were started and fully completed during May. On May 31, there are 400 units in ending working process inventory. Thus, we have, 200 + 4,600 + 400 = 5,200 units all accounted for.

The quantity schedule also shows the computation of the equivalent units of production with respect each of the two cost categories. In the FIFO method, we must calculate equivalent units in beginning work in process inventory in addition to the equivalent units in ending work in process. This recognizes that effort and costs are incurred to bring the units in process at the beginning to completion. Remember that when applying the degree of completion percentage to units in beginning work in process inventory, it has to be

**Exhibit 4–13**
Production Report—FIFO Method

| DOUBLE DIAMOND SKIS |
|---|
| **Shaping and Milling Department—Production Report** |
| **(FIFO Method)** |

| Quantity Schedule and Equivalent Units |
|---|

| | Quantity Schedule |
|---|---|
| Units to be accounted for: | |
| Work in process, May 1 (50% materials, 30% conversion added last month) . . . . . . . . . . . . . . . . . . | 200 |
| Started into production . . . . . . . . . . . . . . . . . . . . . . | 5,000 |
| Total Units (gallons) | 5,200 |

continued

**Exhibit 4–13 continued**

**Equivalent Units (EU)**

| | Physical Units | Equivalent Units | |
|---|---|---|---|
| | | Materials | Conversion |
| Units accounted for: | | | |
| Work in process, May 1 (50% materials, 70% conversion added this month)* ..... | 200 | 100[†] | 140[‡] |
| Units brought into production and fully completed during May ................ | 4,600[§] | 4,600 | 4,600 |
| Work in process, May 31 (40% materials, 25% conversion added this month) ..... | 400 | 160[‖] | 100[#] |
| Total units and equivalent units of production ............................. | 5,200 | 4,860 | 4,840 |

*From the quantity schedule, work in process, May 1 was 50% complete with respect to materials, therefore during May, 100 − 50 = 50% materials was added. Similarly 100 − 30 = 70% of conversion was added during May.

[†]50% × 200 units = 100 equivalent units.

[‡]70% × 200 units = 140 equivalent units.

[§]Units started minus units in work in process May 31 = 5,000 − 400 = 4,600 units or alternatively Units completed in May minus units in work in process May 1 = 4,800 − 200 = 4,600 units.

[‖]40% × 400 units = 160 equivalent units.

[#]25% × 400 units = 100 equivalent units.

**Cost per Equivalent Unit**

| | Total costs | Materials | Conversion | Whole Unit |
|---|---|---|---|---|
| Costs to be accounted for: | | | | |
| Prior period cost in work in process, May 1 ......... | $4,000 | $3,000 | $1,000 | |
| Costs incurred during May (a) ................... | 144,000 | 74,000 | 70,000 | |
| Total cost ...................................... | $148,000 | $77,000 | $71,000 | |
| Equivalent units of production (b) ................... | | 4,860 units | 4,840 units | |
| Cost per EU (a) ÷ (b) .............................. | | $15.226 | $14.463 | $29.689 |
| EU = Equivalent unit | | | | |

**Cost Reconciliation**

| | Total Costs | Equivalent Units | |
|---|---|---|---|
| | | Materials | Conversion |
| Cost accounted for: | | | |
| Prior period cost in work in process, May 1 (1) ....... | $4,000 | | |
| Cost incurred during May: | | | |
| To complete units in work in process, May 1 | | | |
| Direct material at $15.226 per EU .............. | 1,522.60 | 100 | |
| Conversion at $14.463 per EU ................. | 2,024.82 | | 140 |
| Total (2) ................................. | $3,547.42 | | |
| To bring into production and fully complete 4,600 units during May at $29.689 per unit (3) .......... | $136,569.40 | | |
| To partially complete units in work in process, May 31 | | | |
| Direct material at $15.226 per EU .............. | 2,436.16 | 160 | |
| Conversion at $14.463 per EU ................. | 1,446.30 | | 100 |
| Total (4) ................................. | $3882.46 | | |
| Total cost .................................... | $147,999.28* | | |
| Cost transferred out to Graphics Application Department, May 31 (1) + (2) + (3) ............. | $144,116.82 | | |

*Total does not add up to $148,000 due to rounding.

ensured that it represents the work *to be done* in the current period (May) and not the work that was *already done* in the previous period (April).

The calculation proceeds as follows. First, we take the 200 units in beginning work in process and express these as equivalent units of production for each cost category. The percentage completion for the current period is obtained as 100% minus the percentage completed in the previous period. For materials, the percentage completion for the current period is 100% − 50% = 50%; and for conversion, it is 100% − 30% = 70%. The equivalent units in beginning work in process for direct materials is 200 units × 50% = 100. The equivalent units in beginning work in process for conversion is 200 units × 70% = 140.

Second, we calculate the units that were started and fully completed in the current period. This is 4,600 units (5,000 units started − 400 units in ending work in process or 4,800 units completed and transferred out − 200 units in beginning work in process). These represent equivalent units for both cost categories.

Third, we calculate the equivalent units corresponding to the 400 physical units in ending work in process for each cost category. For direct materials, the number of equivalent units in ending work in process is 400 units × 40% = 160. For conversion, the number of equivalent units in ending work in process is 400 units × 25% = 100.

Combining the three calculations, the total equivalent units of production for direct materials and conversion are 4,860 (100 + 4,600 + 160) and 4,840 (140 + 4,600 + 100), respectively.

## Step 2: Compute Costs per Equivalent Unit

The second part of the production report shows the calculation of cost per equivalent unit. Only the current period costs enter into this calculation. We ignore the $4,000 ($3,000 direct materials cost plus $1,000 conversion cost) incurred in the previous period. Double Diamond incurred direct materials cost of $74,000 during May. Given the 4,860 equivalent units of production for direct materials, the direct material cost per equivalent unit is $74,000 ÷ 4,860 = $15.226. For conversion cost the cost per equivalent is $70,000 ÷ 4,840 = $14.463. The total cost per unit of product is $15.226 + $14.463 = $29.689.

## Step 3: Prepare a Cost Reconciliation

The purpose of a cost reconciliation is to show how the costs that have been charged to the department are accounted for. The costs charged to a department will consist of the following:

- Cost in the beginning work in process inventory.
- Materials and conversion costs added during the period.
- Cost (if any) transferred in from the preceding department.

In the FIFO method, we account for the above costs as follows:

1. Costs in the beginning work in process inventory.
2. Materials and conversion costs added to complete the units in beginning work in process inventory.
3. Materials and conversion costs incurred to start and fully complete units in the current period.
4. Materials and conversion costs added to partially complete the units in ending work in process inventory.

The costs transferred out to the next department (or to Finished Goods) will be the sum of the costs (1) + (2) + (3). The cost in (4) will remain with the units in ending work in process inventory and will flow into the following period as the cost of the beginning work in process inventory.

The cost reconciliation is the final part of the production report in Exhibit 4–13. This section provides an accounting of the total incurred cost itemized in the quantity schedule. Remember, the costs to account for are an itemization by cost category and by period.

The costs are accounted for by itemizing by category and by the type of the work done to incur the cost.

We begin by recording the prior period cost (1). Next, we determine the material costs and conversion costs incurred to complete the units in process at the start of May by valuing the equivalent units in beginning work in process inventory using the rate per equivalent unit, with respect to each category. This gives us the cost in (2). Next, the cost of completing 4,600 units from scratch is calculated by multiplying 4,600 by the total cost per equivalent unit, $29.689—this gives us the cost in (3) in the above list. Finally, the equivalent units in ending work in process are valued with respect to each cost category using the cost per equivalent unit. This is the cost in (4). The total of the costs in (1) through (4) agrees with the amount that we had to account for. Thus, the cost reconciliation is complete. The last line shows that the costs that are transferred out to the Graphics Application Department, which is the next department in the production process. This cost is in the amount of $144,116.82.

---

*Jerry:* Here are two examples of the kind of report I can put together for you every month. These particular reports are for the Shaping and Milling Department. Each report follows a fairly standard format for industries like ours and is called a production report. I hope that the information they provide is what you had in mind.

*Samantha:* The quantity schedule makes sense to me. I can see we had a total of 5,200 units to account for in the department for May. We completed 4,800 units and had 400 units remaining to be finished in April. I can also see from the FIFO-based report that we completed the 200 units that were in process at the beginning of May and then began processing 5,000 units from scratch in May. So, we must have started and completed 4,600 units during May. What are these "equivalent units?"

*Jerry:* That is the problem I mentioned earlier. The 400 units still in process at the end of May, for example, are far from complete. When we compute unit costs, it wouldn't make sense to count each of these as a whole unit.

*Samantha:* I suppose not. Since the 400 units in process at May end are only 25% complete with respect to our conversion costs, we should count these as 100 units when we compute the conversion cost per unit.

*Jerry:* That's right. I hope the rest of each of the reports is clear.

*Samantha:* Yes, they seem pretty clear, although I need to study each of them to decide which method I prefer. It appears that the weighted average method calculates the costs per unit by including the prior period costs with the current period costs, whereas the FIFO method only considers the current period costs when determining the cost per unit.

*Jerry:* You are right again! The FIFO method gives you a better idea of how the work done and the costs incurred as a result, in a period, are allocated between units in process at the beginning, units brought into production and completed, and units in process at the end of the period. But the weighted average method is less complicated and depending on your specific needs it may be sufficient. The less inventory we have in our system at the end of each month, the less it will matter as to which method we use.

*Samantha:* In any event, I think I have enough information to help me understand our cost side better. I can focus my efforts on cost control knowing more about how our costs are determined. This information will also help me for planning purposes. Thanks, Jerry.

**MANAGERIAL ACCOUNTING IN ACTION**

## A Comparison of Costing Methods

This chapter has presented two methods of determining the cost of output in a processing department: the weighted average method and the FIFO method. Which method is better? The answer, not surprisingly, is "it depends." The weighted average method is slightly less complicated, but it combines the cost incurred in the prior period that is attached to the units in beginning Work in Process inventory with those incurred in the present period and the entire total is assigned to the units processed by the department. This lack of detail might be undesirable for some managers. The FIFO method keeps prior period costs in the beginning Work in Process inventory separate from the costs incurred in the current period. Only current period costs are assigned to the units that were processed during the period. The FIFO method is also more intuitive in that the physical flow of units is easier to follow. The idea that work done by a department in a period, logically, has to be for completing units from beginning Work in Process, for starting and finishing units, and for starting some units is very appealing. This more detailed accounting of the costs is attractive. But the method is more involved. Ultimately, it all comes down to how much inventory remains in the department at the end of each period. If these inventories are insignificant, it will not matter which method is chosen. But if Work in Process inventories are substantial, the FIFO method, despite its greater complexity, might well be preferred for its more detailed accounting of the costs.

## A Comment about Rounding Errors

If you use a calculator or computer spreadsheet and do not round off the costs per equivalent unit, there should not be any discrepancy between the "Cost to be accounted for" and the "Cost accounted for" in the cost reconciliation. However, if you round off the costs per equivalent unit, the two figures will not always exactly agree. In all of the homework assignments and other materials, we follow two rules: (1) all the costs per equivalent unit are rounded off to three decimal places, and (2) any adjustment needed to reconcile the "Cost accounted for" with the "Cost to be accounted for" is made to the cost "transferred" amount, rather than to the ending inventory (weighted average method), or to the cost of "bringing into production and fully complete" amount (FIFO).

# Summary

**LO1  Prepare journal entries to record the flow of materials, labour, and overhead through a process costing system.**
The journal entries to record the flow of costs in process costing are basically the same as in job-order costing. Direct materials costs are debited to Work in Process when they are released for use in production. Direct labour costs are debited to Work in Process as incurred. Manufacturing overhead costs are applied to Work in Process using predetermined overhead rates. Costs are accumulated by department in process costing and by job in job-order costing. In addition, each department will have its own predetermined overhead rate in process costing.

**LO2  Compute the equivalent units of production using the weighted average method.**
To compute unit costs for a department, the department's output in terms of equivalent units must be determined. In the weighted average method, the equivalent units for a period are the sum of the units transferred out of the department during the period and the equivalent units in ending work in process inventory at the end of the period.

**LO3  Compute the equivalent units of production using the FIFO method.**
The equivalent units of production in the FIFO method is sum of the number of equivalent units in beginning work in process inventory and the number of units started and fully completed during the period and the number of equivalent units in ending work in process inventory. The number of equivalent units in beginning work in process inventory is the number of physical units in process times the degree of work remaining to be done.

**LO4  Prepare a quantity schedule using the weighted average method.**
The activity in a department is summarized on a production report which has three separate (though highly inter-related) parts. The first part is a quantity schedule, which includes a computation of equivalent units and shows the flow of units through the department during the period. The quantity schedule shows the units to be accounted for—the units in beginning Work in Process inventory and the units started into

production. These units are accounted for by detailing the units transferred to the next department and the units still in process in the department at the end of the period. This part of the report also shows the equivalent units of production for the units still in process.

**LO5 Compute the costs per equivalent unit using the weighted average method.**
The cost per equivalent unit is computed by dividing the total cost for a particular cost category, such as conversion costs, by the equivalent units of production for that cost category.

**LO6 Prepare a cost reconciliation using the weighted average method.**
In the cost reconciliation report, the costs of beginning Work in Process inventory and the costs added during the period are reconciled with the costs of the units transferred out of the department and the costs of ending Work in Process inventory.

**LO7 Prepare a quantity schedule using the FIFO method.**
In the FIFO method, the quantity schedule breaks down the units to account for into units in process at the start of the period and the units brought into production during the period. These units are accounted for as the number of units brought into production *and* completed during the period plus the number of equivalent units in process at the beginning of the period plus the number of equivalent units in process at the end of the period.

**LO8 Compute the costs per equivalent unit using the FIFO method.**
The cost per equivalent unit is the total cost incurred during the period for a particular cost category divided by the equivalent units of production for the cost category.

**LO9 Prepare a cost reconciliation using the FIFO method.**
In the FIFO method, the costs contained in the units in beginning work in process are treated separately from the costs incurred during the period. The cost reconciliation report provides an accounting for these latter costs only. The total period costs for a given cost category are broken down into the costs incurred to complete the units that were in process at the start of the period; the costs incurred to start and fully complete units during the period and the costs incurred to partially complete the units in process at the end of the period. The total costs of the units transferred out of the department is the sum of the prior period costs in the units in beginning work in process, the costs to bring to completion these units, and the costs to start and fully complete units introduced during the period.

# Guidance Answers to You Decide and Decision Maker

**WRITER OF TERM PAPERS** (p. 130)
You wrote a total of 15 pages (5 + 5 + 2.5 + 2.5) this month. If you had placed all of your efforts into starting *and* completing papers, you could have written three complete five-page papers.

|  | Quantity Schedule |
| --- | --- |
| Units (papers) to be accounted for: | |
| Work in process, beginning of month | |
| Started into production . . . . . . . . . . . . . . . . . . . . . . | 4 |
| Total units . . . . . . . . . . . . . . . . . . . . . . . . . . . . . . . . . | 4 |

|  | Quantity Schedule | Equivalent Units Labour |
| --- | --- | --- |
| Units accounted for as follows: | | |
| Transferred (handed in) to instructors . . . . . . . . . . . . | 2 | 2 |
| Work in process, end of month (all materials and 50% of labour and overhead added this month) . . | 2 | 1* |
| Total units and equivalent units of production . . . . . | 4 | 3 |

*2 units (papers) × 50% (or 2.5 pages out of 5) = 1

**COST ANALYST** (p. 131)

The Rawlings baseball production facility in Costa Rica might include the following production departments: winding, cutting, stitching, rolling, drying, stamping, inspecting, and packaging. Each department would have its own production report.

# Review Problem: Process Cost Flows and Reports

Luxguard Home Paint Company produces exterior latex paint, which it sells in four-litre containers. The company has two processing departments—Base Fab and Finishing. White paint, which is used as a base for all the company's paints, is mixed from raw ingredients in the Base Fab Department. Pigments are added to the basic white paint, the pigmented paint is squirted under pressure into four-litre containers, and the containers are labelled and packed for shipping in the Finishing Department. Information relating to the company's operations for April follows:

a. Raw materials were issued for use in production: Base Fab Department, $851,000; and Finishing Department, $629,000.

b. Direct labour costs were incurred: Base Fab Department, $330,000; and Finishing Department, $270,000.

c. Manufacturing overhead cost was applied: Base Fab Department, $665,000; and Finishing Department, $405,000.

d. The cost of basic white paint transferred from the Base Fab Department to the Finishing Department was $1,850,000.

e. Paint that had been prepared for shipping was transferred from the Finishing Department to Finished Goods. Its cost according to the company's cost system was $3,200,000.

***Required:***

1. Prepare journal entries to record items (a) through (e) above.

2. Post the journal entries from (1) above to T-accounts. The balance in the Base Fab Department's Work in Process account on April 1 was $150,000; the balance in the Finishing Department's Work in Process account was $70,000. After posting entries to the T-accounts, find the ending balance in each department's Work in Process account.

3. Prepare a production report (weighted average method) for the Base Fab Department for April using the additional information given below:

| | |
|---|---:|
| Production data: | |
|   Units* in process, April 1: 100% complete as to materials, | |
|     60% complete as to labour and overhead . . . . . . . . . . . . . . . . . . . . . . . . . . . . . . | 30,000 |
|   Units started into production during April . . . . . . . . . . . . . . . . . . . . . . . . . . . . . . | 420,000 |
|   Units completed and transferred to the Finishing Department . . . . . . . . . . . . . . . | 370,000 |
|   Units in process, April 30: 50% complete as to materials, | |
|     25% complete as to labour and overhead . . . . . . . . . . . . . . . . . . . . . . . . . . . . . . | 80,000 |
| Cost data: | |
|   Work in process inventory, April 1: | |
|     Materials . . . . . . . . . . . . . . . . . . . . . . . . . . . . . . . . . . . . . . . . . . . . . . . . . . . . . | $ 92,000 |
|     Labour . . . . . . . . . . . . . . . . . . . . . . . . . . . . . . . . . . . . . . . . . . . . . . . . . . . . . . | 21,000 |
|     Overhead . . . . . . . . . . . . . . . . . . . . . . . . . . . . . . . . . . . . . . . . . . . . . . . . . . . . | 37,000 |
|     Total cost . . . . . . . . . . . . . . . . . . . . . . . . . . . . . . . . . . . . . . . . . . . . . . . . . . . . | $ 150,000 |
| Cost added during April: | |
|     Materials . . . . . . . . . . . . . . . . . . . . . . . . . . . . . . . . . . . . . . . . . . . . . . . . . . . . . | $ 851,000 |
|     Labour . . . . . . . . . . . . . . . . . . . . . . . . . . . . . . . . . . . . . . . . . . . . . . . . . . . . . . | 330,000 |
|     Overhead . . . . . . . . . . . . . . . . . . . . . . . . . . . . . . . . . . . . . . . . . . . . . . . . . . . . | 665,000 |
|     Total cost . . . . . . . . . . . . . . . . . . . . . . . . . . . . . . . . . . . . . . . . . . . . . . . . . . . . | $1,846,000 |

*One unit represents four litres.

4. Prepare an FIFO-based production report after combining labour and manufacturing overhead into conversion costs.

*SOLUTION TO REVIEW PROBLEM*

1. a. Work in Process—Base Fab Department . . . . . . . . . . . . . . . . . . . . 851,000
      Work in Process—Finishing Department . . . . . . . . . . . . . . . . . . . . 629,000
        Raw Materials . . . . . . . . . . . . . . . . . . . . . . . . . . . . . . . . . . . . . 1,480,000
   b. Work in Process—Base Fab Department . . . . . . . . . . . . . . . . . . . . 330,000
      Work in Process—Finishing Department . . . . . . . . . . . . . . . . . . . . 270,000
        Salaries and Wages Payable . . . . . . . . . . . . . . . . . . . . . . . . . . . 600,000
   c. Work in Process—Base Fab Department . . . . . . . . . . . . . . . . . . . . 665,000
      Work in Process—Finishing Department . . . . . . . . . . . . . . . . . . . . 405,000
        Manufacturing Overhead . . . . . . . . . . . . . . . . . . . . . . . . . . . . 1,070,000
   d. Work in Process—Finishing Department . . . . . . . . . . . . . . . . . . . . 1,850,000
        Work in Process—Base Fab Department . . . . . . . . . . . . . . . . . 1,850,000
   e. Finished Goods . . . . . . . . . . . . . . . . . . . . . . . . . . . . . . . . . . . . . . . 3,200,000
        Work in Process—Finishing Department . . . . . . . . . . . . . . . . . 3,200,000

2.

| Raw Materials | | | | Salaries and Wages Payable | | |
|---|---|---|---|---|---|---|
| Bal. | XXX | (a) | 1,480,000 | | (b) | 600,000 |

| Work in Process—Base Fab Department | | | | Manufacturing Overhead | | |
|---|---|---|---|---|---|---|
| Bal. | 150,000 | (d) | 1,850,000 | (Various actual | (c) | 1,070,000 |
| (a) | 851,000 | | | costs) | | |
| (b) | 330,000 | | | | | |
| (c) | 665,000 | | | | | |
| Bal. | 146,000 | | | | | |

| Work in Process—Finishing Department | | | | Finished Goods | | |
|---|---|---|---|---|---|---|
| Bal. | 70,000 | (e) | 3,200,000 | Bal. | XXX | |
| (a) | 629,000 | | | (e) | 3,200,000 | |
| (b) | 270,000 | | | | | |
| (c) | 405,000 | | | | | |
| (d) | 1,850,000 | | | | | |
| Bal. | 24,000 | | | | | |

## LUXGUARD HOME PAINT COMPANY
### Production Report—Base Fab Department
### For the Month Ended April 30

**Quantity Schedule and Equivalent Units**

| | Quantity Schedule |
|---|---|
| Units to be accounted for: | |
| Work in process, April 1 (all materials, 60% labour and overhead added last month) . . . . . . . | 30,000 |
| Started into production . . . . . . . . . . . . . | 420,000 |
| Total units . . . . . . . . . . . . . . . . . . . . . | 450,000 |

| | | Equivalent Units (EU) | | |
| --- | --- | --- | --- | --- |
| | | **Materials** | **Labour** | **Overhead** |
| Units accounted for as follows: | | | | |
| Transferred to Finishing Department . . . . . . . . . . . . . . . . . . . | 370,000 | 370,000 | 370,000 | 370,000 |
| Work in process, April 30 (50% materials, 25% labour and overhead added this month) . . . . . . . | 80,000 | 40,000* | 20,000* | 20,000* |
| Total units and equivalent units of production . . . . . . . . . . . . . | 450,000 | 410,000 | 390,000 | 390,000 |

### Costs per Equivalent Unit

| | Total Cost | Materials | Labour | Overhead | Whole Unit |
| --- | --- | --- | --- | --- | --- |
| Cost to be accounted for: | | | | | |
| Work in process, April 1 . . . . . . . . . . . . | $ 150,000 | $ 92,000 | $ 21,000 | $ 37,000 | |
| Cost added by the Base Fab Department . . . . . . . . . . . . . . . . . . . | 1,846,000 | 851,000 | 330,000 | 665,000 | |
| Total cost (a) . . . . . . . . . . . . . . . . . . . . . | $1,996,000 | $943,000 | $351,000 | $702,000 | |
| Equivalent units of production (b) . . . . . . | | 410,000 | 390,000 | 390,000 | |
| Cost per EU, (a) ÷ (b) . . . . . . . . . . . . . . | | $2.30 + | $0.90 + | $1.80 = | $5.00 |

### Cost Reconciliation

| | Total Cost | Equivalent Units (above) | | |
| --- | --- | --- | --- | --- |
| | | **Materials** | **Labour** | **Overhead** |
| Cost accounted for as follows: | | | | |
| Transferred to Finishing Department: | | | | |
| 370,000 units × $5.00 each . . . . . . . | $1,850,000 | 370,000 | 370,000 | 370,000 |
| Work in process, April 30: | | | | |
| Materials, at $2.30 per EU . . . . . . . . | 92,000 | 40,000 | | |
| Labour, at $0.90 per EU . . . . . . . . . | 18,000 | | 20,000 | |
| Overhead, at $1.80 per EU . . . . . . . . | 36,000 | | | 20,000 |
| Total work in process . . . . . . . . . . . . | 146,000 | | | |
| Total cost . . . . . . . . . . . . . . . . . . . . . | $1,996,000 | | | |

*Materials: 80,000 units × 50% = 40,000 equivalent units; labour and overhead: 80,000 units × 25% = 20,000 equivalent units.
EU = Equivalent unit.

# Production Report—FIFO Method

## LUXGUARD HOME PAINT COMPANY
### Base Fab Department Production Report
### (FIFO Method)

### Quantity Schedule and Equivalent Units

| | Quantity Schedule |
|---|---|
| **Units to be accounted for:** | |
| Work in process, April 1 (all materials, 60% conversion added last month) .......... | 30,000 |
| Started into production ................. | 420,000 |
| Total Units (litres) ..................... | 450,000 |

### Equivalent Units (EU)

| | Physical Units | Equivalent Units | |
|---|---|---|---|
| | | Materials | Conversion |
| **Units accounted for:** | | | |
| Work in process, April 1 (0% materials, 40% conversion added this month) ........... | 30,000 | 0* | 12,000[†] |
| Units brought into production and fully complete during April ....................... | 340,000[‡] | 340,000 | 340,000 |
| Work in process, April 30 (50% materials, 25% conversion added this month) ........... | 80,000 | 40,000[§] | 20,000[‖] |
| Total units and equivalent units of production ...................... | 450,000 | 380,000 | 372,000 |

*Work in process on April 1 was fully complete with respect to materials and 60% complete with respect to conversion. Therefore, no work related to materials was performed (100 − 100 = 0%) and 100 − 60 = 40% conversion was added.
[†]40% × 30,000 units = 12,000 equivalent units.
[‡]Units started minus units in work in process April 30 = 420,000 − 80,000 = 340,000 units, or Units completed in April minus units in work in process April 1 = 370,000 − 30,000 = 340,000 units
[§]50% × 80,000 units = 40,000 equivalent units.
[‖]25% × 80,000 units = 20,000 equivalent units.

### Cost per Equivalent Unit

| | Total Cost | Materials | Conversion | Whole Unit |
|---|---|---|---|---|
| **Cost to be accounted for:** | | | | |
| Prior period cost in work in process, April 1 | $ 150,000 | $ 92,000 | $ 58,000 | |
| Costs incurred during April (a) ........... | 1,846,000 | 851,000 | 995,000 | |
| Total cost ........................... | $1,996,000 | $943,000 | $1,053,000 | |
| Equivalent units of production (b) ........... | | 380,000 units | 372,000 units | |
| Cost per equivalent unit (a) ÷ (b) ........... | | $2.24 | $2.675 | $4.915 |

**Cost Reconciliation**

| | Total Costs | Equivalent Units | |
| | | Materials | Conversion |
| --- | --- | --- | --- |
| Cost accounted for: | | | |
| Prior period cost in work in process, April 1 (1) | $150,000 | | |
| Cost incurred during April: ............... | | | |
| To complete units in work in process, April 1 | | | |
|     Direct material at $2.24 per EU ......... | 0 | 0 | |
|     Conversion at $2.675 per EU ............ | 32,100 | | 12,000 |
|         Total (2) ......................... | $32,100 | | |
| To bring into production and fully complete 340,000 | | | |
|     units during April at $4.915 per unit (3) | $1,671,100 | | |
| To partially complete units in work in process, | | | |
| April 30 | | | |
|     Direct material at $2.24 per EU .......... | 89,600 | 40,000 | |
|     Conversion at $2.675 per EU ........... | 53,500 | | 20,000 |
|         Total (4) ........................ | $143,100 | | |
| Total cost ......................... | $1,996,300* | | |
| Cost transferred out to Graphics Application | | | |
|     Department, April 30 (1) + (2) + (3)  .... | $1,853,200 | | |

*Total exceeds $1,996,000 due to rounding errors.

# Glossary

**Conversion cost** Direct labour cost plus manufacturing overhead cost. (p. 121)

**Cost reconciliation** The part of a department's production report that shows the cost to be accounted for during a period and how those costs are accounted for. (p. 133)

**Equivalent units** The product of the number of partially completed units and their percentage of completion with respect to a particular cost. Equivalent units are the number of complete whole units one could obtain from the materials and effort contained in partially completed units. (p. 125)

**Equivalent units of production (weighted-average method)** The units transferred to the next department (or to finished goods) during the period plus the equivalent units in the department's ending work in process inventory. (p. 127)

**FIFO method** A method of accounting for cost flows in a process costing system in which equivalent units and unit costs relate only to work done during the current period. (p. 126)

**Percentage completion** Describes the extent to which a physical unit is complete for each cost category. (p. 125)

**Process costing** A costing method used in situations where essentially homogeneous products are produced on a continuous basis. (p. 118)

**Processing department** Any location in an organization where work is performed on a product and where materials, labour, or overhead costs are added to the product. (p. 119)

**Production report** A report that summarizes all activity in a department's Work in Process account during a period and that contains three parts: a quantity schedule and a computation of equivalent units, a computation of total and unit costs, and a cost reconciliation. (p. 118)

**Quantity schedule** The part of a production report that shows the flow of units through a department during a period and a computation of equivalent units. (p. 132)

**Transferred-in cost** The cost attached to products that have been received from a prior processing department. (p. 121)

**Weighted average method** A method of process costing that blends together units and costs from both the current and prior periods. (p. 126)

**4–1**   Under what conditions would it be appropriate to use a process costing system?

**4–2**   In what ways are job-order and process costing similar?

**4–3**   Costs are accumulated by job in a job-order costing system; how are costs accumulated in a process costing system?

**4–4**   Why is cost accumulation easier under a process costing system than it is under a job-order costing system?

**4–5**   How many Work in Process accounts are maintained in a company using process costing?

**4–6**   Assume that a company has two processing departments, Mixing and Firing. Prepare a journal entry to show a transfer of partially completed units from the Mixing Department to the Firing Department.

**4–7**   Assume again that a company has two processing departments, Mixing and Firing. Explain what costs might be added to the Firing Department's Work in Process account during a period.

**4–8**   What is meant by the term *equivalent units of production* when the weighted average method is used?

**4–9**   What is a quantity schedule, and what purpose does it serve?

**4–10**   Under process costing, it is often suggested that a product is like a rolling snowball as it moves from department to department. Why is this an apt comparison?

**4–11**   Watkins Trophies, Inc. produces thousands of medallions made of bronze, silver, and gold. The medallions are identical except for the materials used in their manufacture. What costing system would you advise the company to use?

# Brief Exercises

**BRIEF EXERCISE 4–1   Process Costing Journal Entries** (LO1)
Quality Brick Company produces bricks in two processing departments—moulding and firing. Information relating to the company's operations in March follows:

a. Raw materials were issued for use in production: Moulding Department, $23,000; and Firing Department, $8,000.

b. Direct labour costs were incurred: Moulding Department, $12,000; and Firing Department, $7,000.

c. Manufacturing overhead was applied: Moulding Department, $25,000; and Firing Department, $37,000.

d. Unfired, moulded bricks were transferred from the Moulding Department to the Firing Department. According to the company's process costing system, the cost of the unfired, moulded bricks was $57,000.

e. Finished bricks were transferred from the Firing Department to the finished goods warehouse. According to the company's process costing system, the cost of the finished bricks was $103,000.

f. Finished bricks were sold to customers. According to the company's process costing system, the cost of the finished bricks sold was $101,000.

*Required:*
Prepare journal entries to record items (a) through (f) above.

**BRIEF EXERCISE 4–2   Computation of Equivalent Units—Weighted Average Method** (LO2)
Clonex Labs, Inc. uses a process costing system. The following data are available for one department for October:

| | | Percent Completed | |
| --- | --- | --- | --- |
| | Units | Materials | Conversion |
| Work in process, October 1 ......... | 30,000 | 65% | 30% |
| Work in process, October 31 ........ | 15,000 | 80% | 40% |

The department started 175,000 units into production during the month and transferred 190,000 completed units to the next department.

*Required:*
Compute the equivalent units of production for October assuming that the company uses the weighted average method of accounting for units and costs.

**BRIEF EXERCISE 4–3    Preparation of Quantity Schedule—Weighted Average Method** (LO3)

Hielta Oy, a Finnish company, processes wood pulp for various manufacturers of paper products. Data relating to tonnes of pulp processed during June are provided below:

|  | Tonnes of Pulp | Percent Completed | |
|---|---|---|---|
|  |  | Materials | Labour and Overhead |
| Work in process, June 1 . . . . . . . . . . . . . . . . . . | 20,000 | 90% | 80% |
| Work in process, June 30 . . . . . . . . . . . . . . . . | 30,000 | 60% | 40% |
| Started into processing during June . . . . . . . . | 190,000 | — | — |

*Required:*
1. Compute the number of tonnes of pulp completed and transferred out during June.
2. Prepare a quantity schedule for June assuming that the company uses the weighted average method.

**BRIEF EXERCISE 4–4    Preparation of Quantity Schedule—FIFO Method** (LO7)

Refer back to the data in Brief Exercise 4–3. Prepare a quantity schedule for June assuming that Hielta Oy Company uses the FIFO method.

**BRIEF EXERCISE 4–5    Cost per Equivalent Unit—Weighted Average Method** (LO5)

Superior Micro Products uses the weighted average method in its process costing system. Data for the Assembly Department for May appear below:

|  | Materials | Labour | Overhead |
|---|---|---|---|
| Work in process, May 1 . . . . . . . . . . . . . | $18,000 | $5,500 | $27,500 |
| Cost added during May . . . . . . . . . . . . . . | $238,900 | $80,300 | $401,500 |
| Equivalent units of production . . . . . . . . | 35,000 | 33,000 | 33,000 |

*Required:*
1. Compute the cost per equivalent unit for materials, for labour, and for overhead.
2. Compute the total cost per equivalent whole unit.

**BRIEF EXERCISE 4–6    Cost Reconciliation—Weighted Average Method** (LO6)

Superior Micro Products uses the weighted average method in its process costing system. During January, the Delta Assembly Department completed its processing of 25,000 units and transferred them to the next department. The cost of beginning inventory and the costs added during January amounted to $599,780 in total. The ending inventory in January consisted of 3,000 units, which were 80% complete with respect to materials and 60% complete with respect to labour and overhead. The costs per equivalent unit for the month were as follows:

|  | Materials | Labour | Overhead |
|---|---|---|---|
| Cost per equivalent unit . . . . . . . . | $12.50 | $3.20 | $6.40 |

*Required:*
1. Compute the total cost per equivalent unit for the month.
2. Compute the equivalent units of material, of labour, and of overhead in the ending inventory for the month.
3. Prepare the cost reconciliation portion of the department's production report for January.

# Exercises

**EXERCISE 4–1    Process Costing Journal Entries** (LO1)

Chocolaterie de Geneve, SA, is located in a French-speaking canton in Switzerland. The company makes chocolate truffles that are sold in popular embossed tins. The company has two processing departments—Cooking and Moulding. In the Cooking Department, the raw ingredients for the truffles are mixed and then cooked in special candy-making vats. In the Moulding Department, the melted chocolate and other ingredients from the Cooking Department are carefully poured into moulds and decorative flourishes are applied by hand. After cooling, the truffles are packed for sale. The company uses a process costing system. The T- accounts below show the flow of costs through the two departments in April (all amounts are in Swiss francs):

**Work in Process—Cooking**

| | | | |
|---|---|---|---|
| Bal. 4/1 | 8,000 | Transferred out | 160,000 |
| Direct materials | 42,000 | | |
| Direct labour | 50,000 | | |
| Overhead | 75,000 | | |

**Work in Process—Moulding**

| | | | |
|---|---|---|---|
| Bal. 4/1 | 4,000 | Transferred out | 240,000 |
| Transferred in | 160,000 | | |
| Direct labour | 36,000 | | |
| Overhead | 45,000 | | |

*Required:*
Prepare journal entries showing the flow of costs through the two processing departments during April.

**EXERCISE 4–2   Quantity Schedule and Equivalent Units—Weighted Average Method (LO2, LO4)**
The Alaskan Fisheries, Inc. processes salmon for various distributors. Two departments are involved—Department 1 and Department 2. Data relating to pounds of salmon processed in Department 1 during July are presented below:

| | Pounds of Salmon | Percent Completed* |
|---|---|---|
| Work in process, July 1 . . . . . . . . . . . . . . . | 20,000 | 30% |
| Started into processing during July . . . . . . . | 380,000 | — |
| Work in process, July 31 . . . . . . . . . . . . . . | 25,000 | 60% |

*Labour and overhead only.

All materials are added at the beginning of processing in Department 1. Labour and overhead (conversion) costs are incurred uniformly throughout processing.

*Required:*
Prepare quantity schedules and a computation of equivalent units for July for Department 1 according to the weighted average method of accounting for units.

**EXERCISE 4–3   Quantity Schedule and Equivalent Units—FIFO Method (LO4, LO7)**
Refer to the data in Exercise 4–2. Prepare a quantity schedule and a computation of equivalent units for July for Department 1 assuming that the company uses the FIFO method of accounting for units.

**EXERCISE 4–4   Equivalent Units and Cost per Equivalent Unit—Weighted Average Method (LO2, LO4)**
Helox, Inc. manufactures a product that passes through two production processes. A quantity schedule for a recent month for the first process follows:

| | Quantity Schedule |
|---|---|
| Units to be accounted for: | |
| Work in process, May 1 (all materials, 40% conversion cost added last month) . . . | 5,000 |
| Started into production . . . . . . . . . . . . . . . . . | 180,000 |
| Total units . . . . . . . . . . . . . . . . . . . . . . . . . . . | 185,000 |

|  | | Equivalent Units | |
| --- | --- | --- | --- |
|  | | **Materials** | **Conversion** |
| Units accounted for as follows: | | | |
| Transferred to the next process . . . . . . . . . . . . | 175,000 | ? | ? |
| Work in process, May 31 (all materials, | | | |
| 30% conversion cost added this month) . . . | 10,000 | ? | ? |
| Total units . . . . . . . . . . . . . . . . . . . . . . . . . . . | 185,000 | ? | ? |

Costs in the beginning work in process inventory of the first processing department were: materials, $1,200; and conversion cost, $3,800. Costs added during the month were: materials, $54,000; and conversion cost, $352,000.

***Required:***
1. Assume that the company uses the weighted average method of accounting for units and costs. Determine the equivalent units for the month for the first process.
2. Compute the costs per equivalent unit for the month for the first process.

**EXERCISE 4–5    Cost Reconciliation—Weighted Average Method (LO6)**
(This exercise should be assigned only if Exercise 4–4 is also assigned.) Refer to the data for Helox, Inc. in Exercise 4–4 and to the equivalent units and costs per equivalent unit you have computed there.

***Required:***
Complete the following cost reconciliation for the first process:

**Cost Reconciliation**

|  | Total Cost | Equivalent Units | |
| --- | --- | --- | --- |
|  | | **Materials** | **Conversion** |
| Cost accounted for as follows: | | | |
| Transferred to the next process: (? units × $?) . . . . . | $? | | |
| Work in process, May 31: | | | |
| Materials, at _____ per EU . . . . . . . . . . . . . . . . . . | ? | ? | |
| Conversion, at _____ per EU . . . . . . . . . . . . . . . | ? | | ? |
| Total work in process . . . . . . . . . . . . . . . . . . . . . | ? | | |
| Total cost . . . . . . . . . . . . . . . . . . . . . . . . . . . . . . . . | $? | | |

**EXERCISE 4–6    Quantity Schedule, Equivalent Units, and Cost per Equivalent Unit—Weighted Average Method and FIFO Method (LO2, LO4)**
Pureform, Inc. manufactures a product that passes through two departments. Data for a recent month for the first department follow:

|  | Units | Materials | Labour | Overhead |
| --- | --- | --- | --- | --- |
| Work in process, beginning . . . . . | 5,000 | $ 4,500 | $ 1,250 | $ 1,875 |
| Units started in process . . . . . . . . | 45,000 | | | |
| Units transferred out . . . . . . . . . . . | 42,000 | | | |
| Work in process, ending . . . . . . . . | 8,000 | | | |
| Cost added during the month . . . . | — | 52,800 | 21,500 | 32,250 |

The beginning work in process inventory was 80% complete as to materials and 60% complete as to processing. The ending work in process inventory was 75% complete as to materials and 50% complete as to processing.

***Required:***

1. Assume that the company uses the weighted average method of accounting for units and costs. Prepare a quantity schedule and a computation of equivalent units for the month.
2. Determine the costs per equivalent unit for the month.
3. Repeat the requirements of parts 1 and 2 assuming the FIFO method of accounting is used.

## Problems

**PROBLEM 4–1  Equivalent Units; Cost Reconciliation—Weighted Average Method and FIFO Method (LO2, LO3)**

CHECK FIGURE
(2) 6/30 WIP: $4,510

Martin Company manufactures a single product. The company uses the weighted average method in its process costing system. Activity for June has just been completed. An incomplete production report for the first processing department follows:

### Quantity Schedule and Equivalent Units

| | Quantity Schedule | | | |
|---|---|---|---|---|
| Units to be accounted for: | | | | |
| Work in process, June 1 (all materials, 75% labour and overhead added last month) ....... | 8,000 | | | |
| Started into production ............ | 45,000 | | | |
| Total units ...................... | 53,000 | | | |

| | | Equivalent Units (EU) | | |
|---|---|---|---|---|
| | | Materials | Labour | Overhead |
| Units accounted for as follows: | | | | |
| Transferred to the next department ................... | 48,000 | ? | ? | ? |
| Work in process, June 30 (all materials, 40% labour and overhead added this month)....... | 5,000 | ? | ? | ? |
| Total units...................... | 53,000 | ? | ? | ? |

### Costs per Equivalent Unit

| | Total Cost | Materials | Labour | Overhead | Whole Unit |
|---|---|---|---|---|---|
| Cost to be accounted for: | | | | | |
| Work in process, June 1 ............ | $ 7,130 | $ 5,150 | $  660 | $ 1,320 | |
| Cost added by the department ....... | 58,820 | 29,300 | 9,840 | 19,680 | |
| Total cost (a) ...................... | $65,950 | $34,450 | $10,500 | $21,000 | |
| Equivalent units (b) ................ | | 53,000 | 50,000 | 50,000 | |
| Cost per EU, (a) ÷ (b) .............. | | $0.65  + | $0.21  + | $0.42  = | $1.28 |

### Cost Reconciliation

| | Total Cost | | |
|---|---|---|---|
| Cost accounted for as follows: | | | |
| ? | ? | | |

*Required:*

1. Prepare a schedule showing how the equivalent units were computed for the first processing department.
2. Complete the "Cost Reconciliation" part of the production report for the first processing department.
3. Repeat requirements 1 and 2 assuming that the company uses the FIFO method of accounting.

CHECK FIGURE
(1) Materials: 220,000 equivalent units
(2) Conversion: $1.30 per unit
(3) 160,000 units

**PROBLEM 4–2    Interpreting a Production Report—Weighted Average Method** (LO2, LO4, LO5)

Cooperative San José of southern Sonora state in Mexico makes a unique syrup using cane sugar and local herbs. The syrup is sold in small bottles and is prized as a flavouring for drinks and for use in desserts. The bottles are sold for $12 each. (The Mexican currency is the peso and is denoted by $.) The first stage in the production process is carried out in the Mixing Department, which removes foreign matter from the raw materials and mixes them in the proper proportions in large vats. The company uses the weighted average method in its process costing system.

A hastily prepared report for the Mixing Department for April appears below:

### Quantity Schedule

Units to be accounted for:

| | |
|---|---:|
| Work in process, April 1 (90% materials, 80% conversion cost added last month) ........ | 30,000 |
| Started into production ...................... | 200,000 |
| Total units ................................. | 230,000 |

Units accounted for as follows:

| | |
|---|---:|
| Transferred to the next department .............. | 190,000 |
| Work in process, April 30 (75% materials, 60% conversion cost added this month) ........ | 40,000 |
| Total units ................................. | 230,000 |

### Total Cost

Cost to be accounted for:

| | |
|---|---:|
| Work in process, April 1 ...................... | $ 98,000 |
| Cost added during the month .................. | 827,000 |
| Total cost .................................. | $925,000 |

### Cost Reconciliation

Cost accounted for as follows:

| | |
|---|---:|
| Transferred to the next department .............. | $805,600 |
| Work in process, April 30 ..................... | 119,400 |
| Total cost .................................. | $925,000 |

Cooperative San José has just been acquired by another company, and the management of the acquiring company wants some additional information about Cooperative San José's operations.

*Required:*

1. What were the equivalent units for the month?
2. What were the costs per equivalent unit for the month? The beginning inventory consisted of the following costs: materials, $67,800; and conversion cost, $30,200. The costs added during the month consisted of: materials, $579,000; and conversion cost, $248,000.
3. How many of the units transferred to the next department were started and completed during the month?
4. The manager of the Mixing Department, anxious to make a good impression on the new owners, stated, "Materials prices jumped from about $2.50 per unit in March to $3 per unit in April, but due to good cost control, I was able to hold our materials cost to less than $3 per unit for the month." Should this manager be rewarded for good cost control? Explain.

**PROBLEM 4–3   Production Report—Weighted Average Method** (LO2, LO4, LO5, LO6)
Sunspot Beverages, Ltd. of Fiji makes blended tropical fruit drinks in two stages. Fruit juices are extracted from fresh fruits and then blended in the Blending Department. The blended juices are then bottled and packed for shipping in the Bottling Department. The following information pertains to the operations of the Blending Department for June. (The currency in Fiji is the Fijian dollar.)

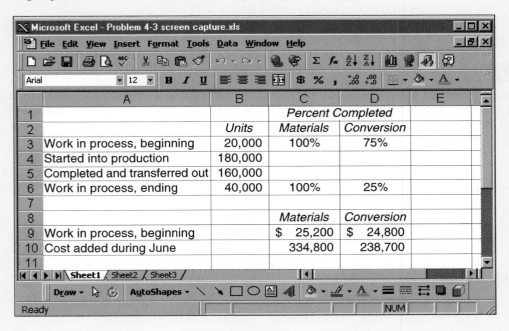

| | A | B | C | D | E |
|---|---|---|---|---|---|
| 1 | | | *Percent Completed* | | |
| 2 | | *Units* | *Materials* | *Conversion* | |
| 3 | Work in process, beginning | 20,000 | 100% | 75% | |
| 4 | Started into production | 180,000 | | | |
| 5 | Completed and transferred out | 160,000 | | | |
| 6 | Work in process, ending | 40,000 | 100% | 25% | |
| 7 | | | | | |
| 8 | | | *Materials* | *Conversion* | |
| 9 | Work in process, beginning | | $ 25,200 | $ 24,800 | |
| 10 | Cost added during June | | 334,800 | 238,700 | |
| 11 | | | | | |

*Required:*
Prepare a production report for the Blending Department for June assuming that the company uses the weighted average method.

**PROBLEM 4–4   Step-by-Step Production Report—Weighted Average Method and FIFO Method**
(LO2, LO4, LO5, LO6)
Builder Products, Inc. manufactures a caulking compound that goes through three processing stages prior to completion. Information on work in the first department, Cooking, is given below for May:

Production data:
   Units in process, May 1: 100% complete
     as to materials and 80% complete
     as to labour and overhead .................... 10,000
   Units started into production during May .......... 100,000
   Units completed and transferred out ............. 95,000
   Units in process, May 31: 60% complete
     as to materials and 20% complete
     as to labour and overhead .................... ?
Cost data:
   Work in process inventory, May 1:
     Materials cost ............................. $ 1,500
     Labour cost ............................... 1,800
     Overhead cost ............................. 5,400
   Cost added during May:
     Materials cost ............................. 154,500
     Labour cost ............................... 22,700
     Overhead cost ............................. 68,100

Materials are added at several stages during the cooking process, whereas labour and overhead costs are incurred uniformly. The company uses the weighted average method.

*Required:*

Prepare a production report for the Cooking Department for May. Use the following three steps in preparing your report:

1. Prepare a quantity schedule and a computation of equivalent units.
2. Compute the costs per equivalent unit for the month.
3. Using the data from (1) and (2) above, prepare a cost reconciliation.
4. Prepare a production report for the cooking department for May assuming the company uses the FIFO method. Follow steps 1 to 3 above.

### PROBLEM 4–5   Preparation of Production Report from Analysis of Work in Process—Weighted Average Method (LO2, LO4, LO5, LO6)

Weston Products manufactures an industrial cleaning compound that goes through three processing departments—Grinding, Mixing, and Cooking. All raw materials are introduced at the start of work in the Grinding Department, with conversion costs being incurred evenly throughout the grinding process. The Work in Process T-account for the Grinding Department for a recent month is given below:

**Work in Process—Grinding Department**

| | | | |
|---|---|---|---|
| Inventory, May 1 (18,000 kgs., 1/3 processed) | $21,800 | Completed and transferred to mixing ( ? kgs.) | $? |
| May costs added: | | | |
| Raw materials (167,000 kgs.) | 133,400 | | |
| Labour and overhead | 226,800 | | |
| Inventory, May 31 (15,000 kgs., 2/3 processed) | $? | | |

The May 1 work in process inventory consists of $14,600 in materials cost and $7,200 in labour and overhead cost. The company uses the weighted average method to account for units and costs.

*Required:*

1. Prepare a production report for the Grinding Department for the month.
2. What criticism can be made of the unit costs that you have computed on your production report?

### PROBLEM 4–6   Costing Inventories; Journal Entries; Cost of Goods Sold—Weighted Average Method (LO1, LO2, LO5, LO6)

You are employed by Spirit Company, a manufacturer of digital watches. The company's chief financial officer is trying to verify the accuracy of the ending work in process and finished goods inventories prior to closing the books for the year. You have been asked to assist in this verification. The year-end balances shown on Spirit Company's books are as follows:

| | Units | Costs |
|---|---|---|
| Work in process, December 31 (50% complete as to labour and overhead) | 300,000 | $660,960 |
| Finished goods, December 31 | 200,000 | 1,009,800 |

Materials are added to production at the beginning of the manufacturing process, and overhead is applied to each product at the rate of 60% of direct labour cost. There was no finished goods inventory at the beginning of the year. A review of Spirit Company's inventory and cost records has disclosed the following data, all of which are accurate:

| | | Costs | |
|---|---|---|---|
| | Units | Materials | Labour |
| Work in process, January 1 (80% complete as to labour and overhead) | 200,000 | $ 200,000 | $ 315,000 |
| Units started into production | 1,000,000 | | |

| | | |
|---|---|---|
| Cost added during the year: | | |
| Materials cost . . . . . . . . . . . . . . . . . . . | 1,300,000 | |
| Labour cost . . . . . . . . . . . . . . . . . . . . . | | 1,995,000 |
| Units completed during the year . . . . . . . | 900,000 | |

The company uses the weighted average cost method.

**Required:**
1. Determine the equivalent units and costs per equivalent unit for materials, labour, and overhead for the year.
2. Determine the amount of cost that should be assigned to the ending work in process and finished goods inventories.
3. Prepare the necessary correcting journal entry to adjust the work in process and finished goods inventories to the correct balances as of December 31.
4. Determine the cost of goods sold for the year assuming there is no under- or over-applied overhead.

(CPA, adapted)

CHECK FIGURE
(2) 3/31 Refining Dept.
WIP: $46,000

**PROBLEM 4–7    Comprehensive Process Costing Problem—Weighted Average Method and FIFO Method** (LO1, LO2, LO4, LO5, LO6)
Lubricants, Inc. produces a special kind of grease that is widely used by race car drivers. The grease is produced in two processes: refining and blending.

Raw oil products are introduced at various points in the Refining Department; labour and overhead costs are incurred evenly throughout the refining operation. The refined output is then transferred to the Blending Department.

The following incomplete Work in Process account is available for the Refining Department for March:

**Work in Process—Refining Department**

| | | | |
|---|---|---|---|
| March 1 inventory (20,000 litres; 100% complete as to materials; 90% complete as to labour and overhead) | 38,000 | Completed and transferred to blending ( ? litres) | ? |
| March costs added: | | | |
| Raw oil materials (390,000 litres) | 495,000 | | |
| Direct labour | 72,000 | | |
| Overhead | 181,000 | | |
| March 31 inventory (40,000 litres; 75% complete as to materials; 25% complete as to labour and overhead) | ? | | |

The March 1 work in process inventory in the Refining Department consists of the following cost elements: raw materials, $25,000; direct labour, $4,000; and overhead, $9,000.

Costs incurred during March in the Blending Department were: materials used, $115,000; direct labour, $18,000; and overhead cost applied to production, $42,000. The company accounts for units and costs by the weighted average method.

**Required:**
1. Prepare journal entries to record the costs incurred in both the Refining Department and Blending Department during March. Key your entries to the items (a) through (g) below.
   a. Raw materials were issued for use in production.
   b. Direct labour costs were incurred.
   c. Manufacturing overhead costs for the entire factory were incurred, $225,000. (Credit Accounts Payable.)
   d. Manufacturing overhead cost was applied to production using a predetermined overhead rate.
   e. Units that were complete as to processing in the Refining Department were transferred to the Blending Department, $740,000.
   f. Units that were complete as to processing in the Blending Department were transferred to Finished Goods, $950,000.

g. Completed units were sold on account, $1,500,000. The Cost of Goods Sold was $900,000.
2. Post the journal entries from (1) above to T-accounts. The following account balances existed at the beginning of March. (The beginning balance in the Refining Department's Work in Process account is given above.)

| | |
|---|---|
| Raw Materials | $618,000 |
| Work in Process—Blending Department | 65,000 |
| Finished Goods | 20,000 |

After posting the entries to the T-accounts, find the ending balance in the inventory accounts and the manufacturing overhead account.
3. Prepare a production report for the Refining Department for March.
4. Prepare a production report for the Refining Department for March assuming that the company uses the FIFO method.

CHECK FIGURE
(2) 5/31 Cooking
Dept. WIP:
$66,000

**PROBLEM 4–8  Comprehensive Process Costing Problem—Weighted Average Method and FIFO Method** (LO1, LO2, LO4, LO5, LO6)
Hilox, Inc. produces an antacid product that goes through two departments—Cooking and Bottling. The company has recently hired a new assistant accountant, who has prepared the following summary of production and costs for the Cooking Department for May using the weighted average method.

Cooking Department costs:

| | |
|---|---|
| Work in process inventory, May 1: 70,000 litres, 60% complete as to materials and 30% complete as to labour and overhead | $ 61,000* |
| Materials added during May | 570,000 |
| Labour added during May | 100,000 |
| Overhead applied during May | 235,000 |
| Total departmental costs | $966,000 |

Cooking Department costs assigned to:

| | |
|---|---|
| Litres completed and transferred to the Bottling Department: 400,000 litres at ? per litre | $ ? |
| Work in process inventory, May 31: 50,000 litres, 70% complete as to materials and 40% complete as to labour and overhead | ? |
| Total departmental costs assigned | $ ? |

*Consists of materials, $39,000; labour, $5,000; and overhead, $17,000.

The new assistant accountant has determined the cost per litre transferred to be $2.415, as follows:

$$\frac{\text{Total departmental costs, \$966,000}}{\text{Litres completed and transferred, 400,000}} = \$2.415 \text{ per litre}$$

However, the assistant accountant is unsure how to use this unit cost figure in assigning cost to the ending work in process inventory. In addition, the company's general ledger shows only $900,000 in cost transferred from the Cooking Department to the Bottling Department, which does not agree with the $966,000 figure above.

The general ledger also shows the following costs incurred in the Bottling Department during May: materials used, $130,000; direct labour cost incurred, $80,000; and overhead cost applied to products, $158,000.

*Required:*
1. Prepare journal entries as follows to record activity in the company during May. Key your entries to the letters (a) through (g) below.
   a. Raw materials were issued to the two departments for use in production.
   b. Direct labour costs were incurred in the two departments.

c. Manufacturing overhead costs were incurred, $400,000. (Credit Accounts Payable.) The company maintains a single Manufacturing Overhead account for the entire plant.

d. Manufacturing overhead cost was applied to production in each department using predetermined overhead rates.

e. Units completed as to processing in the Cooking Department were transferred to the Bottling Department, $900,000.

f. Units completed as to processing in the Bottling Department were transferred to Finished Goods, $1,300,000.

g. Units were sold on account, $2,000,000. The Cost of Goods Sold was $1,250,000.

2. Post the journal entries from (1) above to T-accounts. Balances in selected accounts on May 1 are given below:

| | |
|---|---|
| Raw Materials ................................. | $710,000 |
| Work in Process—Bottling Department ............ | 85,000 |
| Finished Goods ................................ | 45,000 |

After posting the entries to the T-accounts, find the ending balance in the inventory accounts and the Manufacturing Overhead account.

3. Prepare a production report for the Cooking Department for May.

4. Prepare a production report for the Cooking Department for May assuming that the company uses the FIFO method.

# Building Your Skills

**ANALYTICAL THINKING**  (LO2, LO4, LO5, LO6)

"I think we goofed when we hired that new assistant controller," said Ruth Scarpino, president of Provost Industries. "Just look at this production report that he prepared for last month for the Finishing Department. I can't make heads or tails out of it."

| | |
|---|---|
| Finishing Department costs: | |
| Work in process inventory, April 1, 450 units; 100% complete as to materials; 60% complete as to conversion costs .............. | $ 8,208* |
| Costs transferred in during the month from the preceding department, 1,950 units ............. | 17,940 |
| Materials cost added during the month (materials are added when processing is 50% complete in the Finishing Department) ................... | 6,210 |
| Conversion costs incurred during the month .......... | 13,920 |
| Total departmental costs ......................... | $46,278 |
| | |
| Finishing Department costs assigned to: | |
| Units completed and transferred to finished goods, 1,800 units at $25.71 per unit .............. | $46,278 |
| Work in process inventory, April 30, 600 units; 0% complete as to materials; 35% complete as to processing ................. | –0– |
| Total departmental costs assigned ................. | $46,278 |

*Consists of: cost transferred in, $4,068; materials cost, $1,980; and conversion cost, $2,160.

"He's struggling to learn our system," replied Frank Harrop, the operations manager. "The problem is that he's been away from process costing for a long time, and it's coming back slowly."

"It's not just the format of his report that I'm concerned about. Look at that $25.71 unit cost that he's come up with for April. Doesn't that seem high to you?" said Ms. Scarpino.

"Yes, it does seem high; but on the other hand, I know we had an increase in materials prices during April, and that may be the explanation," replied Mr. Harrop. "I'll get someone else to redo this report and then we may be able to see what's going on."

Provost Industries manufactures a ceramic product that goes through two processing departments—Moulding and Finishing. The company uses the weighted average method to account for units and costs.

***Required:***
1. Prepare a revised production report for the Finishing Department.
2. Explain to the president why the unit cost on the new assistant controller's report is so high.

## COMMUNICATING IN PRACTICE   (LO6)
Assume that you are the cost analyst who prepared the Production Report that appears in Exhibit 4–12. You receive a call from Minesh Patel, a new hire in the company's accounting staff who is not sure what needs to be done with the cost reconciliation portion of the report. He wants to know what journal entries should be prepared and what balances need to be checked in the company's accounts.

***Required:***
Write a memorandum to Mr. Patel that explains the steps that should be taken. Refer to specific amounts on the Cost Reconciliation portion of the Production Report to ensure that he properly completes the steps.

## ETHICS CHALLENGE   (LO2, LO5, LO6)
Gary Stevens and Mary James are production managers in the Consumer Electronics Division of General Electronics Company, which has several dozen plants scattered in locations throughout the world. Mary manages the plant located in Hamilton, Ontario, while Gary manages the plant in El Segundo, California. Production managers are paid a salary and get an additional bonus equal to 5% of their base salary if the entire division meets or exceeds its target profits for the year. The bonus is determined in March after the company's annual report has been prepared and issued to shareholders.

Shortly after the beginning of the new year, Mary received a phone call from Gary that went like this:

***Gary:*** How's it going, Mary?
***Mary:*** Fine, Gary. How's it going with you?
***Gary:*** Great! I just got the preliminary profit figures for the division for last year and we are within $200,000 of making the year's target profits. All we have to do is to pull a few strings, and we'll be over the top!
***Mary:*** What do you mean?
***Gary:*** Well, one thing that would be easy to change is your estimate of the percentage completion of your ending work in process inventories.
***Mary:*** I don't know if I can do that, Gary. Those percentage completion figures are supplied by Tom Winthrop, my lead supervisor, who I have always trusted to provide us with good estimates. Besides, I have already sent the percentage completion figures to the corporate headquarters.
***Gary:*** You can always tell them there was a mistake. Think about it, Mary. All of us managers are doing as much as we can to pull this bonus out of the hat. You may not want the bonus cheque, but the rest of us sure could use it.

The final processing department in Mary's production facility began the year with no work in process inventories. During the year, 210,000 units were transferred in from the prior processing department and 200,000 units were completed and sold. Costs transferred in from the prior department totalled $39,375,000. No materials are added in the final processing department. A total of $20,807,500 of conversion cost was incurred in the final processing department during the year.

***Required:***
1. Tom Winthrop estimated that the units in ending inventory in the final processing department were 30% complete with respect to the conversion costs of the final processing department. If this estimate of the percentage completion is used, what would be the Cost of Goods Sold for the year?
2. Does Gary Stevens want the estimated percentage completion to be increased or decreased? Explain why.
3. What percentage completion would result in increasing reported net income by $200,000 over the net income that would be reported if the 30% figure were used?
4. Do you think Mary James should go along with the request to alter estimates of the percentage completion?

**TAKING IT TO THE NET**

Remember to take it to the Net (www.mcgrawhill.ca/college/Garrison).

**TEAMWORK IN ACTION**   (LO2, LO3, LO4, LO5)

The production report includes a quantity schedule, the computation of equivalent costs and costs per equivalent units, and a cost reconciliation.

*Required:*

1. *Learning teams* of three (or more) members should be formed. Each team member must select one of the following sections of the production report (as illustrated in Exhibit 4–9) as an area of expertise (each team must have at least one expert in each section).
   a. Quantity Schedule and Equivalent Units.
   b. Costs per Equivalent Unit.
   c. Cost Reconciliation.
2. *Expert teams* should be formed from the individuals who have selected the same area of expertise. Expert teams should discuss and write up a brief summary that each expert will present to his/her learning team that addresses the following:
   a. The purpose of the section of the production report.
   b. The manner in which the amounts appearing in this section of the report are determined.
3. Each expert should return to his/her learning team. In rotation, each member should present his/her expert team's report to the learning team.

# Chapter *Five*

# Activity-Based Costing

## A Look Back

The previous two chapters introduced two contrasting systems: job-order and process costing. The approach in both the systems to overhead allocation was the use of a single plantwide overhead rate.

## A Look at This Chapter

Chapter 5 continues the discussion of overhead cost allocation; it introduces the concept of activity-based costing, a technique that uses a number of allocation bases to assign overhead costs to cost objects.

## A Look Ahead

Chapter 6 builds on the introduction to cost behaviour in Chapter 2. We will further describe variable and fixed costs and introduce the concept of mixed costs. We will also introduce the contribution format income statement.

## Chapter Outline

# DECISION FEATURE e-Cycling to Profitability

MAXUS Technology Inc. offers a one-stop-shop asset recovery and e-waste recycling solution for end-of-life electronic equipment, with special expertise in telecommunications.

Increased technology use and new laws governing disposal are realities that all citizens and companies will soon face. E-waste disposal has the potential to bring financial liability to a company if not handled properly and can seriously damage carefully cultivated reputations, market shares, and sales.

This is because e-waste is the fastest growing waste stream in North America, and obviously, these products do not biodegrade—a problem in and of itself. In addition, e-waste can also contain hazardous goods. A computer monitor, for example, contains up to eight pounds of lead. Increasing product obsolescence only aggravates the situation.

Shelley Whatmore of Calgary founded MAXUS in 1994, which has been in operation ever since. Initially an asset recovery company (buying and selling old assets), MAXUS has, in recent years, moved into total technology solutions in response to a growing problem—what to do with equipment that cannot be resold. MAXUS has found that clients using its services can generate new revenue through selling their old equipment in markets around the world and thus obtain peace of mind through recycling. Essentially, MAXUS will squeeze as much value as possible from client equipment while ensuring the rest is recycled properly.

Needless to say, e-cycling poses its own environmental challenges which MAXUS has decided to face head on. It designed a unique recycling system that ensures that no harmful components from anything it processes are landfills and no harmful waste is shipped overseas for disposal. From the beginning, MAXUS has followed leading-edge environmental practices and is moving toward ISO 14001 certification.

Clayton Miller, MAXUS's Communications Coordinator, says that finding a way to make e-waste recycling profitable is a trial-and-error process that involves many sleepless nights. For one, the equipment required does not come cheap, and most of it must be designed from the ground up. Second, transportation of e-waste is prohibitive because weights are often high. Other issues include the wide range of possible products—literally every electronic device under the sun—and differing expectations and needs of clients. Activity-based costing is the only way MAXUS runs a successful business.

The time to perform every business activity, from dismantling to packing to preparing proposals, has been measured to figure out the true cost. This allows MAXUS to adjust its rates on a client-by-client basis in order to ensure break-even pricing. Without careful attention to overhead, MAXUS could find itself in a situation where growth in market share actually costs money.

## Learning Objectives

*After studying Chapter 5, you should be able to:*

**LO1** Understand the basic approach in activity-based costing and how it differs from traditional costing.

**LO2** Compute product costs using activity-based costing and compare them with costs under a traditional costing system.

**LO3** Describe the use of activity-based costing in service settings.

**LO4** Understand the benefits and limitations of activity-based costing systems.

**LO5** Record the flow of costs in an activity-based costing system.

Source: http://www.maxustech.com and personal communication with Clayton Miller.

**A**s discussed the earlier chapters, direct materials and direct labour costs can be easily traced to the desired cost object (e.g., product, job, or process). Overhead costs, on the other hand, cannot be traced to cost objects and must be allocated. Chapter 3 introduced the concept of allocation using direct labour as an allocation base. This chapter further elaborates on the concept and process of cost allocation. In doing so, it questions the practice described in Chapter 3 (allocation using a plantwide overhead rate) and introduces activity-based costing (ABC).

# Assigning Overhead Costs to Cost Objects

Companies must find an appropriate method to assign overhead costs to cost objects. The most common cost object to which costs are assigned is product (or service). Other cost objects may include process, customer, distribution channel, and product line. Regardless of the cost object, overhead costs cannot be directly traced to them and must therefore be allocated (or assigned) to the cost object. This section describes three different methods to overhead cost allocation (the focus of this chapter is on the third method). The discussion of overhead allocation is largely couched within a manufacturing context, although the principles can easily be applied to a service setting, too, as we will see later in this chapter.

## Plantwide Overhead Rate

The simplest method of assigning overhead, introduced in Chapter 3, involved using a single allocation base and rate, known as a plantwide overhead rate. This method is based on the convenience it offers in that the cost accounting system must capture only two pieces of information: total overhead costs and the volume of the allocation base (such as total labour-hours). As suggested in Chapter 3, direct labour-hours was widely used largely because direct labour was a significant component of the total conversion costs (i.e., materials and labour) and the designers of cost accounting systems believed that direct labour influenced overhead costs.

Conceptually, the use of a plantwide rate assumes the following: (1) all overhead costs in the organization are *driven* (or caused) by the single allocation base that is used, and (2) products consume overhead resources in the same proportion in which they consume the allocation base. Both assumptions are weak; therefore, using a single plantwide overhead rate has serious limitations, which can lead to cost distortions. A manager using distorted cost information can make flawed decisions that may have serious implications for the future of the organization.

## Departmental Overhead Rate

As a first step to improving the allocation method, many companies use multiple overhead rates along departmental lines. As an example, consider a manufacturing company with three departments: materials, machining, and assembly. Overhead costs *within* each department are accumulated in a single *overhead cost pool*; thus, there will be three overhead cost pools in our example. An appropriate allocation base for each pool must then be identified and a predetermined overhead rate computed for each of the three pools. The allocation bases typically depend upon the nature of the work performed in each department. For example, direct material costs may be used to assign overhead incurred by the materials department, whereas direct labour may be used to allocate the assembly department's overhead costs.

Unfortunately, even departmental overhead allocation makes the same assumptions made in the case of plantwide overhead allocation (but at a departmental, rather than a plantwide, level). These assumptions may not hold true in situations where a company offers a diverse product range and has a complex set of overhead costs. As a result, this method of overhead allocation can also lead to product cost distortions.

## Activity-Based Costing

A serious limitation in the case of both plantwide and departmental overhead allocation is that both the methods fail to recognize two facts: (1) the total overhead cost pool in an organization is an accumulation of the costs of numerous resources that are consumed by the organization to serve its customers, and (2) the individual overhead costs are driven by different factors. While some overhead costs may be caused by the level of production or service volume, others may be caused by the number of transactions processed, and yet others may be caused by other drivers. Second, the two previous methods also fail to recognize that different cost objects (products, services, customers) may consume resources in different proportions. For example, assume that a bank has two customer groups: senior citizens and students. It is not unreasonable to assume that students are likely to be more in tune with the latest technology and use automated banking services more than the senior citizens do. A good cost allocation system must recognize these differences and must consider them when assigning costs.

> **Learning Objective 1**
> Understand the basic approach in activity-based costing and how it differs from traditional costing.

Also, as explained in Chapter 1, the business environment has changed considerably over the last 25 years. In adopting the lean business model, many organizations have automated their operations to a significant extent. This has resulted in a shift in the cost structure within organizations—the proportion of overhead costs has increased at the expense of direct labour costs. Therefore, it is essential that managers reconsider using traditional cost accounting systems that allocate overhead costs using a plantwide rate or even departmental rates. Moreover, increased competition has resulted in organizations offering a diverse range of products and services to their customers. Often, these diverse products/services consume overhead resources in different proportions; this diversity cannot be captured by traditional costing systems.

**Activity-based costing** (ABC) is a method of cost allocation that attempts to assign overhead costs to cost objects more accurately than the methods discussed so far. The basic idea underlying ABC is illustrated in Exhibit 5–1. A customer order for a product or a service triggers a number of activities. For example, if Nordstrom orders a line of women's skirts from Calvin Klein, a production order is generated, materials are ordered, patterns are created, textiles are cut to pattern and then sewn, and the finished products are packed for shipping. These activities consume resources. For example, ordering the appropriate materials consumes clerical time—a resource the company must pay for. In activity-based costing, an attempt is made to trace these costs directly to the activities that cause them.

Rather than a single allocation base, such as direct labour-hours or machine-hours, in activity-based costing, a company uses a number of allocation bases for assigning costs to products. Each allocation base in an activity-based costing system represents a major *activity* that causes overhead costs. An **activity** in activity-based costing is an event that causes the consumption of overhead resources. Examples of activities in various organizations include the following:

- Setting up machines.
- Admitting patients to a hospital.
- Ordering materials or supplies.
- Stocking shelves at a store.

**Exhibit 5–1**
The Activity-Based Costing
Model

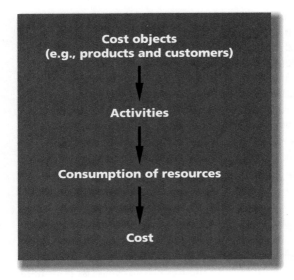

- Scheduling production.
- Performing blood tests at a clinic.
- Billing customers.
- Maintaining equipment.

- Meeting with clients at a law firm.
- Preparing shipments.
- Inspecting materials for defects.
- Opening an account at a bank.

Activity-based costing centres on these activities. Each major activity has its own overhead cost pool (also known as an *activity cost pool*), its own *activity measure*, and its own predetermined overhead rate (also known as an *activity rate*). An **activity cost pool** is a "cost bucket" in which costs related to a particular activity are accumulated. The **activity measure** expresses how much of the activity is carried out, and it is used as the allocation base for applying overhead costs to products and services. For example, *the number of patients admitted* is a natural choice of an activity measure for the activity *admitting patients to the hospital*. An **activity rate** is a predetermined overhead rate in an activity-based costing system. Each activity has its own activity rate that is used to apply overhead costs.

For example, the activity *setting up machines* to process a batch of 100 units of a product would have its own activity cost pool. If the total cost in this activity cost pool is $150,000 and the total expected activity is 1,000 machine setups, the predetermined overhead rate (i.e., activity rate) for this activity would be $150 per machine setup ($150,000 ÷ 1,000 machine setups = $150 per machine setup). Note that this amount does not depend on how many units are produced after the machine is set up. A small job requiring a machine setup would be charged $150—just the same as a large job.

Taking each activity in isolation, this system works exactly like the job-order costing system described in Chapter 3. A predetermined overhead rate is computed for each activity and then applied to cost objects based on the amount of activity required by that cost object. The ABC system can be used by organizations with a job-order costing system or a process costing system. In job-order costing, the desired cost object is a specific job, whereas in a process-costing system, it is a process (or a department).

# Designing an Activity-Based Costing System

In most companies, hundreds or even thousands of different activities cause overhead costs. These activities range from taking a telephone order to training new employees. Setting up and maintaining a complex costing system that includes all of these activities would be prohibitively expensive. The challenge in designing an activity-based costing system is to identify a reasonably small number of activities that explain the bulk of the variation in overhead costs. This is usually done by interviewing a broad range of managers in the organization to find out what activities they think are important and that consume most of the resources they manage. This often results in a long list of potential activities that could be included in the activity-based costing system. This list is refined and pruned in consultation with top managers. Related activities are frequently combined to reduce the amount of detail and record-keeping cost. For example, several actions may be involved in handling and moving raw materials, but these may be combined into a single activity titled *materials handling*. The end result of this stage of the design process is an *activity dictionary* that defines each of the activities that will be included in the activity-based costing system and how the activities will be measured.

## Hierarchy of Activities

Some of the activities commonly found in activity-based costing systems in manufacturing companies are listed in Exhibit 5–2. In the exhibit, activities have been grouped into a four-level hierarchy: *unit-level activities*, *batch-level activities*, *product-level activities*, and *facility-level activities*. This cost hierarchy is useful in understanding the impact of activity-based costing. It also serves as a guide in simplifying an activity-based costing system. In general, activities and costs should be combined in the activity-based costing system only if they fall within the same level in the cost hierarchy.

**Unit-level activities** are performed each time a unit is produced. The costs of unit-level activities should be proportional to the number of units produced. For example, providing power to run processing equipment would be a unit-level activity, since power tends to be consumed in proportion to the number of units produced.

**Batch-level activities** consist of tasks that are performed each time a batch is processed, such as processing purchase orders, setting up equipment, packing shipments to customers, and handling material. Costs at the batch level depend on *the number of batches processed*, rather than on the number of units produced. For example, the cost of processing a purchase order is the same, regardless of whether one unit or 5,000 units of an item are ordered. Thus, the total cost of a batch-level activity, such as purchasing, is a function of the *number* of orders placed.

**Product-level activities** (sometimes called *product-sustaining activities*) relate to specific products and typically must be carried out regardless of how many batches or units of the product are manufactured. Product-level activities include maintaining inventories of parts for a product (also known as parts administration), issuing engineering change

| Level | Activities | Activity Measures |
|---|---|---|
| *Unit-level* | Processing units on machines | Machine-hours |
| | Processing units by hand | Direct labour-hours |
| | Consuming factory supplies | Units produced |
| *Batch-level* | Processing purchase orders | Purchase orders processed |
| | Processing production orders | Production orders processed |
| | Setting up equipment | Number of setups; setup hours |
| | Handling material | Kilograms of material handled; number of times material moved |
| *Product-level* | Testing new products | Hours of testing time |
| | Administering parts inventories | Number of part types |
| | Designing products | Hours of design time |
| *Facility-level* | General factory administration | Direct labour-hours* |
| | Plant building and grounds | Direct labour-hours* |

**Exhibit 5–2**
Examples of Activities and Activity Measures in Manufacturing Companies

*Facility-level costs cannot be traced on a cause-and-effect basis to individual products. Nevertheless, these costs are usually allocated to products using some arbitrary basis, such as direct labour-hours. Note, however, that these costs will represent a small portion of the total overhead costs. Therefore, the distortion which might result from the use of an arbitrary basis for allocating these costs will not be significant.

notices to modify a product to meet a customer's specifications, and developing special test routines when a product is first placed into production. These activities generally depend on the number of different products that a company produces.

**Facility-level activities** (also called *organization-sustaining activities*) are activities that are carried out regardless of which products are produced, how many batches are run, or how many units are made. Facility-level costs include such items as factory management salaries, insurance, property taxes, and building depreciation. The costs of facility-level activities are often combined into a single cost pool and allocated to products using an arbitrary base such as direct labour-hours. As we will see later in the book, allocating such costs to products will result in misleading data that can lead to bad decisions. However, facility-level costs must be allocated to meet external reporting requirements.

## An Example of Activity-Based Costing System Design

Exhibit 5–3 illustrates an ABC system, which consists of a two-stage allocation procedure. The first stage includes the following steps:

- Estimated costs of the various overhead resources are assigned (or allocated) to each of the eight activity cost pools.
- Activity measure for each pool is identified.
- Total activity volume for each activity measure is estimated.
- Predetermined overhead allocation rate (i.e., activity rate) for each pool is computed.

**Exhibit 5–3**

Graphic Example of Activity-Based Costing

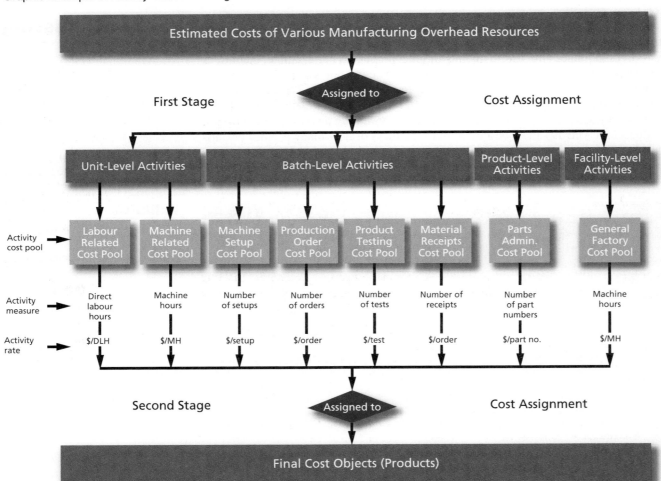

In the second stage, costs from the different pools are allocated to the desired cost objects using the activity rate and the volume of activity measure consumed by that cost object.

As an example, consider the Materials Receipt cost pool. The resources consumed by the activities included in this pool would be manpower (receiving clerks), supplies (shipping documents), and equipment (computers and other material tracking devices). There may be other "common" resources that are consumed by multiple activities, such as the building, central information system, and so on. *In this book, we will not go into the details of how these resource costs are assigned to activity cost pools. Note that in all the examples and assignments, these cost assignments have already been made.*

Once the amount of cost assigned to the Materials Receipt cost pool is known, we must identify an activity measure; in Exhibit 5–3, the activity measure chosen is Number of Receipts. Next, we estimate the total volume for this measure for a given period of time, and then compute a predetermined activity rate as explained on page 73. The procedure for computing a predetermined activity rate is the same as that explained in Chapter 3. Assume that an amount of $50,000 was allocated to the Materials Receipt cost pool at the beginning of the period and that the total activity volume was estimated at 2,500 receipts. The predetermined activity rate is then computed as $20 per receipt ($50,000 ÷ 2,500).

In the second stage, the $20 rate is used to assign costs to the desired cost objects (say, products). If Product A required three shipments of incoming raw materials (i.e., 3 material receipts), $60 will be assigned to this product ($20 × 3). Note that this two-stage procedure is similar to what was explained in Chapter 3; the only difference is that the ABC system has multiple overhead cost pools that are based on activities.

# Using Activity-Based Costing

Different products place different demands on overhead resources. This difference in demand on resources is not recognized by traditional costing systems, which assume that overhead resources are consumed in direct proportion to a single allocation base, such as direct labour hours. The following example illustrates the distortions in product costs that can result from using a traditional costing system and the improvements made possible by ABC.

> **Learning Objective 2**
> Compute product costs using activity-based costing and compare them with costs under a traditional costing system.

Comtek Sound, Inc. makes two products, a radio with a built-in tape player (called a *tape unit*) and a radio with a built-in compact disc player (called a *CD unit*). Both these products are sold to automobile manufacturers for installation in new vehicles. The president of the company, Sarah Kastler, recently returned from a management conference at which activity-based costing was discussed. Following the conference, she called a meeting of the top managers in the company to discuss what she had learned. Attending the meeting were the production manager, Frank Hines; the marketing manager, Nicole Sermone; and the accounting manager, Tom Frazier.

*Sarah:* I learned some things at the conference I just attended that may help resolve some long-standing puzzles here at Comtek Sound.

*Nicole:* Did they tell you why we've been losing all those bids lately on our bread-and-butter tape units and winning every bid on our specialty CD units?

*Sarah:* Nicole, you probably weren't expecting this answer, but yes, there may be a simple explanation. We may have been shooting ourselves in the foot.

*Nicole:* How so? I don't know about anyone else, but we have been hustling like crazy to get more business for the company.

*Sarah:* Nicole, when you talk with our customers, what reasons do they give for taking their tape unit business to our competitors? Is it a problem with quality or on-time delivery?

**MANAGERIAL ACCOUNTING IN ACTION**

The Issue

comtek
SOUND, INC.

*Nicole:* No, our customers readily admit that we're among the best in the business.

*Sarah:* Then what's the problem?

*Nicole:* Price. The competition is undercutting our price on the tape units and then bidding high on the CD units. As a result, they're stealing our high-volume tape business and leaving us with just the low-volume CD business.

*Sarah:* Why is our price so high for the tape units that the competition is able to undercut us?

*Nicole:* Our price isn't too high. Theirs is too low. Our competitors must be pricing below their costs on the tape units.

*Sarah:* Why do you think that?

*Nicole:* Well, if we charged the prices for our tape units that our competitors are quoting, we'd be pricing below *our* cost, and I know we're just as efficient as any competitor.

*Frank:* Nicole, why would our competitors price below their cost?

*Nicole:* They're out to grab market share.

*Frank:* Does that make any sense? What good does more market share do them if they're pricing below their cost?

*Sarah:* I think Frank has a point. Tom, you're the expert with the numbers. Can you suggest another explanation?

*Tom:* I was hoping you'd ask that. Those product cost figures my department reports to you are primarily intended to be used to value inventories and determine cost of goods sold for our external financial statements. I am awfully uncomfortable about using them for bidding. In fact, I have mentioned this several times, but no one was interested.

*Sarah:* Now I'm interested. Tom, are you telling us that the product cost figures we have been using for bidding may be wrong? Are you suggesting that we really don't know what the manufacturing cost is for either the tape units or the CD units?

*Tom:* Yes, that could be the problem. Our cost system isn't designed to recognize that our two products place different demands on our resources, especially overhead. The tape units are simple to manufacture, and the CD units are more complex. We need a cost system that recognizes this difference in demand on resources.

*Sarah:* That's exactly the point made at the conference. The conference speakers suggested we recost our products using something called activity-based costing. Tom, can we do this?

*Tom:* You bet! But we need to do it as a team. Can each person in the room appoint one of their top people to work with me?

*Sarah:* Let's do it! I'd like the special ABC team to report back to this group as soon as possible. If there's a problem with our costs, we need to know it before the competition plows us under.

## Comtek Sound Inc.'s Basic Data

Tom Frazier and the ABC team immediately began gathering basic information relating to the company's two products. As a basis for its study, the team decided to use the cost and other data planned for the current year. A summary of some of this information follows. For the current year, the company's budget provides for selling 50,000 CD units and 200,000 tape units. Both products require two direct labour-hours to complete. Therefore, the company plans to work 500,000 direct labour-hours (DLHs) during the current year, computed as follows:

|  | Hours |
|---|---|
| CD units: 50,000 units × 2 DLHs per unit . . . . . . . . . . | 100,000 |
| Tape units: 200,000 units × 2 DLHs per unit . . . . . . . . | 400,000 |
| Total direct labour-hours . . . . . . . . . . . . . . . . . . . . . . | 500,000 |

Costs for materials and labour for one unit of each product are given below:

| | CD Units | Tape Units |
|---|---|---|
| Direct materials . . . . . . . . . . . . . . . . . | $90 | $50 |
| Direct labour (at $10 per DLH) . . . . | 20 | 20 |

The company's estimated manufacturing overhead costs for the current year total $10,000,000. The ABC team discovered that although the same amount of direct labour time is required for each product, the more complex CD units require more machine time, more machine setups, and more testing than the tape units. Also, the team found that it is necessary to manufacture the CD units in smaller lots, and so they require a relatively large number of production orders as compared with the tape units.

The company has always used direct labour-hours as the base for assigning overhead costs to its products.

With these data in hand, the ABC team was prepared to begin the design of the new activity-based costing system. But first, they wanted to compute the cost of each product using the company's existing cost system.

## Direct Labour-Hours as a Base

Under the company's existing costing system, the company's predetermined overhead rate would be $20 per direct labour-hour. The rate is computed as follows:

$$\frac{\text{Predetermined}}{\text{overhead rate}} = \frac{\text{Estimated total manufacturing overhead}}{\text{Estimated total direct labour-hours (DLHs)}}$$

$$= \frac{\$10,000,000}{500,000 \text{ DLHs}} = \$20 \text{ per DLH}$$

Using this rate, the ABC team then computed the unit product costs as given below:

| | CD Units | Tape Units |
|---|---|---|
| Direct materials (above) . . . . . . . . . . . . . . . . . . . . . . . . . . | $90 | $50 |
| Direct labour (above) . . . . . . . . . . . . . . . . . . . . . . . . . . . . | 20 | 20 |
| Manufacturing overhead (2 DLHs × $20 per DLH) . . . . . . | 40 | 40 |
| Unit product cost . . . . . . . . . . . . . . . . . . . . . . . . . . . . . . . . | $150 | $110 |

Tom Frazier explained to the ABC team that the problem with this costing approach is that it relies entirely on labour time in assigning overhead cost to products and does not consider the impact of other factors—such as setups and testing—on the overhead costs of the company. Since these other factors are being ignored and the two products require equal amounts of labour time, they are assigned equal amounts of overhead cost.

Tom explained that while this method of computing costs is fast and simple, it is accurate only in those situations where other factors affecting overhead costs are not significant. Tom stated that he believed these other factors are significant in the case of Comtek Sound, Inc., and he was anxious for the team to analyze the various activities of the company to see what impact they have on costs.

## Computing Activity Rates

The ABC team then analyzed Comtek Sound, Inc.'s operations and identified eight major activities to be included in the new activity-based costing system. (These eight activities are identical to those illustrated earlier in Exhibit 5–3.) Cost and other data relating to the activities are presented in Exhibit 5–4.

**Exhibit 5–4**
Comtek Sound's Activity-Based Costing System

### Basic Data

| Activities and Activity Measures | Estimated Overhead Cost | Expected Activity | | |
| --- | --- | --- | --- | --- |
| | | Total | CD Units | Tape Units |
| Labour related (direct labour-hours) ..... | $ 800,000 | 500,000 | 100,000 | 400,000 |
| Machine related (machine-hours) ....... | 2,100,000 | 1,000,000 | 300,000 | 700,000 |
| Machine setups (setups) ............... | 1,600,000 | 4,000 | 3,000 | 1,000 |
| Production orders (orders) ............. | 450,000 | 1,200 | 400 | 800 |
| Product testing (tests) ................. | 1,700,000 | 20,000 | 16,000 | 4,000 |
| Material receipts (receipts) ............. | 1,000,000 | 5,000 | 1,800 | 3,200 |
| Parts administration (part types) ........ | 350,000 | 700 | 400 | 300 |
| General factory (machine-hours) ........ | 2,000,000 | 1,000,000 | 300,000 | 700,000 |
| | $10,000,000 | | | |

### Computation of Activity Rates

| Activities | (a) Estimated Overhead Cost | (b) Total Expected Activity | (a) ÷ (b) Activity Rate |
| --- | --- | --- | --- |
| Labour related ...................$ | 800,000 | 500,000 DLHs | $ 1.60 per DLH |
| Machine related ................. | 2,100,000 | 1,000,000 MHs | 2.10 per MH |
| Machine setups .................. | 1,600,000 | 4,000 setups | 400.00 per setup |
| Production orders ............... | 450,000 | 1,200 orders | 375.00 per order |
| Product testing ................. | 1,700,000 | 20,000 tests | 85.00 per test |
| Material receipts ................ | 1,000,000 | 5,000 receipts | 200.00 per receipt |
| Parts administration ............. | 350,000 | 700 part numbers | 500.00 per part no. |
| General factory ................. | 2,000,000 | 1,000,000 MHs | 2.00 per MH |

### Computation of the Overhead Cost per Unit of Product

| Activities and Activity Rates | CD Units | | Tape Units | |
| --- | --- | --- | --- | --- |
| | Expected Activity | Amount | Expected Activity | Amount |
| Labour related, at $1.60 per DLH ........... | 100,000 DLH | $ 160,000 | 400,000 DLH | $ 640,000 |
| Machine related, at $2.10 per MH .......... | 300,000 MH | 630,000 | 700,000 MH | 1,470,000 |
| Machine setups, at $400 per setup .......... | 3,000 setups | 1,200,000 | 1,000 setups | 400,000 |
| Production orders, at $375 per order ........ | 400 orders | 150,000 | 800 orders | 300,000 |
| Product testing, at $85 per test ............. | 16,000 tests | 1,360,000 | 4,000 tests | 340,000 |
| Materials receipts, at $200 per receipt ....... | 1,800 receipts | 360,000 | 3,200 receipts | 640,000 |
| Parts administration, at $500 per part no. .... | 400 part nos. | 200,000 | 300 part nos. | 150,000 |
| General factory, at $2.00 per MH ........... | 300,000 MH | 600,000 | 700,000 MH | 1,400,000 |
| Total overhead costs assigned (a) ........... | | $4,660,000 | | $5,340,000 |
| Number of units produced (b) .............. | | 50,000 | | 200,000 |
| Overhead cost per unit (a) ÷ (b) ............ | | $93.20 | | $26.70 |

As shown in the Basic Data panel at the top of Exhibit 5–4, the ABC team estimated the amount of overhead cost for each activity cost pool, along with the expected amount of activity for the current year. The machine setups activity cost pool, for example, has been assigned $1,600,000 in overhead cost. The company expects to complete 4,000 setups during the year, of which 3,000 will be for CD units and 1,000 will be for tape units. Data for other activities are also shown in the exhibit.

The ABC team then computed an activity rate for each activity. (See the middle panel in Exhibit 5–4.) The rate for machine setups, for example, was computed by dividing the total estimated overhead cost in the activity cost pool, $1,600,000, by the expected amount of activity, 4,000 setups. The result was the activity rate of $400 per setup. This process was repeated for each of the other activities in the activity-based costing system.

## Computing Product Costs

Once the activity rates were determined, it was then an easy matter to compute the overhead cost that would be allocated to each product. (See the bottom panel of Exhibit 5–4.) For example, the amount of machine setup cost allocated to CD units was determined by multiplying the activity rate of $400 per setup by the 3,000 expected setups for CD units during the year. This yielded a total of $1,200,000 in machine setup costs to be assigned to the CD units.

Note from the exhibit that the use of an activity approach has resulted in $93.20 in overhead cost being assigned to each CD unit and $26.70 to each tape unit. The ABC team then used these amounts to determine unit product costs under activity-based costing, as presented in the table below. For comparison, the table also shows the unit costs derived earlier when direct labour was used as the base for assigning overhead costs to the products.

| | Activity-Based Costing | | Direct-Labour Based Costing | |
|---|---|---|---|---|
| | **CD Units** | **Tape Units** | **CD Units** | **Tape Units** |
| Direct materials ......... | $ 90.00 | $50.00 | $ 90.00 | $ 50.00 |
| Direct labour ........... | 20.00 | 20.00 | 20.00 | 20.00 |
| Manufacturing overhead .. | 93.20 | 26.70 | 40.00 | 40.00 |
| Unit product cost ........ | $203.20 | $96.70 | $150.00 | $110.00 |

The ABC team members were shocked by their findings, which Tom Frazier summarized as follows in the team's report:

> In the past, the company has been charging $40 in overhead cost to a unit of either product, whereas it should have been charging $93.20 in overhead cost to each CD unit and only $26.70 to each tape unit. Thus, as a result of using direct labour as the base for overhead costing, unit product costs had been badly distorted. The company may even have been suffering a loss on the CD units without knowing it because the cost of these units has been so vastly understated. Through activity-based costing, we have been able to better identify the overhead costs of each product and thus derive more accurate cost data.

The pattern of cost distortion shown by the ABC team's findings is quite common. Such distortion can happen in any company that relies on a single allocation base in assigning overhead cost to products and ignores other significant factors affecting overhead cost incurrence. When a company implements activity-based costing, overhead cost often shifts from high-volume products to low-volume products, with a higher unit product cost resulting for the low-volume products. This results from the existence of batch-level and product-level costs which do not vary with the number of units produced.

The ABC team presented the results of its work in a meeting attended by all of the top managers of Comtek Sound including the president, Sarah Kastler; the production manager, Frank Hines; the marketing manager, Nicole Sermone; and the accounting manager, Tom Frazier. After the formal presentation by the ABC team, the following discussion took place:

**Sarah:** I would like to personally thank the ABC team for all the work they have done. I am now beginning to wonder about some of the decisions we have made in the past using our old cost accounting system.

**Nicole:** It's obvious from this activity-based costing information that we had everything backwards. We thought the competition was pricing below cost on the tape units, but in fact, *we* were overcharging for these units because our costs were overstated. And we thought the competition was overpricing CD units, but in fact, *our* prices were way too low because our costs for these units were understated. I'll bet the competition has really been laughing behind our backs!

**Sarah:** You can bet they won't be laughing when they see our next bids.

## Activity-Based Costing in Service Settings

**Learning Objective 3**
Describe the use of activity-based costing in service settings.

Although initially developed as a tool for computing product costs in manufacturing companies, activity-based costing is now also being used to assign their marketing and administrative costs to desired cost objects. For example, many companies assign marketing costs to different customer groups to analyze customer profitability. Activity-based costing has also been implemented by various service organizations, such as banks, hospitals, cities, and data service companies. Successful implementation of an activity-based costing system depends on identifying the key activities that generate costs and tracking how many of those activities are performed for each service the organization provides.

### An Example of Using Activity-Based Costing in a Bank[1]

Royal Bank of Canada, one of the largest banks in this country, uses activity-based costing to assign its costs to various cost objects, such as products, customers, distribution channels, and regions. An example of a service provided is a mortgage. Exhibit 5–5 maps the typical high-level activities involved in approving a mortgage to a client. The mortgage approval process consists mainly of four activities:

1. Client interview in branch—branch staff discuss mortgage needs with clients, answer questions, prepare documentation, and send it to the mortgage processing centre.
2. Adjudication—mortgage processing centre analyzes to determine the creditworthiness of the client and decides whether the mortgage should be approved.
3. Processing and due diligence—ensuring everything is in order.
4. Completion—clients sign final mortgage documents.

An additional activity—contacting the client—may be involved in the process if errors or omissions are detected during the mortgage processing activity (this is essentially a quality problem and necessitates rework, which consists of obtaining the required information from the client). Exhibit 5–6 lists the activities using the hierarchy of activities described earlier, the resource requirements for each activity, the allocation basis, and the amount allocated to the service provided (i.e., mortgage). Note that all of the four activities listed in Exhibit 5–6 are unit-level activities; mortgages cannot be processed in batches. Regardless of the fact that all of the activities are unit-based, costs are assigned using three different allocation bases (and not one like in a traditional costing system). Doing so enhances the accuracy of cost allocation.

---

[1]The authors would like to thank RBC Financial Group for its assistance in providing this example. All the numbers presented in the example are fictitious.

**Exhibit 5–5**

Activities Involved in Processing a Mortgage

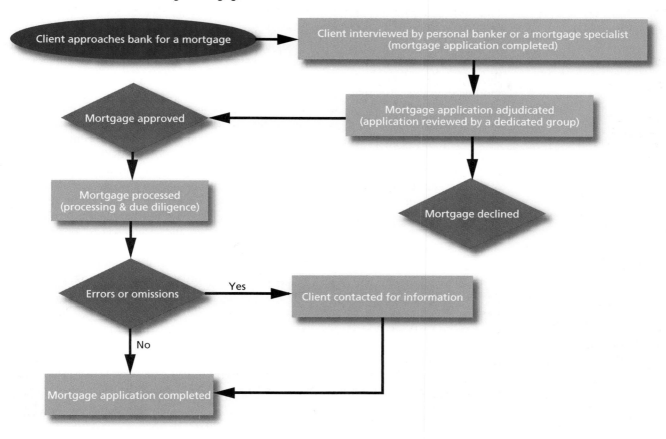

**Exhibit 5–6**

Activities and Costs for Mortgages Processed in a Quarter

| Activity Hierarchy | Activity | Resource(s) Required | Allocation Basis | Amount Allocated |
|---|---|---|---|---|
| Unit-level | Client interview | Branch labour (personal banker) | Time | $40,000 |
| Unit-level | Adjudication | Direct labour (mortgage group) | Direct cost (average cost) | $22,500 |
| Unit-level | Processing & due diligence | Direct labour (mortgage group) | Direct cost (average cost) | $25,000 |
| Unit-level | Completion | Branch labour (personal banker) | Time | $15,500 |
| | | | | $102,500 |

In addition to the amounts shown in Exhibit 5–6, the following costs are also assigned to the product (mostly facility-level costs):

- Business development costs—advertising costs
  - costs of specific mortgage-related advertisements are directly traced to the product
  - costs of general advertisements are allocated on the basis of product mix (% of product mix represented by each product).
- Rework costs—allocated on the basis of time devoted to this activity by the branch staff.

- Branch support costs (utilities, furniture, computer equipment, receptionist)—allocated on the basis of the branch employee costs assigned to the product.
- Corporate overhead costs—allocated on the basis of the operating expenses assigned to the product.

Suppose the facility-level costs assigned to mortgages during the quarter amount to $58,000 and that 250 mortgages were processed. The total (full) costs of $160,500 are then divided by the number of mortgages processed to compute the average unit cost per mortgage; in this case, it amounts to $642 per mortgage.

Unlike in manufacturing, where it is easy to measure activity volume (e.g., machine-hours, number of setups), it may not be easy to accurately record the time that branch employees spend in carrying out each individual activity (such as client interview). In such situations, employees are surveyed to determine the portion of the time that they spend on different activities (e.g., 15% on client interviews) during a representative 40-hour week. This information is then used to assign employee costs to activities.

Royal Bank devotes considerable resources to accurately collecting activity cost information, which they use to assign costs to different cost objects, conduct profitability analyses, and make decisions to increase efficiencies and reduce costs. For example managers can compare the unit cost of $642 with industry data to know how they rank in relation to competing financial institutions. Once they know, they can initiate improvement processes, such as total quality management or process re-engineering, to increase efficiencies and decrease errors, thereby reducing costs.

# Evaluating Activity-Based Costing

**Learning Objective 4**
Understand the benefits and limitations of activity-based costing systems.

Although the prior discussion of activity-based costing appears to suggest that it might be a useful tool for managers, it is important to examine this in greater detail, along with its potential limitations.

## Benefits of Activity-Based Costing

There are at least three different benefits of implementing an activity-based costing system; these are discussed below.

**ACCURATE COSTING**   The initial purpose of implementing an activity-based costing system was to improve the accuracy of costs assigned to cost objects (say, product costs). Activity-based costing improves the accuracy of product costs in three ways. First, activity-based costing usually accumulates overhead costs in multiple activity cost pools which represent the major activities instead of just one or two pools. As a result, the allocation is based on a better matching of the consumption of resources by cost objects.

Second, the activity cost pools are more homogeneous than departmental cost pools. In principle, all of the costs in a single activity cost pool pertain to a single activity. In the event that multiple activities are grouped in a single cost pool, these activities are usually related and, therefore, homogeneous. In contrast, departmental cost pools contain costs of many different activities carried out in a department.

Third, activity-based costing does not rely just on *volume-based* allocation bases (such as direct labour-hours or machine-hours) to assign overhead. Instead, managers use a combination of *volume-based* and *non–volume-based* activity measures to assign overhead costs to cost objects. The non–volume-based activity measures include the batch-level and product-level activity measures illustrated earlier in the chapter. The focus of activity-based costing is to identify the activities or factors that cause or drive costs and use them as allocation bases. In doing so, the system attempts to establish a *cause-effect* relationship between the overhead costs and the allocation bases.

**COST ESTIMATION**   Increased accuracy in overhead allocation means that companies can do a better job of estimating costs. In today's competitive world, many companies are finding that they have less flexibility in setting their prices; they are largely market driven. Consequently, managers in these companies must identify a target cost which they can work toward to generate a desired profit margin. Activity-based costing can be a valuable tool in providing relevant cost information to managers in identifying the target costs and also in monitoring a company's progress toward achieving the target costs. It can also help in estimating costs related to quality. See Appendix 5A at the Online Learning Centre at www.mcgrawhill.ca/college/garrison.

**ACTIVITY-BASED MANAGEMENT**   An important benefit from using activity-based costing is that it allows managers to identify activities that would benefit from improvement, thereby resulting in greater efficiency and lower costs. Indeed, this is the most widely cited benefit of activity-based costing by managers.[2] When used in this manner, it is often called *activity-based management*. Essentially, **activity-based management (ABM)** involves focusing on activities to eliminate waste. In other words, ABM is a tool that can supplement management practices, such as total quality management and process re-engineering described in Chapter 1.

## ABM in the Service Industry                              *in business* | *today*

Reducing the costs to serve clients is a prime objective when using ABM. Mutual Life of Canada decided to use ABM to improve its understanding of the costs of its shared services which provide valuable service to internal customers (departments), such as finance, corporate affairs, strategic development, and human resources. Prior to the implementation, the shared services function for the retail insurance company accounted for one-third of total non–sales-related costs. In addition, many of the internal customers questioned the cost-benefit of the shared services. Mutual Life went through an activity identification process and then mapped those activities to products provided: for example, mapping payroll activity to the payroll product. But more detail was required. ABM revealed where activities could be combined, eliminated, or outsourced. As a result of the ABM effort, service-level agreements were set up with internal customers, along with monthly invoices to bill back to business units for services provided.

Source: Leahy, Tad. "Beyond Traditional Product Costing," 2003. *Business Finance Magazine* Website: http://www.businessfinancemag.com/archives. Rep rinted with permission from *Controller Magazine*.

The first step in any improvement program is to decide what to improve. The theory of constraints (TOC) approach discussed in Chapter 1 is a powerful tool for targeting the area in an organization whose improvement will yield the greatest benefit. An ABC system can provide valuable information. For example, Comtek's managers may wonder why it costs $375, on average, to process a purchase order (see Exhibit 5–4). Such a question arises when organizations decide on **benchmarking** their costs against the costs of similar organizations known for their outstanding performance. Once the activity is targeted for improvement, managers can use the ABM approach to study the activity in greater detail and identifying ways to eliminate the wasteful consumption of resources. Some activities that are deemed to not add any value are targeted for elimination. However, managers must be careful to ensure that eliminating a certain activity does not negatively impact other activities.

---

[2]Swenson, D. "The Benefits of Activity-Based Cost Management to the Manufacturing Industry," *Journal of Management Accounting Research* 7, Fall 1995, pp. 167–80.

Molson Inc. completed an intensive five-month global benchmarking study in December 2001 to measure its corporate performance globally against other brewers. Areas that were measured included packaging line productivity, maintenance costs, utilities consumption, and product shrinkage. The company's representatives examined over 20 manufacturing facilities and compared its performance with that of eight global brewers. In order to be "the best in its class around the world," Molson had to significantly reduce costs and identified that it could potentially save $50 million, as follows:

- $18 million by reducing maintenance costs,
- $14 million by improving bottling line productivity, and
- $9 million each by lowering utilities consumption and reducing shrinkage.

Source: 2002 Annual Report. http://media.integratir.com/T.MOL.A/financials/2002CorpOverview eng.pdf.

## Limitations of Activity-Based Costing

Any discussion of activity-based costing is incomplete without some cautionary warnings. First, the cost of implementing and maintaining an activity-based costing system may outweigh the benefits. Second, it would be naïve to assume that product costs provided even by an activity-based costing are always relevant when making decisions. These limitations are discussed below.

**THE COST OF IMPLEMENTING ACTIVITY-BASED COSTING**   Implementing ABC is a major project that involves a great deal of effort. First, the cost system must be designed—preferably—by a cross-functional team. This requires taking valued employees away from other tasks for a major project. In addition, the data used in the activity-based costing system must be collected and verified. In some cases, this requires collecting data that have never been collected before. In short, implementing and maintaining an activity-based costing system can present a formidable challenge, and management may decide that the costs are too great to justify the expected benefits. Nevertheless, it should be kept in mind that the costs of collecting and processing data have dropped dramatically over the last several decades due to bar coding and other technologies, and these costs can be expected to continue to fall.

When are the benefits of activity-based costing most likely to be worth the cost? Companies that have some of the following characteristics are most likely to benefit from activity-based costing:

1. Products differ substantially in volume, lot size, and in the activities they require.
2. Conditions have changed substantially since the existing cost system was established.
3. Overhead costs are high and increasing, and no one seems to understand why.
4. Management does not trust the existing cost system and ignores cost data from the system when making decisions.

**LIMITATIONS OF THE ABC MODEL**   The activity-based costing model relies on a number of critical assumptions. Perhaps the most important of these assumptions is that the cost in each activity cost pool is strictly proportional to its activity measure. The issue of whether overhead costs are proportional to the driver is of universal concern. What little evidence we have on this issue suggests that overhead costs are less than proportional to activity.[3] As a practical matter, this means that product costs will be overstated for the purposes of making decisions. The product costs generated by activity-based costing are almost certainly more accurate than those generated by a conventional costing system, but the product costs should nevertheless be viewed with caution. Managers should be particularly alert to product costs that contain allocations of facility-level costs. As we shall see later in the book, such product costs can easily lead managers astray in decisions.

**MODIFYING THE ABC MODEL** The discussion in this chapter has assumed that the primary purpose of the activity-based costing system is to provide more accurate product costs for inventory valuation in external reports. If the product costs are to be used by managers for internal decisions, some modifications should be made. For example, for decision-making purposes, the distinction between manufacturing costs on the one hand and selling and general administrative expenses on the other hand is unimportant. Managers need to know what costs a product causes, and it does not matter whether the costs are manufacturing costs or selling and general administrative expenses. Consequently, for decision-making purposes, some selling and general administrative expenses should be assigned to products. Moreover, as mentioned above, facility-level costs should be removed from product costs when making decisions. Nevertheless, the techniques covered in this chapter provide a good basis for understanding the mechanics of activity-based costing. For a more complete coverage of the use of activity-based costing in decisions, see more advanced texts.

## City Controller

*decision* *maker*

You are the controller of your city office. The managers responsible for utilities and property taxes have complained to you regarding the charges from support services departments, such as information systems and maintenance. The city recently decided to "charge" the internal users of support services an "appropriate" amount to reflect the cost of these services. After meeting with the cost analyst for the city, you discover that the city uses a single "citywide" rate to allocate overhead costs. You are puzzled because you know that the support services departments are quite different from one another and that it does not make sense to combine the overhead costs into one single pool. How do you proceed to resolve the issue?

## Cost Flows in an Activity-Based Costing System

In Chapter 3, we discussed the flow of costs in a job-order costing system. The flow of costs through Raw Materials, Work in Process, and other accounts is the same under activity-based costing. The only difference in activity-based costing is that more than one predetermined overhead rate is used to apply overhead costs to products. Our purpose in this section is to provide a detailed example of cost flows in an activity-based costing system.

**Learning Objective 5**
Record the flow of costs in an activity-based costing system.

---

[3]Eric Noreen and Naomi Soderstrom, "The Accuracy of Proportional Cost Models: Evidence from Hospital Service Departments," *Review of Accounting Studies* 2, 1997; and Eric Noreen and Naomi Soderstrom, "Are Overhead Costs Proportional to Activity? Evidence from Hospital Service Departments," *Journal of Accounting and Economics*, January 1994, pp. 253–278.

## An Example of Cost Flows

The company in the following example has five activity cost pools and therefore must compute five predetermined overhead rates (i.e., activity rates). Except for that detail, the journal entries, T-accounts, and general cost flows are the same as described in Chapter 3.

**BASIC DATA**   Consider the following data for Sarvik Company.

At the beginning of the year, the company had inventory balances as follows:

| | |
|---|---|
| Raw materials | $3,000 |
| Work in process | 4,000 |
| Finished goods | –0– |

Selected transactions recorded by the company during the year are given below:

a. Raw materials were purchased on account, $915,000.
b. Raw materials were requisitioned for use in production, $900,000 ($810,000 direct and $90,000 indirect).
c. Labour costs were incurred in the factory, $370,000 ($95,000 direct labour and $275,000 indirect labour).
d. Depreciation was recorded on factory assets, $180,000.
e. Miscellaneous manufacturing overhead costs were incurred, $230,000.
f. The company uses an activity-based costing system to apply manufacturing overhead costs to products. The following data are available pertaining to overhead allocation:

| Activity Cost Pool (1) | Activity Measure (2) | Activity Rate (3) | Actual Activity (4) | Applied Overhead Cost (3) × (4) |
|---|---|---|---|---|
| Machine related | Machine-hours | $35 per MH | 4,600 MHs | $161,000 |
| Purchase orders | Number of orders | $90 per order | 800 orders | 72,000 |
| Machine setups | Number of setups | $200 per setup | 500 setups | 100,000 |
| Product testing | Number of tests | $800 per test | 190 tests | 152,000 |
| General factory | Direct labour-hours | $12 per DLH | 23,000 DLHs | 276,000 |
| | | | | $761,000 |

g. Goods costing $1,650,000 to manufacture were completed during the year.

**TRACKING THE FLOW OF COSTS**   The following journal entries would be used to record transactions (a) through (g) above:

| | | | |
|---|---|---|---|
| a. | Raw Materials | 915,000 | |
| | Accounts Payable | | 915,000 |
| b. | Work in Process | 810,000 | |
| | Manufacturing Overhead | 90,000 | |
| | Raw Materials | | 900,000 |
| c. | Work in Process | 95,000 | |
| | Manufacturing Overhead | 275,000 | |
| | Salaries and Wages Payable | | 370,000 |
| d. | Manufacturing Overhead | 180,000 | |
| | Accumulated Depreciation | | 180,000 |
| e. | Manufacturing Overhead | 230,000 | |
| | Accounts Payable | | 230,000 |
| f. | Work in Process | 761,000 | |
| | Manufacturing Overhead | | 761,000 |
| g. | Finished Goods | 1,650,000 | |
| | Work in Process | | 1,650,000 |

The T-accounts corresponding to the above journal entries appear below:

| Raw Materials | | | |
|---|---|---|---|
| Bal. | 3,000 | (b) | 900,000 |
| (a) | 915,000 | | |
| Bal. | 18,000 | | |

| Work in Process | | | |
|---|---|---|---|
| Bal. | 4,000 | (g) | 1,650,000 |
| (b) | 810,000 | | |
| (c) | 95,000 | | |
| (f) | 761,000 | | |
| Bal. | 20,000 | | |

| Finished Goods | | | |
|---|---|---|---|
| Bal. | –0– | | |
| (g) | 1,650,000 | | |

| Accumulated Depreciation | | | |
|---|---|---|---|
| | | (d) | 180,000 |

| Accounts Payable | | | |
|---|---|---|---|
| | | (a) | 915,000 |
| | | (e) | 230,000 |

| Salaries and Wages Payable | | | |
|---|---|---|---|
| | | (c) | 370,000 |

| Manufacturing Overhead | | | |
|---|---|---|---|
| (b) | 90,000 | (f) | 761,000 |
| (c) | 275,000 | | |
| (d) | 180,000 | | |
| (e) | 230,000 | | |
| | 775,000 | | 761,000 |
| Bal. | 14,000 | | |

The overhead is under-applied by $14,000. This can be determined directly, as shown below, or by reference to the balance in the Manufacturing Overhead T-account above.

| | |
|---|---|
| Actual manufacturing overhead incurred .......... | $775,000 |
| Manufacturing overhead applied ................ | 761,000 |
| Overhead under-applied ...................... | $ 14,000 |

## Entrepreneur

*you decide*

You are the owner of a small manufacturing firm. You are implementing a cost account-ing system and wondering whether you should use direct labour as the base for assigning overhead or implement activity-based costing. How would you go about making this decision?

## Summary

**LO1 Understand the basic approach in activity-based costing and how it differs from traditional costing.**

Activity-based costing was developed as a way of more accurately assigning overhead to products. Activity-based costing differs from traditional costing as described in Chapter 3 in two major ways. First, in activity-based costing, each major activity that consumes overhead resources has its own cost pool and its own activity rate, whereas in Chapter 3 there was only a single overhead cost pool and a single predetermined overhead rate. Second, the allocation bases (or activity measures) in activity-based costing are diverse. They usually include volume-based and non–volume-based activity measures (e.g., machine-hours, number of purchase orders). Nevertheless, within each activity cost pool, the mechanics of computing overhead rates and of applying overhead to products are the same as described in Chapter 3. However, the increase in the number of cost pools and the use of better measures of activity generally result in more accurate product costs.

**LO2   Compute product costs using activity-based costing and compare them with costs under a traditional costing system.**

The allocation of overhead costs under activity-based costing involves a two-stage process. In the first stage, costs of overhead resources are assigned to activities, activity measures are identified and activity rates are computed. These activity rates are used in the second stage to assign costs to cost objects (e.g., products). Activities are generally classified as unit-level, batch-level, product-level, and facility-level. In contrast, traditional costing systems usually assign overhead costs using a single allocation base, such as direct labour-hours or machine-hours, or a departmental overhead allocation system. The change in the allocation bases results shifting overhead costs from high-volume products to low-volume products.

**LO3   Describe the use of activity-based costing in service settings.**

Just like manufacturing companies, service organizations can also use activity-based costing to assign costs to cost objects and use the system for cost estimation and cost management. Many service organizations, such as banks and hospitals, use activity-based costing.

**LO4   Understand the benefits and limitations of activity-based costing systems.**

Activity-based costing (ABC) systems offer a number of benefits, such as more accurate costs, better cost estimation, and above all cost management (called activity-based management). However, ABC is not without its limitations. The major limitation pertains to the implementation challenges. Another limitation is even under this system, overhead costs must allocated. Therefore, although the use of ABC might result in more accurate costs, it still cannot provide the true costs.

**LO5   Record the flow of costs in an activity-based costing system.**

The journal entries and general flow of costs in an activity-based costing system are the same as they are in a traditional costing system. The only difference is the use of more than one predetermined overhead rate (i.e., activity rate) to apply overhead to products.

# Guidance Answers to Decision Maker and You Decide

**CITY CONTROLLER** (p. 177)

You already took the first step by talking to the cost analyst. Your next step is to get a small four- to six-person team consisting of individuals from support services, user departments, and the cost accounting department. You should instruct the team to do a special overhead cost accounting project consisting of at least three major steps: (1) compiling a list of overhead cost items and the factors that cause them, (2) analyzing the data to identify appropriate allocation bases, and (3) testing the system by applying it to one user department. Whether you implement activity-based costing citywide will depend on such issues as cost-benefit and behavioural consequences of the new system.

**ENTREPRENEUR** (p. 179)

You are a small firm, which likely means that your overhead costs are less complex than those of a large firm. However, your firm's overhead may still account for a significant portion of your total costs. This, in itself, may require you to think twice about using a plantwide overhead rate. You must also consider the diversity of your product line and whether individual products consume overhead resources differently. If your products are diverse, using a plantwide overhead rate can lead to product cost distortions. Moreover, regularly adding new products will increase your overhead costs. It is perhaps best for you to implement an activity-based costing system that allows the flexibility of adding new overhead cost items and activity measures, as needed. Of course, implementing such a system will be initially expensive because you may not fully use the system. Therefore, you must carefully weigh all the factors before implementing a system (once implemented, it may take extra effort to change).

# Review Problem: Activity-Based Costing

Aerodec, Inc. manufactures and sells two types of wooden deck chairs: Deluxe and Tourist. Annual sales in units, direct labour-hours (DLHs) per unit, and total direct labour-hours per year are provided below:

| | Total Hours |
|---|---|
| Deluxe deck chair: 2,000 units × 5 DLHs per unit . . . . . . . . . . . . . | 10,000 |
| Tourist deck chair: 10,000 units × 4 DLHs per unit . . . . . . . . . . . . | 40,000 |
| Total direct labour-hours . . . . . . . . . . . . . . . . . . . . . . . . . . . . . . . . | 50,000 |

Costs for materials and labour for one unit of each product are given below:

| | Deluxe | Tourist |
|---|---|---|
| Direct materials . . . . . . . . . . . . . . . . . . . . . . . | $25 | $17 |
| Direct labour (at $12 per DLH) . . . . . . . . . . . | 60 | 48 |

Manufacturing overhead costs total $800,000 each year. The breakdown of these costs among the company's six activity cost pools is given below. The activity measures are shown in parentheses.

| Activities and Activity Measures | Estimated Overhead Cost | Expected Activity | | |
|---|---|---|---|---|
| | | Total | Deluxe | Tourist |
| Labour related (direct labour-hours) . . . . . . . . . . . . | $ 80,000 | 50,000 | 10,000 | 40,000 |
| Machine setups (number of setups) . . . . . . . . . . . . | 150,000 | 5,000 | 3,000 | 2,000 |
| Parts administration (number of parts) . . . . . . . . . . | 160,000 | 80 | 50 | 30 |
| Production orders (number of orders) . . . . . . . . . . | 70,000 | 400 | 100 | 300 |
| Material receipts (number of receipts) . . . . . . . . . . | 90,000 | 750 | 150 | 600 |
| General factory (machine-hours) . . . . . . . . . . . . . . | 250,000 | 40,000 | 12,000 | 28,000 |
| | $800,000 | | | |

*Required:*

1. Classify each of Aerodec's activities as either a unit-level, batch-level, product-level, or facility-level activity.
2. Assume that the company applies overhead cost to products on the basis of direct labour-hours.
   a. Compute the predetermined overhead rate that would be used.
   b. Determine the unit product cost of each product, using the predetermined overhead rate computed in (2)(a) above.
3. Assume that the company uses activity-based costing to compute overhead rates.
   a. Compute the activity rate (i.e., predetermined overhead rate) for each of the six activity centres listed above.
   b. Using the rates developed in (3)(a) above, determine the amount of overhead cost that would be assigned to a unit of each product.
   c. Determine the unit product cost of each product and compare this cost with the cost computed in (2)(b) above.

## SOLUTION TO REVIEW PROBLEM

1.

| Activity Cost Pool | Type of Activity |
|---|---|
| Labour related . . . . . . . . . . . . . . . . . . . . . . . . . . . . . . | Unit level |
| Machine setups . . . . . . . . . . . . . . . . . . . . . . . . . . . . . . | Batch level |
| Parts administration . . . . . . . . . . . . . . . . . . . . . . . . . . | Product level |
| Production orders . . . . . . . . . . . . . . . . . . . . . . . . . . . . . | Batch level |
| Material receipts . . . . . . . . . . . . . . . . . . . . . . . . . . . . | Batch level |
| General factory . . . . . . . . . . . . . . . . . . . . . . . . . . . . . . | Facility level |

2. a.

$$\text{Predetermined overhead rate} = \frac{\text{Estimated total manufacturing overhead}}{\text{Estimated total direct labour-hours (DLHs)}} = \frac{\$800,000}{50,000 \text{ DLHs}} = \$16 \text{ per DLH}$$

b.

|  | Deluxe | Tourist |
|---|---|---|
| Direct materials ..................... | $ 25 | $ 17 |
| Direct labour ....................... | 60 | 48 |
| Manufacturing overhead applied: |  |  |
| Deluxe: 5 DLHs × $16 per DLH ...... | 80 |  |
| Tourist: 4 DLHs × $16 per DLH ...... |  | 64 |
| Unit product cost .................... | $165 | $129 |

3. a.

| Activities | (a) Estimated Overhead Cost | (b) Total Expected Activity | (a) ÷ (b) Activity Rate |
|---|---|---|---|
| Labour related ................. | $ 80,000 | 50,000 DLHs | $1.60 per DLH |
| Machine setups ................ | 150,000 | 5,000 setups | $30.00 per setup |
| Parts administration ............. | 160,000 | 80 parts | $2,000.00 per part |
| Production orders ............... | 70,000 | 400 orders | $175.00 per order |
| Material receipts ............... | 90,000 | 750 receipts | $120.00 per receipt |
| General factory ................ | 250,000 | 40,000 MHs | $6.25 per MH |

b.

| Activities and Activity Rates | Deluxe Expected Activity | Deluxe Amount | Tourist Expected Activity | Tourist Amount |
|---|---|---|---|---|
| Labour related, at $1.60 per DLH ............ | 10,000 | $ 16,000 | 40,000 | $ 64,000 |
| Machine setups, at $30 per setup ............ | 3,000 | 90,000 | 2,000 | 60,000 |
| Parts administration, at $2,000 per part ........ | 50 | 100,000 | 30 | 60,000 |
| Production orders, at $175 per order ........... | 100 | 17,500 | 300 | 52,500 |
| Material receipts, at $120 per receipt .......... | 150 | 18,000 | 600 | 72,000 |
| General factory, at $6.25 per MH ............ | 12,000 | 75,000 | 28,000 | 175,000 |
| Total overhead cost assigned (a) ............. |  | $316,500 |  | $483,500 |
| Number of units produced (b) ............... |  | 2,000 |  | 10,000 |
| Overhead cost per unit, (a) ÷ (b) ............ |  | $158.25 |  | $48.35 |

c.

|  | Deluxe | Tourist |
|---|---|---|
| Direct materials .................... | $ 25.00 | $ 17.00 |
| Direct labour ..................... | 60.00 | 48.00 |
| Manufacturing overhead (see above) .... | 158.25 | 48.35 |
| Unit product cost .................. | $243.25 | $113.35 |

Under activity-based costing, the unit product cost of the Deluxe deck chair is much greater than the cost computed in (2)(b) above, and the unit product cost of the Tourist deck chair is much less. Using volume (direct labour-hours) in (2)(b) as a basis for applying overhead cost to products has resulted in too little overhead cost being applied to the Deluxe deck chair (the low-volume product) and too much overhead cost being applied to the Tourist deck chair (the high-volume product).

# Glossary

**Activity** An event that causes the consumption of overhead resources in an organization. (p. 163)

**Activity-based costing (ABC)** A two-stage costing method in which overhead costs are assigned to products on the basis of the activities they require. (p. 163)

**Activity-based management (ABM)** A management approach that focuses on managing activities as a way of eliminating waste and reducing delays and defects. (p. 175)

**Activity cost pool** A "bucket" in which costs are accumulated that relate to a single activity in the activity-based costing system. (p. 164)

**Activity measure** An allocation base in an activity-based costing system; ideally, a measure of whatever causes the costs in an activity cost pool. (p. 164)

**Activity rate** A predetermined overhead rate in activity-based costing. Each activity cost pool has its own activity rate which is used to apply overhead to products and services. (p. 164)

**Batch-level activities** Activities that are performed each time a batch of goods is handled or processed, regardless of how many units are in a batch. The amount of resources consumed depends on the number of batches run, rather than on the number of units in the batch. (p. 165)

**Benchmarking** A systematic approach to identifying the activities with the greatest room for improvement. It is based on comparing the performance in an organization with the performance of other, similar organizations known for their outstanding performance. (p. 175)

**Facility-level activities** Activities that relate to overall production and therefore cannot be traced to specific products. Costs associated with these activities pertain to a plant's general manufacturing process. (p. 166)

**Product-level activities** Activities that relate to specific products that must be carried out regardless of how many units are produced and sold or batches run. (p. 165)

**Unit-level activities** Activities that arise as a result of the total volume of goods and services that are produced and that are performed each time a unit is produced. (p. 165)

# Questions

**5–1** What are the three common approaches for assigning overhead costs to products?

**5–2** Why is activity-based costing growing in popularity?

**5–3** Why do departmental overhead rates sometimes result in inaccurate product costs?

**5–4** What are the four hierarchical levels of activity discussed in the chapter?

**5–5** Why is activity-based costing described as a "two-stage" costing method?

**5–6** Why do overhead costs often shift from high-volume products to low-volume products when a company switches from a traditional costing method to activity-based costing?

**5–7** What are the three major ways in which activity-based costing improves the accuracy of product costs?

**5–8** What are the major limitations of activity-based costing?

# Brief Exercises

**BRIEF EXERCISE 5–1   ABC Cost Hierarchy (LO1)**

The following activities occur at Greenwich Corporation, a company that manufactures a variety of products.

a. Receive raw materials from suppliers.

b. Manage parts inventories.

c. Do rough milling work on products.

d. Interview and process new employees in the human resources department.

e. Design new products.

f. Perform periodic preventative maintenance on general-use equipment.

g. Use the general factory building.

h. Issue purchase orders for a job.

*Required:*

Classify each of the activities above as either a unit-level, batch-level, product-level, or facility-level activity.

**BRIEF EXERCISE 5–2    Compute Activity Rates** (LO2)

Kramer Corporation is a diversified manufacturer of consumer goods. The company's activity-based costing system has the following seven activity cost pools:

| Activity Cost Pool | Estimated Overhead Cost | Expected Activity |
|---|---|---|
| Labour related ............ | $ 48,000 | 20,000 direct labour-hours |
| Machine related ........... | 67,500 | 45,000 machine-hours |
| Machine setups ............ | 84,000 | 600 setups |
| Production orders .......... | 112,000 | 400 orders |
| Product testing ............ | 58,500 | 900 tests |
| Packaging ................ | 90,000 | 6,000 packages |
| General factory ............ | 672,000 | 20,000 direct labour-hours |

*Required:*

1. Compute the activity rate for each activity cost pool.
2. Compute the company's predetermined overhead rate, assuming that the company uses a single plantwide predetermined overhead rate based on direct labour-hours.

**BRIEF EXERCISE 5–3    Compute ABC Product Costs** (LO2)

Klumper Corporation is a diversified manufacturer of industrial goods. The company's activity-based costing system has the following six activity cost pools and activity rates:

| Activity Cost Pool | Activity Rates |
|---|---|
| Labour related ..................... | $ 6.00 per direct labour-hour |
| Machine related ................... | 4.00 per machine-hour |
| Machine setups .................... | 50.00 per setup |
| Production orders .................. | 90.00 per order |
| Shipments ........................ | 14.00 per shipment |
| General factory .................... | 9.00 per direct labour-hour |

Cost and activity data have been supplied for the following products:

| | K425 | M67 |
|---|---|---|
| Direct materials cost per unit ............ | $13.00 | $56.00 |
| Direct labour cost per unit .............. | $5.60 | $3.50 |
| Number of units produced per year ....... | 200 | 2,000 |

| | Total Expected Activity | |
|---|---|---|
| | K425 | M67 |
| Direct labour-hours ................... | 80 | 500 |
| Machine-hours ....................... | 100 | 1,500 |
| Machine setups ...................... | 1 | 4 |
| Production orders .................... | 1 | 4 |
| Shipments .......................... | 1 | 10 |

*Required:*

Compute the unit product cost of each of the products listed above.

**BRIEF EXERCISE 5–4    Contrast ABC and Traditional Product Costs** (LO2)

Midwest Industrial Products Corporation makes two products, Product H and Product L. Product H is expected to sell 50,000 units next year and Product L is expected to sell 10,000 units. A unit of either product requires 0.2 direct labour-hours.

The company's total manufacturing overhead for the year is expected to be $1,920,000.

***Required:***

1. The company currently applies manufacturing overhead to products using direct labour-hours as the allocation base. If this method is followed, how much overhead cost would be applied to each product? Compute both the overhead cost per unit and the total amount of overhead cost that would be applied to each product. (In other words, how much overhead cost is applied to a unit of Product H? Product L? How much overhead cost is applied in total to all the units of Product H? Product L?)

2. Management is considering an activity-based costing system and would like to know what impact this change might have on product costs. For purposes of discussion, it has been suggested that all of the manufacturing overhead be treated as a product-level cost. The total manufacturing overhead would be divided in half between the two products, with $960,000 assigned to Product H and $960,000 assigned to Product L.

    If this suggestion is followed, how much overhead cost per unit would be applied to each product?

3. Explain the impact on unit product costs of the switch in costing systems.

**BRIEF EXERCISE 5–5    Cost Flows in an ABC System** (LO5)

Larker Corporation implemented activity-based costing several years ago and uses it for its external financial reports. The company has four activity cost pools, which are listed below.

| Activity Cost Pool | Activity Rate |
|---|---|
| Machine related .................. | $24 per MH |
| Purchase orders ................. | $85 per order |
| Machine setups ................. | $175 per setup |
| General factory ................. | $16 per DLH |

At the beginning of the year, the company had inventory balances as follows:

| | |
|---|---|
| Raw materials ................... | $18,000 |
| Work in process ................ | 24,000 |
| Finished goods ................. | 46,000 |

Selected transactions recorded by the company during the year are given below:

a. Raw materials were purchased on account, $854,000.
b. Raw materials were requisitioned for use in production, $848,000 ($780,000 direct and $68,000 indirect).
c. Labour costs were incurred in the factory, $385,000 ($330,000 direct labour and $55,000 indirect labour).
d. Depreciation was recorded on factory assets, $225,000.
e. Miscellaneous manufacturing overhead costs were incurred, $194,000.
f. Manufacturing overhead cost was applied to production. Actual activity during the year was as follows:

| Activity Cost Pool | Actual Activity |
|---|---|
| Machine related .......... | 3,800 MHs |
| Purchase orders .......... | 700 orders |
| Machine setups........... | 400 setups |
| General factory........... | 22,000 DLHs |

g. Completed products were transferred to the company's finished goods warehouse. According to the company's costing system, these products cost $1,690,000.

***Required:***

1. Prepare journal entries to record transactions (a) through (g) above.

2. Post the entries in (1) above to T–accounts, and calculate the ending balance for each T–account.
3. Compute the under-applied or over-applied overhead cost in the Manufacturing Overhead account.

# Exercises

### EXERCISE 5–1   ABC Cost Hierarchy (LO1)
The following activities are carried out in Greenberry Company, a manufacturer of consumer goods.
a. Direct labour workers assemble a product.
b. Engineers design a new product.
c. A machine is set up to process a batch.
d. Numerically controlled machines cut and shape materials.
e. The HR department trains new employees concerning company policies.
f. Raw materials are moved from the receiving dock to the production line.
g. A random sample of 10 units is inspected for defects in each batch.

*Required:*
1. Classify each activity as a unit-level, batch-level, product-level, or facility-level cost.
2. Provide at least one example of an allocation base (i.e., activity measure) that could be used to allocate the cost of each activity listed above.

### EXERCISE 5–2   Contrast ABC and Traditional Product Costs (LO2)
Harrison Company makes two products and uses a conventional costing system in which a single plantwide predetermined overhead rate is computed based on direct labour-hours. Data for the two products for the upcoming year follow:

|  | Rascon | Parcel |
|---|---|---|
| Direct materials cost per unit . . . . . . . . . . | $13.00 | $22.00 |
| Direct labour cost per unit . . . . . . . . . . . . | $6.00 | $3.00 |
| Direct labour-hours per unit . . . . . . . . . . . | 0.40 | 0.20 |
| Number of units produced . . . . . . . . . . . . | 20,000 | 80,000 |

These products are customized to some degree for specific customers.

*Required:*
1. The company's manufacturing overhead costs for the year are expected to be $576,000. Using the company's traditional costing system, compute the unit product costs for the two products.
2. Management is considering an activity-based costing system in which half of the overhead would continue to be allocated on the basis of direct labour-hours and half would be allocated on the basis of engineering design time. This time is expected to be distributed as follows during the upcoming year:

|  | Rascon | Parcel | Total |
|---|---|---|---|
| Engineering design time (in hours) . . . . . . | 3,000 | 3,000 | 6,000 |

Compute the unit product costs for the two products using the proposed ABC system.

3. Explain why the product costs differ between the two systems.

### EXERCISE 5–3   Cost Flows in Activity-Based Costing (LO2, LO5)
Sylvan Company uses activity-based costing to determine product costs for external financial reports. Some of the entries have been completed to the Manufacturing Overhead account for the current year, as shown by entry (a) below:

**Manufacturing Overhead**

| (a) | 1,302,000 | |
|---|---|---|

*Required:*
1. What does the entry (a) above represent?
2. At the beginning of the year, the company made the following estimates of cost and activity for its five activity cost pools:

| Activity Cost Pool | Activity Measure | Estimated Overhead Cost | Expected Activity |
|---|---|---|---|
| Labour related ....... | Direct labour-hours | $280,000 | 40,000 DLHs |
| Purchase orders ...... | Number of orders | 90,000 | 1,500 orders |
| Parts management .... | Number of part types | 120,000 | 400 part types |
| Board etching ....... | Number of boards | 360,000 | 2,000 boards |
| General factory ...... | Machine-hours | 400,000 | 80,000 MHss |

Compute the activity rate (i.e., predetermined overhead rate) for each of the activity cost pools.
3. During the year, actual activity was recorded as follows:

| Activity Cost Pool | Actual Activity |
|---|---|
| Labour related ........... | 41,000 DLHs |
| Purchase orders .......... | 1,300 orders |
| Parts management ........ | 420 part types |
| Board etching ........... | 2,150 boards |
| General factory .......... | 82,000 MHs |

Determine the amount of manufacturing overhead cost applied to production for the year.
4. Determine the amount of under-applied or over-applied overhead cost for the year.

**EXERCISE 5–4  Assigning Overhead to Products in ABC** (LO2)
Refer to the data in Exercise 5–3 for Sylvan Company. The activities during the year were distributed across the company's four products as follows:

| Activity Cost Pool | Actual Activity | Product A | Product B | Product C | Product D |
|---|---|---|---|---|---|
| Labour related ... | 41,000 DLHs | 8,000 | 12,000 | 15,000 | 6,000 |
| Purchase orders .. | 1,300 orders | 100 | 300 | 400 | 500 |
| Parts management | 420 part types | 20 | 90 | 200 | 110 |
| Board etching .... | 2,150 boards | –0– | 1,500 | 650 | –0– |
| General factory ... | 82,000 MHs | 16,000 | 24,000 | 30,000 | 12,000 |

*Required:*
Compute the amount of overhead cost applied to each product during the year.

**EXERCISE 5–5  Activity-based Costing in Marketing and Sales** (LO2, LO3)
Kramer Corporation is an office supplier dealing in a number of different products. It currently allocates its ordering and delivery costs to its residential and business customer groups on the basis of order value. However, the company has recently decided to implement activity-based costing starting in 2005 to assign these costs to customers. Key data for 2004 are as follows:

| Activity | Activity Cost | Activity Base | Activity Volume Residential | Activity Volume Business | Total Activity Volume |
|---|---|---|---|---|---|
| Sales (order value) | | | $2,400,000 | $1,880,000 | $4,280,000 |
| Order processing | $ 480,000 | # of orders | 8,000 | 2,000 | 10,000 |
| Getting sales | 1,000,000 | # of sales calls | 1,000 | 4,000 | 5,000 |
| Sales follow-up | 540,000 | # of follow-ups | 100 | 500 | 600 |
| Processing change orders | 120,000 | # of change orders | 200 | 100 | 300 |
| Delivery | 850,000 | # of deliveries | 8,000 | 2,000 | 10,000 |

Kramer has 2,000 residential customers and 500 business customers.

*Required:*
1. Compute the cost per customer for residential and business customers for 2004, using the current system of cost allocation.
2. Assume that the 2004 data will hold for 2005. Compute the cost per customer for residential and business customers for 2005, using the proposed system of cost allocation. In doing so, compute the overhead allocation rate for each activity, and use these rates to assign costs to the two customer groups.
3. Explain the difference between the two cost allocation systems.

# Problems

### PROBLEM 5–1　ABC Cost Hierarchy (LO1)
Juneau Company manufactures a variety of products in a single facility. Consultants hired by the company to do an activity-based costing analysis have identified the following activities carried out in the company on a routine basis:
a. Machines are set up between batches of different products.
b. The company's grounds crew maintains planted areas surrounding the factory.
c. A percentage of all completed goods are inspected on a random basis.
d. Milling machines are used to make components for products.
e. Employees are trained in general procedures.
f. Purchase orders are issued for materials required in production.
g. The maintenance crew does routine periodic maintenance on general-purpose equipment.
h. The plant controller prepares periodic accounting reports.
i. Material is received on the receiving dock and moved to the production area.
j. The engineering department makes modifications in the designs of products.
k. The human resources department screens and hires new employees.
l. Production orders are issued for jobs.

*Required:*
1. Classify each of the above activities as a unit-level, batch-level, product-level, or facility-level activity.
2. For each of the above activities, suggest an activity measure that could be used to allocate its costs to products.

CHECK FIGURE
(3b) Regular: $152 per unit

### PROBLEM 5–2　Contrasting ABC and Traditional Product Costs (LO2)
Siegel Corporation manufactures a product that is available in both a deluxe and a regular model. The company has made the regular model for years; the deluxe model was introduced several years ago to tap a new segment of the market. Since the introduction of the deluxe model, the company's profits have steadily declined, and management has become concerned about the accuracy of its costing system. Sales of the deluxe model have been increasing rapidly.

Overhead is applied to products on the basis of direct labour-hours. At the beginning of the current year, management estimated that $2,000,000 in overhead costs would be incurred and the company would produce and sell 5,000 units of the deluxe model and 40,000 units of the regular model. The deluxe model requires 1.6 hours of direct labour time per unit, and the regular model requires 0.8 hours. Materials and labour costs per unit are given below:

|  | Deluxe | Regular |
|---|---|---|
| Direct materials cost per unit ......... | $150 | $112 |
| Direct labour cost per unit ........... | 16 | 8 |

*Required:*
1. Compute the predetermined overhead rate using direct labour-hours as the basis for allocating overhead costs to products. Compute the unit product cost for one unit of each model.

2. An intern suggested that the company use activity-based costing to cost its products. A team was formed to investigate this idea, and it came back with the recommendation that four activity cost pools be used. These cost pools and their associated activities are listed below:

| Activity Cost Pool and Activity Measure | Estimated Overhead Cost | Activity | | |
| --- | --- | --- | --- | --- |
| | | Total | Deluxe | Regular |
| Purchase orders (number of orders) . . . . . | $    84,000 | 1,200 | 400 | 800 |
| Rework requests (number of requests) . . . | 216,000 | 900 | 300 | 600 |
| Product testing (number of tests) . . . . . . . | 450,000 | 15,000 | 4,000 | 11,000 |
| Machine-related (machine-hours) . . . . . . | 1,250,000 | 50,000 | 20,000 | 30,000 |
| | $2,000,000 | | | |

Compute the activity rate (i.e., predetermined overhead rate) for each of the activity cost pools.
3. Assume that actual activity is as expected for the year. Using activity-based costing, do the following:
   a. Determine the total amount of overhead that would be applied to each model for the year.
   b. Compute the unit product cost for one unit of each model.
4. Can you identify a possible explanation for the company's declining profits? If so, what is it?

**PROBLEM 5–3   Cost Flows and Unit Product Costs in Activity-Based Costing (LO2, LO5)**
Hunter Corporation uses activity-based costing to determine product costs for external financial reports. At the beginning of the year, management made the following estimates of cost and activity in the company's five activity cost pools:

CHECK FIGURE
(2d) Total overhead
over-applied:
$15,000

| Activity Cost Pool | Activity Measure | Estimated Overhead Cost | Expected Activity |
| --- | --- | --- | --- |
| Labour related . . . . . . . . | Direct labour-hours | $270,000 | 30,000 DLHs |
| Production orders . . . . . | Number of orders | 60,000 | 750 orders |
| Material receipts . . . . . . | Number of receipts | 180,000 | 1,200 receipts |
| Relay assembly . . . . . . . | Number of relays | 320,000 | 8,000 relays |
| General factory . . . . . . . | Machine-hours | 840,000 | 60,000 MHs |

*Required:*
1. Compute the activity rate (i.e., predetermined overhead rate) for each of the activity cost pools.
2. During the year, actual overhead cost and activity were recorded as follows:

| Activity Cost Pool | Actual Overhead Cost | Actual Activity |
| --- | --- | --- |
| Labour related . . . . . . . . . . . . . . | $   279,000 | 32,000 DLHs |
| Production orders . . . . . . . . . . . | 58,000 | 700 orders |
| Material receipts . . . . . . . . . . . . | 190,000 | 1,300 receipts |
| Relay assembly . . . . . . . . . . . . . | 320,000 | 7,900 relays |
| General factory . . . . . . . . . . . . . | 847,000 | 61,000 MHs |
| Total overhead cost . . . . . . . . . . | $1,694,000 | |

   a. Prepare a journal entry to record the incurrence of actual manufacturing overhead cost for the year (credit Accounts Payable). Post the entry to the company's Manufacturing Overhead T-account.
   b. Determine the amount of overhead cost applied to production during the year.
   c. Prepare a journal entry to record the application of manufacturing overhead cost to work in process for the year. Post the entry to the company's Manufacturing Overhead T-account.
   d. Determine the amount of under-applied or over-applied manufacturing overhead for the year.

3.  The actual activity for the year was distributed among the company's four products as follows:

| Activity Cost Pool | Actual Activity | Product A | Product B | Product C | Product D |
|---|---|---|---|---|---|
| Labour related . . . . . . . . . | 32,000 DLHs | 8,000 | 11,000 | 4,000 | 9,000 |
| Production orders . . . . . . | 700 orders | 160 | 200 | 130 | 210 |
| Materials receipts . . . . . . | 1,300 receipts | 100 | 460 | 240 | 500 |
| Relay assembly . . . . . . . . | 7,900 relays | 2,700 | –0– | 5,200 | –0– |
| General factory . . . . . . . . | 61,000 MHs | 13,000 | 18,000 | 14,000 | 16,000 |

a.  Determine the total amount of overhead cost applied to each product.
b.  Does the total amount of overhead cost applied to the products above "tie in" to the T-accounts in any way? Explain.

CHECK FIGURE
(2b) X200 unit product
cost: $213

**PROBLEM 5–4   Contrast Activity-Based Costing and Traditional Product Costs (LO2)**
Ellix Company manufactures two models of ultra-high-fidelity speakers, the X200 model and the X99 model. Data regarding the two products follow:

| | Direct Labour-Hours per Unit | Annual Production | Total Direct Labour-Hours |
|---|---|---|---|
| Model X200 . . . . . . . . . | 1.8 | 5,000 units | 9,000 |
| Model X99 . . . . . . . . . . | 0.9 | 30,000 units | 27,000 |
| | | | 36,000 |

Additional information about the company follows:
a.  Model X200 requires $72 in direct materials per unit, and model X99 requires $50.
b.  The direct labour wage rate is $10 per hour.
c.  The company has always used direct labour-hours as the base for applying manufacturing overhead cost to products.
d.  Model X200 is more complex to manufacture than model X99 and requires the use of special equipment. Consequently, the company is considering the use of activity-based costing to apply manufacturing overhead cost to products for external financial reports. Three activity cost pools have been identified as follows:

| Activity Cost Pool | Activity Measure | Estimated Overhead Cost |
|---|---|---|
| Machine setups . . . . . . . . . . . | Number of setups | $   360,000 |
| Special processing . . . . . . . . | Machine-hours | 180,000 |
| General factory . . . . . . . . . . | Direct labour-hours | 1,260,000 |
| | | $1,800,000 |

| | Expected Activity | | |
|---|---|---|---|
| Activity Measure | Model X200 | Model X99 | Total |
| Number of setups . . . . . . . . | 50 | 100 | 150 |
| Machine-hours . . . . . . . . . . | 12,000 | –0– | 12,000 |
| Direct labour-hours . . . . . . | 9,000 | 27,000 | 36,000 |

*Required:*
1.  Assume that the company continues to use direct labour-hours as the base for applying overhead cost to products.
    a.  Compute the predetermined overhead rate.

b. Compute the unit product cost of each model.
2. Assume that the company decides to use activity-based costing to apply manufacturing overhead cost to products.
   a. Compute the predetermined overhead rate for each activity cost pool and determine the amount of overhead cost that would be applied to each model using the activity-based costing system.
   b. Compute the unit product cost of each model.
3. Explain why the manufacturing overhead cost shifts from Model X99 to Model X200 under activity-based costing.

## PROBLEM 5–5   Activity-Based Costing Cost Flows (LO2, LO5)

Munoz Corporation uses activity-based costing to determine product costs for external financial reports. At the beginning of the year, management made the following estimates of cost and activity in the company's five activity cost pools:

CHECK FIGURE
(2d) Total overhead
under-applied:
$17,000

| Activity Cost Pool | Activity Measure | Estimated Overhead Cost | Expected Activity |
|---|---|---|---|
| Labour related ...... | Direct labour-hours | $210,000 | 35,000 DLHs |
| Purchase orders ..... | Number of orders | 72,000 | 900 orders |
| Product testing ...... | Number of tests | 168,000 | 1,400 tests |
| Template etching .... | Number of templates | 315,000 | 10,500 templates |
| General factory ..... | Machine-hours | 840,000 | 70,000 MHs |

### Required:
1. Compute the activity rate (i.e., predetermined overhead rate) for each of the activity cost pools.
2. During the year, actual overhead cost and activity were recorded as follows:

| Activity Cost Pool | Actual Overhead Cost | Actual Activity |
|---|---|---|
| Labour related ..................... | $ 205,000 | 32,000 DLHs |
| Purchase orders .................... | 74,000 | 950 orders |
| Product testing ................... | 160,000 | 1,300 tests |
| Template etching ................... | 338,000 | 11,500 relays |
| General factory .................... | 825,000 | 68,000 MHs |
| Total overhead cost ................. | $1,602,000 | |

a. Prepare a journal entry to record the incurrence of actual manufacturing overhead cost for the year (credit Accounts Payable). Post the entry to the company's Manufacturing Overhead T-account.
b. Determine the amount of overhead cost applied to production during the year.
c. Prepare a journal entry to record the application of manufacturing overhead cost to work in process for the year. Post the entry to the company's Manufacturing Overhead T-account.
d. Determine the amount of under-applied or over-applied manufacturing overhead for the year.
3. The actual activity for the year was distributed among the company's four products as follows:

| Activity Cost Pool | Actual Activity | Product A | Product B | Product C | Product D |
|---|---|---|---|---|---|
| Labour related ...... | 32,000 DLHs | 6,000 | 7,500 | 10,000 | 8,500 |
| Purchase orders ...... | 950 orders | 150 | 300 | 100 | 400 |
| Product testing ....... | 1,300 tests | 400 | 175 | 225 | 500 |
| Template etching ..... | 11,500 templates | –0– | 4,500 | –0– | 7,000 |
| General factory ...... | 68,000 MHs | 10,000 | 20,000 | 17,000 | 21,000 |

a. Determine the total amount of overhead cost applied to each product.
b. Does the total amount of overhead cost applied to the products above "tie in" to the T-accounts in any way? Explain.

**PROBLEM 5–6    Activity-Based Costing Cost Flows and Income Statement (LO2, LO5)**

Aucton Corporation is a manufacturing company that uses activity-based costing for its external financial reports. The company's activity cost pools and associated data for the coming year appear below:

| Activity Cost Pool | Activity Measure | Estimated Overhead Cost | Expected Activity |
|---|---|---|---|
| Machining . . . . . . . . . | Machine-hours | $180,000 | 1,000 MHs |
| Purchase orders . . . . . . | Number of orders | 90,000 | 600 orders |
| Parts management . . . . | Number of part types | 60,000 | 300 part types |
| Testing . . . . . . . . . . . . | Number of tests | 150,000 | 250 tests |
| General factory . . . . . . | Direct labour-hours | 280,000 | 20,000 DLHs |

At the beginning of the year, the company had inventory balances as follows:

| | |
|---|---|
| Raw materials . . . . . . . . . . . . . . . . . . . . . . | $ 7,000 |
| Work in process . . . . . . . . . . . . . . . . . . . . | 6,000 |
| Finished goods . . . . . . . . . . . . . . . . . . . . . | 10,000 |

The following transactions were recorded for the year:

a. Raw materials were purchased on account, $595,000.
b. Raw materials were withdrawn from the storeroom for use in production, $600,000 ($560,000 direct and $40,000 indirect).
c. The following costs were incurred for employee services: direct labour, $90,000; indirect labour, $300,000; sales commissions, $85,000; and administrative salaries, $245,000.
d. Sales travel costs were incurred, $38,000.
e. Various factory overhead costs were incurred, $237,000.
f. Advertising costs were incurred, $190,000.
g. Depreciation was recorded for the year, $270,000 ($210,000 related to factory operations and $60,000 related to selling and administrative activities).
h. Manufacturing overhead was applied to products. Actual activity for the year was as follows:

| Activity Cost Pool | Actual Activity |
|---|---|
| Machining . . . . . . . . . . . . . . . . . . . | 1,050 MHs |
| Purchase orders . . . . . . . . . . . . . . | 580 orders |
| Parts management . . . . . . . . . . . . | 330 part types |
| Testing . . . . . . . . . . . . . . . . . . . . . | 265 tests |
| General factory . . . . . . . . . . . . . . . | 21,000 DLHs |

i. Goods were completed and transferred to the finished goods warehouse. According to the company's activity-based costing system, these finished goods cost $1,450,000 to manufacture.
j. Goods were sold on account to customers during the year for a total of $2,100,000. According to the company's activity-based costing system, the goods cost $1,400,000 to manufacture.

*Required:*
1. Compute the predetermined overhead rate (i.e., activity rate) for each activity cost pool.
2. Prepare journal entries to record transactions (a) through (j) above.
3. Post the entries in (2) above to T-accounts.
4. Compute the under-applied or over-applied manufacturing overhead cost. Prepare a journal entry to close any balance in the Manufacturing Overhead account to Cost of Goods Sold. Post the entry to the appropriate T-accounts.
5. Prepare an income statement for the year.

**PROBLEM 5–7    Contrasting ABC and Traditional Product Costs (LO2)**

For many years, Zapro Company manufactured a single product called a mono-relay. Then, three years ago, the company automated a portion of its plant and at the same time introduced a second product called a bi-relay that has become increasingly popular. The bi-relay is a more complex product, requiring one hour of direct labour time per unit to manufacture and extensive machining in the automated portion of the plant. The mono-relay requires only 0.75 hour of direct labour time per unit and only a small amount of machining. Manufacturing overhead costs are currently assigned to products on the basis of direct labour-hours.

Despite the growing popularity of the company's new bi-relay, profits have been declining steadily. Management is beginning to believe that there may be a problem with the company's costing system. Material and labour costs per unit are as follows:

| | Mono-Relay | Bi-Relay |
|---|---|---|
| Direct materials | $35 | $48 |
| Direct labour (0.75 hour and 1.0 hour @ $12 per hour) | 9 | 12 |

Management estimates that the company will incur $1,000,000 in manufacturing overhead costs during the current year and 40,000 units of the mono-relay and 10,000 units of the bi-relay will be produced and sold.

*Required:*

1. Compute the predetermined manufacturing overhead rate assuming that the company continues to apply manufacturing overhead cost on the basis of direct labour-hours. Using this rate and other data from the problem, determine the unit product cost of each product.

2. Management is considering using activity-based costing to apply manufacturing overhead cost to products for external financial reports. The activity-based costing system would have the following four activity cost pools:

| Activity Cost Pool | Activity Measure | Estimated Overhead Cost |
|---|---|---|
| Maintaining parts inventory | Number of part types | $ 180,000 |
| Processing purchase orders | Number of purchase orders | 90,000 |
| Quality control | Number of tests run | 230,000 |
| Machine related | Machine-hours | 500,000 |
| | | $1,000,000 |

| | Expected Activity | | |
|---|---|---|---|
| Activity Measure | Mono-Relay | Bi-Relay | Total |
| Number of part types | 75 | 150 | 225 |
| Number of purchase orders | 800 | 200 | 1,000 |
| Number of tests run | 2,500 | 3,250 | 5,750 |
| Machine-hours | 4,000 | 6,000 | 10,000 |

Determine the activity rate (i.e., predetermined overhead rate) for each of the four activity cost pools.

3. Using the activity rates you computed in (2) above, do the following:
   a. Compute the total amount of manufacturing overhead cost that would be applied to each product using the activity-based costing system. After these totals have been computed, determine the amount of manufacturing overhead cost per unit of each product.
   b. Compute the unit product cost of each product.

4. From the data you have developed in (1) through (3) above, identify factors that may account for the company's declining profits.

**PROBLEM 5–8   Compute and Use Activity Rates to Determine the Costs of Serving Customers (LO2, LO3)**

CHECK FIGURE
(3b) $11.95 per diner

Jordan's Lakeside is a popular restaurant located on Lake Muskoka in Ontario. The owner of the restaurant has been trying to better understand costs at the restaurant and has hired a student intern to conduct an activity-based costing study. The intern, in consultation with the owner, identified the following major activities:

| Activity Cost Pool | Activity Measure |
|---|---|
| Serving a party of diners | Number of parties served |
| Serving a diner | Number of diners served |
| Serving drinks | Number of drinks ordered |

A group of diners who ask to sit at the same table are counted as a party. Some costs, such as the costs of cleaning linen, are the same whether one person is at a table or the table is full. Other costs, such as washing dishes, depend on the number of diners served.

Data concerning these activities are displayed below.

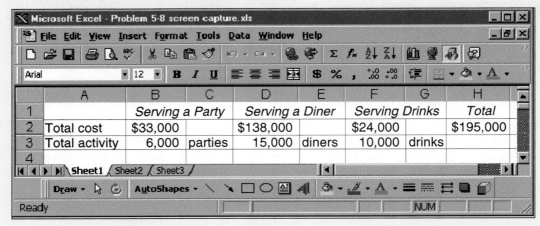

| | A | B | C | D | E | F | G | H |
|---|---|---|---|---|---|---|---|---|
| 1 | | *Serving a Party* | | *Serving a Diner* | | *Serving Drinks* | | *Total* |
| 2 | Total cost | $33,000 | | $138,000 | | $24,000 | | $195,000 |
| 3 | Total activity | 6,000 | parties | 15,000 | diners | 10,000 | drinks | |
| 4 | | | | | | | | |

Prior to the activity-based costing study, the owner knew very little about the costs of the restaurant. She knew that the total cost for the month was $195,000 and that 15,000 diners had been served. Therefore, the average cost per diner was $13 ($195,000 ÷ 15,000 diners = $13 per diner).

***Required:***

1. Compute the activity rates for each of the three activities.
2. According to the activity-based costing system, what is the total cost of serving each of the following parties of diners?
   a. A party of four diners who order three drinks in total.
   b. A party of two diners who do not order any drinks.
   c. A lone diner who orders two drinks.
3. Convert the total costs you computed in (1) above to costs per diner. In other words, what is the average cost per diner for serving each of the following parties of diners?
   a. A party of four diners who order three drinks in total.
   b. A party of two diners who do not order any drinks.
   c. A lone diner who orders two drinks.
4. Why do the costs per diner for the three different parties differ from each other and from the overall average cost of $13 per diner?

# Building Your Skills

CHECK FIGURE
(2) Standard model unit
    product cost: $29.98
    per unit

**ANALYTICAL THINKING\***   (LO2)

"A dollar of gross margin per briefcase? That's ridiculous!" roared Art Dejans, president of CarryAll, Inc. "Why do we go on producing those standard briefcases when we're able to make over $15 per unit on our specialty items? Maybe it's time to get out of the standard line and focus the whole plant on specialty work."

Mr. Dejans is referring to a summary of unit costs and revenues that he had just received from the company's Accounting Department:

| | Standard Briefcases | Specialty Briefcases |
|---|---|---|
| Selling price per unit ............ | $36 | $40 |
| Unit product cost .............. | 35 | 25 |
| Gross margin per unit ............ | $ 1 | $15 |

---

\*Adapted from a case written by Harold P. Roth and Imogene Posey, "Management Accounting Case Study: CarryAll Company," *Management Accounting Campus Report*, Institute of Management Accountants (Fall 1991), p. 9. Used by permission.

CarryAll produces briefcases from leather, fabric, and synthetic materials in a single plant. The basic product is a standard briefcase that is made from leather lined with fabric. The standard briefcase is a high-quality item and has sold well for many years.

Last year, the company decided to expand its product line and produce specialty briefcases for special orders. These briefcases differ from the standard in that they vary in size, they contain the finest synthetic materials, and they are imprinted with the buyer's name. To reduce labour costs on the specialty briefcases, most of the cutting and stitching is done by automated machines. These machines are used to a much lesser degree in the production of standard briefcases.

"I agree that the specialty business is looking better and better," replied Sally Henrie, the company's marketing manager. "And there seems to be plenty of specialty work out there, particularly since the competition hasn't been able to touch our price. Did you know that Armor Company, our biggest competitor, charges over $50 a unit for its specialty items? Now that's what I call gouging the customer!"

A breakdown of the manufacturing cost for each of CarryAll's product lines is given below:

|  | Standard Briefcases | | Specialty Briefcases | |
|---|---|---|---|---|
| Units produced each month .. | | 10,000 | | 2,500 |
| Direct materials: | | | | |
| Leather ................ | 1.0 sq. yd. | $15.00 | 0.5 sq. yd. | $ 7.50 |
| Fabric ................. | 1.0 sq. yd. | 5.00 | 1.0 sq. yd. | 5.00 |
| Synthetic ............. | | — | | 5.00 |
| Total materials ........ | | 20.00 | | 17.50 |
| Direct labour ............ | 0.5 hr. @ $12 | 6.00 | 0.25 hr. @ $12 | 3.00 |
| Manufacturing overhead .... | 0.5 hr. @ $18 | 9.00 | 0.25 hr. @ $18 | 4.50 |
| Unit product cost ...... | | $35.00 | | $25.00 |

Manufacturing overhead is applied to products on the basis of direct labour-hours. The rate of $18 per direct labour-hour is determined by dividing the total manufacturing overhead cost for a month by the direct labour-hours:

$$\frac{\text{Manufacturing overhead cost, } \$101{,}250}{\text{Direct labour-hours, } 5{,}625} = \$18 \text{ per DLH}$$

The following additional information is available about the company and its products:

a. Standard briefcases are produced in batches of 200 units, and specialty briefcases are produced in batches of 25 units. Thus, the company does 50 setups for the standard items each month and 100 setups for the specialty items. A setup for the standard items requires one hour of time, whereas a setup for the specialty items requires two hours of time.

b. All briefcases are inspected to ensure that quality standards are met. A total of 300 hours of inspection time is spent on the standard briefcases and 500 hours of inspection time is spent on the specialty briefcases each month.

c. A standard briefcase requires 0.5 hour of machine time, and a specialty briefcase requires two hours of machine time.

d. The company is considering the use of activity-based costing as an alternative to its traditional costing system for computing unit product costs. Since these unit product costs will be used for external financial reporting, all manufacturing overhead costs are to be allocated to products and nonmanufacturing costs are to be excluded from product costs. The activity-based costing system has already been designed and costs allocated to the activity cost pools. The activity cost pools and activity measures are detailed below:

| Activity Cost Pool | Activity Measure | Estimated Overhead Cost |
|---|---|---|
| Purchasing ......................... | Number of orders | $ 12,000 |
| Material handling ................... | Number of receipts | 15,000 |
| Production orders and setup ........... | Setup hours | 20,250 |
| Inspection ......................... | Inspection-hours | 16,000 |
| Frame assembly .................... | Assembly-hours | 8,000 |
| Machine related ................... | Machine-hours | 30,000 |
| | | $101,250 |

| Activity Measure | Expected Activity | | |
| | Standard Briefcase | Specialty Briefcase | Total |
| --- | --- | --- | --- |
| Number of orders: | | | |
| Leather . . . . . . . . . . . . . . . . . . | 34 | 6 | 40 |
| Fabric . . . . . . . . . . . . . . . . . . | 48 | 12 | 60 |
| Synthetic material . . . . . . . . . | — | 100 | 100 |
| Number of receipts: | | | |
| Leather . . . . . . . . . . . . . . . . . . | 52 | 8 | 60 |
| Fabric . . . . . . . . . . . . . . . . . . | 64 | 16 | 80 |
| Synthetic material . . . . . . . . . | — | 160 | 160 |
| Setup hours . . . . . . . . . . . . . . . | ? | ? | ? |
| Inspection-hours . . . . . . . . . . . . | ? | ? | ? |
| Assembly-hours . . . . . . . . . . . . | 800 | 800 | 1,600 |
| Machine-hours . . . . . . . . . . . . . | ? | ? | ? |

*Required:*
1. Using activity-based costing determine the amount of manufacturing overhead cost that would be applied to each standard briefcase and each specialty briefcase.
2. Using the data computed in (1) above and other data from the case as needed, determine the unit product cost of each product line from the perspective of the activity-based costing system.
3. Within the limitations of the data that have been provided, evaluate the president's concern about the profitability of the two product lines. Would you recommend that the company shift its resources entirely to production of specialty briefcases? Explain.
4. Sally Henrie stated that "the competition hasn't been able to touch our price" on specialty business. Why do you suppose the competition has not been able to touch CarryAll's price?

### COMMUNICATING IN PRACTICE   (LO1, LO2)
You often provide advice to Maria Graham, a client who is interested in diversifying her company. Maria is considering the purchase of a small manufacturing concern that assembles and packages its many products by hand. She plans to automate the factory and her projections indicate that the company will once again be profitable within two to three years. During her review of the company's records, she discovered that the company currently uses direct labour-hours to allocate overhead to its products. Because of its simplicity, Maria hopes that this approach can continue to be used.

*Required:*
Write a memorandum to Maria that addresses whether or not direct labour should continue to be used as an allocation base for overhead.

### ETHICS CHALLENGE   (LO1, LO3)
You and your friends go to a restaurant as a group. At the end of the meal, the issue arises of how the bill for the group should be shared. One alternative is to figure out the cost of what each individual consumed and divide up the bill accordingly. Another alternative is to split the bill equally among the individuals.

*Required:*
Which system for dividing the bill is more equitable? Which system is easier to use? How does this issue relate to the material covered in this chapter?

### TEAMWORK IN ACTION   (LO1)
This activity requires teamwork to reinforce the understanding of the hierarchy of activities commonly found in activity-based costing systems in manufacturing companies.

*Required:*
1. The team should discuss and then write up a brief description of how the activity-based costing allocates overhead to products. All team members should agree with and understand the description.

2. Without referring to the related section in the text, each member of the team should choose one of the following levels of activities, define the level of activity chosen and provide one or more examples of the tasks that are performed at that level of activity in a manufacturing firm:
   a. Unit-level activities.
   b. Batch-level activities.
   c. Product-level activities.
   d. Facility-level activities.
3. Each team member should present his or her answers from part 2 to the other teammates who should confirm or correct those answers.

Do not forget to check out Taking It to the Net as well as all the other quizzes and resources at the Online Learning Centre at www.mcgrawhill.ca/college/garrison.

# Chapter Six

# Cost Behaviour: Analysis and Use

## A Look Back

We provided overviews of the systems that are used to accumulate product costs in Chapters 3, 4, and 5.

## A Look at This Chapter

After reviewing the behaviour of variable and fixed costs, in Chapter 6 we discuss mixed costs, a third type of behavioural pattern, and overview the methods that can be used to break a mixed cost into its variable and fixed components. We also introduce the contribution format income statement, which is used inside companies for decision making.

## A Look Ahead

Chapter 7 describes the basics of cost-volume-profit analysis, a tool that helps managers understand the inter-relationships among cost, volume, and profit.

## Chapter Outline

**Types of Cost Behaviour Patterns**
- Variable Costs
- True Variable versus Step-Variable Costs
- The Linearity Assumption and the Relevant Range
- Fixed Costs
- Types of Fixed Costs
- Fixed Costs and the Relevant Range
- Mixed Costs

**The Analysis of Mixed Costs**
- The High-Low Method
- The Scattergraph Method
- The Least-Squares Regression Method

**The Contribution Format**
- Why a New Income Statement Format?
- The Contribution Approach

# DECISION FEATURE Back on Track

Imagine a company operating in the railroad industry derailing. After suffering a loss in 2001, management at Calgary-based Global Railway Industries Limited knew it was time to get back on track.

Global Railway is a fast-growing company that has pursued an aggressive "growth by acquisition" strategy; it offers its products and services to rail and transit carriers through its four businesses: three Canadian and one American. This acquisition strategy allowed Global to expand its offerings and its customer base. Needless to say, this strategy has delivered the results. Sales increased from $7.1 million in 2001 to $12.6 million in 2002, and $20.2 million in the first nine months of 2003.

Just increasing sales was not enough to remain on track, and Mike Kohut, President and CEO, recognized this fact. With a view to increasing the gross margin, he encouraged his company to convert to a largely variable cost structure. This could translate into higher efficiencies because the company did not have a large amount of fixed resources, and what it had was not be fully utilized. A thorough understanding of costs with a focus on cost behaviour can position the company to better understand the implications of fixed versus variable cost structures on profitability. Kohut was bang on target; net income came in at 11.7% of sales in 2002 and 12.2% in the first nine months of 2003!

Sources: Yturralde, L., "Bay Street's Boarding Global Railway," www.investorfile.com, Special Report, November 7, 2003; Financial Reports of Global Railway available at www.globalrailway.com.

## Learning Objectives

*After studying Chapter 6, you should be able to:*

**LO1** Understand how fixed and variable costs behave and how to use them to predict costs.

**LO2** Analyze a mixed cost using the high-low method.

**LO3** Analyze a mixed cost using the scattergraph method.

**LO4** Analyze a mixed cost using least-squares regression.

**LO5** Prepare and interpret an income statement using the contribution format.

In our discussion of cost terms and concepts in Chapter 2, we stated that one way in which costs can be classified is by behaviour. We defined cost behaviour as the way a cost reacts or changes as changes take place in the level of business activity. An understanding of cost behaviour is the key to many decisions in an organization. Managers who understand how costs behave are better able to predict costs under various operating circumstances. Attempts at decision making without a thorough understanding of the costs involved—and how these costs may change with the activity level—can lead to disaster. For example, a decision to cut back a particular product line might result in far less cost savings than managers had assumed if they confuse variable and fixed costs—leading to a decline in profits. To avoid such problems, a manager must be able to accurately predict what costs will be at various activity levels. In this chapter, we shall find that the key to effective cost prediction lies in understanding variable and fixed costs.

We briefly review in this chapter the definitions of variable costs and fixed costs and then discuss the behaviour of these costs in greater depth than we were able to do in Chapter 2. After this review and discussion, we turn our attention to the analysis of mixed costs. We conclude the chapter by introducing a new income statement format—called the contribution format—in which costs are organized by behaviour rather than by the traditional functions of production, sales, and administration.

## Types of Cost Behaviour Patterns

Concept 6–1

In Chapter 2, we mentioned only variable and fixed costs. In this chapter, we will discuss a third behaviour pattern, generally known as a *mixed* cost. All three cost behaviour patterns—variable, fixed, and mixed—are found in most organizations. The relative proportion of each type of cost present in a firm is known as the firm's **cost structure.** For example, a firm might have many fixed costs but few variable or mixed costs. Alternatively, it might have many variable costs but few fixed or mixed costs. A firm's cost structure can have a significant impact on decisions. In this chapter, we will concentrate on getting a better understanding of the behaviour of each type of cost. In the next chapter, we will discuss more fully how cost structure impacts decisions.

# Variable Costs

We explained in Chapter 2 that a variable cost is a cost whose total dollar amount varies in direct proportion to changes in the activity level. If the activity level doubles, the total dollar amount of the variable cost also doubles. If the activity level increases by only 10%, then the total dollar amount of the variable cost increases by 10% as well.

We also found in Chapter 2 that a variable cost remains constant when expressed on a *per-unit* basis. To provide an example, consider 50 Plus Expeditions, a Toronto-based company that organizes adventure travel for people over 50. Among other things, the company provides all of the necessary equipment and experienced guides and serves meals to its guests. Assume that the meals cost $30 per person for a daylong excursion. If we look at the cost of the meals on a *per-person* basis, the cost remains constant at $30. This unit cost of $30 per person will not change, regardless of how many people participate in a daylong excursion. The behaviour of this variable cost, on both per-unit and total bases, is tabulated below:

| Number of Guests | Cost of Meals per Guest | Total Cost of Meals |
|---|---|---|
| 250 .......... | $30 | $ 7,500 |
| 500 .......... | 30 | 15,000 |
| 750 .......... | 30 | 22,500 |
| 1,000 .......... | 30 | 30,000 |

The idea that a variable cost is constant per unit but varies in total with the activity level is crucial to an understanding of cost behaviour patterns. We shall rely on this concept again and again in this chapter and in the chapters ahead.

Exhibit 6–1 provides a graphic illustration of variable cost behaviour. Note that the graph of the total cost of the meals slants upward to the right. This is because the total cost of the meals is directly proportional to the number of guests. In contrast, the graph of the per unit cost of meals is flat. This is because the cost of the meals per guest is constant at $30 per guest.

**Learning Objective 1**
Understand how fixed and variable costs behave and how to use them to predict costs.

## Exhibit 6–1
Variable Cost Behaviour

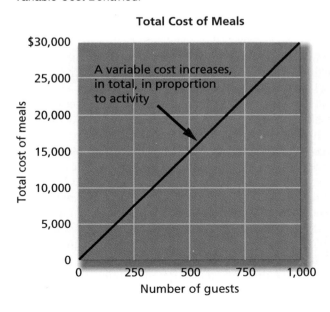

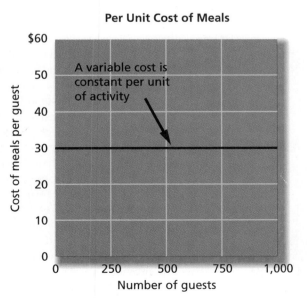

**THE ACTIVITY BASE**   For a cost to be variable, it must be variable *with respect to something*. That "something" is its *activity base*. An **activity base** is a measure of whatever causes the incurrence of variable cost. An activity base is also sometimes referred to as a *cost driver*. Some of the most common activity bases are direct labour-hours, machine-hours, units produced, volume of goods sold or services provided, and number of customers served. Other activity bases (cost drivers) might include the number of miles driven by salespersons, the number of kilograms of laundry cleaned by a hotel, the number of letters typed by a secretary, and the number of beds occupied in a hospital.

To plan and control variable costs, a manager must be well acquainted with the various activity bases within the firm. People sometimes get the notion that if a cost does not vary with production or with sales, then it is not really a variable cost. This is not correct. As suggested by the range of bases listed above, costs are caused by many different activities within an organization. Whether a cost is considered to be variable depends on whether it is caused by the activity under consideration. For example, if a manager is analyzing the cost of service calls under a product warranty, the relevant activity measure will be the number of service calls made. Those costs that vary in total with the number of service calls made are the variable costs of making service calls.

Nevertheless, unless stated otherwise, you can assume that the activity base under consideration is the total volume of goods and services provided by the organization. So, for example, if we ask whether direct materials at Ford is a variable cost, the answer is yes, since the cost of direct materials is variable with respect to Ford's total volume of output. We will specify the activity base only when it is something other than total output.

*decision* | *maker*          **Budget Analyst**

You are the budget analyst for a firm that provides janitorial services to other companies. You have been asked to estimate the costs that will be incurred on the janitorial jobs that will be performed next year. What types of costs would you expect? How would you characterize these costs in terms of behaviour? What activity would you need to measure in order to estimate the costs?

**EXTENT OF VARIABLE COSTS**   The number and type of variable costs present in an organization will depend in large part on the organization's structure and purpose. A public utility, such as B C Hydro, with large investments in equipment will tend to have few variable costs. Most of the costs are associated with its plant, and these costs tend to be insensitive to changes in levels of service provided. A manufacturing company, such as Black and Decker, in contrast, will often have many variable costs; these costs will be associated with both the manufacture and distribution of its products to customers.

A merchandising company, such as Wal-Mart or Safeway will usually have a high proportion of variable costs in its cost structure. In most merchandising companies, the cost of merchandise purchased for resale, a variable cost, constitutes a very large component of total cost. Service companies, by contrast, have diverse cost structures. Some service companies, such as the Boston Pizza restaurant chain, have fairly large variable costs because of the costs of their raw materials. On the other hand, service companies involved in consulting, auditing, engineering, dental, medical, and architectural activities have very large fixed costs in the form of expensive facilities and highly trained salaried employees.

Some of the more frequently encountered variable costs are listed in Exhibit 6–2. This exhibit is not a complete listing of all costs that can be considered variable. Moreover, some of the costs listed in the exhibit may behave more like fixed than variable costs in some firms. We will see some examples of this later in the chapter. Nevertheless, Exhibit 6–2 provides a useful listing of many of the costs that normally would be considered variable with respect to the volume of output.

**Exhibit 6–2**
Examples of Variable Costs

| Type of Organization | Costs that Are Normally Variable with Respect to Volume of Output |
|---|---|
| Merchandising company | Cost of goods (merchandise) sold |
| Manufacturing company | Manufacturing costs: |
| |    Direct materials |
| |    Direct labour* |
| | Variable portion of manufacturing overhead: |
| |    Indirect materials |
| |    Lubricants |
| |    Supplies |
| Both merchandising and manufacturing companies | Selling, general, and administrative costs: |
| |    Commissions |
| |    Clerical costs, such as invoicing |
| |    Shipping costs |
| Service organizations | Supplies, travel, clerical |

*Direct labour may or may not be variable in practice. See the discussion later in this chapter.

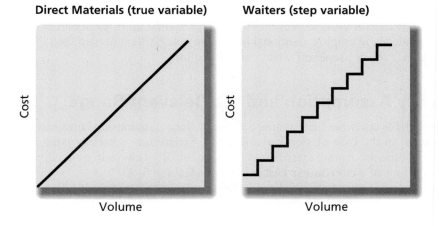

**Direct Materials (true variable)**     **Waiters (step variable)**

**Exhibit 6–3**
True Variable versus Step-Variable Costs

## True Variable versus Step-Variable Costs

Not all variable costs have exactly the same behaviour pattern. Some variable costs behave in a *true variable* or *proportionately variable* pattern. Other variable costs behave in a *step-variable* pattern. Let us examine these costs using Boston Pizza as an example.

**TRUE VARIABLE COSTS**   Direct materials is a true or proportionately variable cost because the amount used during a period will vary in direct proportion to the number of customers served or pizzas served. Moreover, any amounts purchased but not used can be stored and carried forward to the next period as inventory (remember that JIT purchasing is extremely important in the restaurant business because direct materials are perishable items).

**STEP-VARIABLE COSTS**   A cost that is obtainable only in large chunks and that increases or decreases only in response to fairly wide changes in the activity level is known as a **step-variable cost.** The behaviour of a step-variable cost, contrasted with the behaviour of a true variable cost, is illustrated in Exhibit 6–3.

For example, the need for waiters changes only with fairly wide changes in the number of customers, and when additional waiter time is obtained, it comes in large, indivisible chunks. The strategy of management in dealing with step-variable costs must

**Exhibit 6–4**
Curvilinear Costs and the
Relevant Range

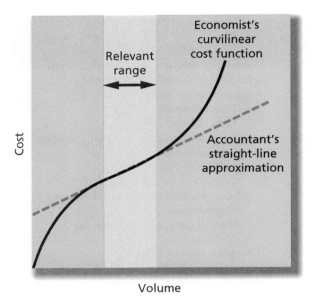

be to obtain the fullest use of services possible for each step. Great care must be taken in working with these kinds of costs to prevent "fat" from building up in an organization. There may be a tendency to employ additional help more quickly than needed, and there is a natural reluctance to lay people off when volume declines.

## The Linearity Assumption and the Relevant Range

In dealing with variable costs, we have assumed a strictly linear relationship between cost and volume, except in the case of step-variable costs. Economists correctly point out that many costs that the accountant classifies as variable actually behave in a *curvilinear* fashion. The behaviour of a **curvilinear cost** is shown in Exhibit 6–4.

Although many costs are not strictly linear when plotted as a function of volume, a curvilinear cost can be satisfactorily approximated with a straight line within a narrow band of activity known as the *relevant range*. The **relevant range** is that range of activity within which the assumptions made about cost behaviour by the manager are valid. For example, note that the dashed line in Exhibit 6–4 can be used as an approximation to the curvilinear cost with very little loss of accuracy within the shaded relevant range. However, outside of the relevant range, this particular straight line is a poor approximation to the curvilinear cost relationship. Managers should always keep in mind that a particular assumption made about cost behaviour may be very inappropriate if activity falls outside of the relevant range.

## Fixed Costs

In our discussion of cost behaviour patterns in Chapter 2, we stated that fixed costs remain constant in total dollar amount within the relevant range of activity. To continue the 50 Plus Expeditions example, assume the company decides to rent a building for $500 per month to store its equipment. The *total* amount of rent paid is the same, regardless of the number of guests the company takes on its expeditions during any given month. This cost behaviour pattern is shown graphically in Exhibit 6–5.

Since fixed costs remain constant in total, the amount of fixed cost computed on a *per-unit* basis becomes progressively smaller as the level of activity increases. If 50 Plus Expeditions has only 250 guests in a month, the $500 fixed rental cost would amount to $2 per guest. If there are 1,000 guests, the fixed rental cost would amount to only 50 cents per guest. This aspect of the behaviour of fixed costs is also displayed in Exhibit 6–5.

**Exhibit 6–5**

Fixed Cost Behaviour

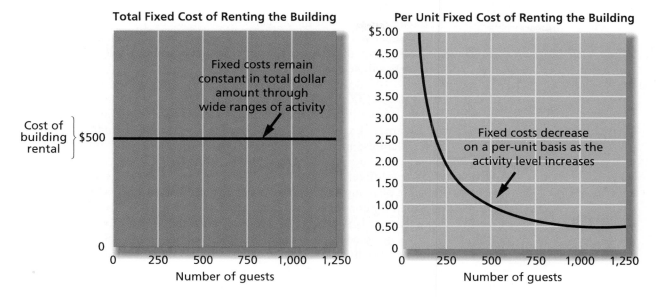

Note that as the number of guests increases, the average unit cost drops, but it drops at a decreasing rate. The first guests have the biggest impact on unit costs.

As we noted in Chapter 2, this aspect of fixed costs can be confusing, although it is necessary in some contexts to express fixed costs on an average per-unit basis. Fixed costs are sometimes expressed on a per-unit basis (i.e., unitized). In such situations, users of the information must be cautioned that fixed costs have been unitized and should not be mistaken for variable costs. For example, if Boston Pizza allocates building rent at $0.25 per pizza, this does not mean that rent cost will increase by $0.25 each time a pizza is served. The amount of $0.25 per pizza is simply an average cost based on a certain volume of pizzas served and really has no meaning for decision-making purposes. This amount is allocated so that managers understand that the total cost of a pizza is *more than* the sum of all the variable costs. From a decision-making angle, this information can be useful for pricing purposes; and from an analysis perspective, total cost information is useful to understand profitability.

## Types of Fixed Costs

Fixed costs are sometimes referred to as capacity costs, since they result from outlays made for buildings, equipment, skilled professional employees, and other items needed to provide the basic capacity for sustained operations. For planning purposes, fixed costs can be viewed as being either *committed* or *discretionary*.

**COMMITTED FIXED COSTS**   **Committed fixed costs** relate to the investment in facilities, equipment, and the basic organizational structure of a firm. Examples of such costs include depreciation of buildings and equipment, taxes on real estate, insurance, and salaries of top management and operating personnel.

Committed fixed costs are long term in nature and cannot be reduced to zero even for short periods of time without seriously impairing the profitability or long-term goals of the organization. Even if operations are interrupted or cut back, the committed fixed costs will still continue largely unchanged. During a recession, for example, a firm will not usually discharge key executives or sell off key facilities. The basic organizational structure and facilities ordinarily are kept intact. The costs of restoring them later are likely to be far greater than any short-term savings that might be realized.

Since it is difficult to change a committed fixed cost once the commitment has been made, management should approach these decisions with particular care. Decisions to acquire major equipment or to take on other committed fixed costs involve a long planning horizon. Management should make such commitments only after careful analysis of the available alternatives. Once a decision is made to build a certain size facility, a firm becomes locked into that decision for many years to come. Decisions relating to committed fixed costs will be examined in Chapter 12.

**DISCRETIONARY FIXED COSTS** **Discretionary fixed costs** (often referred to as *managed fixed costs*) usually arise from *annual* decisions by management to spend in certain fixed cost areas. Examples of discretionary fixed costs include advertising, research, public relations, management development programs, and internships for students.

Basically, two key differences exist between discretionary fixed costs and committed fixed costs. First, the planning horizon for a discretionary fixed cost is fairly short term— usually a single year. By contrast, as we indicated earlier, committed fixed costs have a planning horizon that encompasses many years. Second, discretionary fixed costs can be cut for short periods of time with minimal damage to the long-term goals of the organization. For example, spending on management development programs can be cut back because of poor economic conditions. Although some unfavourable consequences may result from the cutback, it is doubtful that these consequences would be as great as those that would result if the company decided to economize during the year by laying off key personnel.

Whether a particular cost is regarded as committed or discretionary may depend on management's strategy. For example, during recessions when the level of home building is down, many construction companies lay off most of their workers and virtually disband operations. Other construction companies retain large numbers of employees on the payroll, even though the workers have little or no work to do. While these latter companies may be faced with short-term cash flow problems, it will be easier for them to respond quickly when economic conditions improve. And the higher morale and loyalty of their employees may give these companies a significant competitive advantage.

The most important characteristic of discretionary fixed costs is that management is not locked into a decision regarding such costs. They can be adjusted from year to year or even perhaps during the course of a year if circumstances demand such a modification.

**THE TREND TOWARD FIXED COSTS** The trend in many industries is toward greater fixed costs relative to variable costs. Chores that used to be performed by hand have been taken over by machines. For example, an H & R Block employee used to fill out tax returns for customers by hand and the advice given to a customer largely depended on the knowledge of that particular employee. Now, sophisticated computer software is used to complete tax returns, and the software provides the customer with tax planning and other advice tailored to the customer's needs on the basis of the accumulated knowledge of many experts. The move towards online banking and shopping has also necessitated these organizations to invest more in technology and support structure.

As machines take over more and more of the tasks that were performed by humans, the overall demand for human workers has not diminished. The demand for "knowledge" workers—those who work primarily with their minds, rather than their muscles—has grown tremendously. And knowledge workers tend to be salaried, highly trained, and difficult to replace. As a consequence, the costs of compensating knowledge workers are often relatively fixed and are committed, rather than discretionary, costs.

**IS LABOUR A VARIABLE OR A FIXED COST?** As the preceding discussion suggests, wages and salaries may be fixed or variable. The behaviour of wage and salary costs will differ from one country to another, depending on labour regulations, labour contracts, and custom. In some countries, such as France, Germany, China, and Japan, management has little flexibility in adjusting the labour force to changes in business activity. In such countries as Canada, management typically has much greater latitude. However, even in these less restrictive environments, managers may choose to treat employee compensation as a fixed cost for several reasons.

First, many companies have become much more reluctant to adjust the workforce in response to short-term fluctuations in sales. Most companies realize that their employees are a very valuable asset. More and more, highly skilled and trained employees are required to run a successful business, and these workers are not easy to replace. Trained workers who are laid off may never return, and layoffs undermine the morale of those workers who remain.

In addition, managers do not want to be caught with a bloated payroll in an economic downturn. Therefore, there is an increased reluctance to add workers when sales activity picks up. Many companies are turning to temporary and part-time workers to pick up the slack when their permanent, full-time employees are unable to handle all of the demand for the company's products and services. In such companies, labour costs are a mixture of fixed and variable costs.

Many major companies have undergone waves of downsizing in recent years in which large numbers of employees—particularly middle managers—have lost their jobs. It may seem that this downsizing proves that even management salaries should be regarded as variable costs, but this would not be a valid conclusion. Downsizing has been the result of attempts to re-engineer business processes and cut costs, rather than a response to a decline in sales activity. This underscores an important, but subtle, point. Fixed costs can change—they just do not change in response to small changes in activity.

In sum, we cannot provide a clear-cut answer to the question "Is labour a variable or fixed cost?" It depends on how much flexibility management has and management's strategy. *Nevertheless, we will assume in this text that, unless otherwise stated, direct labour is a variable cost*. This assumption is less likely to be valid for companies in countries where employment laws permit much less flexibility.

## Labour Laws and Cost Behaviour

*in business | today*

The labour laws in the country in which the company operates often affect whether employee staff costs are fixed or variable. In Europe, banks have historically had very large numbers of branches, some of which serve very small villages. These branches are expensive to staff and maintain, and banks have argued that they are a drain on profits. In Denmark and the United Kingdom, the number of branches were cut by 34% and 22%, respectively, over a span of 10 years. In both cases, this led to a 15% reduction in staff employees. In contrast, countries with more restrictive labour laws that make it difficult to lay off workers have been unable to reduce staff or the number of branches significantly. For example, in Germany the number of branches was reduced by only 2% and the number of staff by only two-tenths of a percent during the same period.

Source: Charles Fleming, "Kinder Cuts: Continental Banks Seek to Expand Their Way Out of Retail Trouble," *The Wall Street Journal Europe*, March 11, 1997, pp. 1 and 8.

## Fixed Costs and the Relevant Range

The concept of the relevant range, which was introduced in the discussion of variable costs, is also important in understanding fixed costs—particularly discretionary fixed costs. The levels of discretionary fixed costs are typically decided at the beginning of the year and depend on the support needs of planned programs, such as advertising and training. The scope of these programs will depend, in turn, on the overall anticipated level of activity for the year. At very high levels of activity, programs are usually broadened or

**Exhibit 6–6**
Fixed Costs and the Relevant
Range

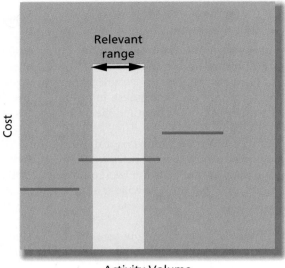

expanded. For example, if a law firm hopes to increase revenues by 25%, it would proba-bly plan for much larger advertising costs than if no increase were planned. So, the *planned* level of activity might affect total discretionary fixed costs. However, once the total discretionary fixed costs have been budgeted, they are unaffected by the *actual* level of activity. For example, once the advertising budget has been decided and has been spent, it will not be affected by the actual increase in revenues. Therefore, the cost is fixed with respect to the *actual* revenues.

Discretionary fixed costs are easier to adjust than committed fixed costs. They also tend to be less "lumpy." Committed fixed costs consist of such costs such as buildings, equipment, and the salaries of key personnel. It is difficult to buy half a piece of equip-ment or to hire a quarter of a sales manager, and so the step pattern depicted in Exhibit 6–6 is typical for such costs. The relevant range of activity for a fixed cost is the range of activity over which the graph of the cost is flat as in Exhibit 6–6. As a company expands its level of activity, it may outgrow its present facilities, or the key management team may need to be expanded. The result, of course, will be increased committed fixed costs as larger facilities are built and as new management positions are created.

One reaction to the step pattern depicted in Exhibit 6–6 is to say that discretionary and committed fixed costs are really just step-variable costs. To some extent, this is true, since almost *all* costs can be adjusted in the long run. There are two major differences, however, between the step-variable costs depicted earlier in Exhibit 6–3 and the fixed costs depicted in Exhibit 6–6.

The first difference is that the step-variable costs can often be adjusted quickly as conditions change, whereas once fixed costs have been set, they often cannot be changed easily. A step-variable cost, such as waiters, can be adjusted upward or downward by hiring and laying off waiters. By contrast, once a company has signed a lease for a build-ing, it is locked into that level of lease cost for the life of the contract.

The second difference is that the *width of the steps* depicted for step-variable costs is much narrower than the width of the steps depicted for the fixed costs in Exhibit 6–6. The width of the steps relates to volume or level of activity. For step-variable costs, the width of a step might be 40 hours of activity or less if one is dealing, for example, with clerical labour cost. For fixed costs, however, the width of a step might be *thousands* or even *tens of thousands* of hours of activity. In essence, the width of the steps for step-variable costs is generally so narrow that these costs can be treated essentially as variable costs for most purposes. The width of the steps for fixed costs, on the other hand, is so wide that these costs must generally be treated as being entirely fixed within the relevant range.

Core Emballage Limited, based in western India, is a manufacturer and exporter of packaging materials—corrugated boxes, trays, and sheets—catering to varying packaging needs of customers. As with every organization, Core has also been finding ways to reduce costs across various functions. A thorough cost analysis suggested that there was some scope for reducing sales and marketing costs by at least 25%. After some analysis, Core decided to close its sales offices in some locations and employ sales agents on a commission basis. As a result, the company eliminated the large fixed costs of maintaining sales offices. It now incurs only variable costs by way of commissions paid to the sales agents on the basis of sales revenues. Core saved about Rupees (Rs.) 23,000 per month on sales of Rs. 200,000 (One dollar = approx. Rs. 34), which translated into a reduction of about 31%. Core has not stopped its cost reduction efforts with these savings; instead, it continues to find other areas where costs can be saved.

Source: Personal correspondence with the Managing Director of Core Emballage Limited.

## Mixed Costs

A **mixed cost** is one that contains both variable and fixed cost elements. Mixed costs are also known as semivariable costs. To continue the 50 Plus Expeditions example, assume that the company must pay a licence fee of $25,000 per year plus $3 per rafting party to provincial authorities. If the company runs 1,000 rafting parties this year, then the total fees paid to the state would be $28,000, made up of $25,000 in fixed cost plus $3,000 in variable cost. The behaviour of this mixed cost is shown graphically in Exhibit 6–7.

Even if 50 Plus fails to attract any customers, the company will still have to pay the licence fee of $25,000. This is why the cost line in Exhibit 6–7 intersects the vertical cost axis at the $25,000 point. For each rafting party the company organizes, the total cost of the provincial fees will increase by $3. Therefore, the total cost line slopes upward as the variable cost element is added to the fixed cost element.

Since the mixed cost in Exhibit 6–7 is represented by a straight line, the following equation for a straight line can be used to express the relationship between mixed cost and the level of activity:

$$Y = a + bX$$

In this equation,

$Y$ = The total mixed cost
$a$ = The total fixed cost (the vertical intercept of the line)
$b$ = The variable cost per unit of activity (the slope of the line)
$X$ = The level of activity

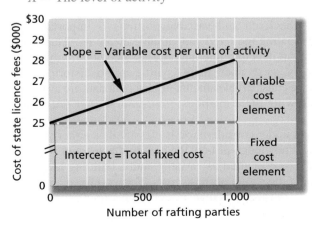

**Exhibit 6–7**
Mixed Cost Behaviour

In the case of the state fees paid by 50 Plus Expeditions, the equation is written as follows:

$$Y = \$25{,}000 + \$3.00X$$

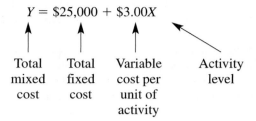

| Total | Total | Variable | Activity |
|---|---|---|---|
| mixed | fixed | cost per | level |
| cost | cost | unit of | |
| | | activity | |

This equation makes it very easy to calculate what the total mixed cost would be for any level of activity within the relevant range. For example, suppose that the company expects to organize 800 rafting parties in the next year. Then the total state fees would be $27,400 calculated as follows:

$$Y = \$25{,}000 + (\$3.00 \text{ per rafting party} \times 800 \text{ rafting parties})$$

$$= \$27{,}400$$

## The Analysis of Mixed Costs

In practice, mixed costs are very common. For example, the cost of providing X-ray services to patients at the Toronto General Hospital is a mixed cost. There are substantial fixed costs for equipment depreciation and for salaries for radiologists and technicians, but there are also variable costs for X-ray film, power, and supplies. At WestJet Airlines, maintenance costs are mixed costs. The company must incur fixed costs for renting maintenance facilities and for keeping skilled mechanics on the payroll, but the costs of replacement parts, lubricating oils, tires, and so on, are variable with respect to how often and how far the company's aircraft are flown.

The fixed portion of a mixed cost represents the basic, minimum cost of just having a service *ready and available* for use. The variable portion represents the cost incurred for *actual consumption* of the service. The variable element varies in proportion to the amount of service that is consumed.

Why should management be interested in separating the fixed and variable portions of a mixed cost? The simple answer is that a mixed cost is a combination of two cost types with exactly opposite behaviours. While one cost increases in total to changes in activity volume, the other does not. Therefore, when activity levels change within the organization, only the variable portion of the mixed cost will be affected (in terms of total cost going up or down). Approximating a mixed cost to one or the other will distort planning and decision making (for example, cost estimates will be incorrect). Managers may take decisions that result in undesirable consequences.

Now we know why separating the fixed and variable portions is important, but how does management go about estimating the fixed and variable elements? That really depends on the availability of historical data to guide the process. *Account analysis* and *engineering approach* are commonly used when there is little or no historical data available for analysis. However, when a considerable amount of historical data are available, managers can choose from the following three methods: *high-low*, *scatter graph*, and *regression analysis*.

In **account analysis,** each account under consideration is classified as either variable or fixed on the basis of the analyst's knowledge of how the cost in the account behaves. For example, direct materials would be classified as variable, and a building lease cost would be classified as fixed because of the nature of those costs. The total fixed cost of an organization is the sum of the costs for the accounts that have been classified as fixed. The variable cost per unit is estimated by dividing the sum of the costs for the accounts that have been classified as variable by the total activity.

Account analysis works best when analyzing costs at a fairly aggregated level, such as the cost of serving patients in the emergency room (ER) of your local hospital. The costs of drugs, supplies, forms, wages, equipment, and so on, can be roughly classified as variable or fixed, and a mixed cost formula for the overall cost of the emergency room can be estimated fairly quickly.

The **engineering approach** to cost analysis involves a detailed analysis of what cost behaviour should be, based on an industrial engineer's evaluation of the production methods to be used, the materials specifications, labour requirements, equipment usage, efficiency of production, power consumption, and so on. For example, Pizza Hut might use the engineering approach to estimate the cost of serving a particular take-out pizza. The cost of the pizza would be estimated by carefully costing the specific ingredients used to make the pizza, the power consumed to cook the pizza, and the cost of the container the pizza is delivered in. The engineering approach must be used in those situations where no past experience is available concerning activity and costs. In addition, it is sometimes used together with other methods to improve the accuracy of cost analysis.

The remainder of this section will focus on how to estimate fixed and variable costs using past data.

---

Dr. Derek Chalmers, the chief executive officer of Mid-Town Medical Centre (MMC), motioned Kinh Nguyen, the chief financial officer of the hospital, into his office.

*Derek:* Kinh, come on in.

**Kinh:** What can I do for you?

*Derek:* Actually, I wanted to talk to you about our maintenance expenses. I don't usually pay attention to such things, but these expenses seem to be bouncing around a lot. Over the last half year or so, they have been as low as $7,400 and as high as $9,800 per month.

**Kinh:** Actually, that's a pretty normal variation in those expenses.

*Derek:* Well, we budgeted a constant $8,400 a month. Can't we do a better job of predicting what these costs are going to be? And how do we know when we've spent too much in a month? Shouldn't there be some explanation for these variations?

**Kinh:** Now that you mention it, we are in the process right now of tightening up our budgeting process. Our first step is to break all of our costs down into fixed and variable components.

*Derek:* How will that help?

**Kinh:** Well, that will permit us to predict what the level of costs will be. Some costs are fixed and shouldn't change much. Other costs go up and down as our activity level goes up and down. The trick is to figure out what is driving the variable component of the costs.

*Derek:* What about the maintenance costs?

**Kinh:** My guess is that the variations in maintenance costs are being driven by our overall level of activity. When we treat more patients, our equipment is used more intensively, which leads to more maintenance expense.

*Derek:* How would you measure the level of overall activity? Would you use patient-days?

**Kinh:** I think so. Each day a patient is in the hospital counts as one patient-day. The greater the number of patient-days in a month, the busier we are. Besides, our budgeting is all based on projected patient-days.

*Derek:* Okay, so suppose you are able to break the maintenance costs down into fixed and variable components. What will that do for us?

**Kinh:** Basically, I will be able to predict what maintenance costs should be as a function of the number of patient-days.

*Derek:* I can see where that would be useful. We could use it to predict costs for budgeting purposes.

**MANAGERIAL ACCOUNTING IN ACTION**

**The Issue**

MID-TOWN MEDICAL CENTRE

*Kinh:* We could also use it as a benchmark. On the basis of the actual number of patient-days for a period, I can predict what the maintenance costs should have been. We can compare this with the actual spending on maintenance.
*Derek:* Sounds good to me. Let me know when you get the results.

We will examine three methods that Kinh Nguyen might use to break down mixed costs into their fixed and variable elements—the *high-low method*, the *scattergraph method*, and the *least-squares regression method*. All three methods are based on analyzing cost and activity records from a number of prior periods. In the case of MMC, we will use the following records of maintenance costs and patient-days for the first seven months of the year to estimate the fixed and variable elements of maintenance costs:

| Month | Activity Level: Patient-Days | Maintenance Cost Incurred |
|---|---|---|
| January ........ | 5,600 | $7,900 |
| February ....... | 7,100 | 8,500 |
| March ......... | 5,000 | 7,400 |
| April .......... | 6,500 | 8,200 |
| May ........... | 7,300 | 9,100 |
| June ........... | 8,000 | 9,800 |
| July .......... | 6,200 | 7,800 |

## The High-Low Method

To analyze mixed costs with the **high-low method,** you begin by identifying the period with the lowest level of activity and the period with the highest level of activity. The difference in cost corresponding to the two extreme activity levels is divided by the difference between the high and low activity levels to estimate the variable cost per unit of activity.

Since total maintenance cost at MMC appears to generally increase as the activity level increases, it is likely that some variable cost element is present. Using the high-low method, we first identify the periods with the highest and lowest *activity*—in this case, June and March. We then use the activity and cost data from these two periods to estimate the variable cost component as follows:

| | Patient-Days | Maintenance Cost Incurred |
|---|---|---|
| High activity level (June) ........... | 8,000 | $9,800 |
| Low activity level (March) .......... | 5,000 | 7,400 |
| Change ...................... | 3,000 | $2,400 |

$$\text{Variable cost} = \frac{\text{Change in cost}}{\text{Change in activity}} = \frac{\$2,400}{3,000 \text{ patient-days}} = \$0.80 \text{ per patient-day}$$

Having determined that the variable rate for maintenance cost is 80 cents per patient-day, we can now determine the amount of fixed cost. This is done by taking total cost at *either* the high or the low activity level and deducting the variable cost element. In the computation below, total cost at the high activity level is used in computing the fixed cost element:

Fixed cost element = Total cost − Variable cost element

$$= \$9,800 - (\$0.80 \text{ per patient-day} \times 8,000 \text{ patient-days})$$

$$= \$3,400$$

Both the variable and fixed cost elements have now been isolated. The cost of maintenance can be expressed as \$3,400 per month plus 80 cents per patient-day.

The cost of maintenance can also be expressed in terms of the equation for a straight line as follows:

$$Y = \$3,400 + \$0.80X$$

Total
maintenance
cost

Total
patient-days

The data used in this illustration are shown graphically in Exhibit 6–8. Three things should be noted in relation to this exhibit:

1. The total maintenance cost, $Y$, is plotted on the vertical axis. Cost is known as the **dependent variable,** since the amount of cost incurred during a period depends on the level of activity for the period. (That is, as the level of activity increases, total cost will also increase.)
2. The activity, $X$ (patient-days in this case), is plotted on the horizontal axis. Activity is known as the **independent variable,** since it causes variations in the cost.
3. A straight line has been drawn through the points corresponding to the low and high levels of activity. In essence, that is what the high-low method does—it draws a straight line through those two points.[1]

Sometimes, the high and low levels of activity do not coincide with the high and low amounts of cost. For example, the period that has the highest level of activity may not have the highest amount of cost. Nevertheless, the highest and lowest levels of *activity* and the corresponding costs are used to analyze a mixed cost under the high-low method. The reason is that the activity presumably causes costs, and so the analyst would like to use data that reflect the greatest possible variation in activity.

The high-low method is very simple to apply, but it suffers from a major (and sometimes critical) defect—it utilizes only two data points. Generally, two points are not enough to produce accurate results in cost analysis work. Additionally, periods in which the activity level is unusually low or unusually high will tend to produce inaccurate results. A cost formula that is estimated solely using data from these unusual periods may seriously misrepresent the true cost relationship that holds during normal periods. Such a distortion is evident in Exhibit 6–8. The straight line should probably be shifted down somewhat so that it is closer to more of the data points. For these reasons, other methods of cost analysis that utilize a greater number of points will generally be more accurate than the high-low method. If a manager chooses to use the high-low method, he or she should do so with a full awareness of the method's limitations.

---

[1] The formula for the variable cost, $\dfrac{\text{Change in cost (i.e., change in } Y)}{\text{Change in activity (i.e., change in } X)}$, is basically the same as the

formula for the slope of the line, $\dfrac{\text{Rise (i.e., change in } Y)}{\text{Run (i.e., change in } X)}$, that you are familiar with from high school algebra. This is because the slope of the line is the variable cost per unit. The higher the variable cost per unit, the steeper is the line.

**Exhibit 6–8**
High-Low Method of Cost
Analysis

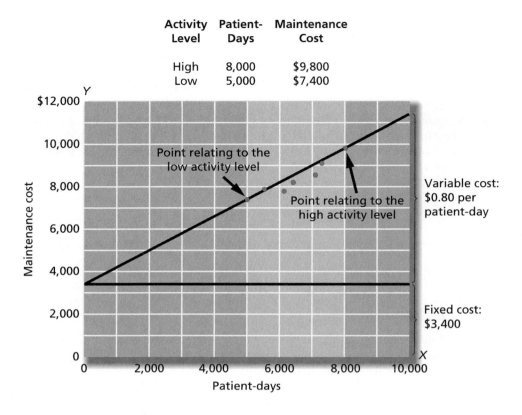

| Activity Level | Patient-Days | Maintenance Cost |
|---|---|---|
| High | 8,000 | $9,800 |
| Low | 5,000 | $7,400 |

## The Scattergraph Method

**Learning Objective 3**
Analyze a mixed cost using
the scattergraph method.

A more accurate way of analyzing mixed costs is to use the **scattergraph method,** which takes into account all of the cost data. A graph like the one that we used in Exhibit 6–8 is constructed, in which cost is shown on the vertical axis and the level of activity is shown on the horizontal axis. Costs observed at various levels of activity are then plotted on the graph, and a line is fitted to the plotted points. However, rather than just fitting the line to the high and low points, all points are considered when the line is drawn. This is done through simple visual inspection of the data, with the analyst taking care that the placement of the line is representative of all points, not just the high and low ones. Typically, the line is placed so that approximately equal numbers of points fall above and below it. A graph of this type is known as a *scattergraph,* and the line *fitted* to the plotted points is known as a **regression line.**

The scattergraph approach using the MMC maintenance data is illustrated in Exhibit 6–9. Note that the regression line has been placed in such a way that approximately equal numbers of points fall above and below it. Also note that the line has been drawn so that it goes through one of the points. This is not absolutely necessary, but it makes subsequent calculations a little easier.

Since the regression line strikes the vertical cost axis at $3,300, that amount represents the fixed cost element. The variable cost element can be computed by subtracting the fixed cost of $3,300 from the total cost for any point lying on the regression line. Since the point representing 7,300 patient-days lies on the regression line, we can use it. The variable cost (to the nearest tenth of a cent) would be 79.5 cents per patient-day, computed as follows:

| | |
|---|---|
| Total cost for 7,300 patient-days (a point falling on the regression line) ....... | $9,100 |
| Less fixed cost element ..................... | 3,300 |
| Variable cost element ..................... | $5,800 |

$5,800 ÷ 7,300 patient-days = $0.795 per patient-day

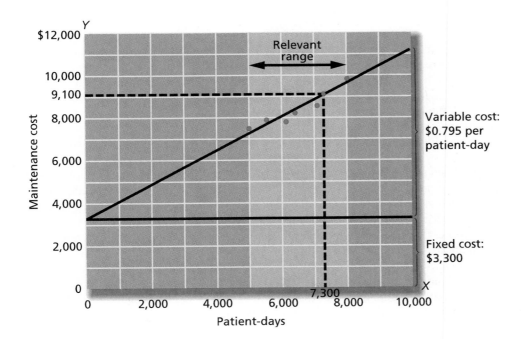

**Exhibit 6–9**
Scattergraph Method of Cost
Analysis

Thus, the cost formula using the regression line in Exhibit 6–9 would be $3,300 per month plus 79.5 cents per patient-day. In terms of the linear equation $Y = a + bX$, the cost formula can be written as:

$$Y = \$3,300 + \$0.795X$$

where activity $(X)$ is expressed in patient-days.

In this example, there is not a great deal of difference between the cost formula derived using the high-low method and the cost formula derived using the scattergraph method. However, sometimes, there *will* be a big difference. In those situations, more reliance should ordinarily be placed on the results of the scattergraph approach.

Also note that all of the points in Exhibit 6–9 lie reasonably close to the straight line. In other words, the estimates of the fixed and variable costs are reasonably accurate within this range of activity, and so the relevant range extends at least from 5,000 to 8,000 patient-days. It may also be accurate below 5,000 patient-days and above 8,000 patient-days—we cannot tell for sure without looking at more data.

A scattergraph can be an extremely useful tool in the hands of an experienced analyst. Quirks in cost behaviour due to strikes, bad weather, breakdowns, and so on, become immediately apparent to the trained observer, who can make appropriate adjustments to the data when fitting the regression line. Some cost analysts would argue that a scattergraph should be the beginning point in all cost analyses, due to the benefits to be gained from having the data visually available in graph form.

However, the scattergraph method has two major drawbacks. First, it is subjective. No two analysts who look at the same scattergraph are likely to draw exactly the same regression line. Second, the estimates are not as precise as they are with other methods. Some managers are uncomfortable with these elements of subjectivity and imprecision and desire a method that will yield a precise answer that will be the same no matter who does the analysis. Fortunately, modern computer software makes it very easy to use sophisticated statistical methods, such as *least-squares regression*, that are capable of providing much more information than just the estimates of variable and fixed costs. The details of these statistical methods are beyond the scope of this text, but the basic approach is discussed below. Nevertheless, even if the least-squares regression approach is used, it is always a good idea to plot the data in a scattergraph. By simply looking at the scattergraph, you can quickly verify whether it makes sense to fit a straight line to the data using least-squares regression or some other method.

## The Least-Squares Regression Method

The **least-squares regression method** is a more objective and precise approach to estimating the regression line than the scattergraph method. Rather than fitting a regression line through the scattergraph data by visual inspection, the least-squares regression method uses mathematical formulas to fit the regression line. Also, unlike the high-low method, the least-squares regression method takes all of the data into account when estimating the cost formula.

The basic idea underlying the least-squares regression method is illustrated in Exhibit 6–10 using hypothetical data points. Note from the exhibit that the deviations from the plotted points to the regression line are measured vertically on the graph. These vertical deviations are called the regression errors and are the key to understanding what least-squares regression does. There is nothing mysterious about the least-squares regression method. It simply computes the regression line that minimizes the sum of these squared errors. The formulas that accomplish this are fairly complex and involve numerous calculations, but the principle is simple.

Fortunately, computers are adept at carrying out the computations required by the least-squares regression formulas. The data—the observed values of X and Y—are entered into the computer, and software does the rest. In the case of MMC's maintenance cost data, we used a statistical software package. Most spreadsheet package can also be used to carry out regression analysis on a personal computer to calculate the following least-squares regression estimates of the total fixed cost ($a$) and the variable cost per unit of activity ($b$):

$$a = \$3,431$$
$$b = \$0.759$$

Therefore, using the least-squares regression method, the fixed element of the maintenance cost is $3,431 per month and the variable portion is 75.9 cents per patient-day.

In terms of the linear equation $Y = a + bX$, the cost formula can be written as

$$Y = \$3,431 + \$0.759X$$

where activity ($X$) is expressed in patient-days.

One very important statistic generated as part of the regression analysis is $R^2$. The $R^2$ in this example is 0.896 or 89.6%. This simply means that 89.6% of the variation in maintenance cost is accounted for (or explained) by the variation in patient-days. In other words, only 10.4% of the variation in maintenance cost is not explained by the variation in patient-days. Knowing this is important to the managers to decide whether the basis

**Exhibit 6–10**
The Concept of Least-Squares Regression

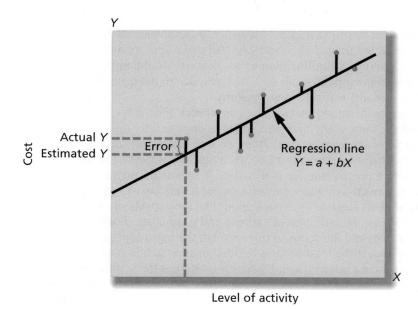

upon which the cost estimates are developed (e.g., patient-days) is reliable. In other words, if the $R^2$ is low, the manager must look for some other base to estimate costs.

---

After completing the analysis of maintenance costs, Kinh Nguyen met with Dr. Derek Chalmers to discuss the results.

**Kinh:** We used least-squares regression analysis to estimate the fixed and variable components of maintenance costs. According to the results, the fixed cost per month is $3,431 and the variable cost per patient-day is 75.9 cents.
**Derek:** Okay, so if we plan for 7,800 patient-days next month, what is your estimate of the maintenance costs?
**Kinh:** That will take just a few seconds to figure out. [Kinh wrote the following calculations on a pad of paper.]

| | |
|---|---:|
| Fixed costs ................................... | $3,431 |
| Variable costs: | |
| 7,800 patient-days × $0.759 per patient-day ....... | 5,920 |
| Total expected maintenance costs ................ | $9,351 |

**Derek:** Nine thousand three hundred and fifty *one* dollars; isn't that a bit *too* precise?
**Kinh:** Sure. I don't really believe the maintenance costs will be exactly this figure. However, based on the information we have, this is the best estimate we can come up with.
**Derek:** Don't let me give you a hard time. Even though it is an estimate, it will be a lot better than just guessing like we have done in the past. It will surely help us in our budgeting efforts. Thanks. I hope to see more of this kind of analysis.

**MANAGERIAL ACCOUNTING IN ACTION**

**The Wrap-Up**

MID-TOWN MEDICAL CENTRE

---

# The Contribution Format

Once the manager has separated costs into fixed and variable elements, what is done with the data? We have already answered this question somewhat by showing how a cost formula can be used to predict costs. To answer this question more fully will require most of the remainder of this text, since much of what the manager does rests in some way on an understanding of cost behaviour. One immediate and very significant application of the ideas we have developed, however, is found in a new income statement format known as the **contribution approach.** The unique thing about the contribution approach is that it provides the manager with an income statement geared directly to cost behaviour.

**Learning Objective 5**
Prepare and interpret an income statement using the contribution format.

## Why a New Income Statement Format?

An income statement prepared using the *traditional approach*, as illustrated in Chapter 2, is not organized in terms of cost behaviour. Rather, it is organized in a "functional" format—emphasizing the functions of production, administration, and sales in the classification and presentation of cost data. No attempt is made to distinguish between the behaviour of costs included under each functional heading. Under the heading "Administrative expense," for example, one can expect to find both variable and fixed costs lumped together.

Although an income statement prepared in the functional format may be useful for external reporting purposes, it has serious limitations when used for internal purposes. Internally, the manager needs cost data organized in a format that will facilitate planning, control, and decision making. As we shall see in the chapters ahead, these tasks are much easier when cost data are available in fixed and variable formats. The contribution approach to the income statement has been developed in response to this need.

## The Contribution Approach

Concept 6–2

Exhibit 6–11 illustrates the contribution approach to the income statement with a simple example, along with the traditional approach discussed in Chapter 2.

Note that the contribution approach separates costs into fixed and variable categories, first deducting variable expenses from sales to obtain what is known as the *contribution margin*. The **contribution margin** is the amount remaining from sales revenues after variable expenses have been deducted. This amount *contributes* toward covering fixed expenses and then toward profits for the period.

The contribution approach to the income statement is used as an internal planning and decision-making tool. Its emphasis on costs by behaviour facilitates cost-volume-profit analysis, which we shall be doing in the next chapter. The approach is also very useful in appraising management performance, in segmented reporting of profit data, and in budgeting. Moreover, the contribution approach helps managers organize data pertinent to all kinds of special decisions, such as product-line analysis, pricing, use of scarce resources, and make or buy analysis. All of these topics are covered in later chapters.

## Exhibit 6–11

Comparison of the Contribution Income Statement with the Traditional Income Statement

| Traditional Approach (costs organized by function) | | | Contribution Approach (costs organized by behaviour) | | |
|---|---|---|---|---|---|
| Sales ...................... | | $12,000 | Sales ...................... | | $12,000 |
| Less cost of goods sold .......... | | 6,000* | Less variable expenses: | | |
| Gross margin ................. | | 6,000 | Variable production ............ | $2,000 | |
| Less operating expenses: | | | Variable selling .............. | 600 | |
| Selling ...................... | $3,100* | | Variable administrative ......... | 400 | 3,000 |
| Administrative ................ | 1,900* | 5,000 | Contribution margin ........... | | 9,000 |
| Net income ................... | | $ 1,000 | | | |
| | | | Less fixed expenses: | | |
| | | | Fixed production .............. | 4,000 | |
| | | | Fixed selling ................. | 2,500 | |
| | | | Fixed administrative ........... | 1,500 | 8,000 |
| | | | Net income ................... | | $ 1,000 |

*Contains both variable and fixed expenses. This is the income statement for a manufacturing company; thus, when the income statement is placed in the contribution format, the "cost of goods sold" figure is divided between variable production costs and fixed production costs. If this were the income statement for a *merchandising* company (which simply purchases completed goods from a supplier), then the cost of goods sold would *all* be variable.

*you decide*      **Entrepreneur**

You are the owner of a small manufacturing firm. You are in the process of applying for a loan. The loan officer would like to compare your company to others in the industry and has requested a copy of your company's income statement. Should you submit an income statement prepared using the traditional approach or the contribution approach?

**LO1** **Understand how fixed and variable costs behave and how to use them to predict costs.**

A variable cost is proportional to the level of activity within the relevant range. The cost per unit of activity for a variable cost is constant as the level of activity changes.

A fixed cost is constant in total for changes of activity within the relevant range. The cost per unit of activity decreases as the level of activity increases since a constant amount is divided by a larger number.

To predict costs at a new level of activity, multiply the variable cost per unit by the new level of activity and then add to the result the constant fixed cost.

**LO2** **Analyze a mixed cost using the high-low method.**

To use the high-low method, first identify the periods in which the highest and the lowest levels of activity have occurred. Second, estimate the variable cost element by dividing the change in total cost by the change in activity for these two periods. Third, estimate the fixed cost element by subtracting the total variable cost from the total cost at either the highest or the lowest level of activity.

The high-low method relies on the two extreme, data points, rather than all of the available data, and therefore may provide misleading estimates of variable and fixed costs.

**LO3** **Analyze a mixed cost using the scattergraph method.**

The scattergraph method begins with plotting the available cost and activity data. Activity is plotted on the horizontal, $X$, axis and cost is plotted on the vertical, $Y$, axis. The analyst then draws a straight line that is representative of the relation between cost and activity revealed by the pattern of points on the plot.

The scattergraph method is criticized because it is subjective and is relatively imprecise. However, a scattergraph is an excellent means of gaining insight into the behaviour of the cost under investigation.

**LO4** **Analyze a mixed cost using least-squares regression.**

This is a more objective method than the scattergraph, which uses a statistical approach to estimating the regression line. Unlike the high-low method, least-squares regression uses all the data points to estimate the cost formula.

**LO5** **Prepare and interpret an income statement using the contribution format.**

Managers use costs organized by behaviour for planning and decision making. To help managers carry out these functions, the income statement can be prepared in a contribution format. The traditional income statement format emphasizes the purposes for which costs were incurred (i.e., to manufacture the product, to sell the product, or to administer the organization). In contrast, the contribution format classifies costs on the income statement by cost behaviour (i.e., variable versus fixed).

## Guidance Answers to Decision Maker and You Decide

**BUDGET ANALYST** (p. 202)

A janitorial service company is likely to incur most of the following types of costs:

| Cost | Type | Activity Base (if variable) |
|------|------|------------------------------|
| Cleaning supplies .................... | Variable | Square footage of client's spaces |
| Depreciation (vacuum cleaners, etc.) ...... | Fixed | Not applicable |
| Reimbursement of employee mileage ..... | Variable | Distance (kilometres) to client |
| Salary of supervisor(s) ................ | Fixed | Not applicable |
| Wages of janitorial employees ........... | Variable | Square footage of client's spaces |

**ENTREPRENEUR** (p. 218)

In order to make useful comparisons to financial information published by other companies, the loan officer would expect an income statement prepared using the approach used for external reporting purposes. As such, you should provide an income statement prepared using the traditional approach. The information that can be obtained from an income statement prepared using the contribution approach would normally only be used internally for planning and decision making. Such income statements are not normally distributed outside of the company.

# Review Problem 1: Cost Behaviour

Neptune Rentals offers a boat rental service. Consider the following costs of the company over the relevant range of 5,000 to 8,000 hours of operating time for its boats:

| | Hours of Operating Time | | | |
|---|---|---|---|---|
| | **5,000** | **6,000** | **7,000** | **8,000** |
| **Total costs:** | | | | |
| Variable costs ............. | $ 20,000 | $ ? | $ ? | $ ? |
| Fixed costs ............... | 168,000 | ? | ? | ? |
| Total costs ............... | $188,000 | $ ? | $ ? | $ ? |
| **Cost per hour:** | | | | |
| Variable cost ............. | $ ? | $ ? | $ ? | $ ? |
| Fixed cost ............... | ? | ? | ? | ? |
| Total cost per hour ........ | $ ? | $ ? | $ ? | $ ? |

**Required:**

Compute the missing amounts, assuming that cost behaviour patterns remain unchanged within the relevant range of 5,000 to 8,000 hours.

**SOLUTION TO REVIEW PROBLEM 1**

The variable cost per hour can be computed as follows:

$$\$20,000 \div 5,000 \text{ hours} = \$4 \text{ per hour}$$

Therefore, in accordance with the behaviour of variable and fixed costs, the missing amounts are as follows:

| | Hours of Operating Time | | | |
|---|---|---|---|---|
| | **5,000** | **6,000** | **7,000** | **8,000** |
| **Total costs:** | | | | |
| Variable costs ........ | $ 20,000 | $ 24,000 | $ 28,000 | $ 32,000 |
| Fixed costs .......... | 168,000 | 168,000 | 168,000 | 168,000 |
| Total costs ......... | $188,000 | $192,000 | $196,000 | $200,000 |
| **Cost per hour:** | | | | |
| Variable cost ........ | $ 4.00 | $ 4.00 | $ 4.00 | $ 4.00 |
| Fixed cost .......... | 33.60 | 28.00 | 24.00 | 21.00 |
| Total cost per hour .... | $37.60 | $32.00 | $28.00 | $25.00 |

Observe that the total variable costs increase in proportion to the number of hours of operating time, but that these costs remain constant at $4 if expressed on a per-hour basis.

In contrast, the total fixed costs do not change with changes in the level of activity. They remain constant at $168,000 within the relevant range. With increases in activity, however, the fixed costs decrease on a per-hour basis, dropping from $33.60 per hour when the boats are operated 5,000 hours a period to only $21 per hour when the boats are operated 8,000 hours a period. *Because of this troublesome aspect of fixed costs, they are most easily (and most safely) dealt with on a total basis, rather than on a unit basis, in cost analysis work.*

# Review Problem 2: High-Low Method

The manager of Golf Warehouse would like a cost formula linking the costs involved in processing orders to the number of orders received during a month. The order entry department's costs and the number of orders received during the immediately preceding eight months are given in the following table:

| Month | Number of Orders Received | Order Entry Department Costs |
|---|---|---|
| May | 1,800 | $14,700 |
| June | 1,900 | 15,200 |
| July | 1,700 | 13,700 |
| August | 1,600 | 14,000 |
| September | 1,500 | 14,300 |
| October | 1,300 | 13,100 |
| November | 1,100 | 12,800 |
| December | 1,500 | 14,600 |

*Required:*
1. Use the high-low method to establish the fixed and variable components of order processing costs.
2. Express the fixed and variable components of order processing costs as a cost formula in the linear equation form $Y = a + bX$.

## SOLUTION TO REVIEW PROBLEM 2
1. The first step in the high-low method is to identify the periods of the lowest and highest activity. Those periods are November (1,100 orders received) and June (1,900 orders received).

   The second step is to compute the variable cost per unit using those two points:

| Month | Number of Orders Received | Order Entry Department Costs |
|---|---|---|
| High activity level (June) | 1,900 | $15,200 |
| Low activity level (November) | 1,100 | 12,800 |
| Change | 800 | $ 2,400 |

$$\text{Variable cost} = \frac{\text{Change in cost}}{\text{Change in activity}} = \frac{\$2,400}{800 \text{ orders received}} = \$3 \text{ per order received}$$

The third step is to compute the fixed cost element by deducting the variable cost element from the total cost at either the high or low activity. In the computation below, the high point of activity is used:

Fixed cost element = Total cost − Variable cost element
   = $15,200 − ($3 per patient admitted × 1,900 orders received)
   = $9,500

2. The cost formula expressed in the linear equation form is $Y = \$9,500 + \$3X$.

# Glossary

**Account analysis** A method for analyzing cost behaviour in which each account is classified as either variable or fixed on the basis of the analyst's knowledge of how the cost in the account behaves. (p. 210)
**Activity base** A measure of whatever causes the incurrence of a variable cost. For example, the total cost of X-ray film in a hospital will increase as the number of X-rays taken increases. Therefore, the number of X-rays is an activity base for explaining the total cost of X-ray film. (p. 202)
**Committed fixed costs** Those fixed costs that are difficult to adjust and that relate to the investment in facilities, equipment, and the basic organizational structure of a firm. (p. 205)
**Contribution approach** An income statement format that is geared to cost behaviour in that costs are separated into variable and fixed categories, rather than being separated according to the functions of production, sales, and administration. (p. 217)
**Contribution margin** The amount remaining from sales revenues after all variable expenses have been deducted. (p. 218)
**Cost structure** The relative proportion of fixed, variable, and mixed costs found within an organization. (p. 200)

**Curvilinear costs** A relation between cost and activity that is a curve, rather than a straight line. (p. 204)

**Dependent variable** A variable that reacts or responds to some causal factor; total cost is the dependent variable, as represented by the letter $Y$, in the equation $Y = a + bX$. (p. 213)

**Discretionary fixed costs** Those fixed costs that arise from annual decisions by management to spend in certain fixed cost areas, such as advertising and research. (p. 206)

**Engineering approach** A detailed analysis of cost behaviour based on an industrial engineer's evaluation of the inputs that are required to carry out a particular activity and of the prices of those inputs. (p. 211)

**High-low method** A method of separating a mixed cost into its fixed and variable elements by analyzing the change in cost between the high and low levels of activity. (p. 212)

**Independent variable** A variable that acts as a causal factor; activity is the independent variable, as represented by the letter $X$, in the equation $Y = a + bX$. (p. 213)

**Least-squares regression method** A method of separating a mixed cost into its fixed and variable elements by fitting a regression line that minimizes the sum of the squared errors. (p. 216)

**Mixed cost** A cost that contains both variable and fixed cost elements. (p. 209)

**Regression line** A line fitted to an array of plotted points. The slope of the line, denoted by the letter $b$ in the linear equation $Y = a + bX$, represents the variable cost per unit of activity. The point where the line intersects the cost axis, denoted by the letter $a$ in the above equation, represents the total fixed cost. (p. 214)

**Relevant range** The range of activity within which assumptions about variable and fixed cost behaviour are valid. (p. 204)

**Scattergraph method** A method of separating a mixed cost into its fixed and variable elements. Under this method, a regression line is fitted to an array of plotted points by drawing a line with a straight-edge. (p. 214)

**Step-variable cost** A cost (such as the cost of a maintenance worker) that is obtainable only in large chunks and that increases and decreases only in response to fairly wide changes in activity. (p. 203)

# Questions

**6–1**    Distinguish among (a) a variable cost, (b) a fixed cost, and (c) a mixed cost.

**6–2**    What effect does an increase in volume have on—

  a.    Unit fixed costs?

  b.    Unit variable costs?

  c.    Total fixed costs?

  d.    Total variable costs?

**6–3**    Define the following terms: (a) cost behaviour, and (b) relevant range.

**6–4**    What is meant by an *activity base* when dealing with variable costs? Give several examples of activity bases.

**6–5**    Distinguish between (a) a variable cost, (b) a mixed cost, and (c) a step-variable cost. Chart the three costs on a graph, with activity plotted horizontally and cost plotted vertically.

**6–6**    Managers often assume a strictly linear relationship between cost and volume. How can this practice be defended in light of the fact that many costs are curvilinear?

**6–7**    Distinguish between discretionary fixed costs and committed fixed costs.

**6–8**    Classify the following fixed costs as normally being either committed or discretionary:

  a.    Depreciation on buildings.

  b.    Advertising.

  c.    Research.

  d.    Long-term equipment leases.

  e.    Pension payments to the firm's retirees.

  f.    Management development and training.

**6–9**    Does the concept of the relevant range apply to fixed costs? Explain.

**6–10**    What is the major disadvantage of the high-low method?

**6–11**    What methods are available for separating a mixed cost into its fixed and variable elements using past records of cost and activity data? Which method is considered to be most accurate? Why?

**6–12**    What is meant by a regression line? Give the general formula for a regression line. Which term represents the variable cost? The fixed cost?

**6–13**    Once a regression line has been drawn, how does one determine the fixed cost element? The variable cost element?

**6–14**    What is meant by the term *least-squares regression?*

**6–15**    What is the difference between the contribution approach to the income statement and the traditional approach to the income statement?

**6–16**    What is the contribution margin?

# Brief Exercises

**BRIEF EXERCISE 6–1   Fixed and Variable Cost Behaviour (LO1)**
Espresso Express operates a number of espresso coffee stands in busy suburban malls. The fixed weekly expense of a coffee stand is $1,200 and the variable cost per cup of coffee served is $0.22.

*Required:*
1. Fill in the following table with your estimates of total costs and cost per cup of coffee at the indicated levels of activity for a coffee stand. Round off the cost of a cup of coffee to the nearest tenth of a cent.

| | Cups of Coffee Served in a Week | | |
| --- | --- | --- | --- |
| | **2,000** | **2,100** | **2,200** |
| Fixed cost ......................... | ? | ? | ? |
| Variable cost ...................... | ? | ? | ? |
| Total cost ......................... | ? | ? | ? |
| Cost per cup of coffee served .......... | ? | ? | ? |

2. Does the cost per cup of coffee served increase, decrease, or remain the same as the number of cups of coffee served in a week increases? Explain.

**BRIEF EXERCISE 6–2   High-Low Method (LO2)**
The Royal Canadian Lodge in Banff, Alberta, has accumulated records of the total electrical costs of the hotel and the number of occupancy-days over the last year. An occupancy-day represents a room rented out for one day. The hotel's business is highly seasonal, with peaks occurring during the ski season and in the summer.

| Month | Occupancy-Days | Electrical Costs |
| --- | --- | --- |
| January .............. | 1,736 | $4,127 |
| February ............. | 1,904 | 4,207 |
| March ............... | 2,356 | 5,083 |
| April ............... | 960 | 2,857 |
| May ................. | 360 | 1,871 |
| June ................ | 744 | 2,696 |
| July ................ | 2,108 | 4,670 |
| August .............. | 2,406 | 5,148 |
| September ........... | 840 | 2,691 |
| October ............. | 124 | 1,588 |
| November ............ | 720 | 2,454 |
| December ............ | 1,364 | 3,529 |

*Required:*
1. Using the high-low method, estimate the fixed cost of electricity per month and the variable cost of electricity per occupancy-day. Round off the fixed cost to the nearest whole dollar and the variable cost to the nearest whole cent.
2. What other factors other than occupancy-days are likely to affect the variation in electrical costs from month to month?

**BRIEF EXERCISE 6–3   Scattergraph Analysis (LO3)**
Oki Products, Ltd. has observed the following processing costs at various levels of activity over the last 15 months:

| Month | Units Produced | Processing Cost |
| --- | --- | --- |
| 1 ........... | 4,500 | $38,000 |
| 2 ........... | 11,000 | 52,000 |

| | | |
|---|---|---|
| 3 . . . . . . . . . . . | 12,000 | 56,000 |
| 4 . . . . . . . . . . . | 5,500 | 40,000 |
| 5 . . . . . . . . . . . | 9,000 | 47,000 |
| 6 . . . . . . . . . . . | 10,500 | 52,000 |
| 7 . . . . . . . . . . . | 7,500 | 44,000 |
| 8 . . . . . . . . . . . | 5,000 | 41,000 |
| 9 . . . . . . . . . . . | 11,500 | 52,000 |
| 10 . . . . . . . . . . | 6,000 | 43,000 |
| 11 . . . . . . . . . . | 8,500 | 48,000 |
| 12 . . . . . . . . . . | 10,000 | 50,000 |
| 13 . . . . . . . . . . | 6,500 | 44,000 |
| 14 . . . . . . . . . . | 9,500 | 48,000 |
| 15 . . . . . . . . . . | 8,000 | 46,000 |

*Required:*
1. Prepare a scattergraph by plotting the above data on a graph. Plot cost on the vertical axis and activity on the horizontal axis. Fit a line to your plotted points by visual inspection.
2. What is the approximate monthly fixed cost? The approximate variable cost per unit processed? Show your computations.

**BRIEF EXERCISE 6–4   Least-squares Regression (LO4)**
Using the data in the previous exercise, repeat #2 using least-squares regression (using any spread-sheet software). Is Units Produced a reliable basis for estimating processing costs?

**BRIEF EXERCISE 6–5   Contribution Format Income Statement (LO5)**
The Alpine House, Inc. is a large retailer of winter sports equipment. An income statement for the company's Ski Department for a recent quarter is presented below:

**THE ALPINE HOUSE, INC.**
**Income Statement—Ski Department**
**For the Quarter Ended March 31**

| | | |
|---|---|---|
| Sales . . . . . . . . . . . . . . . . . . . . . . . . | | $150,000 |
| Less cost of goods sold . . . . . . . . . | | 90,000 |
| Gross margin . . . . . . . . . . . . . . . . . | | 60,000 |
| Less operating expenses: | | |
|    Selling expenses . . . . . . . . . . . . . | $30,000 | |
|    Administrative expenses . . . . . . | 10,000 | 40,000 |
| Net income . . . . . . . . . . . . . . . . . . | | $ 20,000 |

Skis sell, on the average, for $750 per pair. Variable selling expenses are $50 per pair of skis sold. The remaining selling expenses are fixed. The administrative expenses are 20% variable and 80% fixed. The company does not manufacture its own skis; it purchases them from a supplier for $450 per pair.

*Required:*
1. Prepare an income statement for the quarter using the contribution approach.
2. For every pair of skis sold during the quarter, what was the contribution toward covering fixed expenses and toward earning profits?

# Exercises

**EXERCISE 6–1   High-Low Method; Predicting Cost (LO1, LO2)**
The Lakeshore Hotel's guest-days of occupancy and custodial supplies expense over the last seven months were:

| Month | Guest-Days of Occupancy | Custodial Supplies Expense |
|---|---|---|
| March ............ | 4,000 | $ 7,500 |
| April ............ | 6,500 | 8,250 |
| May ............. | 8,000 | 10,500 |
| June ............. | 10,500 | 12,000 |
| July ............. | 12,000 | 13,500 |
| August ........... | 9,000 | 10,750 |
| September ........ | 7,500 | 9,750 |

Guest-days is a measure of the overall activity at the hotel. For example, a guest who stays at the hotel for three days is counted as three guest-days.

*Required:*
1. Using the high-low method, estimate a cost formula for custodial supplies expense.
2. Using the cost formula you derived above, what amount of custodial supplies expense would you expect to be incurred at an occupancy level of 11,000 guest-days?

### EXERCISE 6–2   Least-Squares Regression (LO4)
Repeat 1 and 2 in Exercise 6–1 using least-squares regression (you may use a spreadsheet to compute the fixed and variable costs). Comment on the reliability of the guest-days as an allocation base.

### EXERCISE 6–3   High-Low Analysis and Scattergraph Analysis (LO2, LO3)
Refer to the data in Exercise 6–1.

*Required:*
1. Prepare a scattergraph using the data from Exercise 6–1. Plot cost on the vertical axis and activity on the horizontal axis. Fit a regression line to your plotted points by visual inspection.
2. What is the approximate monthly fixed cost? The approximate variable cost per guest-day?
3. Scrutinize the points on your graph, and explain why the high-low method would or would not yield an accurate cost formula in this situation.

### EXERCISE 6–4   High-Low Analysis and Scattergraph Analysis (LO2, LO3)
The following data relating to units shipped and total shipping expense have been assembled by Archer Company, a manufacturer of large, custom-built air-conditioning units for commercial buildings:

| Month | Units Shipped | Total Shipping Expense |
|---|---|---|
| January ........... | 3 | $1,800 |
| February .......... | 6 | 2,300 |
| March ............ | 4 | 1,700 |
| April ............. | 5 | 2,000 |
| May ............. | 7 | 2,300 |
| June ............. | 8 | 2,700 |
| July ............. | 2 | 1,200 |

*Required:*
1. Using the high-low method, estimate a cost formula for shipping expense.
2. For the scattergraph method, do the following:
   a. Prepare a scattergraph, using the data given above. Plot cost on the vertical axis and activity on the horizontal axis. Fit a regression line to your plotted points by visual inspection.
   b. Using your scattergraph, estimate the approximate variable cost per unit shipped and the approximate fixed cost per month.

3.  What factors, other than the number of units shipped, are likely to affect the company's total shipping expense? Explain.

**EXERCISE 6–5    High-Low Method; Predicting Cost** (LO1, LO2)

Hoi Chong Transport, Ltd. operates a fleet of delivery trucks in Singapore. The company has determined that if a truck is driven 105,000 kilometres during a year, the average operating cost is 11.4 cents per kilometre. If a truck is driven only 70,000 kilometres during a year, the average operating cost increases to 13.4 cents per kilometre. (The Singapore dollar is the currency used in Singapore.)

*Required:*

1.  Using the high-low method, estimate the variable and fixed cost elements of the annual cost of truck operation.
2.  Express the variable and fixed costs in the form $Y = a + bX$.
3.  If a truck were driven 80,000 kilometres during a year, what total cost would you expect to be incurred?

**EXERCISE 6–6    Cost Behaviour and Contribution Format Income Statement** (LO1, LO5)

Harris Company manufactures and sells a single product. A partially completed schedule of the company's total and per unit costs over the relevant range of 30,000 to 50,000 units produced and sold annually is given below:

|  | Units Produced and Sold | | |
| --- | --- | --- | --- |
|  | 30,000 | 40,000 | 50,000 |
| Total costs: | | | |
| Variable costs . . . . . . . . . . . . | $180,000 | ? | ? |
| Fixed costs . . . . . . . . . . . . . . | 300,000 | ? | ? |
| Total costs . . . . . . . . . . . . . . | $480,000 | ? | ? |
| Cost per unit: | | | |
| Variable cost . . . . . . . . . . . . | ? | ? | ? |
| Fixed cost . . . . . . . . . . . . . . | ? | ? | ? |
| Total cost per unit . . . . . . . . . | ? | ? | ? |

*Required:*

1.  Complete the schedule of the company's total and unit costs above.
2.  Assume that the company produces and sells 45,000 units during a year at a selling price of $16 per unit. Prepare an income statement in the contribution format for the year.

# Problems

CHECK FIGURE
(1) $270,000 per month
    plus $7 per bed-day

**PROBLEM 6–1    High-Low Method and Predicting Cost** (LO1, LO2)

St. Mark's Hospital contains 450 beds. The average occupancy rate is 80% per month. In other words, on average, 80% of the hospital's beds are occupied by patients. At this level of occupancy, the hospital's operating costs are $32 per occupied bed per day, assuming a 30-day month. This $32 figure contains both variable and fixed cost elements.

During June, the hospital's occupancy rate was only 60%. A total of $326,700 in operating cost was incurred during the month.

*Required:*

1.  Using the high-low method, estimate:
    a.  The variable cost per occupied bed on a daily basis.
    b.  The total fixed operating costs per month.

CHECK FIGURE
(1) Net income is $8,000

2.  Assume an occupancy rate of 70% per month. What amount of total operating cost would you expect the hospital to incur?

**PROBLEM 6–2    Contribution Format Income Statement** (LO5)

Marwick's Pianos, Inc. purchases pianos from a large manufacturer and sells them at the retail level. The pianos cost, on the average, $2,450 each from the manufacturer. Marwick's Pianos, Inc. sells the pianos to its customers at an average price of $3,125 each. The selling and administrative costs that the company incurs in a typical month are presented below:

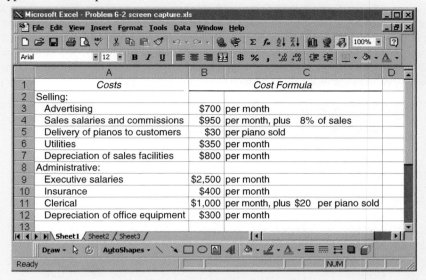

| | A | B | C | D |
|---|---|---|---|---|
| 1 | *Costs* | | *Cost Formula* | |
| 2 | Selling: | | | |
| 3 | Advertising | $700 | per month | |
| 4 | Sales salaries and commissions | $950 | per month, plus   8% of sales | |
| 5 | Delivery of pianos to customers | $30 | per piano sold | |
| 6 | Utilities | $350 | per month | |
| 7 | Depreciation of sales facilities | $800 | per month | |
| 8 | Administrative: | | | |
| 9 | Executive salaries | $2,500 | per month | |
| 10 | Insurance | $400 | per month | |
| 11 | Clerical | $1,000 | per month, plus $20   per piano sold | |
| 12 | Depreciation of office equipment | $300 | per month | |
| 13 | | | | |

During August, Marwick's Pianos, Inc. sold and delivered 40 pianos.

***Required:***

1. Prepare an income statement for Marwick's Pianos, Inc. for August. Use the traditional format, with costs organized by function.
2. Redo (1) above, this time using the contribution format, with costs organized by behaviour. Show costs and revenues on both total and a per-unit basis down through contribution margin.
3. Refer to the income statement you prepared in (2) above. Why might it be misleading to show the fixed costs on a per-unit basis?

## PROBLEM 6–3   Scattergraph Analysis (LO3)

Molina Company is a value-added computer resaler that specializes in providing services to small companies. The company owns and maintains several autos for use by the sales staff. All expenses of operating these autos have been entered into an Automobile Expense account on the company's books. Along with this record of expenses, the company has also kept a careful record of the number of kilometres the autos have been driven each month.

The company's records of miles driven and total auto expenses over the past 10 months are given below:

| Month | Total Mileage (000) | Total Cost |
|---|---|---|
| January | 4 | $3,000 |
| February | 8 | 3,700 |
| March | 7 | 3,300 |
| April | 12 | 4,000 |
| May | 6 | 3,300 |
| June | 11 | 3,900 |
| July | 14 | 4,200 |
| August | 10 | 3,600 |
| September | 13 | 4,100 |
| October | 15 | 4,400 |

Molina Company's president wants to know the cost of operating the fleet of cars in terms of the fixed monthly cost and the variable cost per mile driven.

***Required:***

1. Prepare a scattergraph using the data given above. Place cost on the vertical axis and activity (kilometres driven) on the horizontal axis. Fit a regression line to the plotted points by simple visual inspection.
2. By analyzing your scattergraph, estimate fixed cost per month and the variable cost per kilometre driven.

## PROBLEM 6–4   High-Low; Scattergraph Analysis; Least-Squares Regression (LO2, LO3, LO4)

Pleasant View Hospital of British Columbia has just hired a new chief administrator who is anxious to employ sound management and planning techniques in the business affairs of the hospital. Accordingly,

CHECK FIGURE
(1) $1,000 per month plus
$20 per scan

she has directed her assistant to summarize the cost structure existing in the various departments so that data will be available for planning purposes.

The assistant is unsure how to classify the utilities costs in the Radiology Department, since these costs do not exhibit either strictly variable or fixed cost behaviour. Utilities costs are very high in the department due to a CAT scanner that draws a large amount of power and is kept running at all times. The scanner cannot be turned off due to the long warm-up period required for its use. When the scanner is used to scan a patient, it consumes an additional burst of power. The assistant has accumulated the following data on utilities costs and use of the scanner since the first of the year.

| Month | Number of Scans | Utilities Cost |
|---|---|---|
| January | 60 | $2,200 |
| February | 70 | 2,600 |
| March | 90 | 2,900 |
| April | 120 | 3,300 |
| May | 100 | 3,000 |
| June | 130 | 3,600 |
| July | 150 | 4,000 |
| August | 140 | 3,600 |
| September | 110 | 3,100 |
| October | 80 | 2,500 |

The chief administrator has informed her assistant that the utilities cost is probably a mixed cost that will have to be broken down into its variable and fixed cost elements by use of a scattergraph. The assistant feels, however, that if an analysis of this type is necessary, then the high-low method should be used, since it is easier and quicker. The controller has suggested that there may be a better approach.

### Required:

1. Using the high-low method, estimate a cost formula for utilities. Express the formula in the form $Y = a + bX$. (The variable rate should be stated in terms of cost per scan.)
2. Prepare a scattergraph by plotting the above data on a graph. (The number of scans should be placed on the horizontal axis, and utilities cost should be placed on the vertical axis.) Fit a regression line to the plotted points by visual inspection and estimate a cost formula for utilities.
3. Estimate a cost formula using least-squares regression (use a spread-sheet).
4. Comment on the differences between the three cost formulas estimated above. Which one would you use?

CHECK FIGURE
(2) Shipping: A$18,000 per month plus A$4 per unit

### PROBLEM 6–5    Cost Behaviour; High-Low Analysis; Contribution Format Income Statement (LO1, LO2, LO5)

Morrisey & Brown, Ltd., of Sydney, is a merchandising firm that is the sole distributor of a product that is increasing in popularity among Australian consumers. The company's income statements for the three most recent months follow:

| MORRISEY & BROWN, LTD. Income Statements For the Three Months Ending September 30 | | | |
|---|---|---|---|
| | July | August | September |
| Sales in units | 4,000 | 4,500 | 5,000 |
| Sales revenue | A$400,000 | A$450,000 | A$500,000 |
| Less cost of goods sold | 240,000 | 270,000 | 300,000 |
| Gross margin | 160,000 | 180,000 | 200,000 |
| Less operating expenses: | | | |
| Advertising expense | 21,000 | 21,000 | 21,000 |
| Shipping expense | 34,000 | 36,000 | 38,000 |
| Salaries and commissions | 78,000 | 84,000 | 90,000 |
| Insurance expense | 6,000 | 6,000 | 6,000 |
| Depreciation expense | 15,000 | 15,000 | 15,000 |
| Total operating expenses | 154,000 | 162,000 | 170,000 |
| Net income | A$ 6,000 | A$ 18,000 | A$ 30,000 |

(Note: Morrisey & Brown, Ltd.'s Australian-formatted income statement has been recast in the format common in Canada. The Australian dollar is denoted by A$.)

***Required:***
1. Identify each of the company's expenses (including cost of goods sold) as being either variable, fixed, or mixed.
2. By use of the high-low method, separate each mixed expense into variable and fixed elements. State the cost formula for each mixed expense.
3. Redo the company's income statement at the 5,000-unit level of activity using the contribution format.

## PROBLEM 6–6   Identifying Cost Behaviour Patterns (LO1)

A number of graphs displaying cost behaviour patterns that might be found in a company's cost structure are shown below. The vertical axis on each graph represents total cost and the horizontal axis represents the level of activity (volume).

***Required:***
1. For each of the following situations, identify the graph below that illustrates the cost pattern involved. Any graph may be used more than once.
   a. Cost of raw materials used.
   b. Electricity bill—a flat fixed charge, plus a variable cost after a certain number of kilowatt-hours are used.
   c. City water bill, which is computed as follows:

   | | |
   |---|---|
   | First 1,000,000 litres or less .......... | $1,000 flat fee |
   | Next 10,000 litres ................. | 0.003 per litre used |
   | Next 10,000 litres ................. | 0.006 per litre used |
   | Next 10,000 litres ................. | 0.009 per litre used |
   | Etc. ........................... | Etc. |

   d. Depreciation of equipment, where the amount is computed by the straight-line method. When the depreciation rate was established, it was anticipated that the obsolescence factor would be greater than the wear-and-tear factor.
   e. Rent on a factory building donated by the city, where the agreement calls for a fixed fee payment unless 200,000 labour-hours or more are worked, in which case no rent need be paid.
   f. Salaries of maintenance workers, where one maintenance worker is needed for every 1,000 hours of machine-hours or less (that is, 0 to 1,000 hours requires one maintenance worker, 1,001 to 2,000 hours requires two maintenance workers, etc.)
   g. Cost of raw materials, where the cost starts at $7.50 per unit and then decreases by 5 cents per unit for each of the first 100 units purchased, after which it remains constant at $2.50 per unit.
   h. Rent on a factory building donated by the county, where the agreement calls for rent of $100,000 less $1 for each direct labour-hour worked in excess of 200,000 hours, but a minimum rental payment of $20,000 must be paid.
   i. Use of a machine under a lease, where a minimum charge of $1,000 is paid for up to 400 hours of machine time. After 400 hours of machine time, an additional charge of $2 per hour is paid up to a maximum charge of $2,000 per period.

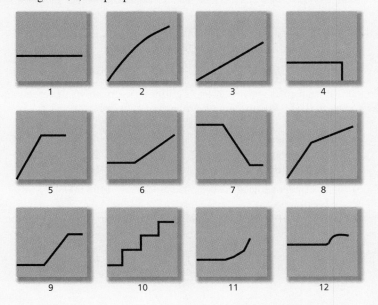

2. How would a knowledge of cost behaviour patterns, such as those above, be of help to a manager in analyzing the cost structure of his or her firm?

(CPA, adapted)

CHECK FIGURE
(2) ¥1,500,000 per year
plus ¥35 per DLH

**PROBLEM 6–7   High-Low Analysis and Cost Behaviour (LO1, LO2)**

Sawaya Co., Ltd., of Japan, is a manufacturing company whose total factory overhead costs fluctuate considerably from year to year according to increases and decreases in the number of direct labour-hours worked in the factory. Total factory overhead costs (in Japanese yen, denoted ¥) at high and low levels of activity for recent years are given below:

|  | Level of Activity | |
| --- | --- | --- |
|  | **Low** | **High** |
| Direct labour-hours . . . . . . . . . . . . . . | 50,000 | 75,000 |
| Total factory overhead costs . . . . . . . . | ¥14,250,000 | ¥17,625,000 |

The factory overhead costs above consist of indirect materials, rent, and maintenance. The company has analyzed these costs at the 50,000-hour level of activity as follows:

| | |
| --- | --- |
| Indirect materials (V) . . . . . . . . . . . . . . | ¥ 5,000,000 |
| Rent (F) . . . . . . . . . . . . . . . . . . . . . . . | 6,000,000 |
| Maintenance (M) . . . . . . . . . . . . . . . . . | 3,250,000 |
| Total factory overhead costs . . . . . . . . | ¥14,250,000 |

V = variable; F = fixed; M = mixed.

To have data available for planning, the company wants to break down the maintenance cost into its variable and fixed cost elements.

***Required:***

1. Estimate how much of the ¥17,625,000 factory overhead cost at the high level of activity consists of maintenance cost. (Hint: To do this, it may be helpful to first determine how much of the ¥17,625,000 consists of indirect materials and rent. Think about the behaviour of variable and fixed costs!)
2. By means of the high-low method of cost analysis, estimate a cost formula for maintenance.
3. What total factory overhead costs would you expect the company to incur at an operating level of 70,000 direct labour-hours?

CHECK FIGURE
(2) $9,000 per month
plus $1.60 per
machine-hour

**PROBLEM 6–8   High-Low Analysis and Predicting Cost (LO1, LO2)**

Nova Company's total overhead costs at various levels of activity are presented below:

| **Month** | **Machine-Hours** | **Total Overhead Costs** |
| --- | --- | --- |
| April . . . . . . . . . . . . . | 70,000 | $198,000 |
| May . . . . . . . . . . . . . . | 60,000 | 174,000 |
| June . . . . . . . . . . . . . . | 80,000 | 222,000 |
| July . . . . . . . . . . . . . . | 90,000 | 246,000 |

Assume that the total overhead costs above consist of utilities, supervisory salaries, and maintenance. The breakdown of these costs at the 60,000 machine-hour level of activity is:

| | |
| --- | --- |
| Utilities (V) . . . . . . . . . . . . . . . . . . | $ 48,000 |
| Supervisory salaries (F) . . . . . . . . . | 21,000 |
| Maintenance (M) . . . . . . . . . . . . . . | 105,000 |
| Total overhead costs . . . . . . . . . . . | $174,000 |

V = variable; F = fixed; M = mixed.

Nova Company's management wants to break down the maintenance cost into its basic variable and fixed cost elements.

*Required:*
1. As shown above, overhead costs in July amounted to $246,000. Determine how much of this consisted of maintenance cost. (Hint: To do this, it may be helpful to first determine how much of the $246,000 consisted of utilities and supervisory salaries. Think about the behaviour of variable and fixed costs!)
2. By means of the high-low method, estimate a cost formula for maintenance.
3. Express the company's *total* overhead costs in the linear equation form $Y = a + bX$.
4. What *total* overhead costs would you expect to be incurred at an operating activity level of 75,000 machine-hours?

**PROBLEM 6–9   High-Low Analysis; Cost of Goods Manufactured (LO1, LO2)**

CHECK FIGURE
(2) $30,000 per month
plus $8 per unit

Amfac Company manufactures a single product. The company keeps careful records of manufacturing activities from which the following information has been extracted:

| | Level of Activity | |
| --- | --- | --- |
| | March-Low | June-High |
| Number of units produced .............. | 6,000 | 9,000 |
| Cost of goods manufactured ............. | $168,000 | $257,000 |
| Work in process inventory, beginning ...... | 9,000 | 32,000 |
| Work in process inventory, ending ......... | 15,000 | 21,000 |
| Direct materials cost per unit ............. | 6 | 6 |
| Direct labour cost per unit ............... | 10 | 10 |
| Manufacturing overhead cost, total ........ | ? | ? |

The company's manufacturing overhead cost consists of both variable and fixed cost elements. To have data available for planning, management wants to determine how much of the overhead cost is variable with units produced and how much of it is fixed per month.

*Required:*
1. For both March and June, determine the amount of manufacturing overhead cost added to production. The company had no under- or over-applied overhead in either month. (Hint: A useful way to proceed might be to construct a schedule of cost of goods manufactured.)
2. By means of the high-low method of cost analysis, estimate a cost formula for manufacturing overhead. Express the variable portion of the formula in terms of a variable rate per unit of product.
3. If 7,000 units are produced during a month, what would be the cost of goods manufactured? (Assume that work in process inventories do not change and that there is no under- or over-applied overhead cost for the month.)

# Building Your Skills

**ANALYTICAL THINKING   (LO2, LO3)**

CHECK FIGURE
Cost formula,
$Y = \$41,500 + \$2.30X$

The Ramon Company manufactures a wide range of products at several plant locations. The Franklin plant, which manufactures electrical components, has been experiencing difficulties with fluctuating monthly overhead costs. The fluctuations have made it difficult to estimate the level of overhead that will be incurred for any one month.

Management wants to be able to estimate overhead costs accurately in order to better plan its operational and financial needs. A trade association publication to which Ramon Company subscribes indicates that for companies manufacturing electrical components, overhead tends to vary with direct labour-hours.

One member of the accounting staff has proposed the cost behaviour pattern of the overhead costs be determined. Then overhead costs could be predicted from the budgeted direct labour-hours.

Another member of the accounting staff has suggested that a good starting place for determining the cost behaviour pattern of overhead costs would be an analysis of historical data. The historical cost behaviour pattern would provide a basis for estimating future overhead costs. Ramon Company has decided to employ the high-low method and the scattergraph method. Data on direct labour-hours and the respective overhead costs incurred have been collected for the past two years. The raw data are as follows:

| | Prior Year | | Current Year | |
|---|---|---|---|---|
| Month | Direct Labour-Hours | Overhead Costs | Direct Labour-Hours | Overhead Costs |
| January | 20,000 | $84,000 | 21,000 | $86,000 |
| February | 25,000 | 99,000 | 24,000 | 93,000 |
| March | 22,000 | 89,500 | 23,000 | 93,000 |
| April | 23,000 | 90,000 | 22,000 | 87,000 |
| May | 20,000 | 81,500 | 20,000 | 80,000 |
| June | 19,000 | 75,500 | 18,000 | 76,500 |
| July | 14,000 | 70,500 | 12,000 | 67,500 |
| August | 10,000 | 64,500 | 13,000 | 71,000 |
| September | 12,000 | 69,000 | 15,000 | 73,500 |
| October | 17,000 | 75,000 | 17,000 | 72,500 |
| November | 16,000 | 71,500 | 15,000 | 71,000 |
| December | 19,000 | 78,000 | 18,000 | 75,000 |

All equipment in the Franklin plant is leased under an arrangement calling for a flat fee up to 19,500 direct labour-hours of activity in the plant, after which lease charges are assessed on an hourly basis. Lease expense is a major item of overhead cost.

***Required:***
1.  Using the high-low method, estimate the cost formula for overhead in the Franklin plant.
2.  Prepare a scattergraph, including on it all data for the two-year period. Fit a regression line or lines to the plotted points by visual inspection. In this part, it is not necessary to compute the fixed and variable cost elements.
3.  Assume that the Franklin plant works 22,500 direct labour-hours during a month. Compute the expected overhead cost for the month using the cost formulas developed above with:
    a.  The high-low method.
    b.  The scattergraph method [read the expected costs directly off the graph prepared in (2) above].
4.  Of the two proposed methods, which one should the Ramon Company use to estimate monthly overhead costs in the Franklin plant? Explain fully, indicating the reasons why the other method is less desirable.
5.  Would a relevant range concept probably be more or less important in the Franklin plant than in most companies?

(CMA, adapted)

**COMMUNICATING IN PRACTICE**   (LO1, LO4)
Maria Chavez owns a catering company that serves food and beverages at parties and business functions. Chavez's business is seasonal, with a heavy schedule during the summer months and holidays and a lighter schedule at other times.

One of the major events requested by Chavez's customers is a cocktail party. She offers a standard cocktail party and has estimated the total cost per guest as follows:

| | |
|---|---|
| Food and beverages | $15.00 |
| Labour (0.5 hours @ $10.00 per hour) | 5.00 |
| Overhead (0.5 hours @ $13.98 per hour) | 6.99 |
| Total cost per guest | $26.99 |

The standard cocktail party lasts three hours, and she hires one worker for every six guests, which works out to one-half hour of direct labour per guest. The servers work only as needed and are paid only for the hours they actually work.

When bidding on cocktail parties, Chavez adds a 15% markup to yield a price of $31 per guest. Chavez is confident about her estimates of the costs of food and beverages and labour but is not as comfortable with the estimate of overhead cost. The overhead cost per guest was determined by dividing total over-head expenses for the last 12 months by total labour hours for the same period. Her overhead includes such costs as annual rent for office space, administrative costs (including those relating to hiring and paying workers), and so on.

Chavez has received a request to bid on a large fund-raising cocktail party to be given next month by an important local charity. (The party would last three hours.) She would really like to win this contract—the guest list for this charity event includes many prominent individuals she would like to land as future clients. Other caterers have also been invited to bid on the event, and she believes that one, if not more, of those companies will bid less than $31 per guest. She is not willing to lose money on the event and needs your input before making any decisions.

*Required:*
Write a memorandum to Ms. Chavez that addresses the validity of her concern about her estimate of over-head costs and whether or not she should base her bid on the estimated cost of $26.99 per guest. (Hint: Start by discussing the need to consider cost behaviour when estimating costs. You can safely assume that she will not incur any additional fixed costs if she wins the bid on this cocktail party.)

## TEAMWORK IN ACTION  (LO1)

Assume that your team is going to form a company that will manufacture chocolate chip cookies. The team is responsible for preparing a list of all product components and costs necessary to manufacture this product.

*Required:*
1. The team should discuss and then write up a brief description of the definitions of variable, fixed, and mixed costs. All team members should agree with and understand the definitions.
2. After preparing a list of all product components and costs necessary to manufacture your cookies, identify each of the product costs as direct materials, direct labour, or factory overhead. Then, identify each of those costs as variable, fixed, or mixed.
3. Prepare to report this information in class. (Each teammate can assume responsibility for a different part of the presentation.)

Do not forget to check out Taking It to the Net as well as other quizzes and resources at the Online Learn-ing Centre at www.mcgrawhill.ca/college/garrison.

# Chapter Seven

# Cost-Volume-Profit Relationships

## A Look Back

After noting the importance of understanding cost behaviour in Chapter 6, we described variable, fixed, and mixed costs and overviewed the methods that can be used to break a mixed cost into its variable and fixed components. We also introduced the contribution format income statement.

## A Look at This Chapter

Chapter 7 describes the basics of cost-volume-profit analysis, an essential tool for decision making. Cost-volume-profit analysis helps managers understand the inter-relationships among cost, volume, and profit.

## A Look Ahead

Chapter 8 describes the process used to create a basic budget, a key element of the profit planning process.

## Chapter Outline

## DECISION FEATURE  One More Airline

Who needs a new airline in Canada? The fiercely competitive industry is in its third straight year of decline, and on average, one airline per year has gone broke over the past 25 years. But David Ho, a multimillionaire Vancouver entrepreneur, strongly believes that HMY Airways can be successful in this industry.

Tired of unpleasant flying experiences, Ho's 10-year old daughter wanted her father to do something about it, and he did! After launching HMY Airways on February 28, 2002, Ho quickly got down to business and started recruiting key operating personnel. After obtaining all required government clearances, HMY's first flight hit the sky from Vancouver to Mexico on November 22 that same year.

Whether the airline will survive is anybody's guess, but according to some experts, HMY certainly enjoys some cost advantages because of its size. It offers the lowest fares from Vancouver to Toronto (less than $400) plus a hot meal, free wine and entertainment, and more leg room for the bigger-sized travellers. Pricing the travel low means that HMY cannot earn hefty margins and must pay close attention to two factors: (1) controlling costs, and (2) attracting passengers.

Has HMY succeeded in its efforts? Within a year of its first flight, the company launched an online booking service, and the airline now offers two flights daily between Vancouver and Toronto, as well as regular flights to Los Angeles and Las Vegas. In October 2003, Ho claimed that the airline's load factor (occupancy rate) had risen to 75% and that HMY would break even by the end of the year. Whether HMY will be a force to reckon with for Air Canada and WestJet remains to be seen.

Source: Seccombe. W. Bird of Pray. www.canadianbusiness.com, 2003-10-27. Reprinted with permission from *Canadian Business*.

## Learning Objectives

*After studying Chapter 7, you should be able to:*

**LO1** Explain how changes in activity affect contribution margin and net operating income..

**LO2** Use the contribution margin ratio (CM ratio) to compute changes in contribution margin and net operating income resulting from changes in sales volume.

**LO3** Prepare and interpret a cost-volume-profit (CVP) graph.

**LO4** Show the effects on contribution margin of changes in variable costs, fixed costs, selling price, and volume.

**LO5** Compute the break-even point.

**LO6** Determine the level of sales needed to achieve a desired target profit.

**LO7** Compute the margin of safety and explain its significance.

**LO8** Compute the degree of operating leverage at a particular level of sales and explain how the degree of operating leverage can be used to predict changes in net operating income.

**LO9** Compute the break-even point for a multiple-product company and explain the effects of shifts in the sales mix on contribution margin and the break-even point.

**C**ost-volume-profit (CVP) analysis is one of the most powerful tools that managers have at their command. It helps them understand the inter-relationship between cost, volume, and profit in an organization so that they can determine, for example, what products to manufacture or sell, what pricing policy to follow, what marketing strategy to employ, and what type of production facilities to acquire. To help understand the role of CVP analysis in business decisions, consider the case of Acoustic Concepts, Inc., a company founded by Prem Narayan.

## MANAGERIAL ACCOUNTING IN ACTION

### The Issue

Accoustic Concepts, Inc.

Prem, an engineer, started Acoustic Concepts to market a radically new speaker he had designed for automobile sound systems. The speaker, called the Sonic Blaster, uses an advanced microprocessor chip to boost amplification to awesome levels. Prem contracted with a Taiwanese electronics manufacturer to produce the speaker. With seed money provided by his family, Prem placed an order with the manufacturer and ran advertisements in auto magazines.

The Sonic Blaster was a success. Sales grew to the point that Prem moved the company's headquarters out of his apartment and into rented quarters in a neighbouring industrial park. He also hired a receptionist, an accountant, a sales manager, and a small sales staff to sell the speakers to retail stores. The accountant, Bob Luchinni, had worked for several small companies where he had acted as a business advisor as well as accountant and bookkeeper. The following discussion occurred soon after Bob was hired:

*Prem:* Bob, I've got a lot of questions about the company's finances that I hope you can help answer.
*Bob:* We're in great shape. The loan from your family will be paid off within a few months.
*Prem:* I know, but I am worried about the risks I've assumed by expanding operations. What would happen if a competitor entered the market and our sales slipped? How far could sales drop before we start to lose money? Another question I've been trying to resolve is how much our sales would have to increase in order to justify the big marketing campaign the sales staff is pushing for.
*Bob:* Marketing always wants more money for advertising.
*Prem:* And they are always pushing me to drop the selling price on the speaker. I agree with them that a lower price will boost our volume, but I'm not sure the increased volume will offset the loss in revenue from the lower price.
*Bob:* It sounds like these questions all are related in some way to the relationships between our selling prices, our costs, and our volume. We shouldn't have a problem coming up with some answers. I'll need a day or two, though, to gather some data.
*Prem:* Why don't we set up a meeting for three days from now? That would be Thursday.
*Bob:* That'll be fine. I'll have some preliminary answers for you as well as a model you can use for answering similar questions in the future.
*Prem:* Good. I'll be looking forward to seeing what you come up with.

## The Basics of Cost-Volume-Profit (CVP) Analysis

Bob Luchinni's preparation for the Thursday meeting begins where our study of cost behaviour in the preceding chapter left off—with the contribution income statement. The contribution income statement emphasizes the behaviour of costs and therefore is extremely helpful to a manager in judging the impact on profits of changes in selling price, cost, or volume. Bob will base his analysis on the following contribution income statement he prepared last month:

| ACOUSTIC CONCEPTS, INC.<br>Contribution Income Statement<br>For the Month of June | | |
|---|---|---|
| | **Total** | **Per Unit** |
| Sales (400 speakers) . . . . . . . . . . . | $100,000 | $250 |
| Less variable expenses . . . . . . . . . | 60,000 | 150 |
| Contribution margin . . . . . . . . . . . | 40,000 | $100 |
| Less fixed expenses . . . . . . . . . . . | 35,000 | |
| Net income . . . . . . . . . . . . . . . . . | $ 5,000 | |

Note that sales, variable expenses, and contribution margin are expressed on a per-unit basis as well as in total. This is a good idea on income statements prepared for management's own use, since it facilitates profitability analysis.

## Contribution Margin

Contribution margin is the amount remaining from sales revenue after variable expenses have been deducted. Thus, it is the amount available to cover fixed expenses and then to provide profits for the period. Note the sequence here—contribution margin is used *first* to cover the fixed expenses, and then whatever remains goes toward profits. If the contribution margin is not sufficient to cover the fixed expenses, then a loss occurs for the period. To illustrate with an extreme example, assume that Acoustic Concepts sells only one speaker during a particular month. Then, the company's income statement will appear as follows:

**Learning Objective 1**
Explain how changes in activity affect contribution margin and net operating income.

| | **Total** | **Per Unit** |
|---|---|---|
| Sales (1 speaker) . . . . . . . . . . . . . . | $ 250 | $250 |
| Less variable expenses . . . . . . . . . | 150 | 150 |
| Contribution margin . . . . . . . . . . . | 100 | $100 |
| Less fixed expenses . . . . . . . . . . . | 35,000 | |
| Net loss . . . . . . . . . . . . . . . . . . . . | $(34,900) | |

For each additional speaker that the company is able to sell during the month, $100 more in contribution margin will become available to help cover the fixed expenses. If a second speaker is sold, for example, then the total contribution margin will increase by $100 (to a total of $200) and the company's loss will decrease by $100, to $34,800:

| | **Total** | **Per Unit** |
|---|---|---|
| Sales (2 speakers) . . . . . . . . . . . . . | $ 500 | $250 |
| Less variable expenses . . . . . . . . . | 300 | 150 |
| Contribution margin . . . . . . . . . . . | 200 | $100 |
| Less fixed expenses . . . . . . . . . . . | 35,000 | |
| Net loss . . . . . . . . . . . . . . . . . . . . | $(34,800) | |

If enough speakers can be sold to generate $35,000 in contribution margin, then all of the fixed costs will be covered and the company will have managed to at least *break even* for the month—that is, to show neither profit nor loss but just cover all of its costs. This is the *concept* of "breaking even." In order to break even, the company will have to sell 350 speakers in a month, since each speaker sold yields $100 in contribution margin:

| | Total | Per Unit |
|---|---|---|
| Sales (350 speakers) . . . . . . . . . . . | $87,500 | $250 |
| Less variable expenses . . . . . . . . . | 52,500 | 150 |
| Contribution margin . . . . . . . . . . . | 35,000 | $100 |
| Less fixed expenses . . . . . . . . . . . | 35,000 | |
| Net income . . . . . . . . . . . . . . . . . | $ –0– | |

The quantity, 350, is the company's **break-even point.** That is, it is the level of sales at which profit (net income) is zero. Computation of the break-even point is discussed in detail later in the chapter.

*Once the break-even point has been reached, net income will increase by the amount of the unit contribution margin for each additional unit sold.* For example, if 351 speakers are sold in a month, then we can expect that the net income for the month will be $100, since the company will have sold one speaker more than the number needed to break even:

| | Total | Per Unit |
|---|---|---|
| Sales (351 speakers) . . . . . . . . . . . | $87,750 | $250 |
| Less variable expenses . . . . . . . . . | 52,650 | 150 |
| Contribution margin . . . . . . . . . . . | 35,100 | $100 |
| Less fixed expenses . . . . . . . . . . . | 35,000 | |
| Net income . . . . . . . . . . . . . . . . . | $ 100 | |

If 352 speakers are sold (two speakers above the break-even point), then we can expect that the net income for the month will be $200, and so on. To know what the profits will be at various levels of activity, therefore, it is not necessary to prepare a whole series of income statements. The manager can, instead, simply take the number of units to be sold over the break-even point and multiply that number by the unit contribution margin. The result represents the anticipated profits for the period. Or, to estimate the effect of a planned increase in sales on profits, the manager can simply multiply the increase in units sold by the unit contribution margin. The result will be the expected increase in profits. To illustrate, if Acoustic Concepts is currently selling 400 speakers per month and plans to increase sales to 425 speakers per month, the anticipated impact on profits can be computed as follows:

| | |
|---|---|
| Increased number of speakers to be sold . . . . . . . | 25 |
| Contribution margin per speaker . . . . . . . . . . . . . | × $100 |
| Increase in net income . . . . . . . . . . . . . . . . . . . . | $2,500 |

These calculations can be verified as follows:

| | Sales Volume | | | |
| --- | --- | --- | --- | --- |
| | **400 Speakers** | **425 Speakers** | **Difference 25 Speakers** | **Per Unit** |
| Sales . . . . . . . . . . . . . . . . | $100,000 | $106,250 | $6,250 | $250 |
| Less variable expenses . . . | 60,000 | 63,750 | 3,750 | 150 |
| Contribution margin . . . . . | 40,000 | 42,500 | 2,500 | $100 |
| Less fixed expenses . . . . . | 35,000 | 35,000 | –0– | |
| Net income . . . . . . . . . . . | $  5,000 | $  7,500 | $2,500 | |

To summarize these examples, if there were no sales, the company's loss would equal its fixed expenses. Each unit that is sold reduces the loss by the amount of the unit contribution margin. Once the break-even point has been reached, each additional unit sold increases the company's profit by the amount of the unit contribution margin.

## Contribution Margin Ratio (CM Ratio)

In addition to being expressed on a per-unit basis, sales revenues, variable expenses, and contribution margin for Acoustic Concepts can also be expressed as a percentage of sales:

| | Total | Per Unit | Percent of Sales |
| --- | --- | --- | --- |
| Sales (400 speakers) | $100,000 | $250 | 100% |
| Less variable expenses | 60,000 | 150 | 60 |
| Contribution margin | 40,000 | $100 | 40% |
| Less fixed expenses | 35,000 | | |
| Net income | $  5,000 | | |

**Learning Objective 2**
Use the contribution margin ratio (CM ratio) to compute changes in contribution margin and net operating income resulting from changes in sales volume.

The contribution margin as a percentage of total sales is referred to as the **contribution margin ratio (CM ratio).** This ratio is computed as follows:

$$\text{CM ratio} = \frac{\text{Contribution margin}}{\text{Sales}}$$

For Acoustic Concepts, the computations are as follows:

$$\frac{\text{Total contribution margin, \$40,000}}{\text{Total sales, \$100,000}} = 40\%$$

In a company such as Acoustic Concepts that has only one product, the CM ratio can also be computed as follows:

$$\frac{\text{Per-unit contribution margin, \$100}}{\text{Per-unit sales, \$250}} = 40\%$$

The CM ratio is extremely useful, since it shows how the contribution margin will be affected by a change in total sales. To illustrate, note that Acoustic Concepts has a CM ratio of 40%. This means that for each dollar increase in sales, total contribution margin will increase by 40 cents ($1 sales × CM ratio of 40%). As this illustration suggests, *the impact on contribution margin of any given dollar change in total sales can be computed in seconds by simply applying the CM ratio to the dollar change.* If Acoustic Concepts plans a $30,000 increase in sales during the coming month, for example, management can expect contribution margin to increase by $12,000 ($30,000 increased sales × CM ratio of 40%).

If fixed costs do not change, then the change in the contribution margin will flow through to change net income. Each dollar increase in sales will increase net income by 40 cents ($1 sales × CM ratio of 40%). And a $30,000 increase in sales will increase net income by $12,000.

This is verified by the following table:

| | Sales Volume | | | Percent of Sales |
| --- | --- | --- | --- | --- |
| | **Percent** | **Expected** | **Increase** | |
| Sales . . . . . . . . . . . . . . . . . . | $100,000 | $130,000 | $30,000 | 100% |
| Less variable expenses . . . . | 60,000 | 78,000* | 18,000 | 60 |
| Contribution margin . . . . . . | 40,000 | 52,000 | 12,000 | 40% |
| Less fixed expenses . . . . . . | 35,000 | 35,000 | –0– | |
| Net income . . . . . . . . . . . . | $ 5,000 | $ 17,000 | $12,000 | |

*$130,000 expected sales ÷ $250 per unit = 520 units. 520 units × $150 per unit = $78,000.

The CM ratio is particularly valuable in those situations where the manager must make trade-offs between more dollar sales of one product versus more dollar sales of another. Generally speaking, when trying to increase sales, products that yield the greatest amount of contribution margin per dollar of sales should be emphasized.

## CVP Relationships in Graphic Form

Concept 7–1

The relations among revenue, cost, profit, and volume can be expressed graphically by preparing a **cost-volume-profit (CVP) graph.** A CVP graph highlights CVP relationships over wide ranges of activity and can give managers a perspective that can be obtained in no other way. To help explain his analysis to Prem Narayan, Bob Luchinni decided to prepare a CVP graph for Acoustic Concepts.

**PREPARING THE CVP GRAPH** In a CVP graph (sometimes called a *break-even chart*), unit volume is commonly represented on the horizontal (X) axis and dollars on the vertical (Y) axis. Preparing a CVP graph involves three steps. These steps are keyed to the graph in Exhibit 7–1:

1. Draw a line parallel to the volume axis to represent total fixed expenses. For Acoustic Concepts, total fixed expenses are $35,000.
2. Choose some volume of sales and plot the point representing total expenses (fixed and variable) at the activity level you have selected. In Exhibit 7–1, Bob Luchinni chose a volume of 600 speakers. Total expenses at that activity level would be as follows:

| | |
| --- | --- |
| Fixed expenses . . . . . . . . . . . . . . . . . . . . . . . . . . . . . . . . . . . . . | $ 35,000 |
| Variable expenses (600 speakers × $150 per speaker) . . . | 90,000 |
| Total expenses . . . . . . . . . . . . . . . . . . . . . . . . . . . . . . . . . . . . | $125,000 |

After the point has been plotted, draw a line through it back to the point where the fixed expenses line intersects the dollars axis.

3.  Again choose some volume of sales and plot the point representing total sales dollars at the activity level you have selected. In Exhibit 7–1, Bob Luchinni again chose a volume of 600 speakers. Sales at that activity level total $150,000 (600 speakers × $250 per speaker). Draw a line through this point back to the origin.

The interpretation of the completed CVP graph is given in Exhibit 7–2. The anticipated profit or loss at any given level of sales is measured by the vertical distance between the total revenue line (sales) and the total expenses line (variable expenses plus fixed expenses).

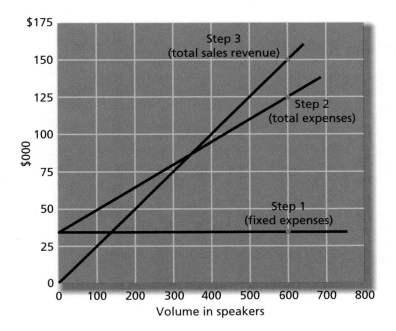

**Exhibit 7–1**
Preparing the CVP Graph

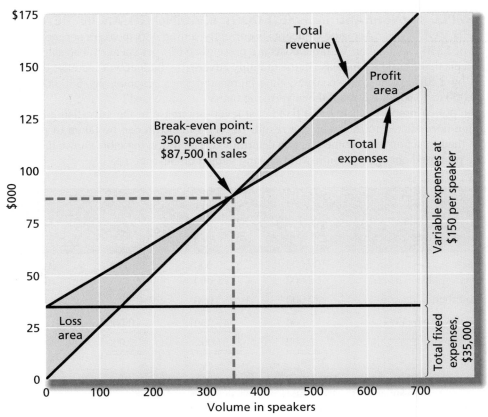

**Exhibit 7–2**
The Completed CVP Graph

The break-even point is where the total revenue and total expenses lines cross. The break-even point of 350 speakers in Exhibit 7–2 agrees with the break-even point computed earlier.

As discussed earlier, when sales are below the break-even point—in this case, 350 units—the company suffers a loss. Note that the loss (represented by the vertical distance between the total expense and total revenue lines) gets worse as sales decline. When sales are above the break-even point, the company earns a profit and the size of the profit (represented by the vertical distance between the total revenue and total expense lines) increases as sales increase.

## Some Applications of CVP Concepts

Bob Luchinni, the accountant at Acoustic Concepts wanted to demonstrate to the company's president, Prem Narayan, how the CVP concepts developed so far can be used in planning and decision making. The CVP framework provides management with the following *levers*: unit variable costs, fixed costs, and selling price. These levers can be used either singly or in combination to influence the sales volume. In so doing, the company's profitability will be affected. The objective of CVP analysis is to determine this impact on the profits. The impact on profits will depend on the effect of the policy on total contribution margin and how that effect flows through to profits. The challenge for managers is that many policies that are proposed can involve changes to both revenues and costs. The ultimate impact on the bottom line—the company's profits—is rarely transparent without a careful analysis. In the following examples, try to identify which combination of levers management is proposing to pull, the nature of trade-offs facing management, and the effect of a proposed policy on the company's profits.

The following approach will be followed. First, the impact of a proposed policy on the *total* contribution margin will be determined. Second, the impact of a proposed policy on fixed costs will be determined, if necessary. By comparing these two impacts, it will be possible to determine the impact on the company's profits, that is, net income.

**EXAMPLE 1: INCREASE IN FIXED COST LEADING TO AN INCREASE IN SALES VOLUME**    Acoustic Concepts is currently selling 400 speakers per month at a price of $250 per speaker. Variable costs are presently $150 per speaker. The sales manager feels that a $10,000 increase in the monthly advertising budget will increase monthly sales by 120 units to 520 speakers, thus increasing sales revenues by $30,000 from $100,000 to $130,000. Should the advertising budget be increased?

The policy proposes to pull the fixed cost lever—increase in the advertising budget. Volume is predicted to increase as a result. Before a decision can be taken to pull the lever, the impact on net income must be determined. The following table shows the effect of the proposed change in monthly advertising budget on net income:

|  | Current Sales | Sales with Additional Advertising Budget | Difference | Percent of Sales |
|---|---|---|---|---|
| Sales . . . . . . . . . . . . . . | $100,000 | $130,000 | $30,000 | 100% |
| Less variable expenses . . | 60,000 | 78,000* | 18,000 | 60 |
| Contribution margin . . . . | 40,000 | 52,000 | 12,000 | 40% |
| Less fixed expenses . . . . . | 35,000 | 45,000† | 10,000 | |
| Net income . . . . . . . . . . | $ 5,000 | $ 7,000 | $ 2,000 | |

*520 units × $150 per unit = $78,000.
†$35,000 plus additional $10,000 monthly advertising budget = $45,000.

The increase in the advertising budget should be approved, since it would lead to an increase in net income of $2,000. There are two shorter ways to present this solution. The first alternative solution follows:

### ALTERNATIVE SOLUTION 1

| | |
|---|---|
| Expected total contribution margin: | |
| $130,000 × 40% CM ratio .............. | $52,000 |
| Present total contribution margin: | |
| $100,000 × 40% CM ratio .............. | 40,000 |
| Incremental contribution margin ............ | 12,000 |
| Change in fixed costs: | |
| Less incremental advertising expense ....... | 10,000 |
| Increased net income ..................... | $ 2,000 |

Since in this case only the fixed costs and the sales volume change, the solution can be presented in an even shorter format, as follows:

### ALTERNATIVE SOLUTION 2

| | |
|---|---|
| Incremental contribution margin: | |
| $30,000 × 40% CM ratio ................ | $12,000 |
| Less incremental advertising expense ......... | 10,000 |
| Increased net income ..................... | $ 2,000 |

Note that this approach does not depend on a knowledge of previous sales. Also note that it is unnecessary under either shorter approach to prepare an income statement. Both of the solutions above involve an **incremental analysis** in that they consider only those items of revenue, cost, and volume that will change if the new program is implemented. Although in each case a new income statement could have been prepared, most managers would prefer the incremental approach. It is simpler and more direct and focuses attention on the specific items involved in the decision. Finally, note that the expected impact on volume from the change in the advertising budget must be provided before you can decide to implement the proposed change to the advertising budget.

## EXAMPLE 2: INCREASE IN UNIT VARIABLE COSTS LEADING TO AN INCREASE IN SALES VOLUME

Acoustic Concepts is currently selling 400 speakers per month at a unit price of $250. Management is contemplating the use of higher-quality components, which would increase variable costs per unit from $150 to $160 (and thereby reducing the unit contribution by $10 per speaker). The sales manager predicts that the higher quality would increase sales to 480 speakers per month. Should the higher-quality components be used?

In this example, the proposal is to pull the variable cost per unit lever. The predicted impact on sales is an increase of 80 units. Now management must determine the impact on net income of the proposed policy. The way to do this is to determine the impact on total contribution and then the impact on fixed costs and then compare the two impacts.

The $10 increase in the unit variable costs will cause the unit contribution margin to go down from $100 to $90. The total contribution margin is expected to change as follows:

| | |
|---|---|
| Expected total contribution margin with higher-quality components: | |
| 480 speakers × $90 contribution margin per speaker ............ | $43,200 |
| Present total contribution margin: | |
| 400 speakers × $100 contribution margin per speaker ........... | $40,000 |
| Increase in total contribution margin ............................ | $ 3,200 |

Since fixed costs will not change, net income should increase by the $3,200 increase in total contribution shown above. The higher-quality components should be used.

### EXAMPLE 3: INCREASE IN FIXED COST, DECREASE IN SELLING PRICE, LEADING TO AN INCREASE IN SALES VOLUME

Acoustic Concepts is currently selling 400 speakers per month at a price of $250 per speaker. The variable costs are $150 per speaker. The sales manager would like to cut the selling price by $20 per speaker to $220 and increase the advertising budget by $15,000 per month. The sales manager argues that if these two steps are taken, unit sales will increase by 200 speakers (50%) to 600 speakers per month. Should the changes be made?

Management is proposing to pull two levers—sales price and fixed costs—together to increase sales. A decrease of $20 per speaker in the selling price will reduce the unit contribution margin from $100 to $80. The increase in the advertising budget by $15,000 will cause fixed cost to increase by this amount. To determine the impact of these changes on net income, the effect on total contribution margin must be compared with the effect on fixed cost. This is shown in the following table:

| | |
|---|---:|
| Expected total contribution margin with higher volume due to a lower selling price and increase in the advertising budget: | |
| 600 speakers × $80 contribution margin per speaker .............. | $48,000 |
| Present total contribution margin: | |
| 400 speakers × $100 contribution margin per speaker ............. | $40,000 |
| Incremental contribution margin (1) ............................. | $ 8,000 |
| Change in fixed costs: | |
| Increase in advertising budget (2) ............................. | $15,000 |
| Increase (reduction) in net income (1) – (2) ...................... | ($7,000) |

On the basis of the information above, the changes should not be made.

### EXAMPLE 4: INCREASE IN VARIABLE COST PER UNIT AND DECREASE IN FIXED COST LEADING TO AN INCREASE IN SALES VOLUME

Acoustic Concepts is currently selling 400 speakers at a price of $250 per speaker. The variable costs are $150 per speaker. Fixed cost is $35,000. The sales manager would like to pay sales staff a commission of $15 per speaker sold, rather than pay them flat salaries that now total $6,000 per month. The sales manager is confident that the change will increase monthly sales by 60 speakers (15%) to 460 speakers. Should the change be made?

In this example, management proposes to pull the variable cost and fixed cost levers which is predicted to lead to an increase in sales. Paying a commission for each speaker sold instead of a flat salary will increase variable cost per speaker by $15 to $165 per speaker and reduce fixed cost by $6,000. Unit contribution margin will decrease by $15 to $85 per speaker. The impact of the these changes on total contribution margin and fixed cost is shown in the following table:

| | |
|---|---:|
| Expected total contribution margin with higher volume due to a higher variable cost per unit and decrease in fixed cost: | |
| 460 speakers × $85 contribution margin per speaker ............. | $39,100 |
| Present total contribution margin: | |
| 400 speakers × $100 contribution margin per speaker ........... | $40,000 |
| Incremental contribution margin (1) ........................... | ($900) |
| Change in fixed costs: | |
| Decrease in fixed cost from salaries avoided (2) ................ | ($6,000) |
| Increase (reduction) in net income (1) – (2) ...................... | $5,100 |

On the basis of the analysis above, the changes should be made. The company stands to increase net income by $5,100 by switching to a commission-based compensation system from the present policy of paying flat salaries.

The same conclusion can be obtained by preparing comparative income statements. This approach is shown in the table below:

| | Present 400 Speakers per Month | | Expected 460 Speakers per Month | | Difference: Increase or (Decrease) in Net Income |
|---|---|---|---|---|---|
| | Total | Per Unit | Total | Per Unit | |
| Sales ............... | $100,000 | $250 | $115,000 | $250 | $15,000 |
| Less variable expenses .. | 60,000 | 150 | 75,900 | 165 | (15,900) |
| Contribution margin .... | 40,000 | $100 | 39,100 | $ 85 | (900) |
| Less fixed expenses .... | 35,000 | | 29,000 | | 6,000 |
| Net income .......... | $  5,000 | | $ 10,100 | | $ 5,100 |

## EXAMPLE 5: CALCULATION OF SELLING PRICE TO MEET PROFIT TARGET

Acoustics Concepts has an opportunity to make a special-order bulk sale of 150 speakers to a wholesaler if an acceptable price can be worked out. This sale will not affect the company's regular sales or its fixed cost. Variable cost is $150 per speaker. Acoustic Concepts would like to make a profit of $3,000 from this sale. What price per speaker should be quoted?

Since the special sale will not affect fixed costs, the company's profits from the sale will be $3,000 if the total contribution margin from the sale is also $3,000. Since the sale is for 150 speakers, the contribution margin per speaker has to be $3,000 ÷ 150 = $20. Given a variable cost of $150 per speaker, the desired selling price per speaker will be the variable cost per speaker plus the contribution margin per speaker, that is, $150 + $20 = $170. The company should quote a price of $170 per speaker. The calculation is summarized below:

| | |
|---|---|
| Variable cost per speaker .................... | $150 |
| Desired profit per speaker: | |
| $3,000 ÷ 150 speakers .................... | 20 |
| Quoted price per speaker .................... | $170 |

This example is different from the earlier examples. It does not involve tracing the impact of pulling a combination of levers on profits. Instead, it illustrates the use of the CVP framework to determine a pricing policy for a special sales order, given costs and a profit target. The CVP framework is a flexible framework that can aid management in planning and decision making.

## Importance of the Contribution Margin

CVP analysis seeks the most profitable combination of variable cost per unit, fixed cost, and selling price. These are levers available for management to pull to influence first volume and ultimately the company's profits. The examples just presented show that without a framework to analyze the effect of pulling the levers, management cannot determine if a proposed policy to improve profits should be adopted.

The challenge is that using a combination of levers involves trade-offs: you have to spend money to make money. Whether you come out ahead at the end will depend on whether the incremental total contribution compares favourably with the incremental fixed cost. Exhibit 7–3, a summary of the examples, illustrates this point.

## Exhibit 7–3
Summary of CVP Examples Illustrating the Use CVP Framework for Decision Making

|  | Example 1 | Example 2 | Example 3 | Example 4 |
|---|---|---|---|---|
| Revenue lever: Selling price | Unchanged | Unchanged | Decrease by $20 per speaker | Unchanged |
| Cost lever: Variable cost per unit | Unchanged | Increase by $10 per speaker | Unchanged | Increase by $15 per speaker |
| Cost lever: Fixed cost | Increase by $10,000 | Unchanged | Increase by $15,000 | Decrease by $6,000 |
| *Predicted* impact on volume | Increase by 120 speakers | Increase by 80 speakers | Increase by 200 speakers | Increase by 60 speakers |
| *Calculated* impact on total contribution margin | Increase by $12,000 | Increase by $3,200 | Increase by $8,000 | Decrease by $900 |
| *Calculated* impact on net income | Increase by $2,000 | Increase by $3,200 | Decrease by $7,000 | Increase by $5,100 |

In the first example, management predicts an increase in volume from increasing the fixed cost. The increase in volume causes the total contribution margin to increase. Profits increased because this increase is greater that the increase in the fixed cost. In this example, management spends money (increases fixed cost) to make money (increase profits).

In the second example, a volume increase is obtained by an increase in variable cost per unit. Although the unit contribution margin decreased, the *total* contribution margin increased because of the increase in volume. The increase in the total contribution margin flows through to the bottom line because the fixed costs are unchanged.

In the third example, management decreases unit price and increases fixed cost. The increase in volume from taking these steps does not increase the total contribution margin sufficiently to cover the increase in fixed costs. Profits are reduced. Therefore, the proposed policy is rejected. Note here that simply looking at the total contribution margin alone is not enough if fixed costs are also changed. It is only from a comparison of the impact on the total contribution margin with the impact on fixed cost can the correct conclusion be reached.

In the fourth example, management decreases fixed expenses and simultaneously increases variable cost per unit. The unit contribution margin is reduced. Management predicts an increase in volume from the steps taken. But the total contribution margin *decreases* from its current level because the increase in volume cannot offset the effect of the reduction in the unit contribution margin. Nonetheless, profits increase because fixed expense is reduced by more than the decrease in the total contribution margin. This example illustrates that a decline in contribution margin need not cause too much distress, provided fixed costs are reduced by even more.

In general, these examples illustrate that it is important to carefully analyze a policy using the CVP framework to determine the impact on profits, especially when there are increases (or decreases) to both costs and revenue. The key is that the effect of a policy on the total contribution margin must be compared with the effect of the policy on fixed cost. This is clear from the exhibit, where you can see that the impact on the bottom line follows from subtracting the impact on the total contribution margin from the impact on the fixed cost.

Finally, note that the size of the unit contribution margin (or the size of the CM ratio) will heavily influence the steps a company is willing to take to improve profits. For example, the greater the unit contribution margin for a product, the greater is the amount that a company will spend in order to increase sales volume by a given percentage (look at example 1 again). This explains why companies with high unit contribution margins (like car makers) advertise so heavily, while companies with low unit contribution margins (such as appliance makers) tend to spend much less on advertising.

# Break-Even Analysis

CVP analysis is sometimes referred to simply as break-even analysis. This is unfortunate because break-even analysis is only one element of CVP analysis—although an important element. Break-even analysis is designed to answer such questions as those asked by Prem Narayan, the president of Acoustic Concepts, concerning how far sales could drop before the company begins to lose money.

Concept 7–2

## Break-Even Computations

Earlier in the chapter, we defined the break-even point to be the level of sales at which the company's profit is zero. The break-even point can be computed using either the *equation method* or the *contribution margin method*—the two methods are equivalent.

> **Learning Objective 5**
> Compute the break-even point.

**THE EQUATION METHOD** The **equation method** centres on the contribution approach to the income statement illustrated earlier in the chapter. The format of this income statement can be expressed in equation form as follows:

$$\text{Profits} = \text{Sales} - (\text{Variable expenses} + \text{Fixed expenses})$$

Rearranging this equation slightly yields the following equation, which is widely used in CVP analysis:

$$\text{Sales} = \text{Variable expenses} + \text{Fixed expenses} + \text{Profits}$$

At the break-even point, profits are zero. Therefore, the break-even point can be computed by finding that point where sales just equal the total of the variable expenses plus the fixed expenses. For Acoustic Concepts, the break-even point in unit sales, $Q$, can be computed as follows:

$$\text{Sales} = \text{Variable expenses} + \text{Fixed expenses} + \text{Profits}$$

$$\$250Q = \$150Q + \$35,000 + \$0$$
$$\$100Q = \$35,000$$
$$Q = \$35,000 \div \$100 \text{ per speaker}$$
$$Q = 350 \text{ speakers}$$

where:

$Q$ = Number (quantity) of speakers sold
$\$250$ = Unit sales price
$\$150$ = Unit variable expenses
$\$35,000$ = Total fixed expenses

The break-even point in sales dollars can be computed by multiplying the break-even level of unit sales by the selling price per unit:

$$350 \text{ speakers} \times \$250 \text{ per speaker} = \$87,500$$

The break-even in total sales dollars, $X$, can also be directly computed as follows:

$$\text{Sales} = \text{Variable expenses} + \text{Fixed expenses} + \text{Profits}$$
$$X = 0.60X + \$35,000 + \$0$$
$$0.40X = \$35,000$$
$$X = \$35,000 \div 0.40$$
$$X = \$87,500$$

where:

$X$ = Total sales dollars

0.60 = Variable expense ratio (Variable expenses ÷ Sales)

$35,000 = Total fixed expenses

Firms often have data available only in percentage or ratio form, and the approach we have just illustrated must then be used to find the break-even point. Note that use of ratios in the equation yields a break-even point in sales dollars, rather than in units sold. The break-even point in units sold is the following:

$$\$87,500 \div \$250 \text{ per speaker} = 350 \text{ speakers}$$

---

*you* *decide*                    **Recruit**

S

Assume that you are being recruited by the ConneXus Corp. and have an interview scheduled later this week. You are interested in working for this company for a variety of reasons. In preparation for the interview, you did some research at your local library and gathered the following information about the company. ConneXus is a company set up by two young engineers, George Searle and Humphrey Chen, to allow consumers to order music CDs on their cell phones. Suppose you hear on the radio a cut from a CD that you would like to own. If you subscribe to their service, you would pick up your cell phone, punch "*CD," and enter the radio station's frequency and the time you heard the song, and the CD would be on its way to you.

ConneXus charges about $17 for a CD, including shipping. The company pays its supplier about $13, leaving a contribution margin of $4 per CD. Because of the fixed costs of running the service (about $1,850,000 a year), Searle expects the company to lose about $1.5 million in its first year of operations on sales of 88,000 CDs.

What are your initial impressions of this company based on the information you gathered? What other information would you want to obtain during the job interview?

Adapted from: Peter Kafka, "Play It Again," *Forbes*, July 26, 1999, p. 94.

---

**THE CONTRIBUTION MARGIN METHOD**   The **contribution margin method** is actually just a shortcut version of the equation method already described. The approach centres on the idea discussed earlier that each unit sold provides a certain amount of contribution margin that goes toward covering fixed costs. To find how many units must be sold to break even, divide the total fixed expenses by the unit contribution margin:

$$\text{Break-even point in units sold} = \frac{\text{Fixed expenses}}{\text{Unit contribution margin}}$$

Each speaker generates a contribution margin of $100 ($250 selling price, less $150 variable expenses). Since the total fixed expenses are $35,000, the break-even point is computed as follows:

$$\frac{\text{Fixed expenses}}{\text{Unit contribution margin}} = \frac{\$35,000}{\$100 \text{ per speaker}} = 350 \text{ speakers}$$

A variation of this method uses the CM ratio instead of the unit contribution margin. The result is the break-even in total sales dollars, rather than in total units sold.

$$\text{Break-even point in total sales dollars} = \frac{\text{Fixed expenses}}{\text{CM ratio}}$$

In the Acoustic Concepts example, the calculations are as follows:

$$\frac{\text{Fixed expenses}}{\text{CM ratio}} = \frac{\$35,000}{0.40} = \$87,500$$

This approach, based on the CM ratio, is particularly useful in those situations where a company has multiple product lines and wishes to compute a single break-even point for the company as a whole. More is said on this point in a later section titled The Concept of Sales Mix.

## Operating on a Shoestring

*in business today*

Hesh Kestin failed in his attempt at publishing an English-language newspaper in Israel in the 1980s. His conclusion: "Never start a business with too many people or too much furniture." Kestin's newest venture is *The American,* a Sunday-only newspaper for overseas Americans. His idea is to publish *The American* on the one day of the week that the well-established *International Herald Tribune* (circulation, 190,000 copies) does not publish. But following what he learned from his first failed venture, he is doing it on a shoestring.

In contrast to the Paris-based *International Herald Tribune* with its eight-story office tower and staff of 250, Kestin has set up business in a small clapboard building on Long Island. Working at desks purchased from a thrift shop, Kestin's staff of 12 assembles the tabloid from stories pulled off wire services. The result of this frugality is that *The American*'s break-even point is only 14,000 copies. Sales topped 20,000 copies just two months after the paper's first issue.

Source: Jerry Useem, "American Hopes to Conquer the World—from Long Island," *Inc*, December 1996, p. 23.

## Target Profit Analysis

CVP formulas can be used to determine the sales volume needed to achieve a target profit. Suppose that Prem Narayan of Acoustic Concepts would like to earn a target profit of $40,000 per month. How many speakers would have to be sold?

**Learning Objective 6**
Determine the level of sales needed to achieve a desired target profit.

**THE CVP EQUATION**    One approach is to use the equation method. Instead of solving for the unit sales where profits are zero, you solve for the unit sales where profits are $40,000.

$$\text{Sales} = \text{Variable expenses} + \text{Fixed expenses} + \text{Profits}$$
$$\$250Q = \$150Q + \$35,000 + \$40,000$$
$$\$100Q = \$75,000$$
$$Q = \$75,000 \div \$100 \text{ per speaker}$$
$$Q = 750 \text{ speakers}$$

where:

$Q$ = Number of speakers sold
$250 = Unit sales price
$150 = Unit variable expenses
$35,000 = Total fixed expenses
$40,000 = Target profit

Thus, the target profit can be achieved by selling 750 speakers per month, which represents \$187,500 in total sales (\$250 per speaker × 750 speakers).

**THE CONTRIBUTION MARGIN APPROACH**  A second approach involves expanding the contribution margin formula to include the target profit:

$$\text{Unit sales to attain the target profit} = \frac{\text{Fixed expenses} + \text{Target profit}}{\text{Unit contribution margin}}$$

$$= \frac{\$35,000 + \$40,000}{\$100 \text{ per speaker}}$$

$$= 750 \text{ speakers}$$

This approach gives the same answer as the equation method, since it is simply a shortcut version of the equation method. Similarly, the dollar sales needed to attain the target profit can be computed as follows:

$$\text{Dollar sales to attain target profit} = \frac{\text{Fixed expenses} + \text{Target profit}}{\text{CM ratio}}$$

$$= \frac{\$35,000 + \$40,000}{0.40}$$

$$= \$187,500$$

Likewise, this approach gives the same answer as the equation method, since it is simply a shortcut version of the equation method.

## The Margin of Safety

The **margin of safety** is the excess of budgeted (or actual) sales over the break-even volume of sales. It states the amount by which sales can drop before losses begin to be incurred. The higher the margin of safety, the lower is the risk of not breaking even. The formula for its calculation is:

$$\text{Margin of safety} = \text{Total budgeted (or actual) sales} - \text{Break-even sales}$$

The margin of safety can also be expressed in percentage form. This percentage is obtained by dividing the margin of safety in dollar terms by total sales:

$$\text{Margin of safety percentage} = \frac{\text{Margin of safety in dollars}}{\text{Total budgeted (or actual) sales}}$$

The calculations for the margin of safety for Acoustic Concepts are as follows:

| | |
|---|---|
| Sales (at the current volume of 400 speakers) (a) . . . . . . . . | \$100,000 |
| Break-even sales (at 350 speakers) . . . . . . . . . . . . . . . . . . . | 87,500 |
| Margin of safety (in dollars) (b) . . . . . . . . . . . . . . . . . . . . . | \$ 12,500 |
| Margin of safety as a percentage of sales, (b) ÷ (a) . . . . . . . | 12.5% |

This margin of safety means that at the current level of sales and with the company's current prices and cost structure, a reduction in sales of \$12,500, or 12.5%, would result in just breaking even.

In a single-product firm like Acoustic Concepts, the margin of safety can also be expressed in terms of the number of units sold by dividing the margin of safety in dollars by the selling price per unit. In this case, the margin of safety is 50 speakers ($12,500 ÷ $250 per speaker = 50 speakers).

## Loan Officer

*decision* *maker*

Pak Melwani and Kumar Hathiramani, former silk merchants from Mumbai, opened a soup store in Manhattan after watching a Seinfeld episode featuring the "soup Nazi." The episode parodied a real-life soup vendor, Ali Yeganeh, whose loyal customers put up with hour-long lines and "snarling customer service." Melwani and Hathiramani approached Yeganeh about turning his soup kitchen into a chain, but they were gruffly rebuffed. Instead of giving up, the two hired a French chef with a repertoire of 500 soups and opened a store called Soup Nutsy. For $6 per serving, Soup Nutsy offers 12 homemade soups each day, such as sherry crab bisque and Thai coconut shrimp. Melwani and Hathiramani report that in their first year of operation, they netted $210,000 on sales of $700,000. They report that it costs about $2 per serving to make the soup.

Assume that Melwani and Hathiramani have approached your bank for a loan. As the loan officer, you should consider a variety of factors, including the company's margin of safety. Assuming that other information about the company is favourable, would you consider Soup Nutsy's margin of safety to be comfortable enough to extend the loan?

Adapted from: Silva Sansoni, "The Starbucks of Soup?" *Forbes*, July 7, 1997, pp. 90–91.

---

It is Thursday morning, and Prem Narayan and Bob Luchinni are discussing the results of Bob's analysis.

*Prem:* Bob, everything you have shown me is pretty clear. I can see what impact some of the sales manager's suggestions would have on our profits. Some of those suggestions are quite good, and some are not so good. I also understand that our break-even is 350 speakers, and so we have to make sure we don't slip below that level of sales. What really bothers me is that we are only selling 400 speakers a month now. What did you call the 50-speaker cushion?

*Bob:* That's the margin of safety.

*Prem:* Such a small cushion makes me very nervous. What can we do to increase the margin of safety?

*Bob:* We have to increase total sales or decrease the break-even point or both.

*Prem:* And to decrease the break-even point, we have to either decrease our fixed expenses or increase our unit contribution margin?

*Bob:* Exactly.

*Prem:* And to increase our unit contribution margin, we must either increase our selling price or decrease the variable cost per unit?

*Bob:* Correct.

*Prem:* So, what do you suggest?

*Bob:* Well, the analysis doesn't tell us which of these to do, but it does indicate we have a potential problem here.

*Prem:* If you don't have any immediate suggestions, I would like to call a general meeting next week to discuss ways we can work on increasing the margin of safety. I think everyone will be concerned about how vulnerable we are to even small downturns in sales.

*Bob:* I agree. This is something everyone will want to work on.

**MANAGERIAL ACCOUNTING IN ACTION**

**The Wrap Up**

Accoustic Concepts, Inc.

# CVP Considerations in Choosing a Cost Structure

As stated in the preceding chapter, cost structure refers to the relative proportion of fixed and variable costs in an organization. An organization often has some latitude in trading off between these two types of costs. For example, fixed investments in automated equipment can reduce variable labour costs. In this section, we discuss the choice of a cost structure. We focus on the impact of cost structure on profit stability, in which *operating leverage* pays a key role.

## Cost Structure and Profit Stability

When a manager has some latitude in trading off between fixed and variable costs, which cost structure is better—high variable costs and low fixed costs, or the opposite? No single answer to this question is possible; there may be advantages either way, depending on the specific circumstances. To show what we mean by this statement, refer to the income statements given below for two blueberry farms. Flat Farm depends on migrant workers to pick its berries by hand, whereas Balloon Farm has invested in expensive berry-picking machines. Consequently, Flat Farm has higher variable costs, but Balloon Farm has higher fixed costs:

|  | Flat Farm | | Balloon Farm | |
|---|---|---|---|---|
|  | Amount | Percent | Amount | Percent |
| Sales ..................... | $100,000 | 100% | $100,000 | 100% |
| Less variable expenses ....... | 60,000 | 60 | 30,000 | 30 |
| Contribution margin ......... | 40,000 | 40% | 70,000 | 70% |
| Less fixed expenses ......... | 30,000 | | 60,000 | |
| Net income ............... | $ 10,000 | | $ 10,000 | |

The question as to which farm has the better cost structure depends on many factors, including the long-term trend in sales, year-to-year fluctuations in the level of sales, and the attitude of the owners toward risk. If sales are expected to be above $100,000 in the future, then Balloon Farm probably has the better cost structure. The reason is that its CM ratio is higher, and its profits will therefore increase more rapidly as sales increase. To illustrate, assume that each farm experiences a 10% increase in sales without any increase in fixed costs. The new income statements would be as follows:

|  | Flat Farm | | Balloon Farm | |
|---|---|---|---|---|
|  | Amount | Percent | Amount | Percent |
| Sales ................ | $110,000 | 100% | $110,000 | 100% |
| Less variable expenses ... | 66,000 | 60 | 33,000 | 30 |
| Contribution margin ..... | 44,000 | 40% | 77,000 | 70% |
| Less fixed expenses ...... | 30,000 | | 60,000 | |
| Net income ........... | $ 14,000 | | $ 17,000 | |

Balloon Farm has experienced a greater increase in net income due to its higher CM ratio even though the increase in sales was the same for both farms.

What if sales drop below $100,000 from time to time? What are the break-even points of the two farms? What are their margins of safety? The computations needed to answer these questions are carried out below using the contribution margin method:

| | Flat Farm | Balloon Farm |
|---|---|---|
| Fixed expenses | $ 30,000 | $ 60,000 |
| Contribution margin ratio | ÷ 40% | ÷ 70% |
| Break-even in total sales dollars | $ 75,000 | $ 85,714 |
| Total current sales (a) | $100,000 | $100,000 |
| Break-even sales | 75,000 | 85,714 |
| Margin of safety in sales dollars (b) | $ 25,000 | $ 14,286 |
| Margin of safety as a percentage of sales, (b) ÷ (a) | 25.0% | 14.3% |

This analysis makes it clear that Flat Farm is less vulnerable to downturns than Balloon Farm. We can identify two reasons why it is less vulnerable. First, due to its lower fixed expenses, Flat Farm has a lower break-even point and a higher margin of safety, as shown by the computations above. Therefore, it will not incur losses as quickly as Balloon Farm in periods of sharply declining sales. Second, due to its lower CM ratio, Flat Farm will not lose contribution margin as rapidly as Balloon Farm when sales fall off. Thus, Flat Farm's income will be less volatile. We saw earlier that this is a drawback when sales increase, but it provides more protection when sales drop.

To summarize, without knowing the future, it is not obvious which cost structure is better. Both have advantages and disadvantages. Balloon Farm, with its higher fixed costs and lower variable costs, will experience wider swings in net income as changes take place in sales, with greater profits in good years and greater losses in bad years. Flat Farm, with its lower fixed costs and higher variable costs, will enjoy greater stability in net income and will be more protected from losses during bad years, but at the cost of lower net income in good years.

## Operating Leverage

A lever is a tool for multiplying force. Using a lever, a massive object can be moved with only a modest amount of force. In business, *operating leverage* serves a similar purpose. **Operating leverage** is a measure of how sensitive net income is to percentage changes in sales. Operating leverage acts as a multiplier. If operating leverage is high, a small percentage increase in sales can produce a much larger percentage increase in net income.

Operating leverage can be illustrated by returning to the data given above for the two blueberry farms. We previously showed that a 10% increase in sales (from $100,000 to $110,000 in each farm) results in a 70% increase in the net income of Balloon Farm (from $10,000 to $17,000) and only a 40% increase in the net income of Flat Farm (from $10,000 to $14,000). Thus, for a 10% increase in sales, Balloon Farm experiences a much greater percentage increase in profits than does Flat Farm. Therefore, Balloon Farm has greater operating leverage than Flat Farm.

The **degree of operating leverage** at a given level of sales is computed by the following formula:

$$\text{Degree of operating leverage} = \frac{\text{Contribution margin}}{\text{Net income}}$$

> **Learning Objective 8**
> Compute the degree of operating leverage at a particular level of sales and explain how the degree of operating leverage can be used to predict changes in net operating income.

*The degree of operating leverage is a measure, at a given level of sales, of how a percentage change in sales volume will affect profits.* To illustrate, the degree of operating leverage for the two farms at a $100,000 sales level would be computed as follows:

$$\text{Flat Farm:} \quad \frac{\$40,000}{\$10,000} = 4$$

$$\text{Balloon Farm:} \quad \frac{\$70,000}{\$10,000} = 7$$

Since the degree of operating leverage for Flat Farm is 4, the farm's net income grows four times as fast as its sales. Similarly, Balloon Farm's net income grows seven times as fast as its sales. Thus, if sales increase by 10%, then we can expect the net income of Flat Farm to increase by four times this amount, or by 40%, and the net income of Balloon Farm to increase by seven times this amount, or by 70%.

| | (1) Percent Increase in Sales | (2) Degree of Operating Leverage | (3) Percent Increase in Net Income (1) × (2) |
|---|---|---|---|
| Flat Farm .......... | 10% | 4 | 40% |
| Balloon Farm ....... | 10% | 7 | 70% |

What is responsible for the higher operating leverage at Balloon Farm? The only difference between the two farms is their cost structure. If two companies have the same total revenue and same total expense but different cost structures, then the company with the higher proportion of fixed costs in its cost structure will have higher operating leverage. Referring back to the original example on page 252, when both farms have sales of $100,000 and total expenses of $90,000, one-third of Flat Farm's costs are fixed but two-thirds of Balloon Farm's costs are fixed. As a consequence, Balloon's degree of operating leverage is higher than Flat's.

The degree of operating leverage is not constant; it is greatest at sales levels near the break-even point and decreases as sales and profits rise. This can be seen from the tabulation below, which shows the degree of operating leverage for Flat Farm at various sales levels. (Data used earlier for Flat Farm are shown in colour.)

| | | | | | |
|---|---|---|---|---|---|
| Sales .................. | $75,000 | $80,000 | $100,000 | $150,000 | $225,000 |
| Less variable expenses ..... | 45,000 | 48,000 | 60,000 | 90,000 | 135,000 |
| Contribution margin (a) ..... | 30,000 | 32,000 | 40,000 | 60,000 | 90,000 |
| Less fixed expenses ........ | 30,000 | 30,000 | 30,000 | 30,000 | 30,000 |
| Net income (b) ............ | $ -0- | $ 2,000 | $ 10,000 | $ 30,000 | $ 60,000 |
| Degree of operating leverage, (a) ÷ (b) .............. | ∞ | 16 | 4 | 2 | 1.5 |

Thus, a 10% increase in sales would increase profits by only 15% (10% × 1.5) if the company were operating at a $225,000 sales level, as compared with the 40% increase we computed earlier at the $100,000 sales level. The degree of operating leverage will continue to decrease the farther the company moves from its break-even point. At the break-even point, the degree of operating leverage will be infinitely large ($30,000 contribution margin ÷ $0 net income = ∞).

A manager can use the degree of operating leverage to quickly estimate what impact various percentage changes in sales will have on profits, without the necessity of preparing detailed income statements. As shown by our examples, the effects of operating leverage can be dramatic. If a company is near its break-even point, then even small percentage increases in sales can yield large percentage increases in profits. *This explains why management will often work very hard for only a small increase in sales volume.* If the degree of operating leverage is 5, then a 6% increase in sales would translate into a 30% increase in profits.

## Fan Appreciation

*in business* | *today*

Operating leverage can be a good thing when business is booming but can turn the situation ugly when sales slacken. Jerry Colangelo, the managing partner of the Arizona Diamondbacks professional baseball team, spent over $100 million to sign six free agents—doubling the team's payroll cost—on top of the costs of operating and servicing the debt on the team's new stadium. With annual expenses of about $100 million, the team needs to average 40,000 fans per game to just break even.

Faced with a financially risky situation, Colangelo decided to raise ticket prices by 12%. And he did it during Fan Appreciation Weekend! Attendance for the season dropped by 15%, turning what should have been a $20 million profit into a loss of over $10 million for the year. Note that a drop of attendance of 15% did not cut profit by just 15%—that is the magic of operating leverage at work.

Source: Mary Summers, "Bottom of the Ninth, Two Out," *Forbes*, November 1, 1999, pp. 69–70.

## The Concept of Sales Mix

Before concluding our discussion, it will be helpful to consider one additional application of the ideas that we have developed—the use of CVP concepts in analyzing sales mix.

> **Learning Objective 9**
> Compute the break-even point for a multiple product company and explain the effects of shifts in the sales mix on contribution margin and the break-even point.

### The Definition of Sales Mix

The term **sales mix** refers to the relative proportions in which a company's products are sold. Managers try to achieve the combination, or mix, that will yield the greatest amount of profits. Most companies have many products, and often these products are not equally profitable. In these companies, profits will depend to some extent on the company's sales mix. Profits will be greater if high-margin, rather than low-margin, items make up a relatively large proportion of total sales.

Once again the concept of contribution margin is the key. In a multiple product setting, managers who focus solely on increasing the total sales volume in an effort to improve the profitability of their companies can cause the profits to decline. If the increase in volume was obtained by shifting the sales mix from high-margin items to low-margin items, then total profits will decrease. On the other hand, if a shift in sales mix from low margin items to high-margin items occurs, total profits can increase, even though total sales decrease. It is one thing to achieve a particular sales volume; it is quite a different thing to sell the most profitable mix of products.

### Sales Mix and Break-Even Analysis

If a company sells more than one product, break-even analysis is somewhat more complex than discussed earlier in the chapter. The reason is that different products will have different selling prices, different costs, and different contribution margins. To illustrate, consider Sound Unlimited, a small company that imports DVD-ROM drives from France for use in personal computers. At present, the company distributes the following two models to retail computer stores: the Le Louvre DVD-ROM drive and the Le Vin DVD-ROM drive. The company's September sales, expenses, and break-even point are shown in Exhibit 7–4.

## Exhibit 7–4
Multiple-Product Break-Even Analysis

**SOUND UNLIMITED**
**Contribution Income Statement**
**For the Month of September**

| | Le Louvre DVD-ROM Drive | | Le Vin DVD-ROM Drive | | Total | |
|---|---|---|---|---|---|---|
| | Amount | Percent | Amount | Percent | Amount | Percent |
| Sales | $20,000 | 100% | $80,000 | 100% | $100,000 | 100% |
| Less variable expenses | 15,000 | 75 | 40,000 | 50 | 55,000 | 55 |
| Contribution margin | $ 5,000 | 25% | $40,000 | 50% | 45,000 | 45% |
| Less fixed expenses | | | | | 27,000 | |
| Net income | | | | | $ 18,000 | |

Computation of the break-even point:

$$\frac{\text{Fixed expenses, }\$27,000}{\text{Overall CM ratio, }45\%} = \$60,000$$

Verification of the breakeven:

| | Le Louvre DVD-ROM Drive | Le Vin DVD-ROM Drive | Total |
|---|---|---|---|
| Current dollar sales | $20,000 | $80,000 | $100,000 |
| Percentage of total dollar sales | 20% | 80% | 100% |
| Sales at break-even | $12,000 | $48,000 | $60,000 |

| | Le Louvre DVD-ROM | | Le Vin DVD-ROM | | Total | |
|---|---|---|---|---|---|---|
| | Amount | Percent | Amount | Percent | Amount | Percent |
| Sales | $12,000 | 100% | $48,000 | 100% | $60,000 | 100% |
| Less variable expenses | 9,000 | 75 | 24,000 | 50 | 33,000 | 55 |
| Contribution margin | $ 3,000 | 25% | $24,000 | 50% | 27,000 | 45% |
| Less fixed expenses | | | | | 27,000 | |
| Net income | | | | | $ –0– | |

As shown in the exhibit, the break-even point is $60,000 in sales. This is computed by dividing the fixed costs by the company's *overall* CM ratio of 45%. The sales mix is currently 20% for the Le Louvre model and 80% for the Le Vin model. If this sales mix is constant, then at the break-even total sales of $60,000, the sales of the Le Louvre model would be $12,000 (20% of $60,000) and the sales of the Le Vin model would be $48,000 (80% of $60,000). As shown in Exhibit 7–4, at these levels of sales, the company would indeed break even. But $60,000 in sales represents the break-even point for the company only so long as the sales mix does not change. *If the sales mix changes, then the break-even point will also change.* This is illustrated by the results for October in which the sales mix shifted away from the more profitable Le Vin model (which has a 50% CM ratio) toward the less profitable Le Louvre model (which has only a 25% CM ratio). These results appear in Exhibit 7–5.

Although sales have remained unchanged at $100,000, the sales mix is exactly the reverse of what it was in Exhibit 7–4, with the bulk of the sales now coming from the less profitable Le Louvre model. Note that this shift in the sales mix has caused both the overall CM ratio and total profits to drop sharply from the prior month—the overall CM ratio has dropped from 45% in September to only 30% in October, and net income has dropped

## Exhibit 7–5

Multiple-Product Break-Even Analysis: A Shift in Sales Mix (see Exhibit 7–4)

| | Le Louvre DVD-Rom Drive | | Le Vin DVD-Rom Drive | | Total | |
|---|---|---|---|---|---|---|
| | **Amount** | **Percent** | **Amount** | **Percent** | **Amount** | **Percent** |
| Sales ........................ | $80,000 | 100% | $20,000 | 100% | $100,000 | 100% |
| Less variable expenses .......... | 60,000 | 75 | 10,000 | 50 | 70,000 | 70 |
| Contribution margin ............ | $20,000 | 25% | $10,000 | 50% | 30,000 | 30% |
| Less fixed expenses ............. | | | | | 27,000 | |
| Net income .................... | | | | | $ 3,000 | |
| Computation of the break-even point: | | | | | | |

**SOUND UNLIMITED**
**Contribution Income Statement**
**For the Month of October**

$$\frac{\text{Fixed expenses, \$27,000}}{\text{Overall CM ratio, 30\%}} = \$90,000$$

from $18,000 to only $3,000. In addition, with the drop in the overall CM ratio, the company's break-even point is no longer $60,000 in sales. Since the company is now realizing less average contribution margin per dollar of sales, it takes more sales to cover the same amount of fixed costs. Thus, the break-even point has increased from $60,000 to $90,000 in sales per year.

In preparing a break-even analysis, some assumptions must be made concerning the sales mix. Usually, the assumption is that it will not change. However, if the manager knows that shifts in various factors (consumer tastes, market share, and so on) are causing shifts in the sales mix, then these factors must be explicitly considered in any CVP computations. Otherwise, the manager may make decisions on the basis of outmoded or faulty data.

## Going Up in Smoke

*in business today*

Despite the common rationale that cigarette companies are a good buy due to their steady cash cow status, recent industry trends have dictated that smokers are either quitting or becoming more cost conscious due to the heavy increases in tobacco taxes. Rothmans Inc. is no exception to the rule. Its customers have resorted to discount brands or cheaper alternatives, such as self-rolling cigarettes. During the first six months in 2002, cigarette volume purchases dropped by an average of 10.7% among three of Canada's largest tobacco companies. The considerable shift in sales mix for Rothmans has enabled the company to be profitable and gaining market share in the price-sensitive tobacco segment. In an effort to post profit growth, the company had effectively cut costs in 2001. Yet, considering the effects of continuous antismoking campaigns, how long can tobacco companies like Rothmans last?

Source: Chow, Jason, "Cash Cow Choking on Cheaper Cigarettes: Rothmans Inc.," *Financial Post (National Post)*, November 6, 2002, p. IN3. Material reprinted with the express permission of: "The CanWest News Service," a CanWest Partnership.

## Assumptions of CVP Analysis

A number of assumptions underlie CVP analysis:

1. Selling price is constant. The price of a product or service will not change as volume changes.

2. Costs are linear and can be accurately divided into variable and fixed elements. The variable element is constant per unit, and the fixed element is constant in total over the entire relevant range.
3. In multiproduct companies, the sales mix is constant.
4. In manufacturing companies, inventories do not change. The number of units produced equals the number of units sold.

While some of these assumptions may be violated in practice, the violations are usually not serious enough to call into question the basic validity of CVP analysis. For example, in most multiproduct companies, the sales mix is constant enough so that the results of CVP analysis are reasonably valid.

Perhaps the greatest danger lies in relying on simple CVP analysis when a manager is contemplating a large change in volume that lies outside of the relevant range. For example, a manager might contemplate increasing the level of sales far beyond what the company has ever experienced before. However, even in these situations, a manager can adjust the model, as we have done in this chapter, to take into account anticipated changes in selling prices, fixed costs, and the sales mix that would otherwise violate the assumptions. For example, in a decision that would affect fixed costs, the change in fixed costs can be explicitly taken into account as illustrated earlier in the chapter in the Acoustic Concepts example.

# Summary

**LO1  Explain how changes in activity affect contribution margin and net income.**
The unit contribution margin, which is the difference between a unit's selling price and its variable cost, indicates how net income will change as the result of selling one more or one fewer unit. For example, if a product's unit contribution margin is $10, then selling one more unit will add $10 to the company's profit.

**LO2  Use the contribution margin ratio (CM ratio) to compute changes in contribution margin and net operating income resulting from changes in sales volume.**
The contribution margin ratio is computed by dividing the unit contribution margin by the unit selling price or by dividing the total contribution margin by the total sales.

The contribution margin ratio shows by how much a dollar increase in sales will affect the total contribution margin and net income. For example, if a product has a 40% contribution margin ratio, then a $100 increase in sales should result in a $40 increase in contribution margin and in net income.

**LO3  Prepare a cost-volume-profit (CVP) graph and explain the significance of each of its components.**
A cost-volume-profit graph displays sales revenues and expenses as a function of unit sales. Revenue is depicted as a straight line slanting upward to the right from the origin. Total expenses consist of both a fixed element and a variable element. The fixed element is flat on the graph. The variable element slants upward to the right. The break-even point is the point at which the total sales revenue and total expenses lines intersect on the graph.

**LO4  Show the effects on contribution margin of changes in variable costs, fixed costs, selling price, and volume.**
Contribution margin concepts can be used to estimate the effects of changes in various parameters, such as variable costs, fixed costs, selling prices, and volume on the total contribution margin and net income.

**LO5  Compute the break-even point by both the equation method and the contribution margin method.**
The break-even point is the level of sales at which profits are zero. It can be computed using several methods. The break-even in units can be determined by dividing total fixed expenses by the unit contribution margin. The break-even in sales dollars can be determined by dividing total fixed expenses by the contribution margin ratio.

**LO6**  **Use the CVP formulas to determine the level of sales needed to achieve a desired target profit.**

The sales, in units, required to attain a desired target profit can be determined by summing the total fixed expenses and the desired target profit and then dividing the result by the unit contribution margin.

**LO7**  **Compute the margin of safety and explain its significance.**

The margin of safety is the difference between the total budgeted (or actual) sales of a period and the break-even sales. It expresses how much cushion there is in the current level of sales above the break-even point.

**LO8**  **Compute the degree of operating leverage at a particular level of sales and explain how the degree of operating leverage can be used to predict changes in net operating income.**

The degree of operating leverage is computed by dividing the total contribution margin by net income. The degree of operating leverage can be used to determine impact a given percentage change in sales would have on net income. For example, if a company's degree of operating leverage is 2.5, then a 10% increase in sales from current levels of sales should result in a 25% increase in net income.

**LO9**  **Compute the break-even point for a multiple product company and explain the effects of shifts in the sales mix on contribution margin and the break-even point.**

The break-even for a multiproduct company can be computed by dividing the company's total fixed expenses by the overall contribution margin ratio.

This method for computing the break-even assumes that the sales mix is constant. If the sales mix shifts toward products with a lower contribution margin ratio, then more total sales are required to attain any given level of profits.

# Guidance Answers to You Decide and Decision Maker

**RECRUIT** (p. 248)

You can get a feel for the challenges that this company will face by determining its break-even point. Start by estimating the company's variable expense ratio:

$$\text{Variable cost per unit} \div \text{Selling price per unit} = \text{Variable expense ratio}$$
$$\$13 \div \$17 = 76.5\%$$

Then, estimate the company's variable expenses:

$$\text{Sales} \times \text{Variable expense ratio} = \text{Estimated amount of variable expenses}$$
$$\$1,500,000 \times 0.765 = \$1,147,500$$

Next, put the contribution format income statement into an equation format to estimate the company's current level of fixed expenses:

$$\text{Sales} = \text{Variable expenses} + \text{Fixed expenses} + \text{Net income (loss)}$$
$$\$1,500,000 = \$1,147,500 + X + (\$1,500,000)$$
$$X = \$1,500,000 - \$1,147,500 + \$1,500,000$$
$$X = \$1,852,500$$

Finally, use the equation approach to estimate the company's break-even point:

$$\text{Sales} = \text{Variable expenses} + \text{Fixed expenses} + \text{Profits}$$
$$\$17Q = \$13Q + \$1,852,500 + \$0$$
$$\$4Q = \$1,852,500$$
$$Q = 463,125$$

Assuming that its cost structure stays the same, ConneXus needs to increase its sales by 527%—from 88,000 to 463,125 CDs—just to break even. After it reaches that break-even point, net income will increase by $4 (the contribution margin) for each additional CD that it sells. Joining the company would be a risky proposition; you should be prepared with some probing questions when you arrive for your interview. (For example, what steps does the company plan to take to increase sales? How might the company reduce its fixed and/or variable expenses so as to lower its break-even point?)

**LOAN OFFICER** (p. 251)

To determine the company's margin of safety, you need to determine its break-even point. Start by estimating the company's variable expense ratio:

$$\text{Variable cost per unit} \div \text{Selling price per unit} = \text{Variable expense ratio}$$
$$\$2 \div \$6 = 33.3\% \text{ or } \frac{1}{3}$$

Then, estimate the company's variable expenses:

$$\text{Sales} \times \text{Variable expense ratio} = \text{Estimated amount of variable expenses}$$
$$\$700,000 \times \frac{1}{3} = \$233,333$$

Next, put the contribution format income statement into an equation format to estimate the company's current level of fixed expenses:

$$\text{Sales} = \text{Variable expenses} + \text{Fixed expenses} + \text{Net income}$$
$$\$700,000 = \$233,333 + X + \$210,000$$
$$X = \$700,000 - \$233,333 - \$210,000$$
$$X = \$256,667$$

Use the equation approach to estimate the company's break-even point:

$$\text{Sales} = \text{Variable expenses} + \text{Fixed expenses} + \text{Profits}$$
$$X = \frac{1}{3}X + \$256,667 + \$0$$
$$\frac{2}{3}X = \$256,667$$
$$X = \$385,000$$

Finally, compute the company's margin of safety:

$$\text{Margin of safety} = (\text{Sales} - \text{Break-even sales}) \div \text{Sales}$$
$$= (\$700,000 - \$385,000) \div \$700,000$$
$$= 45\%$$

The margin of safety appears to be adequate; so, if the other information about the company is favourable, a loan would seem to be justified.

# Review Problem: CVP Relationships

Voltar Company manufactures and sells a telephone answering machine. The company's contribution format income statement for the most recent year is given below:

|  | Total | Per Unit | Percent of Sales |
|---|---|---|---|
| Sales (20,000 units) .......... | $1,200,000 | $60 | 100% |
| Less variable expenses ........ | 900,000 | 45 | ?% |
| Contribution margin .......... | 300,000 | $15 | ?% |
| Less fixed expenses .......... | 240,000 | | |
| Net operating income ........ | $ 60,000 | | |

Management is anxious to improve the company's profit performance and has asked for an analysis of a number of items.

*Required:*
1. Compute the company's CM ratio and variable expense ratio.
2. Compute the company's break-even point in both units and sales dollars. Use the equation method.
3. Assume that sales increase by $400,000 next year. If cost behaviour patterns remain unchanged, by how much will the company's net operating income increase? Use the CM ratio to determine your answer.
4. Refer to the original data. Assume that next year management wants the company to earn a minimum profit of $90,000. How many units will have to be sold to meet this target profit figure?
5. Refer to the original data. Compute the company's margin of safety in both dollar and percentage forms.

6. _a._ Compute the company's degree of operating leverage at the present level of sales.
   _b._ Assume that through a more intense effort by the sales staff the company's sales increase by 8% next year. By what percentage would you expect net income to increase? Use the operating leverage concept to obtain your answer.
   _c._ Verify your answer to (_b_) by preparing a new income statement showing an 8% increase in sales.
7. In an effort to increase sales and profits, management is considering the use of a higher-quality speaker. The higher-quality speaker would increase variable costs by $3 per unit, but management could eliminate one quality inspector who is paid a salary of $30,000 per year. The sales manager estimates that the higher-quality speaker would increase annual sales by at least 20%.
   _a._ Assuming that changes are made as described above, prepare a projected income statement for next year. Show data on total, per-unit, and percentage bases.
   _b._ Compute the company's new break-even point in both units and dollars of sales. Use the contribution margin method.
   _c._ Would you recommend that the changes be made?

## SOLUTION TO REVIEW PROBLEM

1.
$$\text{CM ratio} = \frac{\text{Contribution margin}}{\text{Selling price}} = \frac{\$15}{\$60} = 25\%$$

$$\text{Variable expense ratio} = \frac{\text{Variable expense}}{\text{Selling price}} = \frac{\$45}{\$60} = 75\%$$

2. Sales = Variable expenses + Fixed expenses + Profits

   $60Q = $45Q + $240,000 + $0

   $15Q = $240,000

   $\quad Q = $240,000 \div $15 per unit

   $\quad Q = 16,000$ units; or at $60 per unit, $960,000

   Alternative solution:

   $X = 0.75X + $240,000 + $0

   $0.25X = $240,000

   $\quad X = $240,000 \div 0.25

   $\quad X = $960,000; or at $60 per unit, 16,000 units

3. Increase in sales ........................ $400,000
   Multiply by the CM ratio ................. × 25%
   Expected increase in contribution margin .... $100,000

   Since the fixed expenses are not expected to change, net operating income will increase by the entire $100,000 increase in contribution margin computed above.

4. Equation method:

   Sales = Variable expenses + Fixed expenses + Profits

   $60Q = $45Q + $240,000 + $90,000

   $15Q = $330,000

   $\quad Q = $330,000 \div $15 per unit

   $\quad Q = 22,000$ units

   Contribution margin method:

   $$\frac{\text{Fixed expenses} + \text{Target profit}}{\text{Contribution margin per unit}} = \frac{\$240,000 + \$90,000}{\$15 \text{ per unit}} = 22,000 \text{ units}$$

5. Margin of safety in dollars = Total sales − Break-even sales

   $$= \$1,200,000 - \$960,000 = \$240,000$$

   $$\text{Margin of safety percentage} = \frac{\text{Margin of safety in dollars}}{\text{Total sales}} = \frac{\$240,000}{\$1,200,000} = 20\%$$

6. *a.* Degree of operating leverage $= \dfrac{\text{Contribution margin}}{\text{Net operating income}} = \dfrac{\$300,000}{\$60,000} = \underline{\underline{5}}$

  *b.*

| | |
|---|---:|
| Expected increase in sales ............... | 8% |
| Degree of operating leverage ............. | ×5 |
| Expected increase in net operating income ... | 40% |

  *c.* If sales increase by 8%, then 21,600 units (20,000 × 1.08 = 21,600) will be sold next year. The new income statement will be as follows:

| | Total | Per Unit | Percent of Sales |
|---|---:|---:|---:|
| Sales (21,600 units) ......... | $1,296,000 | $60 | 100% |
| Less variable expenses ....... | 972,000 | 45 | 75% |
| Contribution margin ........ | 324,000 | $15 | 25% |
| Less fixed expenses ......... | 240,000 | | |
| Net operating income ....... | $ 84,000 | | |

Thus, the $84,000 expected net operating income for next year represents a 40% increase over the $60,000 net operating income earned during the current year:

$$\frac{\$84,000 - \$60,000}{\$60,000} = \frac{\$24,000}{\$60,000} = \underline{\underline{40\% \text{ increase}}}$$

Note from the income statement above that the increase in sales from 20,000 to 21,600 units has resulted in increases in *both* total sales and total variable expenses. It is a common error to overlook the increase in variable expenses when preparing a projected income statement.

7. *a.* A 20% increase in sales would result in 24,000 units being sold next year: 20,000 units × 1.20 = 24,000 units.

| | Total | Per Unit | Percent of Sales |
|---|---:|---:|---:|
| Sales (24,000 units) ......... | $1,440,000 | $60 | 100% |
| Less variable expenses ....... | 1,152,000 | 48* | 80 |
| Contribution margin ........ | 288,000 | $12 | 20% |
| Less fixed expenses ......... | 210,000† | | |
| Net operating income ....... | $ 78,000 | | |

*$45 + $3 = $48; $48 ÷ $60 = 80%.
†$240,000 − $30,000 = $210,000.

Note that the change in per-unit variable expenses results in a change in both the per-unit contribution margin and the CM ratio.

  *b.*    Break-even point in unit sales $= \dfrac{\text{Fixed expenses}}{\text{Contribution margin per unit}}$

$$= \frac{\$210,000}{\$12 \text{ per unit}} = \underline{\underline{17,500 \text{ units}}}$$

Break-even point in dollar sales $= \dfrac{\text{Fixed expenses}}{\text{CM ratio}}$

$$= \frac{\$210,000}{0.20} = \underline{\underline{\$1,050,000}}$$

  *c.* Yes, on the basis of these data, the changes should be made. The changes will increase the company's net operating income from the present $60,000 to $78,000 per year. Although the changes will also result in a higher break-even point (17,500 units as compared with the present 16,000 units), the company's margin of safety will actually be wider than before:

$$\text{Margin of safety in dollars} = \text{Total sales} - \text{Break-even sales}$$
$$= \$1,440,000 - \$1,050,000 = \$390,000$$

As shown in (5) above, the company's present margin of safety is only $240,000. Thus, several benefits will result from the proposed changes.

## Glossary

**Break-even point** The level of sales at which profit is zero. The break-even point can also be defined as the point where total sales equals total expenses or as the point where total contribution margin equals total fixed expenses. (p. 238)

**Contribution margin method** A method of computing the break-even point in which the fixed expenses are divided by the contribution margin per unit. (p. 248)

**Contribution margin ratio (CM ratio)** The contribution margin as a percentage of total sales. (p. 239)

**Cost-volume-profit (CVP) graph** The relationships among revenues, costs, and level of activity in an organization presented in graphic form. (p. 240)

**Degree of operating leverage** A measure, at a given level of sales, of how a percentage change in sales volume will affect profits. The degree of operating leverage is computed by dividing contribution margin by net income. (p. 253)

**Equation method** A method of computing the break-even point that relies on the equation Sales = Variable expenses + Fixed expenses + Profits. (p. 247)

**Incremental analysis** An analytical approach that focuses only on those items of revenue, cost, and volume that will change as a result of a decision. (p. 243)

**Margin of safety** The excess of budgeted (or actual) sales over the break-even volume of sales. (p. 250)

**Operating leverage** A measure of how sensitive net income is to a given percentage change in sales. It is computed by dividing the contribution margin by net income. (p. 253)

**Sales mix** The relative proportions in which a company's products are sold. Sales mix is computed by expressing the sales of each product as a percentage of total sales. (p. 255)

## Questions

**7–1**    What is meant by a product's CM ratio? How is this ratio useful in planning business operations?

**7–2**    Often, the most direct route to a business decision is to make an incremental analysis on the basis of  the information available. What is meant by an *incremental analysis?*

**7–3**    Company A's cost structure includes costs that are mostly variable, whereas Company B's cost structure includes costs that are mostly fixed. In a time of increasing sales, which company will tend to realize the most rapid increase in profits? Explain.

**7–4**    What is meant by the term *operating leverage?*

**7–5**    A 10% decrease in the selling price of a product will have the same impact on net income as a 10% increase in the variable expenses. Do you agree? Why, or why not?

**7–6**    What is meant by the term *break-even point?*

**7–7**    Name three approaches to break-even analysis. Briefly explain how each approach works.

**7–8**    In response to a request from your immediate supervisor, you have prepared a CVP graph portraying the cost and revenue characteristics of your company's product and operations. Explain how the lines on the graph and the break-even point would change if (a) the selling price per unit decreased, (b) fixed costs increased throughout the entire range of activity portrayed on the graph, and (c) variable costs per unit increased.

**7–9**    Al's Auto Wash charges $4 to wash a car. The variable costs of washing a car are 15% of sales. Fixed expenses total $1,700 monthly. How many cars must be washed each month for Al to break even?

**7–10**    What is meant by the margin of safety?

**7–11**    What is meant by the term *sales mix?* What assumption is usually made concerning sales mix in CVP analysis?

**7–12**    Explain how a shift in the sales mix could result in both a higher break-even point and a lower net income.

**7–13**    How do absorption costing and variable costing differ in how they treat fixed manufacturing overhead costs?

# Brief Exercises

### BRIEF EXERCISE 7–1    Preparing a Contribution Margin Format Income Statement (LO1)

Whirly Corporation's most recent income statement is shown below:

| | Total | Per Unit |
|---|---|---|
| Sales (10,000 units) . . . . . . . . . | $350,000 | $35.00 |
| Less variable expenses . . . . . . . | 200,000 | 20.00 |
| Contribution margin . . . . . . . . | 150,000 | $15.00 |
| Less fixed expenses . . . . . . . . . | 135,000 | |
| Net income . . . . . . . . . . . . . . | $ 15,000 | |

**Required:**

Prepare a new income statement under each of the following conditions (consider each case independently):

1. The sales volume increases by 100 units.
2. The sales volume decreases by 100 units.
3. The sales volume is 9,000 units.

### BRIEF EXERCISE 7–2    Computing and Using the CM Ratio (LO2)

Last month when Holiday Creations, Inc. sold 50,000 units, total sales were $200,000, total variable expenses were $120,000, and total fixed expenses were $65,000.

**Required:**

1. What is the company's contribution margin (CM) ratio?
2. Estimate the change in the company's net income if it were to increase its total sales by $1,000.

### BRIEF EXERCISE 7–3    Changes in Variable Costs, Fixed Costs, Selling Price, and Volume (LO4)

Data for Hermann Corporation are shown below:

| | Per Unit | Percent of Sales |
|---|---|---|
| Sales price . . . . . . . . . . . . . . . | $90 | 100% |
| Less variable expenses . . . . . . . | 63 | 70 |
| Contribution margin . . . . . . . . | $27 | 30% |

Fixed expenses are $30,000 per month and the company is selling 2,000 units per month.

**Required:**

1. The marketing manager argues that a $5,000 increase in the monthly advertising budget would increase monthly sales by $9,000. Should the advertising budget be increased?
2. Refer to the original data. Management is considering using higher-quality components that would increase the variable cost by $2 per unit. The marketing manager believes the higher-quality product would increase sales by 10% per month. Should the higher-quality components be used?

### BRIEF EXERCISE 7–4    Compute the Break-Even Point (LO5)

Mauro Products has a single product, a woven basket whose selling price is $15 and whose variable cost is $12 per unit. The company's monthly fixed expenses are $4,200.

**Required:**

1. Solve for the company's break-even point in unit sales using the equation method.
2. Solve for the company's break-even point in sales dollars using the equation method and the CM ratio.
3. Solve for the company's break-even point in unit sales using the contribution margin method.
4. Solve for the company's break-even point in sales dollars using the contribution margin method and the CM ratio.

### BRIEF EXERCISE 7–5    Prepare a Cost-Volume-Profit (CVP) Graph (LO3)

Karlik Enterprises has a single product whose selling price is $24 and whose variable cost is $18 per unit. The company's monthly fixed expense is $24,000.

*Required:*
1. Prepare a cost-volume-profit graph for the company up to a sales level of 8,000 units.
2. Estimate the company's break-even point in unit sales using your cost-volume-profit graph.

**BRIEF EXERCISE 7–6    Compute the Level of Sales Required to Attain a Target Profit (LO6)**
Lin Corporation has a single product whose selling price is $120 and whose variable cost is $80 per unit. The company's monthly fixed expense is $50,000.

*Required:*
1. Using the equation method, solve for the unit sales that are required to earn a target profit of $10,000.
2. Using the contribution margin approach, solve for the dollar sales that are required to earn a target profit of $15,000.

**BRIEF EXERCISE 7–7    Compute the Margin of Safety (LO7)**
Molander Corporation sells a sun umbrella used at resort hotels. Data concerning the next month's budget appear below:

| | |
|---|---|
| Selling price | $ 30 per unit |
| Variable expense | $ 20 per unit |
| Fixed expense | $7,500 per month |
| Unit sales | 1,000 units per month |

*Required:*
1. Compute the company's margin of safety.
2. Compute the company's margin of safety as a percentage of its sales.

**BRIEF EXERCISE 7–8    Compute and Use the Degree of Operating Leverage (LO8)**
Engberg Company's most recent monthly income statement appears below:

| | Amount | Percent of Sales |
|---|---|---|
| Sales | $80,000 | 100% |
| Less variable expenses | 32,000 | 40 |
| Contribution margin | 48,000 | 60% |
| Less fixed expenses | 38,000 | |
| Net income | $10,000 | |

*Required:*
1. Compute the company's degree of operating leverage.
2. Using the degree of operating leverage, estimate the impact on net income of a 5% increase in sales.
3. Verify your estimate from part (2) above by constructing a new income statement for the company assuming a 5% increase in sales.

**BRIEF EXERCISE 7–9    Compute the Break-Even Point for a Multiproduct Company (LO9)**
Lucido Products markets two computer games: Claimjumper and Makeover. A contribution margin income statement for a recent month for the two games appears below:

| | Claimjumper | Makeover | Total |
|---|---|---|---|
| Sales | $30,000 | $70,000 | $100,000 |
| Less variable expenses | 20,000 | 50,000 | 70,000 |
| Contribution margin | $10,000 | $20,000 | 30,000 |
| Less fixed expenses | | | 24,000 |
| Net income | | | $ 6,000 |

*Required:*
1. Compute the overall contribution margin (CM) ratio for the company.
2. Compute the overall break-even for the company in sales dollars.
3. Verify the overall break-even for the company by constructing an income statement showing the appropriate levels of sales for the two products.

# Exercises

**EXERCISE 7–1   Using a Contribution Margin Format Income Statement** (LO1, LO4)
Miller Company's most recent income statement is shown below:

|                          | Total      | Per Unit |
| ------------------------ | ---------- | -------- |
| Sales (20,000 units) ......... | $300,000   | $15.00   |
| Less variable expenses ....... | 180,000    | 9.00     |
| Contribution margin  ........ | 120,000    | $ 6.00   |
| Less fixed expenses ......... | 70,000     |          |
| Net income  ............. | $ 50,000   |          |

*Required:*
Prepare a new income statement under each of the following conditions (consider each case independently):
1. The sales volume increases by 15%.
2. The selling price decreases by $1.50 per unit, and the sales volume increases by 25%.
3. The selling price increases by $1.50 per unit, fixed expenses increase by $20,000, and the sales volume decreases by 5%.
4. The selling price increases by 12%, variable expenses increase by 60 cents per unit, and the sales volume decreases by 10%.

**EXERCISE 7–2   Break-Even and Target Profit Analysis** (LO4, LO5, LO6)
Lindon Company is the exclusive distributor for an automotive product. The product sells for $40 per unit and has a CM ratio of 30%. The company's fixed expenses are $180,000 per year.

*Required:*
1. What are the variable expenses per unit?
2. Using the equation method:
    a. What is the break-even point in units and sales dollars?
    b. What sales level in units and in sales dollars is required to earn an annual profit of $60,000?
    c. Assume that by using a more efficient shipper, the company is able to reduce its variable expenses by $4 per unit. What is the company's new break-even point in units and sales dollars?
3. Repeat (2) above using the unit contribution method.

**EXERCISE 7–3   Operating Leverage** (LO1, LO8)
Magic Realm, Inc. has developed a new fantasy board game. The company sold 15,000 games last year at a selling price of $20 per game. Fixed costs associated with the game total $182,000 per year, and variable costs are $6 per game. Production of the game is entrusted to a printing contractor. Variable costs consist mostly of payments to this contractor.

*Required:*
1. Prepare an income statement for the game last year and compute the degree of operating leverage.
2. Management is confident that the company can sell 18,000 games next year (an increase of 3,000 games, or 20%, over last year). Compute:
    a. The expected percentage increase in net income for next year.
    b. The expected total dollar net income for next year. (Do not prepare an income statement; use the degree of operating leverage to compute your answer.)

**EXERCISE 7–4   Break-Even Analysis and CVP Graphing** (LO3, LO4, LO5)

The Hartford Symphony Guild is planning its annual dinner-dance. The dinner-dance committee has assembled the following expected costs for the event:

| | |
|---|---:|
| Dinner (per person) ......................... | $ 18 |
| Favours and program (per person) ............. | 2 |
| Band ...................................... | 2,800 |
| Rental of ballroom ......................... | 900 |
| Professional entertainment during intermission ... | 1,000 |
| Tickets and advertising ..................... | 1,300 |

The committee members would like to charge $35 per person for the evening's activities.

*Required:*

1. Compute the break-even point for the dinner-dance (in terms of the number of persons that must attend).
2. Assume that last year only 300 persons attended the dinner-dance. If the same number attend this year, what price per ticket must be charged in order to break even?
3. Refer to the original data ($35 ticket price per person). Prepare a CVP graph for the dinner-dance from a zero level of activity up to 700 tickets sold. Number of persons should be placed on the horizontal (X) axis, and dollars should be placed on the vertical (Y) axis.

**EXERCISE 7–5   Break-Even Analysis, Target Profit Analysis, Margin of Safety, CM Ratio** (LO2, LO5, LO6, LO7)

Menlo Company manufactures and sells a single product. The company's sales and expenses for last quarter follow:

| | Total | Per Unit |
|---|---:|---:|
| Sales ..................... | $450,000 | $30 |
| Less variable expenses ....... | 180,000 | 12 |
| Contribution margin ........ | 270,000 | $18 |
| Less fixed expenses ......... | 216,000 | |
| Net income ............... | $ 54,000 | |

*Required:*

1. What is the quarterly break-even point in units sold and in sales dollars?
2. Without resorting to computations, what is the total contribution margin at the break-even point?
3. How many units would have to be sold each quarter to earn a target profit of $90,000? Use the unit contribution method. Verify your answer by preparing a contribution income statement at the target level of sales.
4. Refer to the original data. Compute the company's margin of safety in both dollar and percentage terms.
5. What is the company's CM ratio? If sales increase by $50,000 per quarter and there is no change in fixed expenses, by how much would you expect quarterly net income to increase? (Do not prepare an income statement; use the CM ratio to compute your answer.)

**EXERCISE 7–6   Break-Even and Target Profit Analysis** (LO4, LO5, LO6)

Outback Outfitters manufactures and sells recreational equipment. One of the company's products, a small camp stove, sells for $50 per unit. Variable expenses are $32 per stove, and fixed expenses associated with the stove total $108,000 per month.

*Required:*

1. Compute the break-even point in number of stoves and in total sales dollars.
2. If the variable expenses per stove increase as a percentage of the selling price, will it result in a higher or a lower break-even point? Why? (Assume that the fixed expenses remain unchanged.)
3. At present, the company is selling 8,000 stoves per month. The sales manager is convinced that a 10% reduction in the selling price would result in a 25% increase in monthly sales of stoves. Prepare two

contribution income statements, one under present operating conditions, and one as operations would appear after the proposed changes. Show both total and per-unit data on your statements.

4. Refer to the data in (3) above. How many stoves would have to be sold at the new selling price to yield a minimum net income of $35,000 per month?

**EXERCISE 7–7    Multiproduct Break-Even Analysis (LO1, LO9)**
Olongapo Sports Corporation is the distributor in the Philippines of two premium golf balls—the Flight Dynamic and the Sure Shot. Monthly sales and the contribution margin ratios for the two products follow:

| | Product | | |
|---|---|---|---|
| | Flight Dynamic | Sure Shot | Total |
| Sales ......... | P150,000 | P250,000 | P400,000 |
| CM ratio ...... | 80% | 36% | ? |

Fixed expenses total P183,750 per month. (The currency in the Philippines is the peso, which is denoted by P. )

***Required:***
1. Prepare an income statement for the company as a whole. Carry computations to one decimal place.
2. Compute the break-even point for the company based on the current sales mix.
3. If sales increase by P100,000 a month, by how much would you expect net income to increase? What are your assumptions?

**EXERCISE 7–8    Interpretation of the CVP Graph (LO3, LO5)**
A CVP graph, such as the one shown below, is a useful technique for showing relationships among costs, volume, and profits in an organization.

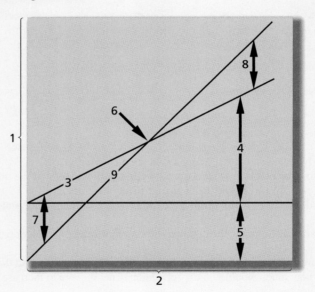

***Required:***
1. Identify the numbered components in the CVP graph.
2. State the effect of each of the following actions on line 3, line 9, and the break-even point. For line 3 and line 9, state whether the action will cause the line to:

    Remain unchanged.
    Shift upward.
    Shift downward.
    Have a steeper slope (i.e., rotate upward).
    Have a flatter slope (i.e., rotate downward).
    Shift upward *and* have a steeper slope.
    Shift upward *and* have a flatter slope.

Shift downward *and* have a steeper slope.
Shift downward *and* have a flatter slope.

In the case of the break-even point, state whether the action will cause the break-even point to:

Remain unchanged.
Increase.
Decrease.
Probably change, but the direction is uncertain.

Treat each case independently.

> x. *Example.* Fixed costs are reduced by $5,000 per period.
> *Answer* (see choices above): Line 3: Shift downward.
> Line 9: Remain unchanged.
> Break-even point: Decrease.

a. The unit selling price is increased from $18 to $20.
b. Unit variable costs are decreased from $12 to $10.
c. Fixed costs are increased by $3,000 per period.
d. Two thousand more units are sold during the period than were budgeted.
e. Due to paying salespersons a commission, rather than a flat salary, fixed costs are reduced by $8,000 per period and unit variable costs are increased by $3.
f. Due to an increase in the cost of materials, both unit variable costs and the selling price are increased by $2.
g. Advertising costs are increased by $10,000 per period, resulting in a 10% increase in the number of units sold.
h. Due to automating an operation previously done by workers, fixed costs are increased by $12,000 per period and unit variable costs are reduced by $4.

# Problems

**PROBLEM 7–1 Basic CVP Analysis** (LO1, LO2, LO4, LO5, LO6, LO8)

CHECK FIGURE
(2) Break-even: $300,000

Feather Friends, Inc. makes a high-quality wooden birdhouse that sells for $20 per unit. Variable costs are $8 per unit, and fixed costs total $180,000 per year.

*Required:*
Answer the following independent questions:
1. What is the product's CM ratio?
2. Use the CM ratio to determine the break-even point in sales dollars.
3. Due to an increase in demand, the company estimates that sales will increase by $75,000 during the next year. By how much should net income increase (or net loss decrease) assuming that fixed costs do not change?
4. Assume that the operating results for last year were:

| Sales | $400,000 |
|---|---|
| Less variable expenses | 160,000 |
| Contribution margin | 240,000 |
| Less fixed expenses | 180,000 |
| Net income | $ 60,000 |

a. Compute the degree of operating leverage at the current level of sales.
b. The president expects sales to increase by 20% next year. By what percentage should net income increase?
5. Refer to the original data. Assume that the company sold 18,000 units last year. The sales manager is convinced that a 10% reduction in the selling price, combined with a $30,000 increase in advertising, would cause annual sales in units to increase by one-third. Prepare two contribution income statements, one showing the results of last year's operations and one showing the results of operations if these changes are made. Would you recommend that the company do as the sales manager suggests?
6. Refer to the original data. Assume again that the company sold 18,000 units last year. The president does not want to change the selling price. Instead, he wants to increase the sales commission by $1 per unit. He thinks that this move, combined with some increase in advertising, would increase annual

sales by 25%. By how much could advertising be increased with profits remaining unchanged? Do not prepare an income statement; use the incremental analysis approach.

**PROBLEM 7–2    Basic CVP Analysis; Cost Structure (LO2, LO4, LO5, LO6)**

Due to erratic sales of its sole product—a high-capacity battery for laptop computers—PEM, Inc. has been experiencing difficulty for some time. The company's income statement for the most recent month is given below:

| | |
|---|---:|
| Sales (19,500 units × $30 per unit) . . . . . . . . . . | $585,000 |
| Less variable expenses . . . . . . . . . . . . . . . . . . . . . | 409,500 |
| Contribution margin . . . . . . . . . . . . . . . . . . . . . . . | 175,500 |
| Less fixed expenses . . . . . . . . . . . . . . . . . . . . . . . | 180,000 |
| Net loss  . . . . . . . . . . . . . . . . . . . . . . . . . . . . . . . . | $  (4,500) |

*Required:*
1. Compute the company's CM ratio and its break-even point in both units and dollars.
2. The president believes that a $16,000 increase in the monthly advertising budget, combined with an intensified effort by the sales staff, will result in an $80,000 increase in monthly sales. If the president is right, what will be the effect on the company's monthly net income or loss? (Use the incremental approach in preparing your answer.)
3. Refer to the original data. The sales manager is convinced that a 10% reduction in the selling price, combined with an increase of $60,000 in the monthly advertising budget, will cause unit sales to double. What will the new income statement look like if these changes are adopted?
4. Refer to the original data. The Marketing Department thinks that a fancy new package for the laptop computer battery would help sales. The new package would increase packaging costs by 75 cents per unit. Assuming no other changes, how many units would have to be sold each month to earn a profit of $9,750?
5. Refer to the original data. By automating certain operations, the company could reduce variable costs by $3 per unit. However, fixed costs would increase by $72,000 each month.
   a. Compute the new CM ratio and the new break-even point in both units and dollars.
   b. Assume that the company expects to sell 26,000 units next month. Prepare two income statements, one assuming that operations are not automated and one assuming that they are. (Show data on per-unit and percentage bases, as well as in total, for each alternative.)
   c. Would you recommend that the company automate its operations? Explain.

**PROBLEM 7–3    Basic CVP Analysis; Graphing (LO2, LO3, LO4, LO5)**

The Fashion Shoe Company operates a chain of women's shoe shops around the country. The shops carry many styles of shoes that are all sold at the same price. Sales personnel in the shops are paid a substantial commission on each pair of shoes sold (in addition to a small basic salary) in order to encourage them to be aggressive in their sales efforts.

The following cost and revenue data relate to Shop 48 and are typical of one of the company's many outlets:

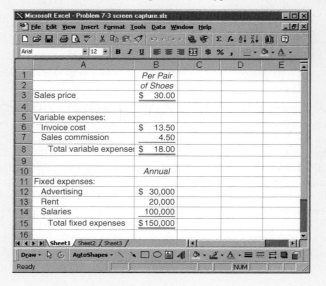

| | Per Pair of Shoes |
|---|---:|
| Sales price | $   30.00 |
| **Variable expenses:** | |
| Invoice cost | $   13.50 |
| Sales commission | 4.50 |
| Total variable expenses | $   18.00 |
| | **Annual** |
| **Fixed expenses:** | |
| Advertising | $  30,000 |
| Rent | 20,000 |
| Salaries | 100,000 |
| Total fixed expenses | $150,000 |

*Required:*

√ 1. Calculate the annual break-even point in dollar sales and in unit sales for Shop 48.
2. Prepare a CVP graph showing cost and revenue data for Shop 48 from a zero level of activity up to 20,000 pairs of shoes sold each year. Clearly indicate the break-even point on the graph.
3. If 12,000 pairs of shoes are sold in a year, what would be Shop 48's net income or loss?
4. The company is considering paying the store manager of Shop 48 an incentive commission of 75 cents per pair of shoes (in addition to the salesperson's commission). If this change is made, what will be the new break-even point in dollar sales and in unit sales?
5. Refer to the original data. As an alternative to (4) above, the company is considering paying the store manager 50 cents commission on each pair of shoes sold in excess of the break-even point. If this change is made, what will be the shop's net income or loss if 15,000 pairs of shoes are sold?
6. Refer to the original data. The company is considering eliminating sales commissions entirely in its shops and increasing fixed salaries by $31,500 annually. If this change is made, what will be the new break-even point in dollar sales and in unit sales for Shop 48? Would you recommend that the change be made? Explain.

**PROBLEM 7–4   Multiproduct Break-Even Analysis** (LO1, LO9)

Fill in the missing amounts in each of the eight case situations below. Each case is independent of the others. (Hint: One way to find the missing amounts would be to prepare a contribution income statement for each case, enter the known data, and then compute the missing items.)

a. Assume that only one product is being sold in each of the four following case situations:

CHECK FIGURE
(a) Case 2 Variable expenses: $60,000
(b) Case 4 Fixed expenses: $185,000

| Case | Units Sold | Sales | Variable Expenses | Contribution Margin per Unit | Fixed Expenses | Net Income (Loss) |
|---|---|---|---|---|---|---|
| 1 .... | 15,000 | $180,000 | $120,000 | $ ? | $ 50,000 | $ ? |
| 2 .... | ? | 100,000 | ? | 10 | 32,000 | 8,000 |
| 3 .... | 10,000 | ? | 70,000 | 13 | ? | 12,000 |
| 4 .... | 6,000 | 300,000 | ? | ? | 100,000 | (10,000) |

b. Assume that more than one product is being sold in each of the four following case situations:

| Case | Sales | Variable Expenses | Average Contribution Margin (percent) | Fixed Expenses | Net Income (Loss) |
|---|---|---|---|---|---|
| 1 .............. | $500,000 | $ ? | 20 | $ ? | $ 7,000 |
| 2 .............. | 400,000 | 260,000 | ? | 100,000 | ? |
| 3 .............. | ? | ? | 60 | 130,000 | 20,000 |
| 4 .............. | 600,000 | 420,000 | ? | ? | (5,000) |

**PROBLEM 7–5   Sales Mix; Multiproduct Break-Even Analysis** (LO1, LO5, LO9)

Gold Star Rice, Ltd., of Thailand, exports Thai rice throughout Asia. The company grows three varieties of rice—Fragrant, White, and Loonzain. (The currency in Thailand is the baht, which is denoted by B.) Budgeted sales by product and in total for the coming month are shown below:

CHECK FIGURE
(2) Break-even: B864,000

| | Product | | | | | | Total | |
|---|---|---|---|---|---|---|---|---|
| | White | | Fragrant | | Loonzain | | Total | |
| Percentage of total sales .. | 20% | | 52% | | 28% | | 100% | |
| Sales ................ | B150,000 | 100% | B390,000 | 100% | B210,000 | 100% | B750,000 | 100% |
| Less variable expenses ... | 108,000 | 72 | 78,000 | 20 | 84,000 | 40 | 270,000 | 36 |
| Contribution margin ..... | B 42,000 | 28% | B312,000 | 80% | B126,000 | 60% | 480,000 | 64% |
| Less fixed expenses ...... | | | | | | | 449,280 | |
| Net income ........... | | | | | | | B 30,720 | |

$$\text{Break-even sales: } \frac{\text{Fixed expenses, B449,280}}{\text{CM ratio, 0.64}} = \text{B702,000}$$

As shown by these data, net income is budgeted at B30,720 for the month and break-even sales at B702,000.

Assume that actual sales for the month total B750,000 as planned. Actual sales by product are: White, B300,000; Fragrant, B180,000; and Loonzain, B270,000.

***Required:***

1. Prepare a contribution income statement for the month on the basis of actual sales data. Present the income statement in the format shown above.
2. Compute the break-even sales for the month on the basis of your actual data.
3. Considering the fact that the company met its B750,000 sales budget for the month, the president is shocked at the results shown on your income statement in (1) above. Prepare a brief memo for the president explaining why both the operating results and break-even sales are different from what was budgeted.

CHECK FIGURE
(1) 300 sweatshirts

**PROBLEM 7–6    Break-Even and Target Profit Analysis (LO5, LO6)**
The Shirt Works sells a large variety of tee shirts and sweatshirts. Steve Hooper, the owner, is thinking of expanding his sales by hiring local high school students, on a commission basis, to sell sweatshirts bearing the name and mascot of the local high school.

These sweatshirts would have to be ordered from the manufacturer six weeks in advance, and they could not be returned because of the unique printing required. The sweatshirts would cost Mr. Hooper $8 each with a minimum order of 75 sweatshirts. Any additional sweatshirts would have to be ordered in increments of 75.

Since Mr. Hooper's plan would not require any additional facilities, the only costs associated with the project would be the costs of the sweatshirts and the costs of the sales commissions. The selling price of the sweatshirts would be $13.50 each. Mr. Hooper would pay the students a commission of $1.50 for each shirt sold.

***Required:***

 1. To make the project worthwhile, Mr. Hooper would require a $1,200 profit for the first three months of the venture. What level of sales in units and in dollars would be required to reach this target net income? Show all computations.
2. Assume that the venture is undertaken and an order is placed for 75 sweatshirts. What would be Mr. Hooper's break-even point in units and in sales dollars? Show computations and explain the reasoning behind your answer.

CHECK FIGURE
(1) Break-even:
      21,000 units

**PROBLEM 7–7    Changes in Fixed and Variable Costs; Break-Even and Target Profit Analysis (LO4, LO5, LO6)**
Neptune Company produces toys and other items for use in beach and resort areas. A small, inflatable toy has come on the market that the company is anxious to produce and sell. Enough capacity exists in the company's plant to produce 16,000 units of the toy each month. Variable costs to manufacture and sell one unit would be $1.25, and fixed costs associated with the toy would total $35,000 per month.

The company's Marketing Department predicts that demand for the new toy will exceed the 16,000 units that the company is able to produce. Additional manufacturing space can be rented from another company at a fixed cost of $1,000 per month. Variable costs in the rented facility would total $1.40 per unit, due to somewhat less efficient operations than in the main plant. The new toy will sell for $3 per unit.

***Required:***

1. Compute the monthly break-even point for the new toy in units and in total dollar sales. Show all computations in good form.
2. How many units must be sold each month to make a monthly profit of $12,000?
3. If the sales manager receives a bonus of 10 cents for each unit sold in excess of the break-even point, how many units must be sold each month to earn a return of 25% on the monthly investment in fixed costs?

CHECK FIGURE
(1b) Break-even: $732,000
(2b) Margin of safety: 22%

**PROBLEM 7–8    Sales Mix; Break-Even Analysis; Margin of Safety (LO1, LO5, LO7, LO9)**
Island Novelties, Inc., of Palau, makes two products, Hawaiian Fantasy and Tahitian Joy. Present revenue, cost, and sales data on the two products follow:

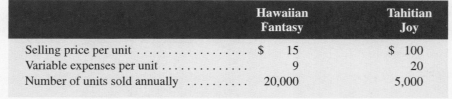

|  | Hawaiian Fantasy | Tahitian Joy |
|---|---|---|
| Selling price per unit ................. | $    15 | $   100 |
| Variable expenses per unit ............. | 9 | 20 |
| Number of units sold annually .......... | 20,000 | 5,000 |

Fixed expenses total $475,800 per year. The Republic of Palau uses the U.S. dollar as its currency.

**Required:**
1. Assuming the sales mix given above, do the following:
   a. Prepare a contribution income statement as in Exhibit 7–3 showing both dollar and percent columns for each product and for the company as a whole.
   b. Compute the break-even point in dollars for the company as a whole and the margin of safety in both dollars and percent.
2. Another product, Samoan Delight, has just come on the market. Assume that the company could sell 10,000 units at $45 each. The variable expenses would be $36 each. The company's fixed expenses would not change.
   a. Prepare another contribution income statement, including sales of Samoan Delight (sales of the other two products would not change). Carry percentage computations to one decimal place.
   b. Compute the company's new break-even point in dollars and the new margin of safety in both dollars and percent.
3. The president of the company examines your figures and says, "There's something strange here. Our fixed costs haven't changed and you show greater total contribution margin if we add the new product, but you also show our break-even point going up. With greater contribution margin, the break-even point should go down, not up. You've made a mistake somewhere." Explain to the president what has happened.

**PROBLEM 7–9   Graphing; Incremental Analysis; Operating Leverage** (LO3, LO4, LO5, LO6, LO8)
Angie Silva has recently opened The Sandal Shop in Brisbane, Australia, a store that specializes in fashionable sandals. Angie has just received a degree in business, and she is anxious to apply the principles she has learned to her business. In time, she hopes to open a chain of sandal shops. As a first step, she has prepared the following analysis for her new store:

CHECK FIGURE
(1) Break-even: 2,500 pairs
(5a) Leverage: 6

| | |
|---|---:|
| Sales price per pair of sandals . . . . . . . . . . . | $40 |
| Variable expenses per pair of sandals . . . . . | 16 |
| Contribution margin per pair of sandals . . . | $24 |
| | |
| Fixed expenses per year: | |
|    Building rental . . . . . . . . . . . . . . . . . . . . . | $15,000 |
|    Equipment depreciation . . . . . . . . . . . . . | 7,000 |
|    Selling . . . . . . . . . . . . . . . . . . . . . . . . . . | 20,000 |
|    Administrative . . . . . . . . . . . . . . . . . . . . . | 18,000 |
| Total fixed expenses . . . . . . . . . . . . . . . . . | $60,000 |

**Required:**
1. How many pairs of sandals must be sold each year to break even? What does this represent in total dollar sales?
2. Prepare a CVP graph for the store from a zero level of activity up to 5,000 pairs of sandals sold each year. Indicate the break-even point on your graph.
3. Angie has decided that she must earn at least $18,000 the first year to justify her time and effort. How many pairs of sandals must be sold to reach this target profit?
4. Angie now has two salespersons working in the store—one full time and one part time. It will cost her an additional $8,000 per year to convert the part-time position to a full-time position. Angie believes that the change would bring in an additional $25,000 in sales each year. Should she convert the position? Use the incremental approach (do not prepare an income statement).
5. Refer to the original data. During the first year, the store sold only 3,000 pairs of sandals and reported the following operating results:

| | |
|---|---:|
| Sales (3,000 pair) . . . . . . . . . . | $120,000 |
| Less variable expenses . . . . . | 48,000 |
| Contribution margin . . . . . . . | 72,000 |
| Less fixed expenses . . . . . . . . | 60,000 |
| Net income . . . . . . . . . . . . . | $ 12,000 |

   a. What is the store's degree of operating leverage?
   b. Angie is confident that with a more intense sales effort and with a more creative advertising program she can increase sales by 50% next year. What would be the expected percentage increase in net income? Use the degree of operating leverage to compute your answer.

# Building Your Skills

### ANALYTICAL THINKING (LO4, LO5, LO9)

Cheryl Montoya picked up the phone and called her boss, Wes Chan, the vice-president of marketing at Piedmont Fasteners Corporation: "Wes, I'm not sure how to go about answering the questions that came up at the meeting with the president yesterday."

"What's the problem?"

"The president wanted to know each product's break-even, but I am having trouble figuring them out."

"I'm sure you can handle it, Cheryl. And, by the way, I need your analysis on my desk tomorrow morning at 8:00 sharp in time for the follow-up meeting at 9:00."

Piedmont Fasteners Corporation makes three different clothing fasteners in its manufacturing facility in Quebec. Data concerning these products appear below:

|  | Velcro | Metal | Nylon |
|---|---|---|---|
| Normal annual sales volume ...... | 100,000 | 200,000 | 400,000 |
| Unit selling price ............... | $1.65 | $1.50 | $0.85 |
| Variable cost per unit ............ | $1.25 | $0.70 | $0.25 |

Total fixed expenses are $400,000 per year.

All three products are sold in highly competitive markets, and so the company is unable to raise its prices without losing unacceptable numbers of customers.

The company has an extremely effective just-in-time manufacturing system, and so there are no beginning or ending work in process or finished goods inventories.

### Required:

1. What is the company's overall break-even in total sales dollars?
2. Of the total fixed costs of $400,000, $20,000 could be avoided if the Velcro product were dropped, $80,000 if the Metal product were dropped, and $60,000 if the Nylon product were dropped. The remaining fixed costs of $240,000 consist of common fixed costs, such as administrative salaries and rent on the factory building, that could be avoided only by going out of business entirely.
   a. What is the break-even quantity of each product?
   b. If the company sells exactly the break-even quantity of each product, what will be the overall profit of the company?

CHECK FIGURE
(1a) Break-even:
$12,000,000

### COMMUNICATING IN PRACTICE (LO3, LO4, LO6, LO8)

Pittman Company is a small but growing manufacturer of telecommunications equipment. The company has no sales force of its own; rather, it relies completely on independent sales agents to market its products. These agents are paid a commission of 15% of selling price for all items sold.

Barbara Cheney, Pittman's controller, has just prepared the company's budgeted income statement for next year. The statement follows:

**PITTMAN COMPANY**
**Budgeted Income Statement**
**For the Year Ended December 31**

| | | |
|---|---|---|
| Sales .................................... | | $16,000,000 |
| Manufacturing costs: | | |
|   Variable ........................ | $7,200,000 | |
|   Fixed overhead ................... | 2,340,000 | 9,540,000 |
| Gross margin ...................... | | 6,460,000 |
| Selling and administrative costs: | | |
|   Commissions to agents ............. | 2,400,000 | |
|   Fixed marketing costs .............. | 120,000* | |
|   Fixed administrative costs ........... | 1,800,000 | 4,320,000 |
| Net operating income ................. | | 2,140,000 |
| Less fixed interest cost ............... | | 540,000 |
| Income before income taxes ........... | | 1,600,000 |
| Less income taxes (30%) .............. | | 480,000 |
| Net income ........................ | | $ 1,120,000 |

*Primarily depreciation on storage facilities.

As Barbara handed the statement to Karl Vecci, Pittman's president, she commented, "I went ahead and used the agents' 15% commission rate in completing these statements, but we've just learned that they refuse to handle our products next year unless we increase the commission rate to 20%."

"That's the last straw," Karl replied angrily. "Those agents have been demanding more and more, and this time they've gone too far. How can they possibly defend a 20% commission rate?"

"They claim that after paying for advertising, travel, and the other costs of promotion, there's nothing left over for profit," replied Barbara.

"I say it's just plain robbery," retorted Karl. "And I also say it's time we dumped those guys and got our own sales force. Can you get your people to work up some cost figures for us to look at?"

"We've already worked them up," said Barbara. "Several companies we know about pay a 7.5% commission to their own salespeople, along with a small salary. Of course, we would have to handle all promotion costs, too. We figure our fixed costs would increase by $2,400,000 per year, but that would be more than offset by the $3,200,000 (20% × $16,000,000) that we would avoid on agents' commissions."

The breakdown of the $2,400,000 cost figure follows:

| Salaries: | |
|---|---|
| Sales manager .............. | $ 100,000 |
| Salespersons ............... | 600,000 |
| Travel and entertainment ....... | 400,000 |
| Advertising ................. | 1,300,000 |
| Total ...................... | $2,400,000 |

"Super," replied Karl. "And I note that the $2,400,000 is just what we're paying the agents under the old 15% commission rate."

"It's even better than that," explained Barbara. "We can actually save $75,000 a year because that's what we're having to pay the auditing firm now to check out the agents' reports. So, our overall administrative costs would be less."

"Pull all of these numbers together, and we'll show them to the executive committee tomorrow," said Karl. "With the approval of the committee, we can move on the matter immediately."

***Required:***
1. Compute Pittman Company's break-even point in sales dollars for next year assuming:
   a. That the agents' commission rate remains unchanged at 15%.
   b. That the agents' commission rate is increased to 20%.
   c. That the company employs its own sales force.
2. Assume that Pittman Company decides to continue selling through agents and pays the 20% commission rate. Determine the volume of sales that would be required to generate the same net income as contained in the budgeted income statement for next year.
3. Determine the volume of sales at which net income would be equal, regardless of whether Pittman Company sells through agents (at a 20% commission rate) or employs its own sales force.
4. Compute the degree of operating leverage that the company would expect to have on December 31 at the end of next year assuming:
   a. That the agents' commission rate remains unchanged at 15%.
   b. That the agents' commission rate is increased to 20%.
   c. That the company employs its own sales force.
   Use income *before* income taxes in your operating leverage computation.
5. On the basis of the data in (1) through (4) above, draft a memorandum to Barbara Cheney that sets forth your recommendation as to whether the company should continue to use sales agents (at a 20% commission rate) or employ its own sales force. Give reasons for your recommendation.

(CMA, adapted)

**SKILLS CHALLENGER** (LO5, LO6)

CHECK FIGURE
(2) 15,820 patient-days

Wymont Hospital operates a general hospital with separate departments, such as Pediatrics, Maternity, and Surgery. Wymont Hospital charges each separate department for services to its patients, such as meals and laundry, and for administrative services, such as billing and collections. Space and bed charges are fixed for the year.

Last year, the Pediatrics Department at Wymont Hospital charged its patients an average of $65 per day, had a capacity of 80 beds, operated 24 hours per day for 365 days, and had total revenue of $1,138,800.

Expenses charged by the hospital to the Pediatrics Department for the year were as follows:

| | Basis for Allocation | |
|---|---|---|
| | Patient-Days (variable) | Bed Capacity (fixed) |
| Dietary | $ 42,952 | |
| Janitorial | | $ 12,800 |
| Laundry | 28,000 | |
| Laboratory | 47,800 | |
| Pharmacy | 33,800 | |
| Repairs and maintenance | 5,200 | 7,140 |
| General administrative services | | 131,760 |
| Rent | | 275,320 |
| Billings and collections | 87,000 | |
| Other | 18,048 | 25,980 |
| | $262,800 | $453,000 |

The only personnel directly employed by the Pediatrics Department are supervising nurses, nurses, and aides. The hospital has minimum personnel requirements for Pediatrics based on total annual patient-days in Pediatrics. Hospital requirements, beginning at the minimum expected level of operation, follow:

| Annual Patient-Days | Aides | Nurses | Supervising Nurses |
|---|---|---|---|
| 10,000–14,000 | 21 | 11 | 4 |
| 14,001–17,000 | 22 | 12 | 4 |
| 17,001–23,725 | 22 | 13 | 4 |
| 23,726–25,550 | 25 | 14 | 5 |
| 25,551–27,375 | 26 | 14 | 5 |
| 27,376–29,200 | 29 | 16 | 6 |

These staffing levels represent full-time equivalents, and it should be assumed that the Pediatrics Department always employs only the minimum number of required full-time equivalent personnel.

Annual salaries for each class of employee are: supervising nurses, $18,000; nurses, $13,000; and aides, $5,000. Salary expense for last year was $72,000, $169,000, and $110,000 for supervising nurses, nurses, and aides, respectively.

*Required:*
1. Compute the following:
   a. The number of patient-days in the Pediatrics Department for last year. (Each day a patient is in the hospital is known as a *patient-day.*)
   b. The variable cost per patient-day for last year.
   c. The total fixed costs, including both allocated fixed costs and personnel costs, in the Pediatrics Department for each level of operation shown above (i.e., total fixed costs at the 10,000–14,000 patient-day level of operation, total fixed costs at the 14,001–17,000 patient-day level of operation, and so on).
2. Using the data computed in (1) above and any other data as needed, compute the *minimum* number of patient-days required for the Pediatrics Department to break even. You may assume that variable and fixed cost behaviour and that revenue per patient-day will remain unchanged in the future.
3. Determine the minimum number of patient-days required for the Pediatrics Department to earn an annual "profit" of $200,000.

(CPA, adapted)

**TEAMWORK IN ACTION   (LO1)**
The cost structure of the airline industry can serve as the basis for a discussion of a number of different cost concepts. Airlines also provide an excellent illustration of the concept of operating leverage, the sensitivity

of a firm's operating profits to changes in demand, and the opportunities and risks presented by such a cost structure. Airline profits and share prices are among some of the most volatile on Wall Street. A recent study of the U.S. airline industry disclosed the following operating cost categories and their percentage of total operating cost:*

| Uniform System of Accounts Required by the Department of Transportation | Mean Percentage of Operating Cost, 1981–85 |
|---|---|
| Fuel and oil | 24.3% |
| Flying operations labour (flight crews—pilots, co-pilots, navigators, and flight engineers) | 8.6 |
| Passenger service labour (flight attendants) | 4.6 |
| Aircraft traffic and servicing labour (personnel servicing aircraft and handling passengers at gates, baggage, and cargo) | 8.9 |
| Promotions and sales labour (reservations and sales agents, advertising and publicity) | 9.0 |
| Maintenance labour (maintenance of flight equipment and ground property and equipment) | 7.0 |
| Maintenance materials and overhead | 2.1 |
| Ground property and equipment (landing fees, and rental expenses and depreciation for ground property and equipment) | 12.5 |
| Flight equipment (rental expenses and depreciation on aircraft frames and engines) | 8.4 |
| General overhead (administrative personnel, utilities, insurance, communications, etc.) | 14.6 |
| Total | 100.0% |

***Required:***

1. Your team should discuss and then write up a brief description of the objectives of airline cost accounting systems. All team members should agree with and understand the description.
2. Each member of the team should present an answer to one of the following questions to the other team members, who should confirm or correct the answer.
   a. For each of the accounts listed above, indicate whether the costs in the account are mainly fixed or variable with respect to the number of flights flown—irrespective of how many passengers are carried on the flights. For purposes of thinking about this assignment, assume that all flights always fly nearly full and the airline already operates out of the airport. On the basis of this analysis, estimate the percentage of costs that are fixed with respect to the number of flights flown.
   b. For each of the accounts listed above, indicate whether the costs in the account are mainly fixed or variable with respect to the number of passengers carried on a particular scheduled flight. On the basis of this analysis, estimate the percentage of costs that are fixed with respect to the number of passengers carried on a particular scheduled flight.
3. The team should discuss and then write up brief answers to the questions listed below. All team members should agree with and understand the answers.
   a. What conclusions do you draw about the nature of fixed and variable costs on the basis of your analysis in question 2 above?
   b. Why are profits more sensitive (more variable) to changes in demand when the cost structure contains a high proportion of fixed costs? What is probably a more effective way to improve the profitability of an airline—increase the number of flights or increase the average number of passengers on flights the airline already flies?

Do not forget to check out Taking It to the Net as well as other quizzes and resources at the Online Learning Centre at www.mcgrawhill.ca/college/garrison.

---

*R. D. Banker and H. H. Johnson, "An Empirical Study of Cost Drivers in the U.S. Airline Industry," *The Accounting Review*, July 1993, pp. 576–601.

# *Chapter Eight*

# Budgeting

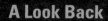

## A Look Back
In Chapter 7, we explained how to compute a break-even point and how to determine the activity level needed to achieve a desired profit. We also described how to compute and assess the significance of the margin of safety and of operating leverage.

## A Look at This Chapter
After discussing why organizations prepare budgets, Chapter 8 overviews each of the individual budgets that constitute a firm's master budget. We also address the preparation of the cash budget, the budgeted income statement, and the budgeted balance sheet. The chapter concludes with a discussion of the processes organizations use to create budgets and some of the issues which arise in practice.

## A Look Ahead
We turn our attention from the planning process to management control and performance measures in Chapter 9 by focusing on the use of standard costs and variance analysis.

## Chapter Outline

**Budgets and Budgeting**
- Budgets: Planning versus Control
- Advantages of Budgeting
- An Overview of the Master Budget
- Choosing a Budget Period
- Zero-Based Budgeting

**Preparing the Master Budget**
- The Sales Budget
- The Production Budget
- Inventory Purchases—Merchandising Firm
- The Direct Materials Budget
- The Direct Labour Budget
- The Manufacturing Overhead Budget
- The Ending Finished Goods Inventory Budget
- The Selling and Administrative Expense Budget

- The Cash Budget
- The Budgeted Income Statement
- The Budgeted Balance Sheet

**Practical Issues in Budgeting: Use and Abuse**
- The Self-Imposed Budget
- The Matter of Human Relations
- The Budget Committee
- Beyond Budgeting

(See the Online Learning Centre at www.mcgrawhill.ca/college/garrison.)

## DECISION FEATURE Budgets Can Point the Way to Improving Financial Health

Grant MacEwan College in Edmonton, Alberta, is faced with higher operating costs than it can handle. Government financing has been tight, and the college must find ways to increase its revenues by June 2003 in order to avoid cost overruns, which has been rising faster than government grants received. The anticipated $2 million shortfall, which represents about 2% of the college's total annual budget of $115 million, must be recovered to avoid shrinking faculty and programs. The college has already taken steps by increasing the tuition fees for the coming year by 9.7%. Junior colleges, such as Grant MacEwan, are strictly prohibited by law to run deficits, unlike their university counterparts, such as the University of Alberta and University of Calgary. The college is expected to recover the $2 million shortfall when submitting its budget to the Alberta Learning Department by the end of June.

Source: "Cash-strapped Edmonton College Must Come Up with Money or Make Cuts," *Canadian Press Newswire*, March 8, 2003. Reprinted with permission from Press News Limited, a division of the Canadian Press.

### Learning Objectives

*After studying Chapter 8, you should be able to:*

**LO1** Understand why organizations budget.

**LO2** Prepare a sales budget, including a schedule of expected cash receipts.

**LO3** Prepare a production budget.

**LO4** Prepare a direct materials budget, including a schedule of expected cash disbursements for purchases of materials.

**LO5** Prepare a direct labour budget.

**LO6** Prepare a manufacturing overhead budget.

**LO7** Prepare a selling and administrative expense budget.

**LO8** Prepare a cash budget.

**LO9** Prepare a budgeted income statement.

**LO10** Prepare a budgeted balance sheet.

**LO11** Understand the processes organizations use to create budgets and the practical issues raised.

**LO12** Understand the Beyond Budgeting Model and its approach to budgeting.

In a **mission, vision, and values statement,** an organization captures the answers to such questions as: Where do we want to be five years from now? What should we be to our customers, our employees, and other stakeholders? Which markets do we want to dominate? The broad intent and aims stated in a mission statement are translated into specific goals and objectives to be achieved by the organization in the next few years by the process of **strategic planning.** Strategic planning involves making decisions about how the organization should position itself in the marketplace to compete successfully with its rivals for customers and resources. These decisions and their implications for resource acquisition and deployment are captured in the **strategic plan,** which is the principal output from the strategic planning process. The strategic plan is then used to develop the specific tactics that will be used to guide the short-term operations of the organization. This process of **operational planning** is where the process of *budgeting* enters the picture. Budgeting is the process used by businesses to describe, in financial terms, how they intend to achieve their desired financial and nonfinancial objectives.

In this chapter, we focus on budgeting. Budgeting is accomplished through the preparation of a number of budgets, which collectively form an integrated business plan known as the **master budget.** The budgeting process culminates with the preparation of a cash budget, detailing the planned cash receipts and disbursements, including short-term borrowing requirements, a budgeted income statement, and a budgeted balance sheet.

# Budgets and Budgeting

The key tool in the budgeting process is the **budget.** A budget is a quantitative plan for acquiring and using financial and other resources. It is a medium to communicate, quantitatively, management's objectives for sales, production, purchasing, distribution, and financing activities. It is also the instrument that guides and coordinates the firm's activities among all of these areas. Exhibit 8–1 provides a context to understand this role of budgeting. As you can see, the budget gives voice to what the organization intends to achieve, financially, during the upcoming operations period. And in doing so, it becomes the basis for management actions and the reference point for performance measurement (what is measured) and performance evaluation (how the measures are used).

## Budgets: Planning versus Control

**Planning** involves developing objectives and the various budgets to achieve these objectives. Budgeting serves to flesh out the conceptual plans and strategies by expressing the plans in financial terms. The use of budgets to guide and coordinate activities across the firm to ensure that objectives are attained is called *budgetary control.* The concept of **control** refers to the steps taken to increase the likelihood that the objectives and targets described in the budgets are attained and all parts of the organization function in a manner consistent with organizational policies.

Planning and control are distinct concepts that are often confused and thought to suggest the same thing. The confusion arises from the fact that budgets are common to both. To avoid confusion, keep in mind that budgets are the *result* of planning and the *basis* for control. To be effective a good budgeting system must provide for both planning and control. Good planning without effective control is time wasted.

## Advantages of Budgeting

**Learning Objective 1**
Understand why organizations budget.

Why should we budget? The simplest answer is scarcity of resources. If resources were unlimited and free, we would be unconcerned about waste and there would be no need for planning and control. There would be no need for communication of plans throughout the

**Exhibit 8–1**
The Budget in the Context of
Strategy and Planning

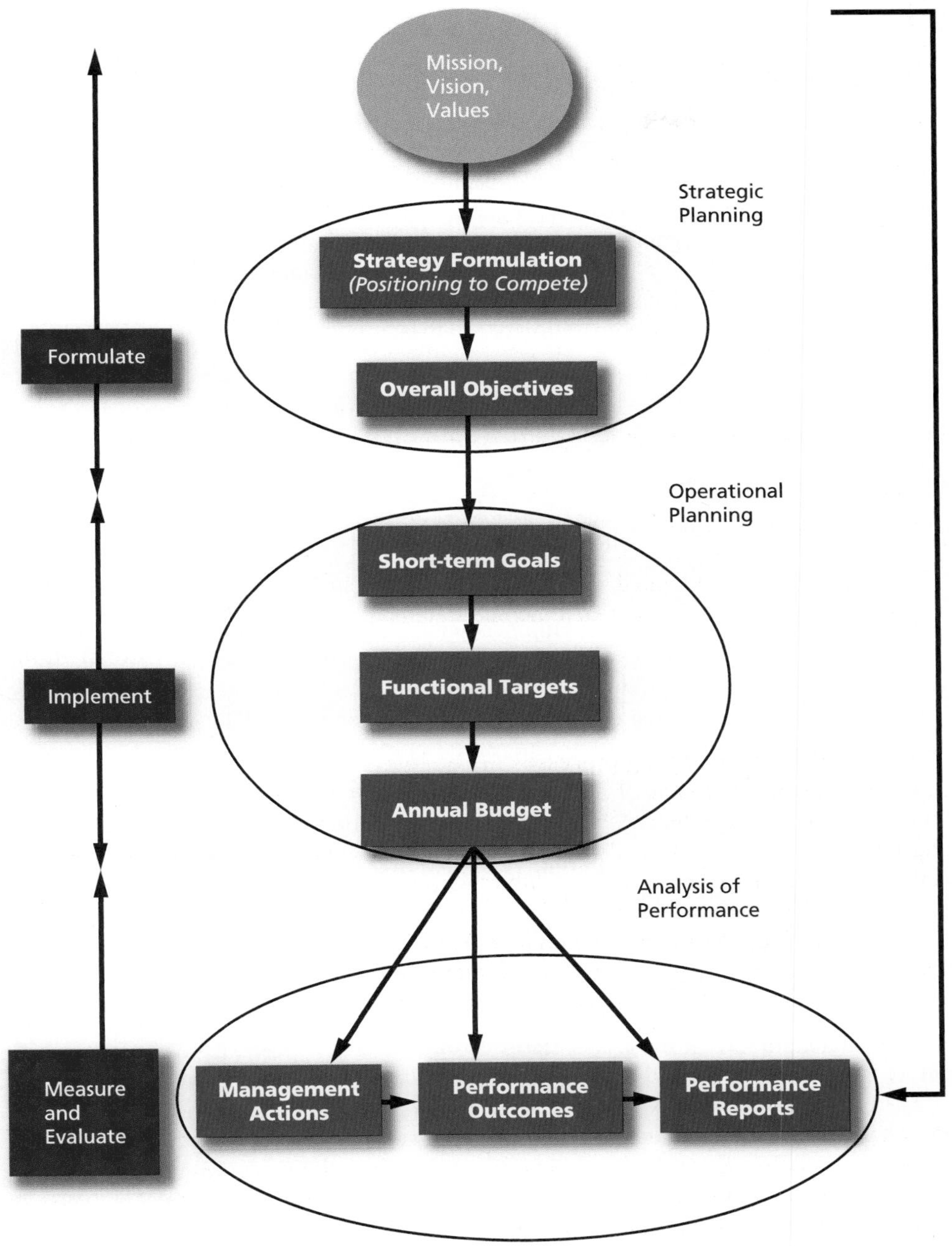

organization. Nothing would impede achieving our objectives. In short, there would be no need to think about how to achieve our objectives in a systematic, organized, and coordinated manner.

But, scarcity of resources is a fundamental reality confronting businesses and individuals. Therefore, organizations and individuals must:

- Think about and plan for the future systematically.
- Uncover potential impediments to achieving goals and objectives, such as resource constraints and bottlenecks.
- Communicate plans carefully and clearly.
- Coordinate the planned actions across the various parts of the organization.
- Ensure that scarce resources are employed to best benefit the organization.

- Define goals and objectives that can serve as benchmarks for subsequent performance.

Budgeting and budgets enable organizations to accomplish all of the above.

How can organizations ensure that the potential benefits from budgeting and preparing budgets are actually realized? This is an extremely important question, the answer to which requires us to consider the *individuals* involved in budgeting, the *steps* taken to accomplish the budgeting, and how the organization intends to *use* the budgets. We must also consider how the organization communicates those intentions and whether the budgets are, in fact, used in the way intended. To fully appreciate these important issues, it will help to go through an example of budgeting. Therefore, we will address these issues after we have illustrated the preparation of the master budget.

---

*in business | today*    **Budgets Can Suggest What Must Be Controlled to Improve the Bottom Line**

With the technology industry in decline, Nortel Networks Corporation (Nortel) realized that it needed to make to some changes to halt the rapid slide toward extinction. Until it was toppled from its position as an industry leader, Nortel was a major player in the telecommunications industry, providing a wide range of products and services that support communication through networks. However, a major misreading of the future growth in demand for its products led Nortel to invest in excess network capacity. Unfortunately, the unanticipated economic downturn caused Nortel's customers to reduce their capital spending significantly. The result? Nortel's shares plummeted from a high of $124.50 to a mere 67¢. Nortel restructured drastically to reduce overhead and make operations more efficient.

Nortel was able to reduce its selling, general, and administrative expenses by $257 million, from $744 million to $487 million, from the first quarter of 2002 to the first quarter of 2003. In all segments of the business, Nortel reduced its workforce by more than 60%, from 96,000 to only 36,000. Nortel further streamlined operations by selling off certain optical components assets and terminating and expiring certain credit facilities and amendments to its security agreements.

Research and Development (R&D) was refocused toward investments that would allow Nortel to maintain its industry leader status. Nortel lowered its R&D expenditures by $106 million in one year to bring them in line with the overall cost structure of the company.

The newly restructured Nortel has already seen an 800% increase in its share price in the last year and is continually looking for ways to reduce costs. Unfortunately, at the time of this writing (Spring 2004), Nortel is again in the financial news, with both the RCMP and the United States Securities and Exchanges Commission (SEC) launching separate investigations into Nortel's financial affairs.

Sources: Nortel Networks Corporation. *2003 First Quarter Shareholders Report*, Brampton, ON. 2003; and Wahl, Andrew. "Groovin' up quickly," *Canadian Business*, September 29–October 14, 2003, pp. 37–39. Reprinted with permission from *Canadian Business*.

---

## An Overview of the Master Budget

The master budget is the principal output of the budgeting process. Exhibit 8–2 provides an overview of the various parts of the master budget and how they are related. The type of organization—is it a manufacturer or a merchandiser or a service provider?—will determine if some of the component budgets are necessary. A merchandiser will not require a production budget, for example. Instead, the merchandising company will prepare a merchandise purchases budget. A service provider will not require either a production

**Exhibit 8–2**
The Master Budget Inter-relationships

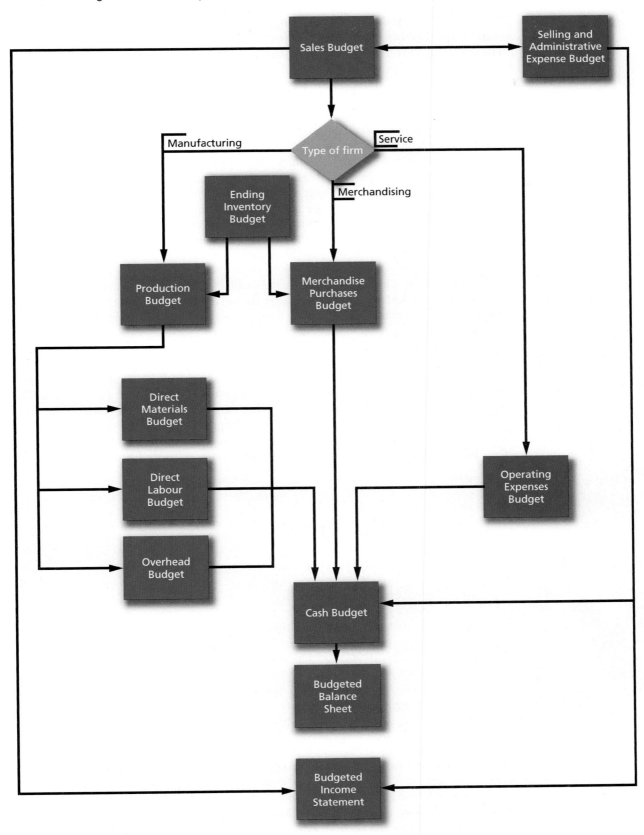

budget or a merchandise purchases budget. Service organizations, such as law offices or a health services department, will rely on the operating expenses budget.

**THE SALES BUDGET**     A **sales budget** is a detailed schedule showing the expected sales—expressed both in dollars and units of product (or service)—for the budget period. The sales budget is usually based on the company's *sales forecast*. In addition, the manager may examine the company's unfulfilled back orders, the company's pricing policy and marketing plans, trends in the industry, and general economic conditions. Sophisticated statistical tools may be used to analyze the data and to build models that are helpful in predicting key factors influencing the company's sales. These tools and models are more appropriately covered in marketing courses, and so we will not go into the details of how the sales forecasts are made.

Service organizations must estimate the demand for their services. Professional accountants, for example, have to estimate the revenues they expect to earn from their consulting practice. These estimates are typically derived from projections of the number of consulting engagements and the nature (tax advice, auditing engagements, business consulting) of the service to be provided. The projections will also depend on the rates to be charged. These rates, in turn, might be established on a cost-plus basis where the exact figure is set on the basis of the desired margin over the costs. In such cases, cost measurement, management, and control will be critical.

An accurate sales budget is the key to the entire budgeting process in for-profit organizations. All of the other parts of the master budget are dependent on the sales budget in some way, as illustrated in Exhibit 8–2. Thus, if the sales budget is sloppily done, then the rest of the budgeting process is largely a waste of time.

Not-for-profit organizations face different challenges. In many of these organizations, the concept of revenue generated from "selling" services will not be relevant. Many of these organizations rely on external sources of funding, such as a parent organization, individual and corporate donors, and/or local and higher levels of government. The programs and services these organizations offer consume financial resources. Budgeting for these organizations controls their operating expenses by controlling the variety and volume of services—the consumer of financial resources—offered so as to be in line with their financial endowments. See the following In Business Today feature.

## *in business* *today*     **A Looming Financial Crisis**

The Repertory Theatre of St. Louis is a not-for-profit professional theatre that is supported by contributions from donors and by ticket sales. Financially, the theatre appeared to be doing well. However, a five-year budget revealed that within a few years, expenses would exceed revenues and the theatre would be facing a financial crisis. Realistically, additional contributions from donors would not fill the gap. Cutting costs would not work because of the theatre's already lean operations; cutting costs even more would jeopardize the quality of the theatre's productions. Raising ticket prices was ruled out due to competitive pressures and to the belief that this would be unpopular with many donors. The solution was to build a second mainstage performing space that would allow the theatre to put on more performances and thereby sell more tickets. By developing a long-range budget, the management of The Repertory Theatre of St. Louis was able to identify in advance a looming financial crisis and to develop a solution that would avert the crisis in time.

Source: Lawrence P. Carr, ed., "The Repertory Theatre of St. Louis (B): Strategic Budgeting," *Cases from Management Accounting Practice: Volumes 10 and 11*, Institute of Management Accountants, Montvale, NJ, 1997. Reprinted with permission from *Management Accounting*.

The remainder of the discussion will assume that we are concerned with a for-profit manufacturing organization.

**THE INTERDEPENDENCY OF THE BUDGETS**    The sales budget will help determine how many units will have to be produced. Thus, the production budget is prepared after the sales budget. The production budget, in turn, is used to determine the budgets for the manufacturing costs, including the direct materials budget, the direct labour budget, and the manufacturing overhead budget. These budgets are then combined with the data from the sales budget and the selling and administrative expense budget to determine the cash budget.

Concept 8–1

**THE CASH BUDGET**    The term *operating budgets* is used to refer to the budgets that pertain to such activities as sales, production, purchasing, selling, and administration that the firm undertakes in the course of operating the business. A **cash budget** is a *financial* budget. It is a detailed plan showing how cash resources will be acquired and used over some specified time period. Observe from Exhibit 8–2 that all of the operating budgets have an impact on the cash budget. Operations run, ultimately, on money! The sales budget provides the basis for the planned cash receipts from sales. In the case of the other budgets, the impact on the cash budget comes from the planned expenditures with the budgets themselves.

## Choosing a Budget Period

Operating budgets, including the cash budget, ordinarily cover the company's fiscal year. Many companies divide their budget year into four quarters. The first quarter is then subdivided into months, and monthly budgets are developed. The last three quarters are carried in the budget at quarterly totals only. As the year progresses, the figures for the second quarter are broken down into monthly amounts, then the third-quarter figures are broken down, and so on. This approach has the advantage of requiring periodic review and reappraisal of budget data throughout the year.

In this chapter, we will focus on one-year operating budgets. However, using basically the same techniques, operating budgets can be prepared for periods that extend over many years. It may be difficult to accurately forecast sales and required data much beyond a year, but even rough estimates can be invaluable in uncovering potential problems and opportunities that would otherwise be overlooked.

## Zero-Based Budgeting

In the traditional approach to budgeting, the manager starts with last year's budget and adds to it (or subtracts from it) according to anticipated needs. This is an incremental approach to budgeting in which the previous year's budget is taken for granted as a baseline.

Zero-based budgeting is an alternative approach that is sometimes used—particularly in the governmental and not-for-profit sectors of the economy. Under a **zero-based budget,** managers are required to justify *all* budgeted expenditures, not just changes in the budget from the previous year. The baseline is zero, rather than last year's budget.

A zero-based budget requires considerable documentation. In addition to all of the schedules in the usual master budget, the manager must prepare a series of "decision packages" in which all of the activities of the department are ranked according to their relative importance and the cost of each activity is identified. Higher-level managers can then review the decision packages and cut back in those areas that appear to be less critical or whose costs do not appear to be justified.

Nearly everyone would agree that zero-based budgeting is a good idea. The only issue is the frequency with which a zero-based review is carried out. Under zero-based budgeting, the review is performed every year. Critics of zero-based budgeting charge that properly executed zero-based budgeting is too time consuming and too costly to justify on an annual basis. In addition, it is argued that annual reviews soon become mechanical and that the whole purpose of zero-based budgeting is then lost.

Whether or not a company should use an annual review is a matter of judgment. In some situations, annual zero-based reviews may be justified; in other situations, they may not because of the time and cost involved. However, most managers would at least agree that on occasion zero-based reviews can be very helpful.

---

*decision* | *maker*    **Sales Manager**

You were recently hired as the sales manager for a company that designs and manufactures hard-soled casual and dress shoes for sale to department stores. The vice-president of sales recently decided that the company will add athletic footwear to its catalogue, and asked you to prepare a sales budget for that product line for the coming year. How would you forecast sales for this product line?

---

# Preparing the Master Budget

**MANAGERIAL ACCOUNTING IN ACTION**

**The Issue**

Tom Wills is the majority shareholder and chief executive officer of Hampton Freeze, Inc., a company he started in 2003. The company makes premium popsicles using only natural ingredients and featuring exotic flavours, such as tangy tangerine and minty mango. The company's business is highly seasonal, with most of the sales occurring in spring and summer.

In 2004, the company's second year of operations, a major cash crunch in the first and second quarters almost forced the company into bankruptcy. In spite of this cash crunch, 2004 turned out to be a very successful year in terms of both overall cash flow and net income. Partly as a result of that harrowing experience, Tom decided toward the end of 2004 to hire a professional financial manager. Tom interviewed several promising candidates for the job and settled on Larry Giano, who had considerable experience in the packaged foods industry. In the job interview, Tom questioned Larry about the steps he would take to prevent a recurrence of the 2004 cash crunch:

*Tom:* As I mentioned earlier, we are going to wind up 2004 with a very nice profit. What you may not know is that we had some very big financial problems this year.
*Larry:* Let me guess. You ran out of cash sometime in the first or second quarter.
*Tom:* How did you know?
*Larry:* Most of your sales are in the second and third quarters, right?
*Tom:* Sure, everyone wants to buy popsicles in the spring and summer, but nobody wants them when the weather turns cold.
*Larry:* So, you don't have many sales in the first quarter?
*Tom:* Right.
*Larry:* And in the second quarter, which is the spring, you are producing like crazy to fill orders?
*Tom:* Sure.
*Larry:* Do your customers, the grocery stores, pay you the day you make your deliveries?
*Tom:* Are you kidding? Of course not.
*Larry:* So, in the first quarter, you don't have many sales. In the second quarter, you are producing like crazy, which eats up cash, but you aren't paid by your customers until long after you have paid your employees and suppliers. No wonder you had a cash problem. I see this pattern all the time in food processing because of the seasonality of the business.
*Tom:* So, what can we do about it?
*Larry:* The first step is to predict the magnitude of the problem before it occurs. If we can predict early in the year what the cash shortfall is going to be, we can go to the bank and arrange for credit before we really need it. Bankers tend to be leery of panicky people who show up begging for emergency loans. They are much more likely to make

the loan if you look like you know what you are doing, you have done your homework, and you are in control of the situation.

*Tom:* How can we predict the cash shortfall?

*Larry:* You can put together a cash budget. While you're at it, you might as well do a master budget. You'll find it is well worth the effort.

*Tom:* I don't like budgets. They are too confining. My wife budgets everything at home, and I can't spend what I want.

*Larry:* Can I ask a personal question?

*Tom:* What?

*Larry:* Where did you get the money to start this business?

*Tom:* Mainly from our family's savings. I get your point. We wouldn't have had the money to start the business if my wife hadn't been forcing us to save every month.

*Larry:* Exactly. I suggest you use the same discipline in your business. It is even more important here because you can't expect your employees to spend your money as carefully as you would.

*Tom:* I'm sold. Welcome aboard.

With the full backing of Tom Wills, Larry Giano set out to create a master budget for the company for the year 2005. In his planning for the budgeting process, Larry drew up the following list of documents that would be a part of the master budget:

1. A sales budget, including a schedule of expected cash collections.
2. A production budget (a merchandise purchases budget would be used in a merchandising company).
3. A direct materials budget, including a schedule of expected cash disbursements for raw materials (this would not be needed for a merchandising company).
4. A direct labour budget (this would not be needed for a merchandising company).
5. A manufacturing overhead budget.
6. An ending finished goods inventory budget.
7. A selling and administrative expense budget.
8. A cash budget.
9. A budgeted income statement.
10. A budgeted balance sheet.

Larry felt it was important to have everyone's cooperation in the budgeting process, and so he asked Tom to call a companywide meeting in which the budgeting process would be explained. At the meeting, there was initially some grumbling, but Tom was able to convince nearly everyone of the necessity for planning and getting better control over spending. It helped that the cash crisis earlier in the year was still fresh in everyone's minds.

In the months that followed, Larry worked closely with all of the managers involved in the master budget, gathering data from them and making sure that they understood and fully supported the parts of the master budget that would affect them. In subsequent years, Larry hoped to turn the whole budgeting process over to the managers and to take on a more advisory role.

The interdependent documents that Larry Giano prepared for Hampton Freeze are Schedules 1 through 10 of his company's master budget. In this section, we will study these schedules.

## The Sales Budget

The sales budget is the starting point in preparing the master budget. As shown earlier in Exhibit 8–2, all other items in the master budget, including production, purchases, inventories, and expenses, depend on it in some way.

The sales budget is constructed by multiplying the budgeted sales in units by the selling price. Schedule 1 on the next page contains the sales budget for Hampton Freeze for the year 2005, by quarters. Note from the schedule that the company plans to sell 100,000 cases of popsicles during the year, with sales peaking in the third quarter.

**Learning Objective 2**

Prepare a sales budget, including a schedule of expected cash receipts.

## Schedule 1

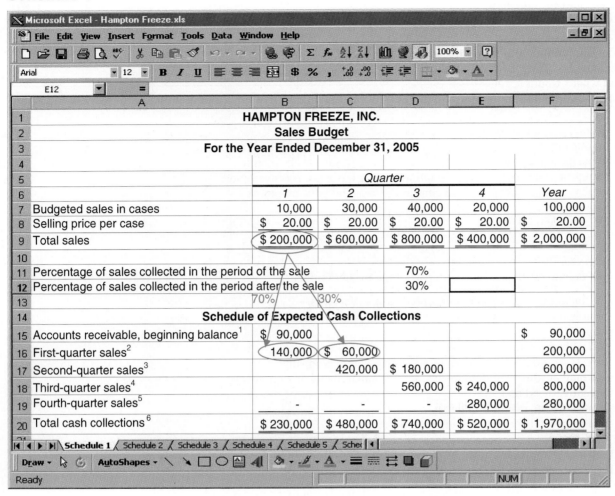

¹Cash collections from last year's fourth-quarter sales. See the beginning-of-year balance sheet on page 299.

²$200,000 × 70%; $200,000 × 30%.

³$600,000 × 70%; $600,000 × 30%.

⁴$800,000 × 70%; $800,000 × 30%.

⁵$400,000 × 70%.

⁶Uncollected fourth-quarter sales appear as accounts receivable on the company's end-of-year balance sheet (see Schedule 10 on page 298).

**SCHEDULE OF EXPECTED CASH COLLECTIONS**  A schedule of expected cash collections, such as the one that appears in Schedule 1 for Hampton Freeze, is prepared after the sales budget. This schedule will be needed later to prepare the cash budget. Cash collections consist of collections on sales made to customers in prior periods plus collections on sales made in the current budget period. At Hampton Freeze, experience has shown that 70% of sales are collected in the quarter in which the sale is made and the remaining 30% are collected in the following quarter. For example, 70% of the first quarter sales of $200,000 (or $140,000) are collected during the first quarter, and 30% (or $60,000) are collected during the second quarter.

## The Production Budget

**Learning Objective 3**

Prepare a production budget.

The production budget is prepared after the sales budget. The **production budget** lists the number of units that must be produced during each budget period to meet sales needs and to provide for the desired ending inventory. Production needs can be determined as follows:

Concept 8–2

| | |
|---|---|
| Budgeted sales in units . . . . . . . . . . . . . . . . . . . . . . . . . | XXXX |
| Add desired ending inventory . . . . . . . . . . . . . . . . . . . | XXXX |
| Total needs . . . . . . . . . . . . . . . . . . . . . . . . . . . . . . . | XXXX |
| Less beginning inventory . . . . . . . . . . . . . . . . . . . . . . | XXXX |
| Required production . . . . . . . . . . . . . . . . . . . . . . . . . . | XXXX |

Schedule 2 contains the production budget for Hampton Freeze.

Note that production requirements for a quarter are influenced by the desired level of the ending inventory. Inventories should be carefully planned. Excessive inventories tie up funds and create storage problems. Insufficient inventories can lead to lost sales or crash production efforts in the following period. At Hampton Freeze, management believes that an ending inventory equal to 20% of the next quarter's sales strikes the appropriate balance.

## Inventory Purchases—Merchandising Firm

Hampton Freeze prepares a production budget, since it is a *manufacturing* firm. If it were a *merchandising* firm, it would prepare a **merchandise purchases budget** showing the amount of goods to be purchased from its suppliers during the period. The merchandise purchases budget follows the same basic format as the production budget, as shown below:

| | |
|---|---|
| Budgeted cost of goods sold (in units or in dollars) . . . . . . . . . . . . | XXXXX |
| Add desired ending merchandise inventory . . . . . . . . . . . . . . . . . | XXXXX |
| Total needs . . . . . . . . . . . . . . . . . . . . . . . . . . . . . . . . . . . . . . . . . . | XXXXX |
| Less beginning merchandise inventory . . . . . . . . . . . . . . . . . . . . . | XXXXX |
| Required purchases (in units or in dollars) . . . . . . . . . . . . . . . . . . | XXXXX |

A merchandising firm would prepare an inventory purchases budget, such as the one above, for each item carried in stock.

## Schedule 2

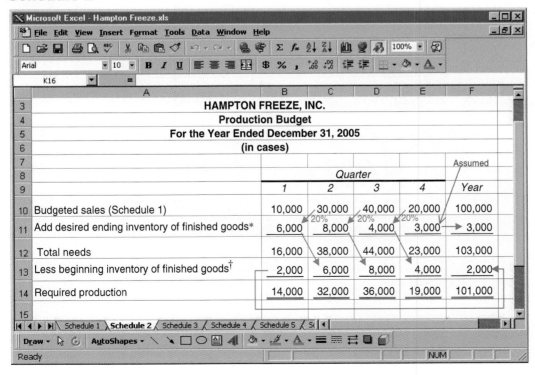

*Twenty percent of the next quarter's sales. The ending inventory of 3,000 cases is assumed.

†The beginning inventory in each quarter is the same as the prior quarter's ending inventory.

# The Direct Materials Budget

Returning to Hampton Freeze, after the production requirements have been computed, a *direct materials budget* can be prepared. The **direct materials budget** details the raw materials that must be purchased to fulfill the production budget and to provide for adequate inventories. The required purchases of raw materials are computed as follows:

| | |
|---|---|
| Raw materials needed to meet the production schedule .......... | XXXXX |
| Add desired ending inventory of raw materials ............... | XXXXX |
|    Total raw materials needs ............................ | XXXXX |
| Less beginning inventory of raw materials .................. | XXXXX |
| Raw materials to be purchased ........................... | XXXXX |

Schedule 3 contains the direct materials budget for Hampton Freeze. The only raw material included in that budget is high-fructose sugar, which is the major ingredient in

## Schedule 3

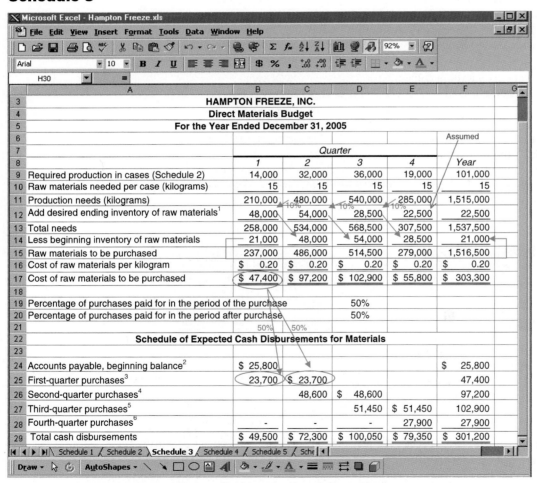

[1]Ten percent of the next quarter's production needs. For example, the second-quarter production needs are 480,000 kilograms. Therefore, the desired ending inventory for the first quarter would be 10% × 480,000 kilograms = 48,000 kilograms. The ending inventory of 22,500 kilograms for the quarter is assumed.

[2]Cash payments for last year's fourth-quarter material purchases. See the beginning-of-year balance sheet on page 299.

[3]$47,400 × 50%; $47,400 × 50%.

[4]$97,200 × 50%; $97,200 × 50%.

[5]$102,900 × 50%; $102,900 × 50%.

[6]$55,800 × 50%. Unpaid fourth-quarter purchases appear as accounts payable on the company's end-of-year balance sheet.

popsicles other than water. The remaining raw materials are relatively insignificant and are included in variable manufacturing overhead. Note that materials requirements are first determined in units (kilograms, litres, and so on) and then translated into dollars by multiplying by the appropriate unit cost. Also note that the management of Hampton Freeze desires to maintain ending inventories of sugar equal to 10% of the following quarter's production needs.

**SCHEDULE OF EXPECTED CASH DISBURSEMENTS FOR RAW MATERIALS**   The direct materials budget is usually accompanied by a schedule of expected cash disbursements for raw materials. This schedule is needed to prepare the overall cash budget. Disbursements for raw materials consist of payments for purchases on account in prior periods plus any payments for purchases in the current budget period. Schedule 3 contains such a schedule of cash disbursements.

## The Direct Labour Budget

The **direct labour budget** is also developed from the production budget. Direct labour requirements must be computed so that the company will know whether sufficient labour time is available to meet production needs. By knowing in advance just what will be needed in the way of labour time throughout the budget year, the company can develop plans to adjust the labour force as the situation may require. Firms that neglect to budget run the risk of facing labour shortages or having to hire and lay off at awkward times. Erratic labour policies lead to insecurity and inefficiency on the part of employees.

> **Learning Objective 5**
> Prepare a direct labour budget.

To compute direct labour requirements, the number of units of finished product to be produced each period (month, quarter, and so on) is multiplied by the number of direct labour-hours required to produce a single unit. The direct labour requirements can then be translated into expected direct labour costs. How this is done will depend on the labour policy of the firm. In Schedule 4, the management of Hampton Freeze has assumed that the direct labour force will be adjusted as the work requirements change from quarter to quarter. In that case, the total direct labour cost is computed by simply multiplying the direct labour-hour requirements by the direct labour rate per hour.

## Schedule 4

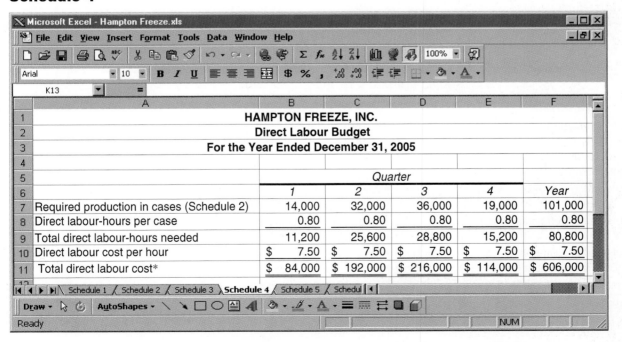

Schedule 4 — HAMPTON FREEZE, INC. — Direct Labour Budget — For the Year Ended December 31, 2005

| | Quarter | | | | |
| --- | --- | --- | --- | --- | --- |
| | 1 | 2 | 3 | 4 | Year |
| Required production in cases (Schedule 2) | 14,000 | 32,000 | 36,000 | 19,000 | 101,000 |
| Direct labour-hours per case | 0.80 | 0.80 | 0.80 | 0.80 | 0.80 |
| Total direct labour-hours needed | 11,200 | 25,600 | 28,800 | 15,200 | 80,800 |
| Direct labour cost per hour | $ 7.50 | $ 7.50 | $ 7.50 | $ 7.50 | $ 7.50 |
| Total direct labour cost* | $ 84,000 | $ 192,000 | $ 216,000 | $ 114,000 | $ 606,000 |

*This schedule assumes that the direct labour workforce will be fully adjusted to the total direct labour-hours needed each quarter.

However, many companies have employment policies or contracts that prevent them from laying off and rehiring workers, as needed. Suppose, for example, that Hampton Freeze has 50 workers who are classified as direct labour and each of them is guaranteed at least 480 hours of pay each quarter at a rate of $7.50 per hour. In that case, the minimum direct labour cost for a quarter would be as follows:

50 workers × 480 hours per worker × $7.50 per hour = $180,000

Note that in Schedule 4, the direct labour costs for the first and fourth quarters would have to be increased to the $180,000 level if Hampton Freeze's labour policy did not allow it to adjust the workforce.

## The Manufacturing Overhead Budget

**Learning Objective 6**
Prepare a manufacturing overhead budget.

The **manufacturing overhead budget** provides a schedule of all costs of production other than direct materials and direct labour. Schedule 5 shows the manufacturing overhead budget for Hampton Freeze. Note how the production costs are separated into variable and fixed components. The variable component is $2 per direct labour-hour. The fixed component is $60,600 per quarter.

Schedule 5 for Hampton Freeze shows its budgeted cash disbursements for manufacturing overhead. Since some of the overhead costs are not cash outflows, the total budgeted manufacturing overhead costs must be adjusted to determine the cash disbursements for manufacturing overhead. At Hampton Freeze, the only significant noncash manufacturing overhead cost is depreciation, which is $15,000 per quarter. These noncash

## Schedule 5

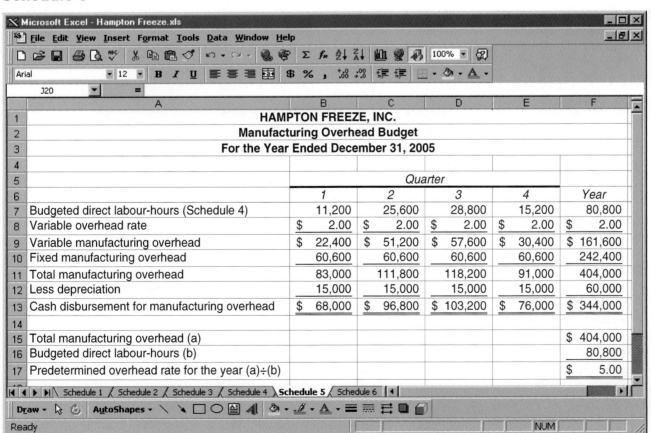

|  |  | Quarter | | | | |
|---|---|---|---|---|---|---|
|  |  | 1 | 2 | 3 | 4 | Year |
| 7 | Budgeted direct labour-hours (Schedule 4) | 11,200 | 25,600 | 28,800 | 15,200 | 80,800 |
| 8 | Variable overhead rate | $ 2.00 | $ 2.00 | $ 2.00 | $ 2.00 | $ 2.00 |
| 9 | Variable manufacturing overhead | $ 22,400 | $ 51,200 | $ 57,600 | $ 30,400 | $ 161,600 |
| 10 | Fixed manufacturing overhead | 60,600 | 60,600 | 60,600 | 60,600 | 242,400 |
| 11 | Total manufacturing overhead | 83,000 | 111,800 | 118,200 | 91,000 | 404,000 |
| 12 | Less depreciation | 15,000 | 15,000 | 15,000 | 15,000 | 60,000 |
| 13 | Cash disbursement for manufacturing overhead | $ 68,000 | $ 96,800 | $ 103,200 | $ 76,000 | $ 344,000 |
| 14 |  |  |  |  |  |  |
| 15 | Total manufacturing overhead (a) |  |  |  |  | $ 404,000 |
| 16 | Budgeted direct labour-hours (b) |  |  |  |  | 80,800 |
| 17 | Predetermined overhead rate for the year (a)÷(b) |  |  |  |  | $ 5.00 |

HAMPTON FREEZE, INC.
Manufacturing Overhead Budget
For the Year Ended December 31, 2005

depreciation charges are deducted from the total budgeted manufacturing overhead to determine the expected cash disbursements. Hampton Freeze pays all overhead costs involving cash disbursements in the quarter incurred. Note that the company's predetermined overhead rate for the year will be $5 per direct labour-hour.

## The Ending Finished Goods Inventory Budget

After completing Schedules 1–5, Larry Giano had all of the data he needed to compute unit product costs. This computation was needed for two reasons: first, to determine cost of goods sold on the budgeted income statement; and second, to know what amount to put on the balance sheet inventory account for unsold units. The carrying cost of the unsold units is computed on the **ending finished goods inventory budget.**

Larry Giano considered using variable costing in preparing Hampton Freeze's budget statements, but he decided to use absorption costing instead, since the bank would very likely require that absorption costing be used. He also knew that it would be easy to convert the absorption costing financial statements to a variable costing basis later. At this point, the primary concern was to determine what financing, if any, would be required in the year 2005 and then to arrange for that financing from the bank.

The unit product cost computations are shown in Schedule 6. For Hampton Freeze, the absorption costing unit product cost is $13 per case of popsicles—consisting of $3 of direct materials, $6 of direct labour, and $4 of manufacturing overhead. Manufacturing overhead is applied to units of product on the basis of direct labour-hours. The budgeted carrying cost of the expected ending inventory is $39,000.

## Schedule 6

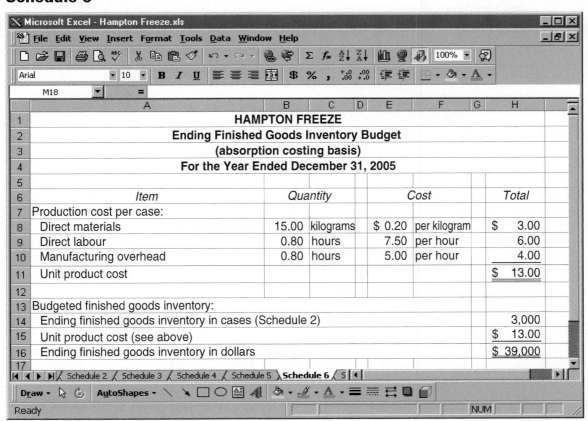

| Item | Quantity | | Cost | | Total | |
|---|---|---|---|---|---|---|
| **HAMPTON FREEZE** | | | | | | |
| **Ending Finished Goods Inventory Budget** | | | | | | |
| **(absorption costing basis)** | | | | | | |
| **For the Year Ended December 31, 2005** | | | | | | |
| | | | | | | |
| Production cost per case: | | | | | | |
| Direct materials | 15.00 | kilograms | $ 0.20 | per kilogram | $ | 3.00 |
| Direct labour | 0.80 | hours | 7.50 | per hour | | 6.00 |
| Manufacturing overhead | 0.80 | hours | 5.00 | per hour | | 4.00 |
| Unit product cost | | | | | $ | 13.00 |
| | | | | | | |
| Budgeted finished goods inventory: | | | | | | |
| Ending finished goods inventory in cases (Schedule 2) | | | | | | 3,000 |
| Unit product cost (see above) | | | | | $ | 13.00 |
| Ending finished goods inventory in dollars | | | | | $ | 39,000 |

## The Selling and Administrative Expense Budget

**Learning Objective 7**

Prepare a selling and administrative expense budget.

The **selling and administrative expense budget** lists the budgeted expenses for areas other than manufacturing. In large organizations, this budget would be a compilation of many smaller, individual budgets submitted by department heads and other persons responsible for selling and administrative expenses. For example, the marketing manager in a large organization would submit a budget detailing the advertising expenses for each budget period.

*in business today*    **Brainwashed Consumers**

Marketing costs are in the range of 25% to 35% of sales in the automotive, consumer packaged goods, pharmaceutical, and telecommunications industries according to a recent PricewaterhouseCoopers survey. Evaluating the effectiveness of marketing costs is much harder than measuring the benefits of costs, such as direct materials. Pricewaterhouse-Coopers consultants suggest that a company's managerial accountants need to work closely with its marketing department to design a system for evaluating marketing costs. In addition to reviewing indicators, such as the number of units sold, criteria might include the extent to which a brand dominates the minds of consumers.

Source: G. K. De Vriend, P. A. von der Heide, and J. C. Steigstra, "Here's a Good Way to Tell If Your Marketing Efforts Are Working," *Strategic Finance*, March 2000, pp. 56–62.

Schedule 7 contains the selling and administrative expense budget for Hampton Freeze.

## Schedule 7

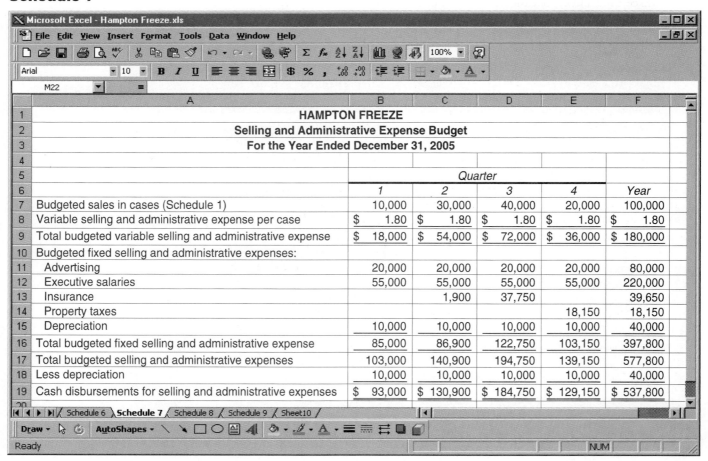

**HAMPTON FREEZE**
**Selling and Administrative Expense Budget**
**For the Year Ended December 31, 2005**

| | | Quarter | | | | |
| A | | 1 | 2 | 3 | 4 | Year |
|---|---|---|---|---|---|---|
| Budgeted sales in cases (Schedule 1) | | 10,000 | 30,000 | 40,000 | 20,000 | 100,000 |
| Variable selling and administrative expense per case | | $ 1.80 | $ 1.80 | $ 1.80 | $ 1.80 | $ 1.80 |
| Total budgeted variable selling and administrative expense | | $ 18,000 | $ 54,000 | $ 72,000 | $ 36,000 | $ 180,000 |
| Budgeted fixed selling and administrative expenses: | | | | | | |
| Advertising | | 20,000 | 20,000 | 20,000 | 20,000 | 80,000 |
| Executive salaries | | 55,000 | 55,000 | 55,000 | 55,000 | 220,000 |
| Insurance | | | 1,900 | 37,750 | | 39,650 |
| Property taxes | | | | | 18,150 | 18,150 |
| Depreciation | | 10,000 | 10,000 | 10,000 | 10,000 | 40,000 |
| Total budgeted fixed selling and administrative expense | | 85,000 | 86,900 | 122,750 | 103,150 | 397,800 |
| Total budgeted selling and administrative expenses | | 103,000 | 140,900 | 194,750 | 139,150 | 577,800 |
| Less depreciation | | 10,000 | 10,000 | 10,000 | 10,000 | 40,000 |
| Cash disbursements for selling and administrative expenses | | $ 93,000 | $ 130,900 | $ 184,750 | $ 129,150 | $ 537,800 |

# The Cash Budget

As illustrated in Exhibit 8–2, the cash budget pulls together much of the data developed in the preceding steps. It is a good idea to restudy Exhibit 8–2 to get the big picture firmly in mind before moving on.

**Learning Objective 8**
Prepare a cash budget.

The cash budget is composed of four major sections:

1. The receipts section.
2. The disbursements section.
3. The cash excess or deficiency section.
4. The financing section.

The receipts section consists of a listing of all of the cash inflows, except for financing, expected during the budget period. Generally, the major source of receipts will be from sales.

The disbursements section consists of all cash payments that are planned for the budget period. These payments will include raw materials purchases, direct labour payments, manufacturing overhead costs, and so on, as contained in their respective budgets. In addition, other cash disbursements, such as equipment purchases, dividends, and other cash withdrawals by owners are listed. For instance, we see in Schedule 8 that management plans to spend $137,000 during the budget period on equipment purchases and $32,000 on dividends to the owners. This is additional information that does not appear on any of the earlier schedules.

The cash excess or deficiency section is computed as follows:

| | |
|---|---|
| Cash balance, beginning | XXXX |
| Add receipts | XXXX |
| Total cash available before financing | XXXX |
| Less disbursements | XXXX |
| Excess (deficiency) of cash available over disbursements | XXXX |

If there is a cash deficiency during any budget period, the company will need to borrow funds. If there is a cash excess during any budget period, funds borrowed in previous periods can be repaid or the excess funds can be invested.

The financing section provides a detailed account of the borrowings and repayments projected to take place during the budget period. It also includes a detail of interest payments that will be due on money borrowed.[1]

Generally speaking, the cash budget should be broken down into time periods that are as short as feasible. Considerable fluctuations in cash balances may be hidden by looking at a longer time period. While a monthly cash budget is most common, many firms budget cash on a weekly or even daily basis. Larry Giano has prepared a quarterly cash budget for Hampton Freeze that can be further refined, as necessary. This budget appears in Schedule 8. Larry has assumed in the budget that an open line of credit can be arranged with the bank that can be used, as needed, to bolster the company's cash position. He has also assumed that any loans taken out with this line of credit would carry an interest rate of 10% per year. Larry has assumed that all borrowings and repayments are in round $1,000 amounts and that all borrowing occurs at the beginning of a quarter and all repayments are made at the end of a quarter. The details on the interest calculation can be found at the Online Learning Centre at www.mcgrawhill.ca/college/garrison.

In the case of Hampton Freeze, all loans have been repaid by year-end. If all loans are not repaid and a budgeted income statement or balance sheet is being prepared, then interest must be accrued on the unpaid loans. This interest will *not* appear on the cash budget (since it has not yet been paid), but it will appear as part of interest expense on the budgeted income statement and as a liability on the budgeted balance sheet.

---

[1]The format for the cash flow statement, which is discussed in Chapter 15, may also be used for the cash budget.

## Schedule 8

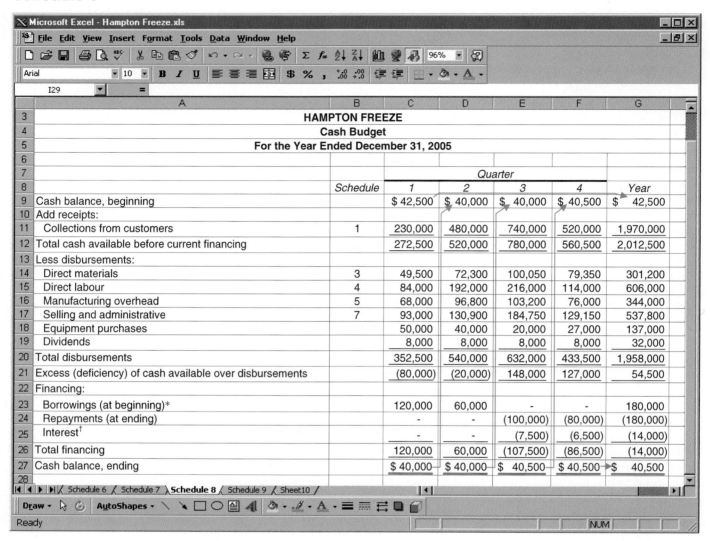

| | Schedule | Quarter 1 | Quarter 2 | Quarter 3 | Quarter 4 | Year |
|---|---|---|---|---|---|---|
| **HAMPTON FREEZE** | | | | | | |
| **Cash Budget** | | | | | | |
| **For the Year Ended December 31, 2005** | | | | | | |
| Cash balance, beginning | | $ 42,500 | $ 40,000 | $ 40,000 | $ 40,500 | $ 42,500 |
| Add receipts: | | | | | | |
| Collections from customers | 1 | 230,000 | 480,000 | 740,000 | 520,000 | 1,970,000 |
| Total cash available before current financing | | 272,500 | 520,000 | 780,000 | 560,500 | 2,012,500 |
| Less disbursements: | | | | | | |
| Direct materials | 3 | 49,500 | 72,300 | 100,050 | 79,350 | 301,200 |
| Direct labour | 4 | 84,000 | 192,000 | 216,000 | 114,000 | 606,000 |
| Manufacturing overhead | 5 | 68,000 | 96,800 | 103,200 | 76,000 | 344,000 |
| Selling and administrative | 7 | 93,000 | 130,900 | 184,750 | 129,150 | 537,800 |
| Equipment purchases | | 50,000 | 40,000 | 20,000 | 27,000 | 137,000 |
| Dividends | | 8,000 | 8,000 | 8,000 | 8,000 | 32,000 |
| Total disbursements | | 352,500 | 540,000 | 632,000 | 433,500 | 1,958,000 |
| Excess (deficiency) of cash available over disbursements | | (80,000) | (20,000) | 148,000 | 127,000 | 54,500 |
| Financing: | | | | | | |
| Borrowings (at beginning)* | | 120,000 | 60,000 | - | - | 180,000 |
| Repayments (at ending) | | - | - | (100,000) | (80,000) | (180,000) |
| Interest† | | - | - | (7,500) | (6,500) | (14,000) |
| Total financing | | 120,000 | 60,000 | (107,500) | (86,500) | (14,000) |
| Cash balance, ending | | $ 40,000 | $ 40,000 | $ 40,500 | $ 40,500 | $ 40,500 |

*The company requires a minimum cash balance of $40,000. Therefore, borrowing must be sufficient to cover the cash deficiency of $80,000 in quarter 1 and to provide for the minimum cash balance of $40,000. All borrowings and repayments of principal are in round $1,000 amounts.

†The interest payments relate only to the principal being repaid at the time it is repaid. For example, the interest in quarter 3 relates only to the interest due on the $100,000 principal being repaid from quarter 1 borrowing: $100,000 × 10% per year × 3/4 year = $7,500. The interest paid in quarter 4 is computed as follows:

$$\$20,000 \times 10\% \text{ per year} \times 1 \text{ year} \dots \quad \$2,000$$
$$\$60,000 \times 10\% \text{ per year} \times 3/4 \text{ year} \dots \quad \underline{4,500}$$
$$\text{Total interest paid} \dots\dots\dots\dots \quad \underline{\underline{\$6,500}}$$

## The Budgeted Income Statement

**Learning Objective 9**
Prepare a budgeted income statement.

A budgeted income statement can be prepared from the data developed in Schedules 1–8. *The budgeted income statement is one of the key schedules in the budget process.* It shows the company's planned profit for the upcoming budget period, and it serves as a benchmark against which subsequent company performance can be measured.

Schedule 9 contains the budgeted income statement for Hampton Freeze. The cost of goods sold is determined from schedules 1 and 6 as follows. Hampton Freeze has planned to sell 100,000 cases during 2005. The cost of each case, from schedule 6 is $13. Therefore, the cost of goods sold is $1,300,000. Although this calculation is simple, it is important to realize it hides many details that may be of interest. For example, detail regarding manufacturing costs incurred and the cost of goods

## Schedule 9

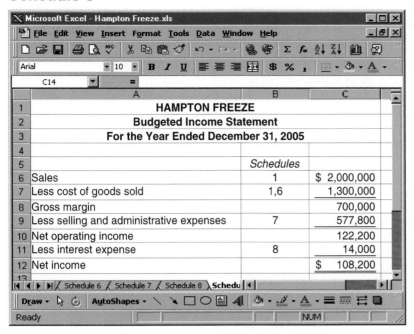

manufactured has been collapsed into the cost of goods sold. It is not difficult to extract this information from the schedules developed. An income statement showing this detail appears below.

### HAMPTON FREEZE, INC.
### Income Statement
### For the year ended December, 2005

| | | |
|---|---:|---:|
| Sales (Schedule 1) | | $2,000,000 |
| Cost of goods sold: | | |
| Beginning finished goods inventory (2,000 cases, Schedule 2 × $13/case, Schedule 6) | | $ 26,000 |
| Add Cost of goods manufactured: | | |
| Total manufacturing costs: | | |
| Direct materials (Schedule 3): | | |
| Beginning inventory of direct materials | $ 4,200 | |
| Add purchases of direct materials | $ 303,300 | |
| Less ending inventory of direct materials | $4,500 | |
| Direct materials used in production | $ 303,000 | |
| Direct labour (Schedule 4) | $ 606,000 | |
| Manufacturing overhead (Schedule 5) | $ 404,000 | |
| Manufacturing costs incurred | $1,313,000 | |
| Cost of goods manufactured: | | $1,313,000 |
| Goods available for sale | | $1,339,000 |
| Less ending finished goods inventory (3,000 cases, Schedule 2 × $13/case, Schedule 6) | | $ 39,000 |
| Cost of goods sold | | $1,300,000 |
| Gross margin | | $ 700,000 |
| Selling and administrative expenses (Schedule 7) | | $ 577,800 |
| Net operating income | | $ 122,200 |
| Interest expense (Schedule 8) | | $ 14,000 |
| Net Income | | $ 108,200 |

Hampton Freeze does not have work in process inventory; therefore, the cost of goods manufactured and manufacturing costs incurred are equal. Study this income statement carefully and make sure you can see how the information from the various schedules has been used in its construction.

## The Budgeted Balance Sheet

The budgeted balance sheet is developed by beginning with the current balance sheet and adjusting it for the data contained in the other budgets. Hampton Freeze's budgeted balance sheet is presented in Schedule 10. Some of the data on the budgeted balance sheet

### Schedule 10

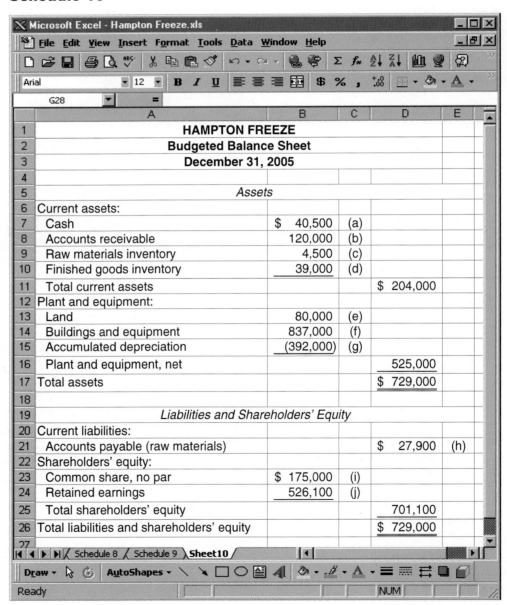

|  | A | B | C | D | E |
|---|---|---|---|---|---|
| 1 | HAMPTON FREEZE | | | | |
| 2 | Budgeted Balance Sheet | | | | |
| 3 | December 31, 2005 | | | | |
| 4 | | | | | |
| 5 | *Assets* | | | | |
| 6 | Current assets: | | | | |
| 7 | Cash | $ 40,500 | (a) | | |
| 8 | Accounts receivable | 120,000 | (b) | | |
| 9 | Raw materials inventory | 4,500 | (c) | | |
| 10 | Finished goods inventory | 39,000 | (d) | | |
| 11 | Total current assets | | | $ 204,000 | |
| 12 | Plant and equipment: | | | | |
| 13 | Land | 80,000 | (e) | | |
| 14 | Buildings and equipment | 837,000 | (f) | | |
| 15 | Accumulated depreciation | (392,000) | (g) | | |
| 16 | Plant and equipment, net | | | 525,000 | |
| 17 | Total assets | | | $ 729,000 | |
| 18 | | | | | |
| 19 | *Liabilities and Shareholders' Equity* | | | | |
| 20 | Current liabilities: | | | | |
| 21 | Accounts payable (raw materials) | | | $ 27,900 | (h) |
| 22 | Shareholders' equity: | | | | |
| 23 | Common share, no par | $ 175,000 | (i) | | |
| 24 | Retained earnings | 526,100 | (j) | | |
| 25 | Total shareholders' equity | | | 701,100 | |
| 26 | Total liabilities and shareholders' equity | | | $ 729,000 | |
| 27 | | | | | |

have been taken from the company's end-of-year balance sheet for 2004 which appears below:

## HAMPTON FREEZE, INC.
### Balance Sheet
### December 31, 2004

### Assets

Current assets:

| | | |
|---|---|---|
| Cash | $42,500 | |
| Accounts receivable | 90,000 | |
| Raw materials inventory (21,000 kilograms) | 4,200 | |
| Finished goods inventory (2,000 cases) | 26,000 | |
| Total current assets | | $162,700 |

Plant and equipment:

| | | |
|---|---|---|
| Land | 80,000 | |
| Buildings and equipment | 700,000 | |
| Accumulated depreciation | (292,000) | |
| Plant and equipment, net | | 488,000 |
| Total assets | | $650,700 |

### Liabilities and Shareholders' Equity

Current liabilities:

| | | |
|---|---|---|
| Accounts payable (raw materials) | | $25,800 |

Shareholders' equity:

| | | |
|---|---|---|
| Common shares, no par | $175,000 | |
| Retained earnings | 449,900 | |
| Total shareholders' equity | | 624,900 |
| Total liabilities and shareholders' equity | | $650,700 |

Explanation of December 31, 2005, balance sheet figures:

a. The ending cash balance, as projected by the cash budget in Schedule 8.
b. Thirty percent of fourth-quarter sales, from Schedule 1 ($400,000 × 30% = $120,000).
c. From Schedule 3, the ending raw materials inventory will be 22,500 kilograms. This material costs $0.20 per kilogram. Therefore, the ending inventory in dollars will be 22,500 kilograms × $0.20 per kilogram = $4,500.
d. From Schedule 6.
e. From the December 31, 2004, balance sheet (no change).
f. The December 31, 2004, balance sheet indicated a balance of $700,000. During 2005, $137,000 additional equipment will be purchased (see Schedule 8), bringing the December 31, 2005, balance to $837,000.
g. The December 31, 2004, balance sheet indicated a balance of $292,000. During 2005, $100,000 of depreciation will be taken ($60,000 on Schedule 5 and $40,000 on Schedule 7), bringing the December 31, 2005, balance to $392,000.
h. One-half of the fourth-quarter raw materials purchases, from Schedule 3.
i. From the December 31, 2004, balance sheet (no change).
j.

| | |
|---|---|
| December 31, 2004 balance | $449,900 |
| Add net income, from Schedule 9 | 108,200 |
| | 558,100 |
| Deduct dividends paid, from Schedule 8 | 32,000 |
| December 31, 2005, balance | $526,100 |

## MANAGERIAL ACCOUNTING IN ACTION

**The Wrap Up**

Freeze, Inc.

After completing the master budget, Larry Giano took the documents to Tom Wills, chief executive officer of Hampton Freeze, for his review.

*Larry:* Here's the budget. Overall, the net income is excellent, and the net cash flow for the entire year is positive.

*Tom:* Yes, but I see on this cash budget that we have the same problem with negative cash flows in the first and second quarters that we had last year.

*Larry:* That's true. I don't see any way around that problem. However, there is no doubt in my mind that if you take this budget to the bank today, they'll approve an open line of credit that will allow you to borrow enough to make it through the first two quarters without any problem.

*Tom:* Are you sure? They didn't seem very happy to see me last year when I came in for an emergency loan.

*Larry:* Did you repay the loan on time?

*Tom:* Sure.

*Larry:* I don't see any problem. You won't be asking for an emergency loan this time. The bank will have plenty of warning. And with this budget, you have a solid plan that shows when and how you are going to pay off the loan. Trust me, they'll go for it.

*Tom:* Fantastic! It would sure make life a lot easier this year.

---

## *you decide*     A Fiscally Responsible Student

You are a new student who will be footing part of the bill for your education. You saved quite a bit of money but are sure that you will need to earn more to cover your expenses. Before you look for a part-time job, you need to decide how many hours per week you will work and what hourly wage you will need in order to pay your expenses. You decide to prepare a budget for your college education. How should you proceed?

---

## Practical Issues in Budgeting: Use and Abuse

**Learning Objective 11**
Understand the processes organizations use to create budgets and the practical issues raised.

How can organizations ensure that the benefits of budgeting and budgets can be attained in practice? This important question suggests that it is possible for budgeting and budgets to have dysfunctional effects on an organization. In this part of the chapter, we will discuss the issues that organizations must consider in order to attain the advantages of budgeting and avoiding the dysfunctional effects.

The example of Larry Giano at Hampton Freeze provides an insightful starting point. Recall how Larry accomplished his mandate to introduce and develop a budgeting system.

1. Larry had the full backing of Tom Wills in developing the budgeting system at Hampton Freeze.
2. At the outset, Larry communicated the need for a budgeting system and obtained the cooperation of those whose involvement was essential to the development and *application* of the budgets.
3. Finally, Larry worked closely with all the managers involved and ensured that they understood and supported the parts of the budget that affected them and prepared them to take ownership of the budgeting system in the future.

Apparently, Larry knows a thing or two about managing. Larry's experience illustrates the importance of top management support, communication, and cooperation for developing budgets that will be accepted by those who will have to follow them. We now examine these aspects further.

# The Self-Imposed Budget

The success of a budget program will be determined, in large part, by the way in which the budget is developed. In the most successful budget programs, managers with cost control responsibilities actively participate in preparing their own budgets. This is in contrast to the approach in which budgets are imposed from above. The participative approach to preparing budgets is particularly important if the budget is to be used to control and evaluate a manager's performance. If a budget is imposed on a manager from above, it will probably generate resentment and ill-will, rather than cooperation and commitment.

This budgeting approach in which managers prepare their own budget estimates— called a *self-imposed budget*—is generally considered to be the most effective method of budget preparation. A **self-imposed budget** or **participative budget** is a budget that is prepared with the full cooperation and participation of managers at all levels. Exhibit 8–3 illustrates this approach to budget preparation.

A number of advantages are commonly cited for such self-imposed budgets:

1. Individuals at all levels of the organization are recognized as members of the team whose views and judgments are valued by top management.
2. Budget estimates prepared by front-line managers can be more accurate and reliable than estimates prepared by top managers who are more remote from day-to-day activities and who have less intimate knowledge of markets and operating conditions.
3. Motivation is generally higher when an individual participates in setting his or her own goals than when management imposes the goals. Self-imposed budgets create commitment.
4. If a manager is not able to meet a budget that has been imposed from above, the manager can always say that the budget was unreasonable or unrealistic to start with and therefore was impossible to meet. With a self-imposed budget, this excuse is not available.

Once self-imposed budgets are prepared, are they subject to any kind of review? The answer is yes. Budget estimates prepared by lower-level managers cannot necessarily be accepted without question by higher levels of management. If no system of checks and balances is present, self-imposed budgets may be too loose and allow too much

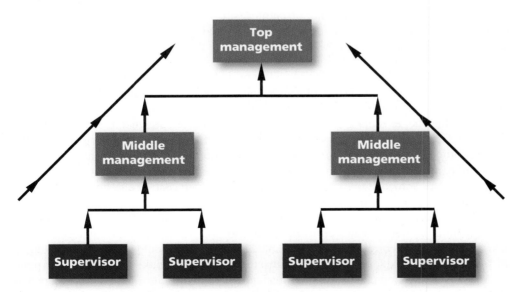

**Exhibit 8–3**
The Initial Flow of Budget Data in a Participative Budgeting System

The initial flow of budget data in a participative system is from lower levels of responsibility to higher levels of responsibility. Each person with responsibility for cost control will prepare his or her own budget estimates and submit them to the next higher level of management. These estimates are reviewed and consolidated as they move upward in the organization.

"budgetary slack." The result will be inefficiency and waste. Therefore, before budgets are accepted, they must be carefully reviewed by immediate superiors. If changes from the original budget seem desirable, the items in question are discussed and modified, as necessary.

In essence, all levels of an organization should work together to produce the budget. Since top management is generally unfamiliar with detailed, day-to-day operations, it should rely on subordinates to provide detailed budget data. On the other hand, top management has a perspective on the company as a whole that is also vital. Each level of responsibility in an organization should contribute in the way that it best can in a *cooperative* effort to develop an integrated budget.

We have described an ideal budgetary process that involves self-imposed budgets prepared by the managers who are directly responsible for revenues and costs. Most companies deviate from this ideal. Typically, top managers initiate the budget process by issuing broad guidelines in terms of overall target profits or sales. Lower-level managers are directed to prepare budgets that meet those targets. The difficulty is that the targets set by top managers may be unrealistically high or may allow too much slack. If the targets are too high and employees know they are unrealistic, motivation will suffer. If the targets allow too much slack, waste will occur. And unfortunately, top managers are often not in a position to know whether the targets they have set are appropriate. Admittedly, however, a pure self-imposed budgeting system may lack sufficient strategic direction, and lower-level managers may be tempted to build into their budgets a great deal of budgetary slack. Nevertheless, because of the motivational advantages of self-imposed budgets, top managers should be cautious about setting inflexible targets.

## The Matter of Human Relations

The success of a budget program also depends on: (1) the degree to which top management accepts the budget program as a vital part of the company's activities, and (2) the way in which top management uses budgeted data.

If a budget program is to be successful, it must have the complete acceptance and support of the persons who occupy key management positions. If lower or middle management personnel sense that top management is lukewarm about budgeting, or if they sense that top management simply tolerates budgeting as a necessary evil, then their own attitudes will reflect a similar lack of enthusiasm. Budgeting is hard work, and if top management is not enthusiastic about and committed to the budget program, then it is unlikely that anyone else in the organization will be either.

**RESPONSIBILITY ACCOUNTING**    The basic idea behind **responsibility accounting** is that a manager should be held responsible for those items—and *only* those items—that the manager can actually control to a significant extent. Each line item (i.e., revenue or cost) in the budget is made the responsibility of a manager, and that manager is held responsible for subsequent deviations between budgeted goals and actual results. In effect, responsibility accounting *personalizes* accounting information by looking at costs from a *personal control* standpoint. This concept is central to any effective profit planning and control system. Someone must be held responsible for each cost, or else no one will be responsible, and the cost will inevitably grow out of control.

Being held responsible for costs does not mean that the manager is penalized if the actual results do not measure up to the budgeted goals. However, the manager should take the initiative to correct any unfavourable discrepancies, should understand the source of significant favourable or unfavourable discrepancies, and should be prepared to explain the reasons for discrepancies to higher management. The point of an effective responsibility system is to make sure that nothing "falls through the cracks," that the organization reacts quickly and appropriately to deviations from its plans, and that the organization learns from the feedback it gets by comparing budgeted goals to actual results. The point is *not* to penalize individuals for missing targets. Top management must not use the budget as a club to pressure employees or as a way to find someone to blame if something goes wrong. Using budgets in such negative ways will simply breed hostility, tension, and mistrust, rather than greater cooperation and productivity. Unfortunately, research suggests that the budget is often used as a pressure device and that great emphasis is placed on "meeting the budget" under all circumstances.[2]

Rather than being used as a pressure device, the budget should be used as a positive instrument to assist in establishing goals, in measuring operating results, and in isolating areas that are in need of extra effort or attention. Any misgivings that employees have about a budget program can be overcome by meaningful involvement at all levels and by proper use of the program over time. Administration of a budget program requires a great deal of insight and sensitivity on the part of management. The budget program should be designed to be a positive aid in achieving both individual and company goals.

Management must keep clearly in mind that the human dimension in budgeting is of key importance. It is easy to become preoccupied with the technical aspects of the budget program to the exclusion of the human aspects. Indeed, the use of budget data in a rigid and inflexible manner is the greatest single complaint of persons whose performance is being evaluated using the budget process.[3] Management should remember that the purposes of the budget are to motivate employees and to coordinate efforts. Preoccupation with the dollars and cents in the budget, or being rigid and inflexible, can only lead to frustration of these purposes.

## Hitting the Target

*in business today*

In establishing a budget, how challenging should budget targets be? In practice, companies typically set their budgets either at a "stretch" level or a "highly achievable" level. A stretch-level budget is one that has only a small chance of being met by even the most capable managers. A highly achievable budget is one that is challenging but is very likely to be met with reasonably hard work. Research shows that managers prefer highly achievable budgets. Such budgets are generally coupled with bonuses that are given when budget targets are met, along with added bonuses when these targets are exceeded. Highly achievable budgets are believed to build a manager's confidence and to generate greater commitment to the budget program.

Source: Kenneth A. Merchant, *Rewarding Results: Motivating Profit Center Managers* (Boston, MA: Harvard Business School Press, 1989). For further discussion of budget targets, see Kenneth A. Merchant, "How Challenging Should Profit Budget Targets Be?" *Management Accounting* 72, no. 5 (November 1990), pp. 46–48.

## The Budget Committee

A standing **budget committee** will usually be responsible for overall policy matters relating to the budget program and for coordinating the preparation of the budget itself. This committee generally consists of the president; vice-presidents in charge of various functions, such as sales, production, and purchasing; and the controller. Difficulties and disputes between segments of the organization in matters relating to the budget are resolved by the budget committee. In addition, the budget committee approves the final budget and receives periodic reports on the progress of the company in attaining budgeted goals.

---

[2]Paul J. Carruth, Thurrell O. McClendon, and Milton R. Ballard, "What Supervisors Don't Like about Budget Evaluations," *Management Accounting* 64, no. 8 (February 1983), p. 42.

[3]Carruth et al., "What Supervisors Don't Like . . . ," p. 91.

Disputes can (and do) erupt over budget matters. Because budgets allocate resources, the budgeting process to a large extent determines which departments get more resources and which get relatively less. Also, the budget sets the benchmarks by which managers and their departments will be at least partially evaluated. Therefore, it should not be surprising that managers take the budgeting process very seriously and invest considerable energy and even emotion in ensuring that their interests and those of their departments are protected. Because of this, the budgeting process can easily degenerate into an interoffice brawl in which the ultimate goal of working together toward common goals is forgotten.

Running a successful budgeting program that avoids interoffice battles requires considerable interpersonal skills in addition to purely technical skills. But even the best interpersonal skills will fail if, as discussed earlier, top management uses the budget process inappropriately as a club or as a way to find blame.

## *in business today* **The Politics of Budgeting**

Budgeting is often an intensely political process in which managers jockey for resources and relaxed goals for the upcoming year. One group of consultants describes the process in this way: Annual budgets "have a particular urgency in that they provide the standard and most public framework against which managers are assessed and judged. It is, therefore, not surprising that budget-setting is taken seriously … Often budgets are a means for managers getting what they want. A relaxed budget will secure a relatively easy twelve months, a tight one means that their names will constantly be coming up in the monthly management review meeting. Far better to shift the burden of cost control and financial discipline to someone else. Budgeting is an intensely political exercise conducted with all the sharper managerial skills not taught at business school, such as lobbying and flattering superiors, forced haste, regretted delay, hidden truth, half-truths, and lies."

Source: Michael Morrow, ed., *Activity-Based Management* (New York: Woodhead-Faulkner, 1992), p. 91.

## Beyond Budgeting*

**Learning Objective 12**
Understand the Beyond Budgeting Model and its approach to budgeting.

Is budgeting worth the trouble that organizations must endure to introduce and apply it successfully? This controversial question is at the heart of a new philosophy about budgeting being developed by the Beyond Budgeting Round Table (BBRT)—a program of a European think tank, the Consortium for Advanced Manufacturing-International (Europe). Traditional budgeting is viewed as a tool more appropriate in "command and control" organizations. Increased globalization, greater customer involvement, and intense competition have required that firms be more flexible and responsive. This, in turn, requires that firms move away from the "command and control" type structures to ones that disperse more authority to the front lines. Traditional budgeting is ill-suited to this type of organizations. It cannot be tweaked or modified. It has to go.

**WEAKNESSES OF TRADITIONAL BUDGETING**   According to the BBRT, the traditional budgeting model has several weaknesses. Managers tend to view a budget as being "cast in stone." Therefore, performance evaluation using the budget as a benchmark is often feared and resented, since the actual performance invariably will differ from planned performance. This fear and resentment can often lead to "gaming." Managers may "lowball" estimates or overstate the funding needs. Meeting the budget becomes an overarching

---

*This section is based on a two-part article "Budgeting—an Unnecessary Evil: How BBRT Envisions a World Without Traditional Budgeting," by Theresa Libby and R. Murray Lindsay, CMA *Management*, March, 2003 and April 2003, www.linkpath.com

objective even at the expense of long-term goals. Unnecessary spending can occur where managers end up spending surpluses to zero out the budget to avoid funding claw-backs for the next operating cycle. Finally, managers might understate the actual performance and profits when they exceed targets to avoid the threat of upward ratcheting of performance targets.

Traditional budgets are considered to be financial representations of operational details of the firm's costs and revenues and, as such, are viewed as having little to do with implementing the firm's strategic objectives. It is argued that the traditional budgeting process disconnects the budget participants from the firm's long-term strategic imperatives. Resource allocation is viewed as a zero-sum game and managers become obsessed with ensuring that they get the funds they need. They end up drowning in the details of the budgeting process and the budgets and lose sight of the goals.

Think back to the master budget for Hampton Freeze. Note that the various budgets comprising the master budget have a *functional* orientation: sales, production, selling and administration, purchasing, and so on. This orientation is considered to be out of step with recent developments in modern management, which emphasizes a *process* orientation. Management of processes is the cornerstone of value creation. Where will budgeting fit in this picture?

Finally, still staying with the Hampton Freeze example, note that Larry Giano could not have created the budget "overnight." Budgets take time and effort to complete. While this is going on, what do you do if the data used as inputs change? Larry required the involvement and cooperation of many individuals throughout the company. This consumes time and attention. BBRT argues that up to 10 to 30% of a senior executives' time can be consumed by the budgeting process. Is this expenditure of resource worthwhile?

So, what is answer? According to the supporters of the Beyond Budgeting Model, the answer simply is, "Get rid of budgets." The argument is that budgets must play many roles: they have to capture plans and act as a coordinating mechanism for actions; they must provide bench marks for evaluation of performance; and they must motivate and guide management actions and behaviour. These are conflicting roles. No one knows how these conflicts can be resolved.

**THE BEYOND BUDGETING MODEL**     If traditional budgeting and budgets are to be done away, what should fill the gap? BBRT has proposed a model that eschews the fixed, performance-contract-based command-and-control framework of traditional budgeting. The BBRT model recommends the use of *relative* performance targets and emphasizes the principles of effective strategic management and empowering employees. The following are the key principles of this new model.

1. *Set challenging relative performance targets.* Benchmarks can be relative to industry, specific competitors, internal business units, and so on. The idea is that there is now a basis for evaluating performance. A manager would be hard pressed to explain away poor performance if targets were attained or exceeded by his or counterparts in similar settings.
2. *Adopt continuous and inclusive planning.* The key here is the "inclusive" aspect. By devolving corporate objectives systematically down the various layers of the organization, a clear link is established between lower level objectives and targets and the overall strategic imperatives. Now lower level units of the organization can see and understand the connection between their actions and the attainment of corporate objectives. Managers at the front line can make better informed decisions because they will be aware of the impact these decisions can have for the organization.
3. *Use rolling forecasts.* Forecasts are updated regularly and frequently. As the environment changes, forecasts are changed to respond to the changes. This allows managers to be aware of the current situation and manage accordingly. In this model, forecasts are separated from performance targets, measures, and rewards.
4. *Use market-like structures for coordination.* The free market structure is still the best coordinating mechanism. The discipline of the market in promoting efficiency and effectiveness is unequalled. The BBRT model proposes that the centralized coordination be replaced by a set of customer–supplier relationships. There is the external

set between the firm and its customers and suppliers. Within the firm, central services serve and support operating units through service agreements often based on market prices. Operating units and service units are subject to the discipline of the market.

5. *Decentralize resource management.* The BBRT model proposes that front-line units be allowed the freedom to manage their own resources and be held accountable for their actions. This eliminates many layers of bureaucracy, speeds up resource and funding approval requests, and enables managers to respond quickly to changing circumstances.

6. *Control through self-regulation and transparent information.* This principle advocates that the managers be provided with strategic, competitive, and market-based information so that they can self-regulate. Information is the basis for making decisions and so should be available to everyone.

7. *Use low-powered incentives lined to group or organizational performance.* Rather than emphasizing individually tailored incentive and compensation schemes based on fixed targets negotiated in advance, this principle recommends the use of collective measures and the inclusion of everyone in the reward program. The idea is to promote a holistic view and teamwork and reduce peer pressure.

There is no doubt that the BBRT model will stimulate lively debate as proponents on both sides try to persuade you and others like you of the merits of their respective positions. Some organizations, such as Borealis, have adopted these principles and have claimed success. There is still a lot to discover and understand about how budgets are prepared and used. Are organizations and individuals prepared to take the leap without the safety parachute of budgets and embrace a management model that does not rely on traditional budgets? The authors of the article on which this discussion has been based have initiated a major research program to improve our understanding of these issues. We invite you to read their article available at the website referenced in the footnote at the beginning of this section.

# Summary

### LO1   Understand why organizations budget.
The purpose in this chapter has been to present an overview of the budgeting process and to show how the various budgets relate to each other.

Organizations budget for a variety of reasons including to communicate management's plans throughout the organization, to force managers to think about and plan for the future, to allocate resources within the organization, to identify bottlenecks before they occur, to coordinate activities, and to provide benchmarks for evaluating subsequent performance.

### LO2   Prepare a sales budget, including a schedule of expected cash receipts.
The sales budget forms the foundation for the master budget. It provides details concerning the anticipated unit and dollar sales for each budget period.

The schedule of expected cash receipts is based on the sales budget, the expected breakdown between cash and credit sales, and the expected pattern of collections on credit sales.

### LO3   Prepare a production budget.
The production budget details how many units must be produced each budget period to satisfy expected sales and to provide for adequate levels of finished goods inventories.

### LO4   Prepare a direct materials budget, including a schedule of expected cash disbursements for purchases of materials.
The direct materials budget shows the materials that must be purchased each budget period to meet anticipated production requirements and to provide for adequate levels of materials inventories.

Cash disbursements for purchases of materials will depend on the amount of materials purchased in each budget period and the company's policies concerning payments to suppliers for materials acquired on credit.

## LO5   Prepare a direct labour budget.

The direct labour budget shows the direct labour-hours that are required to meet the production schedule as detailed in the production budget. The direct labour-hour requirements are used to determine the direct labour cost in each budget period.

## LO6   Prepare a manufacturing overhead budget.

Manufacturing overhead consists of both variable and fixed manufacturing overheads. The variable manufacturing overhead usually depends on the number of units produced from the production budget or the direct labour hours from the direct labour budget. The variable and fixed manufacturing overheads are combined to determine the total manufacturing overhead. Any noncash manufacturing overhead, such as depreciation, is deducted from the total manufacturing overhead to determine the cash disbursements for manufacturing overhead.

## LO7   Prepare a selling and administrative expense budget.

Like manufacturing overhead, selling and administrative expenses consist of both variable and fixed expenses. The variable expenses depend on the number of units sold or some other measure of activity. The variable and fixed expenses are combined to determine the total selling and administrative expense. Any noncash selling and administrative expenses, such as depreciation, are deducted from the total to determine the cash disbursements for selling and administrative expenses.

## LO8   Prepare a cash budget.

The cash budget is a critical element of the master budget. It permits managers to anticipate and plan for cash shortfalls.

The cash budget is organized into a receipts section, a disbursements section, a cash excess or deficiency section, and a financing section. The cash budget draws on information taken from nearly all of the other budgets and schedules, including the schedule of cash receipts, the schedule of cash disbursements for materials, the direct labour budget, the manufacturing overhead budget, and the selling and administrative expense budget.

## LO9   Prepare a budgeted income statement.

The budgeted income statement is constructed using data from the sales budget, the ending finished goods budget, the manufacturing overhead budget, the selling and administrative budget, and the cash budget.

## LO10   Prepare a budgeted balance sheet.

The budgeted balance sheet is constructed using data from virtually all of the other parts of the master budget.

## LO11   Understand the processes organizations use to create budgets and the practical issues raised.

Budgets should be developed with the full participation of all managers who will be subject to budgetary controls. Top management should not use the budget as a club to dominate managers. Managers should be made responsible only to those aspects of the budget that are within their control. Budget committees should oversee the development of policies and guidelines that will govern the budget creation process.

Traditional budgeting processes can be corrupted by organizational politics and management misuse and abuse of budgets. Management must work actively and decisively to avoid the dysfunctional effects of budgets as much as possible. A new management philosophy known as Beyond Budgeting argues that it is very difficult to avoid the dysfunctional effects associated with traditional budgets, and it advocates that traditional budgets be avoided completely. This idea is still the subject of ongoing debate and research.

## LO12   Understand the Beyond Budgeting Model and its approach to budgeting.

The opinion of some managers and academics is that budgets are more trouble than they are worth. Traditional budgets and the budgeting process are viewed as a major source of dysfunctional behaviours in organizations. The model calls for doing away with budgets entirely and relying instead on the principles of empowered employees, effective strategic management, and relative performance targets.

# Guidance Answers to Decision Maker and You Decide

**SALES MANAGER** (p. 286)

You probably cannot rely on the sales forecasts for casual and dress shoes to forecast the sales of athletic footwear. You should meet with the vice-president of sales to become knowledgeable about the factors that were considered when the decision was made to add this product line. Hopefully, the decision-making process included an extensive analysis of that market. If not, such market research will need to be undertaken at this time. In either case, you should review the results of that research to gain a better understanding of the market for athletic footwear. In addition, you should meet with the marketing department to become familiar with their plans for promoting the product and any goals that have been set in terms of unit sales or market share. Because this is a new product line, you should carefully state the assumptions used to forecast the sales.

**A FISCALLY RESPONSIBLE STUDENT** (p. 300)

To prepare a personal budget, start by estimating your expenses. To ensure that you do not overlook any expenses, you can visit your college's financial aid office to request an estimate of student expenses for the coming school year. Your school might also offer a course designed to help students succeed in college. The textbooks for such courses often include strategies for managing money while in college and may include sample budgets. Consider sharing your list of expenses with someone knowledgeable (a faculty member, advisor, or adult relative) and asking for feedback. After you have estimated your expenses, you can determine the amount of income you will need in addition to the money you have saved. (Do not forget to set aside some of your savings for unforeseen emergencies.)

Many, if not most, college professors expect you to put in two to three hours outside of class per week for every hour that you are in class. If you find that the number of hours that you will need to work is excessive, you should consider restricting your spending in some areas. Keep in mind your long-term goal, which is to succeed in college!

# Review Problem: Budget Schedules

Mylar Company manufactures and sells a product that has seasonal variations in demand, with peak sales coming in the third quarter. The following information concerns operations for Year 2—the coming year—and for the first two quarters of Year 3:

a.  The company's single product sells for $8 per unit. Budgeted sales in units for the next six quarters are as follows:

|  | Year 2 Quarter | | | | Year 3 Quarter | |
|---|---|---|---|---|---|---|
|  | 1 | 2 | 3 | 4 | 1 | 2 |
| Budgeted sales in units . . . | 40,000 | 60,000 | 100,000 | 50,000 | 70,000 | 80,000 |

b.  Sales are collected in the following pattern: 75% in the quarter the sales are made and the remaining 25% in the following quarter. On January 1, Year 2, the company's balance sheet showed $65,000 in accounts receivable, all of which will be collected in the first quarter of the year. Bad debts are negligible and can be ignored.

c.  The company desires an ending inventory of finished units on hand at the end of each quarter equal to 30% of the budgeted sales for the next quarter. This requirement was met on December 31, Year 1, in that the company had 12,000 units on hand to start the new year.

d.  Five kilograms of raw materials are required to complete one unit of product. The company requires an ending inventory of raw materials on hand at the end of each quarter equal to 10% of the production needs of the following quarter. This requirement was met on December 31, Year 1, in that the company had 23,000 kilograms of raw materials on hand to start the new year.

e.  The raw material costs $0.80 per kilogram. Purchases of raw material are paid for in the following pattern: 60% paid in the quarter the purchases are made, and the remaining 40% paid in the following quarter. On January 1, Year 2, the company's balance sheet showed $81,500 in accounts payable for raw material purchases, all of which will be paid for in the first quarter of the year.

*Required:*

Prepare the following budgets and schedules for the year, showing both quarterly and total figures:

1.  A sales budget and a schedule of expected cash collections.
2.  A production budget.
3.  A direct materials purchases budget and a schedule of expected cash payments for material purchases.

## SOLUTION TO REVIEW PROBLEM

1. The sales budget is prepared as follows:

| | Year 2 Quarter | | | | Year |
|---|---|---|---|---|---|
| | 1 | 2 | 3 | 4 | |
| Budgeted sales in units .. | 40,000 | 60,000 | 100,000 | 50,000 | 250,000 |
| Selling price per unit .... | × $8 | × $8 | × $8 | × $8 | × $8 |
| Total sales ........... | $320,000 | $480,000 | $800,000 | $400,000 | $2,000,000 |

On the basis of the budgeted sales above, the schedule of expected cash collections is prepared as follows:

| | Year 2 Quarter | | | | Year |
|---|---|---|---|---|---|
| | 1 | 2 | 3 | 4 | |
| Accounts receivable, beginning balance ........ | $ 65,000 | | | | $ 65,000 |
| First-quarter sales ($320,000 × 75%, 25%) ..... | 240,000 | $ 80,000 | | | 320,000 |
| Second-quarter sales ($480,000 × 75%, 25%) ... | | 360,000 | $120,000 | | 480,000 |
| Third-quarter sales ($800,000 × 75%, 25%) .... | | | 600,000 | $200,000 | 800,000 |
| Fourth-quarter sales ($400,000 × 75%) ........ | | | | 300,000 | 300,000 |
| Total cash collections ..................... | $305,000 | $440,000 | $720,000 | $500,000 | $1,965,000 |

2. On the basis of the sales budget in units, the production budget is prepared as follows:

| | Year 2 Quarter | | | | Year | Year 3 Quarter | |
|---|---|---|---|---|---|---|---|
| | 1 | 2 | 3 | 4 | | 1 | 2 |
| Budgeted sales (units) ........................ | 40,000 | 60,000 | 100,000 | 50,000 | 250,000 | 70,000 | 80,000 |
| Add desired ending inventory of finished goods* .. | 18,000 | 30,000 | 15,000 | 21,000† | 21,000 | 24,000 | |
| Total needs ................................ | 58,000 | 90,000 | 115,000 | 71,000 | 271,000 | 94,000 | |
| Less beginning inventory of finished goods ....... | 12,000 | 18,000 | 30,000 | 15,000 | 12,000 | 21,000 | |
| Required production ........................ | 46,000 | 72,000 | 85,000 | 56,000 | 259,000 | 73,000 | |

*30% of the following quarter's budgeted sales in units.
†30% of the budgeted Year 3 first-quarter sales.

3. On the basis of the production budget figures, raw materials will need to be purchased as follows during the year:

| | Year 2 Quarter | | | | Year 2 | Year 3 Quarter |
|---|---|---|---|---|---|---|
| | 1 | 2 | 3 | 4 | | 1 |
| Required production (units) ........................ | 46,000 | 72,000 | 85,000 | 56,000 | 259,000 | 73,000 |
| Raw materials needed per unit (kilograms) ............. | × 5 | × 5 | × 5 | × 5 | × 5 | × 5 |
| Production needs (kilograms) ....................... | 230,000 | 360,000 | 425,000 | 280,000 | 1,295,000 | 365,000 |
| Add desired ending inventory of raw materials (kilograms)* ...................... | 36,000 | 42,500 | 28,000 | 36,500† | 36,500 | |
| Total needs (kilograms) ........................... | 266,000 | 402,500 | 453,000 | 316,500 | 1,331,500 | |
| Less beginning inventory of raw materials (kilograms) ........................... | 23,000 | 36,000 | 42,500 | 28,000 | 23,000 | |
| Raw materials to be purchased (kilograms) ............ | 243,000 | 366,500 | 410,500 | 288,500 | 1,308,500 | |

*Ten percent of the following quarter's production needs in kilograms.
†Ten percent of the Year 3 first-quarter production needs in kilograms.

On the basis of the raw material purchases above, expected cash payments are computed as follows:

| | Year 2 Quarter | | | | |
| --- | --- | --- | --- | --- | --- |
| | 1 | 2 | 3 | 4 | Year 2 |
| Cost of raw materials to be purchased at $0.80 per kilogram .......................... | $194,400 | $293,200 | $328,400 | $230,800 | $1,046,800 |
| Accounts payable, beginning balance ............. | $ 81,500 | | | | $ 81,500 |
| First-quarter purchases ($194,400 × 60%, 40%) .... | 116,640 | $ 77,760 | | | 194,400 |
| Second-quarter purchases ($293,200 × 60%, 40%) .. | | 175,920 | $117,280 | | 293,200 |
| Third-quarter purchases ($328,400 × 60%, 40%) .... | | | 197,040 | $131,360 | 328,400 |
| Fourth-quarter purchases ($230,800 × 60%) ....... | | | | 138,480 | 138,480 |
| Total cash disbursements ...................... | $198,140 | $253,680 | $314,320 | $269,840 | $1,035,980 |

# Glossary

**Budget** A detailed plan for acquiring and using financial and other resources over a specified time period. (p. 280)

**Budget committee** A group of key management persons who are responsible for overall policy matters relating to the budget program and for coordinating the preparation of the budget. (p. 303)

**Cash budget** A detailed plan showing how cash resources will be acquired and used over some specific time period. (p. 285)

**Control** Those steps taken by management to increase the likelihood that the objectives and targets described in the budgeting stage are attained and to ensure that all parts of the organization function in a manner consistent with organizational policies. (p. 280)

**Direct labour budget** A detailed plan showing labour requirements over some specific time period. (p. 291)

**Direct materials budget** A detailed plan showing the amount of raw materials that must be purchased during a period to meet both production and inventory needs. (p. 290)

**Ending finished goods inventory budget** A budget showing the dollar amount of cost expected to appear on the balance sheet for unsold units at the end of a period. (p. 293)

**Manufacturing overhead budget** A detailed plan showing the production costs, other than direct materials and direct labour, that will be incurred over a specified time period. (p. 292)

**Master budget** A summary of a company's plans in which specific targets are set for sales, production, distribution, and financing activities and that generally culminates in a cash budget, budgeted income statement, and budgeted balance sheet. (p. 280)

**Merchandise purchases budget** A budget used by a merchandising company that shows the amount of goods that must be purchased from suppliers during the period. (p. 289)

**Mission, vision, and values statement** A statement that captures the answers to such question as: Where do we want to be five years from now? What should we be to our customers, our employees and other stakeholders? Which markets do we want to dominate? (p. 280)

**Operational planning** This is the process in which the broad goals and objectives of the strategic plan are distilled into specific goals and targets to guide the operations of the organization in the short term (typically one year). (p. 280)

**Participative budget** See *self-imposed budget*. (p. 301)

**Planning** Developing objectives and preparing budgets to achieve these objectives. (p. 280)

**Production budget** A detailed plan showing the number of units that must be produced during a period in order to meet both sales and inventory needs. (p. 288)

**Responsibility accounting** A system of accountability in which managers are held responsible for those items of revenue and cost—and only those items—over which the manager can exert significant control. The managers are held responsible for differences between budgeted goals and actual results. (p. 302)

**Sales budget** A detailed schedule showing the expected sales for coming periods; these sales are typically expressed in both dollars and units. (p. 284)

**Self-imposed budget** A method of preparing budgets in which managers prepare their own budgets. These budgets are then reviewed by the manager's supervisor, and any issues are resolved by mutual agreement. (p. 301)

**Selling and administrative expense budget** A detailed schedule of planned expenses that will be incurred in areas other than manufacturing during a budget period. (p. 294)

**Strategic plan** This is a document that captures the decisions that the organization has made regarding its strategic position in the market place. It is the principal output of the strategic planning process. (p. 280)

**Strategic planning** Strategic planning is the process of making decisions about how the organization should position itself in the marketplace to compete successfully with its rivals for customers and resources. (p. 280)

**Zero-based budget** A method of budgeting in which managers are required to justify all costs as if the programs involved were being proposed for the first time. (p. 285)

# Questions

**8–1** What is a budget? What is budgetary control?

**8–2** What are some of the major benefits to be gained from budgeting?

**8–3** What is meant by the term *responsibility accounting?*

**8–4** What is a master budget? Briefly describe its contents.

**8–5** Why is the sales forecast the starting point in budgeting?

**8–6** "As a practical matter, planning and control mean exactly the same thing." Do you agree? Explain.

**8–7** What is a self-imposed budget? What are the major advantages of self-imposed budgets? What caution must be exercised in their use?

**8–8** How can budgeting assist a firm in its employment policies?

**8–9** "The principal purpose of the cash budget is to see how much cash the company will have in the bank at the end of the year." Do you agree? Explain.

# Brief Exercises

**BRIEF EXERCISE 8–1    Budget Process (LO1, LO11)**
The following terms pertain to the budgeting process:

| | |
|---|---|
| Benchmarks | Bottlenecks |
| Budget | Budget committee |
| Control | Imposed from above |
| Motivation | Planning |
| Responsibility accounting | Self-imposed budget |

*Required:*
Fill in the blanks with the most appropriate word or phrase from the above list.

1. _____ is generally higher when an individual participates in setting his or her own goals than when the goals are imposed from above.

2. If a manager is not able to meet the budget and it has been _____, the manager can always say that the budget was unreasonable or unrealistic to start with and therefore was impossible to meet.

3. A _____ is a detailed quantitative plan for acquiring and using financial and other resources over a specified time period.

4. _____ involves developing objectives and preparing various budgets to achieve those objectives.

5. The budgeting process can uncover potential _____ before they occur.

6. _____ involves the steps taken by management to increase the likelihood that the goals and targets set down in the budgeting stage are attained.

7. Budgets define goals and objectives that can serve as _____ for evaluating subsequent performance.

8. In _____, a manager is held accountable for those items, and only those items, over which he or she has significant control.

9. A _____ is one that is prepared with the full cooperation and participation of managers at all levels of the organization.

10. A _____ is usually responsible for overall policy matters relating to the budget program and for coordinating the preparation of the budget itself.

**BRIEF EXERCISE 8–2    Schedule of Expected Cash Collections** (LO2)

Silver Company makes a product that is very popular as a Mother's Day gift. Thus, peak sales occur in May of each year. These peak sales are shown in the company's sales budget for the second quarter given below:

|  | April | May | June | Total |
|---|---|---|---|---|
| Budgeted sales ...... | $300,000 | $500,000 | $200,000 | $1,000,000 |

From past experience, the company has learned that 20% of a month's sales are collected in the month of sale, that another 70% is collected in the month following sale, and that the remaining 10% is collected in the second month following sale. Bad debts are negligible and can be ignored. February sales totalled $230,000, and March sales totalled $260,000.

*Required:*
1. Prepare a schedule of expected cash collections from sales, by month and in total, for the second quarter.
2. Assume that the company will prepare a budgeted balance sheet as of June 30. Compute the accounts receivable as of that date.

**BRIEF EXERCISE 8–3    Production Budget** (LO3)

Down Under Products, Ltd., of Australia, has budgeted sales of its popular boomerang for the next four months as follows:

|  | Sales in Units |
|---|---|
| April ..................... | 50,000 |
| May .................... | 75,000 |
| June .................... | 90,000 |
| July .................... | 80,000 |

The company is now in the process of preparing a production budget for the second quarter. Past experience has shown that end-of-month inventory levels must equal 10% of the following month's sales. The inventory at the end of March was 5,000 units.

*Required:*

Prepare a production budget for the second quarter; in your budget, show the number of units to be produced each month and for the quarter in total.

**BRIEF EXERCISE 8–4    Materials Purchases Budget** (LO4)

Three grams of musk oil are required for each bottle of Mink Caress, a very popular perfume made by a small company in western Siberia. The cost of the musk oil is 150 roubles per gram. (Siberia is located in Russia, whose currency is the rouble.) Budgeted production of Mink Caress is given below by quarters for Year 2 and for the first quarter of Year 3.

|  | Year 2 Quarter | | | | Year 3 Quarter |
|---|---|---|---|---|---|
|  | First | Second | Third | Fourth | First |
| Budgeted production, in bottles ... | 60,000 | 90,000 | 150,000 | 100,000 | 70,000 |

Musk oil has become so popular as a perfume base that it has become necessary to carry large inventories as a precaution against stockouts. For this reason, the inventory of musk oil at the end of a quarter must be equal to 20% of the following quarter's production needs. Some 36,000 grams of musk oil will be on hand to start the first quarter of Year 2.

*Required:*

Prepare a materials purchases budget for musk oil, by quarter and in total, for Year 2. At the bottom of your budget, show the amount of purchases in roubles for each quarter and for the year in total.

## BRIEF EXERCISE 8–5   Direct Labour Budget (LO5)

The production department of Rordan Corporation has submitted the following forecast of units to be produced by quarter for the upcoming fiscal year.

|  | 1st Quarter | 2nd Quarter | 3rd Quarter | 4th Quarter |
|---|---|---|---|---|
| Units to be produced ..... | 8,000 | 6,500 | 7,000 | 7,500 |

Each unit requires 0.35 direct labour-hours, and direct labour-hour workers are paid $12.00 per hour.

*Required:*
1. Construct the company's direct labour budget for the upcoming fiscal year, assuming that the direct labour workforce is adjusted each quarter to match the number of hours required to produce the forecasted number of units produced.
2. Construct the company's direct labour budget for the upcoming fiscal year, assuming that the direct labour workforce is not adjusted each quarter. Instead, assume that the company's direct labour workforce consists of permanent employees who are guaranteed to be paid for at least 2,600 hours of work each quarter. If the number of required direct labour-hours is less than this number, the workers are paid for 2,600 hours anyway. Any hours worked in excess of 2,600 hours in a quarter are paid at the rate of 1.5 times the normal hourly rate for direct labour.

## BRIEF EXERCISE 8–6   Manufacturing Overhead Budget (LO6)

The direct labour budget of Yuvwell Corporation for the upcoming fiscal year contains the following details concerning budgeted direct labour-hours.

|  | 1st Quarter | 2nd Quarter | 3rd Quarter | 4th Quarter |
|---|---|---|---|---|
| Budgeted direct labour-hours ......... | 8,000 | 8,200 | 8,500 | 7,800 |

The company's variable manufacturing overhead rate is $3.25 per direct labour-hour and the company's fixed manufacturing overhead is $48,000 per quarter. The only noncash item included in the fixed manufacturing overhead is depreciation, which is $16,000 per quarter.

*Required:*
1. Construct the company's manufacturing overhead budget for the upcoming fiscal year.
2. Compute the company's manufacturing overhead rate (including both variable and fixed manufacturing overheads) for the upcoming fiscal year. Round off to the nearest whole cent.

## BRIEF EXERCISE 8–7   Selling and Administrative Budget (LO7)

The budgeted unit sales of Weller Company for the upcoming fiscal year are provided below:

|  | 1st Quarter | 2nd Quarter | 3rd Quarter | 4th Quarter |
|---|---|---|---|---|
| Budgeted unit sales ...... | 15,000 | 16,000 | 14,000 | 13,000 |

The company's variable selling and administrative expense per unit is $2.50. Fixed selling and administrative expenses include advertising expenses of $8,000 per quarter, executive salaries of $35,000 per quarter, and depreciation of $20,000 per quarter. In addition, the company makes insurance payments of $5,000 in the first quarter and $5,000 in the third quarter. Finally, property taxes of $8,000 are paid in the second quarter.

*Required:*
Prepare the company's selling and administrative expense budget for the upcoming fiscal year.

## BRIEF EXERCISE 8–8   Cash Budget (LO8)

Garden Depot is a retailer that is preparing its budget for the upcoming fiscal year. Management has prepared the following summary of its budgeted cash flows:

|  | 1st Quarter | 2nd Quarter | 3rd Quarter | 4th Quarter |
|---|---|---|---|---|
| Total cash receipts ....... | $180,000 | $330,000 | $210,000 | $230,000 |
| Total cash disbursements ......... | $260,000 | $230,000 | $220,000 | $240,000 |

The company's beginning cash balance for the upcoming fiscal year will be $20,000. The company requires a minimum cash balance of $10,000 and may borrow any amount needed from a local bank at an annual interest rate of 12%. The company may borrow any amount at the beginning of any quarter and may repay its loans, or any part of its loans, at the end of any quarter. Interest payments are due on any principal at the time it is repaid.

*Required:*
Prepare the company's cash budget for the upcoming fiscal year.

### BRIEF EXERCISE 8–9   Budgeted Income Statement (LO9)
Gig Harbour Boating is the wholesale distributor of small recreational catamaran sailboats. Management has prepared the following summary data to use in its annual budgeting process:

| | |
|---|---|
| Budgeted sales (in units) | 460 |
| Selling price per unit | $1,950 |
| Cost per unit | $1,575 |
| Variable selling and administrative expenses (per unit) | $75 |
| Fixed selling and administrative expenses (per year) | $105,000 |
| Interest expense for the year | $14,000 |

*Required:*
Prepare the company's budgeted income statement.

### BRIEF EXERCISE 8–10   Budgeted Balance Sheet (LO10)
The management of Mecca Copy, a photocopying centre located on University Avenue, has compiled the following data to use in preparing its budgeted balance sheet for next year:

| | Ending Balances |
|---|---|
| Cash | ? |
| Accounts receivable | $ 8,100 |
| Supplies inventory | 3,200 |
| Equipment | 34,000 |
| Accumulated depreciation | 16,000 |
| Accounts payable | 1,800 |
| Common shares | 5,000 |
| Retained earnings | ? |

The beginning balance of retained earnings was $28,000, net income is budgeted to be $11,500, and dividends are budgeted to be $4,800.

*Required:*
Prepare the company's budgeted balance sheet.

# Exercises

### EXERCISE 8–1   Schedules of Expected Cash Collections and Disbursements (LO2, LO4, LO8)
You have been asked to prepare a December cash budget for Ashton Company, a distributor of exercise equipment. The following information is available about the company's operations:
a. The cash balance on December 1 will be $40,000.
b. Actual sales for October and November and expected sales for December are as follows:

| | October | November | December |
|---|---|---|---|
| Cash sales | $ 65,000 | $ 70,000 | $ 83,000 |
| Sales on account | 400,000 | 525,000 | 600,000 |

Sales on account are collected over a three-month period in the following ratio: 20% collected in the month of sale, 60% collected in the month following sale, and 18% collected in the second month following sale. The remaining 2% is uncollectible.
c. Purchases of inventory will total $280,000 for December. Thirty percent of a month's inventory purchases are paid during the month of purchase. The accounts payable remaining from November's inventory purchases total $161,000, all of which will be paid in December.

d. Selling and administrative expenses are budgeted at $430,000 for December. Of this amount, $50,000 is for depreciation.

e. A new Web server for the Marketing Department costing $76,000 will be purchased for cash during December, and dividends totalling $9,000 will be paid during the month.

f. The company must maintain a minimum cash balance of $20,000. An open line of credit is available from the company's bank to bolster the cash position, as needed.

*Required:*

1. Prepare a schedule of expected cash collections for December.
2. Prepare a schedule of expected cash disbursements for materials during December to suppliers for inventory purchases.
3. Prepare a cash budget for December. Indicate in the financing section any borrowing that will be needed during the month.

**EXERCISE 8–2　Sales and Production Budgets** (LO2, LO3)

The marketing department of Jessi Corporation has submitted the following sales forecast for the upcoming fiscal year.

|  | 1st Quarter | 2nd Quarter | 3rd Quarter | 4th Quarter |
|---|---|---|---|---|
| Budgeted sales (units) .... | 11,000 | 12,000 | 14,000 | 13,000 |

The selling price of the company's product is $18.00 per unit. Management expects to collect 65% of sales in the quarter in which the sales are made, 30% in the following quarter, and 5% of sales are expected to be uncollectible. The beginning balance of accounts receivable, all of which is expected to be collected in the first quarter, is $70,200.

The company expects to start the first quarter with 1,650 units in finished goods inventory. Management desires an ending finished goods inventory in each quarter equal to 15% of the next quarter's budgeted sales. The desired ending finished goods inventory for the fourth quarter is 1,850 units.

*Required:*

1. Prepare the company's sales budget and schedule of expected cash collections.
2. Prepare the company's production budget for the upcoming fiscal year.

**EXERCISE 8–3　Production and Direct Materials Budgets** (LO3, LO4)

The marketing department of Gaeber Industries has submitted the following sales forecast for the upcoming fiscal year.

|  | 1st Quarter | 2nd Quarter | 3rd Quarter | 4th Quarter |
|---|---|---|---|---|
| Budgeted sales (units) .... | 8,000 | 7,000 | 6,000 | 7,000 |

The company expects to start the first quarter with 1,600 units in finished goods inventory. Management desires an ending finished goods inventory in each quarter equal to 20% of the next quarter's budgeted sales. The desired ending finished goods inventory for the fourth quarter is 1,700 units.

In addition, the beginning raw materials inventory for the first quarter is budgeted to be 3,120 kilograms and the beginning accounts payable for the first quarter is budgeted to be $14,820.

Each unit requires two kilograms of raw material that costs $4 per kilogram. Management desires to end each quarter with an inventory of raw materials equal to 20% of the following quarter's production needs. The desired ending inventory for the fourth quarter is 3,140 kilograms. Management plans to pay for 75% of raw material purchases in the quarter acquired and 25% in the following quarter.

*Required:*

1. Prepare the company's production budget for the upcoming fiscal year.
2. Prepare the company's direct materials budget and schedule of expected cash disbursements for materials for the upcoming fiscal year.

**EXERCISE 8–4　Direct Materials and Direct Labour Budgets** (LO4, LO5)

The production department of Hareston Company has submitted the following forecast of units to be produced by quarter for the upcoming fiscal year.

|  | 1st Quarter | 2nd Quarter | 3rd Quarter | 4th Quarter |
|---|---|---|---|---|
| Units to be produced ..... | 7,000 | 8,000 | 6,000 | 5,000 |

In addition, the beginning raw materials inventory for the first quarter is budgeted to be 1,400 kilograms and the beginning accounts payable for the first quarter is budgeted to be $2,940.

Each unit requires two kilograms of raw material that costs $1.40 per kilogram. Management desires to end each quarter with an inventory of raw materials equal to 10% of the following quarter's production needs. The desired ending inventory for the fourth quarter is 1,500 kilograms. Management plans to pay for 80% of raw material purchases in the quarter acquired and 20% in the following quarter. Each unit requires 0.60 direct labour-hours, and direct labour-hour workers are paid $14 per hour.

**Required:**
1. Prepare the company's direct materials budget and schedule of expected cash disbursements for materials for the upcoming fiscal year.
2. Prepare the company's direct labour budget for the upcoming fiscal year, assuming that the direct labour workforce is adjusted each quarter to match the number of hours required to produce the forecasted number of units produced.

**EXERCISE 8–5    Direct Labour and Manufacturing Overhead Budgets** (LO5, LO6)
The production department of Raredon Corporation has submitted the following forecast of units to be produced by quarter for the upcoming fiscal year.

| | 1st Quarter | 2nd Quarter | 3rd Quarter | 4th Quarter |
|---|---|---|---|---|
| Units to be produced ..... | 12,000 | 14,000 | 13,000 | 11,000 |

Each unit requires 0.70 direct labour-hours, and direct labour-hour workers are paid $10.50 per hour.

In addition, the variable manufacturing overhead rate is $1.50 per direct labour-hour. The fixed manufacturing overhead is $80,000 per quarter. The only noncash element of manufacturing overhead is depreciation, which is $22,000 per quarter.

**Required:**
1. Prepare the company's direct labour budget for the upcoming fiscal year, assuming that the direct labour workforce is adjusted each quarter to match the number of hours required to produce the forecasted number of units produced.
2. Prepare the company's manufacturing overhead budget.

**EXERCISE 8–6    Cash Budget Relations** (LO8)
A cash budget, by quarters, is given below for a retail company. Fill in the missing amounts (000 omitted). The company requires a minimum cash balance of at least $5,000 to start each quarter.

| | 1 | 2 | 3 | 4 | Year |
|---|---|---|---|---|---|
| Cash balance, beginning .............. | $ 6 | $ ? | $ ? | $ ? | $ ? |
| Add collections from customers ....... | ? | ? | 96 | ? | 323 |
| Total cash available before current financing ............ | 71 | ? | ? | ? | ? |
| Less disbursements: | | | | | |
| Purchase of inventory .............. | 35 | 45 | ? | 35 | ? |
| Operating expenses ............... | ? | 30 | 30 | ? | 113 |
| Equipment purchases .............. | 8 | 8 | 10 | ? | 36 |
| Dividends ....................... | 2 | 2 | 2 | 2 | ? |
| Total disbursements ................. | ? | 85 | ? | ? | ? |
| Excess (deficiency) of cash available over disbursements .............. | (2) | ? | 11 | ? | ? |
| Financing: | | | | | |
| Borrowings ..................... | ? | 15 | — | — | ? |
| Repayments (including interest)* .... | — | — | (?) | (17) | (?) |
| Total financing ..................... | ? | ? | ? | ? | ? |
| Cash balance, ending ................ | $ ? | $ ? | $ ? | $ ? | $ ? |

*Interest will total $1,000 for the year.

**PROBLEM 8–1   Schedule of Expected Cash Collections; Cash Budget** (LO2, LO8)

CHECK FIGURE
(1) July: $317,500
(2) July 31 cash balance:
$28,000

Herbal Care Corp., a distributor of herb-based sunscreens, is ready to begin its third quarter, in which peak sales occur. The company has requested a $40,000, 90-day loan from its bank to help meet cash requirements during the quarter. Since Herbal Care has experienced difficulty in paying off its loans in the past, the loan officer at the bank has asked the company to prepare a cash budget for the quarter. In response to this request, the following data have been assembled:

a.  On July 1, the beginning of the third quarter, the company will have a cash balance of $44,500.

b.  Actual sales for the last two months and budgeted sales for the third quarter follow:

| | |
|---|---|
| May (actual) . . . . . . . . . . . . . | $250,000 |
| June (actual) . . . . . . . . . . . . . | 300,000 |
| July (budgeted) . . . . . . . . . . . | 400,000 |
| August (budgeted) . . . . . . . . . | 600,000 |
| September (budgeted) . . . . . . | 320,000 |

Past experience shows that 25% of a month's sales are collected in the month of sale, 70% in the month following sale, and 3% in the second month following sale. The remainder is uncollectible.

c.  Budgeted merchandise purchases and budgeted expenses for the third quarter are given below:

| | July | August | September |
|---|---|---|---|
| Merchandise purchases . . . . . . . . . . | $240,000 | $350,000 | $175,000 |
| Salaries and wages . . . . . . . . . . . . . | 45,000 | 50,000 | 40,000 |
| Advertising . . . . . . . . . . . . . . . . . . | 130,000 | 145,000 | 80,000 |
| Rent payments . . . . . . . . . . . . . . . . | 9,000 | 9,000 | 9,000 |
| Depreciation . . . . . . . . . . . . . . . . . | 10,000 | 10,000 | 10,000 |

Merchandise purchases are paid in full during the month following purchase. Accounts payable for merchandise purchases on June 30, which will be paid during July, total $180,000.

d.  Equipment costing $10,000 will be purchased for cash during July.

e.  In preparing the cash budget, assume that the $40,000 loan will be made in July and repaid in September. Interest on the loan will total $1,200.

*Required:*

1.  Prepare a schedule of expected cash collections for July, August, and September and for the quarter in total.

2.  Prepare a cash budget, by month and in total, for the third quarter.

3.  If the company needs a minimum cash balance of $20,000 to start each month, can the loan be repaid as planned? Explain.

**PROBLEM 8–2   Production and Purchases Budgets** (LO3, LO4)

CHECK FIGURE
(1) July: 36,000 units

Pearl Products Limited of Shenzhen, China, manufactures and distributes toys throughout Southeast Asia. Three cubic centimetres (cc) of solvent H300 are required to manufacture each unit of Supermix, one of the company's products. The company is now planning raw materials needs for the third quarter, the quarter in which peak sales of Supermix occur. To keep production and sales moving smoothly, the company has the following inventory requirements:

a.  The finished goods inventory on hand at the end of each month must be equal to 3,000 units of Supermix plus 20% of the next month's sales. The finished goods inventory on June 30 is budgeted to be 10,000 units.

b.  The raw materials inventory on hand at the end of each month must be equal to one-half of the following month's production needs for raw materials. The raw materials inventory on June 30 is budgeted to be 54,000 cc of solvent H300.

c.  The company maintains no work in process inventories.

A sales budget for Supermix for the last six months of the year follows.

| | Budgeted Sales in Units |
|---|---|
| July | 35,000 |
| August | 40,000 |
| September | 50,000 |
| October | 30,000 |
| November | 20,000 |
| December | 10,000 |

*Required:*

1. Prepare a production budget for Supermix for the months July–October.
2. Examine the production budget that you prepared in (1) above. Why will the company produce more units than it sells in July and August, and fewer units than it sells in September and October?
3. Prepare a budget showing the quantity of solvent H300 to be purchased for July, August, and September, and for the quarter in total.

CHECK FIGURE
(1) May 31 cash balance: $8,900
(2) NI: $15,900

**PROBLEM 8–3    Cash Budget; Income Statement; Balance Sheet** (LO4, LO8, LO9, LO10)

Minden Company is a wholesale distributor of premium European chocolates. The company's balance sheet as of April 30 is given below:

**MINDEN COMPANY**
**Balance Sheet**
**April 30**

**Assets**

| | |
|---|---|
| Cash | $ 9,000 |
| Accounts receivable, customers | 54,000 |
| Inventory | 30,000 |
| Buildings and equipment, net of depreciation | 207,000 |
| Total assets | $300,000 |

**Liabilities and Shareholders' Equity**

| | |
|---|---|
| Accounts payable, suppliers | $ 63,000 |
| Note payable | 14,500 |
| Capital shares, no par | 180,000 |
| Retained earnings | 42,500 |
| Total liabilities and shareholders' equity | $300,000 |

The company is in the process of preparing budget data for May. A number of budget items have already been prepared, as stated below:

a. Sales are budgeted at $200,000 for May. Of these sales, $60,000 will be for cash; the remainder will be credit sales. One-half of a month's credit sales are collected in the month the sales are made, and the remainder is collected in the following month. All of the April 30 receivables will be collected in May.

b. Purchases of inventory are expected to total $120,000 during May. These purchases will all be on account. Forty percent of all purchases are paid for in the month of purchase; the remainder is paid in the following month. All of the April 30 accounts payable to suppliers will be paid during May.

c. The May 31 inventory balance is budgeted at $40,000.

d. Operating expenses for May are budgeted at $72,000, exclusive of depreciation. These expenses will be paid in cash. Depreciation is budgeted at $2,000 for the month.

e. The note payable on the April 30 balance sheet will be paid during May, with $100 in interest. (All of the interest relates to May.)

f. New refrigerating equipment costing $6,500 will be purchased for cash during May.

g. During May, the company will borrow $20,000 from its bank by giving a new note payable to the bank for that amount. The new note will be due in one year.

**Required:**

1. Prepare a cash budget for May. Support your budget with schedules showing budgeted cash receipts from sales and budgeted cash payments for inventory purchases.

2. Prepare a budgeted income statement for May. Use the traditional income statement format.

3. Prepare a budgeted balance sheet as of May 31.

### PROBLEM 8–4  Integration of the Sales, Production, and Purchases Budgets  (LO2, LO3, LO4)

CHECK FIGURE
(2) July: 36,000 units

Milo Company manufactures beach umbrellas. The company is now preparing detailed budgets for the third quarter and has assembled the following information to assist in the budget preparation:

a. The Marketing Department has estimated sales as follows for the remainder of the year (in units):

| July | 30,000 | October | 20,000 |
|------|--------|---------|--------|
| August | 70,000 | November | 10,000 |
| September | 50,000 | December | 10,000 |

The selling price of the beach umbrellas is $12 per unit.

b. All sales are on account. On the basis of past experience, sales are collected in the following pattern:

30% in the month of sale
65% in the month following sale
5% uncollectible

Sales for June totalled $300,000.

c. The company maintains finished goods inventories equal to 15% of the following month's sales. This requirement will be met at the end of June.

d. Each beach umbrella requires four metres of Gilden, a material that is sometimes hard to get. Therefore, the company requires that the inventory of Gilden on hand at the end of each month be equal to 50%of the following month's production needs. The inventory of Gilden on hand at the beginning and end of the quarter will be:

June 30 . . . . . . . . . . . .  72,000  metres
September 30 . . . . . . .      ?     metres

e. The Gilden costs $0.80 per metre. One-half of a month's purchases of Gilden is paid for in the month of purchase; the remainder is paid for in the following month. The accounts payable on July 1 for purchases of Gilden during June will be $76,000.

**Required:**

1. Prepare a sales budget, by month and in total, for the third quarter. (Show your budget in both units and dollars.) Also prepare a schedule of expected cash collections, by month and in total, for the third quarter.

2. Prepare a production budget for each of the months July–October.

3. Prepare a materials purchases budget for Gilden, by month and in total, for the third quarter. Also prepare a schedule of expected cash payments for Gilden, by month and in total, for the third quarter.

### PROBLEM 8–5  Cash Budget with Supporting Schedules  (LO2, LO4, LO8)

CHECK FIGURE
(2a) May purchases:
$574,000
(3) June 30 cash balance:
$57,100

Garden Sales, Inc. sells garden supplies. Management is planning its cash needs for the second quarter. The company usually has to borrow money during this quarter to support peak sales of lawn care equipment, which occur during May. The following information has been assembled to assist in preparing a cash budget for the quarter:

a. Budgeted monthly income statements for April–July are:

| | April | May | June | July |
|---|---|---|---|---|
| Sales . . . . . . . . . . . . . . . . . . . . . . | $600,000 | $900,000 | $500,000 | $400,000 |
| Cost of goods sold . . . . . . . . . . . | 420,000 | 630,000 | 350,000 | 280,000 |
| Gross margin . . . . . . . . . . . . . . . | 180,000 | 270,000 | 150,000 | 120,000 |
| Less operating expenses: | | | | |
|    Selling expense . . . . . . . . . . . | 79,000 | 120,000 | 62,000 | 51,000 |
|    Administrative expense* . . . . | 45,000 | 52,000 | 41,000 | 38,000 |
| Total operating expenses . . . . . . | 124,000 | 172,000 | 103,000 | 89,000 |
| Net income . . . . . . . . . . . . . . . . | $ 56,000 | $ 98,000 | $ 47,000 | $ 31,000 |

*Includes $20,000 depreciation each month.

b. Sales are 20% for cash and 80% on account.
c. Sales on account are collected over a three-month period in the following ratio: 10% collected in the month of sale; 70% collected in the first month following the month of sale; and the remaining 20% collected in the second month following the month of sale. February's sales totalled $200,000, and March's sales totalled $300,000.
d. Inventory purchases are paid for within 15 days. Therefore, 50% of a month's inventory purchases are paid for in the month of purchase. The remaining 50% is paid in the following month. Accounts payable at March 31 for inventory purchases during March total $126,000.
e. At the end of each month, inventory must be on hand equal to 20% of the cost of the merchandise to be sold in the following month. The merchandise inventory at March 31 is $84,000.
f. Dividends of $49,000 will be declared and paid in April.
g. Equipment costing $16,000 will be purchased for cash in May.
h. The cash balance at March 31 is $52,000; the company must maintain a cash balance of at least $40,000 at all times.
i. The company can borrow from its bank, as needed, to bolster the Cash account. Borrowings and repayments must be in multiples of $1,000. All borrowings take place at the beginning of a month, and all repayments are made at the end of a month. The annual interest rate is 12%. Compute interest on whole months ($^1/_{12}$, $^2/_{12}$, and so forth).

### Required:

1. Prepare a schedule of expected cash collections from sales for each of the months April, May, and June, and for the quarter in total.
2. Prepare the following for merchandise inventory:
   a. An inventory purchases budget for each of the months April, May, and June.
   b. A schedule of expected cash disbursements for inventory for each of the months April, May, and June, and for the quarter in total.
3. Prepare a cash budget for the third quarter, by month as well as in total for the quarter. Show borrowings from the company's bank and repayments to the bank, as needed, to maintain the minimum cash balance.

CHECK FIGURE
(2) First quarter net
    payments: $75,000
(3) First quarter ending
    cash balance: $12,000

**PROBLEM 8–6**   **Cash Budget with Supporting Schedules**  (LO2, LO4, LO7, LO8)
Westex Products is a wholesale distributor of industrial cleaning products. When the treasurer of Westex Products approached the company's bank in late 2004 seeking short-term financing, he was told that money was very tight and that any borrowing over the next year would have to be supported by a detailed statement of cash receipts and disbursements. The treasurer also was told that it would be very helpful to the bank if borrowers would indicate the quarters in which they would be needing funds, as well as the amounts that would be needed, and the quarters in which repayments could be made.

Since the treasurer is unsure as to the particular quarters in which the bank financing will be needed, he has assembled the following information to assist in preparing a detailed cash budget:

a. Budgeted sales and merchandise purchases for the year 2005, as well as actual sales and purchases for the last quarter of 2004, are:

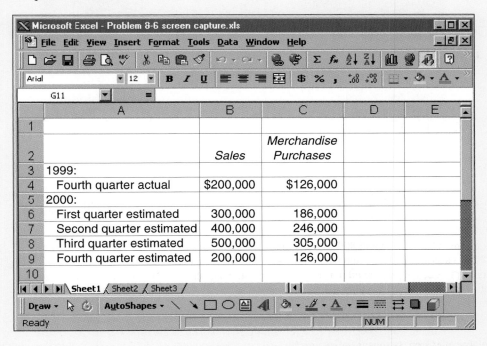

| | Sales | Merchandise Purchases | | |
|---|---|---|---|---|
| **1999:** | | | | |
| Fourth quarter actual | $200,000 | $126,000 | | |
| **2000:** | | | | |
| First quarter estimated | 300,000 | 186,000 | | |
| Second quarter estimated | 400,000 | 246,000 | | |
| Third quarter estimated | 500,000 | 305,000 | | |
| Fourth quarter estimated | 200,000 | 126,000 | | |

b. The company normally collects 65% of a quarter's sales before the quarter ends and another 33% in the following quarter. The remainder is uncollectible. This pattern of collections is now being experienced in the 2004 fourth-quarter actual data.

c. Eighty percent of a quarter's merchandise purchases are paid for within the quarter. The remainder is paid in the following quarter.

d. Operating expenses for the year 2005 are budgeted quarterly at $50,000 plus 15% of sales. Of the fixed amount, $20,000 each quarter is depreciation.

e. The company will pay $10,000 in dividends each quarter.

f. Equipment purchases of $75,000 will be made in the second quarter, and purchases of $48,000 will be made in the third quarter. These purchases will be for cash.

g. The Cash account contained $10,000 at the end of 2004. The treasurer feels that this represents a minimum balance that must be maintained.

h. Any borrowing will take place at the beginning of a quarter, and any repayments will be made at the end of a quarter at an annual interest rate of 10%. Interest is paid only when principal is repaid. All borrowings and all repayments of principal must be in round $1,000 amounts. Interest payments can be in any amount. (Compute interest on whole months, e.g., $1/12$, $2/12$.)

i. At present, the company has no loans outstanding.

**Required:**

1. Prepare the following by quarter and in total for the year 2005:
   a. A schedule of expected cash collections.
   b. A schedule of budgeted cash disbursements for merchandise purchases.
2. Compute the expected cash payments for operating expenses, by quarter and in total, for the year 2005.
3. Prepare a cash budget, by quarter and in total, for the year 2005. Show clearly in your budget the quarter(s) in which borrowing will be necessary and the quarter(s) in which repayments can be made, as requested by the company's bank.

**PROBLEM 8–7   Comprehensive Master Budget** (LO2, LO4, LO7, LO8, LO9, LO10)
Hillyard Company, an office supplies specialty store, prepares its master budget on a quarterly basis. The following data have been assembled to assist in preparation of the master budget for the first quarter:

CHECK FIGURE
(2a) February purchases:
$315,000
(4) February ending cash
balance: $30,800

a. As of December 31 (the end of the prior quarter), the company's general ledger showed the following account balances:

|  | Debits | Credits |
|---|---|---|
| Cash .......................... | $ 48,000 | |
| Accounts Receivable .............. | 224,000 | |
| Inventory ...................... | 60,000 | |
| Buildings and Equipment (net) ....... | 370,000 | |
| Accounts Payable ................ | | $ 93,000 |
| Capital Shares .................. | | 500,000 |
| Retained Earnings ............... | | 109,000 |
| | $702,000 | $702,000 |

b. Actual sales for December and budgeted sales for the next four months are as follows:

| December (actual) .............. | $280,000 |
|---|---|
| January ..................... | 400,000 |
| February .................... | 600,000 |
| March ..................... | 300,000 |
| April ...................... | 200,000 |

c. Sales are 20% for cash and 80% on credit. All payments on credit sales are collected in the month following sale. The accounts receivable at December 31 are a result of December credit sales.
d. The company's gross margin is 40% of sales.
e. Monthly expenses are budgeted as follows: salaries and wages, $27,000 per month: advertising, $70,000 per month; shipping, 5% of sales; depreciation, $14,000 per month; other expenses, 3% of sales.
f. At the end of each month, inventory is to be on hand equal to 25% of the following month's sales needs, stated at cost.
g. One-half of a month's inventory purchases is paid for in the month of purchase; the other half is paid for in the following month.
h. During February, the company will purchase a new copy machine for $1,700 cash. During March, other equipment will be purchased for cash at a cost of $84,500.
i. During January, the company will declare and pay $45,000 in cash dividends.
j. The company must maintain a minimum cash balance of $30,000. An open line of credit is available at a local bank for any borrowing that may be needed during the quarter. All borrowing is done at the beginning of a month, and all repayments are made at the end of a month. Borrowings and repayments of principal must be in multiples of $1,000. Interest is paid only at the time of payment of principal. The annual interest rate is 12%. (Figure interest on whole months, e.g., $1/12$, $2/12$.)

**Required:**
Using the data above, complete the following statements and schedules for the first quarter:
1. Schedule of expected cash collections:

|  | January | February | March | Quarter |
|---|---|---|---|---|
| Cash sales ................... | $ 80,000 | | | |
| Credit sales ................. | 224,000 | | | |
| Total cash collections .......... | $304,000 | | | |

2. a. Inventory purchases budget:

| | January | February | March | Quarter |
|---|---|---|---|---|
| Budgeted cost of goods sold . . . . . | $240,000* | $360,000 | | |
| Add desired ending inventory . . . . | 90,000† | | | |
| Total needs . . . . . . . . . . . . . . . . . . | 330,000 | | | |
| Less beginning inventory . . . . . . . . | 60,000 | | | |
| Required purchases . . . . . . . . . . . | $270,000 | | | |

*For January sales: $400,000 sales × 60% cost ratio = $240,000.
†$360,000 × 25% = $90,000.

b. Schedule of cash disbursements for purchases:

| | January | February | March | Quarter |
|---|---|---|---|---|
| December purchases . . . . . . . . . . . | $ 93,000 | | | $ 93,000 |
| January purchases ($270,000) . . . . | 135,000 | 135,000 | | 270,000 |
| February purchases . . . . . . . . . . . . | | | | |
| March purchases . . . . . . . . . . . . . . | | | | |
| Total cash disbursements for purchases . . . . . . . . . . . . . . | $228,000 | | | |

3. Schedule of cash disbursements for expenses:

| | January | February | March | Quarter |
|---|---|---|---|---|
| Salaries and wages . . . . . . . . . . . . . | $ 27,000 | | | |
| Advertising . . . . . . . . . . . . . . . . . | 70,000 | | | |
| Shipping . . . . . . . . . . . . . . . . . . . | 20,000 | | | |
| Other expenses . . . . . . . . . . . . . . | 12,000 | | | |
| Total cash disbursements for operating expenses . . . . . . . . | $129,000 | | | |

4. Cash budget:

| | January | February | March | Quarter |
|---|---|---|---|---|
| Cash balance, beginning . . . . . . . . | $ 48,000 | | | |
| Add cash collections . . . . . . . . . . . | 304,000 | | | |
| Total cash available . . . . . . . . . . . . | 352,000 | | | |
| Less disbursements: | | | | |
| Purchases of inventory . . . . . . . . | 228,000 | | | |
| Operating expenses . . . . . . . . . . | 129,000 | | | |
| Purchases of equipment . . . . . . . | — | | | |
| Cash dividends . . . . . . . . . . . . . | 45,000 | | | |
| Total disbursements . . . . . . . . . . . | 402,000 | | | |
| Excess (deficiency) of cash . . . . . . | (50,000) | | | |
| Financing: | | | | |
| Etc. | | | | |

5. Prepare an income statement for the quarter ending March 31 as shown in Schedule 9 in the chapter.
6. Prepare a balance sheet as of March 31.

**PROBLEM 8–8  Comprehensive Master Budget** (LO2, LO4, LO7, LO8, LO9, LO10)

Following is selected information relating to the operations of Shilow Company, a wholesale distributor:

| Current assets as of March 31: | |
| --- | --- |
| Cash . . . . . . . . . . . . . . . . . . . | $  8,000 |
| Accounts receivable . . . . . . . | 20,000 |
| Inventory . . . . . . . . . . . . . . . | 36,000 |
| Plant and equipment, net . . . . | 120,000 |
| Accounts payable . . . . . . . . . | 21,750 |
| Capital shares . . . . . . . . . . . . | 150,000 |
| Retained earnings . . . . . . . . . | 12,250 |

a. Gross margin is 25% of sales.
b. Actual and budgeted sales data:

| | |
| --- | --- |
| March (actual) . . . . . . . . . . . . | $50,000 |
| April . . . . . . . . . . . . . . . . . . | 60,000 |
| May . . . . . . . . . . . . . . . . . . . | 72,000 |
| June . . . . . . . . . . . . . . . . . . . | 90,000 |
| July . . . . . . . . . . . . . . . . . . . | 48,000 |

c. Sales are 60% for cash and 40% on credit. Credit sales are collected in the month following sale. The accounts receivable at March 31 are a result of March credit sales.
d. At the end of each month, inventory is to be on hand equal to 80% of the following month's sales needs, stated at cost.
e. One-half of a month's inventory purchases is paid for in the month of purchase; the other half is paid for in the following month. The accounts payable at March 31 are a result of March purchases of inventory.
f. Monthly expenses are as follows: salaries and wages, 12% of sales; rent, $2,500 per month; other expenses (excluding depreciation), 6% of sales. Assume that these expenses are paid monthly. Depreciation is $900 per month (includes depreciation on new assets).
g. Equipment costing $1,500 will be purchased for cash in April.
h. The company must maintain a minimum cash balance of $4,000. An open line of credit is available at a local bank. All borrowing is done at the beginning of a month, and all repayments are made at the end of a month; borrowing must be in multiples of $1,000. The annual interest rate is 12%. Interest is paid only at the time of repayment of principal; figure interest on whole months ($^1/_{12}$, $^2/_{12}$, and so forth).

*Required:*
Using the data above:
1. Complete the following schedule:

**Schedule of Expected Cash Collections**

| | April | May | June | Quarter |
| --- | --- | --- | --- | --- |
| Cash sales . . . . . . . . . . . . . . . . . . . . | $36,000 | | | |
| Credit sales . . . . . . . . . . . . . . . . . . | 20,000 | | | |
| Total collections . . . . . . . . . . . . . . | $56,000 | | | |

2. Complete the following:

**Inventory Purchases Budget**

| | April | May | June | Quarter |
| --- | --- | --- | --- | --- |
| Budgeted cost of goods sold . . . . . . | $45,000* | $54,000 | | |
| Add desired ending inventory . . . . | 43,200† | | | |
| Total needs . . . . . . . . . . . . . . . . . . | 88,200 | | | |
| Less beginning inventory . . . . . . . . | 36,000 | | | |
| Required purchases . . . . . . . . . . . . | $52,200 | | | |

*For April sales: $60,000 sales × 75% cost ratio = $45,000.
†$54,000 × 80% = $43,200.

**Schedule of Expected Cash Disbursements—Purchases**

|  | April | May | June | Quarter |
|---|---|---|---|---|
| March purchases . . . . . . . . . . . . . . | $21,750 |  |  | $21,750 |
| April purchases . . . . . . . . . . . . . . | 26,100 | $26,100 |  | 52,200 |
| May purchases . . . . . . . . . . . . . . . |  |  |  |  |
| June purchases . . . . . . . . . . . . . . . |  |  |  |  |
| Total disbursements . . . . . . . . . . . | $47,850 |  |  |  |

3. Complete the following:

**Schedule of Expected Cash Disbursements—Operating Expenses**

|  | April | May | June | Quarter |
|---|---|---|---|---|
| Salaries and wages . . . . . . . . . . . . . | $ 7,200 |  |  |  |
| Rent . . . . . . . . . . . . . . . . . . . . . . . | 2,500 |  |  |  |
| Other expenses . . . . . . . . . . . . . . . | 3,600 |  |  |  |
| Total disbursements . . . . . . . . . . . | $13,300 |  |  |  |

4. Complete the following cash budget:

**Cash Budget**

|  | April | May | June | Quarter |
|---|---|---|---|---|
| Cash balance, beginning . . . . . . . . . | $ 8,000 |  |  |  |
| Add cash collections . . . . . . . . . . . . | 56,000 |  |  |  |
| Total cash available . . . . . . . . . . . . | 64,000 |  |  |  |
| Less cash disbursements: |  |  |  |  |
|   For inventory . . . . . . . . . . . . . . . | 47,850 |  |  |  |
|   For expenses . . . . . . . . . . . . . . . | 13,300 |  |  |  |
|   For equipment . . . . . . . . . . . . . . | 1,500 |  |  |  |
| Total cash disbursements . . . . . . . . | 62,650 |  |  |  |
| Excess (deficiency) of cash . . . . . . | 1,350 |  |  |  |
| Financing: |  |  |  |  |
| Etc. |  |  |  |  |

5. Prepare an income statement for the quarter ended June 30. (Use the functional format in preparing your income statement, as shown in Schedule 9 in the text.)
6. Prepare a balance sheet as of June 30.

# Building Your Skills

**ANALYTICAL THINKING**   (LO2, LO4, LO8, LO9, LO10)

You have just been hired as a new management trainee by Earrings Unlimited, a distributor of earrings to various retail outlets located in shopping malls across the country. In the past, the company has done very little in the way of budgeting and at certain times of the year has experienced a shortage of cash.

Since you are well trained in budgeting, you have decided to prepare comprehensive budgets for the upcoming second quarter in order to show management the benefits that can be gained from an integrated budgeting program. To this end, you have worked with accounting and other areas to gather the information assembled below.

CHECK FIGURE
(1c) April purchases: 79,000 units
(2) June 30 cash balance: $94,700

The company sells many styles of earrings, but all are sold for the same price—$10 per pair. Actual sales of earrings for the last three months and budgeted sales for the next six months follow (in pairs of earrings):

| | | | |
|---|---|---|---|
| January (actual) . . . . . . . . . . . . | 20,000 | June (budget) . . . . . . . . . . . . . . | 50,000 |
| February (actual) . . . . . . . . . . . | 26,000 | July (budget) . . . . . . . . . . . . . . | 30,000 |
| March (actual) . . . . . . . . . . . . . | 40,000 | August (budget) . . . . . . . . . . . | 28,000 |
| April (budget) . . . . . . . . . . . . . | 65,000 | September (budget) . . . . . . . . . | 25,000 |
| May (budget) . . . . . . . . . . . . . . | 100,000 | | |

The concentration of sales before and during May is due to Mother's Day. Sufficient inventory should be on hand at the end of each month to supply 40% of the earrings sold in the following month.

Suppliers are paid $4 for a pair of earrings. One-half of a month's purchases is paid for in the month of purchase; the other half is paid for in the following month. All sales are on credit, with no discount, and payable within 15 days. The company has found, however, that only 20% of a month's sales are collected in the month of sale. An additional 70% is collected in the following month, and the remaining 10% is collected in the second month following sale. Bad debts have been negligible.

Monthly operating expenses for the company are given below:

| | |
|---|---|
| Variable: | |
| Sales commissions . . . . . . . . . . . . . . . . . . . . . . . . | 4% of sales |
| Fixed: | |
| Advertising . . . . . . . . . . . . . . . . . . . . . . . . . . . . . | $200,000 |
| Rent . . . . . . . . . . . . . . . . . . . . . . . . . . . . . . . . . . . | 18,000 |
| Salaries . . . . . . . . . . . . . . . . . . . . . . . . . . . . . . . . | 106,000 |
| Utilities . . . . . . . . . . . . . . . . . . . . . . . . . . . . . . . . | 7,000 |
| Insurance expired . . . . . . . . . . . . . . . . . . . . . . . . . | 3,000 |
| Depreciation . . . . . . . . . . . . . . . . . . . . . . . . . . . . . | 14,000 |

Insurance is paid on an annual basis, in November of each year.

The company plans to purchase $16,000 in new equipment during May and $40,000 in new equipment during June; both purchases will be for cash. The company declares dividends of $15,000 each quarter, payable in the first month of the following quarter.

A listing of the company's ledger accounts as of March 31 is given below:

### Assets

| | | |
|---|---|---|
| Cash . . . . . . . . . . . . . . . . . . . . . . . . . . . . . . . . . . . | $ | 74,000 |
| Accounts receivable ($26,000 February sales; | | |
| $320,000 March sales) . . . . . . . . . . . . . . . . . . . . . | | 346,000 |
| Inventory . . . . . . . . . . . . . . . . . . . . . . . . . . . . . . . | | 104,000 |
| Prepaid insurance . . . . . . . . . . . . . . . . . . . . . . . . . | | 21,000 |
| Property and equipment (net) . . . . . . . . . . . . . . . . | | 950,000 |
| Total assets . . . . . . . . . . . . . . . . . . . . . . . . . . . . . | | $1,495,000 |

### Liabilities and Shareholders' Equity

| | | |
|---|---|---|
| Accounts payable . . . . . . . . . . . . . . . . . . . . . . . . . | $ | 100,000 |
| Dividends payable . . . . . . . . . . . . . . . . . . . . . . . . | | 15,000 |
| Capital shares . . . . . . . . . . . . . . . . . . . . . . . . . . . . | | 800,000 |
| Retained earnings . . . . . . . . . . . . . . . . . . . . . . . . | | 580,000 |
| Total liabilities and shareholders' equity . . . . . . . . | | $1,495,000 |

Part of the use of the budgeting program will be to establish an ongoing line of credit at a local bank. Therefore, determine the borrowing that will be needed to maintain a minimum cash balance of $50,000. All borrowing will be done at the beginning of a month; any repayments will be made at the end of a month.

The annual interest rate will be 12%. Interest will be computed and paid at the end of each quarter on all loans outstanding during the quarter. Compute interest on whole months ($^1/_{12}$, $^2/_{12}$, and so forth).

### Required:
Prepare a master budget for the three-month period ending June 30. Include the following detailed budgets:
1. a. A sales budget, by month and in total.
   b. A schedule of expected cash collections from sales, by month and in total.
   c. A merchandise purchases budget in units and in dollars. Show the budget by month and in total.
   d. A schedule of expected cash disbursements for merchandise purchases, by month and in total.
2. A cash budget. Show the budget by month and in total.
3. A budgeted income statement for the three-month period ending June 30. Use the contribution approach.
4. A budgeted balance sheet as of June 30.

## COMMUNICATING IN PRACTICE   (LO8)

Risky Rolling, Inc. is a rapidly expanding manufacturer of skateboards that have been modified for use on ski slopes during the off-season. This year's sales are considerably higher than last year's sales, and sales are expected to double next year. The unexpected growth in sales has presented numerous challenges to the company's management team, and the stress is really starting to show. Laura Dennan, the company's president, believes that the management time required to prepare a cash budget should be devoted to other, more pressing matters.

### Required:
Write a memorandum to the president that states why cash budgeting is particularly important to a rapidly expanding company, such as Risky Rolling.

## ETHICS CHALLENGE   (LO1, LO2)

Norton Company, a manufacturer of infant furniture and carriages, is in the initial stages of preparing the annual budget for next year. Scott Ford has recently joined Norton's accounting staff and is interested to learn as much as possible about the company's budgeting process. During a recent lunch with Marge Atkins, sales manager, and Pete Granger, production manager, Ford initiated the following conversation:

*Ford:* Since I'm new around here and am going to be involved with the preparation of the annual budget, I'd be interested to learn how the two of you estimate sales and production numbers.

*Atkins:* We start out very methodically by looking at recent history, discussing what we know about current accounts, potential customers, and the general state of consumer spending. Then, we add that usual dose of intuition to come up with the best forecast we can.

*Granger:* I usually take the sales projections as the basis for my projections. Of course, we have to make an estimate of what this year's ending inventories will be, which is sometimes difficult.

*Ford:* Why does that present a problem? There must have been an estimate of ending inventories in the budget for the current year.

*Granger:* Those numbers aren't always reliable, since Marge makes some adjustments to the sales number before passing them on to me.

*Ford:* What kind of adjustments?

*Atkins:* Well, we don't want to fall short of the sales projections, and so we generally give ourselves a little breathing room by lowering the initial sales projection anywhere from 5% to 10%.

*Granger:* So, you can see why this year's budget is not a very reliable starting point. We always have to adjust the projected production rates as the year progresses, and of course, this changes the ending inventory estimates. By the way, we make similar adjustments to expenses by adding at least 10% to the estimates; I think everyone around here does the same thing.

### Required:
1. Marge Atkins and Pete Granger have described the use of what is sometimes called *budgetary slack*.
   a. Explain why Atkins and Granger behave in this manner and describe the benefits they expect to realize from the use of budgetary slack.
   b. Explain how the use of budgetary slack can adversely affect Atkins and Granger.
2. As a management accountant, Scott Ford believes that the behaviour described by Marge Atkins and Pete Granger may be unethical. Refer to the Standards of Ethical Conduct for Practitioners of Management Accounting and Financial Management in Chapter 1, and explain why the use of budgetary slack may be unethical.

(CMA, adapted)

**TEAMWORK IN ACTION**   (LO1, LO11)

Tom Emory and Jim Morris strolled back to their plant from the administrative offices of Ferguson & Son Mfg. Company. Tom is manager of the machine shop in the company's factory; Jim is manager of the equipment maintenance department.

The men had just attended the monthly performance evaluation meeting for plant department heads. These meetings had been held on the third Tuesday of each month since Robert Ferguson, Jr., the president's son, had become plant manager a year earlier.

As they were walking, Tom Emory spoke: "Boy, I hate those meetings! I never know whether my department's accounting reports will show good or bad performance. I'm beginning to expect the worst. If the accountants say I saved the company a dollar, I'm called 'Sir,' but if I spend even a little too much—boy, do I get into trouble. I don't know if I can hold on until I retire."

Tom had just been given the worst evaluation he had ever received in his long career with Ferguson & Son. He was the most respected of the experienced machinists in the company. He had been with Ferguson & Son for many years and was promoted to supervisor of the machine shop when the company expanded and moved to its present location. The president (Robert Ferguson, Sr.) had often stated that the company's success was due to the high quality of the work of machinists like Tom. As supervisor, Tom stressed the importance of craftsmanship and told his workers that he wanted no sloppy work coming from his department.

When Robert Ferguson, Jr., became the plant manager, he directed that monthly performance comparisons be made between actual and budgeted costs for each department. The departmental budgets were intended to encourage the supervisors to reduce inefficiencies and to seek cost reduction opportunities. The company controller was instructed to have his staff "tighten" the budget slightly whenever a department attained its budget in a given month; this was done to reinforce the plant manager's desire to reduce costs. The young plant manager often stressed the importance of continued progress toward attaining the budget; he also made it known that he kept a file of these performance reports for future reference when he succeeded his father.

Tom Emory's conversation with Jim Morris continued as follows:

*Emory:* I really don't understand. We've worked so hard to get up to budget, and the minute we make it, they tighten the budget on us. We can't work any faster and still maintain quality. I think my men are ready to quit trying. Besides, those reports don't tell the whole story. We always seem to be interrupting the big jobs for all those small rush orders. All that setup and machine adjustment time is killing us. And quite frankly, Jim, you were no help. When our hydraulic press broke down last month, your people were nowhere to be found. We had to take it apart ourselves and got stuck with all that idle time.

*Morris:* I'm sorry about that, Tom, but you know my department has had trouble making budget, too. We were running well behind at the time of that problem, and if we'd spent a day on that old machine, we would never have made it up. Instead, we made the scheduled inspections of the forklift trucks because we knew we could do those in less than the budgeted time.

*Emory:* Well, Jim, at least you have some options. I'm locked into what the scheduling department assigns to me, and you know they're being harassed by sales for those special orders. Incidentally, why didn't your report show all the supplies you guys wasted last month when you were working in Bill's department?

*Morris:* We're not out of the woods on that deal yet. We charged the maximum we could to other work and haven't even reported some of it yet.

*Emory:* Well, I'm glad you have a way of getting out of the pressure. The accountants seem to know everything that's happening in my department, sometimes even before I do. I thought all that budget and accounting stuff was supposed to help, but it just gets me into trouble. It's all a big pain. I'm trying to put out quality work; they're trying to save pennies.

*Required:*

The team should discuss and then respond to the following two questions. All team members should agree with and understand the answers and be prepared to explain the solutions in class. (Each teammate can assume responsibility for a different part of the presentation.)

1. Identify the problems that appear to exist in Ferguson & Son Mfg. Company's budgetary control system, and explain how the problems are likely to reduce the effectiveness of the system.
2. Explain how Ferguson & Son Mfg. Company's budgetary control system could be revised to improve its effectiveness.

                                                                  (CMA, adapted)

Do not forget to check out Taking It to the Net as well as the other quizzes and resources at the Online Learning Centre at www.mcgrawhill.ca/college/garrison.

# Chapter *Nine*

# Standard Costs

## A Look Back

We discussed the budgeting process in Chapter 8 and overviewed each of the budgets that constitute the master budget.

## A Look at This Chapter

We begin a discussion of management control by focusing on standard costing systems in Chapter 9. Management by exception and variance analysis are described, as are the computations of material, labour, and overhead variances.

## A Look Ahead

We compare and contrast the static budget approach and flexible budget approach in Chapter 10 and discuss the preparation of performance reports, using a flexible budget approach, to analyze overhead variances.

## Chapter Outline

**Standard Costs**

**Setting Standard Costs**
- Ideal versus Practical Standards
- Setting Direct Materials Standards
- Setting Direct Labour Standards
- Setting Variable Manufacturing Overhead Standards
- Are Standards the Same as Budgets?

**A General Model for Variance Analysis**
- Price and Quantity Variances

**Using Standard Costs—Direct Materials Variances**
- Materials Price Variance—A Closer Look
- Materials Quantity Variance—A Closer Look

**Using Standard Costs—Direct Labour Variances**
- Labour Rate Variance—A Closer Look
- Labour Efficiency Variance—A Closer Look

**Using Standard Costs—Variable Overhead Variances**
- Overhead Variances—A Closer Look

**Variance Analysis and Management by Exception**

**Evaluation of Controls Based on Standard Costs**
- Advantages of Standard Costs
- Potential Problems with the Use of Standard Costs

(See the Online Learning Centre at www.mcgrawhill.ca/college/garrison.)

# DECISION FEATURE Auto Service Standards

Keith Atchinson and Herb Friesen, two co-workers in a Saskatoon-based auto service business, took over the business in 1961 and renamed it Keith & Herb Alignment and Brake, specializing in brakes, wheel alignments, and front-end repairs. After over 40 years, it is still very much in business and going strong. In 2000, Richard Semchyshen, a young mechanic with eight years of experience at Keith & Herb, bought out the business and is running it successfully with his twin brother Steve.

Richard fully understands the value of the Keith & Herb's reputation and is working hard to maintain is by providing value to the customer—quality service at a reasonable price. At the same time, however, being profitable is also important to Richard, and this is where standards come into the picture. For most jobs (such as a wheel alignment for a four-wheel-drive jeep), his charges to customers are based on standard times that he has developed over the years; for others, he uses the standard times published in labour guides. Richard and his brother pay close attention to the standards—completing a job in less than the standard time means more money for the business.

Given the small size of his business, Richard does not need an elaborate standard costing system to monitor his performance. He has been doing this long enough and just knows when a job takes longer than it is supposed to! However, this does not mean that there are no avenues for improvement to close any gaps between standard and actual times for a job. Although the primary source of learning is "on the job" training and experience, that is, learning by doing more of the same, there are times when he attends training seminars organized by parts dealers and even contacts other mechanics when he needs a second opinion (especially on less frequent jobs). He is very careful about accepting jobs outside of his specialty areas, especially complicated ones, such as replacing a water pump on a Rolls Royce.

According to him, "there is never a dull moment in the shop," as he always has his hands full—literally speaking. Richard is passionate about his work, as he is about hockey and, above all, his family!

## Learning Objectives

*After studying Chapter 9, you should be able to:*

**LO1** Explain how direct materials and direct labour standards are set.

**LO2** Compute and apply the direct materials price and quantity variances and explain their significance.

**LO3** Compute and apply the direct labour rate and efficiency variances and explain their significance.

**LO4** Compute the variable overhead spending and efficiency variances.

**LO5** (Appendix 9A) Prepare journal entries to record standard costs and variances.

**I**n this chapter, we will continue our focus on planning and extend it to control (the other side of the coin). We learned that budgeting can be a useful tool for planning purposes. However, in order to prepare budgets, managers must know how much resources (inputs) are required for carrying out different tasks. For example, the manager of your local Pizza store knows that on average, it takes seven minutes to enter a customer's order on her computer system. She then uses this average time to compute the total time that should be budgeted for the "order-taking" activity during a certain period (week, month, quarter, or year). In other words, she strongly believes that seven minutes is an acceptable *standard* time for the "order-taking" activity. We will explain the concept of standard costs and illustrate how they are useful both in planning and control.

## Standard Costs

A *standard* is a benchmark or "norm" that is used as a basis for determining the quantity of resources required to carry out a certain activity (or set of activities). The same standard is also used as the base against which managers can compare actual performance at the end of the budgeting period. The use of standards is by no means restricted to businesses. Colleges and universities use admission standards to decide which students are eligible for admission into their programs. Your doctor evaluates your weight using standards that have been established for individuals of your age, height, and gender. Similarly, the food we eat in restaurants and the buildings we live in must also conform to certain standards. The absence of standards could result in adverse consequences.

*in business today* | **International and Canadian Standards**

The International Organization for Standardization (ISO) is an organization recognized worldwide that develops standards that are applicable to various organizations. For example, the ISO 9000 and 14000 series of standards pertain to quality management and environmental management systems, respectively. Many businesses prefer dealing with organizations that are ISO certified, as this gives them confidence that the processes existing in these organizations have met, and continue to meet, a certain set of standards. In Canada, the National Standards System is the system for the development, promotion, and implementation of voluntary standards and is monitored by the Standards Council of Canada, a federal crown corporation.

Source: http://www.iso.ch/iso/en/aboutiso/introduction/index.html, and http://www.scc.ca/nss/index_e.html

Managers and administrators of various organizations generally conform to some set of standards for carrying out their activities and defining their output specifications. For example, educational institutions set course completion standards, manufacturing companies set quality standards for their products, and hospital emergency units follow standard operating procedures. Similarly, these organizations develop standards for the inputs required to complete their tasks. For example, the auto service centre of Petro-Canada would set specific labour time standards for the completion of such tasks as replacing the timing belt, performing an oil change, and so on. Manufacturing companies use their product and process knowledge to determine standards for the inputs required to produce the output. These inputs typically consist of raw materials, labour, and manufacturing overhead. Such standards are known as *quantity standards.*

In addition, managers also like to compute the costs associated with the quantity standards; these are known as *cost (or price) standards.* A **standard cost** is computed as the standard quantity of input multiplied by the standard price of the input required to produce one unit of a product or provide one unit of service to a customer. For example, a tax consultant can compute the standard cost of preparing a normal tax return (i.e., without too many complications).

Manufacturing companies often have highly developed standard costing systems in which standards relating to materials, labour, and overhead are developed in detail for each separate product. These standards are listed on a **standard cost card** that provides the manager with a great deal of information concerning the inputs that are required to produce a unit and their costs. We now provide details of setting standards and the preparation of a standard cost card.

# Setting Standard Costs

Setting price and quantity standards is more an art than a science. It requires the combined expertise of all persons who have responsibility over input prices and over the effective use of inputs. In a manufacturing setting, this might include accountants, purchasing managers, engineers, production supervisors, line managers, and production workers. Past records of purchase prices and of input usage can be helpful in setting standards. However, the standards should be designed to encourage efficient *future* operations, not a repetition of past inefficient operations.

## Ideal versus Practical Standards

Should standards be attainable all of the time, should they be attainable only part of the time, or should they be so tight that they become, in effect, "the impossible dream"? Opinions among managers vary, but standards tend to fall into one of two categories—either ideal or practical.

**Ideal standards** are those that can be attained only under the best circumstances. They allow for no machine breakdowns or other work interruptions, and they call for a level of effort that can be attained only by the most skilled and efficient employees working at peak effort 100% of the time. Some managers feel that such standards have a motivational value. These managers argue that even though employees know they will rarely meet the standard, it is a constant reminder of the need for ever-increasing efficiency and effort. For example, many "lean" organizations set "stretch targets" to encourage their employees to "take the extra step" toward achieving perfection. However, managers must make a very conscious effort to ensure that employees are not discouraged by such standards/targets which might otherwise ruin morale within the organization. Deviations from ideal standards may be hard to interpret and must therefore be interpreted with caution.

**Practical standards** are defined as standards that are "tight but attainable." They allow for normal machine downtime and employee rest periods, and they can be attained through reasonable, though highly efficient, efforts by the average worker. Variances from such a standard represent deviations that fall outside of normal operating conditions and signal a need for management attention. Furthermore, practical standards can serve multiple purposes. In addition to signalling abnormal conditions, they can also be used in forecasting cash flows and in planning inventory. By contrast, ideal standards cannot be used in forecasting and planning; they do not allow for normal inefficiencies, and therefore they result in unrealistic planning and forecasting figures.

## Hockey Coach

*you decide*

During the winter, you coach a team of 8 to 10-year-olds, in your neighbourhood. One of the parents has approached you with a list of NHL records that he believes should be used as benchmarks or standards of performance for the kids. The parent suggests that players who meet the benchmarks be recognized and rewarded for their efforts. How do you respond?

Throughout the remainder of this chapter, we will assume the use of practical, rather than ideal, standards.

---

**MANAGERIAL ACCOUNTING**
IN ACTION

**The Issue**

The Colonial Pewter Company was organized a year ago. The company's only product is a reproduction of an 18th century pewter bookend. The bookend is made largely by hand, using traditional metal-working tools. Consequently, the manufacturing process is labour intensive and requires a high level of skill.

Colonial Pewter has recently expanded its workforce to take advantage of unexpected demand for the bookends as gifts. The company started with a small cadre of experienced pewter workers but has had to hire less experienced workers as a result of the expansion. The president of the company, J. D. Wriston, has called a meeting to discuss production problems. Attending the meeting are Tom Kuchel, the production manager; Janet Warner, the purchasing manager; and Terry Sherman, the corporate controller.

*J. D.:* I've got a feeling that we aren't getting the production we should out of our new people.
*Tom:* Give us a chance. Some of the new people have been on board for less than a month.
*Janet:* Let me add that production seems to be wasting an awful lot of material—particularly pewter. That stuff is very expensive.
*Tom:* What about the shipment of defective pewter you bought a couple of months ago—the one with the iron contamination? That caused us major problems.
*Janet:* That's ancient history. How was I to know it was off-grade? Besides, it was a great deal.
*J. D.:* Calm down everybody. Let's get the facts before we start sinking our fangs into each other.
*Tom:* I agree. The more facts, the better.
*J. D.:* Okay, Terry, it's your turn. Facts are the controller's department.
*Terry:* I'm afraid I can't provide the answers off the top of my head, but it won't take me too long to set up a system that can routinely answer questions relating to worker productivity, material waste, and input prices.
*J. D.:* How long is "not too long"?
*Terry:* I will need all of your cooperation, but how about a week from today?
*J. D.:* That's okay with me. What about everyone else?
*Tom:* Sure.
*Janet:* Fine with me.
*J. D.:* Let's mark it on our calendars.

## Setting Direct Materials Standards

**Learning Objective 1**
Explain how direct materials and direct labour standards are set.

Terry Sherman's first task was to prepare price and quantity standards for the company's only significant raw material, pewter ingots. The **standard price per unit** for direct materials should reflect the final, delivered cost of the materials, net of any discounts taken. After consulting with purchasing manager Janet Warner, Terry prepared the following documentation for the standard price of a kilo of pewter in ingot form:

| | |
|---|---|
| Purchase price, top-grade pewter ingots, in 18-kg ingots .......... | $7.90 |
| Freight, by truck, from the supplier's warehouse ................ | 1.00 |
| Receiving and handling ...................................... | 0.10 |
| Less purchase discount ...................................... | (0.20) |
| Standard price per kilogram ................................. | $8.80 |

Note that the standard price reflects a particular grade of material (top grade), purchased in particular lot sizes (18-kg ingots), and delivered by a particular type of carrier (truck).

Allowances have also been made for handling and discounts. If everything proceeds according to these expectations, the net cost of a kilogram of pewter should therefore be $8.80.

The **standard quantity per unit** for direct materials should reflect the amount of material going into each unit of finished product, as well as an allowance for unavoidable waste, spoilage, and other normal inefficiencies. After consulting with the production manager, Tom Kuchel, Terry Sherman prepared the following documentation for the standard quantity of pewter in a pair of bookends:

| | |
|---|---:|
| Material requirements as specified in the bill of materials for a pair of bookends, in kilograms . . . . . . . . . . . . . . . . . . . . . . | 5.95 |
| Allowance for waste and spoilage, in kilograms . . . . . . . . . . . . . . | 0.45 |
| Allowance for rejects, in kilograms . . . . . . . . . . . . . . . . . . . . . . . . | 1.50 |
| Standard quantity per pair of bookends, in kilograms . . . . . . . . . . . | 7.90 |

A **bill of materials** is a list that shows the quantity of each type of material going into a unit of finished product. It is a handy source for determining the basic material input per unit, but it should be adjusted for waste and other factors, as shown above, when determining the standard quantity per unit of product. "Waste and spoilage" in the table above refers to materials that are wasted as a normal part of the production process or that spoil before they are used. "Rejects" refers to the direct material contained in units that are defective and must be scrapped.

Although it is common to recognize allowances for waste, spoilage, and rejects when setting standard costs, this practice is now coming into question. Those involved in TQM (total quality management) and similar improvement programs argue that no amount of waste or defects should be tolerated. If allowances for waste, spoilage, and rejects are built into the standard cost, the levels of those allowances should be periodically reviewed and reduced over time to reflect improved processes, better training, and better equipment.

Once the price and quantity standards have been set, the standard cost of material per unit of finished product can be computed as follows:

$$1.25 \text{ kg per unit} \times \$8.80 \text{ per kg} = \$11 \text{ per unit}$$

This $11 cost figure will appear as one item on the standard cost card of the product.

## "Allowable" Waste

*in business today*

After many years of operating a standard cost system, a major wood products company reviewed the materials standards for its products by breaking each standard down into its basic elements. In doing so, the company discovered that there was a 20% waste factor built into the standard cost for every product. Management was dismayed to learn that the dollar amount of "allowable" waste was so large. Since the quantity standards had not been scrutinized for many years, management was unaware of the existence of this significant cost improvement potential in the company.

Source: James M. Reeve, "The Impact of Variation on Operating System Performance," *Performance Excellence* (Sarasota, FL: American Accounting Association, 1990), p. 77.

## Setting Direct Labour Standards

Direct labour price and quantity standards are usually expressed in terms of a labour rate and labour-hours. The **standard rate per hour** for direct labour should include not only wages earned but also fringe benefits and other labour costs. Using last month's wage records and in consultation with the production manager, Terry determined the standard rate per hour at the Colonial Pewter Company as follows:

| | |
|---|---|
| Basic wage rate per hour ........................... | $10 |
| Employment taxes at 10% of the basic rate ............. | 1 |
| Fringe benefits at 30% of the basic rate ................ | 3 |
| Standard rate per direct labour-hour .................. | $14 |

Many companies prepare a single standard rate for all employees in a department. This standard rate reflects the expected "mix" of workers, even though the actual wage rates may vary somewhat from individual to individual due to differing skills or seniority. A single standard rate simplifies the use of standard costs and also permits the manager to monitor the use of employees within departments. More is said on this point a little later. According to the standard computed above, the direct labour rate for Colonial Pewter should average $14 per hour.

The standard direct labour time required to complete a unit of product (generally called the **standard hours per unit**) is perhaps the single most difficult standard to determine. One approach is to divide each operation performed on the product into elemental body movements (such as reaching, pushing, and turning over). Published tables of standard times for such movements are available. These times can be applied to the movements and then added together to determine the total standard time allowed per operation. Another approach is for an industrial engineer to do a time and motion study, actually clocking the time required for certain tasks. As stated earlier, the standard time should include allowances for breaks, personal needs of employees, cleanup, and machine downtime. After consulting with the production manager, Terry prepared the following documentation for the standard hours per unit:

| | |
|---|---|
| Basic labour time per unit, in hours ................... | 1.9 |
| Allowance for breaks and personal needs .............. | 0.1 |
| Allowance for cleanup and machine downtime .......... | 0.3 |
| Allowance for rejects ............................... | 0.2 |
| Standard labour-hours per unit of product .............. | 2.5 |

Once the rate and time standards have been set, the standard labour cost per unit of product can be computed as follows:

$$2.5 \text{ hours per unit} \times 14 \text{ per hour} = \$35 \text{ per unit}$$

This $35 cost figure appears along with direct materials as one item on the standard cost card of the product. Note that if Colonial Pewter implements lean business practices, managers would strive to reduce the allowances included in computing the labour standards.

## Setting Variable Manufacturing Overhead Standards

As with direct labour, the price and quantity standards for variable manufacturing overhead are generally expressed in terms of rate and hours. The rate represents *the variable portion of the predetermined overhead rate* discussed in Chapter 3; the hours represent whatever hours base is used to apply overhead to units of product (usually machine-hours or direct labour-hours, as we learned in Chapter 3). At Colonial Pewter, the variable portion of the predetermined overhead rate is $3 per direct labour-hour. Therefore, the standard variable manufacturing overhead cost per unit is computed as follows:

$$2.5 \text{ hours per unit} \times \$3 \text{ per hour} = \$7.50 \text{ per unit}$$

**Exhibit 9–1**
Standard Cost Card—Variable
Production Cost

| Inputs | (1)<br>Standard<br>Quantity<br>or Hours | (2)<br>Standard<br>Price<br>or Rate | (3)<br>Standard<br>Cost<br>(1) × (2) |
|---|---|---|---|
| Direct materials .................. | 1.25 kg | $ 8.80 | $11.00 |
| Direct labour .................... | 2.5 hours | 14.00 | 35.00 |
| Variable manufacturing overhead .... | 2.5 hours | 3.00 | 7.50 |
| Total standard cost per unit ......... | | | $53.50 |

This $7.50 cost figure appears along with direct materials and direct labour as one item on the standard cost card in Exhibit 9–1. Observe that the **standard cost per unit** is computed by multiplying the standard quantity or hours by the standard price or rate.

## Are Standards the Same as Budgets?

Standards and budgets are very similar. The major distinction between the two terms is that a standard is a *unit* amount, whereas a budget is a *total* amount. The standard cost for materials at Colonial Pewter is $11 per pair of bookends. If 1,000 pairs of bookends are to be manufactured during a budgeting period, then the budgeted cost of materials would be $11,000. In effect, *a standard can be viewed as the budgeted cost for one unit of product.*

## Standard Costing and Process Re-engineering

*in business today*

For Montreal-based Standard Life, tracking the time spent on projects was not easy until it started using the HMS TimeControl software to increase operations efficiency and streamline internal processes. The company uses the software to record time spent on each project and measures the actual hours to budgeted hours to enable managers to make any future adjustments. As well, the software saves the company time in paying external contractors and consultants. Finally, the new software gave managers insights into the inconsistencies related to actual versus budgeted time.

Source: Hilson, Gary, "Watching the Clock: Montreal's Standard Life Keeps a Close Eye on the Fourth Dimension When Managing Myriad Projects," *Computing Canada.* February 1, 2002, Volume 28(3), p. 23.

## A General Model for Variance Analysis

Recall from Chapter 1 that planning and control are important tasks performed by managers; we mentioned that management accounting information is critical for performing these tasks effectively and efficiently. While standard cost information is useful for planning (budgets are prepared using standard cost data), it also provides the basis for control. Most organizations prepare performance reports which compare actual results at the end of a period with the budgeted performance for that period. Any deviation from the budget is called a **variance.** The performance report is a useful tool for managers to monitor activities on a periodic basis.

Although the performance report provides an overview of the actual performance during a period, the report merely *informs* managers of any deviations. Managers often need more details of the deviations (or variances) so that they can get more actionable information which they can then use to make changes, as necessary. The process of computing and interpreting variances is known as *variance analysis.* As a manager, the first thing of importance is to identify the source(s) of the variances. Generally speaking, there are two sources of a variance: (1) difference between the actual and budgeted (standard) price of inputs, and (2) difference between the actual quantity (or volume) of inputs consumed and the standard quantity that was planned.

An important reason for separating standards into two categories—price and quantity—is that different managers are usually responsible for buying and for using inputs and these two activities occur at different points in time. In the case of raw materials, for example, the purchasing manager is responsible for the price, and this responsibility is exercised at the time of purchase. In contrast, the production manager is responsible for the amount of the raw material used, and this responsibility is exercised when the materials are used in production, which may be days or weeks after the purchase date. It is important, therefore, that we cleanly separate discrepancies due to deviations from price standards from those due to deviations from quantity standards.

## Price and Quantity Variances

A general model for computing standard cost variances for variable costs is presented in Exhibit 9–2. This model isolates price variances from quantity variances and shows how each of these variances is computed.[1] We will be using this model throughout the chapter to compute variances for direct materials, direct labour, and variable manufacturing overhead.

Three things should be noted from Exhibit 9–2. First, note that a price variance and a quantity variance can be computed for all three variable cost elements—direct materials, direct labour, and variable manufacturing overhead—even though the variance is not called by the same name in all cases. For example, a price variance is called a *materials price variance* in the case of direct materials but a *labour rate variance* in the case of direct labour and an *overhead spending variance* in the case of variable manufacturing overhead.

Second, note that even though a price variance may be called by different names, it is computed in exactly the same way, regardless of whether one is dealing with direct materials, direct labour, or variable manufacturing overhead. The same is true with the quantity variance.

Third, note that variance analysis is actually a type of input–output analysis. The inputs represent the actual quantity of direct materials, direct labour, and variable manufacturing overhead used; the output represents the good production of the period, expressed in terms of the *standard quantity (or the standard hours) allowed for the actual output* (see column 3 in Exhibit 9–2). By **standard quantity allowed** or **standard hours allowed,** we mean the amount of direct materials, direct labour, or variable manufacturing overhead

**Exhibit 9–2**

A General Model for Variance Analysis—Variable Production Costs

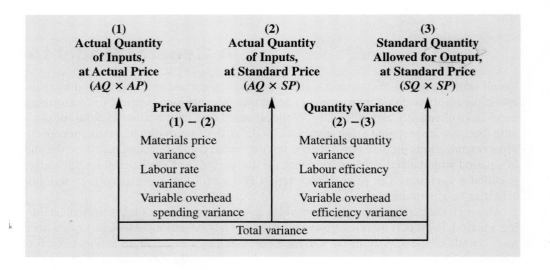

| (1) Actual Quantity of Inputs, at Actual Price ($AQ \times AP$) | (2) Actual Quantity of Inputs, at Standard Price ($AQ \times SP$) | (3) Standard Quantity Allowed for Output, at Standard Price ($SQ \times SP$) |
|---|---|---|
| **Price Variance** (1) − (2) | **Quantity Variance** (2) − (3) | |
| Materials price variance | Materials quantity variance | |
| Labour rate variance | Labour efficiency variance | |
| Variable overhead spending variance | Variable overhead efficiency variance | |
| Total variance | | |

[1]Variance analysis of fixed costs is discussed in the next chapter.

*that should have been used* to produce the actual output of the period. This could be more or could be less materials, labour, or overhead than was *actually* used, depending on the efficiency or inefficiency of operations. The standard quantity allowed is computed by multiplying the actual output in units by the standard input allowed per unit.

It is important to emphasize that a price variance occurs due to the difference between actual price and standard price—the quantity element is kept constant in the computation of this variance. Similarly, the quantity variance occurs due to the difference between actual and standard quantities of inputs used—the price element is kept constant in the computation of this variance. This is explained later in the chapter.

Although the general model for variance analysis is explained in the context of a manufacturing company, it is equally applicable to many service organizations. For example, Taco Time can use this model to compute the materials and labour-related variances pertaining to preparing a Bean Burrito. However, given that each customer order may be different, separately tracking the time for every burrito prepared may not be cost beneficial. In contrast, manufacturing companies usually produce in batches, and it is easier to track the quantity of input resources per batch.

With this general model as a foundation, we will now examine the price and quantity variances in more detail.

## Using Standard Costs—Direct Materials Variances

After determining Colonial Pewter Company's standard costs for direct materials, direct labour, and variable manufacturing overhead, Terry Sherman's next step was to compute the company's variances for June, the most recent month. As discussed in the preceding section, variances are computed by comparing standard costs with actual costs. To facilitate this comparison, Terry referred to the standard cost data contained in Exhibit 9–1. This exhibit shows that the standard cost of direct materials per unit of product is as follows:

1.25 kilograms per unit × \$8.80 per kilogram = \$11 per unit

Colonial Pewter's purchasing records for June showed that 3,000 kg of pewter were purchased at a cost of \$10.50 per kg. This cost figure included freight and handling and was net of the quantity discount. All of the material purchased was used during June to manufacture 2,000 pairs of pewter bookends. Using these data and the standard costs from Exhibit 9–1, Terry computed the price and quantity variances shown in Exhibit 9–3.

> **Learning Objective 2**
> Compute and apply the direct materials price and quantity variances, and explain their significance.

Concept 9–1

**Exhibit 9–3**
Variance Analysis—Direct Materials

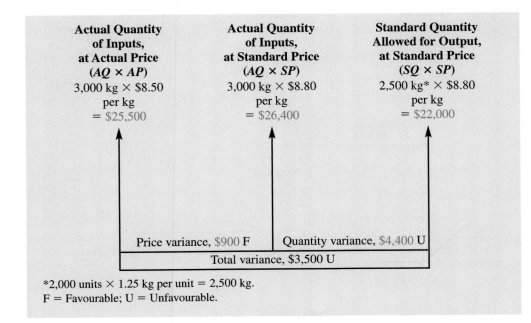

| Actual Quantity of Inputs, at Actual Price ($AQ \times AP$) | Actual Quantity of Inputs, at Standard Price ($AQ \times SP$) | Standard Quantity Allowed for Output, at Standard Price ($SQ \times SP$) |
|---|---|---|
| 3,000 kg × \$8.50 per kg = \$25,500 | 3,000 kg × \$8.80 per kg = \$26,400 | 2,500 kg* × \$8.80 per kg = \$22,000 |

Price variance, \$900 F          Quantity variance, \$4,400 U

Total variance, \$3,500 U

*2,000 units × 1.25 kg per unit = 2,500 kg.
F = Favourable; U = Unfavourable.

The three arrows in Exhibit 9–3 point to three different total cost figures. The first, $25,500, refers to the actual total cost of 3,000 kg of pewter that were purchased during June at a price of $8.50 per kilogram. The second, $26,400, refers to what the pewter would have cost had the company bought it at the standard price of $8.80 per kilogram. The difference of $900 between these two figures is the price variance, and it exists due to the difference between the actual and standard purchase prices ($0.30 × 3,000 kg = $900). Also note that because the actual price is less than the standard price, this represents a favourable (F) situation because it contributes toward an *increase* in income compared with the budget. If the actual price had been higher than the standard price, this would represent an unfavourable (U) situation because that would have contributed toward a *decrease* in income compared with the budgeted income. You can see how variance analysis shows the effect on profitability of each individual variance.

The third cost figure in Exhibit 9–3, $22,000, is the standard cost of the pewter. According to the standard cost card in Exhibit 9–1, Colonial Pewter should have consumed a total of 2,500 kg of pewter to produce 2,000 book-case ends (1.25 kg × 2,000 = 2,500 kg) at a price of $8.80 per kilogram (the figure of 2,500 kilograms is known as the standard quantity of materials allowed for the actual output of 2,000 book-case ends). Alternatively, Exhibit 9–1 suggests that the standard cost of pewter for one book-case end is $11. Therefore, the total standard cost of pewter for 2,000 book-case ends is $22,000 ($11 × 2,000). The difference of $4,400 between the second and third figures in Exhibit 9–3, ($26,400 − $22,000) is known as the quantity (or usage) variance. Note that this quantity variance arises because Colonial Pewter used 500 kg more than planned ($8.80 × 500 = $4,400). Because the company used more materials than planned, the resulting variance is unfavourable (U).

The computations in Exhibit 9–3 reflect the fact that all of the material purchased during June was also used during June. How are the variances computed if the amount of material is purchased is different from what is used? To illustrate, assume that during June, the company purchased 3,000 kilos of materials, as before, but that it used only 2,100 kg of material during the month and produced only 1,600 units. In this case, the price variance and quantity variance would be as shown in Exhibit 9–4.

**Exhibit 9–4**

Variance Analysis—Direct Materials, When the Amount Purchased Differs from the Amount Used

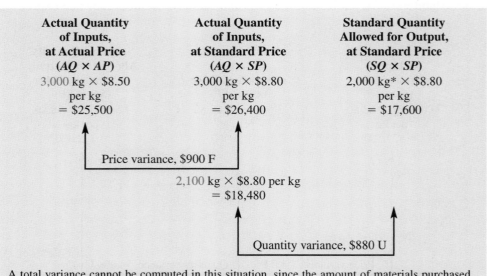

| Actual Quantity of Inputs, at Actual Price ($AQ \times AP$) | Actual Quantity of Inputs, at Standard Price ($AQ \times SP$) | Standard Quantity Allowed for Output, at Standard Price ($SQ \times SP$) |
|---|---|---|
| 3,000 kg × $8.50 per kg = $25,500 | 3,000 kg × $8.80 per kg = $26,400 | 2,000 kg* × $8.80 per kg = $17,600 |

Price variance, $900 F

2,100 kg × $8.80 per kg = $18,480

Quantity variance, $880 U

A total variance cannot be computed in this situation, since the amount of materials purchased differs from the amount used in production.

*1,600 units × 1.25 kg per unit = 2,000 kg.

Most firms compute the materials price variance when materials *are purchased*, rather than when the materials are placed into production.[2] This permits earlier isolation of the variance, since materials may remain in storage some time before being used in production.

Note from the exhibit that the price variance is computed on the entire amount of material purchased, as before, whereas the quantity variance is computed only on the portion of this material used in production during the month. A quantity variance on the 900 kg of material that was purchased during the month but *not* used in production will be computed in a future period when these materials are drawn out of inventory and used in production. The situation illustrated in Exhibit 9–4 is common in companies that purchase materials well in advance of use and store the materials in warehouses while awaiting the production process. In companies that use a just-in-time purchasing policy, there would be no difference between the quantity purchased and the quantity used.

## Materials Price Variance—A Closer Look

A **materials price variance** measures the difference between the actual price paid for a given quantity of materials and what should have been paid according to the standard set by the managers. From Exhibit 9–3, this difference can be expressed by the following formula:

$$\text{Materials price variance} = (AQ \times AP) - (AQ \times SP)$$

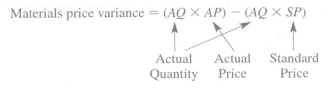

Actual Quantity    Actual Price    Standard Price

The formula can be factored into simpler form as follows:

$$\text{Materials price variance} = AQ(AP - SP)$$

Some managers prefer this simpler formula, since it permits variance computations to be made very quickly. Using the data from Exhibit 9–3 in this formula, we have the following:

$$3{,}000 \text{ kg } (\$8.50 \text{ per kilogram} - \$8.80 \text{ per kilogram}) = \$900 \text{ F}$$

Note that the answer is the same as that yielded in Exhibit 9–3. If the company wanted to put these data into a performance report, the data might appear as follows:

| | | | | | | |
|---|---|---|---|---|---|---|
| **COLONIAL PEWTER COMPANY** Performance Report—Purchasing Department | | | | | | |
| | **(1)** | **(2)** | **(3)** | **(4)** Difference in Price **(2) − (3)** | **(5)** Total Price Variance **(1) × (4)** | |
| **Item Purchased** | **Quantity Purchased** | **Actual Price** | **Standard Price** | | | **Explanation** |
| Pewter ...... | 3,000 kg | $8.50 | $8.80 | $0.30 | $900 F | Bargained for an especially favourable price |

F = Favourable; U = Unfavourable.

[2]Max Laudeman and F. W. Schaeberle, "The Cost Accounting Practices of Firms Using Standard Costs," *Cost and Management* 57, no. 4 (July–August 1983), p. 24.

**ISOLATION OF VARIANCES** At what point should variances be isolated and brought to the attention of management? The answer is, the earlier the better. The sooner deviations from standard are brought to the attention of management, the sooner problems can be evaluated and corrected.

Once a performance report has been prepared, what does management do with the price variance data? The most significant variances should be viewed as "red flags," calling attention to the fact that an exception has occurred that will require some explanation and perhaps follow-up effort. Normally, the performance report itself will contain some explanation of the reason for the variance, as shown above. In the case of Colonial Pewter Company, the purchasing manager, Janet Warner, said that the favourable price variance resulted from bargaining for an especially favourable price.

**RESPONSIBILITY FOR THE VARIANCE** Who is responsible for the materials price variance? Generally speaking, the purchasing manager has control over the price paid for goods and is therefore responsible for any price variances. Many factors influence the prices paid for goods, including how many units are ordered in a lot, how the order is delivered, whether the order is a rush order, and the quality of materials purchased. A deviation in any of these factors from what was assumed when the standards were set can result in a price variance. For example, purchase of second-grade materials, rather than top-grade materials, may result in a favourable price variance, since the lower-grade materials would generally be less costly (but perhaps less suitable for production). Although this may result in a favourable purchase price variance, it can lead to an unfavourable quantity variance, as explained later.

There may be times, however, when someone other than the purchasing manager is responsible for a materials price variance. Production may be scheduled in such a way, for example, that the purchasing manager must request express delivery. In these cases, the production manager would bear responsibility for the resulting price variances.

A word of caution is in order. Variance analysis should not be used as an excuse to conduct witch-hunts or as a means of beating line managers and workers over the head. The emphasis must be on the control function in the sense of *supporting* the line managers and *assisting* them in meeting the goals that they have participated in setting for the company. In short, the emphasis should be positive, rather than negative. Excessive dwelling on what has already happened, particularly in terms of trying to find someone to blame, can destroy morale and kill any cooperative spirit.

## Materials Quantity Variance—A Closer Look

The **materials quantity variance** measures the difference between the actual quantity of materials used in production and the quantity that should have been used according to the standard set by managers. Although the variance is concerned with the physical usage of materials, it is generally stated in dollar terms, as shown in Exhibit 9–3. The formula for the materials quantity variance is as follows:

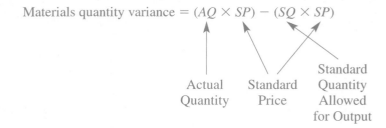

$$\text{Materials quantity variance} = (AQ \times SP) - (SQ \times SP)$$

Actual Quantity — Standard Price — Standard Quantity Allowed for Output

Again, the formula can be factored into simpler terms:

$$\text{Materials quantity variance} = SP(AQ - SQ)$$

Using the data from Exhibit 9–3 in the formula, we have the following:

$$\$8.80 \text{ per kg } (3,000 \text{ kg } - 2,500 \text{ kg*}) = \$4,400 \text{ U}$$

$$\text{*2,000 units} \times 1.25 \text{ kg per unit} = 2,500 \text{ kg.}$$

The answer, of course, is the same as that yielded in Exhibit 9–3. The data might appear as follows if a formal performance report were prepared:

| | (1) | (2) | (3) | (4) | (5) | |
|---|---|---|---|---|---|---|
| | | | | | **Total** | |
| | | | **Standard** | **Difference** | **Quantity** | |
| | **Standard** | **Actual** | **Quantity** | **in Quantity** | **Variance** | |
| **Type of Materials** | **Price** | **Quantity** | **Allowed** | **(2) − (3)** | **(1) × (4)** | **Explanation** |
| Pewter ...... | $8.80 | 3,000 kg | 2,500 kg | 500 kg | $4,400 U | Second-grade materials unsuitable for production |

**COLONIAL PEWTER COMPANY**
**Performance Report—Production Department**

F = Favourable; U = Unfavourable.

The materials quantity variance is best isolated at the time that materials are placed into production. Materials are drawn for the number of units to be produced, according to the standard bill of materials for each unit. Any additional materials are usually drawn with an excess materials requisition slip, which is different in colour from the normal requisition slips. This procedure calls attention to the excessive usage of materials *while production is still in process* and provides an opportunity for early control of any developing problem.

Excessive usage of materials can result from many factors, including faulty machines, inferior quality of materials, untrained workers, and poor supervision. Generally speaking, it is the responsibility of the production department to see that material usage is kept in line with standards. There may be times, however, when the *purchasing* department may be responsible for an unfavourable materials quantity variance. If the purchasing department obtains inferior quality materials in an effort to economize on price, the materials may be unsuitable for use and may result in excessive waste. Thus, purchasing, rather than production, would be responsible for the quantity variance. At Colonial Pewter, the production manager, Tom Kuchel, said that second-grade materials were the cause of the unfavourable materials quantity variance for June.

## Using Standard Costs—Direct Labour Variances

Terry's next step in determining Colonial Pewter's variances for June was to compute the direct labour variances for the month. Recall from Exhibit 9–1 that the standard direct labour cost per unit of product is $35, computed as follows:

$$2.5 \text{ hours per unit} \times \$14 \text{ per hour} = \$35 \text{ per unit}$$

During June, the company paid its direct labour workers $74,250, including employment taxes and fringe benefits, for 5,400 hours of work. This was an average of $13.75 per hour. Using these data and the standard costs from Exhibit 9–1, Terry computed the direct labour rate and efficiency variances that appear in Exhibit 9–5.

Note that the column headings in Exhibit 9–5 are the same as those used in the prior two exhibits, except that in Exhibit 9–5 the terms *hours* and *rate* are used in place of the terms *quantity* and *price*.

**Learning Objective 3**
Compute and apply the direct labour rate and efficiency variances and explain their significance.

Concept 9–2

**Exhibit 9–5**
Variance Analysis—Direct
Labour

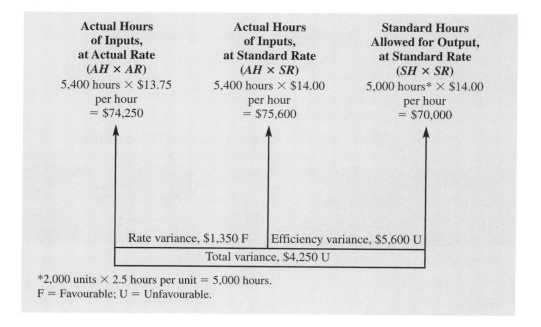

| Actual Hours of Inputs, at Actual Rate ($AH \times AR$) | Actual Hours of Inputs, at Standard Rate ($AH \times SR$) | Standard Hours Allowed for Output, at Standard Rate ($SH \times SR$) |
|---|---|---|
| 5,400 hours × $13.75 per hour = $74,250 | 5,400 hours × $14.00 per hour = $75,600 | 5,000 hours* × $14.00 per hour = $70,000 |

Rate variance, $1,350 F | Efficiency variance, $5,600 U

Total variance, $4,250 U

*2,000 units × 2.5 hours per unit = 5,000 hours.
F = Favourable; U = Unfavourable.

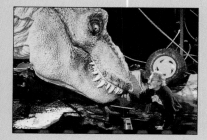

## *in business today*    Controlling the Costs of Visual Effects

Special effects, such as the computed-generated action shots of dinosaurs in Jurassic Park, are expensive to produce. A single visual effect, lasting three to seven seconds, can cost up to $50,000, and a high-profile film may contain hundreds of these shots. Since visual effects are produced under fixed-price contracts, visual-effects companies must carefully estimate their costs. Once a bid has been accepted, costs must be zealously monitored to make sure they do not spin out of control.

Buena Vista Visual Effects, a part of Walt Disney Studios, uses a standard cost system to estimate and control costs. A "storyboard" is created for each special effects shot. The storyboard sketches the visual effect, details the length of the shot, which is measured in frames (24 frames equals one second of film), and describes the work that will need to be done to create the effect. A detailed budget is then prepared using standard costs. As the project progresses, actual costs are compared with the standard cost, and significant cost overruns are investigated.

Source: Ray Scalice, "Lights! Cameras! ... Accountants," *Management Accounting,* June 1996, pp. 42–46. Reprinted with permission from *Management Accounting.*

## Labour Rate Variance—A Closer Look

As explained earlier, the price variance for direct labour is commonly termed a **labour rate variance.** This variance measures any deviation from standard in the average hourly rate paid to direct labour workers. The formula for the labour rate variance is expressed as follows:

$$\text{Labour rate variance} = (AH \times AR) - (AH \times SR)$$

Actual Hours    Actual Rate    Standard Rate

The formula can be factored into simpler form as follows:

$$\text{Labour rate variance} = AH(AR - SR)$$

Using the data from Exhibit 9–5 in the formula, we have the following:

$$5,400 \text{ hours } (\$13.75 \text{ per hour} - \$14.00 \text{ per hour}) = \$1,350 \text{ F}$$

In most firms, the rates paid to workers are quite predictable. Nevertheless, rate variances can arise through the way labour is used. Skilled workers with high hourly rates of pay may be given duties that require little skill and call for low hourly rates of pay. This will result in unfavourable labour rate variances, since the actual hourly rate of pay will exceed the standard rate specified for the particular task being performed. A reverse situation exists when unskilled or untrained workers are assigned to jobs that require some skill or training. The lower pay scale for these workers will result in favourable rate variances, although the workers may be inefficient. Finally, unfavourable rate variances can arise from overtime work at premium rates if any portion of the overtime premium is added to the direct labour account.

Who is responsible for controlling the labour rate variance? Since rate variances generally arise as a result of how labour is used, supervisors bear responsibility for seeing that labour rate variances are kept under control.

## Labour Efficiency Variance—A Closer Look

The quantity variance for direct labour, more commonly called the **labour efficiency variance,** measures the productivity of labour time. No variance is more closely watched by management, since it is widely believed that increasing the productivity of direct labour time is vital to reducing costs. This is particularly true in the case of labour-intensive operations but may not be relevant in highly automated environments. The formula for the labour efficiency variance is expressed as follows:

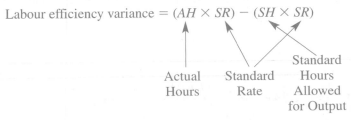

$$\text{Labour efficiency variance} = (AH \times SR) - (SH \times SR)$$

Actual Hours    Standard Rate    Standard Hours Allowed for Output

Factored into simpler terms, the formula is as follows:

$$\text{Labour efficiency variance} = SR(AH - SH)$$

Using the data from Exhibit 9–5 in the formula, we have the following:

$$\$14.00 \text{ per hour } (5,400 \text{ hours} - 5,000 \text{ hours*}) = \$5,600 \text{ U}$$

*2,000 units × 2.5 hours per unit = 5,000 hours.

Possible causes of an unfavourable labour efficiency variance include poorly trained or motivated workers; poor quality materials, requiring more labour time in processing; faulty equipment, causing breakdowns and work interruptions; poor supervision of workers; and inaccurate standards. The managers in charge of production would generally be responsible for control of the labour efficiency variance. However, the variance might be chargeable to purchasing if the acquisition of poor materials resulted in excessive labour processing time.

When the labour force is essentially fixed in the short term, another important cause of an unfavourable labour efficiency variance is insufficient demand for the output of the factory. In some firms, the actual labour-hours worked is basically fixed—particularly in the short term. It is difficult, and perhaps even unwise, to constantly adjust the workforce in response to changes in the work load. Therefore, the only way a work centre manager can avoid an unfavourable labour efficiency variance in such firms is by keeping everyone busy all of the time. The option of reducing the number of workers on hand is not available.

Thus, if customer orders are insufficient to keep the workers busy, the work centre manager has two options—either accept an unfavourable labour efficiency variance or build inventory.[3] A central lesson of just-in-time (JIT) is that building inventory with no immediate prospect of sale is a bad idea. Inventory—particularly work in process inventory—can lead to high defect rates, obsolete goods, and generally inefficient operations. As a consequence, when the workforce is basically fixed in the short term, managers must be cautious about how labour efficiency variances are used. Some managers advocate dispensing with labour efficiency variances entirely in such situations—at least for the purposes of motivating and controlling workers on the shop floor.

## *decision* | *maker*

### Department Resources Manager

You are the manager of the computer-generated special effects department for a company that produces special effects for high-profile films. You receive a copy of this month's performance report for your department and discover a large labour efficiency variance that is unfavourable. What factors might have contributed to this unfavourable variance?

## Using Standard Costs—Variable Overhead Variances

**Learning Objective 4**

Compute the variable overhead spending and efficiency variances.

The final step in Terry's analysis of Colonial Pewter's variances for June was to compute the variable manufacturing overhead variances. The variable portion of manufacturing overhead can be analyzed using the same basic formulas that are used to analyze direct materials and direct labour. Recall from Exhibit 9–1 that the standard variable manufacturing overhead is $7.50 per unit of product, computed as follows:

$$2.5 \text{ hours per unit} \times \$3 \text{ per hour} = \$7.50 \text{ per unit}$$

Colonial Pewter's cost records showed that the total actual variable manufacturing overhead cost for June was $15,390. Recall from the earlier discussion of the direct labour variances that 5,400 hours of direct labour time were recorded during the month and that the company produced 2,000 pairs of bookends. Terry's analysis of this overhead data appears in Exhibit 9–6.

**Exhibit 9–6**

Variance Analysis—Variable Manufacturing Overhead

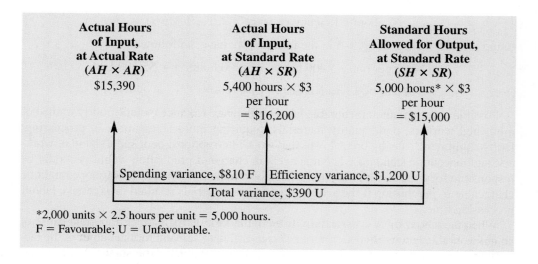

*2,000 units × 2.5 hours per unit = 5,000 hours.
F = Favourable; U = Unfavourable.

---

[3]For further discussion, see Eliyahu M. Goldratt and Jeff Cox, *The Goal*, 2nd rev. ed. (Croton-on-Hudson, NY: North River Press, 1992).

Note the similarities between Exhibits 9–5 and 9–6. These similarities arise from the fact that direct labour-hours are being used as a base for allocating overhead cost to units of product; thus, the same hourly figures appear in Exhibit 9–6 for variable manufacturing overhead as in Exhibit 9–5 for direct labour. The main difference between the two exhibits is in the standard hourly rate being used, which in this company is much lower for variable overhead.

Our example in this chapter uses direct labour as the only base to allocate overhead. Using a single allocation base certainly makes the variance computations much simpler. However, information about the variable overhead variances may not be very useful to managers, particularly if direct labour is not a representative allocation base. Using activity cost pools as in activity-based costing will require managers to establish standards for the different allocation bases corresponding to the activity cost pools and to track the information required to compute variances pertaining to the different allocation bases.

## Overhead Variances—A Closer Look

The formula for the **variable overhead spending variance** is expressed as follows:

$$\text{Variable overhead spending variance} = (AH \times AR) - (AH \times SR)$$

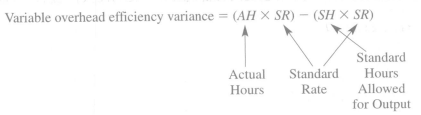

| Actual | Actual | Standard |
| Hours | Rate | Rate |

Or, factored into simpler terms:

$$\text{Variable overhead spending variance} = AH(AR - SR)$$

Using the data from Exhibit 9–6 in the formula, we have the following:

$$5{,}400 \text{ hours } (\$2.85 \text{ per hour*} - \$3 \text{ per hour}) = \$810 \text{ F}$$

*$15,390 ÷ 5,400 hours = $2.85 per hour.

The formula for the **variable overhead efficiency variance** is expressed as follows:

$$\text{Variable overhead efficiency variance} = (AH \times SR) - (SH \times SR)$$

| Actual | Standard | Standard |
| Hours | Rate | Hours |
| | | Allowed |
| | | for Output |

Or, factored into simpler terms:

$$\text{Variable overhead efficiency variance} = SR(AH - SH)$$

Again using the data from Exhibit 9–6, the computation of the variance would be as follows:

$$\$3.00 \text{ per hour } (5{,}400 \text{ hours} - 5{,}000 \text{ hours*}) = \$1{,}200 \text{ U}$$

*2,000 units × 2.5 hours per unit = 5,000 hours.

We will reserve further discussion of the variable overhead spending and efficiency variances until the next chapter, where overhead analysis is discussed in depth.

Before proceeding further, it might be useful to summarize the standard and actual costs and the variances for Colonial Pewter Company; this is done in Exhibit 9–7. Comparing the total actual and standard costs for 2,000 units simply tells us that Colonial incurred an additional cost of $8,140 (>7.6% of standard cost). The numbers in Exhibit 9–7 clearly indicate that the cost increase was due to excess usage of the two inputs: direct

**Exhibit 9–7**

Summary of Standard Costs and Variances for Colonial Pewter Company

| | Direct Materials | Direct Labour | Variable Overhead | Total |
|---|---|---|---|---|
| Standard cost/unit . . . . . . . . . . . . . | $11.00 | $35.00 | $7.50 | $53.50 |
| Standard cost/2,000 units . . . . . . . . | $22,000 | $70,000 | $15,000 | $107,000 |
| Actual cost/2,000 units . . . . . . . . . | $25,500 | $74,250 | $15,390 | $115,140 |
| Price-related variance . . . . . . . . . . | $900 F | $1,350 F | $810 F | $3,060 F |
| Quantity-related variance . . . . . . . . | $4,400 U | $5,600 U | $1,200 U | $11,200 U |
| Total variance . . . . . . . . . . . . . . . . | $3,500 U | $4,250 U | $390 U | $8,140 U |

materials and direct labour. Remember that variable overhead is allocated using direct labour as the base; therefore, the variable overhead efficiency variance is a result of the additional labour hours. Note also that managers at Colonial were able to acquire all three inputs at lower than the standard prices. It may be useful to examine the implications of variances in a little more detail.

**MANAGERIAL ACCOUNTING IN ACTION**

**The Wrap-Up**

In preparation for the scheduled meeting to discuss his analysis of Colonial Pewter's standard costs and variances, Terry distributed Exhibits 9–1 through 9–7, with supporting explanations, to the management group of Colonial Pewter. This included J. D. Wriston, the president of the company; Tom Kuchel, the production manager; and Janet Warner, the purchasing manager. J. D. Wriston opened the meeting with the following question:

*J. D.:* Terry, I think I understand the report you distributed, but just to make sure, would you mind summarizing the highlights of what you found?

*Terry:* As you can see, the biggest problems are the unfavourable materials quantity variance of $4,400 and the unfavourable labour efficiency variance of $5,600.

*J. D.:* Tom, you're the production boss. What do you think is responsible for the unfavourable labour efficiency variance?

*Tom:* It pretty much has to be the new production workers. Our experienced workers shouldn't have much problem meeting the standard of 2.5 hours per unit. We all knew that there would be some inefficiency for a while as we brought new people on board.

*J. D.:* No one is disputing that, Tom. However, $5,600 is a lot of money. Is this problem likely to go away very soon?

*Tom:* I hope so. If we were to contrast the last two weeks of June with the first two weeks, I'm sure we would see some improvement.

*J. D.:* I don't want to beat up on you, Tom, but this is a significant problem. Can you do something to accelerate the training process?

*Tom:* Sure. I could pair up each of the new guys with one of our old-timers and have them work together for a while. It would slow down our older guys a bit, but I'll bet the new workers would learn a lot.

*J. D.:* Let's try it. Now, what about that $4,400 unfavourable materials quantity variance?

*Tom:* Are you asking me?

*J. D.:* Well, I would like someone to explain it.

*Tom:* Don't look at me. It's that iron-contaminated pewter that Janet bought on her "special deal."

*Janet:* We got rid of that stuff months ago.

*J. D.:* Hold your horses. We're not trying to figure out who to blame here. I just want to understand what happened. If we can understand what happened, maybe we can fix it.

*Terry:* Tom, are the new workers generating a lot of scrap?

*Tom:* Yeah, I guess so.

*J. D.:* I think that could be part of the problem. Can you do anything about it?

*Tom:* I can watch the scrap real closely for a few days to see where it's being generated. If it is the new workers, I can have the old-timers work with them on the problem when I team them up.

*J. D.:* Good. Let's reconvene in a few weeks and see what has happened. Hopefully, we can get those unfavourable variances under control.

# Variance Analysis and Management by Exception

The budgets and standard costs discussed in this and the preceding chapters reflect management's plans. If actual performance is close to the plans, there is little cause for immediate worry. What is important in such a context is to examine the standards (and budgets). Organizations that embrace lean business practices continuously look for ways to improve; a significant benefit of improvements is that they can result in reducing the level of input resources required by the organization (e.g., less materials, labour, and overhead). Any reduction in input requirements will directly impact standard costs; organizations must revise the standard costs to reflect such improvements.

What happens when actual results are different from the plan? More often than not, actual results *are* different from the plan, which means that management often ends up investigating the variances. However, are all variances worth investigating? The answer is no. Variances almost always occur because plans are prepared on the basis of certain assumptions that may not hold. Also, there are unforeseen events that one simply cannot consider during planning (economic downturns or upturns, natural or man-made disasters, exchange rate fluctuations, and so on).

How should managers decide which variances are worth investigating? One clue is the size of the variance either in absolute dollar figures or as percentage figures. For example, it is simply not worth management's time to spend time on a 0.5% variance from the standard. This is where the concept of *management by exception* is useful. Simply put, **management by exception** is a management philosophy where a manager directs attention toward those parts of the organization where the variances are significant (say, 5% or more, or $5,000 or more). By focusing on the more significant variances, managers can hope to achieve significant gains from any improvements. Investigating a direct materials quantity variance of $500 is a mere waste of time when the total materials consumed cost over $1,000,000 during a given period. Time spent on investigating small variances often means that other (sometimes larger) variances may be neglected.

In addition to watching for large variances, managers must also pay attention to the pattern of variances. For example, if the labour efficiency variance is steadily increasing period after period, that should trigger an investigation, even though none of the variances is large enough by itself to warrant investigation. Timely attention to the pattern of variances can help in arresting the situation before problems get out of hand. For example, a rising trend of materials quantity and labour efficiency variances may suggest the existence of problems with the process or equipment used, which need to be looked into. In summary, variance analysis is a useful tool for managers and facilitates management by exception.

# Evaluation of Controls Based on Standard Costs

## Advantages of Standard Costs

Standard cost systems have a number of advantages.

1.  As stated earlier, the use of standard costs is a key element in a management by exception approach. So long as costs remain within the standards, managers can focus on other issues. When costs fall significantly outside the standards, managers are alerted that there may be problems requiring attention. This approach helps managers focus on important issues.

2. So long as standards are viewed by employees as being reasonable, they can promote economy and efficiency. They provide benchmarks that individuals can use to judge their own performance.
3. Standard costs can greatly simplify bookkeeping. Instead of recording actual costs for each job, the standard costs for materials, labour, and overhead can be charged to jobs.
4. Standard costs fit naturally in an integrated system of "responsibility accounting." The standards establish what costs should be, who should be responsible for them, and whether actual costs are under control.

## Potential Problems with the Use of Standard Costs

The use of standard costs can present a number of potential problems. Most of these problems result from improper use of standard costs and the management by exception principle or from using standard costs in situations in which they are not appropriate.

1. Standard cost variance reports are usually prepared on a monthly basis and often are released days or even weeks after the end of the month. As a consequence, the information in the reports may be so stale that it is almost useless. Timely, frequent reports that are approximately correct are better than infrequent reports that are very precise but out of date by the time they are released. Some companies are now reporting variances and other key operating data daily or even more frequently.
2. If managers are insensitive and use variance reports as a club, morale may suffer. Employees should receive positive reinforcement for work well done. Management by exception, by its nature, tends to focus on the negative. If variances are used as a club, subordinates may be tempted to cover up unfavourable variances or take actions that are not in the best interests of the company to make sure the variances are favourable. For example, workers may put on a crash effort to increase output at the end of the month to avoid an unfavourable labour efficiency variance. In the rush to produce output, quality may suffer.
3. Labour quantity standards and efficiency variances make two important assumptions. First, they assume that the production process is labour-paced; if labour works faster, output will go up. However, output in many companies is no longer determined by how fast labour works; rather, it is determined by the processing speed of machines. Second, the computations assume that labour is a variable cost. However, direct labour may be essentially fixed. If labour is fixed, then an undue emphasis on labour efficiency variances creates pressure to build excess work in process and finished goods inventories.
4. In some cases, a "favourable" variance can be as bad or worse than an "unfavourable" variance. For example, McDonald's has a standard for the amount of hamburger meat that should be in a Big Mac. A "favourable" variance means that less meat was used than the standard specifies. The result is a substandard Big Mac and possibly a dissatisfied customer.
5. There may be a tendency with standard cost reporting systems to emphasize meeting the standards to the exclusion of other important objectives, such as maintaining and improving quality, on-time delivery, and customer satisfaction. This tendency can be reduced by using supplemental performance measures that focus on these other objectives (this is discussed in Chapter 11).
6. Just meeting standards may not be sufficient; continual improvement may be necessary to survive in the current competitive environment. For this reason, some companies focus on the trends in the standard cost variances—aiming for continual improvement, rather than just meeting the standards. In other companies, engineered standards are being replaced either by a rolling average of actual costs, which is expected to decline, or by very challenging target costs.

In sum, managers should exercise considerable care in their use of a standard cost system. It is particularly important that managers go out of their way to focus on the positive, rather than just on the negative, and to be aware of possible unintended consequences.

# Summary

**LO1    Explain how direct materials standards and direct labour standards are set.**
Each direct cost has both a price and a quantity standard. The standard price for an input is the price that should be paid for a single unit of the input. In the case of direct materials, the price should include shipping and receiving costs and should be net of quantity and other discounts. In the case of direct labour, the standard rate should include wages, fringe benefits, and employment taxes.

**LO2    Compute and apply the direct materials price and quantity variances and explain their significance.**
The materials price variance is the difference between the actual price paid for materials and the standard price, multiplied by the quantity purchased. An unfavourable variance occurs whenever the actual price exceeds the standard price. A favourable variance occurs when the actual price is less than the standard price for the input.

The materials quantity variance is the difference between the amount of materials actually used and the amount that should have been used to produce the actual good output of the period, multiplied by the standard price per unit of the input. An unfavourable materials quantity variance occurs when the amount of materials actually used exceeds the amount that should have been used according to the materials quantity standard. A favourable variance occurs when the amount of materials actually used is less than the amount that should have been used according to the standard.

**LO3    Compute and apply the direct labour rate and efficiency variances and explain their significance.**
The direct labour rate variance is the difference between the actual wage rate paid and the standard wage rate, multiplied by the hours worked. An unfavourable variance occurs whenever the actual wage rate exceeds the standard wage rate. A favourable variance occurs when the actual wage rate is less than the standard wage rate.

The labour efficiency variance is the difference between the hours actually worked and the hours that should have been used to produce the actual good output of the period, multiplied by the standard wage rate. An unfavourable labour efficiency variance occurs when the hours actually worked exceed the hours allowed for the actual output. A favourable variance occurs when the hours actually worked are less than hours allowed for the actual output.

**LO4    Compute the variable overhead spending and efficiency variances.**
The variable overhead spending variance is the difference between the actual variable overhead cost incurred and the actual hours worked multiplied by the variable overhead rate. The variable overhead efficiency variance is the difference between the hours actually worked and the hours that should have been used to produce the actual good output of the period, multiplied by the standard variable overhead rate.

# Guidance Answers to You Decide and Decision Maker

**HOCKEY COACH** (p. 333)
NHL records would be similar to ideal standards. They call for levels of effort and skill that have been attained only by professional baseball players under the best circumstances. Even though such standards might have a motivational value to professional hockey players, they would probably tend to discourage the players on your team if you told them that they needed to meet those expectations to receive recognition.

Practical standards are tight but can be attained through reasonable, though highly efficient, efforts by the average worker. Practical standards might motivate your players to do their best on the field and might help you identify problems requiring additional coaching or practice. Given the differing athletic abilities and skill levels among the players on your team, it might be best to start with each player's statistics from last season and then make adjustments to create benchmarks for each player.

After acknowledging your gratitude for the parent's interest in the team, you might remind the parents that the kids are playing on the team to have fun and develop their skills and self-confidence. Then, after explaining the pros and cons of each of the two types of standards, you can address how you set benchmarks for the players.

**DEPARTMENT RESOURCES MANAGER** (p. 346)
An unfavourable labour efficiency variance in the computer-generated special effects department might have been caused by inexperienced, poorly trained, or unmotivated employees, faulty hardware and/or

software that may have caused work interruptions, and/or poor supervision of the employees in this department. In addition, it is possible that there was insufficient demand for the output of this department—resulting in idle time—or that the standard (or benchmark) for this department is inaccurate.

# Review Problem: Standard Costs

Xavier Company produces a single product. Variable manufacturing overhead is applied to products on the basis of direct labour-hours. The standard costs for one unit of product are as follows:

| | |
|---|---|
| Direct material: 6 grams at $0.50 per gram ............................ | $ 3 |
| Direct labour: 1.8 hours at $10 per hour ............................. | 18 |
| Variable manufacturing overhead: 1.8 hours at $5 per hour ............... | 9 |
| Total standard variable cost per unit ................................. | $30 |

During June, 2,000 units were produced. The costs associated with June's operations were as follows:

| | |
|---|---|
| Material purchased: 18,000 grams at $0.60 per gram ................. | $10,800 |
| Material used in production: 14,000 grams ......................... | — |
| Direct labour: 4,000 hours at $9.75 per hour ....................... | 39,000 |
| Variable manufacturing overhead costs incurred ..................... | 20,800 |

*Required:*
Compute the materials, labour, and variable manufacturing overhead variances.

*SOLUTION TO THE REVIEW PROBLEM*

**Materials Variances**

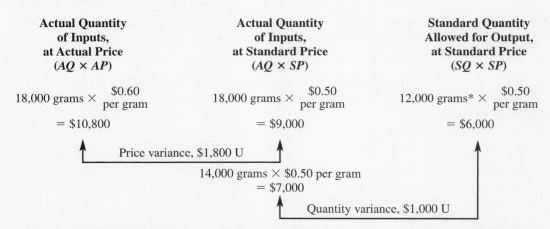

A total variance cannot be computed in this situation, since the amount of materials purchased (18,000 grams) differs from the amount of materials used in production (14,000 grams).
   *2,000 units × 6 grams per unit = 12,000 grams.

Using the formulas in the chapter, the same variances would be computed as:

$$\text{Materials price variance} = AQ(AP - SP)$$
$$18{,}000 \text{ grams } (\$0.60 \text{ per gram} - \$0.50 \text{ per gram}) = \$1{,}800 \text{ U}$$

$$\text{Materials quantity variance} = SP(AQ - SQ)$$
$$\$0.50 \text{ per gram } (14{,}000 \text{ grams} - 12{,}000 \text{ grams}) = \$1{,}000 \text{ U}$$

**Labour Variances**

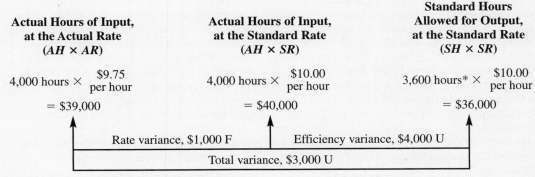

$$\text{4,000 hours} \times \frac{\$9.75}{\text{per hour}} \qquad \text{4,000 hours} \times \frac{\$10.00}{\text{per hour}} \qquad \text{3,600 hours*} \times \frac{\$10.00}{\text{per hour}}$$

= \$39,000      = \$40,000      = \$36,000

Rate variance, \$1,000 F     Efficiency variance, \$4,000 U

Total variance, \$3,000 U

*2,000 units × 1.8 hours per unit = 3,600 hours.

Using the formulas in the chapter, the same variances would be computed as:

$$\text{Labour rate variance} = AH(AR - SR)$$
$$\text{4,000 hours (\$9.75 per hour} - \text{\$10.00 per hour)} = \$1,000 \text{ F}$$

$$\text{Labour efficiency variance} = SR(AH - SH)$$
$$\text{\$10.00 per hour (4,000 hours} - \text{3,600 hours)} = \$4,000 \text{ U}$$

**Variable Manufacturing Overhead Variances**

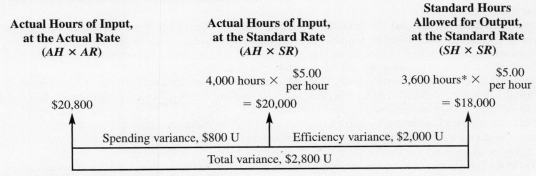

$$\text{4,000 hours} \times \frac{\$5.00}{\text{per hour}} \qquad \text{3,600 hours*} \times \frac{\$5.00}{\text{per hour}}$$

\$20,800      = \$20,000      = \$18,000

Spending variance, \$800 U     Efficiency variance, \$2,000 U

Total variance, \$2,800 U

*2,000 units × 1.8 hours per unit = 3,600 hours.

Using the formulas in the chapter, the same variances would be computed as:

$$\text{Variable overhead spending variance} = AH(AR - SR)$$
$$\text{4,000 hours (\$5.20 per hour*} - \text{\$5.00 per hour)} = \$800 \text{ U}$$

$$\text{*\$20,800} \div \text{4,000 hours} = \$5.20 \text{ per hour.}$$

$$\text{Variable overhead efficiency variance} = SR(AH - SH)$$
$$\text{\$5.00 per hour (4,000 hours} - \text{3,600 hours)} = \$2,000 \text{ U}$$

# Glossary

**Bill of materials** A listing of the quantity of each type of material required to manufacture a unit of product. (p. 335)

**Ideal standards** Standards that allow for no machine breakdowns or other work interruptions and that require peak efficiency at all times. (p. 333)

**Labour efficiency variance** A measure of the difference between the actual hours taken to complete a task and the standard hours allowed, multiplied by the standard hourly labour rate. (p. 345)

**Labour rate variance** A measure of the difference between the actual hourly labour rate and the standard rate, multiplied by the number of hours worked during the period. (p. 344)

**Management by exception** A system of management in which standards are set for various operating activities, with actual results then compared with these standards. Any differences that are deemed significant are brought to the attention of management as "exceptions." (p. 349)

**Materials price variance** A measure of the difference between the actual unit price paid for an item and the standard price, multiplied by the quantity purchased. (p. 341)

**Materials quantity variance** A measure of the difference between the actual quantity of materials used in production and the standard quantity allowed, multiplied by the standard price per unit of materials. (p. 342)

**Practical standards** Standards that allow for normal machine downtime and other work interruptions and that can be attained through reasonable, though highly efficient, efforts by the average worker. (p. 333)

**Standard cost** Computed by standard quantity of input multiplied by the standard price of the input required to produce one unit of product or provide one unit of service to a customer. (p. 332)

**Standard cost card** A detailed listing of the standard amounts of materials, labour, and overhead that should go into a unit of product, multiplied by the standard price or rate that has been set for each cost element. (p. 333)

**Standard cost per unit** The standard cost of a unit of product as shown on the standard cost card; it is computed by multiplying the standard quantity or hours by the standard price or rate for each cost element. (p. 337)

**Standard hours allowed** The time that should have been taken to complete the period's output as computed by multiplying the actual number of units produced by the standard hours per unit. (p. 338)

**Standard hours per unit** The amount of labour time that should be required to complete a single unit of product, including allowances for breaks, machine downtime, cleanup, rejects, and other normal inefficiencies. (p. 336)

**Standard price per unit** The price that should be paid for a single unit of materials, including allowances for quality, quantity purchased, shipping, receiving, and other such costs, net of any discounts allowed. (p. 334)

**Standard quantity allowed** The amount of materials that should have been used to complete the period's output as computed by multiplying the actual number of units produced by the standard quantity per unit. (p. 338)

**Standard quantity per unit** The amount of materials that should be required to complete a single unit of product, including allowances for normal waste, spoilage, rejects, and similar inefficiencies. (p. 335)

**Standard rate per hour** The labour rate that should be incurred per hour of labour time, including employment taxes, fringe benefits, and other such labour costs. (p. 335)

**Variable overhead efficiency variance** The difference between the actual activity (direct labour-hours, machine-hours, or some other base) of a period and the standard activity allowed, multiplied by the variable part of the predetermined overhead rate. (p. 347)

**Variable overhead spending variance** The difference between the actual variable overhead cost incurred during a period and the standard cost that should have been incurred based on the actual activity of the period. (p. 347)

**Variance** The difference between standard prices and quantities on the one hand and actual prices and quantities on the other hand. (p. 337)

# Questions

**9–1**  What is a quantity standard? What is a price standard?

**9–2**  Distinguish between ideal and practical standards.

**9–3**  What is meant by the term *variance*?

**9–4**  What is meant by the term *management by exception*?

**9–5**  Who is generally responsible for the materials price variance? The materials quantity variance? The labour efficiency variance?

**9–6**  The materials price variance can be computed at what two different points in time? Which point is better? Why?

**9–7**  What dangers lie in using standards as punitive tools?

**9–8**  What effect, if any, would you expect poor quality materials to have on direct labour variances?

**9–9**  If variable manufacturing overhead is applied to production on the basis of direct labour-hours and the direct labour efficiency variance is unfavourable, will the variable overhead efficiency variance be favourable or unfavourable, or could it be either? Explain.

**9–10**  Why can undue emphasis on labour efficiency variances lead to excess work in process inventories?

# Brief Exercises

**BRIEF EXERCISE 9–1  Setting Standards (LO1)**

Victoria Chocolates, Ltd. makes premium handcrafted chocolate confections in London. The owner of the company is setting up a standard cost system and has collected the following data for one of the company's products, the Empire Truffle. This product is made with the finest white chocolate and various fillings. The data below pertain only to the white chocolate used in the product:

| | |
|---|---|
| Material requirements, kilograms of white chocolate per dozen truffles .. | 0.70 kilogram |
| Allowance for waste, kilograms of white chocolate per dozen truffles ... | 0.03 kilogram |
| Allowance for rejects, kilograms of white chocolate per dozen truffles .. | 0.02 kilogram |
| Purchase price, finest grade white chocolate ...................... | £7.50 per kilogram |
| Purchase discount ................................ | 8% of purchase price |
| Shipping cost from the supplier in Belgium ....................... | £0.30 per kilogram |
| Receiving and handling cost .................................... | £0.04 per kilogram |

*Required:*
1. Determine the standard price of a kilogram of white chocolate.
2. Determine the standard quantity of white chocolate for a dozen truffles.
3. Determine the standard cost of the white chocolate in a dozen truffles.

### BRIEF EXERCISE 9–2   Materials Variance (LO2)
Bandar Industries Berhad of Malaysia manufactures sporting equipment. One of the company's products, a football helmet for the North American market, requires a special plastic. During the quarter ending June 30, the company manufactured 35,000 helmets, using 22,500 kilograms of plastic in the process. The plastic cost the company RM 171,000. (The currency in Malaysia is the ringgit, which is denoted here by RM.)

According to the standard cost card, each helmet should require 0.6 kilograms of plastic, at a cost of RM 8 per kilogram.

*Required:*
1. What cost for plastic should have been incurred in the manufacture of the 35,000 helmets? How much greater or less is this than the cost that was incurred?
2. Break down the difference computed in (1) above into a materials price variance and a materials quantity variance.

### BRIEF EXERCISE 9–3   Direct Labour Variances (LO3)
SkyChefs, Inc. prepares in-flight meals for a number of major airlines. One of the company's products is grilled salmon in dill sauce with baby new potatoes and spring vegetables. During the most recent week, the company prepared 4,000 of these meals using 960 direct labour-hours. The company paid these direct labour workers a total of $9,600 for this work, or $10 per hour.

According to the standard cost card for this meal, it should require 0.25 direct labour-hours at a cost of $9.75 per hour.

*Required:*
1. What direct labour cost should have been incurred to prepare the 4,000 meals? How much greater or less is this than the direct labour cost that was incurred?
2. Break down the difference computed in (1) above into a labour rate variance and a labour efficiency variance.

### BRIEF EXERCISE 9–4   Variable Overhead Variances (LO4)
Logistics Solutions provides order fulfillment services for dot.com merchants. The company maintains warehouses that stock items carried by its dot.com clients. When a client receives an order from a customer, the order is forwarded to Logistics Solutions, which pulls the item from storage, packs it, and ships it to the customer. The company uses a predetermined variable overhead rate based on direct labour-hours.

In the most recent month, 120,000 items were shipped to customers using 2,300 direct labour-hours. The company incurred a total of $7,360 in variable overhead costs.

According to the company's standards, 0.02 direct labour-hour is required to fulfill an order for one item and the variable overhead rate is $3.25 per direct labour-hour.

*Required:*
1. What variable overhead cost should have been incurred to fill the orders for the 120,000 items? How much greater or less is this than the variable overhead cost that was incurred?
2. Break down the difference computed in (1) above into a variable overhead spending variance and a variable overhead efficiency variance.

**BRIEF EXERCISE 9–5    Recording Variances in the General Ledger** (LO5)

(Appendix 9A) Bliny Corporation makes a product with the following standard costs for direct material and direct labour:

| | |
|---|---|
| Direct material: 2.00 metres at $3.25 per metre ...................... | $6.50 |
| Direct labour: 0.40 hours at $12.00 per hour .......................... | $4.80 |

During the most recent month, 5,000 units were produced. The costs associated with the month's production of this product were as follows:

| | |
|---|---|
| Material purchased: 12,000 metres at $3.15 per metre ................. | $37,800 |
| Material used in production: 10,500 metres ......................... | — |
| Direct labour: 1,975 hours at $12.20 per hour ....................... | $24,095 |

The standard cost variances for direct material and direct labour have been computed to be:

| | |
|---|---|
| Materials price variance: 12,000 metres at $0.10 per metre F ........... | $1,200 F |
| Materials quantity variance: 500 metres at $3.25 per metre U .......... | $1,625 U |
| Labour rate variance: 1,975 hours at $0.20 per hour U ................ | $395 U |
| Labour efficiency variance: 25 hours at $12.00 per hour F ............. | $300 F |

*Required:*
1. Prepare the general ledger entry to record the purchase of materials on account for the month.
2. Prepare the general ledger entry to record the use of materials for the month.
3. Prepare the general ledger entry to record the incurrence of direct labour cost for the month.

# Exercises

**EXERCISE 9–1    Setting Standards; Preparing a Standard Cost Card** (LO1)

Martin Company manufactures a powerful cleaning solvent. The main ingredient in the solvent is a raw material called Echol. Information on the purchase and use of Echol follows:

*Purchase of Echol*    Echol is purchased in 60-litre containers at a cost of $115 per container. A discount of 2% is offered by the supplier for payment within 10 days, and Martin Company takes all discounts. Shipping costs, which Martin Company must pay, amount to $130 for an average shipment of 100 sixty-litre containers of Echol.

*Use of Echol*    The bill of materials calls for 7.6 litres of Echol per bottle of cleaning solvent. About 5% of all Echol used is lost through spillage or evaporation (the 7.6 litres above is the *actual* content per bottle). In addition, statistical analysis has shown that every 41st bottle is rejected at final inspection because of contamination.

*Required:*
1. Compute the standard purchase price for one litre of Echol.
2. Compute the standard quantity of Echol (in litres) per saleable bottle of cleaning solvent.
3. Using the data from (1) and (2) above, prepare a standard cost card showing the standard cost of Echol per bottle of cleaning solvent.

**EXERCISE 9–2    Material and Labour Variances** (LO2, LO3)

Huron Company produces a commercial cleaning compound known as Zoom. The direct materials and direct labour standards for one unit of Zoom are given below:

| | Standard Quantity or Hours | Standard Price or Rate | Standard Cost |
|---|---|---|---|
| Direct materials .......... | 2.1 kilograms | $ 5.50 per kilogram | $11.55 |
| Direct labour ............. | 0.2 hour | 12.00 per hour | 2.40 |

During the most recent month, the following activity was recorded:
a.  Nine thousand kilograms of material were purchased at a cost of $5.20 per kilogram.
b.  All of the material purchased was used to produce 4,000 units of Zoom.
c.  A total of 750 hours of direct labour time was recorded at a total labour cost of $10,425.

*Required:*
1.  Compute the direct materials price and quantity variances for the month.
2.  Compute the direct labour rate and efficiency variances for the month.

## EXERCISE 9–3   Material Variances (LO2)

Refer to the data in Exercise 9–2. Assume that instead of producing 4,000 units during the month, the company produced only 3,000 units, using 6,700 kilograms of material in the production process. (The rest of the material purchased remained in inventory.)

*Required:*
Compute the direct materials price and quantity variances for the month.

## EXERCISE 9–4   Labour and Variable Overhead Variances (LO3, LO4)

Erie Company manufactures a small cassette player called the Jogging Mate. The company uses standards to control its costs. The labour standards that have been set for one Jogging Mate cassette player are as follows:

| Standard Hours | Standard Rate per Hour | Standard Cost |
|---|---|---|
| 18 minutes | $12.00 | $3.60 |

During August, 5,750 hours of direct labour time were recorded in the manufacture of 20,000 units of the Jogging Mate. The direct labour cost totalled $73,600 for the month.

*Required:*
1.  What direct labour cost should have been incurred in the manufacture of the 20,000 units of the Jogging Mate? By how much does this differ from the cost that was incurred?
2.  Break down the difference in cost from (1) above into a labour rate variance and a labour efficiency variance.
3.  The budgeted variable manufacturing overhead rate is $4 per direct labour-hour. During August, the company incurred $21,850 in variable manufacturing overhead cost. Compute the variable overhead spending and efficiency variances for the month.

## EXERCISE 9–5   Materials and Labour Variances (LO2, LO3)

Dawson Toys, Ltd. produces a toy called the Maze. The company has recently established a standard cost system to help control costs and has established the following standards for the Maze toy:

Direct materials: 6 microns per toy at $0.50 per micron
Direct labour: 1.3 hours per toy at $8 per hour

During July, the company produced 3,000 Maze toys. Production data for the month on the toy follow:

Direct materials: 25,000 microns were purchased for use in production at a cost of $0.48 per micron. Some 5,000 of these microns were still in inventory at the end of the month.
Direct labour: 4,000 direct labour-hours were worked at a cost of $36,000.

*Required:*
1.  Compute the following variances for July:
    a.  Direct materials price and quantity variances.
    b.  Direct labour rate and efficiency variances.
2.  Prepare a brief explanation of the significance and possible causes of each variance.

## EXERCISE 9–6   Material and Labour Variances; Journal Entries (LO2, LO3, LO5)

(Appendix 9A) Genola Fashions began production of a new product on June 1. The company uses a standard cost system and has established the following standards for one unit of the new product:

| | Standard Quantity or Hours | Standard Price or Rate | Standard Cost |
|---|---|---|---|
| Direct materials . . . . . . . . . . . | 7.0 feet | $5 per foot | $35.00 |
| Direct labour . . . . . . . . . . . . | 1.6 hours | 8 per hour | 12.80 |

During June, the following activity was recorded relative to the new product:

a. Purchasing acquired 30,000 feet of material at a cost of $4.60 per foot.

b. Production used 24,000 feet of the material to manufacture 3,000 units of the new product.

c. Production reported 5,000 hours of labour time worked directly on the new product; the cost of this labour time was $43,000.

***Required:***

1. For materials:
   a. Compute the direct materials price and quantity variances.
   b. Prepare journal entries to record the purchase of materials and the use of materials in production.
2. For direct labour:
   a. Compute the direct labour rate and efficiency variances.
   b. Prepare a journal entry to record the incurrence of direct labour cost for the month.
3. Post the entries you have prepared to the following T-accounts:

| Raw Materials | | Accounts Payable |
|---|---|---|
| ? | ? | 138,000 |
| Bal.  ? | | |

| Materials Price Variance | | Wages Payable |
|---|---|---|
| | | 43,000 |

| Materials Quantity Variance | | Labour Rate Variance |
|---|---|---|
| | | |

| Work in Process | | Labour Efficiency Variance |
|---|---|---|
| Materials used   ? | | |
| Labour cost       ? | | |

# Problems

**PROBLEM 9–1    Variance Analysis in a Hospital (LO2, LO3, LO4)**

John Fleming, chief administrator for a district hospital, is concerned about costs for tests in the hospital's lab. Mr. Fleming has asked you to evaluate costs in the hospital's lab for the past month. The following information is available:

a. Basically, two types of tests are performed in the lab—blood tests and smears. During the past month, 1,800 blood tests and 2,400 smears were performed in the lab.

b. Small glass plates are used in both types of tests. During the past month, the hospital purchased 12,000 plates at a cost of $28,200. This cost is net of a 6% quantity discount. Some 1,500 of these plates were still on hand unused at the end of the month; there were no plates on hand at the beginning of the month.

c. During the past month, 1,150 hours of labour time were recorded in the lab. The cost of this labour time was $13,800.

d. Variable overhead cost last month in the lab for utilities and supplies totalled $7,820.

The hospital has never used standard costs. By searching industry literature, however, you have determined the following nationwide averages for hospital labs:

*Plates:* Two plates are required per lab test. These plates cost $2.50 each and are disposed of after the test is completed.

*Labour:* Each blood test should require 0.3 hour to complete, and each smear should require 0.15 hour to complete. The average cost of this lab time is $14 per hour.

*Overhead:* Overhead cost is based on direct labour-hours. The average rate for variable overhead is $6 per hour.

Mr. Fleming would like a complete analysis of the cost of plates, labour, and overhead in the lab for the last month so that he can get to the root of the lab's cost problem.

*Required:*
1. Compute a materials price variance for the plates purchased last month and a materials quantity variance for the plates used last month.
2. For labour cost in the lab:
   a. Compute a labour rate variance and a labour efficiency variance.
   b. In most hospitals, one-half of the workers in the lab are senior technicians and one-half are assistants. In an effort to reduce costs, the hospital employs only one-fourth senior technicians and three-fourths assistants. Would you recommend that this policy be continued? Explain.
3. Compute the variable overhead spending and efficiency variances. Is there any relationship between the variable overhead efficiency variance and the labour efficiency variance? Explain.

## PROBLEM 9–2   Basic Variance Analysis (LO2, LO3, LO4)

Becton Labs Inc. produces various chemical compounds for industrial use. One compound, called Fludex, is prepared by means of an elaborate distilling process. The company has developed standard costs for one unit of Fludex, as follows:

CHECK FIGURE
(1a) Materials price variance: $15,000 F
(2a) Labour efficiency variance: $4,375 U

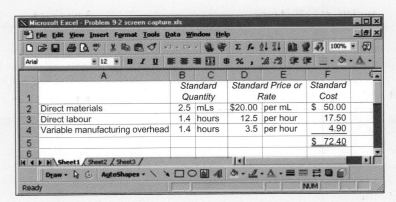

| | Standard Quantity | Standard Price or Rate | Standard Cost |
|---|---|---|---|
| Direct materials | 2.5 mLs | $20.00 per mL | $ 50.00 |
| Direct labour | 1.4 hours | 12.5 per hour | 17.50 |
| Variable manufacturing overhead | 1.4 hours | 3.5 per hour | 4.90 |
| | | | $ 72.40 |

During November, the following activity was recorded by the company relative to production of Fludex:

a. Materials purchased, 12,000 mL at a cost of $225,000.
b. There was no beginning inventory of materials on hand to start the month; at the end of the month, 2,500 mL of material remained in the warehouse unused.
c. The company employs 35 lab technicians to work on the production of Fludex. During November, each worked an average of 160 hours at an average rate of $12 per hour.
d. Variable manufacturing overhead is assigned to Fludex on the basis of direct labour-hours. Variable manufacturing overhead costs during November totalled $18,200.
e. During November, 3,750 good units of Fludex were produced.

The company's management is anxious to determine the efficiency of the activities surrounding the production of Fludex.

*Required:*
1. For materials used in the production of Fludex:
   a. Compute the price and quantity variances.
   b. The materials were purchased from a new supplier who is anxious to enter into a long-term purchase contract. Would you recommend that the company sign the contract? Explain.
2. For direct labour employed in the production of Fludex:
   a. Compute the rate and efficiency variances.

b. In the past, the 35 technicians employed in the production of Fludex consisted of 20 senior technicians and 15 assistants. During November, the company experimented with only 15 senior technicians and 20 assistants in order to save costs. Would you recommend that the new labour mix be continued? Explain.

3. Compute the variable overhead spending and efficiency variances. What relationship can you see between this efficiency variance and the labour efficiency variance?

CHECK FIGURE
(1a) Materials price
      variance: $3,000 F
(2) Net variance: $16,290 U

**PROBLEM 9–3   Comprehensive Variance Analysis (LO2, LO3, LO4)**

Miller Toy Company manufactures a plastic swimming pool at its Westwood Plant. The plant has been experiencing problems for some time as shown by its June income statement below:

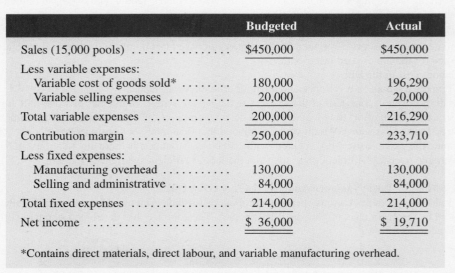

|  | Budgeted | Actual |
|---|---|---|
| Sales (15,000 pools) . . . . . . . . . . . . . . . . | $450,000 | $450,000 |
| Less variable expenses: |  |  |
|    Variable cost of goods sold* . . . . . . . . | 180,000 | 196,290 |
|    Variable selling expenses . . . . . . . . . | 20,000 | 20,000 |
| Total variable expenses . . . . . . . . . . . . . | 200,000 | 216,290 |
| Contribution margin . . . . . . . . . . . . . . . | 250,000 | 233,710 |
| Less fixed expenses: |  |  |
|    Manufacturing overhead . . . . . . . . . . . | 130,000 | 130,000 |
|    Selling and administrative . . . . . . . . . . | 84,000 | 84,000 |
| Total fixed expenses . . . . . . . . . . . . . . . | 214,000 | 214,000 |
| Net income . . . . . . . . . . . . . . . . . . . . . | $ 36,000 | $ 19,710 |

*Contains direct materials, direct labour, and variable manufacturing overhead.

Janet Dunn, who has just been appointed general manager of the Westwood Plant, has been given instructions to "get things under control." Upon reviewing the plant's income statement, Ms. Dunn has concluded that the major problem lies in the variable cost of goods sold. She has been provided with the following standard cost per swimming pool:

| | Standard Quantity or Hours | Standard Price or Rate | Standard Cost |
|---|---|---|---|
| Direct materials . . . . . . . . . . . | 1.5 kilograms | $4.00 per kilogram | $ 6.00 |
| Direct labour . . . . . . . . . . . . . | 0.8 hours | 6.00 per hour | 4.80 |
| Variable manufacturing overhead . . . . . . . . . . . . . | 0.4 hours* | 3.00 per hour | 1.20 |
| Total standard cost . . . . . . . . | | | $12.00 |

*Based on machine-hours.

Ms. Dunn has determined that during June the plant produced 15,000 pools and incurred the following costs:

a. Purchased 30,000 kilograms of materials at a cost of $3.90 per kilogram.
b. Used 24,600 kilograms of materials in production. (Finished goods and work-in-process inventories are insignificant and can be ignored.)
c. Worked 11,800 direct labour-hours at a cost of $7.00 per hour.
d. Incurred variable manufacturing overhead cost totalling $18,290 for the month. A total of 5,900 machine-hours was recorded.

It is the company's policy to close all variances to cost of goods sold on a monthly basis.

*Required:*

1. Compute the following variances for June:
   a. Direct materials price and quantity variances.

b. Direct labour rate and efficiency variances.

c. Variable overhead spending and efficiency variances.

2. Summarize the variances that you computed in (1) above by showing the net overall favourable or unfavourable variance for the month. What impact did this figure have on the company's income statement? Show computations.

3. Pick out the two most significant variances that you computed in (1) above. Explain to Ms. Dunn possible causes of these variances.

**PROBLEM 9–4   Comprehensive Variance Analysis; Journal Entries** (LO2, LO3, LO4, LO5)
(Appendix 9A) Trueform Products Inc. produces a broad line of sports equipment and uses a standard cost system for control purposes. Last year, the company produced 8,000 of its varsity footballs. The standard costs associated with this football, along with the actual costs incurred last year, are given below (per football):

CHECK FIGURE
(2a) Labour rate
    variance: $3,200 U
(3) Variable overhead
    efficiency variance:
    $2,000 F

|  | Standard Cost | Actual Cost |
|---|---|---|
| Direct materials: |  |  |
| Standard: 3.7 feet at $5 per foot | $18.50 |  |
| Actual: 4.0 feet at $4.80 per foot |  | $19.20 |
| Direct labour: |  |  |
| Standard: 0.9 hour at $7.50 per hour | 6.75 |  |
| Actual: 0.8 hour at $8 per hour |  | 6.40 |
| Variable manufacturing overhead: |  |  |
| Standard: 0.9 hour at $2.50 per hour | 2.25 |  |
| Actual: 0.8 hour at $2.75 per hour |  | 2.20 |
| Total cost per football | $27.50 | $27.80 |

The president was elated when he saw that actual costs exceeded standard costs by only $0.30 per football. He stated, "I was afraid that our unit cost might get out of hand when we gave out those raises last year in order to stimulate output. But it's obvious our costs are well under control."

There was no inventory of materials on hand to start the year. During the year, 32,000 feet of materials were purchased and used in production.

***Required:***

1. For direct materials:
   a. Compute the price and quantity variances for the year.
   b. Prepare journal entries to record all activity relating to direct materials for the year.
2. For direct labour:
   a. Compute the rate and efficiency variances.
   b. Prepare a journal entry to record the incurrence of direct labour cost for the year.
3. Compute the variable overhead spending and efficiency variances.
4. Was the president correct in his statement that "our costs are well under control"? Explain.
5. State possible causes of each variance that you have computed.

**PROBLEM 9–5   Setting Standards** (LO1)
Danson Company is a chemical manufacturer that supplies various products to industrial users. The company plans to introduce a new chemical solution, called Nysap, for which it needs to develop a standard product cost. The following information is available on the production of Nysap:

CHECK FIGURE
(1) Nyclyn: 18.0 kg
(3) Standard cost: $97.20

a. Nysap is made by combining a chemical compound (nyclyn) and a solution (salex), and boiling the mixture. A 20% loss in volume occurs for both the salex and the nyclyn during boiling. After boiling, the mixture consists of 9.6 litres of salex and 12 kilograms of nyclyn per 10-litre batch of Nysap.

b. After the boiling process is complete, the solution is cooled slightly before five kilograms of protet are added per 10-litre batch of Nysap. The addition of the protet does not affect the total liquid volume. The resulting solution is then bottled in 10-litre containers.

c. The finished product is highly unstable, and one 10-litre batch out of six is rejected at final inspection. Rejected batches have no commercial value and are thrown out.

d. It takes a worker 35 minutes to process one 10-litre batch of Nysap. Employees work an eight-hour day, including one hour per day for rest breaks and cleanup.

*Required:*

1. Determine the standard quantity for each of the raw materials needed to produce an acceptable 10-litre batch of Nysap.
2. Determine the standard labour time to produce an acceptable 10-litre batch of Nysap.
3. Assuming the following purchase prices and costs, prepare a standard cost card for materials and labour for one acceptable 10-litre batch of Nysap:

| | |
|---|---|
| Salex ..................... | $1.50 per litre |
| Nyclyn .................... | 2.80 per kilogram |
| Protet ..................... | 3.00 per kilogram |
| Direct labour cost ........... | 9.00 per hour |

(CMA, adapted)

CHECK FIGURE
(1) Actual hours: 145

### PROBLEM 9–6    Working Backwards from Labour Variances (LO3)

The auto repair shop of Quality Motor Company uses standards to control the labour time and labour cost in the shop. The standard labour cost for a motor tune-up is given below:

| Job | Standard Hours | Standard Rate | Standard Cost |
|---|---|---|---|
| Motor tune-up ............... | 2.5 | $9 | $22.50 |

The record showing the time spent in the shop last week on motor tune-ups has been misplaced. However, the shop supervisor recalls that 50 tune-ups were completed during the week, and the controller recalls the following variance data relating to tune-ups:

| | |
|---|---|
| Labour rate variance .................... | $87 F |
| Total labour variance ................... | 93 U |

*Required:*

1. Determine the number of actual labour-hours spent on tune-ups during the week.
2. Determine the actual hourly rate of pay for tune-ups last week.

(Hint: A useful way to proceed would be to work from known to unknown data either by using the variance formulas or by using the columnar format shown in Exhibit 9–5.)

CHECK FIGURE
(1) Standard cost: $31.50
(3) 2.8 metres

### PROBLEM 9–7    Comprehensive Variance Problem (LO1, LO2, LO3, LO4)

Highland Company produces a lightweight backpack that is popular with college students. Standard variable costs relating to a single backpack are given below:

| | Standard Quantity or Hours | Standard Price or Rate | Standard Cost |
|---|---|---|---|
| Direct materials ..................... | ? | $6 per metre | $? |
| Direct labour ........................ | ? | ? | ? |
| Variable manufacturing overhead ......... | ? | $3 per hour | ? |
| Total standard cost ..................... | | | $? |

During March, 1,000 backpacks were manufactured and sold. Selected information relating to the month's production is given below:

| | Materials Used | Direct Labour | Variable Manufacturing Overhead |
|---|---|---|---|
| Total standard cost allowed* ............. | $16,800 | $10,500 | $4,200 |
| Actual costs incurred .................. | 15,000 | ? | 3,600 |
| Materials price variance ................ | ? | | |

| | | | |
|---|---|---|---|
| Materials quantity variance .............. | 1,200 U | | |
| Labour rate variance ................... | | ? | |
| Labour efficiency variance ............. | | ? | |
| Variable overhead spending variance ..... | | | ? |
| Variable overhead efficiency variance ..... | | | ? |

*For the month's production.

The following additional information is available for March's production:

| | |
|---|---|
| Actual direct labour-hours ..................................................... | 1,500 |
| Standard overhead rate per hour ............................................... | $3.00 |
| Standard price of one metre of materials ...................................... | 6.00 |
| Difference between standard and actual cost per backpack produced during March .... | 0.15 F |

Overhead is applied to production on the basis of direct labour-hours.

*Required:*
1. What is the standard cost of a single backpack?
2. What was the actual cost per backpack produced during March?
3. How many metres of material are required at standard per backpack?
4. What was the materials price variance for March?
5. What is the standard direct labour rate per hour?
6. What was the labour rate variance for March? The labour efficiency variance?
7. What was the variable overhead spending variance for March? The variable overhead efficiency variance?
8. Prepare a standard cost card for one backpack.

**PROBLEM 9–8   Computations from Incomplete Data (LO2, LO3)**
Sharp Company manufactures a product for which the following standards have been set:

CHECK FIGURE
(1a) Actual cost: $5.30/ft.
(2a) Standard labour
rate: $8

| | Standard Quantity or Hours | Standard Price or Rate | Standard Cost |
|---|---|---|---|
| Direct materials ........... | 3 feet | $5 per foot | $15 |
| Direct labour ............. | ? hours | ? per hour | ? |

During March, the company purchased direct materials at a cost of $55,650, all of which were used in the production of 3,200 units of product. In addition, 4,900 hours of direct labour time were worked on the product during the month. The cost of this labour time was $36,750. The following variances have been computed for the month:

| | |
|---|---|
| Materials quantity variance ..................... | $4,500 U |
| Total labour variance .......................... | 1,650 F |
| Labour efficiency variance ..................... | 800 U |

*Required:*
1. For direct materials:
   a. Compute the actual cost per foot for materials for March.
   b. Compute the materials price variance and a total variance for materials.
2. For direct labour:
   a. Compute the standard direct labour rate per hour.
   b. Compute the standard hours allowed for the month's production.
   c. Compute the standard hours allowed per unit of product.

(Hint: In completing the problem, it may be helpful to move from known to unknown data either by using the columnar format shown in Exhibits 9–3 and 9–5 or by using the variance formulas.)

### PROBLEM 9–9  Variance Analysis with Multiple Lots (LO2, LO3)

Hillcrest Leisure Wear Inc. manufactures men's clothing. The company has a single line of slacks that is produced in lots, with each lot representing an order from a customer. As a lot is completed, the customer's store label is attached to the slacks before shipment.

Hillcrest has a standard cost system and has established the following standards for a dozen slacks:

| | Standard Quantity or Hours | Standard Price or Rate | Standard Cost |
|---|---|---|---|
| Direct materials . . . . . . . . . . . | 32 metres | 2.40 per metre | $76.80 |
| Direct labour . . . . . . . . . . . . . | 6 hours | 7.50 per hour | 45.00 |

During October, Hillcrest worked on three orders for slacks. The company's job cost records for the month reveal the following:

| Lot | Units in Lot (dozens) | Materials Used (metres) | Hours Worked |
|---|---|---|---|
| 48 . . . . . . . . . . . . . . . | 1,500 | 48,300 | 8,900 |
| 49 . . . . . . . . . . . . . . . | 950 | 30,140 | 6,130 |
| 50 . . . . . . . . . . . . . . . | 2,100 | 67,250 | 10,270 |

The following additional information is available:

a. Hillcrest purchased 180,000 metres of material during October at a cost of $424,800.
b. Direct labour cost incurred during the month for production of slacks amounted to $192,280.
c. There was no work in process inventory on October 1. During October, lots 48 and 49 were completed, and lot 50 was 100% complete as to materials and 80% complete as to labour.

*Required:*
1. Compute the materials price variance for the materials purchased during October.
2. Determine the materials quantity variance for October in both metres and dollars:
   a. For each lot worked on during the month.
   b. For the company as a whole.
3. Compute the labour rate variance for October.
4. Determine the labour efficiency variance for the month in both hours and dollars:
   a. For each lot worked on during the month.
   b. For the company as a whole.
5. In what situations might it be better to express variances in units (hours, metres, and so on), rather than in dollars? In dollars, rather than in units?

(CPA, adapted)

### PROBLEM 9–10  Comprehensive Variance Analysis with Incomplete Data; Journal Entries (LO1, LO2, LO3, LO4, LO5)

(Appendix 9A) Maple Products Ltd. manufactures hockey sticks that are used worldwide. The standard cost of one hockey stick is:

| | Standard Quantity or Hours | Standard Price or Rate | Standard Cost |
|---|---|---|---|
| Direct materials . . . . . . . . . . . | ? feet | $3.00 per foot | $ ? |
| Direct labour . . . . . . . . . . . . . | 2 hours | ? per hour | ? |
| Variable manufacturing overhead . . . . . . . . . . . . . . | ? hours | 1.30 per hour | ? |
| Total standard cost . . . . . . . . | | | $27.00 |

Last year, 8,000 hockey sticks were produced and sold. Selected cost data relating to last year's operations follow:

| | Dr. | Cr. |
|---|---|---|
| Direct materials purchased (60,000 feet) ............. | $174,000 | |
| Wages payable (? hours) .......................... | | $79,200* |
| Work in process—direct materials ................. | 115,200 | |
| Direct labour rate variance ....................... | | 3,300 |
| Variable overhead efficiency variance .............. | 650 | |

*Relates to the actual direct labour cost for the year.

The following additional information is available for last year's operations:

a. No materials were on hand at the start of last year. Some of the materials purchased during the year were still on hand in the warehouse at the end of the year.
b. The variable manufacturing overhead rate is based on direct labour-hours. Total actual variable manufacturing overhead cost for last year was $19,800.
c. Actual direct materials usage for last year exceeded the standard by 0.2 foot per stick.

*Required:*
1. For direct materials:
   a. Compute the price and quantity variances for last year.
   b. Prepare journal entries to record all activities relating to direct materials for last year.
2. For direct labour:
   a. Verify the rate variance given above and compute the efficiency variance for last year.
   b. Prepare a journal entry to record activity relating to direct labour for last year.
3. Compute the variable overhead spending variance for last year and verify the variable overhead efficiency variance given above.
4. State possible causes of each variance that you have computed.
5. Prepare a completed standard cost card for one hockey stick.

### PROBLEM 9–11   Developing Standard Costs (LO1)

ColdKing Company is a small producer of fruit-flavoured frozen desserts. For many years, ColdKing's products have had strong regional sales on the basis of brand recognition; however, other companies have begun marketing similar products in the area, and price competition has become increasingly important. John Wakefield, the company's controller, is planning to implement a standard cost system for ColdKing and has gathered considerable information from his co-workers on production and material requirements for ColdKing's products. Wakefield believes that the use of standard costing will allow ColdKing to improve cost control and make better pricing decisions.

ColdKing's most popular product is raspberry sherbet. The sherbet is produced in 40-litre batches, and each batch requires 24 litres of good raspberries. The fresh raspberries are sorted by hand before they enter the production process. Because of imperfections in the raspberries and normal spoilage, one litre of berries is discarded for every four litres of acceptable berries. One minute is the standard direct labour time for the sorting that is required to obtain one litre of acceptable raspberries. The acceptable raspberries are then blended with the other ingredients; blending requires 12 minutes of direct labour time per batch. After blending, the sherbet is packaged in litre containers. Wakefield has gathered the following pricing information:

a. ColdKing purchases raspberries at a cost of $0.20 per litre. All other ingredients cost a total of $0.45 per four litres of sherbert.
b. Direct labour is paid at the rate of $9 per hour.
c. The total cost of material and labour required to package the sherbet is $0.38 per litre.

*Required:*
1. Develop the standard cost for the direct cost components (materials, labour, and packaging) of a 40-litre batch of raspberry sherbet. The standard cost should identify the standard quantity, standard rate, and standard cost per batch for each direct cost component of a batch of raspberry sherbet.

CHECK FIGURE
(1) Standard cost: $30.20

2. As part of the implementation of a standard cost system at ColdKing, John Wakefied plans to train those responsible for maintaining the standards on how to use variance analysis. Wakefield is particularly concerned with the causes of unfavourable variances.

     a. Discuss possible causes of unfavourable materials price variances and identify the individual(s) who should be held responsible for these variances.

     b. Discuss possible causes of unfavourable labour efficiency variances and identify the individual(s) who should be held responsible for these variances.

(CMA, adapted)

# Building Your Skills

CHECK FIGURE
(1) 120 batches
(2a) Actual cost: $7,700

**ANALYTICAL THINKING**    (LO2, LO3, LO4, LO5)

(Appendix 9A) You are employed by Olster Company, which manufactures products for the senior citizen market. As a rising young executive in the company, you are scheduled to make a presentation in a few hours to your superior. This presentation relates to last week's production of Maxitol, a popular health tonic that is manufactured by Olster Company. Unfortunately, while studying ledger sheets and variance summaries by the poolside in the company's fitness area, you were bumped and dropped the papers into the pool. In desperation, you fished the papers from the water, but you have discovered that only the following fragments are readable:

Maxitol—Standard Cost Card

| | Standard Quantity or Hours | Standard Price or Rate | Standard Cost |
|---|---|---|---|
| Material A . . . . . . . . . . . . . . . | 24 litres | $2 per litr | $ 48 |
| Material B . . . . . . . . . . . . . . . | | per kilogr | |
| Direct labour . . . . . . . . . . . . . | | per ho | 0 |
| Standard cost per batc . . . . . . | | | $99.50 |

Maxitol—General Ledger Accounts

**Raw Materials—A**

| | | | |
|---|---|---|---|
| Bal. 3/1 | 0 | | |
| Bal. 3/7 | 2,000 | | |

**Work in Process**

| | | | |
|---|---|---|---|
| Bal. 3/1 | 0 | | |
| Material A | 5,760 | | |
| Bal. 3/7 | 0 | | |

**Material A—Price Variance**

| | |
|---|---|
| 300 | |

**Wages Payable**

| | |
|---|---|
| | 4,100 |

**Raw Materials—B**

| | | | |
|---|---|---|---|
| Bal. 3/1 | 700 | 2,500 | |
| Bal. 3/7 | 1,400 | | |

**Labour Rate Variance**

| | |
|---|---|
| 500 | |

**Material B—Quantity Variance**

| | |
|---|---|
| 100 | |

**Accounts Payable**

| | |
|---|---|
| | 11,460 |

You remember that the accounts payable are for purchases of both material A and material B. You also remember that only 10 direct labour workers are involved in the production of Maxitol and that each worked 40 hours last week. The wages payable above are for wages earned by these workers.

You realize that to be ready for your presentation, you must reconstruct all data relating to Maxitol very quickly. As a start, you have called purchasing and found that 4,000 litres of material A and 400 kilograms of material B were purchased last week.

*Required:*

✓1. How many batches of Maxitol were produced last week? (This is a key figure; be sure it is right before going on.)
2. For material A:
   ✓a. What was the cost of material A purchased last week? −AP
   b. How many litres were used in production last week? − Qv
   c. What was the quantity variance?
   d. Prepare journal entries to record all activity relating to material A for last week.
3. For material B:
   a. What is the standard cost per pound for material B?
   b. How many kilograms of material B were used in production last week? How many kilograms should have been used at standard?
   c. What is the standard quantity of material B per batch?
   d. What was the price variance for material B last week?
   e. Prepare journal entries to record all activity relating to material B for last week.
4. For direct labour:
   a. What is the standard rate per direct labour-hour?
   b. What are the standard hours per batch?
   c. What were the standard hours allowed for last week's production?
   d. What was the labour efficiency variance for last week?
   e. Prepare a journal entry to record all activity relating to direct labour for last week.
5. Complete the standard cost card shown above for one batch of Maxitol.

## COMMUNICATING IN PRACTICE   (LO1)

Make an appointment to meet with the manager of an auto repair shop that uses standards. In most cases, this would be an auto repair shop that is affiliated with a chain, such as PetroCanada or Canadian Tire, or the service department of a new-car dealer.

*Required:*

At the scheduled meeting, find out the answers to the following questions and write a memo to your instructor describing the information obtained during your meeting.
1. How are standards set?
2. Are standards practical or ideal?
3. Is the actual time taken to complete a task compared with the standard time?
4. What are the consequences of unfavourable variances? Of favourable variances?
5. Do the standards and variances create any potential problems?

## ETHICS CHALLENGE   (LO1)

Stacy Cummins, the newly hired controller at Merced Home Products, Inc., was disturbed by what she had discovered about the standard costs at the Home Security Division. In looking over the past several years of quarterly earnings reports at the Home Security Division, she noticed that the first-quarter earnings were always poor, the second-quarter earnings were slightly better, the third-quarter earnings were again slightly better, and then the fourth quarter and the year always ended with a spectacular performance in which the Home Security Division always managed to meet or exceed its target profit for the year. She also was concerned to find letters from the company's external auditors to top management warning about an unusual use of standard costs at the Home Security Division.

When Ms. Cummins ran across these letters, she asked the assistant controller, Gary Farber, if he knew what was going on at the Home Security Division. Gary said that it was common knowledge in the company that the vice-president in charge of the Home Security Division, Preston Lansing, had rigged the standards at the Home Security Division in order to produce the same quarterly earnings pattern every year. According to company policy, variances are taken directly to the income statement as an adjustment to cost of goods sold.

Favourable variances have the effect of increasing net income, and unfavourable variances have the effect of decreasing net income. Lansing had rigged the standards so that there were always large favourable variances. Company policy was a little vague about when these variances have to be reported on the divisional income statements. While the intent was clearly to recognize variances on the income statement in the period in which they arise, nothing in the company's accounting manuals explicitly required this. So, for many years, Lansing had followed a practice of saving up the favourable variances and using them to create a nice smooth pattern of earnings growth in the first three quarters, followed by a big "Christmas present" of an extremely good fourth quarter. (Financial reporting regulations forbid carrying variances forward from one year to the next on the annual audited financial statements, and so all of the variances must appear on the divisional income statement by the end of the year.)

Ms. Cummins was concerned about these revelations and attempted to bring up the subject with the president of Merced Home Products but was told that "we all know what Lansing's doing, but as long as he continues to turn in such good reports, don't bother him." When Ms. Cummins asked if the board of directors was aware of the situation, the president somewhat testily replied, "Of course, they are aware."

### Required:

1. How did Preston Lansing probably "rig" the standard costs—are the standards set too high or too low? Explain.
2. Should Preston Lansing be permitted to continue his practice of managing reported earnings?
3. What should Stacy Cummins do in this situation?

### TEAMWORK IN ACTION   (LO1)

Terry Travers is the manufacturing supervisor of Aurora Manufacturing Company, which produces a variety of plastic products. Some of these products are standard items that are listed in the company's catalogue, while others are made to customer specifications. Each month, Travers receives a performance report showing the budget for the month, the actual activity, and the variance between budget and actual. Part of Travers' annual performance evaluation is based on his department's performance against budget. Aurora's purchasing manager, Sally Christensen, also receives monthly performance reports, and she, too, is evaluated partly on the basis of these reports.

The monthly reports for June had just been distributed when Travers met Christensen in the hallway outside their offices. Scowling, Travers began the conversation, "I see we have another set of monthly performance reports hand-delivered by that not very nice junior employee in the budget office. He seemed pleased to tell me that I'm in trouble with my performance again."

*Christensen:* I got the same treatment. All I ever hear about are the things I haven't done right. Now I'll have to spend a lot of time reviewing the report and preparing explanations. The worst part is that it's now the 21st of July so the information is almost a month old, and we have to spend all this time on history.

*Travers:* My biggest gripe is that our production activity varies a lot from month to month, but we're given an annual budget that's written in stone. Last month, we were shut down for three days when a strike delayed delivery of the basic ingredient used in our plastic formulation, and we had already exhausted our inventory. You know about that problem, though, because we asked you to call all over the country to find an alternative source of supply. When we got what we needed on a rush basis, we had to pay more than we normally do.

*Christensen:* I expect problems like that to pop up from time to time—that's part of my job—but now we'll both have to take a careful look at our reports to see where the charges are reflected for that rush order. Every month, I spend more time making sure I should be charged for each item reported than I do making plans for my department's daily work. It's really frustrating to see charges for things I have no control over.

*Travers:* The way we get information doesn't help, either. I don't get copies of the reports you get, and yet a lot of what I do is affected by your department and by most of the other departments we have. Why do the budget and accounting people assume that I should only be told about my operations, even though the president regularly gives us pep talks about how we all need to work together as a team?

*Christensen:* I seem to get more reports than I need, and I am never asked to comment on them until top management puts me on the carpet about my department's shortcomings. Do you ever hear comments when your department shines?

*Travers:* I guess they don't have time to review the good news. One of my problems is that all the reports are in dollars and cents. I work with people, machines, and materials. I need information to help me *this* month to solve *this* month's problems—not another report of the dollars expended *last* month or the month before.

*Required:*

Your team should discuss and then respond to the following questions. All team members should agree with and understand the answers and be prepared to report on those answers in class. (Each teammate can assume responsibility for a different part of the presentation.)

1. On the basis of the conversation between Terry Travers and Sally Christensen, describe the likely motivation and behaviour of these two employees as a result of the standard cost and variance reporting system that is used by Aurora Manufacturing Company.

2. List the recommendations that your team would make to Aurora Manufacturing Company to enhance employee motivation as it relates to the company's standard cost and variance reporting system.

(CMA, adapted)

Do not forget to check out Taking It to the Net as well as other quizzes and resources at the Online Learning Centre at www.mcgrawhill.ca/college/garrison.

# Chapter *Ten*

# Flexible Budgets and Overhead Analysis

## A Look Back

We discussed budgeting in Chapter 8—the process that is used by organizations to plan the financial aspects of their operations. We introduced management control and performance measures in Chapter 9 with a discussion of standard costs and variance analysis.

## A Look at This Chapter

Chapter 10 continues our coverage of the budgeting process by presenting the flexible approach to budgeting. In addition to illustrating the use of a flexible budget to control overhead costs, we also expand the study of overhead variance analysis.

## A Look Ahead

We continue the discussion of management control and performance measures in Chapter 11 by focusing on how decentralized organizations are managed.

## Chapter Outline

**Flexible Budgets**
- Characteristics of a Flexible Budget
- Deficiencies of the Static Budget
- How a Flexible Budget Works
- Using the Flexible Budgeting Concept in Performance Evaluation
- The Measure of Activity—A Critical Choice

**Variable Overhead Variances—A Closer Look**
- The Problem of Actual versus Standard Hours
- Spending Variance Alone
- Both Spending and Efficiency Variances
- Activity-Based Costing and the Flexible Budget

**Overhead Rates and Fixed Overhead Analysis**
- Flexible Budgets and Overhead Rates
- Overhead Application in a Standard Cost System
- The Fixed Overhead Variances
- The Budget Variance—A Closer Look
- The Volume Variance—A Closer Look
- Cautions in Fixed Overhead Analysis
- Overhead Variances and Under- or Over-applied Overhead Cost

**Is Variance Analysis a Timely Control Tool?**

## DECISION FEATURE Overhead Costs: Burden or Opportunity?

It is not uncommon for many companies to use the term "burden" to refer to their overhead costs. But, are overhead costs really a burden? That depends. Overhead costs can easily become a burden if they are not checked. This can be very true in certain sectors of the economy, such as health care and manufacturing. Given the increasing share of overhead costs, most organizations are finding ways to get the "best bang for the buck."

Toronto Medical Laboratories (TML), an example of a strategic alliance consisting of three teaching hospitals and the medical services company MDS, Inc., has "invested" in overhead costs to reap big benefits. TML provides services that are of critical importance to hospitals: testing samples, such as blood, urine, sputum, and so on, and sending the results to the doctors. Accuracy and speed are extremely important variables that TML must always monitor. Therefore, the lab has invested in a highly automated and sophisticated lab testing system called ULTRA where robots do most of the repetitive work thereby eliminating any chance of human error. ULTRA also allows TML to be ahead on speed; it allows the lab to deliver results within just two hours!

Has TML cut costs? Well, not directly, but it has added 25% additional capacity without hiring an additional employee. This means it has the potential to increase revenues by 25% with the same level of overhead costs! Is overhead really a burden?

Source: "Vital Signs," www.canadianbusiness.com, 2002-12-09. Reprinted with permission from *Canadian Business.*

### Learning Objectives

*After studying Chapter 10, you should be able to:*

**LO1** Prepare a flexible budget and explain the advantages of the flexible budget approach over the static budget approach.

**LO2** Prepare a performance report for both variable and fixed overhead costs using the flexible budget approach and explain its advantages.

**LO3** Use the flexible budget to prepare a variable overhead performance report containing only a spending variance.

**LO4** Use the flexible budget to prepare a variable overhead performance report containing both a spending and an efficiency variance.

**LO5** Compute the predetermined overhead rate and apply overhead to products in a standard cost system.

**LO6** Compute and interpret the fixed overhead budget and volume variances.

In this chapter, we continue our discussion of variance analysis that we introduced in the previous chapter. However, we will turn our attention to the analysis of overhead costs. Why are overhead costs so important? Overhead is a significant portion of total costs in most types of organizations. For example, pharmaceutical companies spend millions of dollars in research and development (R&D), which is an overhead cost. For such organizations as Petro-Canada, implementing environmental control systems can cost significant amounts of money particularly in light of the Kyoto Accord; once again, these are overhead costs. Similarly, manufacturing overhead as a percentage of total costs has also increased largely due to automation. However, the increase is overhead costs has resulted in reduced labour costs and increased efficiencies.

Controlling overhead costs poses special problems. Such costs as direct materials and direct labour are often easier to understand, and therefore to control, than overhead, which can include everything from the disposable coffee cup in the visitor's waiting area to the president's salary. Overhead is usually made up of many separate costs—many of which may be small. This makes it impractical to control them in the same way that such costs as direct materials and direct labour are controlled. And some overhead costs are variable, some are fixed, and some are a mixture of fixed and variable. These particular problems can be largely overcome by the use of flexible budgets—a topic that was briefly discussed in Chapter 8. In this chapter, we study flexible budgets in greater detail and learn how they can be used to control costs. We also expand the study of overhead variances that we started in Chapter 9.

## *in business today* Reducing Overhead Costs

Overhead costs now account for as much as 66% of the total costs incurred by companies in service industries and up to 37% of the total costs of manufacturers. Because of the magnitude of these costs, overhead cost reduction is now a recurring goal for many organizations. However, the extent of the reductions must be considered in light of competitive pressures to improve fundamental services to customers and product quality. Managers must take care not to cut costs that add value to the company.

Source: Nick Develin, "Unlocking Overhead Value," *Management Accounting*, December 1999, pp. 22–24. Reprinted with permission from *Management Accounting*.

# Flexible Budgets

## Characteristics of a Flexible Budget

**Learning Objective 1**
Prepare a flexible budget and explain the advantages of the flexible budget approach over the static budget approach.

The budgets that we studied in Chapter 8 were *static budgets*. A **static budget** is prepared for only the planned level of activity. This approach is suitable for planning purposes, but it is inadequate for evaluating how well costs are controlled. This is because a variance between actual costs and static budget costs can be due to differences in (1) activity level (e.g., sales being higher or lower than expected), and/or (2) how efficiently resources are used. While a simple performance report as in Exhibit 10–1 provides useful information about differences in activity-level, it fails to inform managers how well they have used input resources. If activity is higher than expected, the variable costs should be higher than expected; and if activity is lower than expected, the variable costs should be lower than expected.

**Exhibit 10–1**

### RICK'S HAIRSTYLING
### Static Budget Performance Report
### For the Month Ended March 31

| | Actual | Budgeted | Variance |
|---|---|---|---|
| Client-visits .................... | 5,200 | 5,000 | 200 F |
| | | | |
| Variable overhead costs: | | | |
| Hairstyling supplies ............. | $ 6,400 | $ 6,000 | $ 400 U* |
| Client gratuities ................ | 22,300 | 20,000 | 2,300 U* |
| Electricity .................... | 1,020 | 1,000 | 20 U* |
| Total variable overhead cost ......... | 29,720 | 27,000 | 2,720 U* |
| | | | |
| Fixed overhead costs: | | | |
| Support staff wages and salaries .... | 8,100 | 8,000 | 100 U |
| Rent ......................... | 12,000 | 12,000 | -0- |
| Insurance ..................... | 1,000 | 1,000 | -0- |
| Utilities other than electricity ...... | 470 | 500 | 30 F |
| Total fixed overhead cost .......... | 21,570 | 21,500 | 70 U |
| Total overhead cost ............... | $51,290 | $48,500 | $2,790 U* |

*The cost variances for variable costs and for total overhead are useless for evaluating how well costs were controlled, since they have been derived by comparing actual costs at one level of activity with budgeted costs at a different level of activity.

In order to better understand how well managers used input resources in a given period, we must prepare flexible budgets which take into account changes in costs that should occur as a consequence of changes in activity level. A **flexible budget** provides estimates of what costs should be for any level of activity within a specified range. When a flexible budget is used in performance evaluation, actual costs are compared with what the *costs should have been for the actual level of activity during the period*, rather than with the budgeted costs from the original static budget. This is a very important distinction—particularly for variable costs. If adjustments for the level of activity are not made, it is very difficult to interpret discrepancies between budgeted and actual costs—this would be like comparing apples to oranges.

Concept 10–1

## Deficiencies of the Static Budget

To illustrate the difference between a static budget and a flexible budget, we will consider the case of Rick's Hairstyling, an upscale hairstyling salon located in Victoria that is owned and managed by Rick Manzi. The salon has very loyal customers—many of whom are wealthy retirees. Despite the glamour associated with his salon, Rick is a very shrewd businessman. Recently, he has been attempting to get better control over his overhead, and at the urging of his accounting and business adviser Victoria Kho, he has begun to prepare monthly budgets.

At the end of February, Rick carefully prepared the March budget for overhead items; he believes that the number of customers served in a month is the best way to measure the overall level of activity in his salon. Rick refers to these visits as client-visits. A customer who comes into the salon and has his or her hair styled is counted as one client-visit. After some discussion with Victoria Kho, Rick identified three major categories of variable overhead costs—hairstyling supplies, client gratuities, and electricity—and four major categories of fixed costs—support staff wages and salaries, rent, insurance, and utilities other than electricity. Client gratuities consist of flowers, candies, and glasses of champagne that Rick offers to his customers while they are in the salon. Rick considers electricity to be a variable cost, since almost all of the electricity in the salon is consumed in running blow-dryers, curling irons, and other hairstyling equipment.

To develop the budget for variable overhead, Rick estimated that the average cost per client-visit should be $1.20 for hairstyling supplies, $4 for client gratuities, and $0.20 for electricity. On the basis of his estimate of 5,000 client-visits in March, Rick budgeted for $6,000 ($1.20 per client-visit $\times$ 5,000 client-visits) in hairstyling supplies, $20,000 ($4 per client-visit $\times$ 5,000 client-visits) in client gratuities, and $1,000 ($0.20 per client-visit $\times$ 5,000 client-visits) in electricity.

The budget for fixed overhead items was based on Rick's records of how much he had spent on these items in the past. The budget included $8,000 for support staff wages and salaries, $12,000 for rent, $1,000 for insurance, and $500 for utilities other than electricity.

At the end of March, Rick prepared a report comparing actual with budgeted costs. That report appears in Exhibit 10–1. The problem with that report, as Rick immediately realized, is that it compares costs at one level of activity (5,200 client-visits) with costs at a different level of activity (5,000 client-visits). Since Rick had 200 more client-visits than expected, his variable costs *should* be higher than budgeted. The static budget performance report confuses control over activity and control over costs. From Rick's standpoint, the increase in activity was good and should be counted as a favourable variance, but the increase in activity has an apparently negative impact on the costs in the report. Rick knew that something would have to be done to make the report more meaningful, but he was unsure of what to do. So, he made an appointment to meet with Victoria Kho to discuss the next step.

---

*Victoria:* How is the budgeting going?

*Rick:* Not bad. I didn't have any trouble putting together the overhead budget for March. I also made out a report comparing the actual costs for March with the budgeted costs, but that report isn't telling me what I really want to know.

*Victoria:* Because your actual level of activity didn't match your budgeted activity?

*Rick:* Right. I know that shouldn't affect my fixed costs, but we had a lot more client-visits than I had expected, and that had to affect my variable costs.

*Victoria:* So, you want to know whether the actual costs are justified by the actual level of activity you had in March?

*Rick:* Precisely.

*Victoria:* If you leave your reports and data with me, I can work on them later today, and by tomorrow I'll have a report to show to you. Actually, I have a styling appointment for later this week. Why don't I move my appointment up to tomorrow, and I will bring along the analysis so we can discuss it.

*Rick:* That's great.

## How a Flexible Budget Works

The basic idea of the flexible budget approach is that a budget does not have to be static. Depending on the actual level of activity, a budget can be adjusted to show what costs *should be* for that specific level of activity. A master budget summarizes a company's plans and indicates how the plans will be accomplished. To simplify the discussion of the budgeting process, only one level of activity was assumed when each of the components of the master budget was illustrated in Chapter 8. However, a master budget can also be developed using a flexible budget approach. Because management places a great deal of significance on the control of overhead costs, the overhead budget is used in this chapter to illustrate the concept of flexible budgeting. However, the flexible budget approach is equally applicable to the other components of the master budget.

**Exhibit 10–2**

Illustration of the Flexible Budgeting Concept

| | | Activity (in client-visits) | | | |
|---|---|---|---|---|---|
| **RICK'S HAIRSTYLING** **Flexible Budget** **For the Month Ended March 31** | | | | | |
| Budgeted number of client-visits . . . . . . . . . . . . . | | 5,000 | | | |
| **Overhead Costs** | **Cost Formula (per client-visit)** | **4,900** | **5,000** | **5,100** | **5,200** |
| Variable overhead costs: | | | | | |
| Hairstyling supplies . . . . . . . . . . . . . . . . . . . | $1.20 | $ 5,880 | $ 6,000 | $ 6,120 | $ 6,240 |
| Client gratuities . . . . . . . . . . . . . . . . . . . . . . | 4.00 | 19,600 | 20,000 | 20,400 | 20,800 |
| Electricity (variable) . . . . . . . . . . . . . . . . . . | 0.20 | 980 | 1,000 | 1,020 | 1,040 |
| Total variable overhead cost . . . . . . . . . . . . . . . | $5.40 | 26,460 | 27,000 | 27,540 | 28,080 |
| Fixed overhead costs: | | | | | |
| Support staff wages and salaries . . . . . . . . . . . | | 8,000 | 8,000 | 8,000 | 8,000 |
| Rent . . . . . . . . . . . . . . . . . . . . . . . . . . . . . . . | | 12,000 | 12,000 | 12,000 | 12,000 |
| Insurance . . . . . . . . . . . . . . . . . . . . . . . . . . . | | 1,000 | 1,000 | 1,000 | 1,000 |
| Utilities other than electricity . . . . . . . . . . . . . | | 500 | 500 | 500 | 500 |
| Total fixed overhead cost . . . . . . . . . . . . . . . . . | | 21,500 | 21,500 | 21,500 | 21,500 |
| Total overhead cost . . . . . . . . . . . . . . . . . . . . . | | $47,960 | $48,500 | $49,040 | $49,580 |

To illustrate how flexible budgets work, Victoria prepared a report as illustrated in (Exhibit 10–2). It shows how overhead costs can be expected to change, depending on the monthly level of activity. Within the activity range of 4,900 to 5,200 client-visits, the fixed costs are expected to remain the same. For the variable overhead costs, Victoria multiplied Rick's per client costs ($1.20 for hairstyling supplies, $4 for client gratuities, and $0.20 for electricity) by the appropriate number of client-visits in each column. For example, the $1.20 cost of hairstyling supplies was multiplied by 4,900 client-visits to give the total cost of $5,880 for hairstyling supplies at that level of activity.

## Using the Flexible Budgeting Concept in Performance Evaluation

To get a better idea of how well Rick's variable overhead costs were controlled in March, Victoria applied the flexible budgeting concept to create a new performance report (Exhibit 10–3). Using the flexible budget approach, Victoria constructed a budget based on the *actual* number of client-visits for the month. The budget is prepared by multiplying the actual level of activity by the cost formula for each of the variable cost categories. For example, using the $1.20 per client-visit for hairstyling supplies, the total cost for this item *should be* $6,240 for 5,200 client-visits ($1.20 × 5,200). Since the actual cost for hairstyling supplies was $6,400, the unfavourable variance was $160.

Compare the flexible budget performance report in Exhibit 10–3 with the static budget performance report in Exhibit 10–1. The static budget performance report shows an unfavourable variance of $2,790 in total. Although this is an accurate reflection of the fact that actual costs were much higher than budgeted costs, it does not properly reflect the effect of the change in activity level during the month (i.e., the additional 200 client-visits).

**Exhibit 10–3**

### RICK'S HAIRSTYLING
### Flexible Budget Performance Report
### For the Month Ended March 31

Budgeted number of client-visits . . . . . . . . . . . . . . .  5,000
Actual number of client-visits. . . . . . . . . . . . . . . . .  5,200

| Overhead Costs | Cost Formula (per client-visit) | Actual Costs Incurred for 5,200 Client-Visits | Budget Based on 5,200 Client-Visits | Variance |
|---|---|---|---|---|
| Variable overhead costs: | | | | |
| Hairstyling supplies . . . . . . . . . . . . . . . . . . . . . . | $1.20 | $ 6,400 | $ 6,240 | $  160 U |
| Client gratuities . . . . . . . . . . . . . . . . . . . . . . . | 4.00 | 22,300 | 20,800 | 1,500 U |
| Electricity (variable) . . . . . . . . . . . . . . . . . . . . . | 0.20 | 1,020 | 1,040 | 20 F |
| Total variable overhead cost . . . . . . . . . . . . . . . . . . | $5.40 | 29,720 | 28,080 | 1,640 U |
| Fixed overhead costs: | | | | |
| Support staff wages and salaries . . . . . . . . . . . . . . | | 8,100 | 8,000 | 100 U |
| Rent . . . . . . . . . . . . . . . . . . . . . . . . . . . . . . . . | | 12,000 | 12,000 | -0- |
| Insurance . . . . . . . . . . . . . . . . . . . . . . . . . . . . . | | 1,000 | 1,000 | -0- |
| Utilities other than electricity . . . . . . . . . . . . . . . . | | 470 | 500 | 30 F |
| Total fixed overhead cost . . . . . . . . . . . . . . . . . . . . | | 21,570 | 21,500 | 70 U |
| Total overhead cost . . . . . . . . . . . . . . . . . . . . . . . . | | $51,290 | $49,580 | $1,710 U |

In contrast, the flexible budget performance report takes this into consideration. Because variable costs should increase with an increase in the activity level, it is only fair that we compare actual costs with the flexible budget amounts corresponding to 5,200 client-visits. Note that the budgeted variable overhead costs in Exhibit 10–3 are higher than the amounts in Exhibit 10–1 by $1,080 ($28,080 − $27,000). This difference accounts for the $5.40 variable overhead costs that should have been budgeted for each of the additional 200 client-visits. Although an unfavourable variance still exists, it is lower by an amount of $1,080 ($2,720 − $1,640). Moreover, the report also suggests that the variance for electricity costs is actually favourable, thereby providing a more accurate picture.

## MANAGERIAL ACCOUNTING IN ACTION

**The Wrap–up**

The following discussion took place the next day at Rick's salon.

*Victoria:* Let me show you what I've got. [Victoria shows the report contained in Exhibit 10–3.] All I did was multiply the costs per client-visit by the number of client-visits you actually had in March for the variable costs. That allowed me to come up with a better benchmark for what the variable costs should have been.

*Rick:* That's what you labelled the "budget based on 5,200 client-visits"?

*Victoria:* That's right. Your original budget was based on 5,000 client-visits, so it understated what the variable overhead costs should be when you actually serve 5,200 customers.

*Rick:* That's clear enough. These variances aren't quite as shocking as the variances on my first report.

*Victoria:* Yes, but you still have an unfavourable variance of $1,500 for client gratuities.

*Rick:* I know how that happened. In March, there was a big fund-raising dinner that I forgot about when I prepared the March budget. Many celebrities came here to attend the event. At any rate, to fit all of our regular clients in, we had to push them through here pretty fast. Everyone still got top-rate service, but I felt pretty bad about not being able to spend as much time with each customer. I wanted to give my customers a little extra something to compensate them for the less personal service, and so I ordered a lot of flowers which I gave away by the bunch.

*Victoria:* With the prices you charge, Rick, I am sure the gesture was appreciated.

*Rick:* One thing bothers me about the report. Why are some of my actual fixed costs different from what I budgeted? Doesn't fixed mean that they are not supposed to change?

*Victoria:* We call these costs *fixed* because they shouldn't be affected by *changes in the level of activity.* However, that doesn't mean that they can't change for other reasons. For example, your utilities bill, which includes natural gas for heating, varies with the weather.

*Rick:* I can see that. March was warmer than normal, and so my utilities bill was lower than I had expected.

*Victoria:* The use of the term *fixed* seems to suggest that the cost can't be controlled, but that isn't true. It is often easier to control fixed costs than variable costs. For example, it would be fairly easy for you to change your insurance bill by adjusting the amount of insurance you carry. It would be much more difficult for you to have much of an impact on the variable electric bill, which is a necessary part of serving customers.

*Rick:* I think I understand, but it *is* confusing.

*Victoria:* Just remember that a cost is called variable if it is proportional to activity; it is called fixed if it does not depend on the level of activity. However, fixed costs can change for reasons having nothing to do with changes in the level of activity. And controllability has little to do with whether a cost is variable or fixed. Fixed costs are often more controllable than variable costs.

The static budget performance report informs a manager about differences in activity-levels (if any). A report like this feeds back to the planning function; for example, Rick did not seem to spend much time on planning. He failed to include the possibility that the fund-raising dinner to be attended by many celebrities could result in additional business. In other words, managers should consider internal and external factors when establishing a budget. A flexible budget performance report, on the other hand, is a good control tool.

Using the flexible budget approach, Rick Manzi now has a much better way of assessing whether overhead costs are under control. The analysis is not so simple, however, in companies that provide a variety of products and services. The number of units produced or customers served may not be an adequate measure of overall activity. For example, does it make sense to count a Sony floppy diskette, worth only a few dollars, as equivalent to a large-screen Sony TV? If the number of units produced is used as a measure of overall activity, then the floppy diskette and the large-screen TV would be counted as equivalent. Clearly, the number of units produced (or customers served) may not be appropriate as an overall measure of activity when the organization has a variety of products or services; a common denominator may be needed.

## The Measure of Activity—A Critical Choice

What should be used as the measure of activity when the company produces a variety of products and services? At least three factors are important in selecting an activity base for an overhead flexible budget:

1.  There should be a causal relationship between the activity base and variable overhead costs. Changes in the activity base should cause, or at least be highly correlated with, changes in the variable overhead costs in the flexible budget. Ideally, the variable overhead costs in the flexible budget should vary in direct proportion to changes in the activity base. For example, in a carpentry shop specializing in handmade wood furniture, the costs of miscellaneous supplies, such as glue, wooden dowels, and sandpaper, can be expected to vary with the number of direct labour-hours. Direct

labour-hours would therefore be a good measure of activity to use in a flexible budget for the costs of such supplies. The use of activity-based costing can greatly help in identifying representative cost drivers (or activity bases).

2. The activity base should not be expressed in dollars or other currency. For example, direct labour cost is usually a poor choice for an activity base in flexible budgets. Changes in wage rates affect the activity base but do not usually result in a proportionate change in overhead. For example, we would not ordinarily expect to see a 5% increase in the consumption of glue in a carpentry shop if the workers receive a 5% increase in pay. Therefore, it is normally best to use physical, rather than financial, measures of activity in flexible budgets.

3. The activity base should be simple and easily understood. Using a base that is not easily understood will probably result in confusion and misunderstanding. It is difficult to control costs if people do not understand the reports or do not accept them as valid.

## *in business today* | Budgeting for Success

What would you do if you wanted to really impress your boss? How does being under budget on more than 500 projects in one year sound? Eugene Roman, the Chief Information Officer of Bell Canada, has created his own success through a unique combination of budgeting skills and being able to bounce from idea to idea. Information technology departments have a habit of running projects over budget, but Roman has been able to gain credibility by generating reliable financial forecasts. Roman attributes his success to superior management control, proper cost management, and the ability to view costs from a different angle. "My groups have always delivered to the numbers. We work to the goal of a budget being met, but not overstepped. It starts with good planning and execution, and considers trade-offs and risk analysis. If there are problems, we find out how to recover and make it work. That's part and parcel of the package."

Source: Cooper, John, "When in Rome . . . Renaissance man Eugene Roman sets the standard for excellence at Bell Canada," *CMA Management,* April, 2002, pp. 37–39. Reprinted with permission from CMA Canada.

# Variable Overhead Variances—A Closer Look

Concept 10–2

A special problem arises when the flexible budget is based on *hours* of activity (such as direct labour-hours), rather than on units of product or number of customers served. The problem relates to whether actual hours or standard hours should be used to develop the flexible budget on the performance report.

## The Problem of Actual versus Standard Hours

The nature of the problem can best be seen through a specific example. MicroDrive Corporation is an automated manufacturer of precision personal computer disk-drive motors. Data concerning the company's variable manufacturing overhead costs are shown in Exhibit 10–4.

MicroDrive Corporation uses machine-hours as the activity base in its flexible budget. Based on the budgeted production of 25,000 motors and the standard of two machine-hours per motor, the budgeted level of activity was 50,000 machine-hours. However, actual production for the year was only 20,000 motors, and 42,000 hours of machine time were used to produce these motors. According to the standard, only 40,000 hours of machine time should have been used (40,000 hours = 2 hours per motor × 20,000 motors).

**Exhibit 10–4**
MicroDrive Corporation Data

| | | |
|---|---|---|
| Budgeted production ........................ | 25,000 | motors |
| Actual production ........................... | 20,000 | motors |
| Standard machine-hours per motor ............. | 2 | machine-hours per motor |
| Budgeted machine-hours (2 × 25,000) .......... | 50,000 | machine-hours |
| Standard machine-hours allowed for the actual production (2 × 20,000) ................... | 40,000 | machine-hours |
| Actual machine-hours ....................... | 42,000 | machine-hours |
| **Variable overhead costs per machine-hour:** | | |
| Indirect labour ........................... | $0.80 | per machine-hour |
| Lubricants ................................ | 0.30 | per machine-hour |
| Power .................................... | 0.40 | per machine-hour |
| **Actual total variable overhead costs:** | | |
| Indirect labour ........................... | $36,000 | |
| Lubricants ................................ | 11,000 | |
| Power .................................... | 24,000 | |
| Total actual variable overhead cost ........... | $71,000 | |

In preparing an overhead performance report for the year, MicroDrive could use the 42,000 machine-hours actually worked during the year *or* the 40,000 machine-hours that should have been worked according to the standard. If the actual hours are used, only a spending variance will be computed. If the standard hours are used, both a spending *and* an efficiency variance will be computed. Both of these approaches are illustrated in the following sections.

## Spending Variance Alone

If MicroDrive Corporation bases its overhead performance report on the 42,000 machine-hours actually worked during the year, then the performance report will show only a spending variance for variable overhead. A performance report prepared in this way is shown in Exhibit 10–5.

The formula for the spending variance was introduced in the preceding chapter. That formula is:

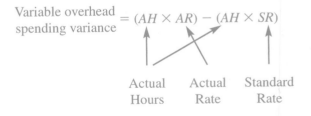

$$\text{Variable overhead spending variance} = (AH \times AR) - (AH \times SR)$$

Actual Hours    Actual Rate    Standard Rate

Or, in factored form:

$$\text{Variable overhead spending variance} = AH\,(AR - SR)$$

The report in Exhibit 10–5 is structured around the first, or unfactored, format.

**INTERPRETING THE SPENDING VARIANCE**  The variable overhead spending variance is useful only if the cost driver for variable overhead really is the actual hours worked. Then the flexible budget based on the actual hours worked is a valid benchmark that tells us how much *should* have been spent in total on variable overhead items during the period. The actual overhead costs would be larger than this benchmark, resulting in an

> **Learning Objective 3**
> Use the flexible budget to prepare a variable overhead performance report containing only a spending variance.

**Exhibit 10–5**

## MICRODRIVE CORPORATION
### Variable Overhead Performance Report
### For the Year Ended December 31

Budget allowances are based on 42,000 machine-hours actually worked

Comparing the budget against actual overhead cost yields only a spending variance

| | |
|---|---|
| Budgeted machine-hours | 50,000 |
| Actual machine-hours | 42,000 |
| Standard machine-hours allowed | 40,000 |

| Overhead Costs | Cost Formula (per machine-hour) | Actual Costs Incurred 42,000 Machine-Hours (AH × AR) | Budget Based on 42,000 Machine-Hours (AH × SR) | Spending Variance |
|---|---|---|---|---|
| Variable overhead costs: | | | | |
| Indirect labour | $0.80 | $36,000 | $33,600* | $2,400 U |
| Lubricants | 0.30 | 11,000 | 12,600 | 1,600 F |
| Power | 0.40 | 24,000 | 16,800 | 7,200 U |
| Total variable overhead cost | $1.50 | $71,000 | $63,000 | $8,000 U |

*42,000 machine-hours × $0.80 per machine-hour = $33,600. Other budget allowances are computed in the same way.

unfavourable variance, if either (1) the variable overhead items cost more to purchase than the standards allow or (2) more variable overhead items were used than the standards allow. Consuming more variable overhead items than the standards allow will result in an increase in variable overhead costs. However, the cost increase has nothing to do with the actual price paid for acquiring individual overhead items (e.g., supplies). In reality, this is a usage issue—more resources have been consumed than planned. Nonetheless, it impacts the amount spent on variable overhead, thereby resulting in a spending variance. To avoid any confusion, it is important to note that variable overhead efficiency variance has nothing to do with how efficiently overhead resources are consumed; this is clarified below.

## Both Spending and Efficiency Variances

If management of MicroDrive Corporation wants both a spending and an efficiency variance for variable overhead, then it should compute budget allowances for *both* the 40,000 machine-hour and the 42,000 machine-hour levels of activity. A performance report prepared in this way is shown in Exhibit 10–6.

Note from Exhibit 10–6 that the spending variance is the same as the spending variance shown in Exhibit 10–5. The performance report in Exhibit 10–6 has simply been expanded to include an efficiency variance as well. Together, the spending and efficiency variances make up the total variance.

INTERPRETING THE EFFICIENCY VARIANCE   From the earlier chapters, we know that overhead costs are assigned or allocated to cost objects using one or more allocation bases (or activity bases). The variable overhead efficiency variance is a measure of

## Exhibit 10–6

**MICRODRIVE CORPORATION**
**Variable Overhead Performance Report**
**For the Year Ended December 31**

Budget allowances are based on 40,000 machine-hours—the time it *should have taken* to produce the year's output of 20,000 motors—as well as on the 42,000 *actual* machine-hours worked

This approach yields both a spending and an efficiency variance

Budgeted machine-hours ................. 50,000
Actual machine-hours .................... 42,000
Standard machine-hours allowed ........... 40,000

| Overhead Costs | Cost Formula (per machine-hour) | (1) Actual Costs Incurred 42,000 Machine-Hours $(AH \times AR)$ | (2) Budget Based on 42,000 Machine-Hours $(AH \times SR)$ | (3) Budget Based on 40,000 Machine-Hours $(SH \times SR)$ | (4) Total Variance $(1) - (3)$ | Breakdown of the Total Variance Spending Variance $(1) - (2)$ | Breakdown of the Total Variance Efficiency Variance $(2) - (3)$ |
|---|---|---|---|---|---|---|---|
| Variable overhead costs: | | | | | | | |
| Indirect labour .............. | $0.80 | $36,000 | $33,600* | $32,000 | $ 4,000 U | $2,400 U | $1,600 U |
| Lubricants ................. | 0.30 | 11,000 | 12,600 | 12,000 | 1,000 F | 1,600 F | 600 U |
| Power .................... | 0.40 | 24,000 | 16,800 | 16,000 | 8,000 U | 7,200 U | 800 U |
| Total variable overhead cost ................... | $1.50 | $71,000 | $63,000 | $60,000 | $11,000 U | $8,000 U | $3,000 U |

*42,000 machine-hours × $0.80 per machine-hour = $33,600. Other budget allowances are computed in the same way.

the impact on variable overhead of how efficiently (or inefficiently) the activity (allocation) bases have been used. In a sense, the term *variable overhead efficiency variance* is a misnomer. It seems to suggest that it measures the efficiency with which variable overhead resources were used. It does not. It is an estimate of the indirect effect on variable overhead costs of inefficiency in the use of the activity base.

Recall from the preceding chapter that the variable overhead efficiency variance is a function of the difference between the actual hours incurred and the hours that should have been used to produce the period's output:

$$\frac{\text{Variable overhead}}{\text{efficiency variance}} = (AH \times SR) - (SH \times SR)$$

Actual Hours

Standard Rate

Standard Hours Allowed for Output

Or, in factored form:

$$\frac{\text{Variable overhead}}{\text{efficiency variance}} = SR(AH - SH)$$

If more hours are worked than are allowed at standard, then the overhead efficiency variance will be unfavourable. However, as discussed above, the inefficiency is not in the use of overhead *but, rather, in the use of the base itself.*

This point can be illustrated by looking again at Exhibit 10–6. Two thousand more machine-hours were used during the period than should have been used to produce the period's output. Each of these hours presumably required the incurrence of $1.50 of variable overhead cost, resulting in an unfavourable variance of $3,000 (2,000 hours $\times$ $1.50 = $3,000). Although this $3,000 variance is called an overhead efficiency variance, it could be better termed a machine-hours efficiency variance, since it results from using too many machine-hours, rather than from inefficient use of overhead resources. However, the term *overhead efficiency variance* is so firmly ingrained in day-to-day use that a change is unlikely. Even so, be careful to interpret the variance with a clear understanding of what it really measures.

**CONTROL OF THE EFFICIENCY VARIANCE**   Who is responsible for control of the overhead efficiency variance? Since the variance really reflects efficiency in the utilization of the base underlying the flexible budget, whoever is responsible for control of this base is responsible for control of the variance. If the base is direct labour-hours, then the supervisor responsible for the use of labour time will be responsible for any overhead efficiency variance.

## Activity-Based Costing and the Flexible Budget

It is unlikely that all of the variable overhead in a complex organization is driven by a single factor, such as the number of units produced or the number of labour-hours or machine-hours. Activity-based costing provides a way of recognizing a variety of overhead cost drivers and thereby increasing the accuracy of the costing system. In activity-based costing, each overhead cost pool has its own measure of activity. The actual spending in each overhead cost pool can be independently evaluated using the techniques discussed in this chapter. The only difference is that the cost formulas for variable overhead costs will be stated in terms of different kinds of activities instead of all being stated in terms of units or a common measure of activity, such as direct labour-hours or machine-hours. If done properly, activity-based costing can greatly enhance the usefulness of overhead performance reports by recognizing multiple causes of overhead costs. But the usefulness of overhead performance reports depends on how carefully the reports are done. In particular, managers must take care to separate the variable from the fixed costs in the flexible budgets.[1]

*in business* *today*   **Pools within Pools**

Caterpillar, Inc., a manufacturer of heavy equipment and a pioneering company in the development and use of activity-based costing, divides its overhead costs into three large pools—the logistics cost pool, the manufacturing cost pool, and the general cost pool. In turn, these three cost pools are subdivided into scores of activity centres, with each centre having its own flexible budget from which variable and fixed overhead rates are developed. In an article describing the company's cost system, the systems manager stated that "the many manufacturing cost centre rates are the unique elements that set Caterpillar's system apart from simple cost systems."

Source: Lou F. Jones, "Product Costing at Caterpillar," *Management Accounting* 72, no. 8 (February 1991), p. 39. Reprinted with permission from *Management Accounting.*

---

[1]See Mak and Roush, "Managing Activity Costs with Flexible Budgeting and Variance Analysis," *Accounting Horizons*, September 1996, pp. 141–146, for an insightful discussion of activity-based costing and overhead variance analysis.

# Overhead Rates and Fixed Overhead Analysis

The detailed analysis of fixed overhead differs considerably from the analysis of variable overhead, simply because of the difference in the nature of the costs involved. To provide a background for our discussion, we will first review briefly the need for, and computation of, predetermined overhead rates. This review will be helpful, since the predetermined overhead rate plays a major role in fixed overhead analysis. We will then show how fixed overhead variances are computed and make some observations as to their usefulness to managers.

## Flexible Budgets and Overhead Rates

Fixed costs come in large, indivisible pieces that by definition do not change with changes in the level of activity within a relevant range. This creates a problem in product costing, since a given level of fixed overhead cost spread over a small number of units will result in a higher cost per unit than if the same amount of cost is spread over a large number of units. Consider the data in the following table:

**Learning Objective 5**
Compute the predetermined overhead rate and apply overhead to products in a standard cost system.

| Month | (1) Fixed Overhead Cost | (2) Number of Units Produced | (3) Unit Cost (1) ÷ (2) |
|---|---|---|---|
| January | $6,000 | 1,000 | $6.00 |
| February | 6,000 | 1,500 | 4.00 |
| March | 6,000 | 800 | 7.50 |

Note that the large number of units produced in February results in a low unit cost ($4), whereas the small number of units produced in March results in a high unit cost ($7.50). This problem arises only in connection with the fixed portion of overhead, since by definition the variable portion of overhead remains constant on a per-unit basis, rising and falling in total proportionately with changes in the activity level. Most managers feel that the fixed portion of unit cost should be stabilized so that a single unit cost figure can be used throughout the year. As we learned in Chapter 3, this stability can be accomplished through use of the predetermined overhead rate.

Throughout the remainder of this chapter, we will be analyzing the fixed overhead costs of MicroDrive Corporation. To assist us in that task, the flexible budget of the company—including fixed costs—is displayed in Exhibit 10–7. Note that the total fixed overhead costs amount to $300,000 within the range of activity in the flexible budget.

DENOMINATOR ACTIVITY    The formula that we used in Chapter 3 to compute the predetermined overhead rate is given below

$$\text{Predetermined overhead rate} = \frac{\text{Estimated total manufacturing overhead cost}}{\text{Estimated total units in the allocation base (MH, DLH, etc.)}}$$

The estimated total units in the base in the formula for the predetermined overhead rate is called the **denominator activity.** Recall from our discussion in Chapter 3 that once an estimated activity level (denominator activity) has been chosen, it remains unchanged throughout the year, even if the actual activity turns out to be different from what was estimated. The reason for not changing the denominator is to maintain stability in the amount of overhead applied to each unit of product, regardless of when it is produced during the year.

**Exhibit 10–7**

### MICRODRIVE CORPORATION
### Flexible Budgets at Various Levels of Activity

| Overhead Costs | Cost Formula (per machine-hour) | Activity (in machine-hours) | | | |
|---|---|---|---|---|---|
| | | 40,000 | 45,000 | 50,000 | 55,000 |
| Variable overhead costs: | | | | | |
|   Indirect labour ........ | $0.80 | $ 32,000 | $ 36,000 | $ 40,000 | $ 44,000 |
|   Lubricants ........... | 0.30 | 12,000 | 13,500 | 15,000 | 16,500 |
|   Power .............. | 0.40 | 16,000 | 18,000 | 20,000 | 22,000 |
| Total variable overhead cost ......... | $1.50 | 60,000 | 67,500 | 75,000 | 82,500 |
| Fixed overhead costs: | | | | | |
|   Depreciation ......... | | 100,000 | 100,000 | 100,000 | 100,000 |
|   Supervisory salaries .... | | 160,000 | 160,000 | 160,000 | 160,000 |
|   Insurance ........... | | 40,000 | 40,000 | 40,000 | 40,000 |
| Total fixed overhead cost ......... | | 300,000 | 300,000 | 300,000 | 300,000 |
| Total overhead cost ...... | | $360,000 | $367,500 | $375,000 | $382,500 |

**COMPUTING THE OVERHEAD RATE**  When we discussed predetermined overhead rates in Chapter 3, we did not explain how the estimated total manufacturing cost was determined. This figure can be derived from the flexible budget. Once the denominator level of activity has been chosen, the flexible budget can be used to determine the total amount of overhead cost that should be incurred at that level of activity. The predetermined overhead rate can then be computed using the following variation on the basic formula for the predetermined overhead rate:

$$\text{Predetermined overhead rate} = \frac{\text{Overhead from the flexible budget at the denominator level of activity}}{\text{Denominator level of activity}}$$

To illustrate, refer to MicroDrive Corporation's flexible budget for manufacturing overhead in Exhibit 10–7. Suppose that the budgeted activity level for the year is 50,000 machine-hours and that this will be used as the denominator activity in the formula for the predetermined overhead rate. The numerator in the formula is the estimated total overhead cost of $375,000 when the activity is 50,000 machine-hours. This figure is taken from the flexible budget in Exhibit 10–7. In sum, the predetermined overhead rate for MicroDrive Corporation will be computed as follows:

$$\frac{\$375,000}{50,000 \text{ MHs}} = \$7.50 \text{ per machine-hour}$$

Or the company can break its predetermined overhead rate down into variable and fixed elements, rather than using a single combined figure:

$$\text{Variable element:} \frac{\$75,000}{50,000 \text{ MHs}} = \$1.50 \text{ per machine-hour (MH)}$$

$$\text{Fixed element:} \frac{\$300,000}{50,000 \text{ MHs}} = \$6 \text{ per machine-hour (MH)}$$

For every standard machine-hour of operation, work in process will be charged with $7.50 of overhead, of which $1.50 will be variable overhead and $6 will be fixed overhead. If a disk-drive motor should take two machine-hours to complete, then its cost will include $3 variable overhead and $12 fixed overhead, as shown on the following standard cost card:

| Standard Cost Card—Per Motor | |
| --- | ---: |
| Direct materials (assumed) ................................... | $14 |
| Direct labour (assumed) ...................................... | 6 |
| Variable overhead (2 machine-hours at $1.50 per machine-hour) ..... | 3 |
| Fixed overhead (2 machine-hours at $6 per machine-hour) .......... | 12 |
| Total standard cost per motor ................................ | $35 |

In sum, the flexible budget provides the estimated overhead cost needed to compute the predetermined overhead rate. Thus, the flexible budget plays a key role in determining the amount of fixed and variable overhead costs that will be charged to units of product.

## Overhead Application in a Standard Cost System

To understand the fixed overhead variances, it is necessary first to understand how overhead is applied to work in process in a standard cost system. In Chapter 3, recall that we applied overhead to work in process on the basis of actual hours of activity (multiplied by the predetermined overhead rate). This procedure was correct, since at the time we were dealing with a normal cost system.[2] However, we are now dealing with a standard cost system. In such a system, overhead is applied to work in process on the basis of the *standard hours allowed for the output of the period,* rather than on the basis of the actual number of hours worked. This point is illustrated in Exhibit 10–8. In a standard cost system, every unit of product moving along the production line bears the same amount of overhead cost, regardless of any variations in efficiency that may have been involved in its production.

| Normal Cost System Manufacturing Overhead | | Standard Cost System Manufacturing Overhead | |
| --- | --- | --- | --- |
| Actual overhead costs incurred | Applied overhead costs: Actual hours × Predetermined overhead rate | Actual overhead costs incurred | Applied overhead costs: Standard hours allowed for actual output × Predetermined overhead rate |
| Under- or over-applied overhead | | Under- or over-applied overhead | |

**Exhibit 10–8**
Applied Overhead Costs: Normal Cost System versus Standard Cost System

---

[2]Normal cost systems are discussed in Chapter 3.

# The Fixed Overhead Variances

**Learning Objective 6**
Compute and interpret the fixed overhead budget and volume variances.

To illustrate the computation of fixed overhead variances, we will refer again to the data for MicroDrive Corporation.

| | |
|---|---|
| Denominator activity in machine-hours .......... | 50,000 |
| Budgeted fixed overhead costs ................. | $300,000 |
| Fixed portion of the predetermined overhead rate (computed earlier) ............. | $6 per machine-hour |

Let us assume that the following actual operating results were recorded for the year:

| | |
|---|---|
| Actual machine-hours ......................... | 42,000 |
| Standard machine-hours allowed* .............. | 40,000 |
| Actual fixed overhead costs: | |
| Depreciation ................................ | $100,000 |
| Supervisory salaries ........................ | 172,000 |
| Insurance ................................... | 36,000 |
| Total actual cost ........................... | $308,000 |

*For the actual production during the year.

From these data, two variances can be computed for fixed overhead—a *budget variance* and a *volume variance*. The variances are shown in Exhibit 10–9.

Note from the exhibit that overhead has been applied to work in process on the basis of 40,000 standard hours allowed for the output of the year, rather than on the basis of 42,000 actual hours worked. As stated earlier, this keeps unit costs from being affected by any variations in efficiency.

# The Budget Variance—A Closer Look

The **budget variance** is the difference between the actual fixed overhead costs incurred during the period and the budgeted fixed overhead costs as contained in the flexible budget. It can be computed as shown in Exhibit 10–9 or by using the following formula:

$$\text{Budget variance} = \text{Actual fixed overhead cost} - \text{Flexible budget fixed overhead cost}$$

Applying this formula to MicroDrive Corporation, the budget variance would be as follows:

$$\$308,000 - \$300,000 = \$8,000 \text{ U}$$

**Exhibit 10–9**
Computation of the Fixed Overhead Variances

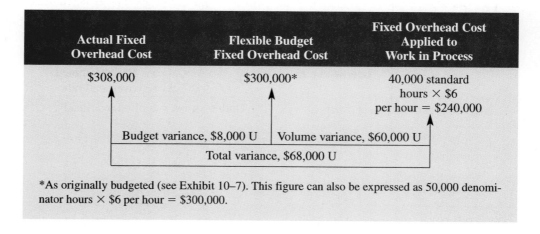

| Actual Fixed Overhead Cost | Flexible Budget Fixed Overhead Cost | Fixed Overhead Cost Applied to Work in Process |
|---|---|---|
| $308,000 | $300,000* | 40,000 standard hours × $6 per hour = $240,000 |
| | Budget variance, $8,000 U | Volume variance, $60,000 U |
| | Total variance, $68,000 U | |

*As originally budgeted (see Exhibit 10–7). This figure can also be expressed as 50,000 denominator hours × $6 per hour = $300,000.

**Exhibit 10–10**
Fixed Overhead Costs on the
Overhead Performance Report

**MICRODRIVE CORPORATION**
**Overhead Performance Report**
**For the Year Ended December 31**

Budgeted machine-hours ............    50,000
Actual machine-hours .............    42,000
Standard machine-hours allowed .....    40,000

| Overhead Costs | Cost Formula (per machine-hour) | Actual Costs 42,000 Machine-Hours | Budget Based on 42,000 Machine-Hours | Spending or Budget Variance |
|---|---|---|---|---|
| Variable overhead costs: | | | | |
| Indirect labour ............ | $0.80 | $ 36,000 | $ 33,600 | $ 2,400 U |
| Lubricants .............. | 0.30 | 11,000 | 12,600 | 1,600 F |
| Power ................. | 0.40 | 24,000 | 16,800 | 7,200 U |
| Total variable overhead cost ............. | $1.50 | 71,000 | 63,000 | 8,000 U |
| Fixed overhead costs: | | | | |
| Depreciation .............. | | 100,000 | 100,000 | — |
| Supervisory salaries ........ | | 172,000 | 160,000 | 12,000 U |
| Insurance ............... | | 36,000 | 40,000 | 4,000 F |
| Total fixed overhead cost ...... | | 308,000 | 300,000 | 8,000 U |
| Total overhead cost .......... | | $379,000 | $363,000 | $16,000 U |

The variances computed for the fixed costs at Rick's Hairstyling in Exhibit 10–3 are all budget variances, since they represent the difference between the actual fixed overhead cost and the budgeted fixed overhead cost from the flexible budget.

An expanded overhead performance report for MicroDrive Corporation appears in Exhibit 10–10. This report now includes the budget variances for fixed overhead as well as the spending variances for variable overhead that were in Exhibit 10–5.

The budget variances for fixed overhead can be very useful, since they represent the difference between how much *should* have been spent (according to the flexible budget) and how much was actually spent. For example, supervisory salaries has a $12,000 unfavourable variance. There should be some explanation for this large variance. Was it due to an increase in salaries? Was it due to overtime? Was another supervisor hired? If so, why was another supervisor hired?—this was not included in the budget when activity for the year was planned. Another factor causing increase in fixed overhead is investments in technology, such as the automated system implemented by TML (see opening decision feature). To the extent that the additional capacity created by the investment is not utilized, it will be seen as a burden despite some gains in efficiency.

## The Volume Variance—A Closer Look

The **volume variance** is a measure of utilization of plant facilities. It can be computed as shown in Exhibit 10–9 or by means of the following formula:

$$\text{Volume variance} = \text{Fixed portion of the predetermined overhead rate} \times \left( \text{Denominator hours} - \text{Standard hours allowed} \right)$$

Applying this formula to MicroDrive Corporation, the volume variance would be computed as follows:

$$\$6 \text{ per MH } (50{,}000 \text{ MH} - 40{,}000 \text{ MH}) = \$60{,}000 \text{ U}$$

Note that this computation agrees with the volume variance as shown in Exhibit 10–9. As stated earlier, the volume variance is a measure of utilization of available plant facilities. An unfavourable variance, as above, means that the company operated at an activity level *below* that planned for the period. A favourable variance would mean that the company operated at an activity level *greater* than that planned for the period.

It is important to note that the volume variance does not measure over- or underspending. The variance arises because 5,000 fewer units were produced during the budget period than planned (see Exhibit 10–4). This means that we spread the total fixed costs over a smaller number of units; each unit of product "absorbs" a greater portion of the overhead than planned. Managers must focus their attention on understanding why 5,000 fewer units were produced. The reasons could be many, such as a decline in orders (perhaps due to a downturn in the economy or due to lack of proper marketing), production problems, labour problems, or other factors. An effort must be made to ensure that planned production levels are achieved.

To summarize:

1. If the planned and actual production levels are the same, then the denominator activity and standard hours allowed for the output of the period are the same, and there is no volume variance.
2. If actual production is less than planned production, then the denominator activity is greater than the standard hours allowed for the output of the period, and the volume variance is unfavourable. This signals that the available facilities are under-utilized.
3. If actual production is greater than planned production, then the denominator activity is less than the standard hours allowed for the output of the period, and the volume variance is favourable. This signals that utilization levels are higher than planned.

*decision* | *maker*      **Vice-President of Production**

One of the company's factories produces a single product. The factory recently reported a significant unfavourable volume variance for the year. Sales for that product were less than anticipated. What should you do?

## Cautions in Fixed Overhead Analysis

The reason we get a volume variance for fixed overhead is that the total fixed cost does not depend on activity; yet when applying the costs to work in process, we act *as if* the fixed costs were variable and depended on activity. This point can be illustrated graphically as in Exhibit 10–11. Note from the graph that the fixed overhead costs are applied to work in process at a rate of $6 per hour *as if* they were variable. Treating these costs as if they were variable is necessary for product costing purposes, but there are some real dangers here. The manager can easily become misled and start thinking of the fixed costs as if they were, *in fact*, variable.

The manager must keep clearly in mind that fixed overhead costs come in large, indivisible pieces. Expressing fixed costs on a unit or per-hour basis, though necessary for product costing for external reports, is artificial. Increases or decreases in activity, in fact, have no effect on total fixed costs within the relevant range of activity. Even though fixed costs are expressed on a unit or per-hour basis, they are *not* proportional to activity. In a sense, the volume variance is the error that occurs as a result of treating fixed costs as variable costs in the costing system.

**Exhibit 10–11**
Graphic Analysis of Fixed
Overhead Variances

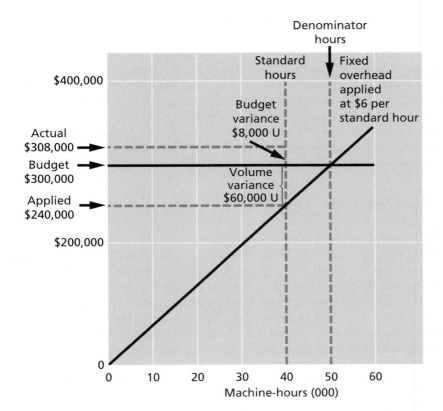

Because of the confusion that can arise concerning the interpretation of the volume variance, some companies present the volume variance in physical units (hours), rather than in dollars. These companies feel that stating the variance in physical units gives management a clearer signal concerning the cause of the variance.

## Overhead Variances and Under- or Over-applied Overhead Cost

Four variances relating to overhead cost have been computed for MicroDrive Corporation in this chapter. These four variances are as follows:

| | |
|---|---:|
| Variable overhead spending variance (p. 380) . . . . . | $ 8,000 U |
| Variable overhead efficiency variance (p. 381) . . . . . | 3,000 U |
| Fixed overhead budget variance (p. 386) . . . . . . . . . | 8,000 U |
| Fixed overhead volume variance (p. 386) . . . . . . . . . | 60,000 U |
| Total overhead variance . . . . . . . . . . . . . . . . . . . . . | $79,000 U |

Recall from Chapter 3 that under- or over-applied overhead is the difference between the amount of overhead applied to products and the actual overhead costs incurred during a period. Basically, the overhead variances we have computed in this chapter break the under- or over-applied overhead down into variances that can be used by managers for control purposes. Consequently, *the sum of the overhead variances equals the under- or over-applied overhead cost for a period.*

Furthermore, in a standard cost system, unfavourable variances are equivalent to underapplied overhead and favourable variances are equivalent to over-applied overhead. Unfavourable variances occur because more was spent on overhead than the standards allow. Under-applied overhead occurs when more was spent on overhead than was applied to products during the period. But in a standard costing system, the standard amount of overhead allowed is exactly the same amount of overhead applied to products. Therefore, in a standard costing system, unfavourable variances and under-applied overhead are the same thing, as are favourable variances and over-applied overhead.

For MicroDrive Corporation, the total overhead variance was $79,000 unfavourable. Therefore, its overhead cost was under-applied by $79,000 for the year. To solidify this point in your mind, *carefully study the review problem at the end of the chapter!* This review problem provides a comprehensive summary of overhead analysis, including the computation of under- or over-applied overhead cost in a standard cost system.

# Is Variance Analysis a Timely Control Tool?

Given the importance of timely information for the purposes of decision making, should managers wait until the end of a period to find out about variances that occurred during that period? The answer really depends on why the flexible budgeting and variance analysis is used in an organization. In most cases, responsible managers will likely be aware of variances prior to the end of the budget period. Production managers can monitor the use of input resources on a daily basis and get an idea whether more or less quantities than planned will be used during the period. They can then take corrective actions even before the end of the budgeting period. In fact, such an action is desirable to avoid excessive deviations/cost over-runs.

However, without formally computing the variances in dollar amounts, they will not know the impact of the deviations on profitability. Organizations that use management by exception also find the variance reports useful for follow-up actions. Preparing variance reports is useful for financial accounting purposes in firms that use a standard cost accounting system. Any deviations can be appropriately closed to the proper accounts.

*you decide*     **Budget Analyst**

Your company is in the process of implementing an activity-based costing program and plans to use the flexible approach to budgeting. To aid in the analysis of the factory overhead once these plans are in place, how should the under- or over-applied overhead be analyzed? Who should be held responsible for each of the variances?

# Summary

**LO1    Prepare a flexible budget and explain the advantages of the flexible budget approach over the static budget approach.**

A flexible budget shows what costs should be as a function of the level of activity. A flexible budget provides a better benchmark for evaluating how well costs have been controlled than the static budget approved at the beginning of the period. Some costs should be different from the amounts budgeted at the beginning of the period simply because the level of activity is different from what was expected. The flexible budget takes this fact into account, whereas the static budget does not.

**LO2    Prepare a performance report for both variable and fixed overhead costs using the flexible budget approach and explain its advantages.**

A flexible budget performance report compares actual costs with what the costs should have been, given the actual level of activity for the period. Variable costs are flexed (i.e., adjusted) for the actual level of activity. This is done by multiplying the cost per unit of activity by the actual level of activity. Fixed costs, at least within the relevant range, are not adjusted for the level of activity. The total cost for a fixed cost item is carried over from the static budget without adjustment.

### LO3  Use the flexible budget to prepare a variable overhead performance report containing only a spending variance.

The spending variance for a variable overhead item is computed by comparing the actual cost incurred to the amount that should have been spent, on the basis of the actual direct labour-hours or machine-hours of the period.

### LO4  Use the flexible budget to prepare a variable overhead performance report containing both a spending and an efficiency variance.

As stated above, the spending variance for a variable overhead item is computed by comparing the actual cost incurred with the amount that should have been spent, on the basis of the actual direct labour-hours or machine-hours of the period. The efficiency variance is computed by comparing the cost that should have been incurred for the actual direct labour-hours or machine-hours of the period with the cost that should have been incurred for the actual level of *output* of the period.

### LO5  Compute the predetermined overhead rate and apply overhead to products in a standard cost system.

In a standard cost system, overhead is applied to products based on the standard hours allowed for the actual output of the period. This differs from a normal cost system in which overhead is applied to products on the basis of the actual hours of the period.

### LO6  Compute and interpret the fixed overhead budget and volume variances.

The fixed overhead budget variance is the difference between the actual total fixed overhead costs incurred for the period and the budgeted total fixed overhead costs. This variance measures how well fixed overhead costs were controlled.

The fixed overhead volume variance is the difference between the fixed overhead applied to production using the predetermined overhead rate and the budgeted total fixed overhead. A favourable variance occurs when the standard hours allowed for the actual output exceed the hours assumed when the predetermined overhead rate was computed. An unfavourable variance occurs when the standard hours allowed for the actual output is less than the hours assumed when the predetermined overhead rate was computed.

# Guidance Answers to You Decide and Decision Maker

**VICE-PRESIDENT OF PRODUCTION** (p. 388)

An unfavourable fixed overhead volume variance means that the factory is operating at an activity level below the level that was planned for the year. You should meet with the vice-president of sales to determine why demand was less than planned. Was production part of the problem? Were orders delivered late? Were customers quoted lead times that were too long? Could production help increase demand by improving the quality of the product and the services provided to customers? If sales are declining and are not expected to rebound, you should consider how to make use of the excess capacity in this factory. You might consider whether the factory could be reconfigured to produce another product or if a section of the factory could be leased to another company.

**BUDGET ANALYST** (p. 390)

The under- or over-applied overhead should be broken into its four components: (1) the variable overhead spending variance, (2) the variable overhead efficiency variance, (3) the fixed overhead budget variance, and (4) the fixed overhead volume variance.

The person who purchases the variable overhead items (such as lubricants) and the supervisor(s) who directs and/or controls the employees who are classified as indirect labour are responsible for the variable overhead spending variance. Whoever is responsible for the control of the activity base that is used to apply overhead should be responsible for the control of the variable overhead efficiency variance. The person(s) responsible for negotiating the purchase of the fixed overhead items (such as rent and insurance) and the supervisor(s) who directs and/or controls the support staff are responsible for the fixed overhead budget variance. The fixed overhead volume variance does not indicate that the company has overspent or underspent; it is a measure of utilization of available plant facilities. As such, the person responsible for determining the level of activity for the plant would be responsible for this variance.

# Review Problem: Overhead Analysis

(This problem provides a comprehensive review of Chapter 10, including the computation of under- or over-applied overhead and its breakdown into the four overhead variances.)

Data for the manufacturing overhead of Aspen Company are given below:

| Overhead Costs | Cost Formula (per machine-hour) | Machine-Hours | | |
|---|---|---|---|---|
| | | 5,000 | 6,000 | 7,000 |
| Variable overhead costs: | | | | |
|   Supplies ..................... | $0.20 | $ 1,000 | $ 1,200 | $ 1,400 |
|   Indirect labour ................ | 0.30 | 1,500 | 1,800 | 2,100 |
| Total variable overhead cost ......... | $0.50 | 2,500 | 3,000 | 3,500 |
| Fixed overhead costs: | | | | |
|   Depreciation ................... | | 4,000 | 4,000 | 4,000 |
|   Supervision ................... | | 5,000 | 5,000 | 5,000 |
| Total fixed overhead cost .......... | | 9,000 | 9,000 | 9,000 |
| Total overhead cost .............. | | $11,500 | $12,000 | $12,500 |

Five hours of machine time are required per unit of product. The company has set denominator activity for the coming period at 6,000 machine-hours (or 1,200 units). The computation of the predetermined overhead rate would be as follows:

$$\text{Total:} \frac{\$12,000}{6,000 \text{ MH}} = \$2.00 \text{ per machine-hour}$$

$$\text{Variable element:} \frac{\$3,000}{6,000 \text{ MH}} = \$0.50 \text{ per machine-hour}$$

$$\text{Fixed element:} \frac{\$9,000}{6,000 \text{ MH}} = \$1.50 \text{ per machine-hour}$$

Assume the following *actual* results for the period:

| | |
|---|---|
| Number of units produced ............ | 1,300 units |
| Actual machine-hours .............. | 6,800 machine-hours |
| Standard machine-hours allowed* ...... | 6,500 machine-hours |
| Actual variable overhead cost ......... | $4,200 |
| Actual fixed overhead cost ............ | 9,400 |

*1,300 units × 5 machine-hours per unit.

Therefore, the company's Manufacturing Overhead account would appear as follows at the end of the period:

**Manufacturing Overhead**

| Actual overhead costs | 13,600* | 13,000† | Applied overhead costs |
|---|---|---|---|
| Under-applied overhead | 600 | | |

*$4,200 variable + $9,400 fixed = $13,600.

†6,500 standard machine-hours × $2 per machine-hour = $13,000.

In a standard cost system, overhead is applied on the basis of standard hours, not actual hours.

*Required:*

Analyze the $600 under-applied overhead in terms of:

1. A variable overhead spending variance.
2. A variable overhead efficiency variance.
3. A fixed overhead budget variance.
4. A fixed overhead volume variance.

## SOLUTION TO REVIEW PROBLEM

### Variable Overhead Variances

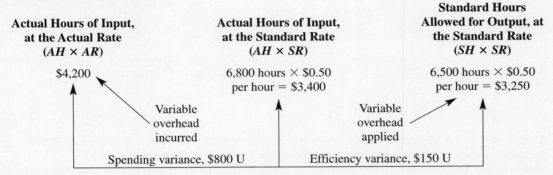

These same variances in the alternative format would be as follows:

Variable overhead spending variance:

$$\text{Spending variance} = (AH \times AR) - (AH \times SR)$$
$$(\$4,200^*) - (6,800 \text{ hours} \times \$0.50 \text{ per hour}) = \$800 \text{ U}$$

*$AH \times AR$ equals the total actual cost for the period.

Variable overhead efficiency variance:

$$\text{Efficiency variance} = SR(AH - SH)$$
$$\$0.50 \text{ per hour} (6,800 \text{ hours} - 6,500 \text{ hours}) = \$150 \text{ U}$$

### Fixed Overhead Variances

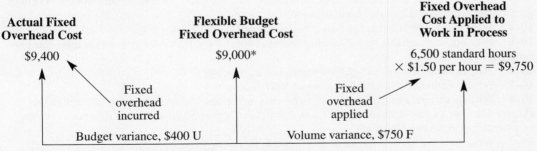

*Can be expressed as: 6,000 denominator hours × $1.50 per hour = $9,000.

These same variances in the alternative format would be as follows:

Fixed overhead budget variance:

$$\frac{\text{Budget}}{\text{variance}} = \frac{\text{Actual fixed}}{\text{overhead cost}} - \frac{\text{Flexible budget}}{\text{fixed overhead cost}}$$

$$\$9,400 - \$9,000 = \$400 \text{ U}$$

Fixed overhead volume variance:

$$\text{Volume variance} = \begin{array}{c} \text{Fixed portion} \\ \text{of the predetermined} \\ \text{overhead rate} \end{array} \times \left(\begin{array}{c} \text{Denominator} \\ \text{hours} \end{array} - \begin{array}{c} \text{Standard} \\ \text{hours} \end{array}\right)$$

$$\$1.50 \text{ per hour} (6,000 \text{ hours} - 6,500 \text{ hours}) = \$750 \text{ F}$$

**Summary of Variances**

A summary of the four overhead variances is given below:

| | |
|---|---|
| Variable overhead: | |
| Spending variance . . . . . . . . | $800 U |
| Efficiency variance . . . . . . . | 150 U |
| Fixed overhead: | |
| Budget variance . . . . . . . . . . | 400 U |
| Volume variance . . . . . . . . . | 750 F |
| Under-applied overhead . . . . . | $600 |

Note that the $600 summary variance figure agrees with the under-applied balance in the company's Manufacturing Overhead account. This agreement verifies the accuracy of our variance analysis.

# Glossary

**Budget variance** A measure of the difference between the actual fixed overhead costs incurred during the period and budgeted fixed overhead costs as contained in the flexible budget. (p. 386)

**Denominator activity** The activity figure used to compute the predetermined overhead allocation rate. (p. 383)

**Flexible budget** A budget that is designed to cover a range of activity and that can be used to develop budgeted costs at any point within that range to compare with actual costs incurred. (p. 373)

**Static budget** A budget designed for only one level of activity. (p. 372)

**Volume variance** The variance that arises when actual output during a period is different from the planned output. It is a measure of how well the organization's facilities are utilized. (p. 387)

# Questions

**10–1**  What is a static budget?

**10–2**  What is a flexible budget, and how does it differ from a static budget?

**10–3**  In comparing flexible budget data with actual data in a performance report for variable overhead, what variance(s) will be produced if the flexible budget data are based on actual hours worked? On both actual hours worked and standard hours allowed?

**10–4**  What is meant by the term *standard hours allowed?*

**10–5**  How does the variable manufacturing overhead spending variance differ from the materials price variance?

**10–6**  Why is the term *overhead efficiency variance* a misnomer?

**10–7**  What is meant by the term *denominator level of activity?*

**10–8**  Why do we apply overhead to work in process on the basis of standard hours allowed in this chapter when we applied it on the basis of actual hours in Chapter 3? What is the difference in costing systems between the two chapters?

**10–9**  What does the fixed overhead budget variance measure?

**10–10**  Under what circumstances would you expect the volume variance to be favourable? Unfavourable? Does the variance measure deviations in spending for fixed overhead items? Explain.

**10–11**  In Chapter 3, you became acquainted with the concept of under- or over-applied overhead. The under- or over-applied overhead can be broken down into what four variances?

**10–12**  If factory overhead is over-applied for August, would you expect the total of the overhead variances to be favourable or unfavourable?

# Brief Exercises

**BRIEF EXERCISE 10–1    Preparing a Flexible Budget** (LO1)

An incomplete flexible budget is given below for Lavage Rapide, a Swiss company that owns and operates a large automatic carwash facility near Geneva. The Swiss currency is the Swiss franc, which is denoted by SFr.

**LAVAGE RAPIDE**
**Flexible Budget**
**For the Month Ended August 31**

| Overhead Costs | Cost Formula (per car) | Activity (cars) | | |
| --- | --- | --- | --- | --- |
| | | 8,000 | 9,000 | 10,000 |
| Variable overhead costs: | | | | |
| Cleaning supplies ............... | ? | ? | 7,200 SFr | ? |
| Electricity ...................... | ? | ? | 2,700 | ? |
| Maintenance .................... | ? | ? | 1,800 | ? |
| Total variable overhead cost .......... | ? | ? | ? | ? |
| Fixed overhead costs: | | | | |
| Operator wages .................. | | ? | 9,000 | ? |
| Depreciation .................... | | ? | 6,000 | ? |
| Rent............................ | | ? | 8,000 | ? |
| Total fixed overhead cost ............ | | ? | ? | ? |
| Total overhead cost ................. | | ? | ? | ? |

*Required:*
Fill in the missing data.

### BRIEF EXERCISE 10–2   Prepare a Static Budget (LO1)

Refer to the data in Brief Exercise 10–1. Lavage Rapide's owner-manager would like to prepare a budget for August assuming an activity level of 8,800 cars.

*Required:*
Prepare a static budget for August. Use Exhibit 10–1 in the chapter as your guide.

### BRIEF EXERCISE 10–3   Flexible Budget Performance Report (LO2)

Refer to the data in Brief Exercise 10–1. Lavage Rapide's actual level of activity during August was 8,900 cars, although the owner had constructed his static budget for the month assuming the level of activity would be 8,800 cars. The actual overhead costs incurred during August are given below:

| | Actual Costs Incurred for 8,900 Cars |
| --- | --- |
| Variable overhead costs: | |
| Cleaning supplies .......... | 7,080 SFr |
| Electricity ................ | 2,460 |
| Maintenance .............. | 1,550 |
| Fixed overhead costs: | |
| Operator wages ............ | 9,100 |
| Depreciation ............. | 7,000 |
| Rent .................... | 8,000 |

*Required:*
Prepare a flexible budget performance report for both the variable and fixed overhead costs for August. Use Exhibit 10–3 in the chapter as your guide.

### BRIEF EXERCISE 10–4   Variable Overhead Performance Report with Just a Spending Variance (LO3)

Yung Corporation bases its variable overhead performance report on the actual direct labour-hours of the period. Data concerning the most recent year that ended on December 31 appear below:

| | |
| --- | --- |
| Budgeted direct labour-hours ........... | 38,000 |
| Actual direct labour-hours ............. | 34,000 |
| Standard direct labour-hours allowed ..... | 35,000 |

Cost formula (per direct labour-hour):

| | |
|---|---|
| Indirect labour . . . . . . . . . . . . . . . . . . . . . . . | $0.60 |
| Supplies . . . . . . . . . . . . . . . . . . . . . . . . . . . | 0.10 |
| Electricity . . . . . . . . . . . . . . . . . . . . . . . . . | 0.05 |

Actual costs incurred:

| | |
|---|---|
| Indirect labour . . . . . . . . . . . . . . . . . . . . . . . | $21,200 |
| Supplies . . . . . . . . . . . . . . . . . . . . . . . . . . . | 3,200 |
| Electricity . . . . . . . . . . . . . . . . . . . . . . . . . | 1,600 |

*Required:*

Prepare a variable overhead performance report using the format in Exhibit 10–5. Compute just the variable overhead spending variances (do not compute the variable overhead efficiency variances).

**BRIEF EXERCISE 10–5    Variable Overhead Performance Report with Both Spending and Efficiency Variances (LO4)**

Refer to the data for Yung Corporation in Brief Exercise 10–4. Management would like to compute both spending and efficiency variances for variable overheads in the company's variable overhead performance report.

*Required:*

Prepare a variable overhead performance report using the format in Exhibit 10–6. Compute both the variable overhead spending variances and the overhead efficiency variances.

**BRIEF EXERCISE 10–6    Applying Overhead in a Standard Costing System (LO5)**

Privack Corporation has a standard cost system in which it applies overhead to products on the basis of the standard direct labour-hours allowed for the actual output of the period. Data concerning the most recent year appear below:

| | |
|---|---|
| Variable overhead cost per direct labour-hour . . . . . . . . . . . . . . . . . . . . . . | $2.00 |
| Total fixed overhead cost per year . . . . . . . . . . . . . . . . . . . . . . . . . . . . . | $250,000 |
| Budgeted standard direct labour-hours (denominator level of activity) . . . | 40,000 |
| Actual direct labour-hours . . . . . . . . . . . . . . . . . . . . . . . . . . . . . . . . . . . | 39,000 |
| Standard direct labour-hours allowed for the actual output . . . . . . . . . . . . | 38,000 |

*Required:*

1. Compute the predetermined overhead rate for the year.
2. Determine the amount of overhead that would be applied to the output of the period.

**BRIEF EXERCISE 10–7    Fixed Overhead Variances (LO6)**

Primara Corporation has a standard cost system in which it applies overhead to products on the basis of the standard direct labour-hours allowed for the actual output of the period. Data concerning the most recent year appear below:

| | |
|---|---|
| Total budgeted fixed overhead cost for the year . . . . . . . . . . . . . . . . . . . . . | $250,000 |
| Actual fixed overhead cost for the year . . . . . . . . . . . . . . . . . . . . . . . . . . . | $254,000 |
| Budgeted standard direct labour-hours (denominator level of activity) . . . | 25,000 |
| Actual direct labour-hours . . . . . . . . . . . . . . . . . . . . . . . . . . . . . . . . . . . | 27,000 |
| Standard direct labour-hours allowed for the actual output . . . . . . . . . . . . | 26,000 |

*Required:*
1. Compute the fixed portion of the predetermined overhead rate for the year.
2. Compute the fixed overhead budget variance and volume variance.

**EXERCISE 10–1    Prepare a Flexible Budget (LO1)**

The cost formulas for Emory Company's manufacturing overhead costs are given below. These cost formulas cover a relevant range of 15,000 to 25,000 machine-hours each year.

| Overhead Costs | Cost Formula |
|---|---|
| Utilities ................... | $0.30 per machine-hour |
| Indirect labour ............. | $52,000 plus $1.40 per machine-hour |
| Supplies .................. | $0.20 per machine-hour |
| Maintenance ............... | $18,000 plus $0.10 per machine-hour |
| Depreciation ............... | $90,000 |

*Required:*
Prepare a flexible budget in increments of 5,000 machine-hours. Include all costs in your budget.

**EXERCISE 10–2    Variable Overhead Performance Report (LO2, LO3)**

The variable portion of Murray Company's flexible budget for manufacturing overhead is given below:

| Variable Overhead Costs | Cost Formula (per machine-hour) | Machine-Hours | | |
|---|---|---|---|---|
| | | 10,000 | 12,000 | 14,000 |
| Supplies ................... | $0.20 | $ 2,000 | $ 2,400 | $ 2,800 |
| Maintenance ................ | 0.70 | 7,000 | 8,400 | 9,800 |
| Utilities ................... | 0.10 | 1,000 | 1,200 | 1,400 |
| Rework time ................ | 0.40 | 4,000 | 4,800 | 5,600 |
| Total variable overhead cost ...... | $1.40 | $14,000 | $16,800 | $19,600 |

During a recent period, the company recorded 11,500 machine-hours of activity. The variable overhead costs incurred were:

| | |
|---|---|
| Supplies ............. | $2,420 |
| Maintenance .......... | 7,000 |
| Utilities ............. | 1,070 |
| Rework time .......... | 5,190 |

The budgeted activity for the period had been 12,000 machine-hours.

*Required:*
1. Prepare a variable overhead performance report for the period. Indicate whether variances are favourable (F) or unfavourable (U). Show only a spending variance on your report.
2. Discuss the significance of the variances. Might some variances be the result of others? Explain.

**EXERCISE 10–3    Variable Overhead Variances with Performance Report** (LO2, LO4)

The cheque-clearing office of your local credit union bank is responsible for processing all cheques that come to the bank for payment. Managers at the bank believe that variable overhead costs are essentially proportional to the number of labour-hours worked in the office, and so labour-hours is used as the activity base for budgeting and for performance reports for variable overhead costs in the department. Data for September, the most recent month, appear below:

| | |
|---|---|
| Budgeted labour-hours . . . . . . . . . . . . . . . . . . . . . . . . . . . . . | 3,050 |
| Actual labour-hours . . . . . . . . . . . . . . . . . . . . . . . . . . . . . . | 3,100 |
| Standard labour-hours allowed for the actual number of cheques processed . . . . . . . . . . . . . . . . . . . . | 3,250 |

| | Cost Formula (per labour-hour) | Actual Costs Incurred in September |
|---|---|---|
| Variable overhead costs: | | |
| Office supplies . . . . . . . . . . . . . . . . . . . . . . . . . . . . . . | $0.10 | $   365 |
| Staff coffee lounge . . . . . . . . . . . . . . . . . . . . . . . . . . . | 0.20 | 520 |
| Indirect labour . . . . . . . . . . . . . . . . . . . . . . . . . . . . . . | 0.90 | 2,710 |
| Total variable overhead cost . . . . . . . . . . . . . . . . . . . . . . | $1.20 | $3,595 |

*Required:*

Prepare a variable overhead performance report for September for the cheque-clearing office that includes both spending and efficiency variances. Use Exhibit 10–6 as a guide.

**EXERCISE 10–4    Predetermined Overhead Rates** (LO5)

Operating at a normal level of 30,000 direct labour-hours, Lasser Company produces 10,000 units of product each period. The direct labour wage rate is $6 per hour. Seven and one-half metres of direct materials go into each unit of product; the material costs $3 per metre. The flexible budget used to plan and control manufacturing overhead costs is given below (in condensed form):

| Overhead Costs | Cost Formula (per direct labour-hour) | Direct Labour-Hours | | |
|---|---|---|---|---|
| | | 20,000 | 30,000 | 40,000 |
| Variable costs . . . . . . . . . . . . | $1.90 | $ 38,000 | $ 57,000 | $ 76,000 |
| Fixed costs . . . . . . . . . . . . . . | | 168,000 | 168,000 | 168,000 |
| Total overhead cost . . . . . . . | | $206,000 | $225,000 | $244,000 |

*Required:*

1. Using 30,000 direct labour-hours as the denominator activity, compute the predetermined overhead rate and break it down into variable and fixed elements.
2. Complete the standard cost card below for one unit of product:

| | |
|---|---|
| Direct materials, 7.5 metres at $3 per metre . . . . . . . . . . . | $22.50 |
| Direct labour,           ? . . . . . . . . . . . . . . . . . . . . . . . . | ? |
| Variable overhead,           ? . . . . . . . . . . . . . . . . . . . . . . | ? |
| Fixed overhead,           ? . . . . . . . . . . . . . . . . . . . . . . . . | ? |
| Total standard cost per unit . . . . . . . . . . . . . . . . . . . . . . | $  ? |

**EXERCISE 10–5  Predetermined Overhead Rates and Overhead Variances** (LO4, LO5, LO6)

Norwall Company's flexible budget for manufacturing overhead (in condensed form) is given below:

| Overhead Costs | Cost Formula (per machine-hour) | Machine-Hours 50,000 | 60,000 | 70,000 |
|---|---|---|---|---|
| Variable costs .......... | $3 | $150,000 | $180,000 | $210,000 |
| Fixed costs ............. | | 300,000 | 300,000 | 300,000 |
| Total overhead cost ....... | | $450,000 | $480,000 | $510,000 |

The following information is available for a recent period:

a.  A denominator activity of 60,000 machine-hours is used to compute the predetermined overhead rate.

b.  At the 60,000 standard machine-hours level of activity, the company should produce 40,000 units of product.

c.  The company's actual operating results were:

| | |
|---|---|
| Number of units produced ...................... | 41,000 |
| Actual machine-hours ......................... | 62,500 |
| Actual variable overhead costs .................. | $181,250 |
| Actual fixed overhead costs .................... | 302,400 |

**Required:**

1.  Compute the predetermined overhead rate and break it down into variable and fixed cost elements.
2.  Compute the standard hours allowed for the actual production.
3.  Compute the variable overhead spending and efficiency variances and the fixed overhead budget and volume variances.

**EXERCISE 10–6  Fixed Overhead Variances** (LO6)

Selected operating information on three different companies for a recent year is given below:

| | Company A | B | C |
|---|---|---|---|
| Full-capacity machine-hours ............. | 10,000 | 18,000 | 20,000 |
| Budgeted machine-hours* ............... | 9,000 | 17,000 | 20,000 |
| Actual machine-hours ................. | 9,000 | 17,800 | 19,000 |
| Standard machine-hours allowed for actual production ................. | 9,500 | 16,000 | 20,000 |

*Denominator activity for computing the predetermined overhead rate.

**Required:**

For each company, state whether the company would have a favourable or unfavourable volume variance and why.

**EXERCISE 10–7  Variable Overhead Performance Report** (LO2, LO4)

The cost formulas for variable overhead costs in a machining operation are given below:

| Variable Overhead Costs | Cost Formula (per machine-hour) |
|---|---|
| Power ........................................ | $0.30 |
| Setup time ............................. | 0.20 |
| Polishing wheels ......................... | 0.16 |
| Maintenance ............................. | 0.18 |
| Total variable overhead cost ................. | $0.84 |

During August, the machining operation was scheduled to work 11,250 machine-hours and to produce 4,500 units of product. The standard machine time per unit of product is 2.5 hours. A strike near the end of the month forced a cutback in production. Actual results for the month were:

| | |
|---|---|
| Actual machine-hours worked | 9,250 |
| Actual number of units produced | 3,600 |

Actual costs for the month were:

| Variable Overhead Costs | Total Actual Costs | Per Machine-Hour |
|---|---|---|
| Power | $2,405 | $0.26 |
| Setup time | 2,035 | 0.22 |
| Polishing wheels | 1,110 | 0.12 |
| Maintenance | 925 | 0.10 |
| Total variable overhead cost | $6,475 | $0.70 |

*Required:*

Prepare an overhead performance report for the machining operation for August. Use column headings in your report as shown below:

| Overhead Item | Cost Formula (per machine-hour) | Actual Costs Incurred 9,250 Machine-Hours | Budget Based on ? Machine-Hours | Budget Based on ? Machine-Hours | Total Variance | Breakdown of the Total Variance | |
|---|---|---|---|---|---|---|---|
| | | | | | | Spending Variance | Efficiency Variance |

# Problems

**PROBLEM 10–1  Preparing a Performance Report** (LO2, LO3, LO6)

Several years ago, Westmont Company developed a comprehensive budgeting system for profit planning and control purposes. The line supervisors have been very happy with the system and with the reports being prepared on their performance, but both middle and upper management have expressed considerable dissatisfaction with the information being generated by the system. A typical manufacturing overhead performance report for a recent period is shown below:

**WESTMONT COMPANY**
**Overhead Performance Report—Assembly Department**
**For the Quarter Ended March 31**

| | Actual | Budget | Variance |
|---|---|---|---|
| Machine-hours | 38,000 | 40,000 | |
| Variable overhead costs: | | | |
| Indirect materials | $ 32,250 | $ 34,000 | $1,750 F |
| Rework time | 8,560 | 9,200 | 640 F |
| Utilities | 56,240 | 60,000 | 3,760 F |
| Machine setup | 12,600 | 13,200 | 600 F |
| Total variable overhead cost | 109,650 | 116,400 | 6,750 F |
| Fixed overhead costs: | | | |
| Maintenance | 79,200 | 80,000 | 800 F |
| Inspection | 60,000 | 60,000 | — |
| Total fixed overhead cost | 139,200 | 140,000 | 800 F |
| Total overhead cost | $248,850 | $256,400 | $7,550 F |

After receiving a copy of this overhead performance report, the supervisor of the Assembly Department stated, "These reports are super. It makes me feel really good to see how well things are going in my department. I can't understand why those people upstairs complain so much."

The budget data above are for the original planned level of activity for the quarter.

*Required:*
1. The company's vice-president is uneasy about the performance reports being prepared and would like you to evaluate their usefulness to the company.
2. What changes, if any, would you recommend be made in the overhead performance report above in order to give better insight into how well the supervisor is controlling costs?
3. Prepare a new overhead performance report for the quarter, incorporating any changes you suggested in (2) above. (Include both the variable and the fixed costs in your report.)

### PROBLEM 10–2  Preparing a Performance Report (LO2, LO3)

The St. Lucia Blood Bank, a private charity partly supported by government grants, is located on the Caribbean island of St. Lucia. The Blood Bank has just finished its operations for September, which was a particularly busy month due to a powerful hurricane that hit neighbouring islands causing many injuries. The hurricane largely bypassed St. Lucia, but residents of St. Lucia willingly donated their blood to help people on other islands. As a consequence, the Blood Bank collected and processed over 20% more blood than had been originally planned for the month.

A report prepared by a government official comparing actual costs to budgeted costs for the Blood Bank appears below. (The currency on St. Lucia is the East Caribbean dollar.) Continued support from the government depends on the Blood Bank's ability to demonstrate control over its costs.

CHECK FIGURE
(1) Flexible budget total cost at 620 litres: $32,290

| ST. LUCIA BLOOD BANK<br>Cost Control Report<br>For the Month Ended September 30 | | | |
|---|---|---|---|
| | **Actual** | **Budget** | **Variance** |
| Litres of blood collected ............. | 620 | 500 | 120 F |
| **Variable costs:** | | | |
| Medical supplies ................. | $ 9,350 | $ 7,500 | $1,850 U |
| Lab tests ....................... | 6,180 | 6,000 | 180 U |
| Refreshments for donors ........... | 1,340 | 1,000 | 340 U |
| Administrative supplies ............ | 400 | 250 | 150 U |
| Total variable cost ................. | 17,270 | 14,750 | 2,520 U |
| **Fixed costs:** | | | |
| Staff salaries ..................... | 10,000 | 10,000 | — |
| Equipment depreciation ............ | 2,800 | 2,500 | 300 U |
| Rent ........................... | 1,000 | 1,000 | — |
| Utilities ........................ | 570 | 500 | 70 U |
| Total fixed cost ..................... | 14,370 | 14,000 | 370 U |
| Total cost ........................ | $31,640 | $28,750 | $2,890 U |

The managing director of the Blood Bank was very unhappy with this report, claiming that his costs were higher than expected due to the emergency on the neighbouring islands. He also pointed out that the additional costs had been fully covered by payments from grateful recipients on the other islands. The government official who prepared the report countered that all of the figures had been submitted by the Blood Bank to the government; he was just pointing out that actual costs were a lot higher than promised in the budget.

*Required:*
1. Prepare a new performance report for September using the flexible budget approach. (Note: Even though some of these costs might be classified as direct costs, rather than as overhead, the flexible budget approach can still be used to prepare a flexible budget performance report.)
2. Do you think any of the variances in the report you prepared should be investigated? Why?

**PROBLEM 10–3   Comprehensive Standard Cost Variances** (LO4, LO6)

Flandro Company uses a standard cost system and sets predetermined overhead rates on the basis of direct labour-hours. The following data are taken from the company's budget for the current year:

| | |
|---|---|
| Denominator activity (direct labour-hours) | 10,000 |
| Variable manufacturing overhead cost | $30,000 |
| Fixed manufacturing overhead cost | 68,000 |

The standard cost card for the company's only product is given below:

| | |
|---|---|
| Direct materials, 3 metres at $4.80 | $14.40 |
| Direct labour, 2 hours at $7 | 14.00 |
| Manufacturing overhead, 140% of direct labour cost | 19.60 |
| Standard cost per unit | $48.00 |

During the year, the company produced 6,000 units of product and incurred the following costs:

| | |
|---|---|
| Materials purchased, 24,000 metres at $5.10 | $122,400 |
| Materials used in production (in metres) | 18,500 |
| Direct labour cost incurred, 11,600 hours at $7.50 | $ 87,000 |
| Variable manufacturing overhead cost incurred | 34,580 |
| Fixed manufacturing overhead cost incurred | 69,400 |

*Required:*

1. Redo the standard cost card in a clearer, more usable format by detailing the variable and fixed overhead cost elements.
2. Prepare an analysis of the variances for materials and labour for the year.
3. Prepare an analysis of the variances for variable and fixed overhead for the year.
4. What effect, if any, does the choice of a denominator activity level have on unit standard costs? Is the volume variance a controllable variance from a spending point of view? Explain.

**PROBLEM 10–4   Applying Overhead; Overhead Variances** (LO4, LO5, LO6)

Chilczuk, S.A., of Gdansk, Poland, is a major producer of classic Polish sausage. The company uses a standard cost system to help in the control of costs. Overhead is applied to production on the basis of labour-hours. According to the company's flexible budget, the following manufacturing overhead costs should be incurred at an activity level of 35,000 labour-hours (the denominator activity level):

| | |
|---|---|
| Variable overhead costs | PZ  87,500 |
| Fixed overhead costs | 210,000 |
| Total overhead cost | PZ297,500 |

The currency in Poland is the zloty, which is denoted here by PZ.

During the most recent year, the following operating results were recorded:

| | |
|---|---|
| Activity: | |
| Actual labour-hours worked | 30,000 |
| Standard labour-hours allowed for output | 32,000 |
| Cost: | |
| Actual variable overhead cost incurred | PZ 78,000 |
| Actual fixed overhead cost incurred | 209,400 |

At the end of the year, the company's Manufacturing Overhead account contained the following data:

**Manufacturing Overhead**

| Actual | 287,400 | Applied | 272,000 |
|--------|---------|---------|---------|
|        | 15,400  |         |         |

Management would like to determine the cause of the PZ15,400 under-applied overhead.

*Required:*
1. Compute the predetermined overhead rate. Break the rate down into variable and fixed cost elements.
2. Show how the PZ272,000 applied figure in the Manufacturing Overhead account was computed.
3. Analyze the PZ15,400 under-applied overhead figure in terms of the variable overhead spending and efficiency variances and the fixed overhead budget and volume variances.
4. Explain the meaning of each variance that you computed in (3) above.

**PROBLEM 10–5   Comprehensive Standard Cost Variances (LO4, LO6)**
"Wonderful! Not only did our salespeople do a good job in meeting the sales budget this year, but our production people did a good job in controlling costs as well," said Kim Clark, president of Martell Company. "Our $18,000 overall manufacturing cost variance is only 1.5% of the $1,200,000 standard cost of products sold during the year. That's well within the 3% parameter set by management for acceptable variances. It looks like everyone will be in line for a bonus this year."
   The company produces and sells a single product. A standard cost card for the product follows:

CHECK FIGURE
(3a) Efficiency variance: $7,500 U
(3b) Volume variance: $42,000 F

| Standard Cost Card—Per Unit of Product | |
|---|---|
| Direct materials, 2 metres at $8.45 per metre .......... | $16.90 |
| Direct labour, 1.4 hours at $8 per hour .............. | 11.20 |
| Variable overhead, 1.4 hours at $2.50 per hour ........ | 3.50 |
| Fixed overhead, 1.4 hours at $6 per hour ............. | 8.40 |
| Standard cost per unit ........................... | $40.00 |

The following additional information is available for the year just completed:
a. The company manufactured 30,000 units of product during the year.
b. A total of 64,000 metres of material was purchased during the year at a cost of $8.55 per metre. All of this material was used to manufacture the 30,000 units. There were no beginning or ending inventories for the year.
c. The company worked 45,000 direct labour-hours during the year at an average cost of $7.80 per hour.
d. Overhead is applied to products on the basis of direct labour-hours. Data relating to manufacturing overhead costs follow:

| | |
|---|---|
| Denominator activity level (direct labour-hours) ..... | 35,000 |
| Budgeted fixed overhead costs (from the overhead flexible budget) ............................ | $210,000 |
| Actual variable overhead costs incurred ............ | 108,000 |
| Actual fixed overhead costs incurred .............. | 211,800 |

*Required:*
1. Compute the direct materials price and quantity variances for the year.
2. Compute the direct labour rate and efficiency variances for the year.
3. For manufacturing overhead compute:
   a. The variable overhead spending and efficiency variances for the year.
   b. The fixed overhead budget and volume variances for the year.
4. Total the variances you have computed, and compare the net amount with the $18,000 mentioned by the president. Do you agree that bonuses should be given to everyone for good cost control during the year? Explain.

CHECK FIGURE
(1) Standard hours allowed:
      28,500 hours

**PROBLEM 10–6   Using Fixed Overhead Variances (LO6)**

The standard cost card for the single product manufactured by Cutter, Inc. is given below:

| Standard Cost Card—Per Unit | |
|---|---:|
| Direct materials, 3 metres at $7.50 per metre ......... | $22.50 |
| Direct labour, 3 hours at $7.75 per hour ............. | 23.25 |
| Variable overhead, 3 hours at $1.50 per hour .......... | 4.50 |
| Fixed overhead, 3 hours at $5 per hour ............. | 15.00 |
| Total standard cost per unit ...................... | $65.25 |

Manufacturing overhead is applied to production on the basis of direct labour-hours. During the year, the company worked 27,000 hours and manufactured 9,500 units of product. Selected data relating to the company's fixed manufacturing overhead cost for the year are shown below:

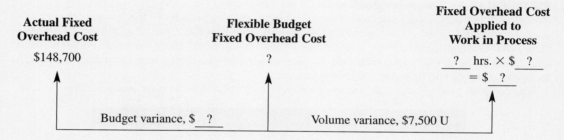

**Required:**
1. What were the standard hours allowed for the year's production?
2. What was the amount of fixed overhead cost contained in the flexible budget for the year?
3. What was the fixed overhead budget variance for the year?
4. What denominator activity level did the company use in setting the predetermined overhead rate for the year?

CHECK FIGURE
(3) Volume variance:
      $18,000 U

**PROBLEM 10–7   Relations among Fixed Overhead Variances (LO6)**

Selected information relating to Yost Company's operations for the most recent year is given below:

| | |
|---|---:|
| Activity: | |
|    Denominator activity (machine-hours) ......... | 45,000 |
|    Standard hours allowed per unit ............. | 3 |
|    Number of units produced ................. | 14,000 |
| Costs: | |
|    Actual fixed overhead costs incurred .......... | $267,000 |
|    Fixed overhead budget variance ............. | 3,000 F |

The company applies overhead cost to products on the basis of machine-hours.

**Required:**
1. What were the standard hours allowed for the actual production?
2. What was the fixed portion of the predetermined overhead rate?
3. What was the volume variance?

CHECK FIGURE
(2) Total of spending and
      budget variances:
      $800 U

**PROBLEM 10–8   Flexible Budget and Overhead Performance Report (LO1, LO2, LO4)**

You have just been hired by FAB Company, the manufacturer of a revolutionary new garage door opening device. John Foster, the president, has asked that you review the company's costing system and "do what you can to help us get better control of our manufacturing overhead costs." You find that the company has never used a flexible budget, and you suggest that preparing such a budget would be an excellent first step in overhead planning and control.

After much effort and analysis, you are able to determine the following cost formulas for the company's normal operating range of 20,000 to 30,000 machine-hours each month:

| Overhead Costs | Cost Formula |
|---|---|
| Utilities ................... | $0.90 per machine-hour |
| Maintenance ............... | $1.60 per machine-hour plus $40,000 per month |
| Machine setup .............. | $0.30 per machine-hour |
| Indirect labour ............. | $0.70 per machine-hour plus $130,000 per month |
| Depreciation ............... | $70,000 per month |

To show the president how the flexible budget concept works, you have gathered the following actual cost data for the most recent month, March, in which the company worked 26,000 machine-hours and produced 15,000 units:

| | |
|---|---|
| Utilities ......................... | $ 24,200 |
| Maintenance ..................... | 78,100 |
| Machine setup ................... | 8,400 |
| Indirect labour .................. | 149,600 |
| Depreciation .................... | 71,500 |
| Total cost ....................... | $331,800 |

The only variance in the fixed costs for the month was with depreciation, which was increased as a result of a purchase of new equipment.

The company had originally planned to work 30,000 machine-hours during March.

**Required:**

1. Prepare a flexible budget for the company in increments of 5,000 hours.
2. Prepare an overhead performance report for the company for March. (Use the format illustrated in Exhibit 10–10.)
3. What additional information would you need to compute an overhead efficiency variance for the company?

**PROBLEM 10–9   Overhead Performance Report** (LO2, LO4)

Frank Western, supervisor of the Machining Department for Freemont Company, was visibly upset after being reprimanded for his department's poor performance over the prior month. The department's performance report is given below:

CHECK FIGURE
(2) Total variance: $6,500 F

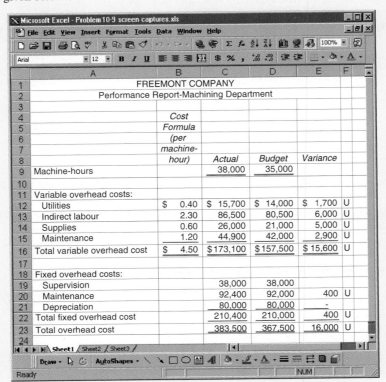

**FREEMONT COMPANY**
**Performance Report-Machining Department**

| | Cost Formula (per machine-hour) | Actual | Budget | Variance | |
|---|---|---|---|---|---|
| Machine-hours | | 38,000 | 35,000 | | |
| | | | | | |
| Variable overhead costs: | | | | | |
| Utilities | $  0.40 | $ 15,700 | $ 14,000 | $ 1,700 | U |
| Indirect labour | 2.30 | 86,500 | 80,500 | 6,000 | U |
| Supplies | 0.60 | 26,000 | 21,000 | 5,000 | U |
| Maintenance | 1.20 | 44,900 | 42,000 | 2,900 | U |
| Total variable overhead cost | $  4.50 | $173,100 | $157,500 | $ 15,600 | U |
| | | | | | |
| Fixed overhead costs: | | | | | |
| Supervision | | 38,000 | 38,000 | | |
| Maintenance | | 92,400 | 92,000 | 400 | U |
| Depreciation | | 80,000 | 80,000 | - | |
| Total fixed overhead cost | | 210,400 | 210,000 | 400 | U |
| Total overhead cost | | 383,500 | 367,500 | 16,000 | U |

"I just can't understand all the red ink," said Western to Sarah Mason, supervisor of another department. "When the boss called me in, I thought he was going to give me a pat on the back because I know for a fact that my department worked more efficiently last month than it has ever worked before. Instead, he tore me apart. I thought for a minute that it might be over the supplies that were stolen out of our warehouse last month. But they only amounted to a couple of thousand dollars, and just look at this report. *Everything* is unfavourable, and I don't even know why."

The budget for the Machining Department had called for production of 14,000 units last month, which is equal to a budgeted activity level of 35,000 machine-hours (at a standard time of 2.5 hours per unit). Actual production in the Machining Department for the month was 16,000 units.

*Required:*
1. Evaluate the overhead performance report given above, and explain why the variances are all unfavourable.
2. Prepare a new overhead performance report that will help Mr. Western's superiors assess efficiency and cost control in the Machining Department. (Hint: Exhibit 10–6 may be helpful in structuring your report; however, the report you prepare should include both variable and fixed costs.)
3. Would the supplies stolen out of the warehouse be included as part of the variable overhead spending variance or as part of the variable overhead efficiency variance for the month? Explain.

**PROBLEM 10–10  Applying Overhead; Overhead Variances (LO4, LO5, LO6)**
Lane Company manufactures a single product that requires a great deal of hand labour. Overhead cost is applied on the basis of direct labour-hours. The company's condensed flexible budget for manufacturing overhead is given below:

| Overhead Costs | Cost Formula (per direct labour-hour) | Direct Labour-Hours | | |
|---|---|---|---|---|
| | | 60,000 | 80,000 | 100,000 |
| Variable costs | $2 | $ 120,000 | $160,000 | $200,000 |
| Fixed costs | | 480,000 | 480,000 | 480,000 |
| Total overhead cost | | $600,000 | $640,000 | $680,000 |

The company's product requires 1.5 kilograms of material that has a standard cost of $14 per kilogram and two hours of direct labour time that has a standard rate of $4.50 per hour.

The company planned to operate at a denominator activity level of 80,000 direct labour-hours and to produce 40,000 units of product during the most recent year. Actual activity and costs for the year were as follows:

| | |
|---|---|
| Number of units produced | 42,000 |
| Actual direct labour-hours worked | 85,000 |
| Actual variable overhead cost incurred | $163,500 |
| Actual fixed overhead cost incurred | 483,000 |

*Required:*
1. Compute the predetermined overhead rate for the year. Break the rate down into variable and fixed elements.
2. Prepare a standard cost card for the company's product; show the details for all manufacturing costs on your standard cost card.
3. Do the following:
   a. Compute the standard hours allowed for the year's production.
   b. Complete the following Manufacturing Overhead T-account for the year:

**Manufacturing Overhead**

| ? | ? |
|---|---|
| ? | ? |

4. Determine the reason for any under- or over-applied overhead for the year by computing the variable overhead spending and efficiency variances and the fixed overhead budget and volume variances.
5. Suppose the company had chosen 85,000 direct labour-hours as the denominator activity, rather than 80,000 hours. State which, if any, of the variances computed in (4) above would have changed, and explain how the variance(s) would have changed. No computations are necessary.

# Building Your Skills

## ANALYTICAL THINKING   (LO4, LO5, LO6)

A company that uses a standard cost system has provided the following data. The company's flexible budget for manufacturing overhead is based on standard machine-hours.

| | |
|---|---|
| 1. Denominator activity in hours | ? |
| 2. Standard hours allowed for units produced | 32,000 |
| 3. Actual hours worked | 30,000 |
| 4. Flexible budget variable overhead per machine-hour | $    ? |
| 5. Flexible budget fixed overhead (total) | ? |
| 6. Actual variable overhead cost incurred | 54,000 |
| 7. Actual fixed overhead cost incurred | 209,400 |
| 8. Variable overhead cost applied to production* | ? |
| 9. Fixed overhead cost applied to production* | 192,000 |
| 10. Variable overhead spending variance | ? |
| 11. Variable overhead efficiency variance | 3,500 F |
| 12. Fixed overhead budget variance | ? |
| 13. Fixed overhead volume variance | 18,000 U |
| 14. Variable portion of the predetermined overhead rate | ? |
| 15. Fixed portion of the predetermined overhead rate | ? |
| 16. Under-applied (or over-applied) overhead | ? |

*Based on standard hours allowed for units produced.

### Required:
Compute the unknown amounts. (Hint: One way to proceed would be to use the format for variance analysis found in Exhibit 9–6 for variable overhead and in Exhibit 10–9 for fixed overhead.)

## COMMUNICATING IN PRACTICE   (LO1)

Use an online yellow pages directory, such as www.comfind.com, or www.athand.com, to find a manufacturer in your area that has a website. Make an appointment with the controller or chief financial officer of the company. Before your meeting, find out as much as you can about the organization's operations from its website.

### Required:
After asking the following questions, write a brief memorandum to your instructor that summarizes the information obtained from the company's website and addresses what you found out during your interview.
1. Are actual overhead costs compared with a static budget, a flexible budget, or something else?
2. Does the organization distinguish between variable and fixed overhead costs in its performance reports?
3. What are the consequences of unfavourable variances? Of favourable variances?

## ETHICS CHALLENGE   (LO2)

Tom Kemper is the controller of the Brandon manufacturing facility of Kingston Enterprises, Incorporated. Among the many reports that must be filed with corporate headquarters is the annual overhead performance report. The report covers an entire fiscal year, which ends on December 31, and is due at corporate headquarters shortly after the beginning of the New Year. Kemper does not like putting work off to the last minute, and so just before Christmas he put together a preliminary draft of the overhead performance report. Some adjustments would be required for transactions that occur between Christmas and New Year's Day, but there are generally very few of these. A copy of the preliminary draft report, which Kemper completed on December 21, follows:

## BRANDON MANUFACTURING FACILITY
### Overhead Performance Report
### December 21 Preliminary Draft

Budgeted machine-hours . . . . . . . . . .     200,000
Actual machine-hours . . . . . . . . . . . .    180,000

| Overhead Costs | Cost Formula (per machine-hour) | Actual Costs 180,000 Machine-Hours | Budget Based on 180,000 Machine-Hours | Spending or Budget Variance |
|---|---|---|---|---|
| Variable overhead costs: | | | | |
| Power . . . . . . . . . . . . . . . . . . . . . . | $0.10 | $    19,750 | $    18,000 | $  1,750 U |
| Supplies . . . . . . . . . . . . . . . . . . . . | 0.25 | 47,000 | 45,000 | 2,000 U |
| Abrasives . . . . . . . . . . . . . . . . . | 0.30 | 58,000 | 54,000 | 4,000 U |
| Total variable overhead cost . . . . . . . | $0.65 | 124,750 | 117,000 | 7,750 U |
| Fixed overhead costs: | | | | |
| Depreciation . . . . . . . . . . . . . . . . . | | 345,000 | 332,000 | 13,000 U |
| Supervisory salaries . . . . . . . . . . . | | 273,000 | 275,000 | 2,000 F |
| Insurance . . . . . . . . . . . . . . . . . . . . | | 37,000 | 37,000 | — |
| Industrial engineering . . . . . . . . . . | | 189,000 | 210,000 | 21,000 F |
| Factory building lease . . . . . . . . . . | | 60,000 | 60,000 | — |
| Total fixed overhead cost  . . . . . . . . | | 904,000 | 914,000 | 10,000 F |
| Total overhead cost . . . . . . . . . . . . . | | $1,028,750 | $1,031,000 | $  2,250 F |

Melissa Ilianovitch, the general manager at the Brandon facility, asked to see a copy of the preliminary draft report at 4:45 P.M. on December 23. Kemper carried a copy of the report to her office where the following discussion took place:

*Ilianovitch:* Ouch! Almost all of the variances on the report are unfavourable. The only thing that looks good at all are the favourable variances for supervisory salaries and for industrial engineering. How did we have an unfavourable variance for depreciation?

*Kemper:* Do you remember that milling machine that broke down because the wrong lubricant was used by the machine operator?

*Ilianovitch:* Only vaguely.

*Kemper:* It turned out we couldn't fix it. We had to scrap the machine and buy a new one.

*Ilianovitch:* This report doesn't look good. I was raked over the coals last year when we had just a few unfavourable variances.

*Kemper:* I'm afraid the final report is going to look even worse.

*Ilianovitch:* Oh?

*Kemper:* The line item for industrial engineering on the report is for work we hired Ferguson Engineering to do for us on a contract basis. The original contract was for $210,000, but we asked them to do some additional work that was not in the contract. Under the terms of the contract, we have to reimburse Ferguson Engineering for the costs of the additional work. The $189,000 in actual costs that appear on the preliminary draft report reflects only their billings up through December 21. The last bill they had sent us was on November 28, and they completed the project just last week. Yesterday, I got a call from Laura Sunder over at Ferguson and she said they would be sending us a final bill for the project before the end of the year. The total bill, including the reimbursements for the additional work, is going to be . . .

*Ilianovitch:* I am not sure I want to hear this.

*Kemper:* $225,000.

*Ilianovitch:* Ouch! Ouch! Ouch!

*Kemper:* The additional work we asked them to do added $15,000 to the cost of the project.

*Ilianovitch:* No way can I turn in a performance report with an overall unfavourable variance. They'll kill me at corporate headquarters. Call up Laura at Ferguson and ask her not to send the bill until after the first of the year. We have to have that $21,000 favourable variance for industrial engineering on the performance report.

**Required:**
What should Tom Kemper do? Explain.

## TEAMWORK IN ACTION  (LO1, LO3, LO5)

Boyne University offers an extensive continuing education program in many cities throughout the state. For the convenience of its faculty and administrative staff and to save costs, the university employs a supervisor to operate a motor pool. The motor pool operated with 20 vehicles until February, when an additional automobile was acquired. The motor pool furnishes gasoline, oil, and other supplies for its automobiles. A mechanic does routine maintenance and minor repairs. Major repairs are done at a nearby commercial garage.

Each year, the supervisor prepares an operating budget that informs the university administration of the funds needed for operating the motor pool. Depreciation (straight line) on the automobiles is recorded in the budget in order to determine the cost per kilometre of operating the vehicles.

The following performance report was prepared by a budget analyst who was recently hired by the university. It presents the operating budget for the current year, which was approved by the university. The performance report also shows actual operating costs for March of the current year compared with one-twelfth of the annual operating budget.

| UNIVERSITY MOTOR POOL Performance Report for March | | | |
|---|---|---|---|
| | Annual Operating Budget | Monthly Budget* | March Actual | (Over) Under Budget |
| Gasoline ................. | $ 70,000 | $ 5,833 | $ 6,633 | $(800) |
| Oil, minor repairs, parts ...... | 3,000 | 250 | 380 | (130) |
| Outside repairs ............. | 2,700 | 225 | 50 | 175 |
| Insurance ................ | 6,000 | 500 | 525 | (25) |
| Salaries and benefits ........ | 30,000 | 2,500 | 2,500 | — |
| Depreciation of vehicles ..... | 26,400 | 2,200 | 2,310 | (110) |
| Total costs ............... | $138,100 | $ 11,508 | $12,398 | $(890) |
| Total kilometres ............ | 1,000,000 | 83,333 | 102,000 | |
| Cost per kilometre .......... | $0.1381 | $0.1381 | $0.1215 | |
| Number of automobiles in use .. | 20 | 20 | 21 | |

*Annual operating budget ÷ 12 months.

The annual operating budget was constructed on the following assumptions:

a. Twenty automobiles in the motor pool.
b. Fifty thousand kilometres driven per year per automobile.
c. Ten kilometres per litre per automobile.
d. $0.70 per litre of gasoline.
e. $0.003 cost per kilometre for oil, minor repairs, and parts.
f. $135 cost per automobile per year for outside repairs.
g. $300 cost per automobile per year for insurance.

The supervisor of the motor pool is unhappy with the monthly performance report comparing budget and actual costs for March, claiming it presents an unfair picture of performance.

### Required:
1. Using a flexible budgeting approach, prepare a new performance report for March showing budgeted costs, actual costs, and variances. All team members should understand how the revised performance report was prepared.
2. The team should discuss and then write up brief answers to the questions listed below. All team members should agree with and understand the answers.
   a. What are the deficiencies in the performance report that was prepared by the budget analyst?
   b. How does the revised performance report, which was prepared using a flexible budget approach, overcome these deficiencies?

(CMA, adapted)

Do not forget to check out Taking It to the Net as well as other quizzes and resources at the Online Learning Centre at www.mcgrawhill.ca/college/garrison.

# Chapter Eleven

# Decentralization and Performance Measurement

## A Look Back

We discussed the budgeting process in Chapter 8. We introduced management control and performance measures in Chapter 9 with a discussion of standard costs and variance analysis. Chapter 10 extended that discussion to overhead costs.

## A Look at This Chapter

Chapter 11 continues our coverage of performance measurement by introducing return on investment and residual income measures to motivate managers and monitor progress toward achieving the company's goals.

## A Look Ahead

After introducing the concept of relevant costs and benefits, we discuss in Chapter 12 how the effectiveness of the decision-making process depends on the correct use of relevant data.

## Chapter Outline

## DECISION FEATURE Decentralization Gone Wrong

Great Canadian Bagel was once one of the fastest growing franchises in Canada. At the pinnacle of the franchise's success, there were more than 150 locations across Canada. In the summer of 2003, there were just 95 stores left, leaving many wondering what went wrong.

Great Canadian Bagel was founded in 1993. By 1996, the chain was named Entrepreneur of the Year by a Canadian hospitality and restaurant magazine, and another US trade magazine dubbed 1996 the "Year of the Bagel."

Each store was considered an independent investment centre because it was the responsibility of the franchise owner to control revenues and costs and budget for future investments. However, decision making was not fully decentralized; each store still relied on head office for numerous decisions, such as national marketing, new store locations, and the choice of suppliers. Indeed, strategy formulation was centralized, but not implementation. However, this level of independence did not work well when selling to large national chains, such as Loblaws and Costco; there was wide variation in quality and service among the franchises. Due to the inconsistency, Loblaws eventually terminated all deals with the company which cost some stores dearly.

"The people at head office now are going in the right direction," says one store owner. "But there's a lot of mistrust between the franchisees and the company." Former franchise owners still get together to lick their wounds, trade horror stories, and swap tales about the latest shutdowns.

Source: Gray, John, "Sour Dough," *Canadian Business*, June 23, 2003, pp. 36–41. Reprinted with permission from *Canadian Business*.

## Learning Objectives

*After studying Chapter 11, you should be able to:*

**LO1** Understand the role of cost, revenue, profit, and investment centres in a decentralized organization.

**LO2** Compute and understand the return on investment (ROI) measure.

**LO3** Understand how changes in sales, expenses, and operating assets affect an organization's ROI.

**LO4** Compute residual income and understand the strengths and weaknesses of this method of measuring performance.

**LO5** Understand the balanced scorecard and its role in implementing an organization's strategies.

**P**erformance management is an important task for managers as it helps them in ensuring that the organization's overall objectives are met (or even exceeded). The previous two chapters introduced variance analysis, which is one tool that can be used by managers for the purposes of performance management. In a broader context, performance management includes specifying how individual units within an organization will be evaluated, what measures will be used to evaluate these units, and what actions will be taken to ensure continuous progress. We will discuss these issues in this chapter.

# Decentralization in Organizations

In small organizations, a single manager or a small management team can usually make most decisions, including strategic and day-to-day operating decisions (this is known as a centralized organization). However, as organizations grow larger, it often becomes impossible for the top manager (or management team) to make decisions regarding all aspects of business. For example, it would be impossible for the top management team of the Real Canadian Superstore to make decisions about hiring a certain job applicant for a store in British Columbia or in Saskatchewan. Such decisions are best left to the individual store manager who knows best what her personnel needs are. Top management would, however, likely be involved in establishing hiring policies and establishing the overall strategic direction for the retailer.

In the above example, the superstore is considered a **decentralized organization,** which is one where decision making is not confined to a few top executives but is spread throughout the organization, with managers at various levels making decisions that pertain to their area of responsibility. Most organizations fall between the two extremes of being fully decentralized or fully centralized. While certain functions/decisions can be carried out efficiently in a centralized setting, others work better in a decentralized setting. Organizational size, in terms of number of employees, is an important determinant of whether an organization should or should not be decentralized.

The decision to decentralize results in an organization being classified into different *segments.* For example, in a university, the first line of segmentation would be the different colleges (such as Business, Nursing, Education, and so on), and the second line of segmentation may be the individual departments within each college (e.g., Accounting, Marketing, and so on within the School of Business). In business organizations, individual segments may represent the different divisions, product lines, market territories, or even individual departments (e.g., Marketing, Purchasing, Accounting, Legal, Production, and so on).

It is important to remember that individual segments within an organization are not usually independent of one another. They must often work closely to achieve the objectives of the organization. Consequently, coordination and communication among the individual segments are important and sometimes challenging issues for top management.

## Advantages and Disadvantages of Decentralization

Decentralization has many benefits, including:

1. Top management is relieved of much day-to-day problem solving and is left free to concentrate on strategy, on higher-level decision making, and on coordinating activities.
2. Decentralization provides lower-level managers with vital experience in making decisions. Without such experience, they would be ill-prepared to make decisions when they are promoted to higher-level positions.

3. Added responsibility and decision-making authority often result in increased job satisfaction. It makes the job more interesting and provides greater incentives for people to put out their best efforts.
4. Lower-level managers generally have more detailed and up-to-date information about conditions in their own area of responsibility than top managers. Therefore, the decisions of lower-level managers are often based on better information.
5. It is difficult to evaluate a manager's performance if the manager is not given much latitude in what he or she can do.

Decentralization has four major disadvantages:

1. Lower-level managers may make decisions without fully understanding the "big picture." While top-level managers typically have less detailed information about operations than the lower-level managers, they usually have more information about the company as a whole and may have a better understanding of the company's strategy.
2. In a truly decentralized organization, there may be a lack of coordination among autonomous managers. This problem can be reduced by clearly defining the company's strategy and communicating it effectively throughout the organization.
3. Lower-level managers may have objectives that are different from the objectives of the entire organization. For example, some managers may be more interested in increasing the sizes of their departments than in increasing the profits of the company.[1] To some degree, this problem can be overcome by designing performance evaluation systems that motivate managers to make decisions that are in the best interests of the company.
4. In a strongly decentralized organization, it may be more difficult to effectively spread innovative ideas. Someone in one part of the organization may have a terrific idea that would benefit other parts of the organization, but without strong central direction the idea may not be shared with, and adopted by, other parts of the organization.

## A Friend

*decision* maker

One of your friends from college started a business that designs web pages, which has become a wildly successful startup. On the way to meet your friend for lunch, you think how great it would be to be your own boss—to be able to come and go as you please. At lunch, you hardly recognize her. She is tired and stressed, complains a lot about the hours she has been putting in to supervise various projects, and is puzzled by the high turnover that she has experienced at the managerial level. After all, as she notes, she keeps her hand in all of the major projects. What advice do you have for her?

## Responsibility Centres

There are two key issues relating to decentralization: (1) clarifying the decentralized segment manager's scope of responsibilities, and (2) deciding how the manager's performance will be evaluated. In order to resolve these issues, top management categorizes the

**Learning Objective 1**
Understand the role of cost, revenue, profit, and investment centres in a decentralized organization

---

[1]There is a similar problem with top-level managers as well. The shareholders of the company have, in effect, decentralized by delegating their decision-making authority to the top managers. Unfortunately, top managers may abuse that trust by spending too much company money on palatial offices, rewarding themselves and their friends too generously, and so on. The issue of how to ensure that top managers act in the best interests of the owners of the company continues to puzzle experts. To a large extent, the owners rely on performance evaluation using return on investment and residual income measures as discussed later in the chapter and on bonuses and stock options. The stock market is also an important disciplining mechanism. If top managers squander the company's resources, the price of the company's shares will almost surely fall—resulting in a loss of prestige, bonuses, and possibly a job.

individual segments into **responsibility centres,** which are segments of an organization whose manager is responsible and accountable for costs, revenues, profits, or investments. We will discuss four types of responsibility centres.

**COST CENTRE**    A **cost centre** is an organizational unit whose manager is responsible for costs but not revenues, profits, or investments. Service departments, such as accounting, finance, general administration, human resources, and so on are usually classified as cost centres. In addition, production departments (or manufacturing facilities) may also be considered as cost centres. Managers of cost centres are expected to minimize costs while ensuring that the outputs they provide to other segments within the organization meet the needs of these "consumer" segments (e.g., quality). Given the scope of responsibility of a cost centre manager, she would find cost variance information—as presented in the previous two chapters—useful for performance management and control.

**REVENUE CENTRE**    A **revenue centre** is an organizational unit whose manager is responsible for meeting revenue targets and is considered to have the authority to strongly influence (if not control) revenues. A typical example of a revenue centre is a sales office. Given the scope of the revenue centre manager's responsibilities, he would find sales variance information useful for performance management and control.

**PROFIT CENTRE**    In contrast to a cost or revenue centre, a **profit centre** is an organizational unit whose manager is responsible for the unit's profitability and has the authority to strongly influence both costs and revenues. This means the manager does not need top management's approval for decisions affecting costs, revenues, or both. Managers of individual stores of a major retail chain would usually be responsible for profits and would likely be evaluated by comparing actual profit with targeted or budgeted profit.

**INVESTMENT CENTRE**    An **investment centre** is similar to a profit centre; in addition to profitability, the manager of an investment centre is also responsible for investing in operating assets. An individual division of a large corporation, such as Honeywell Limited, would have responsibility for initiating investment proposals to fund research and development, modernize production equipment, and for improvement in other areas of the division. Once the proposal is approved, it is the investment centre manager's responsibility to ensure that the assets be utilized in such a manner that they provide the targeted returns. Investment centre managers are usually evaluated using such measures as return on investment (ROI) or residual income (RI).

*in business* *today*    **Law Firms Unite**

Borden Ladner Gervais (BLG) proves just how beneficial a decentralized management style can be. In March 2000, five regional law firms—Ladner Downs in Vancouver, Howard & Mackie in Calgary, Borden & Elliot in Toronto, Scott & Aylen in Ottawa, and McMaster Gervais in Montreal—merged to become a national firm, BLG.

Prior to the merger, the senior partners examined possibilities for a postmerger management structure. They wanted a system that would allow all five firms to maintain their unique culture while reaping the benefits of a national firm. It was decided that all day-to-day decisions would be controlled by the individual firms, while corporate/strategic decisions would be made by a national council. BLG's national council comprises members from all five firms and gives each firm an equal voice, despite differences in firm size. This new decentralized structure has worked wonders. In the aftermath of the merger, the new company boasts increased profits and a larger customer base.

Source: Gray, John, "The Brothers in Law," *Canadian Business.* September 29, 2003, pp. 75–76.

**Exhibit 11–1**

Business Segments Classified as Cost, Profit, and Investment Centres

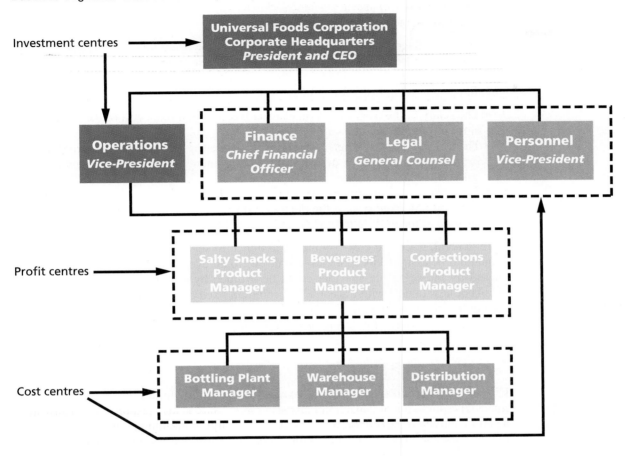

## An Example of Responsibility Centres

A partial organization chart for Universal Foods Corporation, a company in the snack food and beverage industry, appears in Exhibit 11–1. This partial organization chart indicates how the various business segments of the company are classified in terms of responsibility. Note that the cost centres are the departments and work centres that do not generate significant revenues by themselves. These are staff departments, such as finance, legal, and human resources, and operating units, such as the bottling plant, warehouse, and beverage distribution centre. The profit centres are business segments that generate revenues and include the beverage, salty snacks, and confections product segments. The vice-president of operations oversees allocation of investment funds across the product segments and is responsible for revenues and costs, and so it is treated as an investment centre. Finally, corporate headquarters is an investment centre, since it is responsible for all revenues, costs, and investments.

## Traceable and Common Fixed Costs

Performance reports are often compiled for a part of the organization, or segment, such as an investment centre. In such segment reports, a distinction should be drawn between *traceable fixed costs* and *common fixed costs*. A **traceable fixed cost** of a segment is a fixed cost that is incurred because of the existence of the segment and if the segment were eliminated, the fixed cost would disappear. Examples of traceable fixed costs include the following:

- The salary of the Phosphate business manager at IMC Global is a traceable fixed cost of the Phosphate business segment of IMC Global.

• The maintenance cost for the building in which Global Express XRS business jets are assembled is a traceable fixed cost of the aerospace segment of Bombardier.
• The liability insurance at Disney World is a traceable fixed cost of the Disney World business segment of the Disney Corporation.

A **common fixed cost** is a fixed cost that supports the operations of more than one segment but is not traceable in whole or in part to any one segment. Even if the segment were entirely eliminated, there would be no change in a common fixed cost. Examples of common fixed costs include the following:

• The salary of the CEO of Nissan Canada is a common fixed cost of the various divisions of Nissan Canada.
• The cost of the checkout equipment at a Safeway or Extra Foods grocery store is a common fixed cost of the various departments—such as groceries, produce, bakery—in the store.
• The cost of the receptionist's salary at an office shared by a number of doctors is a common fixed cost of the doctors. The cost is traceable to the office but not to any one of the doctors individually.

In general, traceable costs should be assigned to segments, but common fixed costs should not be assigned to segments—to do so would overstate the costs that are actually caused by the segments and that could be avoided by eliminating the segments. The details of how to deal with traceable and common fixed costs in segment reports are covered in more advanced texts. For example, see Chapter 12 of Garrison, Noreen, Chesley, and Carroll, *Managerial Accounting*, 6th Canadian Edition, McGraw-Hill Ryerson, 2004.

## Segmented Reporting

Effective decentralization requires segmented reporting. In addition to companywide financial reports, the organization must also report on individual segments. A **segment** is a part or activity of an organization about which managers would like performance information. A segment's report is extremely important for its manager to plan and make key decisions about its current and future performance. Senior managers like to have individual segment reports to assess the performance and viability of the different segments, to allocate resources, and for strategic planning purposes. Exhibit 11–2 illustrates a segment report that the Vice-President of Operations of Universal Foods Corporation would find useful. The report clearly indicates that all three profit centres generate roughly the same segment margin in absolute dollar amounts. However, Confections generates the best return of 30% on every sales dollar earned ($45,000 / $150,000).

**Exhibit 11–2**

Profit Centre Segmented Report: Universal Foods Corporation

| | | Profit Centres | | |
|---|---|---|---|---|
| | **Total Company** | **Salty Snacks** | **Beverages** | **Confections** |
| Sales .................. | $600,000 | $250,000 | $200,000 | $150,000 |
| Less variable expenses: | | | | |
|   Variable cost of goods sold ... | 200,000 | 80,000 | 70,000 | 50,000 |
|   Other variable expenses ...... | 60,000 | 25,000 | 20,000 | 15,000 |
|     Total variable expenses .... | 260,000 | 105,000 | 90,000 | 65,000 |
| Contribution margin .......... | 340,000 | 145,000 | 110,000 | 85,000 |
| Less traceable fixed expenses ... | 200,000 | 100,000 | 60,000 | 40,000 |
| Segment margin ............. | 140,000 | 45,000 | 50,000 | 45,000 |
| Less common fixed expenses .... | 90,000 | | | |
| Net income ................. | $50,000 | | | |

## Rate of Return for Measuring Managerial Performance

When a company is truly decentralized, managers are given a great deal of autonomy. So great is this autonomy that the various profit and investment centres are often viewed as being virtually independent businesses, with their managers having about the same control over decisions as if they were, in fact, running their own independent firms. With this autonomy, fierce competition often develops among managers, with each striving to make his or her segment the "best" in the company.

Competition between investment centres is particularly keen for investment funds. How do top managers in corporate headquarters go about deciding who gets new investment funds as they become available, and how do these managers decide which investment centres are most profitably using the funds that have already been entrusted to their care? One of the most popular ways of making these judgments is to measure the rate of return that investment centre managers are able to generate on their assets. This rate of return is called the *return on investment (ROI).*

> **Learning Objective 2**
> Compute and understand the return on investment (ROI) measure.

### The Return on Investment (ROI) Formula

The **return on investment (ROI)** is defined as net operating income divided by average operating assets:

$$\text{ROI} = \frac{\text{Net operating income}}{\text{Average operating assets}}$$

Concept 11–1

There are some issues about how to measure net operating income and average operating assets, but this formula seems clear enough. The higher the ROI of a business segment, the greater is the profit generated per dollar invested in the segment's operating assets.

### Net Operating Income and Operating Assets Defined

Note that *net operating income,* rather than net income, is used in the ROI formula. **Net operating income** is income before interest and taxes and is sometimes referred to as

EBIT (earnings before interest and taxes). The reason for using net operating income in the formula is that the income figure used should be consistent with the base to which it is applied. Note that the base (i.e., denominator) consists of *operating assets*. Thus, to be consistent we use net operating income in the numerator.

**Operating assets** include cash, accounts receivable, inventory, plant and equipment, and all other assets held for productive use in the organization. Examples of assets that would not be included in the operating assets category, (i.e., examples of nonoperating assets) would include land held for future use, an investment in another company, or a factory building rented to someone else. The operating assets base used in the formula is typically computed as the average of the operating assets between the beginning and the end of the year.

## Plant and Equipment: Net Book Value or Gross Cost?

A major issue in ROI computations is the dollar amount of plant and equipment that should be included in the operating assets base. To illustrate the problem involved, assume that a company reports the following amounts for plant and equipment on its balance sheet:

| | |
|---|---|
| Plant and equipment | $3,000,000 |
| Less accumulated depreciation | 900,000 |
| Net book value | $2,100,000 |

What dollar amount of plant and equipment should the company include with its operating assets in computing ROI? One widely used approach is to include only the plant and equipment's *net book value*—that is, the plant's original cost less accumulated depreciation ($2,100,000 in the example above). A second approach is to ignore depreciation and include the plant's entire *gross cost* in the operating assets base ($3,000,000 in the example above). Both these approaches are used in actual practice, even though they will obviously yield very different operating asset and ROI figures.

The following arguments can be raised for using net book value to measure operating assets and for using gross cost to measure operating assets in ROI computations:

**Arguments for Using Net Book Value to Measure Operating Assets in ROI Computations:**

1. The net book value method is consistent with how plant and equipment are reported on the balance sheet (i.e., cost less accumulated depreciation to date).
2. The net book value method is consistent with the computation of operating income, which includes depreciation as an operating expense.

**Arguments for Using Gross Cost to Measure Operating Assets in ROI Computations:**

1. The gross cost method eliminates both the age of equipment and the method of depreciation as factors in ROI computations. (Under the net book value method, ROI will tend to increase over time as net book value declines due to depreciation.)
2. The gross cost method does not discourage replacement of old, worn-out equipment. (Under the net book value method, replacing fully depreciated equipment with new equipment can have a dramatic, adverse effect on ROI.)

Managers generally view consistency as the most important of the considerations above. As a result, a majority of companies use the net book value approach in ROI computations. In this text, we will also use the net book value approach unless a specific exercise or problem directs otherwise.

# Controlling the Rate of Return

When we first defined the return on investment, we used the following formula:

$$\text{ROI} = \frac{\text{Net operating income}}{\text{Average operating assets}}$$

**Learning Objective 3**
Understand how changes in sales, expenses, and operating assets affect an organization's ROI.

We can modify this formula slightly by introducing sales as follows:

$$\text{ROI} = \frac{\text{Net operating income}}{\text{Sales}} \times \frac{\text{Sales}}{\text{Average operating assets}}$$

The first term on the right-hand side of the equation is the *margin*, which is defined as follows:

$$\text{Margin} = \frac{\text{Net operating income}}{\text{Sales}}$$

The **margin** is a measure of management's ability to control operating expenses in relation to sales. The lower the operating expenses per dollar of sales, the higher is the margin earned. This, in itself, can be a useful measure even for a profit centre manager.

The second term on the right-hand side of the preceding equation is *turnover* which is defined as follows:

$$\text{Turnover} = \frac{\text{Sales}}{\text{Average operating assets}}$$

**Turnover** is a measure of the sales that are generated for each dollar invested in operating assets.

The following alternative form of the ROI formula, which we will use most frequently, combines margin and turnover:

$$\text{ROI} = \text{Margin} \times \text{Turnover}$$

Which formula for ROI should be used—the original one stated in terms of net operating income and average operating assets or this one stated in terms of margin and turnover? Either can be used—they will always give the same answer. However, the margin and turnover formulation provides some additional insights.

Some managers tend to focus too much on margin and ignore turnover. To some degree at least, the margin can be a valuable indicator of a manager's performance. Standing alone, however, it overlooks one very crucial area of a manager's responsibility—the investment in operating assets. Excessive funds tied up in operating assets, which depresses turnover, can be just as much of a drag on profitability as excessive operating expenses, which depresses margin. One of the advantages of ROI as a performance measure is that it forces the manager to control the investment in operating assets as well as to control expenses and the margin.

Du Pont pioneered the ROI concept and recognized the importance of looking at both margin and turnover in assessing the performance of a manager. The ROI formula is now widely used as the key measure of the performance of an investment centre. The ROI formula blends together many aspects of the manager's responsibilities into a single figure that can be compared with the returns of competing investment centres, with the returns of other firms in the industry, and with the past returns of the investment centre itself.

Du Pont also developed the diagram that appears in Exhibit 11–3. This exhibit helps managers understand how they can control ROI. An investment centre manager can increase ROI in basically three ways:

1. Increase sales.
2. Reduce expenses.
3. Reduce assets.

## Exhibit 11–3
Elements of Return on Investment (ROI)

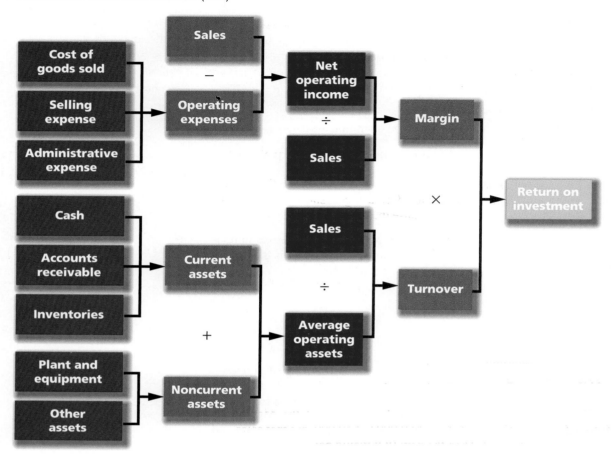

To illustrate how the rate of return can be improved by each of these three actions, consider how the manager of the Monthaven Burger Grill is evaluated. Burger Grill is a small chain of upscale casual restaurants that has been rapidly adding outlets via franchising. The Monthaven franchise is owned by a group of local surgeons who have little time to devote to management and little expertise in business matters. Therefore, they delegate operating decisions—including decisions concerning investment in operating assets, such as inventories—to a professional manager they have hired. The manager is evaluated largely on the basis of the ROI the franchise generates.

The following data represent the results of operations for the most recent month:

| | |
|---|---|
| Net operating income ..................... | $10,000 |
| Sales ................................... | 100,000 |
| Average operating assets ................. | 50,000 |

The rate of return generated by the Monthaven Burger Grill investment centre is as follows:

$$\text{ROI} = \quad \text{Margin} \quad \times \quad \text{Turnover}$$

$$= \quad \frac{\text{Net operating income}}{\text{Sales}} \quad \times \quad \frac{\text{Sales}}{\text{Average operating assets}}$$

$$= \quad \frac{\$10,000}{\$100,000} \quad \times \quad \frac{\$100,000}{50,000}$$

$$= \quad 10\% \quad \times \quad 2 \quad = 20\%$$

As we stated above, to improve the ROI figure, the manager can (1) increase sales, (2) reduce expenses, or (3) reduce the operating assets.

**APPROACH 1: INCREASE SALES**   Assume that the manager of the Monthaven Burger Grill is able to increase sales from $100,000 to $110,000. Given that some expenses are fixed, the increase in sales is likely to result in an increase in net operating income. Assume that the net operating income increases to $12,000. Assume that the operating assets remain constant. Then the new ROI would be:

$$\text{ROI} = \frac{\$12,000}{\$110,000} \times \frac{\$110,000}{\$50,000}$$

$$10.91\% \quad \times \quad 2.2 \quad = 24\% \text{ (as compared with 20\% above)}$$

Note, however, that an increase in sales may be due to additional marketing efforts (which may be costly). This may result in the income decreasing or staying the same. In such situations, the ROI will not increase. This is because the margin will decrease despite an increase in the turnover.

**APPROACH 2: REDUCE EXPENSES**   Assume that the manager of the Monthaven Burger Grill is able to reduce expenses by $1,000 so that net operating income increases from $10,000 to $11,000. Assume that both sales and operating assets remain constant. Then the new ROI would be:

$$\text{ROI} = \frac{\$11,000}{\$100,000} \times \frac{\$100,000}{\$50,000}$$

$$11\% \quad \times \quad 2 \quad = 22\% \text{ (as compared with 20\% above)}$$

**APPROACH 3: REDUCE ASSETS**   Assume that the manager of the Monthaven Burger Grill is able to reduce operating assets from $50,000 to $40,000, but that sales and net operating income remain unchanged. Then the new ROI would be:

$$\text{ROI} = \frac{\$10,000}{\$100,000} \times \frac{\$100,000}{\$40,000}$$

$$10\% \quad \times \quad 2.5 \quad = 25\% \text{ (as compared with 20\% above)}$$

A clear understanding of these three approaches to improving the ROI figure is critical to the effective management of an investment centre. We will now look at each approach in more detail.

## Increase Sales

When first looking at the ROI formula, one is inclined to think that the sales figure is neutral, since it appears as the denominator in the margin computation and as the numerator in the turnover computation. We *could* cancel out the sales figure, but we do not do it for two reasons. First, this would tend to draw attention away from the fact that the rate of return is a function of *two* variables, margin and turnover. And second, it would tend to conceal the fact that a change in sales can affect both the margin and the turnover in an organization. A change in sales can affect the *margin* if expenses increase or decrease at a different rate from sales. For example, a company may be able to keep a tight control on its costs as its sales go up, with the result that net operating income increases more rapidly than sales and increases the margin. Or a company may have fixed expenses that remain constant as sales go up, resulting in an increase in the net operating income and in the margin. Either (or both) of these factors could have been responsible for the increase in the margin percentage from 10% to 10.91% illustrated in approach 1 above.

Further, a change in sales can affect the *turnover* if sales either increase or decrease without a proportionate increase or decrease in the operating assets. In the first approach above, for example, sales increased from $100,000 to $110,000, but the operating assets remained unchanged. As a result, the turnover increased from 2 to 2.2 for the period.

## Reduce Expenses

Often, the easiest route to increased profitability and to a stronger ROI figure is to simply cut the "fat" out of an organization through a concerted effort to control expenses. When margins begin to be squeezed, this is generally the first line of attack by a manager. Discretionary fixed costs (that is, fixed costs that arise from annual decisions by management to spend in certain fixed cost areas) usually come under scrutiny first, and various programs are either curtailed or eliminated in an effort to cut costs. Managers must be careful, however, not to cut out muscle and bone along with the fat. Also, they must remember that frequent cost-cutting binges can destroy morale. Most managers now agree that it is best to stay "lean and mean" all of the time.

## Reduce Operating Assets

Managers have always been sensitive to the need to control sales, operating expenses, and operating margins. However, they have not always been equally sensitive to the need to control investment in operating assets. Firms that have adopted the ROI approach to measuring managerial performance report that one of the first reactions of investment centre managers is to trim their investment in operating assets. Managers soon realize that an excessive investment in operating assets reduces turnover and hurts the ROI. As these managers reduce their investment in operating assets, funds are released that can be used elsewhere in the organization.

How can an investment centre manager control the investment in operating assets? One approach is to eliminate unneeded inventory. Just-in-time (JIT) purchasing and JIT manufacturing have been extremely helpful in reducing inventories of all types, with the result that ROI figures have improved dramatically in some companies. Another approach is to devise various methods of speeding up the collection of receivables. For example, many firms now employ the lockbox technique, which enables customers in distant states to send their payments directly to post office boxes in their area. The funds are received and deposited by a local bank on behalf of the payee firm. This speeds up the collection process, since the payments are not delayed in the postal system. As a result of the speedup in collection, the accounts receivable balance is reduced and the asset turnover is increased.

## Criticisms of ROI

Although ROI is widely used in evaluating performance, it is not a perfect tool. The method is subject to the following criticisms:

1. Just telling managers to increase ROI may not be enough. Managers may not know how to increase ROI; they may increase ROI in a way that is inconsistent with the company's strategy; or they may take actions that increase ROI in the short run but harm the company in the long run (such as cutting back on research and development).
2. A manager who takes over a business segment typically inherits many committed costs over which the manager has no control. These committed costs make it difficult to fairly assess the performance of the manager relative to other managers.
3. As discussed in the next section, a manager who is evaluated on the basis of ROI may reject investment opportunities that are profitable for the company as a whole.

You were recently hired as the manager of a chain of jewellery stores that are located in downtown Toronto. You are excited about the high level of autonomy that you have been given to run the stores but are nervous because you have heard rumours that the previous manager was let go because the return on investment (ROI) of the stores was unacceptable. What steps should you consider to improve ROI?

# Residual Income—Another Measure of Performance

Another approach to measuring an investment centre's performance focuses on a concept known as *residual income*. **Residual income** is the net operating income that an investment centre earns above the minimum required return on its operating assets.

For purposes of illustration, consider the following data for an investment centre—the Lethbridge Division of Western Canada Services Corporation.

**Learning Objective 4**
Compute residual income and understand the strengths and weaknesses of this method of measuring performance.

| WESTERN CANADA SERVICES CORPORATION<br>Lethbridge Division<br>Basic Data for Performance Evaluation | |
| --- | --- |
| Average operating assets | $100,000 |
| Net operating income | $ 20,000 |
| Minimum required rate of return | 15% |

Western Canada Services Corporation has long had a policy of evaluating investment centre managers on the basis of ROI, but it is considering a switch to residual income. The controller of the company, who is in favour of the change to residual income, has provided the following table that shows how the performance of the division would be evaluated under each of the two methods:

| WESTERN CANADA SERVICES CORPORATION<br>Lethbridge Division | Alternative<br>Performance Measures | |
| --- | --- | --- |
| | **ROI** | **Residual<br>Income** |
| Average operating assets (a) | $100,000 | $100,000 |
| Net operating income (b) | $ 20,000 | $ 20,000 |
| ROI, (b) ÷ (a) | 20% | |
| Minimum required return (15% × $100,000) | | 15,000 |
| Residual income | | $ 5,000 |

The reasoning underlying the residual income calculation is straightforward. The company is able to earn a rate of return of at least 15% on its investments. Since the company has invested $100,000 in the Lethbridge Division in the form of operating assets, the company should be able to earn at least $15,000 (15% × $100,000) on this

Concept 11–2

investment. Since the Lethbridge Division's net operating income is $20,000, the residual income above and beyond the minimum required return is $5,000. If residual income is adopted as the performance measure to replace ROI, the manager of the Lethbridge Division would be evaluated on the basis of the growth from year to year in residual income.

**Economic value added (EVA)** is a similar concept that differs in some details from residual income.[2] For example, under the economic value added concept, funds used for research and development are treated as investments rather than as expenses.[3] However, for our purposes, we will not draw any distinction between residual income and economic value added.

When residual income or economic value added is used to measure performance, the objective is to maximize the total amount of residual income or economic value added, not to maximize overall ROI. Organizations as diverse as Coca-Cola, Alcan, Domtar, and Grand and Toy, have embraced some version of EVA/residual income in recent years.

---

## *in business today*    Linking EVA to Bonuses

Daniel O'Neill, a chief executive at Molson Inc., received a bonus that was far more than expected and allowed by the company. His bonus was based on "EVA improvement as well as exceeding the annual business financial target and individual objectives set by the human resources committee," said the management proxy circular. In addition, O'Neill was known for getting Molson out of the slump by refurbishing advertising, firing many employees, reducing overhead costs, and buying a major brewery in Brazil to catapult the company worldwide. O'Neill's compensation at that time was far higher than any other Molson executive.

Source: "Molson Chief Executive O'Neill Gets $2.36 Million Bonus After Dramatic Moves," *Canadian Press Newswire*, May 27, 2002. Reprinted with permission from Press News Limited, a division of *The Canadian Press*.

---

## Motivation and Residual Income

One of the primary reasons why the controller of Western Canada Services Corporation would like to switch from ROI to residual income has to do with how managers view new investments under the two performance measurement schemes. The residual income approach encourages managers to make investments that are profitable for the entire company but that would be rejected by managers who are evaluated by the ROI formula.

To illustrate this problem, suppose that the manager of the Lethbridge Division is considering purchasing a computerized diagnostic machine to aid in servicing marine diesel engines. The machine would cost $25,000 and is expected to generate additional operating income of $4,500 a year. From the standpoint of the company, this would be a good

---

[2]The basic idea underlying residual income and economic value added has been around for over 100 years. In recent years, economic value added has been popularized and trademarked by the consulting firm Stern, Stewart & Co.

[3]Over 100 different adjustments could be made for deferred taxes, LIFO reserves, provisions for future liabilities, mergers and acquisitions, gains or losses due to changes in accounting rules, operating leases, and other accounts, but most companies make only a few. For further details, see John O'Hanlon and Ken Peasnell, "Wall Street's Contribution to Management Accounting: The Stern Stewart EVA® Financial Management System," *Management Accounting Research* 9, 1998, pp. 421–444.

investment, since it promises a rate of return of 18% ($4,500/$25,000), which is in excess of the company's minimum required rate of return of 15%.

If the manager of the Lethbridge Division is evaluated on the basis of residual income, she would be in favour of the investment in the diagnostic machine as shown below:

**WESTERN CANADA SERVICES CORPORATION**
**Lethbridge Division**
**Performance Evaluated Using Residual Income**

|  | Present | New Project | Overall |
|---|---|---|---|
| Average operating assets ...... | $100,000 | $25,000 | $125,000 |
| Net operating income ......... | $ 20,000 | $ 4,500 | $ 24,500 |
| Minimum required return ...... | 15,000 | 3,750* | 18,750 |
| Residual income ............. | $ 5,000 | $ 750 | $ 5,750 |

*$25,000 × 15% = $3,750.

Since the project would increase the residual income of the Lethbridge Division, the manager would want to invest in the new diagnostic machine.

Now suppose that the manager of the Lethbridge Division is evaluated on the basis of ROI. The effect of the diagnostic machine on the division's ROI is computed below:

**WESTERN CANADA SERVICES CORPORATION**
**Lethbridge Division**
**Performance Evaluated Using ROI**

|  | Present | New Project | Overall |
|---|---|---|---|
| Average operating assets (a) .... | $100,000 | $25,000 | $125,000 |
| Net operating income (b) ...... | $20,000 | $4,500 | $24,500 |
| ROI, (b) ÷ (a) .............. | 20% | 18% | 19.6% |

The new project reduces the division's ROI from 20% to 19.6%. This happens because the 18% rate of return on the new diagnostic machine, while above the company's 15% minimum rate of return, is below the division's present ROI of 20%. Therefore, the new diagnostic machine would drag the division's ROI down, even though it would be a good investment from the standpoint of the company as a whole. If the manager of the division is evaluated on the basis of ROI, she will be reluctant to even propose such an investment.

Basically, a manager who is evaluated on the basis of ROI will reject any project whose rate of return is below the division's current ROI, even if the rate of return on the project is above the minimum required rate of return for the entire company. In contrast, any project whose rate of return is above the minimum required rate of return for the company will result in an increase in residual income. Since it is in the best interests of the company as a whole to accept any project whose rate of return is above the minimum required rate of return, managers who are evaluated on the basis of residual income will tend to make better decisions concerning investment projects than managers who are evaluated on the basis of ROI.

## Divisional Comparison and Residual Income

The residual income approach has one major disadvantage. It cannot be used to compare the performance of divisions of different sizes. You would expect larger divisions to have a greater residual income than smaller divisions, not necessarily because they are better managed but simply because of the bigger numbers involved.

As an example, consider the following residual income computations for Division X and Division Y:

|  | Division | |
| --- | --- | --- |
|  | X | Y |
| Average operating assets (a) ................. | $1,000,000 | $250,000 |
| Net operating income ........................ | $ 120,000 | $ 40,000 |
| Minimum required return: 10% × (a) .......... | 100,000 | 25,000 |
| Residual income ........................... | $ 20,000 | $ 15,000 |

Observe that Division X has slightly more residual income than Division Y but that Division X has $1,000,000 in operating assets as compared with only $250,000 in operating assets for Division Y. Thus, Division X's greater residual income is probably more a result of its size than the quality of its management. In fact, it appears that the smaller division is better managed, since it has been able to generate nearly as much residual income with only one-fourth as much in operating assets to work with. This problem can be reduced to some degree by focusing on the percentage change in residual income from year to year, rather than on the absolute amount of the residual income. On the other hand, ROI is a standardized measure and lends itself to comparisons regardless of size.

## Transfer Prices

In some companies, all segments may be classified as profit or investment centres, regardless of whether they can generate revenues. In such companies, one segment may "sell" its services or products to another segment at a predetermined price. In these situations, the organization records such a transaction as an internal transfer. The price at which this transfer is recorded is known as the **transfer price.** For example, the information services (IS) department of a large organization may "sell" its services to user departments. In this setting, the IS department is treated as a profit centre. It is natural to assume that the selling segment would like the transfer price to be as high as possible, while the buying segment would like the price to be as low as possible.

The question of what transfer price to charge is one of the most difficult problems in managerial accounting. The objective in transfer pricing should be to motivate the segment managers to do what is in the best interests of the overall organization. For example, if we want the manager of the passenger car division of Ford to make decisions that are in the best interests of the overall organization, the transfer price charged to the passenger car division for trucks must be the cost incurred by the entire organization up to the point of transfer—including any opportunity costs. If the transfer price is less than this cost, then the manager of the passenger car division will think that the cost of the trucks is lower than it really is and will tend to demand more trucks than would be optimal for the entire company. If the transfer price is greater than the cost incurred by the entire organization up to the point of the transfer, then the passenger car division manager will think the cost of the trucks is higher than it really is and will tend to demand fewer trucks than would be optimal for the entire organization. While this principle may seem clear-cut, as a practical matter, implementing it is very difficult for a variety of reasons. In practice, companies usually adopt a simplified transfer pricing policy based on variable cost, absorption cost, or market prices. All of these approaches have flaws, which are covered in more advanced texts.

Adopting a proactive approach to transfer pricing has never been more important. Companies are increasingly expanding their geographical boundaries resulting in the need for transfer pricing. The Canada Revenue Agency (CRA) has taken steps to ensure that it gets its piece of the pie. In the past year, the federal government hired over 300 auditors to examine transfer pricing practices adopted by these businesses. Transfer prices can no longer be a whimsical number created to "beat the tax man." A company must now be able to validate its chosen transfer prices.

Source: Swaneveld, Hendrik and Martin Przysuski, "Transfer pricing now a Canadian priority," *CMA Management,* April, 2002, pp. 42–44. Reprinted with permission from CMA Canada.

## Balanced Scorecard

An important characteristic of a performance measurement system is that it must aid in the implementation of an organization's strategies. A strategy is a plan of action that organizations adopt to achieve their goals. The performance measures that we have discussed until now (variances, margin, return on investment, residual income) are all financial measures. This approach of measuring performance using financial measures has come under criticism in the last 15 years.

A significant limitation of focusing only on financial measures is that they do not provide information to managers about the organization's performance along other dimensions. More importantly, although tracking financial performance is important, knowing how the organization got where it is is equally important. Managers must know what factors influence performance and establish measures that inform how well the organization is doing with those factors that influence financial performance. Therefore, a performance measurement system must include other "nonfinancial" measures that provide useful information to managers to monitor the progress regarding strategy implementation.

The **balanced scorecard** is a performance measurement system which contains measures along at least four dimensions: (1) financial, (2) customer, (3) internal business process, and (4) learning and growth. Measures pertaining to the learning and growth dimension are supposed to inform managers about the likely performance along the internal business process dimension. Similarly, measures along the internal business process dimension are supposed to inform about potential performance along the customer dimension and ultimately the financial dimension. Thus, a key feature of the scorecard is that measures along the different dimensions are linked to one another or integrated. In this sense, the balanced scorecard is an integrated performance measurement system.

The balanced scorecard provides a way of communicating a company's strategy to managers throughout the organization. A properly designed scorecard should allow managers to answer such questions as: Which customers should be targeted, and how can they be attracted and retained at a profit? Which internal business process must be improved to meet customer requirements? In short, a well constructed balanced scorecard should provide managers with a road map that indicates how the company will achieve its financial objectives. Achieving the financial objectives is important to ensure the long-term viability of the business.

As an example, think of a car dealership that wants to increase its profitability and growth. A balanced scorecard for this dealership would include measures pertaining to the two objectives, and measures that influence the two objectives. Given that the generic profitability equation consists of two variables—sales revenues and costs—the scorecard should measure these two variables. Sales revenue and other sales-related measures, such as customer service, number of referrals, and customer satisfaction, will appear in the customer dimension of the scorecard. Cost and other operational measures that will lead to improvements in the customer and financial measures will appear along the internal business process dimension. These may include costs, quality, and delivery/service time—factors that are important to customers, thereby leading to an improvement in the customer measures. Finally, management of the dealership may believe that learning is very important in improving the other measures. Therefore, they may decide to track training hours within the learning and growth perspective. The key aspect in identifying the right performance measures is that the measures must be linked in a cause–effect relationship. Otherwise, the scorecard is simply a collection of *ad hoc* measures that may result in more confusion, rather than provide any direction to management.

A multidimensional performance measurement system, such as the balanced scorecard, can provide a more complete picture of an organization's performance. Although the concept is very appealing and has been embraced by many types of organizations, including hospitals, universities, government departments and businesses, there are some key issues that managers must keep in mind when implementing a balanced scorecard within their organizations. First and foremost, top managers must fully support its implementation. Second, individual measures within the different dimensions must be well defined and should flow from the goals and objectives established by senior management. Third, the individual measures must be mutually reinforcing to ensure that employees are not pulled in different directions. Finally, the performance measurement system and the employee evaluation and compensation system must be linked. A system that emphasizes A and rewards B is a classic recipe for disaster.

*in business today*   **How the Saskatchewan Transportation Company Defines Success**

The use of a balanced scorecard is not restricted to private businesses only. Many government and not-for-profit organizations have also implemented the balanced scorecard. In 1946, the Saskatchewan Transportation Company (STC) was established by the Government of Saskatchewan to provide intercity bus service within the province. STC, unlike most companies, is in a unique position in that financial performance is not the most important indicator of success. STC is in business to provide a service to the people of Saskatchewan, even when that means operating a bus route that is not profitable. As stated by President and CEO Jim Hadifield, "return on investment is not the reason STC exists. It is in place for the provision of a service."

Since the late 1990s, STC has been using the balanced scorecard to help define overall corporate goals. STC's current balanced scorecard includes measures along the following four quadrants: Public Policy, Customer, Financial, and Innovation and Growth. Currently, STC is working on refurbishing its balanced scorecard to focus even more on customer service.

Source: Saskatchewan Transportation Company, *2002 Annual Report*, Regina, SK, 2002.

# Summary

**LO1   Understand the role of cost, revenue, profit and investment centres in a decentralized organization.**

Decentralized organizations consist of individual segments which are often classified as cost, revenue, profit, or investment centres. A cost centre an organizational unit whose manager is responsible for costs but not revenues, profits, or investments. A revenue centre is an organizational unit whose manager is responsible for meeting revenue targets and is considered to have the authority to strongly influence (if not control) revenues. A profit centre is an organizational unit whose manager is responsible for the segment's profitability and has the authority to strongly influence both costs and revenues. An investment centre is similar to a profit centre; in addition to profitability, the manager of an investment centre is also responsible for investments in operating assets.

### LO2    Compute and understand the return on investment (ROI) measure.

Return on investment (ROI) is computed by dividing net operating income by average operating assets. Alternatively, it can be computed by multiplying the margin (net operating income divided by sales revenue) and turnover (sales revenues divided by average operating assets). The measure provides an evaluation of how well the segment utilized its operating assets to generate returns.

### LO3    Understand how changes in sales, expenses, and operating assets affect and organization's ROI.

The relationships among sales, expenses, assets, and the ROI are complex. The effect of a change in any one variable on the others will depend on the specific circumstances. Nevertheless, an increase in sales often leads to an increase in operating income and therefore the ROI. A decrease (increase) in operating assets will lead to an increase (decrease) in ROI provided the net operating income does not change.

### LO4    Compute residual income and understand the strengths and weaknesses of this method of measuring performance.

Residual income is the difference between net operating income and the minimum required return on average operating assets. The major advantage of residual income over ROI is that it does not discourage investment in projects whose rates of return are above the minimum required rate of return for the entire organization, but below the segment's current ROI.

### LO5    Understand the balanced scorecard and its role in implementing an organization's strategies.

The balanced scorecard is an integrated performance measurement system which consists of measures along at least four dimensions: (1) financial, (2) customer, (3) internal business process, and (4) learning and growth. A well constructed balanced scorecard should provide managers with a road map that indicates how the company will achieve its financial objectives.

# Guidance Answers to you Decide and Decision Maker

**A FRIEND** (p. 413)

It sounds like your friend's business is strongly centralized; that is, she makes all of the major decisions and takes responsibility for all of the major projects. Not only is your friend spreading herself too thin and burning out as a result, her managers seem to have little, if any, freedom. You might propose that she consider decentralizing the organization.

A strongly decentralized organization in which even the lowest-level managers and employees are free to make decisions may not be the answer, but some degree of decentralization would help the current situation. She would be relieved of much of the daily problem solving and could use the time to concentrate on strategy, higher-level decision making, and coordinating the activities of her managers. Not only would her managers become more skilled at making effective decisions, they would probably enjoy their jobs more and should be more willing to remain with the company. If your friend is reluctant to make changes, you might suggest that she interview the managers who have left the company. Their comments may help point your friend in the right direction.

**STORE MANAGER** (p. 423)

Three approaches can be used to increase ROI:

1. Increase sales—An increase in sales will positively impact the margin if expenses increase less than sales. An increase in sales will also affect turnover if there is not a proportionate increase in operating assets.
2. Reduce expenses—This approach is often the first path selected by managers to increase profitability and ROI. You should start by reviewing the stores' discretionary fixed costs (such as advertising). It may be possible to cut some discretionary fixed costs with minimal damage to the long-term goals of the organization. You should also investigate whether there are adequate physical controls over the inventory of jewellery items. Thefts result in an increase in cost of goods sold without a corresponding increase in sales!

3. Reduce operating assets—An excessive investment in operating assets (such as inventory) reduces turnover and hurts ROI. Given the nature of the operations of retail jewellery stores, inventory must be in sufficient quantities at specific times during the year (such as Christmas, Valentine's Day, and Mother's Day) or sales will suffer. However, those levels do not need to be maintained throughout the year.

# Review Problem: Return on Investment (ROI) and Residual Income

The Magnetic Imaging Division of Medical Diagnostics, Inc. has reported the following results for last year's operations:

| | |
|---|---|
| Sales ........................... | $25 million |
| Net operating income ............. | 3 million |
| Average operating assets ........... | 10 million |

**Required:**

1. Compute the margin, turnover, and ROI for the Magnetic Imaging Division.
2. Top management of Medical Diagnostics, Inc. has set a minimum required rate of return on average operating assets of 25%. What is the Magnetic Imaging Division's residual income for the year?

**SOLUTION TO REVIEW PROBLEM**

1. The required calculations appear below:

$$\text{Margin} = \frac{\text{Net operating income, } \$3,000,000}{\text{Sales, } \$25,000,000}$$

$$= 12\%$$

$$\text{Turnover} = \frac{\text{Sales, } \$25,000,000}{\text{Average operating assets, } \$10,000,000}$$

$$= 2.5$$

$$\text{ROI} = \text{Margin} \times \text{Turnover}$$

$$= 12\% \times 2.5$$

$$= 30\%$$

2. The residual income for the Magnetic Imaging Division is computed as follows:

| | |
|---|---|
| Average operating assets ............................... | $10,000,000 |
| Net operating income .................................... | $ 3,000,000 |
| Minimum required return (25% × $10,000,000) ............. | 2,500,000 |
| Residual income ....................................... | $ 500,000 |

# Glossary

**Balanced scorecard** An integrated performance measurement system which contains measures along at least four dimensions: (1) financial, (2) customer, (3) internal business process, and (4) learning and growth. (p. 427)

**Common fixed cost** A fixed cost that supports more than one business segment, but is not traceable in whole or in part to any one of the business segments. (p. 416)

**Cost centre** A business segment whose manager is responsible for costs but not revenues, profits, or investments. (p. 414)

**Decentralized organization** An organization in which decision making is not confined to a few top executives but, rather, is spread throughout the organization. (p. 412)

**Economic value added (EVA)** A concept similar to residual income. (p. 424)

**Investment centre** A business segment similar to the profit centre; in addition to profitability, the manager of an investment centre is also responsible for investments in operating assets. (p. 414)

**Margin** Net operating income divided by sales. (p. 419)

**Net operating income** Income before interest and income taxes have been deducted. (p. 417)

**Operating assets** Cash, accounts receivable, inventory, plant and equipment, and all other assets held for productive use in an organization. (p. 418)

**Profit centre** A business segment whose manager is responsible for the segment's profitability and has the authority to strongly influence both costs and revenues. (p. 414)

**Residual income** The net operating income that an investment centre earns above the required return on its operating assets. (p. 423)

**Responsibility centre** A segment of an organization whose manager is responsible and accountable for costs, revenues, profits, or investments. (p. 414)

**Return on investment (ROI)** Net operating income divided by average operating assets. It also equals margin multiplied by turnover. (p. 417)

**Revenue centre** A business segment whose manager is responsible for meeting revenue targets and is considered to have the authority to strongly influence (if not control) revenues. (p. 414)

**Segment** Any part or activity of an organization about which the manager seeks cost, revenue, or profit data. (p. 416)

**Traceable fixed cost** A fixed cost that is incurred because of the existence of a particular business segment. (p. 415)

**Transfer price** The price charged when one segment of an organization provides goods or services to another. (p. 426)

**Turnover** The amount of sales generated in an investment centre for each dollar invested in operating assets. It is computed by dividing sales by the average operating assets figure. (p. 419)

# Questions

11–1   What is meant by the term *decentralization?*

11–2   What benefits result from decentralization?

11–3   Distinguish between a cost centre, a revenue centre, a profit centre, and an investment centre.

11–4   Define a segment of an organization. Give several examples of segments.

11–5   What is meant by the terms *margin* and *turnover?*

11–6   What are the three basic approaches to improving return on investment (ROI)?

11–7   What is meant by residual income?

11–8   In what way can the use of ROI as a performance measure for investment centres lead to bad decisions? How does the residual income approach overcome this problem?

11–9   What is meant by the term *transfer price*, and why are transfer prices needed?

11–10   Explain the balanced scorecard.

# Brief Exercises

**BRIEF EXERCISE 11–1   Principles of Decentralization (LO1)**

Listed below are a number of terms that are associated with decentralization in organizations.

| | |
|---|---|
| Cost centre | Profit centre |
| Segment | Investment centre |
| Responsibility centre | Transfer price |
| Job satisfaction | |

*Required:*

Fill in the appropriate terms from the above list in the blanks provided.

1. A(n) _____ is a part or activity of an organization about which managers would like cost, revenue, or profit data.

2. Added responsibility and decision-making authority often result in increased _____.

3. A(n) _____ is a business segment whose manager is responsible for both cost and revenue, but not over investment funds.

4. When one segment, such as a division of a company, provides goods or services to another segment of the company, the _____ will determine how much revenue the segment recognizes on the transaction.

5. A(n) _____ is a business segment whose manager is responsible for costs, but not over revenue or investment funds.
6. A(n) _____ is any segment of an organization whose manager is responsible and accountable for cost, revenue, or investment funds.
7. A(n) _____ is a business segment whose manager is responsible for cost, revenue, and investments in operating assets.

**BRIEF EXERCISE 11–2    Compute the Return on Investment (ROI) (LO2)**
Alyeska Services Company, a division of a major oil company, provides various services to the operators of the North Slope oil field in Alaska. Data concerning the most recent year appear below:

| | |
|---|---|
| Sales .............................. | $7,500,000 |
| Net operating income ............... | 600,000 |
| Average operating assets ............. | 5,000,000 |

*Required:*
1. Compute the margin for Alyeska Services Company.
2. Compute the turnover for Alyeska Services Company.
3. Compute the return on investment (ROI) for Alyeska Services Company.

**BRIEF EXERCISE 11–3    Effects of Changes in Sales, Expenses, and Assets on ROI (LO3)**
CommercialServices.com Corporation provides business-to-business services on the Internet. Data concerning the most recent year appear below:

| | |
|---|---|
| Sales .............................. | $3,000,000 |
| Net operating income ............... | 150,000 |
| Average operating assets ............. | 750,000 |

*Required:*
Consider each question below independently. Carry out all computations to two decimal places.
1. Compute the company's return on investment (ROI).
2. The entrepreneur who founded the company is convinced that sales will increase next year by 50% and that net operating income would increase as a result by 200%, with no increase in average operating assets. What would be the company's ROI?
3. The chief financial officer of the company believes a more realistic scenario would be a $1,000,000 increase in sales, requiring a $250,000 increase in average operating assets, with a resulting $200,000 increase in net operating income. What would be the company's ROI in this scenario?

**BRIEF EXERCISE 11–4    Residual income (LO4)**
Juniper Design Ltd. of Manchester, England, is a company specializing in providing design services to residential developers. Last year, the company had net operating income of £600,000 on sales of £3,000,000. The company's average operating assets for the year were £2,800,000 and its minimum required rate of return was 18%. (The currency used in England is the pound sterling, denoted by £.)

*Required:*
Compute the company's residual income for the year.

# Exercises

**EXERCISE 11–1    Computing and Interpreting Return on Investment (ROI) (LO2)**
Selected operating data for two divisions of Outback Brewing, Ltd., of Australia, are given below:

| | Division | |
|---|---|---|
| | Queensland | New South Wales |
| Sales .............................. | $4,000,000 | $7,000,000 |
| Average operating assets ................. | 2,000,000 | 2,000,000 |
| Net operating income .................... | 360,000 | 420,000 |
| Property, plant, and equipment (net) ........ | 950,000 | 800,000 |

*Required:*

1. Compute the rate of return for each division using the return on investment (ROI) formula stated in terms of margin and turnover.
2. So far as you can tell from the data, which divisional manager seems to be doing the better job? Why?

**EXERCISE 11–2   Contrasting Return on Investment (ROI) and Residual Income** (LO2, LO4)

Meiji Isetan Corp. of Japan has two regional divisions with headquarters in Osaka and Yokohama. Selected data on the two divisions follow (in millions of yen, denoted by ¥):

| | Division | |
| --- | --- | --- |
| | Osaka | Yokohama |
| Sales ..................................... | ¥3,000,000 | ¥9,000,000 |
| Net operating income ................... | 210,000 | 720,000 |
| Average operating assets ............... | 1,000,000 | 4,000,000 |

*Required:*

1. For each division, compute the return on investment (ROI) in terms of margin and turnover. Where necessary, carry computations to two decimal places.
2. Assume that the company evaluates performance by use of residual income and that the minimum required return for any division is 15%. Compute the residual income for each division.
3. Is Yokohama's greater amount of residual income an indication that it is better managed? Explain.

**EXERCISE 11–3   Evaluating New Investments with Return on Investment (ROI) and Residual Income** (LO2, LO4)

Selected sales and operating data for three divisions of a multinational structural engineering firm are given below:

| | Division | | |
| --- | --- | --- | --- |
| | Asia | Europe | North America |
| Sales ........................ | $12,000,000 | $14,000,000 | $25,000,000 |
| Average operating assets .......... | 3,000,000 | 7,000,000 | 5,000,000 |
| Net operating income ............ | 600,000 | 560,000 | 800,000 |
| Minimum required rate of return ... | 14% | 10% | 16% |

*Required:*

1. Compute the return on investment (ROI) for each division using the formula stated in terms of margin and turnover.
2. Compute the residual income for each division.
3. Assume that each division is presented with an investment opportunity that would yield a 15% rate of return.
   a. If performance is being measured by ROI, which division or divisions will probably accept the opportunity? Reject? Why?
   b. If performance is being measured by residual income, which division or divisions will probably accept the opportunity? Reject? Why?

**EXERCISE 11–4   Effects of Changes in Profits and Assets on Return on Investment (ROI)** (LO3)

Pecs Alley is a regional chain of health clubs. The managers of the clubs, who have authority to make investments as needed, are evaluated based largely on return on investment (ROI). The Springfield Club reported the following results for the past year:

| | |
| --- | --- |
| Sales ............................ | $1,400,000 |
| Net operating income .............. | 70,000 |
| Average operating assets ............ | 350,000 |

*Required:*

The following questions are to be considered independently. Carry out all computations to two decimal places.

1. Compute the club's return on investment (ROI).

2. Assume that the manager of the club is able to increase sales by $70,000 and that, as a result, net operating income increases by $18,200. Further assume that this is possible without any increase in operating assets. What would be the club's return on investment (ROI)?
3. Assume that the manager of the club is able to reduce expenses by $14,000 without any change in sales or operating assets. What would be the club's return on investment (ROI)?
4. Assume that the manager of the club is able to reduce operating assets by $70,000 without any change in sales or net operating income. What would be the club's return on investment (ROI)?

**EXERCISE 11–5    Cost-Volume-Profit Analysis and Return on Investment (ROI) (LO3)**
Posters.com is a small Internet retailer of high-quality posters. The company has $1,000,000 in operating assets and fixed expenses of $150,000 per year. With this level of operating assets and fixed expenses, the company can support sales of up to $3,000,000 per year. The company's contribution margin ratio is 25%, which means that an additional dollar of sales results in additional contribution margin, and net operating income, of 25 cents.

*Required:*
1. Complete the following table showing the relation between sales and return on investment (ROI).

| Sales | Net Operating Income | Average Operating Assets | ROI |
|---|---|---|---|
| $2,500,000 | $475,000 | $1,000,000 | ? |
| 2,600,000 | ? | 1,000,000 | ? |
| 2,700,000 | ? | 1,000,000 | ? |
| 2,800,000 | ? | 1,000,000 | ? |
| 2,900,000 | ? | 1,000,000 | ? |
| 3,000,000 | ? | 1,000,000 | ? |

2. What happens to the company's return on investment (ROI) as the sales increase? Explain.

# Problems

**PROBLEM 11–1    Return on Investment (ROI) Relations (ROI) (LO2)**
Provide the missing data in the following tabulation:

| | Division | | |
|---|---|---|---|
| | Alpha | Bravo | Charlie |
| Sales ......................... | $  ? | $11,500,000 | $  ? |
| Net operating income ............. | ? | 920,000 | 210,000 |
| Average operating assets .......... | 800,000 | ? | ? |
| Margin ...................... | 4% | ? | 7% |
| Turnover ..................... | 5 | ? | ? |
| Return on investment (ROI) ........ | ? | 20% | 14% |

**PROBLEM 11–2    Return on Investment (ROI) and Residual Income Relations (LO2, LO4)**
A family friend has asked your help in analyzing the operations of three anonymous companies. Supply the missing data in the tabulation below:

| | Company | | |
|---|---|---|---|
| | A | B | C |
| Sales .......................... | $9,000,000 | $7,000,000 | $4,500,000 |
| Net operating income ............... | ? | 280,000 | ? |
| Average operating assets ............. | 3,000,000 | ? | 1,800,000 |
| Return on investment (ROI) .......... | 18% | 14% | ? |
| Minimum required rate of return: | | | |
| Percentage ..................... | 16% | ? | 15% |
| Dollar amount .................. | ? | 320,000 | ? |
| Residual income .................. | ? | ? | 90,000 |

**PROBLEM 11–3  Comparison of Performance Using Return on Investment (ROI)** (LO2)

Comparative data on three companies in the same industry are given below:

| | Company | | |
|---|---|---|---|
| | **A** | **B** | **C** |
| Sales ............................ | $600,000 | $500,000 | $    ? |
| Net operating income ............... | 84,000 | 70,000 | ? |
| Average operating assets ............. | 300,000 | ? | 1,000,000 |
| Margin ......................... | ? | ? | 3.5% |
| Turnover ........................ | ? | ? | 2 |
| ROI ............................ | ? | 7% | ? |

*Required:*
1. What advantages can you see in breaking down the ROI computation into two separate elements, margin and turnover?
2. Fill in the missing information above, and comment on the relative performance of the three companies in as much detail as the data permit. Make *specific recommendations* on steps to be taken to improve the return on investment, where needed.

(Adapted from National Association of Accountants, *Research Report No. 35,* p. 34)

**PROBLEM 11–4  Return on Investment (ROI) and Residual Income** (LO2, LO4)

Financial data for Joel de Paris Inc. for last year follow:

### JOEL DE PARIS INC.
### Balance Sheet

| | Ending Balance | Beginning Balance |
|---|---|---|
| **Assets** | | |
| Cash ....................................... | $   120,000 | $   140,000 |
| Accounts receivable ........................... | 530,000 | 450,000 |
| Inventory ................................... | 380,000 | 320,000 |
| Plant and equipment, net ....................... | 620,000 | 680,000 |
| Investment in Buisson, S.A. ..................... | 280,000 | 250,000 |
| Land (undeveloped) ........................... | 170,000 | 180,000 |
| Total assets ................................. | $2,100,000 | $2,020,000 |
| **Liabilities and Shareholders' Equity** | | |
| Accounts payable ............................. | $   310,000 | $   360,000 |
| Long-term debt .............................. | 1,500,000 | 1,500,000 |
| Shareholders' equity .......................... | 290,000 | 160,000 |
| Total liabilities and shareholders' equity ............ | $2,100,000 | $2,020,000 |

### JOEL DE PARIS INC.
### Income Statement

| | | |
|---|---|---|
| Sales ....................................... | | $4,050,000 |
| Less operating expenses ....................... | | 3,645,000 |
| Net operating income ......................... | | 405,000 |
| Less interest and taxes: | | |
| Interest expense ........................... | $ 150,000 | |
| Tax expense .............................. | 110,000 | 260,000 |
| Net income ................................. | | $   145,000 |

The company paid dividends of $15,000 last year. The "Investment in Buisson, S.A.," on the balance sheet represents an investment in the shares of another company.

*Required:*

1. Compute the company's margin, turnover, and ROI for last year.
2. The board of directors of Joel de Paris Inc. has set a minimum required return of 15%. What was the company's residual income last year?

**PROBLEM 11–5    Return on Investment (ROI) and Residual Income** (LO2, LO4)

"I know headquarters wants us to add on that new product line," said Dell Havasi, manager of Billings Company's Office Products Division. "But I want to see the numbers before I make any move. Our division has led the company for three years, and I don't want any letdown."

Billings Company is a decentralized organization with five autonomous divisions. The divisions are evaluated on the basis of the return that they are able to generate on invested assets, with year-end bonuses given to the divisional managers who have the highest ROI figures. Operating results for the company's Office Products Division for the most recent year are given below:

| | |
|---|---|
| Sales ........................... | $10,000,000 |
| Less variable expenses ............. | 6,000,000 |
| Contribution margin ............... | 4,000,000 |
| Less fixed expenses ............... | 3,200,000 |
| Net operating income ............. | $    800,000 |
| Divisional operating assets .......... | $ 4,000,000 |

The company had an overall ROI of 15% last year (considering all divisions). The Office Products Division has an opportunity to add a new product line that would require an additional investment in operating assets of $1,000,000. The cost and revenue characteristics of the new product line per year would be:

| | |
|---|---|
| Sales ........................... | $2,000,000 |
| Variable expenses ............... | 60% of sales |
| Fixed expenses .................. | $640,000 |

*Required:*

1. Compute the Office Products Division's ROI for the most recent year; also compute the ROI as it will appear if the new product line is added.
2. If you were in Dell Havasi's position, would you be inclined to accept or reject the new product line? Explain.
3. Why do you suppose headquarters is anxious for the Office Products Division to add the new product line?
4. Suppose that the company views a return of 12% on invested assets as being the minimum that any division should earn and that performance is evaluated by the residual income approach.
   a. Compute the Office Products Division's residual income for the most recent year; also compute the residual income as it will appear if the new product line is added.
   b. Under these circumstances, if you were in Dell Havasi's position, would you accept or reject the new product line? Explain.

**PROBLEM 11–6    Return on Investment (ROI) Analysis** (LO2, LO3)

The income statement for Huerra Company for last year is given below:

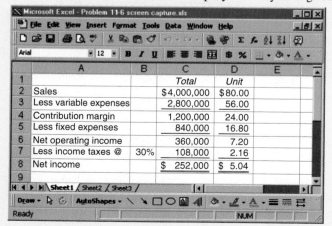

The company had average operating assets of $2,000,000 during the year.

*Required:*

1. Compute the company's ROI for the period using the ROI formula stated in terms of margin and turnover.

For each of the following questions, indicate whether the margin and turnover will increase, decrease, or remain unchanged as a result of the events described, and then compute the new ROI figure. Consider each question separately, starting in each case from the data used to compute the original ROI in (1) above.

2. By use of just-in-time (JIT), the company is able to reduce the average level of inventory by $400,000. (The released funds are used to pay off short-term creditors.)
3. The company achieves a cost savings of $32,000 per year by using less costly materials.
4. The company issues bonds and uses the proceeds to purchase $500,000 in machinery and equipment. Interest on the bonds is $60,000 per year. Sales remain unchanged. The new, more efficient equipment reduces production costs by $20,000 per year.
5. As a result of a more intense effort by salespeople, sales are increased by 20%; operating assets remain unchanged.
6. Obsolete items of inventory carried on the records at a cost of $40,000 are scrapped and written off as a loss since they are unsaleable.
7. The company uses $200,000 of cash (received on accounts receivable) to repurchase and retire some of its common shares.

**PROBLEM 11–7  Return on Investment (ROI); Residual Income; Decentralization** (LO1, LO2, LO4)

Raddington Industries produces tool and die machinery for manufacturers. The company expanded vertically several years ago by acquiring Reigis Steel Company, one of its suppliers of alloy steel plates. Raddington decided to maintain Reigis' separate identity and therefore established the Reigis Steel Division as one of its investment centres.

Raddington evaluates its divisions on the basis of ROI. Management bonuses are also based on ROI. All investments in operating assets are expected to earn a minimum rate of return of 11%.

Reigis' ROI has ranged from 14% to 17% since it was acquired by Raddington. During the past year, Reigis had an investment opportunity that would yield an estimated rate of return of 13%. Reigis' management decided against the investment because it believed the investment would decrease the division's overall ROI.

Last year's income statement for Reigis Steel Division is given below. The division's operating assets employed were $12,960,000 at the end of the year, which represents an 8% increase over the previous year-end balance.

CHECK FIGURE
(1b) Residual income:
$499,200

| REIGIS STEEL DIVISION Divisional Income Statement For the Year Ended December 31 | | |
|---|---|---|
| Sales | | $31,200,000 |
| Cost of goods sold | | 16,500,000 |
| Gross margin | | 14,700,000 |
| Less operating expenses: | | |
| Selling expenses | $5,620,000 | |
| Administrative expenses | 7,208,000 | 12,828,000 |
| Net operating income | | $1,872,000 |

*Required:*

1. Compute the following performance measures for the Reigis Steel Division:
   a. ROI. (Remember, ROI is based on the *average* operating assets, computed from the beginning-of-year and end-of-year balances.) State ROI in terms of margin and turnover.
   b. Residual income.
2. Would the management of Reigis Steel Division have been more likely to accept the investment opportunity it had last year if residual income were used as a performance measure instead of ROI? Explain.
3. The Reigis Steel Division is a separate investment centre within Raddington Industries. Identify the items Reigis must be free to control if it is to be evaluated fairly by either the ROI or residual income performance measures.

(CMA, adapted)

# Building Your Skills

**ANALYTICAL THINKING**   (LO2, LO3, LO4)

The Valve Division of Bendix Inc. produces a small valve that is used by various companies as a component part in their products. Bendix Inc. operates its divisions as autonomous units, giving its divisional managers great discretion in pricing and other decisions. Each division is expected to generate a rate of return of at least 14% on its operating assets. The Valve Division has average operating assets of $700,000. The valves are sold for $5 each. Variable costs are $3 per valve, and fixed costs total $462,000 per year. The division has a capacity of 300,000 valves each year.

*Required:*

1. How many valves must the Valve Division sell each year to generate the desired rate of return on its assets?
   a. What is the margin earned at this level of sales?
   b. What is the turnover at this level of sales?
2. Assume that the Valve Division's current ROI is just equal to the minimum required 14%. In order to increase the division's ROI, the divisional manager wants to increase the selling price per valve by 4%. Market studies indicate that an increase in the selling price would cause sales to drop by 20,000 units each year. However, operating assets could be reduced by $50,000 due to decreased needs for accounts receivable and inventory. Compute the margin, turnover, and ROI if these changes are made.
3. Refer to the original data. Assume again that the Valve Division's current ROI is just equal to the minimum required 14%. Rather than increase the selling price, the sales manager wants to reduce the selling price per valve by 4%. Market studies indicate that this would fill the plant to capacity. In order to carry the greater level of sales, however, operating assets would increase by $50,000. Compute the margin, turnover, and ROI if these changes are made.
4. Refer to the original data. Assume that the normal volume of sales is 280,000 valves each year at a price of $5 per valve. Another division of the company is currently purchasing 20,000 valves each year from an overseas supplier, at a price of $4.25 per valve. The manager of the Valve Division has adamantly refused to meet this price, pointing out that it would result in a loss for his division:

| | | |
|---|---:|---:|
| Selling price per valve . . . . . . . . . . . . . . . . . . . . | | $4.25 |
| Cost per valve: | | |
|   Variable . . . . . . . . . . . . . . . . . . . . . . . . . . . . | $3.00 | |
|   Fixed ($462,000 ÷ 300,000 valves) . . . . . . . . | 1.54 | 4.54 |
| Net loss per valve . . . . . . . . . . . . . . . . . . . . . . . . | | $(0.29) |

The manager of the Valve Division also points out that the normal $5 selling price barely allows his division the required 14% rate of return. "If we take on some business at only $4.25 per unit, then our ROI is obviously going to suffer," he reasons, "and maintaining that ROI figure is the key to my future. Besides, taking on these extra units would require us to increase our operating assets by at least $50,000 due to the larger inventories and receivables we would be carrying." If the manager of the Valve Division accepts the transfer price of $4.25 for 20,000 units, how would that decision impact the Valve Division's ROI? Should the manager of the Valve Division accept the price of $4.25 per valve? Why, or why not?

**COMMUNICATING IN PRACTICE**   (LO1, LO4)

How do the performance measurement and compensation systems of service firms compare with those of manufacturers? To study one well-run service-oriented business, ask the manager of your local Tim Horton's if he or she could spend some time discussing the performance measures that the company uses to evaluate store managers and how the performance measures tie in with their compensation.

*Required:*

After asking the following questions, write a brief memorandum to your instructor that summarizes what you discovered during your interview with the manager of the franchise.

1. What are Tim Horton's goals, that is, the broad, long-range plans of the company (e.g., to increase market share)?

2. What performance measures are used to help motivate the store managers and monitor progress toward achieving the corporation's goals?

3. Are the performance measures consistent with the store manager's compensation plan?

## TEAMWORK IN ACTION  (LO5)

The balanced scorecard is becoming an increasingly popular performance measurement system. Why?

### *Required:*

Form teams and discuss the primary reason why companies might adopt a balanced scorecard type performance measurement system. List the primary advantages that companies have derived from adopting the scorecard. Ensure that all members of the team understand and agree with the team's consensus. Each and every member of the team should be prepared to present the team's conclusions in a class discussion.

(Hint: Look up articles in *CMA Management* and *Harvard Business Review* to guide your thinking.)

Do not forget to check out Taking It to the Net and other quizzes and resources at the Online Learning Centre at www.mcgrawhill.ca/college/garrison.

# Chapter *Twelve*

# Relevant Costs for Decision Making

## A Look Back

We concluded our coverage of performance measures in Chapter 11 by focusing on decentralized organizations. The concepts discussed in that chapter, return on investment (ROI) and residual income, are used to motivate the managers of investment and profit centres and to monitor the performance of these centres.

## A Look at This Chapter

We continue our coverage of the decision-making process in Chapter 12 by focusing on the use of relevant cost data when analyzing alternatives. In general, only those costs and benefits that differ between alternatives are relevant in a decision. This basic idea is applied in a wide variety of situations in this chapter.

## A Look Ahead

The common approaches to making major investment decisions, which can have significant long-term implications for any organization, are discussed in Chapter 13.

## Chapter Outline

**Cost Concepts for Decision Making**
- Identifying Relevant Costs and Benefits
- Different Costs for Different Purposes

**Sunk Costs Are Not Relevant Costs**
- Book Value of Old Equipment

**Future Costs That Do Not Differ Are Not Relevant Costs**
- An Example of Irrelevant Future Costs
- Why Isolate Relevant Costs?

**Adding and Dropping Product Lines and Other Segments**
- An Illustration of Cost Analysis
- A Comparative Format

- Beware of Allocated Fixed Costs
- The Make-or-Buy Decision
- The Matter of Opportunity Cost

**Special Orders**

**Pricing New Products: Target Costing**

**Utilization of a Constrained Resource**
- Contribution in Relation to a Constrained Resource
- Managing Constraints

# DECISION FEATURE Getting the Customer Involved

Special orders are one-time orders. Generally, managers agree to accept special orders that generate additional profits (referred to as incremental net operating income in this chapter) and reject special orders that do not. However, managers sometimes accept a special order that is unprofitable if they believe that the special order will lead to additional future sales of normal items to a customer. This is often the case for book retailers, who can usually afford to stock only a small percentage of the books that are in print.

Processing a special book order requires a lot of work—an employee must locate and order the book from a publisher and then call the customer when it arrives. Special orders are also costly because they often require special shipping and quantity discounts are not available. Moreover, special orders are risky since the customer may never come in to pick up and pay for a book that was ordered. Even so, many book retailers take special orders because they count on an increase in customer loyalty. Canada's leading bookseller, Chapters (chapters.indigo.ca), has taken a different approach.

Chapters Inc. operates more than 200 traditional bookstores (averaging 2,700 square feet in size) and 70 superstores (ranging in size from 16,000 to 46,000 square feet) across Canada. The company also owns 70% of Chapters Online (www.chapters.indigo.ca), an online e-tailer of books and related products. In addition, realizing that many customers do not have Internet access and/or prefer the experience of visiting a bookstore, Chapters has installed e-commerce kiosks in each of its superstores in cooperation with Chapters Online.

Chapters' customers are now able to check the availability of a book using the in-store kiosks, which access a real-time database. If the title is in the store, the customer is directed to the appropriate shelf. If the book is not in stock, the customer can order the book at the kiosk. The kiosks overcome two of the major problems relating to special orders of books discussed above. First, the process is no longer labour-intensive. Customers special order their own books, which are shipped directly to them. Second, rather than being risky, special orders at the kiosks immediately generate cash for the company. The customer either pays online at the kiosk using a credit card or at the register using cash at the time the order is placed. The decision to accept or reject special orders is no longer the issue it once was for

## Learning Objectives

*After studying Chapter 12, you should be able to:*

**LO1** Distinguish between relevant and irrelevant costs in decisions.

**LO2** Prepare an analysis showing whether to keep or replace old equipment.

**LO3** Prepare an analysis showing whether a product line or other organizational segment should be dropped or retained.

**LO4** Prepare a well-organized make-or-buy analysis.

**LO5** Prepare an analysis showing whether a special order should be accepted.

**LO6** Determine the most profitable use of a constrained resource.

**M**aking decisions is one of the basic functions of a manager. Managers are constantly faced with problems of deciding what products to sell, what production methods to use, whether to make or buy component parts, what prices to charge, what channels of distribution to use, whether to accept special orders at special prices, and so forth. Decision making is often a difficult task that is complicated by the existence of numerous alternatives and massive amounts of data, only some of which may be relevant.

Every decision involves choosing from among at least two alternatives. In making a decision, the costs and benefits of one alternative must be compared with the costs and benefits of other alternatives. Costs that differ between alternatives are called **relevant costs.** Distinguishing between relevant and irrelevant cost and benefit data is critical for two reasons. First, irrelevant data can be ignored and need not be analyzed. This can save decision makers tremendous amounts of time and effort. Second, bad decisions can easily result from erroneously including irrelevant cost and benefit data when analyzing alternatives. To be successful in decision making, managers must be able to tell the difference between relevant and irrelevant data and must be able to correctly use the relevant data in analyzing alternatives. The purpose of this chapter is to develop these skills by illustrating their use in a wide range of decision-making situations. We hasten to add that these decision-making skills are as important in your personal life as they are to managers. After completing your study of the material in this chapter, you should be able to think more clearly about decisions in all facets of your life. You may find it helpful to turn back to Chapter 2 and refresh your memory concerning different cost concepts before reading on.

# Cost Concepts for Decision Making

## Identifying Relevant Costs and Benefits

**Learning Objective 1**
Distinguish between relevant and irrelevant costs in decisions.

Only those costs and benefits that differ in total between alternatives are relevant in a decision. If a cost will be the same regardless of the alternative selected, then the decision has no effect on the cost, and it can be ignored. For example, if you are trying to decide whether to go to a movie or to rent a videotape for the evening, the rent on your apartment is irrelevant because regardless of your decision, the rent will be the same. On the other hand, the cost of the movie ticket and the cost of renting the videotape would be relevant in the decision since they are different.

The concept of *avoidable costs* can be helpful when identifying relevant costs and benefits. An **avoidable cost** is a cost that can be eliminated in whole or in part by choosing one alternative over another. By choosing the alternative of going to the movie, the cost of renting the videotape can be avoided. By choosing the alternative of renting the videotape, the cost of the movie ticket can be avoided. Therefore, the cost of the movie ticket and the cost of renting the videotape are both avoidable costs. On the other hand, the rent on the apartment is not an avoidable cost of either alternative. You would continue to rent your apartment under either alternative. Avoidable costs are relevant costs. Unavoidable costs are irrelevant costs.

Two broad categories of costs are never relevant in decisions. These irrelevant costs are:

1. Sunk costs.
2. Future costs that do not differ between the alternatives.

As we learned in Chapter 2, a **sunk cost** is a cost that has already been incurred and that cannot be avoided, regardless of what a manager decides to do. Sunk costs are always the same, no matter what alternatives are being considered, and they are therefore always irrelevant and should be ignored. On the other hand, future costs that do differ between alternatives *are* relevant. For example, when deciding whether to go to a movie or rent a videotape, the cost of buying a movie ticket and the cost of renting a videotape have not yet been incurred. These are future costs that differ between alternatives when the decision is being made and therefore are relevant.

Along with sunk cost, the term **differential cost** was introduced in Chapter 2. In managerial accounting, the terms *avoidable cost*, *differential cost*, *incremental cost*, and *relevant cost* are often used interchangeably. To identify the costs that are avoidable (differential) in a particular decision situation and are therefore relevant, these steps can be followed:

1. Eliminate costs and benefits that do not differ between alternatives. These irrelevant costs consist of (a) sunk costs, and (b) future costs that do not differ between alternatives.
2. Use the remaining costs and benefits that do differ between alternatives in making the decision. The costs that remain are the differential, or avoidable, costs.

## Different Costs for Different Purposes

It is important to recognize that costs that are relevant in one decision situation are not necessarily relevant in another. For example, suppose you have plans to go out for a late evening dinner. The choice between a movie and renting a videotape is not relevant to your choice of restaurant. The cost of the dining out will depend on the choice of the restaurant; therefore, the dining costs at alternative restaurants will be relevant to your choice of the restaurant. But the cost of the movie ticket and the rental cost of the video tape are not relevant in this situation. Simply put, you require *different costs for different purposes*. The costs you require to decide between a movie and renting a video are different from those that you require for deciding which restaurant to go to for a late evening dinner. In *each* decision situation, one must examine the data and isolate the relevant costs. Otherwise, it is easy to become misled by irrelevant data.

The concept of "different costs for different purposes" is basic to managerial accounting; we shall see its application frequently in the pages that follow.

# Sunk Costs Are Not Relevant Costs

One of the most difficult conceptual lessons that managers have to learn is that sunk costs are never relevant in decisions.

## MANAGERIAL ACCOUNTING IN ACTION

**The Issue**

**SOARING**
**WINGS,INC.**

SoaringWings Inc. is a small manufacturer of high-quality hang gliders. The most critical component of a hang glider is its metal frame, which must be very strong and yet very light. The frames are made by brazing together tubes of high-strength, but lightweight, metal alloys. Most of the brazing must be done by hand, but some can be done in an automated process by machine. Pete Kronski, the production manager of SoaringWings Inc., has been trying to convince J. J. Marker, the company's president, to purchase a new brazing machine from Furimoro Industries. This machine would replace an old brazing machine from Bryston Inc. that generates a large amount of scrap and waste.

On a recent blustery morning, Pete and J. J. happened to drive into the company's parking lot at the same time. The following conversation occurred as they walked together into the building.

*Pete:* Morning, J. J. Have you had a chance to look at the specifications on the new brazing machine from Furimoro Industries that I gave you last week?
*J. J.:* Are you still bugging me about the brazing machine?
*Pete:* You know it's almost impossible to keep that old Bryston brazing machine working within tolerances.
*J. J.:* I know, I know. But we're carrying the Bryston machine on the books for $140,000.
*Pete:* That's right. But I've done some investigating, and we could sell it for $90,000 to a plumbing company in town that doesn't require as tight tolerances as we do.
*J. J.:* Pete, that's just brilliant! You want me to sell a $140,000 machine for $90,000 and take a loss of $50,000. Do you have any other great ideas this morning?
*Pete:* J. J., I know it sounds far-fetched, but we would actually save money buying the new machine.
*J. J.:* I'm skeptical. However, if you can show me the hard facts, I'll listen.
*Pete:* Fair enough. I'll do it.

## Book Value of Old Equipment

**Learning Objective 2**
Prepare an analysis showing whether to keep or replace old equipment.

Pete first gathered the following data concerning the old machine and the proposed new machine:

| Old Machine | | Proposed New Machine | |
|---|---|---|---|
| Original cost | $175,000 | List price new | $200,000 |
| Remaining book value | 140,000 | Expected life | 4 years |
| Remaining life | 4 years | Disposal value in four years | $ –0– |
| Disposal value now | $ 90,000 | Annual variable expenses | |
| Disposal value in four years | –0– | to operate | 300,000 |
| Annual variable expenses | | Annual revenue from sales | 500,000 |
| to operate | 345,000 | | |
| Annual revenue from sales | 500,000 | | |

Should the old machine be disposed of and the new machine purchased? The first reaction of SoaringWings' president was to say no, since disposal of the old machine would result in a "loss" of $50,000:

| Old Machine | |
|---|---|
| Remaining book value | $140,000 |
| Disposal value now | 90,000 |
| Loss if disposed of now | $ 50,000 |

This analysis is wrong. The investment that has been made in the old machine is a sunk cost. The portion of this investment that remains on the company's books (the book value of $140,000) should not be considered in a decision about whether to buy the new machine. It is *not* a cost of anykind. The firm has not incurred it. It is merely an artifact of an accounting policy which apportions the original (sunk) cost of $175,000 to future periods. Pete Kronski verified the irrelevance of the book value of the old machine by the following analysis:[1]

| | Total Cost and Revenues—Four Years | | |
| --- | --- | --- | --- |
| | Keep Old Machine | Purchase New Machine | Differential Costs and Benefits |
| Sales . . . . . . . . . . . . . . . . . . . . . . . . | $ 2,000,000 | $ 2,000,000 | $     –0– |
| Variable expenses . . . . . . . . . . . . . . . | (1,380,000) | (1,200,000) | 180,000 |
| Cost of the new machine . . . . . . . . . . | — | (200,000) | (200,000) |
| Depreciation of the old machine or book value write-off . . . . . . . . . | (140,000) | (140,000)* | –0– |
| Disposal value of the old machine . . . . | — | 90,000* | 90,000 |
| Total net operating income over the four years . . . . . . . . . . . . . . . . . | $    480,000 | $    550,000 | $   70,000 |

*For external reporting purposes, the $140,000 remaining book value of the old machine and the $90,000 disposal value would be netted together and deducted as a single $50,000 "loss" figure.

Looking at all four years together, note that the firm will be $70,000 better off by purchasing the new machine. The $140,000 book value of the old machine had *no effect* on the outcome of the analysis. If the old machine is kept and used, then the $140,000 book value is deducted in the form of depreciation. If the old machine is sold, then the $140,000 book value is deducted in the form of a lump-sum write-off. Either way, the differential cost is zero.

**FOCUSING ON RELEVANT COSTS**   What costs in the example above are relevant in the decision concerning the new machine? Looking at the original cost data, we should eliminate (1) the sunk costs, and (2) the future costs and benefits that do not differ between the alternatives at hand.

1. The sunk costs:
    a. The original investment, $175,000. The remaining book value of the old machine ($140,000) is also irrelevant, since it is not a cost as such.
2. The future costs and benefits that do not differ:
    a. The sales revenue ($500,000 per year).
    b. The variable expenses (to the extent of $300,000 per year).

The costs and benefits that remain will form the basis for a decision. The analysis is as follows:

| | Differential Costs and Benefits—Four Years |
| --- | --- |
| Reduction in variable expense promised by the new machine ($45,000* per year × 4 years) . . . . . . . . . . . . . . . . . . . . . . . . . | $ 180,000 |
| Cost of the new machine . . . . . . . . . . . . . . . . . . . . . . . . . . . . . | (200,000) |
| Disposal value of the old machine . . . . . . . . . . . . . . . . . . . . . . | 90,000 |
| Net advantage of the new machine . . . . . . . . . . . . . . . . . . . . . . | $  70,000 |

*$345,000 – $300,000 = $45,000.

---

[1] The analysis of the machine replacement decision makes the following simplifying assumptions: (1) we assume that the depreciation treatment for both machines is identical; 2) there are no taxes; 3) there is no time value of money. The relevance of this concept for decision making is considered in next chapter; and 4) both machines are assumed to last for the same length of time. A separate procedure exists for situations where the useful lives of equipment are different. This book does not consider such situations.

Note that the items above are the same as those in the last column of the earlier analysis and represent those costs and benefits that differ between the two alternatives. Also note that all of these figures represent *cash flows*. The company pays out or receives these amounts. Armed with this analysis, Pete felt confident that he would be able to explain the financial advantages of the new machine to the president of the company.

---

## MANAGERIAL ACCOUNTING IN ACTION

### The Wrap-Up

SOARING WINGS, INC.

Pete Kronski took his analysis to the office of J. J. Marker, the president of SoaringWings, where the following conversation took place.

*Pete:* J. J., do you remember that discussion we had about the proposed new brazing machine?

*J. J.:* Sure I remember. Did you find out that I'm right?

*Pete:* Not exactly. Here's the analysis where I compare the profit with the old machine over the next four years to the profit with the new machine.

*J. J.:* I see you're claiming the profit is $70,000 higher with the new machine. Are you assuming higher sales with the new machine?

*Pete:* No, I have assumed total sales of $2,000,000 over the four years in either situation. The real advantage comes with the reduction in variable expenses of $180,000.

*J. J.:* Where are those reductions going to come from?

*Pete:* The new brazing machine should cut our scrap and rework rate at least in half. That results in substantial savings in materials and labour costs.

*J. J.:* What about the $50,000 loss on the old machine?

*Pete:* What really matters is the $200,000 cost of the new machine and the $90,000 salvage value of the old machine. The book value of the old machine is irrelevant. No matter what we do, it will eventually flow through the income statement as a charge in one form or another.

*J. J.:* I find that hard to accept, but it is difficult to argue with your analysis.

*Pete:* The analysis actually understates the advantages of the new machine. We don't catch all of the defects caused by the old machine, and defective products are sometimes sold to customers. With the new machine, I expect our warranty costs to decrease and our repeat sales to increase. And I would hate to be held responsible for any accidents caused by defective brazing by our old machine.

*J. J.:* Okay, I'm convinced. Put together a formal proposal, and we'll present it at the next meeting of the board of directors.

---

# Future Costs That Do Not Differ Are Not Relevant Costs

We stated above that people often have difficulty accepting the idea that sunk costs are never relevant in a decision. Some people also have difficulty accepting the principle that future costs that do not differ between alternatives are never relevant in a decision. An example will help illustrate how future costs *should* be handled in a decision.

---

*in business today*    **Future Labour Costs That Do Not Differ**

In the early 1990s, General Motors Corp. laid off tens of thousands of its hourly workers who would nevertheless continue to receive full pay under union contracts. GM entered into an agreement with one of its suppliers, Android Industries, Inc., to use laid-off GM workers. GM agreed to pay the wages of the workers who would be supervised by

Android Industries. In return, Android subtracted the wages from the bills it submitted to GM under their current contract. This reduction in contract price is pure profit to GM, since GM would have had to pay the laid-off workers in any case.

Source: "GM Agrees to Allow a Parts Supplier to Use Some of Its Idled Employees," *The Wall Street Journal*, November 30, 1992, p. B3.

## An Example of Irrelevant Future Costs

A company is contemplating the purchase of a new labour-saving machine that will cost $30,000 and have a 10-year useful life. Data concerning the company's annual sales and costs with and without the new machine are shown below:

| | Current Situation | Situation with the New Machine |
|---|---|---|
| Units produced and sold | 5,000 | 5,000 |
| Selling price per unit | $ 40 | $ 40 |
| Direct materials cost per unit | 14 | 14 |
| Direct labour cost per unit | 8 | 5 |
| Variable overhead cost per unit | 2 | 2 |
| Fixed costs, other | 62,000 | 62,000 |
| Fixed costs, new machine | — | 3,000 |

The new machine promises a saving of $3 per unit in direct labour costs ($8 − $5 = $3), but it will increase fixed costs by $3,000 per year. All other costs, as well as the total number of units produced and sold, will remain the same. Following the steps outlined earlier, the analysis is as follows:

1. Eliminate the sunk costs. (No sunk costs are included in this example.)
2. Eliminate the future costs and benefits that do not differ between the alternatives.
   a. The selling price per unit and the number of units sold do not differ between the alternatives. (Therefore, total future sales revenues will not differ.)
   b. The direct materials cost per unit, the variable overhead cost per unit, and the number of units produced do not differ between the alternatives. (Therefore, total future direct materials costs and variable overhead costs will not differ.)
   c. The "Fixed costs, other" do not differ between the alternatives.

The remaining costs—direct labour costs and the fixed costs associated with the new machine—are the only relevant costs.

| | |
|---|---|
| Savings in direct labour costs ($5,000 units at a cost saving of $3 per unit) | $15,000 |
| Less increase in fixed costs | 3,000 |
| Net annual cost savings promised by the new machine | $12,000 |

This solution can be verified by looking at *all* of the cost data (both those that are relevant and those that are not) under the two alternatives. This is done in Exhibit 12–1.

**Exhibit 12–1**
Differential Cost Analysis

| | 5,000 Units Produced and Sold | | |
| --- | --- | --- | --- |
| | **Current Situation** | **Situation with New Machine** | **Differential Costs and Benefits (New – Old)** |
| Sales . . . . . . . . . . . . . . . . . . . . | $200,000 | $200,000 | $ –0– |
| Variable expenses: | | | |
|    Direct materials . . . . . . . . . . . | 70,000 | 70,000 | –0– |
|    Direct labour . . . . . . . . . . . . | 40,000 | 25,000 | 15,000 |
|    Variable overhead . . . . . . . . . | 10,000 | 10,000 | –0– |
| Total variable expenses . . . . . . . | 120,000 | 105,000 | |
| Contribution margin . . . . . . . . . | 80,000 | 95,000 | |
| Less fixed expenses: | | | |
|    Other . . . . . . . . . . . . . . . . . . | 62,000 | 62,000 | –0– |
|    New machine . . . . . . . . . . . . | –0– | 3,000 | (3,000) |
| Total fixed expenses . . . . . . . . . | 62,000 | 65,000 | |
| Net operating income . . . . . . . . | $ 18,000 | $ 30,000 | $12,000 |

Note from the exhibit that the net advantage in favour of buying the machine is $12,000—the same answer we obtained by focusing on just the relevant costs. Thus, we can see that future costs that do not differ between alternatives are, indeed, irrelevant in the decision-making process and can be safely eliminated from the analysis.

## Why Isolate Relevant Costs?

Isolating relevant costs is desirable for at least two reasons. First, only rarely will enough information be available to prepare a detailed income statement for both alternatives. Assume, for example, that you are called on to make a decision relating to a *single operation* of a multi-departmental, multi-product firm. Under these circumstances, it would be virtually impossible to prepare an income statement of any type. You would have to rely on your ability to recognize which costs are relevant and which are not in order to assemble those data necessary to make a decision.

Second, mingling irrelevant costs with relevant costs may cause confusion and distract attention from the matters that are really critical. Furthermore, the danger always exists that an irrelevant piece of information may be used improperly, resulting in an incorrect decision. The best approach is to ignore irrelevant data and base the decision entirely on the relevant data.

Relevant cost analysis, combined with the *contribution approach* to the income statement, provides a powerful tool for making decisions.[2] We will investigate various uses of this tool in the remaining sections of this chapter.

---

[2]Using the contribution margin approach (see Chapter 6), the unit contribution margin (unit price minus unit variable cost) improves by $3 thereby increasing the total contribution margin for a sales volume of 5,000 units by $15,000. Since fixed costs increase by only $3,000, net income will increase by $15,000 − $3,000 = $12,000.

## Costs and Decision Making at Rogers and Lantic Ltd.

Rogers and Lantic Sugar Ltd. has secured contracts with many candy makers, food companies, and other industrial customers. However, the company has faced the choice of becoming a value-added manufacturer by expanding beyond their existing packaging and refining duties.

A lucrative contract proposed from Kraft Foods Inc. has attracted Rogers and Lantic's attention. Basically, Kraft has moved its entire LifeSavers production line to a Montreal plant in an effort to reduce substantial production costs, and a supplier was needed. Since LifeSavers are composed of 99% sugar, the sugar-laden company can anticipate an additional 25,000 tonnes of sugar sales per year. Instead of just supplying sugar to Kraft, Rogers and Lantic has the option to operate and manage the LifeSavers production line from mixing to packaging the candy. The company would have to acquire new facilities in order to carry out this plan. As well, to move up in the value chain, Rogers and Lantic would have to expand their operations.

For Kraft, the decision to allow Rogers and Lantic to take-over the LifeSavers manufacturing and packaging is a make-or-buy decision. For Rogers and Lantic, this is an opportunity to add a new line of business. The disadvantage to Rogers and Lantic is the risk of competing against its own customers in an effort to procure higher profit margins. Furthermore, observers believe that many companies that have gone beyond their core business in hopes of more rewards end up in ruins. If Rogers and Lantic is not careful, it can end up being flattened by their customers-turned-competitors. However, if Rogers and Lantic can find a winning strategy to add value to its products and become a multibillion dollar company, it may have a leading edge in the industry.

Source: Banks, Brian, "How Sweet It Is," *Canadian Business*, April 1, 2002, pp. 54–57. Reprinted with permission from *Canadian Business*.

# Adding and Dropping Product Lines and Other Segments

Decisions relating to whether old product lines or other segments of a company should be dropped and new ones added are among the most difficult that a manager has to make. In such decisions, many qualitative and quantitative factors must be considered. Ultimately, however, any final decision to drop an old segment or to add a new one is going to hinge primarily on the impact the decision will have on net operating income. To assess this impact, it is necessary to make a careful analysis of the costs involved.

**Learning Objective 3**
Prepare an analysis showing whether a product line or other organizational segment should be dropped or retained.

## WestJet Expands Routes

WestJet was founded in 1996 by Clive Beddoe, Mark Hill, Tim Morgan, and Donald Bell, four Calgary entrepreneurs who saw an opportunity to provide low-fare air travel across western Canada. Through researching other successful airlines in North America—and in particular low-cost carriers from throughout the continent—the team followed the primary examples of Southwest Airlines and Morris Air and determined that a similar concept could be successful in western Canada.

On February 29, 1996, the airline started flight operations with 220 employees and three aircraft to the cities of Vancouver, Kelowna, Calgary, Edmonton, and Winnipeg. Since that time, the company has continued to expand, bringing more western cities into

WestJet's world. In 1996, WestJet added Victoria, Regina, and Saskatoon to its route network. Today, WestJet serves markets all across Canada, connecting Canadians from the Maritimes, Quebec, Ontario, and western Canada.

In 2000, WestJet's four founders were honoured as "The Ernst & Young Entrepreneur of the Year" for Canada, in recognition of the contributions they have made to Canadian travellers and the lives of all of WestJet's people and shareholders. In 2003, WestJet celebrated its 27th quarter of profitability with its third quarter 2003 results.

Concept 12–1

## An Illustration of Cost Analysis

Consider the three major product lines of the Discount Drug Company—drugs, cosmetics, and housewares. Sales and cost information for the preceding month for each separate product line and for the store in total are given in Exhibit 12–2.

What can be done to improve the company's overall performance? One product line—housewares—shows a net operating loss for the month. Perhaps dropping this line would cause profits in the company as a whole to improve. In deciding whether the line should be dropped, management should reason as follows:

If the housewares line is dropped, then the company will lose $20,000 per month in contribution margin. By dropping the line, however, it may be possible to avoid some fixed costs. It may be possible, for example, to discharge certain employees, or it may be possible to reduce advertising costs. If by dropping the housewares line the company is able to avoid more in fixed costs than it loses in contribution margin, then it will be better off if the line is eliminated, since overall net income should improve. On the other hand, if the company is not able to avoid as much in fixed costs as it loses in contribution margin, then the housewares line should be retained. In short, the manager should ask, "What costs can I avoid if I drop this product line?"

As we have seen from our earlier discussion, not all costs are avoidable. For example, some of the costs associated with a product line may be sunk costs. Other costs may be

**Exhibit 12–2**
Discount Drug Company
Product Lines

| | | Product Line | | |
|---|---|---|---|---|
| | **Total** | **Drugs** | **Cosmetics** | **Housewares** |
| Sales . . . . . . . . . . . . . . . . . . . . . | $250,000 | $125,000 | $75,000 | $50,000 |
| Less variable expenses . . . . . . . | 105,000 | 50,000 | 25,000 | 30,000 |
| Contribution margin . . . . . . . . . | 145,000 | 75,000 | 50,000 | 20,000 |
| Less fixed expenses: | | | | |
| Salaries . . . . . . . . . . . . . . . . . | 50,000 | 29,500 | 12,500 | 8,000 |
| Advertising . . . . . . . . . . . . . . | 15,000 | 1,000 | 7,500 | 6,500 |
| Utilities . . . . . . . . . . . . . . . . . | 2,000 | 500 | 500 | 1,000 |
| Depreciation—fixtures . . . . . | 5,000 | 1,000 | 2,000 | 2,000 |
| Rent . . . . . . . . . . . . . . . . . . . | 20,000 | 10,000 | 6,000 | 4,000 |
| Insurance . . . . . . . . . . . . . . . | 3,000 | 2,000 | 500 | 500 |
| General administrative . . . . . | 30,000 | 15,000 | 9,000 | 6,000 |
| Total fixed expenses . . . . . . . . | 125,000 | 59,000 | 38,000 | 28,000 |
| Net operating income (loss) . . . | $ 20,000 | $ 16,000 | $12,000 | $ (8,000) |

allocated fixed costs that will not differ in total, regardless of whether the product line is dropped or retained.

To show how the manager should proceed in a product-line analysis, suppose that the management of the Discount Drug Company has analyzed the costs being charged to the three product lines and has determined the following:

1. The salaries expense represents salaries paid to employees working directly in each product-line area. All of the employees working in housewares would be discharged if the line is dropped.

2. The advertising expense represents direct advertising of each product line and is avoidable if the line is dropped.

3. The utilities expense represents utilities costs for the entire company. The amount charged to each product line is an allocation based on space occupied and is not avoidable if the product line is dropped.

4. The depreciation expense represents depreciation on fixtures used for display of the various product lines. Although the fixtures are nearly new, they are custom-built and will have little resale value if the housewares line is dropped.

5. The rent expense represents rent on the entire building housing the company; it is allocated to the product lines on the basis of sales dollars. The monthly rent of $20,000 is fixed under a long-term lease agreement.

6. The insurance expense represents insurance carried on inventories within each of the three product-line areas.

7. The general administrative expense represents the costs of accounting, purchasing, and general management, which are allocated to the product lines on the basis of sales dollars. Total administrative costs will not change if the housewares line is dropped.

With this information, management can identify costs that can and cannot be avoided if the product line is dropped:

|                        | Total Cost | Not Avoidable* | Avoidable |
|------------------------|-----------|----------------|-----------|
| Salaries ............... | $ 8,000   |                | $ 8,000   |
| Advertising ............ | 6,500     |                | 6,500     |
| Utilities ............... | 1,000     | $ 1,000        |           |
| Depreciation—fixtures ....... | 2,000 | 2,000       |           |
| Rent ................... | 4,000     | 4,000          |           |
| Insurance .............. | 500       |                | 500       |
| General administrative ....... | 6,000 | 6,000       |           |
| Total fixed expenses ......... | $28,000 | $13,000    | $15,000   |

*These costs represent either (1) sunk costs or (2) future costs that will not change whether the housewares line is retained or discontinued.

To determine how dropping the line will affect the overall profits of the company, we can compare the contribution margin that will be lost with the costs that can be avoided if the line is dropped:

| | |
|---|---|
| Contribution margin lost if the housewares line is discontinued (see Exhibit 12–2) ....................................................... | $(20,000) |
| Less fixed costs that can be avoided if the housewares line is discontinued (see above) ........................................................ | 15,000 |
| Decrease in overall company net operating income .................... | $ (5,000) |

In this case, the fixed costs that can be avoided by dropping the product line are less than the contribution margin that will be lost. Therefore, on the basis of the data given, the housewares line should not be discontinued unless a more profitable use can be found for the floor and counter space that it is occupying. (The issue of opportunity cost of floor space is considered later in the chapter.)

---

*in business* *today*

## Expansion of Product Lines and Cost Trims Fail to Improve Profit

Royal Group Technologies LTD recently expanded the product line in its Window Coverings Division and initiated new customer programs. The company also made cost cuts to trim its material costs. But the cost savings were not insufficient to offset the costs of product line expansion and new customer programs, including higher manufacturing, inventory, and selling costs. Sales volume did not rise sufficiently to cover the net increase in costs.

Source: "Royal Group Announces Third Quarter Results," News Release, July 30, 2002, CCN Matthews website: http://www2.cdn-news.com/scripts/ccn-release.pl?/2002/07/30/0730005n.html

---

## A Comparative Format

Some managers prefer to approach decisions of this type by preparing comparative income statements showing the effects on the company as a whole of either keeping or dropping the product line in question. A comparative analysis of this type for the Discount Drug Company is shown in Exhibit 12–3.

As shown by column 3 in the exhibit, overall company net operating income will decrease by $5,000 each period if the housewares line is dropped. This is the same answer, of course, as we obtained in our earlier analysis.

**Exhibit 12–3**
A Comparative Format for Product-Line Analysis

| | Keep Housewares | Drop Housewares | Difference: (Drop – Keep) Net Income Increase or (Decrease) |
|---|---|---|---|
| Sales ..................... | $50,000 | $ –0– | $(50,000) |
| Less variable expenses ......... | 30,000 | –0– | 30,000 |
| Contribution margin ........... | 20,000 | –0– | (20,000) |
| Less fixed expenses: | | | |
|   Salaries .................. | 8,000 | –0– | 8,000 |
|   Advertising .............. | 6,500 | –0– | 6,500 |
|   Utilities ................. | 1,000 | 1,000 | –0– |
|   Depreciation—fixtures ....... | 2,000 | 2,000 | –0– |
|   Rent .................... | 4,000 | 4,000 | –0– |
|   Insurance ............... | 500 | –0– | 500 |
|   General administrative ....... | 6,000 | 6,000 | –0– |
| Total fixed expenses ........... | 28,000 | 13,000 | 15,000 |
| Net operating income (loss) ..... | $ (8,000) | $(13,000) | $ (5,000) |

# Beware of Allocated Fixed Costs

Our conclusion that the housewares line should not be dropped seems to conflict with the data shown earlier in Exhibit 12–2. Recall from the exhibit that the housewares line is showing a loss, rather than a profit. Why keep a line that is showing a loss? The explanation for this apparent inconsistency lies, at least in part, with the *common fixed costs* that are being allocated to the product lines. A **common fixed cost** is a fixed cost that supports the operations of more than one segment of an organization and is not avoidable in whole or in part by eliminating any one segment. For example, the salary of the CEO of a company ordinarily would not be cut if any one product line were dropped, and so it is a common fixed cost of the product lines. In fact, if dropping a product line is a good idea that results in higher profits for the company, the compensation of the CEO is likely to increase, rather than decrease, as a result of dropping the product line. One of the great dangers in allocating common fixed costs is that such allocations can make a product line (or other segment of a business) *look* less profitable than it really is. By allocating the common fixed costs among all product lines, the housewares line has been made to *look* as if it were unprofitable, whereas, in fact, dropping the line would result in a decrease in overall company net operating income. This point can be seen clearly if we recast the data in Exhibit 12–2 and eliminate the allocation of the common fixed costs. This recasting of data is shown in Exhibit 12–4.

Note that the common fixed expenses have not been allocated to the product lines in Exhibit 12–4. Only the fixed expenses that are traceable to the product lines and that could be avoided by dropping the product lines are assigned to them. For example, the fixed expenses of advertising the housewares product line can be traced to that product line and can be eliminated if that product line is dropped. However, the general administrative expenses, such as the CEO's salary, cannot be traced to the individual product lines and would not be eliminated if any one product line were dropped. Consequently, these common fixed expenses are not allocated to the product lines in Exhibit 12–4 as they were

**Exhibit 12–4**
Discount Drug Company Product Lines—Recast in Contribution Format (from Exhibit 12–2)

| | | Product Line | | |
|---|---|---|---|---|
| | **Total** | **Drugs** | **Cosmetics** | **Housewares** |
| Sales | $250,000 | $125,000 | $75,000 | $50,000 |
| Less variable expenses | 105,000 | 50,000 | 25,000 | 30,000 |
| Contribution margin | 145,000 | 75,000 | 50,000 | 20,000 |
| Less traceable fixed expenses: | | | | |
| Salaries | 50,000 | 29,500 | 12,500 | 8,000 |
| Advertising | 15,000 | 1,000 | 7,500 | 6,500 |
| Depreciation—fixtures | 5,000 | 1,000 | 2,000 | 2,000 |
| Insurance | 3,000 | 2,000 | 500 | 500 |
| Total traceable fixed expenses | 73,000 | 33,500 | 22,500 | 17,000 |
| Product-line segment margin | 72,000 | $ 41,500 | $27,500 | $ 3,000* |
| Less common fixed expenses: | | | | |
| Utilities | 2,000 | | | |
| Rent | 20,000 | | | |
| General administrative | 30,000 | | | |
| Total common fixed expenses | 52,000 | | | |
| Net operating income | $ 20,000 | | | |

*The impact of dropping the housewares line will be the $3,000 segment margin plus $2,000 representing depreciation expense. The depreciation expense must be added back to obtain the impact on profits because it represents a noncash charge. In other words, the company does not actually *incur* this expense. Thus, it can be seen that if the housewares line is dropped, the company will *lose* $5,000.

in Exhibit 12–2. The allocations in Exhibit 12–2 provide a misleading picture that suggests that portions of the fixed common expenses can be eliminated by dropping individual product lines—which is not the case.

Exhibit 12–4 gives us a much different perspective of the housewares line than does Exhibit 12–2. As shown in Exhibit 12–4, the housewares line is covering all of its own traceable fixed costs and is generating a $3,000 *segment margin* toward covering the common fixed costs of the company. The **segment margin** is the difference between the revenue generated by a segment and its own traceable costs. Unless another product line can be found that will generate more than a $3,000 segment margin, the company would be better off keeping the housewares line. By keeping the line, the company's overall net operating income will be higher than if the product line were dropped.

Additionally, we should note that managers may choose to retain an unprofitable product line (when considered *by itself*) if the line is necessary to the sale of other products or if it serves as a "magnet" to attract customers. Bread, for example, is not an especially profitable line in food stores, but customers expect it to be available, and many would undoubtedly shift their buying elsewhere if a particular store decided to stop carrying it. In other words, bread may be profitable if its impact on sales of other items is included in the analysis. Finally, note that this issue of common fixed cost and the distortions introduced by allocating such costs lie at the heart of the rationale for an ABC management system. This was covered in Chapter 5. You can see that the analysis in Exhibit 12–4 could not have been done if it was not possible to *trace* the fixed expenses to the various segments. The ability to carry out this type of tracing is clearly the key.

*in business today* | **The Trap Laid by Fully Allocated Costs**

A bakery distributed its products through route salespersons, each of whom loaded a truck with an assortment of products in the morning and spent the day calling on customers in an assigned territory. Believing that some items were more profitable than others, management asked for an analysis of product costs and sales. The accountants to whom the task was assigned allocated all manufacturing and marketing costs to products to obtain a net profit for each product. The resulting figures indicated that some of the products were being sold at a loss, and management discontinued these products. However, when this change was put into effect, the company's overall profit declined. It was then seen that by dropping some products, sales revenues had been reduced without commensurate reduction in costs because the common manufacturing costs and route sales costs had to be continued in order to make and sell the remaining products.

## The Make-or-Buy Decision

A decision on whether to produce a fabricated part internally, rather than to buy the part externally from a supplier is called a **make-or-buy decision.** This is also known as the outsourcing or subcontracting decision. To provide an illustration of a make-or-buy decision, consider Mountain Goat Cycles. The company is now producing the heavy-duty gear shifters used in its most popular line of mountain bikes. The company's Accounting Department reports the following costs of producing the shifter internally:

Concept 12–2

| | Per Unit | 8,000 Units |
|---|---|---|
| Direct materials | $ 6 | $ 48,000 |
| Direct labour | 4 | 32,000 |
| Variable overhead | 1 | 8,000 |
| Supervisor's salary | 3 | 24,000 |
| Depreciation of special equipment | 2 | 16,000 |
| Allocated general overhead | 5 | 40,000 |
| Total cost | $21 | $168,000 |

An outside supplier has offered to sell Mountain Goat Cycles 8,000 shifters a year at a price of only $19 each. Should the company stop producing the shifters internally and start purchasing them from the outside supplier? To approach the decision from a financial point of view, the manager should again focus on the differential costs. As we have seen, the differential costs can be obtained by eliminating those costs that are not avoidable—that is, by eliminating (1) the sunk costs, and (2) the future costs that will continue regardless of whether the shifters are produced internally or purchased outside. The costs that remain after making these eliminations are the costs that are avoidable to the company by purchasing outside. If these avoidable costs are less than the outside purchase price, then the company should continue to manufacture its own shifters and reject the outside supplier's offer. That is, the company should purchase outside only if the outside purchase price is less than the costs that can be avoided internally as a result of stopping production of the shifters.

Looking at the cost data for producing the shifter internally, note first that depreciation of special equipment is listed as one of the costs of producing the shifters internally. Since the equipment has already been purchased, this depreciation is a sunk cost and is therefore irrelevant. If the equipment could be sold, its salvage value would be relevant. Or if the machine could be used to make other products, this could be relevant as well. However, we will assume that the equipment has no salvage value and that it has no other use than making the heavy-duty gear shifters.

Also note that the company is allocating a portion of its general overhead costs to the shifters. Any portion of this general overhead cost that would actually be eliminated if the gear shifters were purchased, rather than made, would be relevant in the analysis. However, it is likely that the general overhead costs allocated to the gear shifters are, in fact, common to all items produced in the factory and would continue unchanged even if the shifters are purchased from the outside. Such allocated common costs are not differential costs (since they do not differ between the make or buy alternatives) and should be eliminated from the analysis along with the sunk costs.

The variable costs of producing the shifters (materials, labour, and variable overhead) are differential costs, since they can be avoided by buying the shifters from the outside supplier. If the supervisor can be discharged and his or her salary avoided by buying the shifters, then it too will be a differential cost and relevant to the decision. Assuming that both the variable costs and the supervisor's salary can be avoided by buying from the outside supplier, then the analysis takes the form shown in Exhibit 12–5.

**Exhibit 12–5**
Mountain Goat Cycles
Make-or-Buy Analysis

| | Production "Cost" per Unit | Per-Unit Differential Costs | | Total Differential Costs—8,000 Units | |
|---|---|---|---|---|---|
| | | Make | Buy | Make | Buy |
| Direct materials . . . . . . . . . . . | $ 6 | $ 6 | | $ 48,000 | |
| Direct labour . . . . . . . . . . . . . | 4 | 4 | | 32,000 | |
| Variable overhead . . . . . . . . . | 1 | 1 | | 8,000 | |
| Supervisor's salary . . . . . . . . | 3 | 3 | | 24,000 | |
| Depreciation of special equipment . . . . . . . . . . . . . | 2 | — | | — | |
| Allocated general overhead . . | 5 | — | | — | |
| Outside purchase price . . . . . | | | $19 | | $152,000 |
| Total cost . . . . . . . . . . . . . . . . | $21 | $14 | $19 | $112,000 | $152,000 |
| Difference in favour of continuing to make . . . . . . | | | $ 5 | | $40,000 |

Since it costs $5 less per unit to continue to make the shifters, Mountain Goat Cycles should reject the outside supplier's offer. However, there is one additional factor that the company may wish to consider before coming to a final decision. This factor is the opportunity cost of the space now being used to produce the shifters.

## The Matter of Opportunity Cost

If the space now being used to produce the shifters *would otherwise be idle*, then Mountain Goat Cycles should continue to produce its own shifters and the supplier's offer should be rejected, as stated above. Idle space that has no alternative use has an opportunity cost of zero.

But what if the space now being used to produce shifters could be used for some other purpose? In that case, the space would have an opportunity cost that would have to be considered in assessing the desirability of the supplier's offer. What would this opportunity cost be? It would be the segment margin that could be derived from the best alternative use of the space.

To illustrate, assume that the space now being used to produce shifters could be used to produce a new cross-country bike that would generate a segment margin of $60,000 per year. Under these conditions, Mountain Goat Cycles would be better off to accept the supplier's offer and to use the available space to produce the new product line:

| | Make | Buy |
|---|---|---|
| Differential cost per unit (see prior example) . . . . . . . . . | $ 14 | $ 19 |
| Number of units needed annually . . . . . . . . . . . . . . . . . . | × 8,000 | × 8,000 |
| Total annual cost . . . . . . . . . . . . . . . . . . . . . . . . . . . . . . | 112,000 | 152,000 |
| Opportunity cost—segment margin forgone on a potential new product line . . . . . . . . . . . . . . . . . . . . | 60,000 | |
| Total cost . . . . . . . . . . . . . . . . . . . . . . . . . . . . . . . . . . . . | $172,000 | $152,000 |
| Difference in favour of purchasing from the outside supplier . . . . . . . . . . . . . . . . . . . . . . . . . . . . . . | | $ 20,000 |

Opportunity costs are not recorded in accounts of an organization. They do not represent actual dollar outlays. Rather, they represent economic benefits that are *forgone* as a result of pursuing some course of action. The opportunity costs of Mountain Goat Cycles are sufficiently large in this case to make continued production of the shifters very costly from an economic point of view.

## Vice-President of Production

*decision maker*

You are faced with a make-or-buy decision. The company currently makes a component for one of its products but is considering whether it should instead purchase the component. If the offer from an outside supplier were accepted, the company would no longer need to rent the machinery that is currently being used to manufacture the component. You realize that the annual rental cost is a fixed cost, but recall some sort of warning about fixed costs. Is the annual rental cost relevant to this make-or-buy decision?

## Special Orders

Managers often must evaluate whether a *special order* should be accepted, and if the order is accepted, the price that should be charged. A **special order** is a one-time order that is not considered part of the company's normal ongoing business. To illustrate, Mountain Goat Cycles has just received a request from the Saskatoon Police Department to produce 100 specially modified mountain bikes at a price of $740 each. The bikes would be used to patrol some of the more densely populated residential sections of the city. Mountain Goat Cycles can easily modify its City Cruiser model to fit the specifications of the Saskatoon Police. The normal selling price of the City Cruiser bike is $930, and its unit product cost is $750 as shown below:

| | |
|---|---|
| Direct materials | $ 400 |
| Direct labour | 225 |
| Manufacturing overhead | 125 |
| Unit product cost | $750 |

The variable portion of the above manufacturing overhead is $25 per unit. The order would have no effect on the company's total fixed manufacturing overhead costs.

The modifications to the bikes consist of welded brackets to hold radios, nightsticks, and other gear. These modifications would require $50 in incremental variable costs. In addition, the company would have to pay a graphics design studio $2,000 to design and cut stencils that would be used for spray painting the Saskatoon Police Department's logo and other identifying marks on the bikes.

This order should have no effect on the company's other sales. The production manager says that she can handle the special order without disrupting any of the regular scheduled production.

What effect would accepting this order have on the company's net operating income?

Only the incremental costs and benefits are relevant. Since the existing fixed manufacturing overhead costs would not be affected by the order, they are not incremental costs and are therefore not relevant. The incremental net operating income can be computed as follows:

| | Per Unit | Total 100 Bikes |
|---|---|---|
| Incremental revenue . . . . . . . . . . . . . . . . . . . . | $740 | $74,000 |
| Incremental costs: | | |
| Variable costs: | | |
| Direct materials . . . . . . . . . . . . . . . . . | 400 | 40,000 |
| Direct labour . . . . . . . . . . . . . . . . . . . . . | 225 | 22,500 |
| Variable manufacturing overhead . . . . . . | 25 | 2,500 |
| Special modifications . . . . . . . . . . . . . . | 50 | 5,000 |
| Total variable cost . . . . . . . . . . . . . . . | $700 | 70,000 |
| Fixed cost: | | |
| Purchase of stencils . . . . . . . . . . . . . . . | | 2,000 |
| Total incremental cost . . . . . . . . . . . . . . . . . | | 72,000 |
| Incremental net operating income . . . . . . . . . | | $ 2,000 |

Therefore, even though the price on the special order ($740) is below the normal unit product cost ($750) and the order would require incurring additional costs, the order would result in an increase in net operating income. In general, a special order is profitable as long as the incremental revenue from the special order exceeds the incremental costs of the order. We must note, however, that it is important to make sure that there is, indeed, idle capacity and that the special order does not cut into normal sales. For example, if the company was operating at capacity, opportunity costs would have to be taken into account as well as the incremental costs that have already been detailed above.

# Pricing New Products: Target Costing

When offering a new product or service for the first time, a company must decide on its selling price. A cost-based approach has often been followed in practice. In this approach, the product is first designed and produced, then its cost is determined and its price is computed by adding a markup to the cost. This *cost-plus* approach to pricing suffers from a number of drawbacks—the most obvious being that customers may not be willing to pay the price set by the company. If the price is too high, customers may decide to purchase a similar product from a competitor or, if no similar competing product exists, they may decide not to buy the product at all.

*Target costing* provides an alternative, market-based approach to pricing new products. In the **target costing** approach, management estimates how much the market will be willing to pay for the new product even before the new product has been designed. The company's required profit margin is subtracted from the estimated selling price to determine the target cost for the new product. A cross-functional team consisting of designers, engineers, cost accountants, marketing personnel, and production personnel is charged with the responsibility of ensuring that the cost of the product is ultimately less than the target cost. If at some point in the product development process it becomes clear that it will not be possible to meet the target cost, the new product is abandoned.

The target costing approach to pricing has a number of advantages over the cost-plus approach. First, the target costing approach is focused on the market and the customer. A product is not made unless the company is reasonably confident that customers will be willing to buy the product at a price that provides the company with an adequate profit. Second, the target costing approach instills a much higher level of cost-consciousness than the cost-plus approach and probably results in less expensive products that are more attractive to customers. The target cost lid creates relentless pressure to drive out unnecessary costs. In the cost-plus approach, there is little pressure to control costs, since whatever the costs turn out to be, the price will be higher. This allows designers and engineers to create products with expensive features that customers may not actually be willing to pay for. Because of these advantages, more and more companies are abandoning the cost-plus approach to new product pricing in favour of the target costing approach.

## Tutor

*you* *decide*

Your financial accounting instructor has suggested that you should consider working with selected students in her class as a tutor. Should you adopt a cost-plus or target costing approach to setting your hourly fee?

# Utilization of a Constrained Resource

Managers are routinely faced with the problem of deciding how constrained resources are going to be utilized. A department store, for example, has a limited amount of floor space and therefore cannot stock every product that may be available. A manufacturing firm has a limited number of machine-hours and a limited number of direct labour-hours at its disposal. When a limited resource of some type restricts the company's ability to satisfy demand, the company is said to have a **constraint.** Because of the constrained resource, the company cannot fully satisfy demand, and so the manager must decide how the constrained resource should be used. Fixed costs are usually unaffected by such choices, and so the manager should select the course of action that will maximize the firm's *total* contribution margin.

**Learning Objective 6**
Determine the most profitable use of a constrained resource.

## Contribution in Relation to a Constrained Resource

To maximize total contribution margin, a firm should promote those products or accept those orders that provide the highest unit contribution margin *per unit of the constrained resource.* To illustrate, Mountain Goat Cycles makes a line of paniers—saddlebags for bicycles. There are two models offered—a touring model and a mountain model. Cost and revenue data for each panier model are given below:

| | Model | |
| --- | --- | --- |
| | **Mountain Panier** | **Touring Panier** |
| Selling price per unit .................... | $25 | $30 |
| Variable cost per unit ................... | 10 | 18 |
| Contribution margin per unit ............. | $15 | $12 |
| Contribution margin (CM) ratio .......... | 60% | 40% |

The mountain panier appears to be much more profitable than the touring panier. It has a $15 per unit contribution margin as compared with only $12 per unit for the touring model, and it has a 60% CM ratio as compared with only 40% for the touring model.

But now let us add one more piece of information—the plant that makes the paniers is operating at capacity. At Mountain Goat Cycles, the machine or process that is limiting overall output is called the **bottleneck**—it is the constraint. The bottleneck is a particular stitching machine. The mountain panier requires two minutes of stitching time, and each unit of the touring panier requires one minute of stitching time. In this situation, if additional time becomes available on the stitching machine, which product is more profitable to produce? To answer this question, the manager should look at the *contribution margin per unit of the constrained resource.* This figure is computed by dividing the contribution margin by the amount of the constrained resource a unit of product requires. These calculations are carried out below for the mountain and touring paniers.

| | Model | |
| --- | :---: | :---: |
| | **Mountain Panier** | **Touring Panier** |
| Contribution margin per unit (above) (a) ......... | $15 | $12 |
| Time on the stitching machine required to produce one unit (b) .................... | 2 min. | 1 min. |
| Contribution margin per unit of the constrained resource, (a) ÷ (b) .............. | $7.50/min. | $12/min. |

Each minute of processing time on the stitching machine that is devoted to the touring panier results in an increase of $12 in contribution margin and profits. The comparable figure for the mountain panier is only $7.50 per minute. Therefore, more units of the touring model should be made using the additional time. Even though the mountain model has the larger per-unit contribution margin and the larger CM ratio, the touring model provides the larger contribution margin in relation to the constrained resource.

To verify that the touring model is, indeed, the more profitable product, suppose an hour of additional stitching time is available and that there are unfilled orders for both products. Total contribution margin will increase by $7.50/min. × 60 min. = $450, if the mountain panier is made; and total contribution margin will increase by $12/min. × 60 min. = $720 if the touring panier is made.

This example clearly shows that looking at unit contribution margins alone is not enough; the contribution margin must be viewed in relation to the amount of the constrained resource each product requires.

## Managing Constraints

Profits can be increased by effectively managing the organization's constraints. One aspect of managing constraints is to decide how to utilize them best. As discussed above, if the constraint is a bottleneck in the production process, the manager should select the product mix that maximizes the total contribution margin. In addition, the manager should take an active role in managing the constraint itself. Management should focus efforts on increasing the efficiency of the bottleneck operation and on increasing its capacity. Such efforts directly increase the output of finished goods and will often pay off in an almost immediate increase in profits.

It is often possible for a manager to effectively increase the capacity of the bottleneck, which is called **relaxing (or elevating) the constraint.** For example, the stitching machine operator could be asked to work overtime. This would result in more available stitching time and hence more finished goods that can be sold. The benefits from relaxing the constraint in such a manner are often enormous and can be easily quantified. The manager should first ask, "What would I do with additional capacity at the bottleneck if it were available?" In the example, if there are unfilled orders for both the touring and mountain paniers, the additional capacity would be used to process more touring paniers, since that would be a better use of the additional capacity. In that situation, the additional capacity would be worth $720 per hour. Since overtime pay for the operator is likely to be much less than $720 per hour, running the stitching machine on overtime would be an excellent way to increase the profits of the company while satisfying customers as well.

To reinforce this concept, suppose that making touring paniers has already been given top priority and consequently there are only unfilled orders for the mountain panier. How much would it be worth to the company to run the stitching machine overtime in this situation? Since the additional capacity would be used to make the mountain panier, the value of that additional capacity would drop to $7.50 per minute or $450 per hour. Nevertheless, the value of relaxing the constraint would still be quite high.

These calculations indicate that managers should pay great attention to bottleneck operations. If a bottleneck machine breaks down or is ineffectively utilized, the losses to the company can be quite large. In our example, for every minute the stitching machine is down due to breakdowns or setups, the company loses between $7.50 and $12. The losses on an hourly basis are between $450 and $720! In contrast, there is no such loss of contribution margin if time is lost on a machine that is not a bottleneck—such machines have excess capacity anyway.

The implications are clear. Managers should focus much of their attention on managing bottlenecks. As we have discussed, managers should emphasize products that most profitably utilize the constrained resource. They should also make sure that products are processed smoothly through the bottlenecks, with minimal lost time due to breakdowns and setups. And they should try to find ways to increase the capacity at the bottlenecks.

The capacity of a bottleneck can be effectively increased in a number of ways, including:

- Working overtime on the bottleneck.
- Subcontracting some of the processing that would be done at the bottleneck.
- Investing in additional machines at the bottleneck.
- Shifting workers from processes that are not bottlenecks to the process that is a bottleneck.
- Focusing business process improvement efforts, such as TQM and Business Process Re-engineering on the bottleneck.
- Reducing defective units. Each defective unit that is processed through the bottleneck and subsequently scrapped takes the place of a good unit that could be sold.

The last three methods of increasing the capacity of the bottleneck are particularly attractive, since they are essentially free and may even yield additional cost savings.

Finally, note that the analysis considered a single constraint. When there are multiple bottlenecks, the method of analysis is more complicated. The basic idea, however, is still the same.

## Summary

### LO1   Distinguish between relevant and irrelevant costs in decisions.

Every decision involves a choice from among at least two alternatives. Only those costs and benefits that differ between alternatives are relevant; costs and benefits that are the same for all alternatives are not affected by the decision and can be ignored. Only future costs that differ between alternatives are relevant. Costs that have already been incurred are sunk costs and are always irrelevant. Future costs that do not differ between alternatives are not relevant.

**LO2    Prepare an analysis showing whether to keep or replace old equipment.**

Decisions concerning the replacement of old equipment should focus on the differences in costs and benefits between the old and new equipment. It is particularly important to realize that the original cost and net book value of the old equipment are irrelevant in making such a decision, although the disposal value of the old equipment is relevant.

**LO3    Prepare an analysis showing whether a product line or other organizational segment should be dropped or retained.**

A decision of whether a product line or other segment should be dropped should focus on the differences in the costs and benefits between dropping or retaining the product line or segment. Caution should be exercised when using reports in which common fixed costs have been allocated among segments. If these common fixed costs are unaffected by the decision of whether to drop or retain the segment, they are irrelevant and should be removed before determining the real profitability of a segment.

**LO4    Prepare a well-organized make-or-buy analysis.**

A make-or-buy decision should focus on the costs and benefits that differ between the alternatives of making or buying a component. As in other decisions, sunk costs—such as the depreciation on old equipment—should be ignored. Future costs that do not differ between alternatives—such as allocations of common fixed costs like general overhead—should be ignored.

**LO5    Prepare an analysis showing whether a special order should be accepted.**

When deciding whether to accept or reject a special order, the analyst should focus on the benefits and costs that differ between those two alternatives. Specifically, a special order should be accepted when the incremental revenue from the sale exceeds the incremental cost. As always, sunk costs and future costs that do not differ between the alternatives are irrelevant.

**LO6    Determine the most profitable use of a constrained resource.**

When demand for a company's products and services exceeds its ability to supply them, the company has a bottleneck. The bottleneck, whether it is a particular material, skilled labour, or a specific machine, is a constrained resource. Since the company is unable to make everything it could sell, managers must decide what the company will make and what the company will not make. In this situation, the profitability of a product is best measured by its contribution margin per unit of the constrained resource. The products with the highest contribution margin per unit of the constrained resource should be favoured.

Managers should focus their attention on effectively managing the constraint. This involves making the best use possible of the constrained resource and increasing the amount of the constrained resource that is available.

# Guidance Answers to You Decide and Decision Maker

**VICE-PRESIDENT OF PRODUCTION** (p. 457)

The warning that you recall about fixed costs in decisions relates to *allocated* fixed costs. Allocated fixed costs often make a product line or other segment of a business appear less profitable than it really is. However, in this situation, the annual rental cost for the machinery is an *avoidable* fixed cost, rather than an allocated fixed cost. An avoidable fixed cost is a cost that can be eliminated in whole or in part by choosing one alternative over another. Because the annual rental cost of the machinery can be avoided if the company purchases the components from an outside supplier, it is relevant to this decision.

**TUTOR** (p. 459)

Individuals who provide services to others often struggle to decide how to charge for their services. As a tutor, you probably will not incur any significant costs, unless you agree to provide the supplies (such as paper, pencils, calculators, or study guides) or software that might be required to assist the students you will be tutoring. As such, a cost-plus approach may not be a practical way to set the hourly fee (or price) for your services. On the other hand, if you use a target costing approach, you would estimate how much the market (that is, other students who require tutoring services) would be willing to pay for the tutoring services. How would you obtain this information? You probably should ask your instructor. If your institution offers tutoring services to its students, you should inquire about the fee that is charged by that office or department. You should check the student newspaper (or local newspapers) to determine the going rate for tutors. If you plan to tutor instead of working at a part-time job, you should consider the opportunity cost (that is, the hourly rate that you will be forgoing).

# Review Problem: Relevant Costs

Charter Sports Equipment manufactures round, rectangular, and octagonal trampolines. Data on sales expenses for the past month follow:

| | Total | Trampoline | | |
| | | Round | Rectangular | Octagonal |
|---|---|---|---|---|
| Sales . . . . . . . . . . . . . . . . . . . . | $1,000,000 | $140,000 | $500,000 | $360,000 |
| Less variable expenses . . . . . . | 410,000 | 60,000 | 200,000 | 150,000 |
| Contribution margin . . . . . . . | 590,000 | 80,000 | 300,000 | 210,000 |
| Less fixed expenses: | | | | |
| Advertising—traceable . . . . | 216,000 | 41,000 | 110,000 | 65,000 |
| Depreciation of special | | | | |
| equipment . . . . . . . . . . . . | 95,000 | 20,000 | 40,000 | 35,000 |
| Line supervisors' salaries . . . | 19,000 | 6,000 | 7,000 | 6,000 |
| General factory overhead* . . | 200,000 | 28,000 | 100,000 | 72,000 |
| Total fixed expenses . . . . . . . . | 530,000 | 95,000 | 257,000 | 178,000 |
| Net operating income (loss) . . . $ | 60,000 | $(15,000) | $ 43,000 | $ 32,000 |

*A common cost that is allocated on the basis of sales dollars.

Management is concerned about the continued losses shown by the round trampolines and wants a recommendation as to whether or not the line should be discontinued. The special equipment used to produce the trampolines has no resale value. If the round trampoline model is dropped, the two line supervisors assigned to the model would be discharged.

**Required:**
1. Should production and sale of the round trampolines be discontinued? You may assume that the company has no other use for the capacity now being used to produce the round trampolines. Show computations to support your answer.
2. Recast the above data in a format that would be more usable to management in assessing the long-term profitability of the various product lines.

**SOLUTION TO REVIEW PROBLEM**
1. No, production and sale of the round trampolines should not be discontinued. Computations to support this answer follow:

| | | |
|---|---|---|
| Contribution margin lost if the round trampolines are discontinued . . . | | $(80,000) |
| Less fixed costs that can be avoided: | | |
| Advertising—traceable . . . . . . . . . . . . . . . . . . . . . . . . . . . . . . . . . . . | $41,000 | |
| Line supervisors' salaries . . . . . . . . . . . . . . . . . . . . . . . . . . . . . . . . . | 6,000 | 47,000 |
| Decrease in net operating income for the company as a whole . . . . . . . | | $(33,000) |

The depreciation of the special equipment represents a sunk cost, and therefore, it is not relevant to the decision. The general factory overhead is allocated and will presumably continue regardless of whether or not the round trampolines are discontinued; thus, it also is not relevant to the decision.

*ALTERNATIVE SOLUTION TO QUESTION 1*

| | Keep Round Tramps | Drop Round Tramps | Difference: Net Income Increase or (Decrease) |
|---|---|---|---|
| Sales .............................. | $140,000 | $ –0– | $(140,000) |
| Less variable expenses ................ | 60,000 | –0– | 60,000 |
| Contribution margin ................... | 80,000 | –0– | (80,000) |
| Less fixed expenses: | | | |
|     Advertising—traceable ............... | 41,000 | –0– | 41,000 |
|     Depreciation of special equipment ..... | 20,000 | 20,000 | –0– |
|     Line supervisors' salaries ............ | 6,000 | –0– | 6,000 |
|     General factory overhead ............ | 28,000 | 28,000 | –0– |
| Total fixed expenses ................. | 95,000 | 48,000 | 47,000 |
| Net operating income (loss) ............ | $ (15,000) | $(48,000) | $ (33,000) |

2. If management wants a clear picture of the profitability of the segments, the general factory overhead should not be allocated. It is a common cost and therefore should be deducted from the total product-line segment margin, as shown in Exhibit 12–4. A more useful income statement format would be as follows:

| | Total | Trampoline | | |
| | | Round | Rectangular | Octagonal |
|---|---|---|---|---|
| Sales ...................... | $1,000,000 | $140,000 | $500,000 | $360,000 |
| Less variable expenses ......... | 410,000 | 60,000 | 200,000 | 150,000 |
| Contribution margin ........... | 590,000 | 80,000 | 300,000 | 210,000 |
| Less traceable fixed expenses: | | | | |
|     Advertising—traceable ....... | 216,000 | 41,000 | 110,000 | 65,000 |
|     Depreciation of special | | | | |
|     equipment .............. | 95,000 | 20,000 | 40,000 | 35,000 |
|     Line supervisors' salaries ..... | 19,000 | 6,000 | 7,000 | 6,000 |
| Total traceable fixed expenses ... | 330,000 | 67,000 | 157,000 | 106,000 |
| Product-line segment margin .... | 260,000 | $ 13,000 | $143,000 | $104,000 |
| Less common fixed expenses .... | 200,000 | | | |
| Net operating income (loss) ..... | $ 60,000 | | | |

# Glossary

**Avoidable cost** Any cost that can be eliminated (in whole or in part) by choosing one alternative over another in a decision making situation. In managerial accounting, this term is synonymous with *relevant cost* and *differential cost*. (p. 442)

**Bottleneck** A machine or process that limits total output because it is operating at capacity. (p. 460)

**Common fixed cost** A fixed cost that supports the operations of more than one segment of an organization and is not avoidable in whole or in part by eliminating any one segment. (p. 453)

**Constraint** A limitation under which a company must operate, such as limited machine time available or limited raw materials available that restricts the company's ability to satisfy demand. (p. 459)

**Differential cost** Any cost that differs between alternatives in a decision-making situation. In managerial accounting, this term is synonymous with *avoidable cost* and *relevant cost*. (p. 443)

**Make-or-buy decision** A decision as to whether an item should be produced internally or purchased from an outside supplier. (p. 454)

**Relaxing (or elevating) the constraint** An action that increases the capacity of a bottleneck. (p. 460)

**Relevant cost** A cost that differs between alternatives in a particular decision. In managerial accounting, this term is synonymous with *avoidable cost* and *differential cost*. (p. 442)

**Segment margin** The difference between the revenue generated by a segment and its own traceable cost. (p. 454)

**Special order** A one-time order that is not considered part of the company's normal ongoing business. (p. 457)

**Sunk cost** Any cost that has already been incurred and that cannot be changed by any decision made now or in the future. (p. 443)

**Target costing** Before launching a new product, management estimates how much the market will be willing to pay for the product and then takes steps to ensure that the cost of the product will be low enough to provide an adequate profit margin. (p. 458)

## Questions

**12–1** What is a *relevant cost?*

**12–2** Define the following terms: *incremental cost*, *opportunity cost*, and *sunk cost.*

**12–3** Are variable costs always relevant costs? Explain.

**12–4** The original cost of a machine the company already owns is irrelevant in decision making. Explain why this is so.

**12–5** "Sunk costs are easy to spot—they're simply the fixed costs associated with a decision." Do you agree? Explain.

**12–6** "Variable costs and differential costs mean the same thing." Do you agree? Explain.

**12–7** "All future costs are relevant in decision making." Do you agree? Why?

**12–8** Prentice Company is considering dropping one of its product lines. What costs of the product line would be relevant to this decision? Irrelevant?

**12–9** "If a product line is generating a loss, then that's pretty good evidence that the product line should be discontinued." Do you agree? Explain.

**12–10** What is the danger in allocating common fixed costs among product lines or other segments of an organization?

**12–11** How does opportunity cost enter into the make-or-buy decision?

**12–12** Give four examples of possible constraints.

**12–13** How will relating product contribution margins to the constrained resource they require help a company ensure that profits will be maximized?

**12–14** Airlines sometimes offer reduced rates during certain times of the week to members of a businessperson's family if they accompany him or her on trips. How does the concept of relevant costs enter into the decision to offer reduced rates of this type?

## Brief Exercises

**BRIEF EXERCISE 12–1  Identifying Relevant Costs** (LO1)

Listed below are a number of costs that may be relevant in decisions faced by the management of Svahn, AB, a Swedish manufacturer of sailing yachts:

| | Case 1 | | Case 2 | |
|---|---|---|---|---|
| **Item** | **Relevant** | **Not Relevant** | **Relevant** | **Not Relevant** |
| a.  Sales revenue . . . . . . . . . . . . . . . . . . . . . . | | | | |
| b.  Direct materials . . . . . . . . . . . . . . . . . . . . | | | | |
| c.  Direct labour . . . . . . . . . . . . . . . . . . . . . . | | | | |
| d.  Variable manufacturing overhead . . . . . . . . . | | | | |
| e.  Depreciation—Model B100 machine . . . . . | | | | |
| f.  Book value—Model B100 machine . . . . . . . | | | | |
| g.  Disposal value—Model B100 machine . . . . | | | | |

continued

h. Market value—Model B300
   machine (cost) .......................
i. Depreciation—Model B300 machine .....
j. Fixed manufacturing overhead (general) ...
k. Variable selling expense ...............
l. Fixed selling expense .................
m. General administrative overhead ........

***Required:***
Copy the information above onto your answer sheet and place an X in the appropriate column to indicate whether each item is relevant or not relevant in the following situations (requirement 1 relates to Case 1 above, and requirement 2 relates to Case 2):
1. Management is considering purchasing a Model B300 machine to use in addition to the company's present Model B100 machine. This will increase the company's production and sales. The increase in volume will be large enough to require increases in fixed selling expenses and in general administrative overhead, but not in the fixed manufacturing overhead.
2. Management is instead considering replacing its present Model B100 machine with a new Model B300 machine. The Model B100 machine would be sold. This change will have no effect on production or sales, other than some savings in direct materials costs due to less waste.

### BRIEF EXERCISE 12–2   Equipment Replacement Decision (LO2)
Waukee Railroad is considering the purchase of a powerful, high-speed wheel grinder to replace a standard wheel grinder that is now in use. Selected information on the two machines is given below:

|  | Standard Wheel Grinder | High-Speed Wheel Grinder |
| --- | --- | --- |
| Original cost new ..................... | $20,000 | $30,000 |
| Accumulated depreciation to date ......... | 6,000 | — |
| Current salvage value ................. | 9,000 | — |
| Estimated cost per year to operate ........ | 15,000 | 7,000 |
| Remaining years of useful life ........... | 5 years | 5 years |

***Required:***
Prepare a computation covering the five-year period that will show the net advantage or disadvantage of purchasing the high-speed wheel grinder. Use only relevant costs in your analysis.

### BRIEF EXERCISE 12–3   Dropping or Retaining a Segment (LO3)
Bed & Bath, a retailing company, has two departments, Hardware and Linens. A recent monthly income statement for the company follows:

|  |  | Department | |
| --- | --- | --- | --- |
|  | Total | Hardware | Linens |
| Sales ........................ | $4,000,000 | $3,000,000 | $1,000,000 |
| Less variable expenses ........... | 1,300,000 | 900,000 | 400,000 |
| Contribution margin ............. | 2,700,000 | 2,100,000 | 600,000 |
| Less fixed expenses ............. | 2,200,000 | 1,400,000 | 800,000 |
| Net operating income (loss) ....... | $ 500,000 | $ 700,000 | $ (200,000) |

   A study indicates that $340,000 of the fixed expenses being charged to Linens are sunk costs or allocated costs that will continue even if the Linens Department is dropped. In addition, the elimination of the Linens Department will result in a 10% decrease in the sales of the Hardware Department. If the Linens Department is dropped, what will be the effect on the net operating income of the company as a whole?

### BRIEF EXERCISE 12–4   Make or Buy a Component (LO4)
For many years Futura Company has purchased the starters that it installs in its standard line of farm tractors. Due to a reduction in output of certain of its products, the company has idle capacity that could be

used to produce the starters. The chief engineer has recommended against this move, however, pointing out that the cost to produce the starters would be greater than the current $8.40 per unit purchase price:

| | Per Unit | Total |
|---|---|---|
| Direct materials | $3.10 | |
| Direct labour | 2.70 | |
| Supervision | 1.50 | $60,000 |
| Depreciation | 1.00 | 40,000 |
| Variable manufacturing overhead | 0.60 | |
| Rent | 0.30 | 12,000 |
| Total production cost | $9.20 | |

A supervisor would have to be hired to oversee production of the starters. However, the company has sufficient idle tools and machinery that no new equipment would have to be purchased. The rent charge above is based on space utilized in the plant. The total rent on the plant is $80,000 per period. Depreciation is due to obsolescence, rather than wear and tear. Prepare computations to show the dollar advantage or disadvantage per period of making the starters.

### BRIEF EXERCISE 12–5  Special Order (LO5)

Delta Company produces a single product. The cost of producing and selling a single unit of this product at the company's normal activity level of 60,000 units per year is:

| | |
|---|---|
| Direct materials | $5.10 |
| Direct labour | 3.80 |
| Variable manufacturing overhead | 1.00 |
| Fixed manufacturing overhead | 4.20 |
| Variable selling and administrative expense | 1.50 |
| Fixed selling and administrative expense | 2.40 |

The normal selling price is $21 per unit. The company's capacity is 75,000 units per year. An order has been received from a mail-order house for 15,000 units at a special price of $14 per unit. This order would not affect regular sales.

*Required:*
1. If the order is accepted, by how much will annual profits be increased or decreased? (The order will not change the company's total fixed costs.)
2. Assume the company has 1,000 units of this product left over from last year that are vastly inferior to the current model. The units must be sold through regular channels at reduced prices. What unit cost figure is relevant for establishing a minimum selling price for these units? Explain.

### BRIEF EXERCISE 12–6  Utilization of a Constrained Resource (LO6)

Benoit Company produces three products, A, B, and C. Data concerning the three products follow (per unit):

| | Product | | |
|---|---|---|---|
| | A | B | C |
| Selling price | $80 | $56 | $70 |
| Less variable expenses: | | | |
| Direct materials | 24 | 15 | 9 |
| Other variable expenses | 24 | 27 | 40 |
| Total variable expenses | 48 | 42 | 49 |
| Contribution margin | $32 | $14 | $21 |
| Contribution margin ratio | 40% | 25% | 30% |

Demand for the company's products is very strong, with far more orders each month than the company has raw materials available to produce. The same material is used in each product. The material costs

$3 per pound with a maximum of 5,000 pounds available each month. Which orders would you advise the company to accept first, those for A, for B, or for C? Which orders second? Third?

# Exercises

### EXERCISE 12–1   Identifying Relevant Costs (LO1)

Bill has just returned from a duck hunting trip. He has brought home eight ducks. Bill's friend John disapproves of duck hunting, and to discourage Bill from further hunting, John has presented him with the following cost estimate per duck:

| | |
|---|---:|
| Camper and equipment: | |
| Cost, $12,000; usable for eight seasons; 10 hunting trips per season | $150 |
| Travel expense (pickup truck): | |
| 100 kilometres at $0.12 per kilometres (gas, oil, and tires—$0.07 per kilometres: | |
| depreciation and insurance—$0.05 per kilometres) | 12 |
| Shotgun shells (two boxes) | 20 |
| Boat: | |
| Cost, $2,320, usable for eight seasons; 10 hunting trips per season | 29 |
| Hunting license: | |
| Cost, $30 for the season; 10 hunting trips per season | 3 |
| Money lost playing poker: | |
| Loss, $18 (Bill plays poker every weekend) | 18 |
| A fifth of Old Grandad: | |
| Cost, $8 (used to ward off the cold) | 8 |
| Total cost | $240 |
| Cost per duck ($240 ÷ 8 ducks) | $ 30 |

#### Required:

1. Assuming that the duck hunting trip Bill has just completed is typical, what costs are relevant to a decision as to whether Bill should go duck hunting again this season?
2. Suppose that Bill gets lucky on his next hunting trip and shoots 10 ducks in the amount of time it took him to shoot eight ducks on his last trip. How much would it have cost him to shoot the last two ducks?
3. Which costs are relevant in a decision of whether Bill should give up hunting? Explain.

### EXERCISE 12–2   Identification of Relevant Costs; Equipment Replacement (LO1, LO2)

Hollings Company sells office furniture in the Rocky Mountain area. As part of its service, it delivers furniture to customers.

The costs associated with the acquisition and annual operation of a delivery truck are given below:

| | |
|---|---|
| Insurance | $1,600 |
| Licences | 250 |
| Taxes (vehicle) | 150 |
| Garage rent for parking (per truck) | 1,200 |
| Depreciation ($9,000 ÷ 5 years) | 1,800* |
| Gasoline, oil, tires, and repairs | 0.07 per km |

*Based on obsolescence, rather than on wear and tear.

#### Required:

1. Assume that Hollings Company has purchased one truck and that the truck has been driven 50,000 kilometres during the first year. Compute the average cost per kilometre of owning and operating the truck.
2. At the beginning of the second year, Hollings Company is unsure whether to use the truck or leave it parked in the garage and have all hauling done commercially. (The state requires the payment of vehicle taxes even if the vehicle is not used.) What costs from the previous list are relevant to this decision? Explain.

3. Assume that the company decides to use the truck during the second year. Near year-end an order is received from a customer over 1,000 kilometres away. What costs from the previous list are relevant in a decision between using the truck to make the delivery and having the delivery done commercially? Explain.

4. Occasionally, the company could use two trucks at the same time. For this reason, some thought is being given to purchasing a second truck. The total kilometres driven would be the same as if only one truck were owned. What costs from the previous list are relevant to a decision over whether to purchase the second truck? Explain.

### EXERCISE 12–3 Dropping or Retaining a Segment (LO3)

Thalassines Kataskeves, S.A., of Greece makes marine equipment. The company has been experiencing losses on its bilge pump product line for several years. The most recent quarterly income statement for the bilge pump product line is given below:

**THALASSINES KATASKEVES, S.A.**
**Income Statement—Bilge Pump**
**For the Quarter Ended March 31**

| | | |
|---|---:|---:|
| Sales | | €850,000 |
| Less variable expenses: | | |
|    Variable manufacturing expenses | €330,000 | |
|    Sales commissions | 42,000 | |
|    Shipping | 18,000 | |
| Total variable expenses | | 390,000 |
| Contribution margin | | 460,000 |
| Less fixed expenses: | | |
|    Advertising | 270,000 | |
|    Depreciation of equipment (no resale value) | 80,000 | |
|    General factory overhead | 105,000* | |
|    Salary of product-line manager | 32,000 | |
|    Insurance on inventories | 8,000 | |
|    Purchasing department expenses | 45,000† | |
| Total fixed expenses | | 540,000 |
| Net operating loss | | €(80,000) |

*Common costs allocated on the basis of machine-hours.
†Common costs allocated on the basis of sales dollars.

The currency in Greece is the euro, denoted by €. The discontinuance of the bilge pump product line would not affect sales of other product lines and would have no noticeable effect on the company's total general factory overhead or total Purchasing Department expenses.

*Required:*
Would you recommend that the bilge pump product line be discontinued? Support your answer with appropriate computations.

### EXERCISE 12–4 Make or Buy a Component (LO4)

Han Products manufactures 30,000 units of part S-6 each year for use on its production line. At this level of activity, the cost per unit for part S-6 is as follows:

| | |
|---|---:|
| Direct materials | $ 3.60 |
| Direct labour | 10.00 |
| Variable overhead | 2.40 |
| Fixed overhead | 9.00 |
| Total cost per part | $25.00 |

An outside supplier has offered to sell 30,000 units of part S-6 each year to Han Products for $21 per part. If Han Products accepts this offer, the facilities now being used to manufacture part S-6 could be rented to another company at an annual rental of $80,000. However, Han Products has determined that two-thirds of the fixed overhead being applied to part S-6 would continue even if part S-6 were purchased from the outside supplier.

***Required:***

Prepare computations to show the net dollar advantage or disadvantage of accepting the outside supplier's offer.

### EXERCISE 12–5    Evaluating a Special Order (LO5)

Imperial Jewellers is considering a special order for 20 handcrafted gold bracelets for a major upscale wedding. The gold bracelets are to be given as gifts to members of the wedding party. The normal selling price of a gold bracelet is $189.95 and its unit product cost is $149 as shown below:

| | |
|---|---|
| Materials ............................. | $ 84.00 |
| Direct labour ........................ | 45.00 |
| Manufacturing overhead .............. | 20.00 |
| Unit product cost .................... | $149.00 |

The manufacturing overhead is largely fixed and unaffected by variations in how much jewellery is produced in any given period. However, $4 of the overhead is variable with respect to the number of bracelets produced. The customer who is interested in the special bracelet order would like special filigree applied to the bracelets. This filigree would require additional materials costing $2 per bracelet and would also require acquisition of a special tool costing $250 that would have no other use once the special order is completed. This order would have no effect on the company's regular sales and the order could be fulfilled using the company's existing capacity without affecting any other order.

***Required:***

What effect would accepting this order have on the company's net operating income if a special price of $169.95 is offered per bracelet for this order? Should the special order be accepted at this price?

### EXERCISE 12–6    Utilization of a Constrained Resource (LO6)

Barlow Company manufactures three products: A, B, and C. The selling price, variable costs, and contribution margin for one unit of each product follow:-

| | Product | | |
|---|---|---|---|
| | **A** | **B** | **C** |
| Selling price ................ | $180 | $270 | $240 |
| Less variable expenses: | | | |
|    Direct materials ............ | 24 | 72 | 32 |
|    Other variable expenses ...... | 102 | 90 | 148 |
| Total variable expenses ........ | 126 | 162 | 180 |
| Contribution margin .......... | $ 54 | $108 | $ 60 |
| Contribution margin ratio ...... | 30% | 40% | 25% |

The same raw material is used in all three products. Barlow Company has only 5,000 pounds of material on hand and will not be able to obtain any more material for several weeks due to a strike in its supplier's plant. Management is trying to decide which product(s) to concentrate on next week in filling its backlog of orders. The material costs $8 per pound.

***Required:***

1.  Compute the amount of contribution margin that will be obtained per kilogram of material used in each product.
2.  Which orders would you recommend that the company work on next week—the orders for product A, product B, or product C? Show computations.
3.  A foreign supplier could furnish Barlow with additional stocks of the raw material at a substantial premium over the usual price. If there is unfilled demand for all three products, what is the highest price that Barlow Company should be willing to pay for an additional kilogram of materials?

## PROBLEM 12–1   Equipment Replacement Decision (LO2)

Murl Plastics Inc. purchased a new machine one year ago at a cost of $60,000. Although the machine operates well, the president of Murl Plastics is wondering if the company should replace it with a new electronically operated machine that has just come on the market. The new machine would slash annual operating costs by two-thirds, as shown in the comparative data below:

|  | Present Machine | Proposed New Machine |
|---|---|---|
| Purchase cost new ................ | $60,000 | $90,000 |
| Estimated useful life new ........... | 6 years | 5 years |
| Annual operating costs ............. | $42,000 | $14,000 |
| Annual straight-line depreciation ...... | 10,000 | 18,000 |
| Remaining book value ............. | 50,000 | — |
| Salvage value now ................ | 10,000 | — |
| Salvage value in 5 years ............ | –0– | –0– |

In trying to decide whether to purchase the new machine, the president has prepared the following analysis:

| | |
|---|---|
| Book value of the old machine .......... | $50,000 |
| Less salvage value ................... | 10,000 |
| Net loss from disposal ............... | $40,000 |

"Even though the new machine looks good," said the president, "we can't get rid of that old machine if it means taking a huge loss on it. We'll have to use the old machine for at least a few more years."

Sales are expected to be $200,000 per year, and selling and administrative expenses are expected to be $126,000 per year, regardless of which machine is used.

### Required:

1. Prepare a summary income statement covering the next five years, assuming:
   a. That the new machine is not purchased.
   b. That the new machine is purchased.
2. Determine the desirability of purchasing the new machine using only relevant costs in your analysis.

## PROBLEM 12–2   Dropping or Retaining a Product (LO3)

The Regal Cycle Company manufactures three types of bicycles—a dirt bike, a mountain bike, and a racing bike. Data on sales and expenses for the past quarter follow:

|  | Total | Dirt Bikes | Mountain Bikes | Racing Bikes |
|---|---|---|---|---|
| Sales ............................ | $300,000 | $90,000 | $150,000 | $60,000 |
| Less variable manufacturing and selling expenses ............. | 120,000 | 27,000 | 60,000 | 33,000 |
| Contribution margin ............... | 180,000 | 63,000 | 90,000 | 27,000 |
| Less fixed expenses: |  |  |  |  |
| Advertising, traceable ............ | 30,000 | 10,000 | 14,000 | 6,000 |
| Depreciation of special equipment .. | 23,000 | 6,000 | 9,000 | 8,000 |
| Salaries of product-line managers ... | 35,000 | 12,000 | 13,000 | 10,000 |
| Common allocated costs* ......... | 60,000 | 18,000 | 30,000 | 12,000 |
| Total fixed expenses .............. | 148,000 | 46,000 | 66,000 | 36,000 |
| Net operating income (loss) ........ | $ 32,000 | $17,000 | $ 24,000 | $ (9,000) |

*Allocated on the basis of sales dollars.

Management is concerned about the continued losses shown by the racing bikes and wants a recommendation as to whether or not the line should be discontinued. The special equipment used to produce racing bikes has no resale value and does not wear out.

***Required:***

1. Should production and sale of the racing bikes be discontinued? Show computations to support your answer.
2. Recast the above data in a format that would be more usable to management in assessing the long-term profitability of the various product lines.

CHECK FIGURE
(1) Decrease in profits:
$3,200

### PROBLEM 12–3   Discontinuing a Flight (LO3)

Profits have been decreasing for several years at Pegasus Airlines. In an effort to improve the company's performance, consideration is being given to dropping several flights that appear to be unprofitable.

A typical income statement for one such flight (flight 482) is given below (per flight):

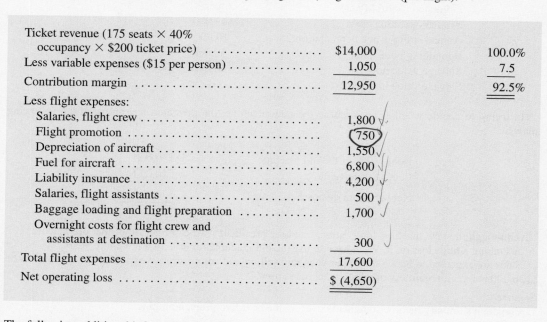

|  |  |  |
|---|---|---|
| Ticket revenue (175 seats × 40% occupancy × $200 ticket price) | $14,000 | 100.0% |
| Less variable expenses ($15 per person) | 1,050 | 7.5 |
| Contribution margin | 12,950 | 92.5% |
| Less flight expenses: |  |  |
|   Salaries, flight crew | 1,800 |  |
|   Flight promotion | 750 |  |
|   Depreciation of aircraft | 1,550 |  |
|   Fuel for aircraft | 6,800 |  |
|   Liability insurance | 4,200 |  |
|   Salaries, flight assistants | 500 |  |
|   Baggage loading and flight preparation | 1,700 |  |
|   Overnight costs for flight crew and assistants at destination | 300 |  |
| Total flight expenses | 17,600 |  |
| Net operating loss | $ (4,650) |  |

The following additional information is available about flight 482:

a. Members of the flight crew are paid fixed annual salaries, whereas the flight assistants are paid by the flight.
b. One-third of the liability insurance is a special charge assessed against flight 482 because in the opinion of the insurance company, the destination of the flight is in a "high-risk" area. The remaining two-thirds would be unaffected by a decision to drop flight 482.
c. The baggage loading and flight preparation expense is an allocation of ground crews' salaries and depreciation of ground equipment. Dropping flight 482 would have no effect on the company's total baggage loading and flight preparation expenses.
d. If flight 482 is dropped, Pegasus Airlines has no authorization at present to replace it with another flight.
e. Depreciation of aircraft is due entirely to obsolescence. Depreciation due to wear and tear is negligible.
f. Dropping flight 482 would not allow Pegasus Airlines to reduce the number of aircraft in its fleet or the number of flight crew on its payroll.

***Required:***

1. Prepare an analysis showing what impact dropping flight 482 would have on the airline's profits.
2. The airline's scheduling officer has been criticized because only about 50% of the seats on Pegasus' flights are being filled compared with an average of 60% for the industry. The scheduling officer has explained that Pegasus' average seat occupancy could be improved considerably by eliminating about 10% of the flights but that doing so would reduce profits. Explain how this could happen.

CHECK FIGURE
(1) The part can be made inside the company for $6 less per unit

### PROBLEM 12–4   Make or Buy a Component (LO4)

Troy Engines Ltd. manufactures a variety of engines for use in heavy equipment. The company has always produced all of the necessary parts for its engines, including all of the carburetors. An outside supplier has offered to produce and sell one type of carburetor to Troy Engines Ltd. for a cost of $35 per unit.

To evaluate this offer, Troy Engines Ltd. has gathered the following information relating to its own cost of producing the carburetor internally:

|  | Per Unit | 15,000 Units per Year |
|---|---|---|
| Direct materials . . . . . . . . . . . . . . . . . . . . . . . . . . | $14 | $210,000 |
| Direct labour . . . . . . . . . . . . . . . . . . . . . . . . . . . . | 10 | 150,000 |
| Variable manufacturing overhead . . . . . . . . . . . . . | 3 | 45,000 |
| Fixed manufacturing overhead, traceable . . . . . . . . | 6* | 90,000 |
| Fixed manufacturing overhead, allocated . . . . . . . . | 9 | 135,000 |
| Total cost . . . . . . . . . . . . . . . . . . . . . . . . . . . . . . | $42 | $630,000 |

*One-third supervisory salaries; two-thirds depreciation of special equipment (no resale value).

**Required:**
1. Assuming that the company has no alternative use for the facilities that are now being used to produce the carburetors, should the outside supplier's offer be accepted? Show all computations.
2. Suppose that if the carburetors were purchased, Troy Engines Ltd. could use the freed capacity to launch a new product. The segment margin of the new product would be $150,000 per year. Should Troy Engines Ltd. accept the offer to buy the carburetors for $35 per unit? Show all computations.

**PROBLEM 12–5   Accept or Reject a Special Order (LO5)**
Polaski Company manufactures and sells a single product called a Ret. Operating at capacity, the company can produce and sell 30,000 Rets per year. Costs associated with this level of production and sales are given below:

CHECK FIGURE
(1) Net increase in profits: $65,000

|  | Unit | Total |
|---|---|---|
| Direct materials . . . . . . . . . . . . . . . . . . . . . . . . . | $15 | $ 450,000 |
| Direct labour . . . . . . . . . . . . . . . . . . . . . . . . . . . | 8 | 240,000 |
| Variable manufacturing overhead . . . . . . . . . . . | 3 | 90,000 |
| Fixed manufacturing overhead . . . . . . . . . . . . . . | 9 | 270,000 |
| Variable selling expense . . . . . . . . . . . . . . . . . . . | 4 | 120,000 |
| Fixed selling expense . . . . . . . . . . . . . . . . . . . . . | 6 | 180,000 |
| Total cost . . . . . . . . . . . . . . . . . . . . . . . . . . . . . | $45 | $1,350,000 |

The Rets normally sell for $50 each. Fixed manufacturing overhead is constant at $270,000 per year within the range of 25,000 through 30,000 Rets per year.

**Required:**
1. Assume that due to a recession, Polaski Company expects to sell only 25,000 Rets through regular channels next year. A large retail chain has offered to purchase 5,000 Rets if Polaski is willing to accept a 16% discount off the regular price. There would be no sales commissions on this order; thus, variable selling expenses would be slashed by 75%. However, Polaski Company would have to purchase a special machine to engrave the retail chain's name on the 5,000 units. This machine would cost $10,000. Polaski Company has no assurance that the retail chain will purchase additional units any time in the future. Determine the impact on profits next year if this special order is accepted.
2. Refer to the original data. Assume again that Polaski Company expects to sell only 25,000 Rets through regular channels next year. The Canadian Army would like to make a one-time-only purchase of 5,000 Rets. The Army would pay a fixed fee of $1.80 per Ret, and in addition it would reimburse Polaski Company for all costs of production (variable and fixed) associated with the units. Since the Army would pick up the Rets with its own trucks, there would be no variable selling expenses of any type associated with this order. If Polaski Company accepts the order, by how much will profits be increased or decreased for the year?
3. Assume the same situation as that described in (2) above, except that the company expects to sell 30,000 Rets through regular channels next year. Thus, accepting the Canadian Army's order would require giving up regular sales of 5,000 Rets. If the Army's order is accepted, by how much will profits be increased or decreased from what they would be if the 5,000 Rets were sold through regular channels?

## PROBLEM 12–6    Utilization of a Constrained Resource (LO6)

The Walton Toy Company manufactures a line of dolls and a doll dress sewing kit. Demand for the dolls is increasing, and management requests assistance from you in determining an economical sales and production mix for the coming year. The company has provided the following information:

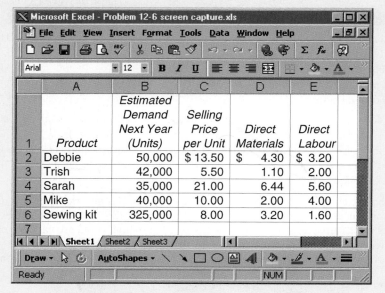

| Product | Estimated Demand Next Year (Units) | Selling Price per Unit | Direct Materials | Direct Labour |
|---|---|---|---|---|
| Debbie | 50,000 | $ 13.50 | $ 4.30 | $ 3.20 |
| Trish | 42,000 | 5.50 | 1.10 | 2.00 |
| Sarah | 35,000 | 21.00 | 6.44 | 5.60 |
| Mike | 40,000 | 10.00 | 2.00 | 4.00 |
| Sewing kit | 325,000 | 8.00 | 3.20 | 1.60 |

The following additional information is available:

a. The company's plant has a capacity of 130,000 direct labour-hours per year on a single-shift basis. The company's present employees and equipment can produce all five products.
b. The direct labour rate is $8 per hour; this rate is expected to remain unchanged during the coming year.
c. Fixed costs total $520,000 per year. Variable overhead costs are $2 per direct labour-hour.
d. All of the company's nonmanufacturing costs are fixed.
e. The company's present inventory of finished products is negligible and can be ignored.

***Required:***
1. Determine the contribution margin per direct labour-hour expended on each product.
2. Prepare a schedule showing the total direct labour-hours that will be required to produce the units estimated to be sold during the coming year.
3. Examine the data you have computed in (1) and (2) above. Indicate how much of each product should be made so that total production time is equal to the 130,000 hours available.
4. What is the highest price, in terms of a rate per hour, that Walton Toy Company would be willing to pay for additional capacity (that is, for added direct labour time)?
5. Assume again that the company does not want to reduce sales of any product. Identify ways in which the company could obtain the additional output.

                                                 (CPA, heavily adapted)

## PROBLEM 12–7    Make-or-Buy Analysis; Equipment Replacement Decision (LO2, LO4)

"In my opinion, we ought to stop making our own drums and accept that outside supplier's offer," said Wim Niewindt, managing director of Antilles Refining, N.V., of Aruba. "At a price of 18 florins per drum, we would be paying 5 florins less than it costs us to manufacture the drums in our own plant. (The currency in Aruba is the florin, denoted below by fl.) Since we use 60,000 drums a year, that would be an annual cost savings of 300,000 florins." Antilles Refining's present cost to manufacture one drum is given below (based on 60,000 drums per year):

| | |
|---|---|
| Direct material . . . . . . . . . . . . . . . . . . . . . . . . . . . . . . . | fl 10.35 |
| Direct labour . . . . . . . . . . . . . . . . . . . . . . . . . . . . . | 6.00 |
| Variable overhead . . . . . . . . . . . . . . . . . . . . . . . . . | 1.50 |
| Fixed overhead (fl 2.80 general company overhead, fl 1.60 depreciation and, fl 0.75 supervision) . . . . . . . . . . . . . . . . . . . . . . | 5.15 |
| Total cost per drum . . . . . . . . . . . . . . . . . . . . . . . . | fl 23.00 |

A decision about whether to make or buy the drums is especially important at this time, since the equipment being used to make the drums is completely worn out and must be replaced. The choices facing the company are:

*Alternative 1:* Purchase new equipment and continue to make the drums. The equipment would cost fl 810,000; it would have a six-year useful life and no salvage value. The company uses straight-line depreciation.

*Alternative 2:* Purchase the drums from an outside supplier at fl 18 per drum under a six-year contract.

The new equipment would be more efficient than the equipment that Antilles Refining has been using and, according to the manufacturer, would reduce direct labour and variable overhead costs by 30%. The old equipment has no resale value. Supervision cost (fl 45,000 per year) and direct materials cost per drum would not be affected by the new equipment. The new equipment's capacity would be 90,000 drums per year. The company has no other use for the space being used to produce the drums.

The company's total general company overhead would be unaffected by this decision.

*Required:*
1. To assist the managing director in making a decision, prepare an analysis showing what the total cost and the cost per drum would be under each of the two alternatives given above. Assume that 60,000 drums are needed each year. Which course of action would you recommend to the managing director?
2. Would your recommendation in (1) above be the same if the company's needs were: (a) 75,000 drums per year or (b) 90,000 drums per year? Show computations to support your answer, with costs presented on both a total and a per-unit basis.
3. What other factors would you recommend that the company consider before making a decision?

### PROBLEM 12–8   Shutting Down or Continuing to Operate a Plant (LO3)

(Note: This type of decision is similar to that of dropping a product line.)

Birch Company normally produces and sells 30,000 units of RG-6 each month. RG-6 is a small electrical relay used in the automotive industry as a component part in various products. The selling price is $22 per unit, variable costs are $14 per unit, fixed manufacturing overhead costs total $150,000 per month, and fixed selling costs total $30,000 per month.

Employment-contract strikes in the companies that purchase the bulk of the RG-6 units have caused Birch Company's sales to temporarily drop to only 8,000 units per month. Birch Company estimates that the strikes will last for about two months, after which time sales of RG-6 should return to normal. Due to the current low level of sales, however, Birch Company is thinking about closing down its own plant during the two months that the strikes are on. If Birch Company does close down its plant, it is estimated that fixed manufacturing overhead costs can be reduced to $105,000 per month and that fixed selling costs can be reduced by 10%. Startup costs at the end of the shutdown period would total $8,000. Since Birch Company uses just-in-time (JIT) production methods, no inventories are on hand.

*Required:*
1. Assuming that the strikes continue for two months, as estimated, would you recommend that Birch Company close its own plant? Show computations in good form.
2. At what level of sales (in units) for the two-month period should Birch Company be indifferent between closing the plant or keeping it open? Show computations. (Hint: This is a type of break-even analysis, except that the fixed cost portion of your break-even computation should include only those fixed costs that are relevant [i.e., avoidable] over the two-month period.)

CHECK FIGURE
(1) Disadvantage to close: $40,000

### PROBLEM 12–9   Relevant Cost Analysis in a Variety of Situations (LO3, LO4, LO5)

Andretti Company has a single product called a Dak. The company normally produces and sells 60,000 Daks each year at a selling price of $32 per unit. The company's unit costs at this level of activity are given below:

| | | |
|---|---|---|
| Direct materials | $10.00 | |
| Direct labour | 4.50 | |
| Variable manufacturing overhead | 2.30 | |
| Fixed manufacturing overhead | 5.00 | ($300,000 total) |
| Variable selling expenses | 1.20 | |
| Fixed selling expenses | 3.50 | ($210,000 total) |
| Total cost per unit | $26.50 | |

CHECK FIGURE
(1) Incremental net income: $130,000
(2) Break-even price: $22.15

A number of questions relating to the production and sale of Daks follow. Each question is independent.

*Required:*

1. Assume that Andretti Company has sufficient capacity to produce 90,000 Daks each year without any increase in fixed manufacturing overhead costs. The company could increase its sales by 25% above the present 60,000 units each year if it were willing to increase the fixed selling expenses by $80,000. Would the increased fixed expenses be justified?

2. Assume again that Andretti Company has sufficient capacity to produce 90,000 Daks each year. A customer in a foreign market wants to purchase 20,000 Daks. Import duties on the Daks would be $1.70 per unit, and costs for permits and licences would be $9,000. The only selling costs that would be associated with the order would be $3.20 per unit shipping cost. You have been asked by the president to compute the per-unit break-even price on this order.

3. The company has 1,000 Daks on hand that have some irregularities and are therefore considered to be "seconds." Due to the irregularities, it will be impossible to sell these units at the normal price through regular distribution channels. What unit cost figure is relevant for setting a minimum selling price?

4. Due to a strike in its supplier's plant, Andretti Company is unable to purchase more material for the production of Daks. The strike is expected to last for two months. Andretti Company has enough material on hand to continue to operate at 30% of normal levels for the two-month period. As an alternative, Andretti could close its plant down entirely for the two months. If the plant were closed, fixed overhead costs would continue at 60% of their normal level during the two-month period; the fixed selling costs would be reduced by 20% while the plant was closed. What would be the dollar advantage or disadvantage of closing the plant for the two-month period?

5. An outside manufacturer has offered to produce Daks for Andretti Company and to ship them directly to Andretti's customers. If Andretti Company accepts this offer, the facilities that it uses to produce Daks would be idle; however, fixed overhead costs would be reduced by 75% of their present level. Since the outside manufacturer would pay for all the costs of shipping, the variable selling costs would be only two-thirds of their present amount. Compute the unit cost figure that is relevant for comparison to whatever quoted price is received from the outside manufacturer.

# Building Your Skills

CHECK FIGURE
(2) Minimum sales: R60,000

**ANALYTICAL THINKING**   (LO3)

Tracey Douglas is the owner and managing director of Heritage Garden Furniture Ltd., a South African company that makes museum-quality reproductions of antique outdoor furniture. Ms. Douglas would like advice concerning the advisability of eliminating the model C3 lawnchair. These lawnchairs have been among the company's best-selling products, but they seem to be unprofitable.

A condensed statement of operating income for the company and for the model C3 lawnchair for the quarter ended June 30 follows:

|  | All Products | Model C3 Lawnchair |
|---|---|---|
| Sales | R2,900,000 | R300,000 |
| Cost of sales: |  |  |
| Direct materials | 759,000 | 122,000 |
| Direct labour | 680,000 | 72,000 |
| Fringe benefits (20% of direct labour) | 136,000 | 14,400 |
| Variable manufacturing overhead | 28,000 | 3,600 |
| Building rent and maintenance | 30,000 | 4,000 |
| Depreciation | 75,000 | 19,100 |
| Total cost of sales | 1,708,000 | 235,100 |
| Gross margin | 1,192,000 | 64,900 |
| Selling and administrative expenses: |  |  |
| Product managers' salaries | 75,000 | 10,000 |
| Sales commissions (5% of sales) | 145,000 | 15,000 |
| Fringe benefits (20% of salaries and commissions) | 44,000 | 5,000 |
| Shipping | 120,000 | 10,000 |
| General administrative expenses | 464,000 | 48,000 |
| Total selling and administrative expenses | 848,000 | 88,000 |
| Net operating income (loss) | R344,000 | R(23,100) |

The currency in South Africa is the rand, denoted here by R.

The following additional data have been supplied by the company:

a. Direct labour is a variable cost at Heritage Garden Furniture.
b. All of the company's products are manufactured in the same facility and use the same equipment. Building rent and maintenance and depreciation are allocated to products using various bases. The equipment does not wear out through use; it eventually becomes obsolete.
c. There is ample capacity to fill all orders.
d. Dropping the model C3 lawnchair would have no effect on sales of other product lines.
e. Inventories of work in process or finished goods are insignificant.
f. Shipping costs are traced directly to products.
g. General administrative expenses are allocated to products on the basis of sales dollars. There would be no effect on the total general administrative expenses if the model C3 lawnchair were dropped.
h. If the model C3 lawnchair were dropped, the product manager would be laid off.

**Required:**
1. Given the current level of sales, would you recommend that the model C3 lawnchair be dropped? Prepare appropriate computations to support your answer.
2. What would sales of the model C3 lawnchair have to be, at minimum, in order to justify retaining the product? (Hint: Set this up as a break-even problem but include only the relevant costs from 1 above.)

## COMMUNICATING IN PRACTICE   (LO4)

CHECK FIGURE
(1) Savings per box
to make: $0.20

Silven Industries, which manufactures and sells a highly successful line of summer lotions and insect repellents, has decided to diversify in order to stabilize sales throughout the year. A natural area for the company to consider is the production of winter lotions and creams to prevent dry and chapped skin.

After considerable research, a winter products line has been developed. However, Bob Murdock, Silven's president, has decided to introduce only one of the new products for this coming winter. If the product is a success, further expansion in future years will be initiated.

The product selected (called Chap-Off) is a lip balm that will be sold in a lipstick-type tube. The product will be sold to wholesalers in boxes of 24 tubes for $8 per box. Because of excess capacity, no additional fixed overhead costs will be incurred to produce the product. However, a $90,000 charge for fixed overhead will be absorbed by the product under the company's absorption costing system.

Using the production and sales estimates of 100,000 boxes of Chap-Off, the Accounting Department has developed the following cost per box:

| | |
|---|---|
| Direct material | $3.60 |
| Direct labour | 2.00 |
| Manufacturing overhead | 1.40 |
| Total cost | $7.00 |

The costs above include costs for producing both the lip balm and the tube into which the lip balm is to be placed. As an alternative to making the tubes, Silven has approached a supplier to discuss the possibility of purchasing the tubes for Chap-Off. The purchase price of the empty tubes from the supplier would be $1.35 per box of 24 tubes. If Silven Industries accepts the purchase proposal, it is predicted that direct labour and variable manufacturing overhead costs per box of Chap-Off would be reduced by 10% and that direct materials costs would be reduced by 25%.

**Required:**
Write a memorandum to the president that answers the following questions. Use headings to organize the information presented in the memorandum. Include computations to support your answers, where appropriate.

1. Should Silven Industries make the tubes for the lip balm or buy them from the supplier? How much would be saved by making this decision?
2. What is the maximum purchase price that would be acceptable to Silven Industries if the tubes for the lip balm were bought from a supplier?
3. As noted above, the Accounting Department assumed that 100,000 boxes of Chap-Off would be produced and sold. However, the vice-president of sales estimates that 120,000 boxes of Chap-Off can be sold. This higher volume would require additional equipment at an annual rental of $40,000. Assuming the company buys the tubes from the supplier at $1.35 per box of 24 tubes and that the supplier will not accept an order for less than 100,000 boxes of tubes, should Silven Industries make the tubes for the lip balm or buy them from the supplier? What are the total costs of producing 120,000 boxes of Chap-Off assuming that the company makes the tubes? What are the total costs assuming that the company buys the tubes? How much would be saved by buying the tubes, rather than making them internally?

4. Refer to the information in (3) above. Assume that a different supplier will accept an order of any size for the tubes at $1.35 per box of 24 tubes. Should Silven Industries make the tubes for the lip balm or buy them from the supplier?

5. What qualitative factors should be considered in this make-or-buy decision?

(CMA, heavily adapted)

### ETHICS CHALLENGE   (LO3)

Haley Romeros had just been appointed vice-president of the Rocky Mountain Region of the Bank Services Corporation (BSC). The company provides cheque-processing services to small banks. The banks send cheques presented for deposit or payment to BSC, which records the data on each cheque in a computerized database. BSC then sends the data electronically to a Canadian Payments Association cheque-clearing centre where the appropriate transfers of funds are made between banks. The Great Lakes Region has three cheque-processing centres, which are located in Burlington, Kingston, and Owen Sound, Ontario. Prior to her promotion to vice-president, Ms. Romeros had been the manager of a cheque-processing centre in Nova Scotia.

Immediately upon assuming her new position, Ms. Romeros requested a complete financial report for the just-ended fiscal year from the region's controller, John Littlebear. Ms. Romeros specified that the financial report should follow the standardized format required by corporate headquarters for all regional performance reports. That report follows:

### BANK SERVICES CORPORATION (BSC)
### Great Lakes Region
### Financial Performance

| | | Cheque-Processing Centres | | |
| --- | --- | --- | --- | --- |
| | Total | Kingston | Burlington | Owen Sound |
| Sales ................... | $50,000,000 | $20,000,000 | $18,000,000 | $12,000,000 |
| Operating expenses: | | | | |
|   Direct labour ........... | 32,000,000 | 12,500,000 | 11,000,000 | 8,500,000 |
|   Variable overhead ....... | 850,000 | 350,000 | 310,000 | 190,000 |
|   Equipment depreciation .. | 3,900,000 | 1,300,000 | 1,400,000 | 1,200,000 |
|   Facility expense ......... | 2,800,000 | 900,000 | 800,000 | 1,100,000 |
|   Local administrative expense* ............ | 450,000 | 140,000 | 160,000 | 150,000 |
|   Regional administrative expense† ............ | 1,500,000 | 600,000 | 540,000 | 360,000 |
|   Corporate administrative expense‡ ............ | 4,750,000 | 1,900,000 | 1,710,000 | 1,140,000 |
| Total operating expense ..... | 46,250,000 | 17,690,000 | 15,920,000 | 12,640,000 |
| Net operating income ...... | $ 3,750,000 | $ 2,310,000 | $ 2,080,000 | $ (640,000) |

*Local administrative expenses are the administrative expenses incurred at the cheque-processing centres.
†Regional administrative expenses are allocated to the cheque-processing centres on the basis of sales.
‡Corporate administrative expenses are charged to segments of the company, such as the Rocky Mountain Region and the cheque-processing centres at the rate of 9.5% of their sales.

Upon seeing this report, Ms. Romeros summoned John Littlebear for an explanation.

*Romeros:* What's the story on Owen Sound? It didn't have a loss the previous year did it?

*Littlebear:* No, the Owen Sound facility has had a nice profit every year since it was opened six years ago, but Owen Sound lost a big contract this year.

*Romeros:* Why?

*Littlebear:* One of our national competitors entered the local market and bid very aggressively on the contract. We couldn't afford to meet the bid. Owen Sound's costs—particularly their facility expenses—are just too high. When Owen Sound lost the contract, we had to lay off a lot of employees, but we could not reduce the fixed costs of the Owen Sound facility.

*Romeros:* Why is Owen Sound's facility expense so high? It's a smaller facility than either Kingston or Burlington and yet its facility expense is higher.

*Littlebear:* The problem is that we are able to rent suitable facilities very cheaply at Kingston and Burlington. No such facilities were available at Owen Sound; we had them built. Unfortunately, there were big cost overruns. The contractor we hired was inexperienced at this kind of work and, in fact, went bankrupt before the project was completed. After hiring another contractor to finish the work, we were way over budget. The large depreciation charges on the facility didn't matter at first because we didn't have much competition at the time and could charge premium prices.

*Romeros:* Well, we can't do that anymore. The Owen Sound facility will obviously have to be shut down. Its business can be shifted to the other two cheque-processing centres in the region.

*Littlebear:* I would advise against that. The $1,200,000 in depreciation at the Owen Sound facility is misleading. That facility should last indefinitely with proper maintenance. And it has no resale value; there is no other commercial activity around Owen Sound.

*Romeros:* What about the other costs at Owen Sound?

*Littlebear:* If we shifted Owen Sound's business over to the other two processing centres in the region, we wouldn't save anything on direct labour or variable overhead costs. We might save $90,000 or so in local administrative expense, but we would not save any regional administrative expense and corporate headquarters would still charge us 9.5% of our sales as corporate administrative expense.

In addition, we would have to rent more space in Kingston and Burlington in order to handle the work transferred from Owen Sound; that would probably cost us at least $600,000 a year. And don't forget that it will cost us something to move the equipment from Owen Sound to Kingston and Burlington. And the move will disrupt service to customers.

*Romeros:* I understand all of that, but a money-losing processing centre on my performance report is completely unacceptable.

*Littlebear:* And if you shut down Owen Sound, you are going to throw some loyal employees out of work.

*Romeros:* That's unfortunate, but we have to face hard business realities.

*Littlebear:* And you would have to write off the investment in the facilities at Owen Sound.

*Romeros:* I can explain a write-off to corporate headquarters; hiring an inexperienced contractor to build the Owen Sound facility was my predecessor's mistake. But they'll have my head at headquarters if I show operating losses every year at one of my processing centres. Owen Sound has to go. At the next corporate board meeting, I am going to recommend that the Owen Sound facility be closed.

### Required:

1. From the standpoint of the company as a whole, should the Owen Sound processing centre be shut down and its work redistributed to other processing centres in the region? Explain.
2. Do you think Haley Romeros's decision to shut down the Owen Sound facility is ethical? Explain.
3. What influence should the depreciation on the facilities at Owen Sound have on prices charged by Owen Sound for its services?

## TEAMWORK IN ACTION   (LO4, LO6)

Sportway Inc. is a wholesale distributor supplying a wide range of moderately priced sporting equipment to large chain stores. About 60% of Sportway's products are purchased from other companies, while the remainder of the products are manufactured by Sportway. The company has a Plastics Department that is currently manufacturing molded fishing tackle boxes. Sportway is able to manufacture and sell 8,000 tackle boxes annually, making full use of its direct labour capacity at available workstations. Presented below are the selling price and costs associated with Sportway's tackle boxes.

| | | |
|---|---:|---:|
| Selling price per box . . . . . . . . . . . . . . . . . . | | $86.00 |
| Cost per box: | | |
|    Moulded plastic . . . . . . . . . . . . . . . . . . . . | $ 8.00 | |
|    Hinges, latches, handle . . . . . . . . . . . . . . | 9.00 | |
|    Direct labour ($15 per hour) . . . . . . . . . . | 18.75 | |
|    Manufacturing overhead . . . . . . . . . . . . . | 12.50 | |
|    Selling and administrative cost . . . . . . . . | 17.00 | 65.25 |
| Net operating income per box . . . . . . . . . . | | $20.75 |

Because Sportway believes it could sell 12,000 tackle boxes if it had sufficient manufacturing capacity, the company has looked into the possibility of purchasing the tackle boxes for distribution. Maple Products, a steady supplier of quality products, would be able to provide up to 9,000 tackle boxes per year at a price of $68 per box delivered to Sportway's facility.

Traci Kader, Sportway's production manager, has suggested that the company could make better use of its Plastics Department by manufacturing skateboards. To support her position, Traci has a market study that indicates an expanding market for skateboards. Traci believes that Sportway could expect to sell 17,500 skateboards annually at a price of $45 per skateboard. Traci's estimate of the costs to manufacture the skateboards is presented below.

| | | |
|---|---:|---:|
| Selling price per skateboard . . . . . . . . . . . . | | $45.00 |
| Cost per skateboard: | | |
|     Moulded plastic . . . . . . . . . . . . . . . . . . . . | $5.50 | |
|     Wheels, hardware . . . . . . . . . . . . . . . . . | 7.00 | |
|     Direct labour ($15 per hour) . . . . . . . . . . | 7.50 | |
|     Manufacturing overhead . . . . . . . . . . . . . | 5.00 | |
|     Selling and administrative cost . . . . . . . . | 9.00 | 34.00 |
| Net operating income per skateboard . . . . . | | $11.00 |

In the Plastics Department, Sportway uses direct labour-hours as the application base for manufacturing overhead. Included in the manufacturing overhead for the current year is $50,000 of fixed overhead costs, of which 40% is traceable to the Plastics Department and 60% is allocated factorywide manufacturing overhead cost. The remaining manufacturing overhead cost is variable with respect to direct labour-hours. The skateboards could be produced with existing equipment and personnel in the Plastics Department.

For each unit of product that Sportway sells, regardless of whether the product has been purchased or is manufactured by Sportway, there is an allocated $6 fixed cost per unit for distribution. This $6 per unit is included in the selling and administrative cost for all products. The remaining amount of selling and administrative cost for all products—purchased or manufactured—is variable. The total selling and administrative cost figure for the purchased tackle boxes would be $10 per unit.

### Required:
Your team should discuss and then respond to the following questions. All team members should agree with and understand the answers (including the calculations supporting the answers) and be prepared to report to the class. (Each teammate can assume responsibility for a different part of the presentation.)

1. Determine the number of direct labour-hours per year being used to manufacture tackle boxes.
2. Compute the contribution margin per unit for:
   a. Purchased tackle boxes.
   b. Manufactured tackle boxes.
   c. Manufactured skateboards.
3. Determine the number of tackle boxes (if any) that Sportway should purchase and the number of tackle boxes and/or skateboards that it should manufacture, and compute the improvement in net income that will result from this product mix over current operations.

(CMA, adapted)

Do not forget to check out Taking It to the Net and other quizzes and resources at the Online Learning Centre at www.mcgrawhill.ca/college/garrison.

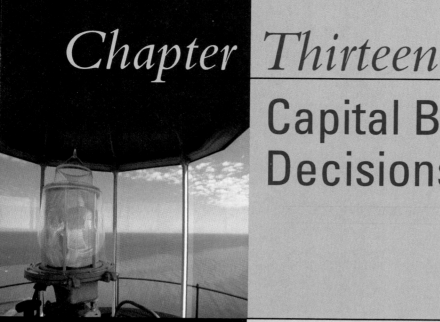

# Chapter Thirteen

# Capital Budgeting Decisions

## A Look Back

A basic framework for the decision-making process centred on the notion of relevant costs and benefits was used in a wide variety of situations in Chapter 12.

## A Look at This Chapter

Chapter 13 expands coverage of the decision-making process by focusing on decisions about significant outlays on long-term projects. A variety of techniques used by managers faced with these decisions are overviewed and illustrated.

## A Look Ahead

Financial statements analysis is covered in Chapter 14. This is the use of financial statements to assess the financial health of a company. The focus in that chapter is on analysis of trends and on the use of financial ratios.

## Chapter Outline

**Capital Budgeting—Planning Investments**
- Typical Capital Budgeting Decisions
- The Time Value of Money

**The Net Present Value Method**
- Emphasis on Cash Flows
- Simplifying Assumptions
- Choosing a Discount Rate
- An Extended Example of the Net Present Value Method

**Expanding the Net Present Value Method**
- The Total-Cost Approach
- The Incremental-Cost Approach
- Least-Cost Decisions

**Preference Decisions—The Ranking of Investment Projects**

**The Internal Rate of Return Method**

**Other Approaches to Capital Budgeting Decisions**
- The Payback Method
- Payback and Uneven Cash Flows

- An Extended Example of Payback
- Evaluation of the Payback Method
- The Simple Rate of Return Method
- Criticisms of the Simple Rate of Return

**Postaudit of Investment Projects**

**Appendix 13A: The Concept of Present Value**
- The Theory of Interest
- Computation of Present Value
- Present Value of a Series of Cash Flows

**Appendix 13B: Future Value and Present Value Tables**

**Appendix 13C: Inflation and Capital Budgeting**

**Appendix 13D: Income Taxes in Capital Budgeting Decisions**

## DECISION FEATURE Funding Only the Best Projects

Steven Burd became the CEO of Safeway, now one of the largest food and drug retailers in North America, in 1992. At the time, Safeway was operating approximately 1,100 stores, which occupied approximately 39 million square feet of retail space. Burd immediately slashed annual capital spending from $550 million to $290 million. He justified the decision as follows: "We had projects that were not returning the cost of money. So, we cut spending back, which made the very best projects come to the surface."

Safeway set a minimum 22.5% pretax return on investment in all new store and remodelling projects. In addition to opening new stores, Burd felt that the company should emphasize expanding existing stores that are in excellent locations so as to pump up sales. With its new approach to capital budgeting firmly in place, Safeway started to steadily increase its capital spending on both new stores and remodelling projects.

Eight years after implementing the new decision-making process, Safeway's 1,665 stores now occupy 70.8 million square feet of retail space. The company's capital budget approached $1.5 billion in 1999, when it opened 67 and remodelled 251 stores. It plans to spend another $1.6 billion to open 70 to 75 stores and remodel 250 others in 2000. Safeway's approach to capital budgeting projects relating to its stores has continued to result in strong returns on investment.

Safeway recently decided to make a significant investment in a different type of capital project. Analysts had been critical of the company's reluctance to enter the online marketplace, but during June 2000, the company announced that it was investing $30 million in GroceryWorks.com, an online grocer. Customers will be able to access the GroceryWorks.com online website via Safeway's home page (www.safeway.com). Safeway's management stressed that they had felt the need to complete a comprehensive analysis of any project of this nature before proceeding. Given the problems that have plagued Peapod.com and Webvan, two major online grocers, Safeway's diligent approach to its decision-making process is being praised.

Sources: Safeway, Inc., website, August 2000; Jessica Materna, "Safeway Rolls into the Web through Online Deliverer," *San Francisco Business Times*, June 23, 2000, p. 26 © *San Francisco Business Times*. Reprinted with the permission of the *San Francisco Business Times*. Robert Berner, "Safeway's Resurgence Is Built on Attention to Detail," *The Wall Street Journal*, October 2, 1998, p. B4.

## Learning Objectives

*After studying Chapter 13, you should be able to:*

**LO1** Determine the acceptability of an investment project using the net present value method.

**LO2** Prepare a net present value analysis of two competing investment projects using either the incremental-cost approach or the total-cost approach.

**LO3** Rank investment projects in order of preference using the profitability index.

**LO4** Compute the internal rate of return of a project and determine its acceptability using the internal rate of return method.

**LO5** Compute the payback period of an investment.

**LO6** Compute the simple rate of return of an investment.

**LO7** (Appendix 13A) Explain the concept of present value and prepare present value computations.

**LO8** (Appendix 13C) Explain the concept of inflation and understand its implications for capital budgeting.

**LO9** (Appendix 13D) Understand the impact of the tax deductibility of depreciation expense on the cash flows of a project.

**LO10** (Appendix 13D) Compute the capital cost allowance of depreciable assets used for a project and incorporate the computations into a net present value analysis of the project.

The term **capital budgeting** is used to describe how managers plan significant outlays on projects that have long-term implications, such as the purchase of new equipment and the introduction of new products. Most companies have many more potential projects than can actually be funded. Hence, managers must carefully select those projects that promise the greatest future return. How well managers make these capital budgeting decisions is a critical factor in the long-term profitability of the company.

Capital budgeting involves *investment*—a company must commit funds now in order to receive a return in the future. Investments are not limited to shares and bonds. Purchase of inventory or equipment is also an investment. For example, Tri-Con Global Restaurants Inc. makes an investment when it opens a new Pizza Hut restaurant. Mountain Equipment Co-op makes an investment when it installs a new computer to handle customer billing. DaimlerChrysler makes an investment when it redesigns a product, such as the Jeep Eagle, and must retool its production lines. Merck & Co. invests in medical research. Amazon.com makes an investment when it redesigns its website. All of these investments are characterized by a commitment of funds today in the expectation of receiving a return in the future in the form of additional cash inflows or reduced cash outflows.

# Capital Budgeting—Planning Investments

## Typical Capital Budgeting Decisions

The types of business decisions that require capital budgeting analysis are virtually any decisions that involve an outlay now in order to obtain some return (increase in revenue or reduction in costs) in the future. Typical capital budgeting decisions include:

1. Cost reduction decisions: Should new equipment be purchased to reduce costs?
2. Expansion decisions: Should a new plant, warehouse, or other facility be acquired to increase capacity and sales?
3. Equipment selection decisions: Which of several available machines would be the most cost effective to purchase?
4. Lease-or-buy decisions: Should new equipment be leased or purchased?
5. Equipment replacement decisions: Should old equipment be replaced now or later?

*in business today*     **The Yukon Goes Online**

Canada's Yukon Territory, which is two-thirds the size of Texas, has only 31,000 residents. Two-thirds of those live in Whitehorse, the territory's capital. All are about to get higher-speed Internet access as part of an ambitious Canadian government program to connect the Yukon with the rest of the world. To date, the Yukon's physical isolation has precluded economic growth in the area. The Internet may change all that. In some ways, it already has. A variety of organizations in the Yukon have made significant outlays on Internet projects that will have long-term implications.

After struggling to stay in business with annual sales of only $10,000, Herbie Croteau, the founder of Midnight Sun Plant Food, spent $1,600 to build a website for the company (www.midnightsunplantfood.com). Just two years later, sales are expected to exceed $65,000. Croteau is in the process of spending another $2,000 to redesign the company's website.

The town of Haines Junction is spending $10,000 to redesign its website. The town's chief administrative officer estimates that printing costs for tourist brochures will drop by 75%, since tourist information can now be obtained online at www.yukon.com/community/kluane/hj.html.

Four years ago, Roland and Susan Shaver started Bear North Adventures to provide guided snowmobile tours. To date, their biggest investment (other than for snowmobiles) has been the $2,000 they spent to create a website packed with photos at www.bearnorth.yukon.net.

Source: David H. Freedman, "Cold Comfort," *Forbes ASAP*, May 29, 2000, pp. 174–182.

---

Capital budgeting decisions tend to fall into two broad categories—*screening decisions* and *preference decisions*. **Screening decisions** are those relating to whether a proposed project meets some preset standard of acceptance. For example, a firm may have a policy of accepting projects only if they promise a return of, say, 20% on the investment. The required rate of return is the minimum rate of return a project must yield to be acceptable.

**Preference decisions,** by contrast, relate to selecting from among several *competing* courses of action. To illustrate, a firm may be considering several different machines to replace an existing machine on the assembly line. The choice of which machine to purchase is a *preference* decision.

In this chapter, we initially discuss ways of making screening decisions. Preference decisions are discussed toward the end of the chapter.

## The Time Value of Money

As stated earlier, business investments commonly involve returns that extend over fairly long periods of time. Therefore, in approaching capital budgeting decisions, it is necessary to employ techniques that recognize the *time value of money*. A dollar today is worth more than a dollar a year from now. The same concept applies in choosing between investment projects. Those projects that promise returns earlier in time are preferable to those that promise returns later in time.

The capital budgeting techniques that recognize the above two characteristics of business investments most fully are those that involve *discounted cash flows*. We will spend most of this chapter illustrating the use of discounted cash flow methods in making capital budgeting decisions. If you are not already familiar with discounting and the use of present value tables, you should read Appendix 13A, The Concept of Present Value, at the end of this chapter before proceeding any further.

Several approaches can be used to evaluate investments using discounted cash flows. The easiest method to use is the *net present value method*, which is the subject of the next several sections.

## The Net Present Value Method

Under the net present value method, the present value of a project's cash inflows is compared with the present value of the project's cash outflows. The difference between the present value of these cash flows, called the **net present value,** determines whether or not the project is an acceptable investment. To illustrate, let us assume the following data:

**Learning Objective 1**
Determine the acceptability of an investment project using the net present value method.

**EXAMPLE A**
Harper Company is contemplating the purchase of a machine capable of performing certain operations that are now performed manually. The machine will cost $5,000, and it will last for five years. At the end of the five-year period, the machine will have a zero scrap value.

Use of the machine will reduce labour costs by $1,800 per year. Harper Company requires a minimum return of 20% before taxes on all investment projects.[1]

Should the machine be purchased? Harper Company must determine whether a cash investment now of $5,000 can be justified if it will result in an $1,800 reduction in cost each year over the next five years. It may appear that the answer is obvious, since the total cost savings is $9,000 (5 × $1,800). However, the company can earn a 20% return by investing its money elsewhere. It is not enough that the cost reductions cover just the original cost of the machine; they must also yield at least a 20% return, or the company would be better off investing the money elsewhere.

To determine whether the investment is desirable, the stream of annual $1,800 cost savings is discounted to its present value and then compared with the cost of the new machine. Since Harper Company requires a minimum return of 20% on all investment projects, this rate is used in the discounting process. Exhibit 13–1 shows how this analysis is done.

According to the analysis, Harper Company should purchase the new machine. The present value of the cost savings is $5,384, as compared with a present value of only $5,000 for the investment required (cost of the machine). Deducting the present value of the investment required from the present value of the cost savings gives a *net present value* of $384. Whenever the net present value is zero or greater, as in our example, an investment project is acceptable. Whenever the net present value is negative (the present value of the cash outflows exceeds the present value of the cash inflows), an investment project is not acceptable. In sum:

| If the Net Present Value Is ... | Then the Project Is ... |
|---|---|
| Positive ............. | Acceptable, since it promises a return greater than the required rate of return. |
| Zero ............... | Acceptable, since it promises a return equal to the required rate of return. |
| Negative ........... | Not acceptable, since it promises a return less than the required rate of return. |

A full interpretation of the solution would be as follows: The new machine promises more than the required 20% rate of return. This is evident from the positive net present value of $384. Harper Company could spend up to $5,384 for the new machine and still obtain the minimum required 20% rate of return. The net present value of $384, therefore, shows the amount of "cushion" or "margin of error." One way to look at this is that the company could underestimate the cost of the new machine by up to $384 or overestimate

**Exhibit 13–1**
Net Present Value Analysis of a Proposed Project

| | |
|---|---|
| Initial cost ......................... | $5,000 |
| Life of the project (years) ............. | 5 |
| Annual cost savings ................. | $1,800 |
| Salvage value ...................... | –0– |
| Required rate of return ............... | 20% |

| Item | Year(s) | Amount of Cash Flow | 20% Factor | Present Value of Cash Flows |
|---|---|---|---|---|
| Annual cost savings .... | 1–5 | $ 1,800 | 2.991* | $5,384 |
| Initial investment ...... | Now | (5,000) | 1.000 | (5,000) |
| Net present value ...... | | | | $ 384 |

*From Table 13B–4 in Appendix 13B at the end of this chapter.

[1]For simplicity, we ignore taxes and inflation.

the net present value of the future cash savings by up to $384, and the project would still be financially attractive.

## Emphasis on Cash Flows

In capital budgeting decisions, the focus is on cash flows and not on accounting net income. The reason is that accounting net income is based on accrual concepts that ignore the timing of cash flows into and out of an organization. From a capital budgeting standpoint, the timing of cash flows is important, since a dollar received today is more valuable than a dollar received in the future. Therefore, even though the accounting net income figure is useful for many things, it is not ordinarily used in discounted cash flow analysis.[2] However, accounting net income can, in some situations, be the starting point for determining the cash flows of a project. In these cases, the manager must make appropriate adjustments to net income (like adding back depreciation) to arrive at the project's cash flows. We will not consider this approach further in this chapter.

What kinds of cash flows should the manager look for? Although they will vary from project to project, certain types of cash flows tend to recur, as explained in the following paragraphs.

**TYPICAL CASH OUTFLOWS**   Most projects will have an immediate cash outflow in the form of an initial investment in equipment or other assets. In addition, some projects require that a company expand its working capital. **Working capital** is current assets (cash, accounts receivable, and inventory) less current liabilities. When a company takes on a new project, the balances in the current asset accounts will often increase. For example, opening a new Ikea store would require additional cash in sales registers, increased accounts receivable for new customers, and more inventory to stock the shelves. These additional working capital needs should be treated as part of the initial investment in a project. Also, many projects require periodic outlays for repairs and maintenance and for additional operating costs. These should all be treated as cash outflows for capital budgeting purposes.

**TYPICAL CASH INFLOWS**   On the cash inflow side, a project will normally either increase revenues or reduce costs. Either way, the amount involved should be treated as a cash inflow for capital budgeting purposes. *A reduction in costs is equivalent to an increase in revenues.* Cash inflows are also frequently realized from salvage of equipment. This can occur at the start of a project when old equipment is replaced and at the end of a project when equipment is sold. In addition, any working capital that was tied up in the project can be released for use elsewhere at the end of the project and should be treated as a cash inflow. Working capital is released, for example, when a company sells off its inventory or collects its receivables.

In summary, the following types of cash flows are common in business investment projects:

Cash outflows:
    Initial investment (including installation costs).
    Increased working capital needs.
    Repairs and maintenance.
    Incremental operating costs.
Cash inflows:
    Incremental revenues.
    Reduction in costs.
    Salvage value.
    Release of working capital.

---

[2]Under certain conditions, capital budgeting decisions can be correctly made by discounting appropriately defined accounting net income. However, this approach requires advanced techniques that are beyond the scope of this book.

## Simplifying Assumptions

There are a number of assumptions that underlie our treatment of the net present value method.

**TIMING OF CASH FLOWS**   The first assumption is that at all cash flows occur at the end of the period. Typically cash flows will occur throughout a period but our assumption will make calculations easier.

**REINVESTMENT OF CASH INFLOWS**   The second assumption is that all surplus cash inflows generated by the project are immediately reinvested at a rate of return equal to the discount rate, until the end of the project. Without this assumption, (say, if the cash flows from a project are simply kept locked up in a safe until the project ends) the net present value will not be accurate.

**PROJECTS ARE CARBON COPIES OF THE FIRM**   The third assumption is that the risk of investing in a project is identical to the risk you would face if you bought the company outright—that is, if you purchased all of the outstanding securities of the company. This means that projects are basically clones of the company in so far as risk is concerned. This assumption is very important to the choice of the discount rate in net present value analysis and to the procedure for handling financing-related cash flows. This is explained below.

**TREATMENT OF INFLATION**   Although somewhat unrealistic, we will assume that there is no inflation. When inflation exists, it will be necessary to either adjust the cash flows or the discount rate. A brief discussion of these adjustments is provided in Appendix 13C.

**INCOME TAXES**   Net present value method usually considers cash flows only on an *after-tax* basis. This, in turn, requires that we use an after tax discount rate and that we focus on after-tax cash flows. The effect of income taxes on revenues and costs should be fully reflected in the analysis. This includes taking into account the tax deductibility of depreciation. Depreciation is itself not a cash flow, but it is treated as an expense when calculating income taxes and hence results in tax savings. These tax savings—called tax shields—are cash inflows and must be treated as such in any net present value analysis involving depreciable property. In Canada, a complex set of rules governs the calculation of depreciation for tax purposes. The amount allowed as a deduction is called the *capital cost allowance* (CCA). These rules as well as the techniques for calculating CCA, after-tax discount rates and after-tax cash flows are discussed briefly in Appendix 13D. A more complete treatment can be found in advanced texts on Corporate Finance.

*in business today*  **A Return on Investment of 100%**

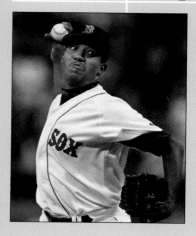

During negotiations to build a replacement for the old Fenway Park in Boston, the Red Sox offered the city approximately $2 million per year over 30 years in exchange for an investment of $150 million by the city for land acquisition and cleanup. In May 2000, after denying his lack of support for the project, Boston Mayor Thomas M. Menino stated that his goal is a 100% rate of return on any investment that is made by the city. Some doubt that the Red Sox would be able to pay players' salaries if the team were required to meet the mayor's goal. The mayor has countered with a list of suggestions for raising private funds (such as selling shares to the public, as the Celtics did in 1986). Private funds would reduce the investment that would need to be made by the city and, as a result, reduce the future payments made to the city by the Red Sox. Negotiations continue.

Source: Meg Vaillancourt, "Boston Mayor Wants High Return on Investment in New Ballpark," *Knight-Ridder/Tribune Business News*, May 11, 2000, pITEM00133018. Reprinted with permission of Knight Ridder/Tribune Information Services.

## Choosing a Discount Rate

The discount rate should be the company's minimum required rate of return. A positive net present value means that the project's return exceeds the minimum required rate of return. A negative net present value means that the project's return is less than the minimum required rate of return.

What is a company's minimum required rate of return? The company's *cost of capital* is usually regarded as the minimum required rate of return. The **cost of capital** is the average rate of return the company must pay to its long-term creditors and to shareholders for the use of their funds. The cost of capital is the minimum required rate of return because if a project's rate of return is less than the cost of capital, the company does not earn enough of a return to compensate its creditors and shareholders. Therefore, any project with a rate of return less than the cost of capital should not be accepted.

The cost of capital serves as a *screening device* in net present value analysis. When the cost of capital is used as the discount rate, any project with a negative net present value does not cover the company's cost of capital and therefore should be discarded as unacceptable.

## Financing-Related Cash Flows

A common source of confusion for students is how to handle cash inflows from borrowing and cash outflows for making interest payments and principal repayments. Given our simplifying assumptions and our choice of the company's cost of capital for the discount rate, the rule is very simple: *ignore all financing-related cash flows*. The impact on the project of the financing decisions made to fund the project is captured in the company's cost of capital—the discount rate. More advanced discussions of this topic will consider specific cases where our simple rule requires modification. For our purposes, this rule will suffice.

---

### Negotiator for the Red Sox

*decision* | *maker*

As stated above, Boston Mayor Thomas M. Menino's goal is a 100% rate of return on any investment that is made by the city to build a new park for the Red Sox. How would you respond to the mayor?

---

## An Extended Example of the Net Present Value Method

To conclude our discussion of the net present value method, we present below an extended example of how it is used to analyze an investment proposal. This example will also help tie together (and to reinforce) many of the ideas developed thus far.

**EXAMPLE B**

Under a special licensing arrangement, Swinyard Company has an opportunity to market a new product in the western Canada for a five-year period. The product would be purchased from the manufacturer, with Swinyard Company responsible for all costs of promotion and distribution. The licensing arrangement could be renewed at the end of the five-year period at the option of the manufacturer. After careful study, Swinyard Company has estimated the following costs and revenues for the new product:

| | |
|---|---|
| Cost of equipment needed . . . . . . . . . . . . . . . . . . . . . . . . . . . . . . . . . . . . . . . | $ 60,000 |
| Working capital needed . . . . . . . . . . . . . . . . . . . . . . . . . . . . . . . . . . . . . . . | 100,000 |
| Overhaul of the equipment in four years . . . . . . . . . . . . . . . . . . | 5,000 |
| Salvage value of the equipment in five years . . . . . . . . . . . . . . . . | 10,000 |
| Annual revenues and costs: | |
| Sales revenues . . . . . . . . . . . . . . . . . . . . . . . . . . . . . . . . . . . . . | 200,000 |
| Cost of goods sold (cash) . . . . . . . . . . . . . . . . . . . . . . . . . . . . | 125,000 |
| Out-of-pocket operating costs (for salaries, advertising, and other direct costs) . . . . . . . . . . . . . . . . . . . . . | 35,000 |

## Exhibit 13–2

The Net Present Value Method—An Extended Example

| | |
|---|---:|
| Sales revenues (cash) .......................................... | $200,000 |
| Less cost of goods sold (cash) ................................ | 125,000 |
| Less out-of-pocket costs for salaries, advertising, etc. ............ | 35,000 |
| Annual net cash inflows ..................................... | $ 40,000 |

| Item | Year(s) | Amount of Cash Flows | 20% Factor | Present Value of Cash Flows |
|---|---|---:|---|---:|
| Purchase of equipment ................ | Now | $ (60,000) | 1.000 | $ (60,000) |
| Working capital needed ................ | Now | (100,000) | 1.000 | (100,000) |
| Overhaul of equipment ................ | 4 | (5,000) | 0.482* | (2,410) |
| Annual net cash inflows from | | | | |
|   sales of the product line ............. | 1–5 | 40,000 | 2.991† | 119,640 |
| Salvage value of the equipment ......... | 5 | 10,000 | 0.402* | 4,020 |
| Working capital released .............. | 5 | 100,000 | 0.402* | 40,200 |
| Net present value .................... | | | | $ 1,450 |

*From Table 13B–3 in Appendix 13B.
†From Table 13B–4 in Appendix 13B.

At the end of the five-year period, the working capital would be released for investment elsewhere if the manufacturer decided not to renew the licensing arrangement. Swinyard Company's discount rate and cost of capital is 20%. Would you recommend that the new product be introduced?

This example involves a variety of cash inflows and cash outflows. The solution is given in Exhibit 13–2.

Note particularly how the working capital is handled in this exhibit. It is counted as a cash outflow at the beginning of the project and as a cash inflow when it is released at the end of the project. Also note how the sales revenues, cost of goods sold, and out-of-pocket costs are handled. **Out-of-pocket costs** are actual cash outlays for salaries, advertising, and other operating expenses. Cost of goods sold are also assumed to be cash costs. Depreciation involves no current cash outlay and hence is not considered here.

Since the overall net present value is positive, the new product should be added assuming the company has no better use for the investment funds.

# Expanding the Net Present Value Method

**Learning Objective 2**

Prepare a net present value analysis of two competing investment projects using either the incremental-cost approach or the total-cost approach.

So far, our examples have involved only a single investment alternative. We will now expand the net present value method to include two alternatives. Note that if all projects have a negative net present value *none* should be accepted. In addition, we will integrate the concept of relevant costs into the discounted cash flow analysis.

The net present value method can be used to compare competing investment projects in two ways. One is the *total-cost approach*, and the other is the *incremental-cost approach*. Each approach is illustrated below.

## The Total-Cost Approach

The total-cost approach is the most flexible method for comparing projects. To illustrate the mechanics of the approach, let us assume the following data:

**EXAMPLE C**

Don Ferry Company provides a ferry service across the Don River. One of its ferryboats is in poor condition. This ferry can be renovated at an immediate cost of $20,000. Further repairs and an overhaul of the motor will be needed five years from now at a cost of $8,000. In all, the ferry will be usable for 10 years if this work is done. At the end of 10 years, the ferry will have to be scrapped at a salvage value of approximately $6,000. The scrap value of the ferry right now is $7,000. It will cost $30,000 each year to operate the ferry, and revenues will total $40,000 annually.

As an alternative, Don Ferry Company can purchase a new ferryboat at a cost of $36,000. The new ferry will have a life of 10 years, but it will require some repairs at the end of 5 years. It is estimated that these repairs will amount to $3,000. At the end of 10 years, it is estimated that the ferry will have a scrap value of $6,000. It will cost $21,000 each year to operate the ferry, and revenues will total $40,000 annually.

Don Ferry Company requires a return of at least 18% before taxes on all investment projects.

Should the company purchase the new ferry or renovate the old ferry? Exhibit 13–3 gives the solution using the total-cost approach.

Two points should be noted from the exhibit. First, observe that *all* cash inflows and *all* cash outflows are included in the solution under each alternative. No effort has been made to isolate those cash flows that are relevant to the decision and those that are not relevant. The inclusion of all cash flows associated with each alternative gives the approach its name—the *total-cost* approach.

Second, note that a net present value figure is computed for each of the two alternatives. This is a distinct advantage of the total-cost approach in that an unlimited number

## Exhibit 13–3

The Total-Cost Approach to Project Selection

| | | | New Ferry | | Old Ferry |
|---|---|---|---|---|---|
| Annual revenues | | | $40,000 | | $40,000 |
| Annual cash operating costs | | | 21,000 | | 30,000 |
| Net annual cash inflows | | | $19,000 | | $10,000 |

| Item | Year(s) | Amount of Cash Flows | 18% Factor* | Present Value of Cash Flows |
|---|---|---|---|---|
| **Buy the new ferry:** | | | | |
| Initial investment | Now | $(36,000) | 1.000 | $(36,000) |
| Repairs in five years | 5 | (3,000) | 0.437 | (1,311) |
| Net annual cash inflows | 1–10 | 19,000 | 4.494 | 85,386 |
| Salvage of the old ferry | Now | 7,000 | 1.000 | 7,000 |
| Salvage of the new ferry | 10 | 6,000 | 0.191 | 1,146 |
| Net present value | | | | 56,221 |
| **Keep the old ferry:** | | | | |
| Initial repairs | Now | (20,000) | 1.000 | (20,000) |
| Repairs in five years | 5 | (8,000) | 0.437 | (3,496) |
| Net annual cash inflows | 1–10 | 10,000 | 4.494 | 44,940 |
| Salvage of the old ferry | 10 | 6,000 | 0.191 | 1,146 |
| Net present value | | | | 22,590 |
| Net present value in favour of buying the new ferry | | | | $ 33,631 |

*All factors are from Tables 13B–3 and 13B–4 in Appendix 13B.

of alternatives can be compared side by side to determine the best action. For example, another alternative for Don Ferry Company would be to get out of the ferry business entirely. If management desired, the net present value of this alternative could be computed to compare with the alternatives shown in Exhibit 13–3. Still other alternatives might be open to the company. Once management has determined the net present value of each alternative, it can select the course of action that promises to be the most profitable. In the case at hand, given only the two alternatives, the best alternative is to purchase the new ferry.[3]

## The Incremental-Cost Approach

When only two alternatives are being considered, the incremental-cost approach offers a simpler and more direct route to a decision. Unlike the total-cost approach, it focuses only on differential costs.[4] The procedure is to include in the discounted cash flow analysis only those costs and revenues that *differ* between the two alternatives being considered. To illustrate, refer again to the data in Example C relating to Don Ferry Company. The solution using only differential costs is presented in Exhibit 13–4.

Two things should be noted from the data in this exhibit. First, note that the net present value in favour of buying the new ferry of $33,631 shown in Exhibit 13–4 agrees with the net present value shown under the total-cost approach in Exhibit 13–3. This agreement should be expected, since the two approaches are just different roads to the same destination.

Second, note that the costs used in Exhibit 13–4 are just the differences between the costs shown for the two alternatives in the prior exhibit. For example, the $16,000 incremental investment required to purchase the new ferry in Exhibit 13–4 is the difference between the $36,000 cost of the new ferry and the $20,000 cost required to renovate the old ferry from Exhibit 13–3. The other figures in Exhibit 13–4 have been computed in the same way.

**Exhibit 13–4**

The Incremental-Cost Approach to Project Selection

| Item | Year(s) | Amount of Cash Flows | 18% Factor* | Present Value of Cash Flows |
|---|---|---|---|---|
| Incremental investment required to purchase the new ferry | Now | $(16,000) | 1.000 | $(16,000) |
| Repairs in five years avoided | 5 | 5,000 | 0.437 | 2,185 |
| Increased net annual cash inflows | 1–10 | 9,000 | 4.494 | 40,446 |
| Salvage of the old ferry | Now | 7,000 | 1.000 | 7,000 |
| Difference in salvage value in 10 years | 10 | –0– | — | –0– |
| Net present value in favour of buying the new ferry | | | | $ 33,631 |

*All factors are from Tables 13B–3 and 13B–4 in Appendix 13B.

[3]The alternative with the highest net present value is not always the best choice, although it is the best choice in this case. For further discussion, see the section Preference Decisions—The Ranking of Investment Projects.

[4]Technically, the incremental-cost approach is misnamed, since it focuses on differential costs (that is, on both cost increases and decreases), rather than just on incremental costs. As used here, the term *incremental costs* should be interpreted broadly to include both cost increases and cost decreases.

# Least-Cost Decisions

Revenues are not directly involved in some decisions. For example, a company that does not charge for delivery service may need to replace an old delivery truck, or a company may be trying to decide whether to lease or to buy its fleet of executive cars. In such situations, where no revenues are involved, the most desirable alternative will be the one that promises the *least total cost* from the present value perspective. Hence, these are known as least-cost decisions. To illustrate a least-cost decision, assume the following data:

**EXAMPLE D**

Val-Tek Company is considering the replacement of an old threading machine. A new threading machine is available that could substantially reduce annual operating costs. Selected data relating to the old and the new machines are presented below:

| | Old Machine | New Machine |
|---|---|---|
| Purchase cost when new . . . . . . . . . . . | $20,000 | $25,000 |
| Salvage value now . . . . . . . . . . . . . . | 3,000 | — |
| Annual cash operating costs . . . . . . . . | 15,000 | 9,000 |
| Overhaul needed immediately . . . . . . . | 4,000 | — |
| Salvage value in six years . . . . . . . . . | –0– | 5,000 |
| Remaining life . . . . . . . . . . . . . . . . . | 6 years | 6 years |

Val-Tek Company's cost of capital is 10%.

Exhibit 13–5 provides an analysis of the alternatives using the total-cost approach.

As shown in the exhibit, the new machine has the lowest total cost when the present value of the net cash outflows is considered. An analysis of the two alternatives using the incremental-cost approach is presented in Exhibit 13–6. As before, the data in this exhibit represent the differences between the alternatives as shown under the total-cost approach.

## Exhibit 13–5

The Total-Cost Approach (Least-Cost Decision)

| Item | Year(s) | Amount of Cash Flows | 10% Factor* | Present Value of Cash Flows |
|---|---|---|---|---|
| **Buy the new machine:** | | | | |
| Initial investment . . . . . . . . . . . . . . . . . . | Now | $(25,000) | 1.000 | $(25,000)† |
| Salvage of the old machine . . . . . . . . . . . | Now | 3,000 | 1.000 | 3,000† |
| Annual cash operating costs . . . . . . . . . . | 1–6 | (9,000) | 4.355 | (39,195) |
| Salvage of the new machine . . . . . . . . . . | 6 | 5,000 | 0.564 | 2,820 |
| Present value of net cash outflows . . . . . | | | | (58,375) |
| **Keep the old machine:** | | | | |
| Overhaul needed now . . . . . . . . . . . . . . . | Now | (4,000) | 1.000 | (4,000) |
| Annual cash operating costs . . . . . . . . . . | 1–6 | (15,000) | 4.355 | (65,325) |
| Present value of net cash outflows . . . . . | | | | (69,325) |
| Net present value in favour of buying the new machine . . . . . . . . . . . . . | | | | $ 10,950 |

*All factors are from Tables 13B–3 and 13B–4 in Appendix 13B.
†These two items could be netted into a single $22,000 incremental-cost figure ($25,000 − $3,000 = $22,000).

## Exhibit 13–6
The Incremental-Cost Approach (Least-Cost Decision)

| Item | Year(s) | Amount of Cash Flows | 10% Factor* | Present Value of Cash Flows |
|---|---|---|---|---|
| Incremental investment required to purchase the new machine ........... | Now | $(21,000) | 1.000 | $(21,000)† |
| Salvage of the old machine ............. | Now | 3,000 | 1.000 | 3,000† |
| Savings in annual cash operating costs .... | 1–6 | 6,000 | 4.355 | 26,130 |
| Difference in salvage value in six years ... | 6 | 5,000 | 0.564 | 2,820 |
| Net present value in favour of buying the new machine ................... | | | | $ 10,950 |

*All factors are from Tables 13B–3 and 13B–4 in Appendix 13B.
†These two items could be netted into a single $18,000 incremental-cost figure ($21,000 − $3,000 = $18,000).

# Preference Decisions—The Ranking of Investment Projects

**Learning Objective 3**
Rank investment projects in order of preference using the profitability index.

Recall that when considering investment opportunities, managers must make two types of decisions—screening decisions and preference decisions. Screening decisions pertain to whether or not some proposed investment is acceptable. Preference decisions come *after* screening decisions and attempt to answer the following question: How do the remaining investment proposals, all of which have been screened and provide an acceptable rate of return, rank in terms of preference? That is, which one(s) would be *best* for the firm to accept?

Preference decisions are more difficult to make than screening decisions because investment funds are usually limited. This often requires that some (perhaps many) otherwise very profitable investment opportunities must be passed up.

Sometimes, preference decisions are called rationing decisions or ranking decisions because they ration limited investment funds among many competing alternatives, or there may be many alternatives that must be ranked.

If the net present value method is used to rank projects, the net present value of one project cannot be compared directly with the net present value of another project unless the investments in the projects are of equal size. For example, assume that a company is considering two competing investments, as shown below:

| | Investment | |
|---|---|---|
| | A | B |
| Investment required ............ | $(80,000) | $(5,000) |
| Present value of cash inflows ..... | 81,000 | 6,000 |
| Net present value ............. | $ 1,000 | $ 1,000 |

Each project has a net present value of $1,000, but the projects are not equally desirable. The project requiring an investment of only $5,000 is much more desirable when funds are limited than the project requiring an investment of $80,000. To compare the two projects on a valid basis, the present value of the cash inflows should be divided by the investment required. The result is called the **profitability index.** The formula for the profitability index follows:

$$\text{Profitability index} = \frac{\text{Present value of cash inflows}}{\text{Investment required}} \tag{1}$$

The profitability indexes for the two investments above would be computed as follows:

|  | Investment | |
| --- | :---: | :---: |
|  | **A** | **B** |
| Present value of cash inflows (a) ....... | $81,000 | $6,000 |
| Investment required (b) ............. | $80,000 | $5,000 |
| Profitability index, (a) ÷ (b) ......... | 1.01 | 1.20 |

When using the profitability index to rank competing investment projects, the preference rule is: *The higher the profitability index, the more desirable is the project.* Applying this rule to the two investments above, investment B should be chosen over investment A.

The profitability index is an application of the techniques for utilizing scarce resources. In this case, the scarce resource is the limited funds available for investment, and the profitability index is similar to the contribution margin per unit of the scarce resource.

A few details should be clarified with respect to the computation of the profitability index. The "Investment required" refers to any cash outflows that occur at the beginning of the project, reduced by any salvage value recovered from the sale of old equipment. The "Investment required" also includes any investment in working capital that the project may need. Finally, we should note that the "Present value of cash inflows" is net of all *out*flows that occur after the project starts.

## Net Present Value and the Kyoto Accord

*in business today*

Since the ratification of the Kyoto Accord by Canada, the amount of risk and uncertainty has many investors and insiders wondering about the future of many oilsands projects, particularly in Alberta. Under the protocol, Canada is expected to reduce greenhouse emissions to "six percent below 1990 levels" by the year 2012 despite the fact that the economy boomed when emissions levels rose throughout the 1990s. A substantial amount of the economic growth stemmed from northern Alberta's oilsands. In a report issued by New York–based Lehman Brothers, many oilsands projects bear the largest amount of reduction in emissions levels, since a huge amount of energy is consumed during the production process. In addition, the share prices of many companies, such as EnCana Corp., Nexen Inc., and Canadian Natural Resources Ltd., are facing the most risk. Lehman estimates that Nexen's $2.5 billion Long Lake oilsands project may face a reduction of estimated net present value by $25 million. Likewise, Canadian Natural Resources can also face a reduction of its estimated net present value by $79 million for its Horizon oilsands project.

Source: "Lehman Brothers Warns Kyoto Could Have Negative Impact on Oilsands Stocks," *Canadian Press Newswire*, December 18, 2002. Reprinted with permission from Press News Limited, a division of The Canadian Press.

# The Internal Rate of Return Method

The **internal rate of return** of a project is defined as the discount rate that makes the net present value of the project equal zero. The internal rate of return is sometimes referred to as the *yield* of the project. It is interpreted as the rate of return promised by the project over the project's useful life. We will consider three aspects of the internal rate of return: (1) its calculation, (2) its interpretation, and (3) its usefulness for decision making about projects as compared with the net present value rule.

**Learning Objective 4**
Compute the internal rate of return of a project and determine its acceptability using the internal rate of return method.

## Calculating the Internal Rate of Return of a Project

To illustrate the calculation of the internal rate of return assume the following data:

**EXAMPLE E**

Chantal Enterprises is planning to add a new line of clothes for sale through its retail outlets during the summer. The cost of the clothing will be $142,514. The net cash inflow from the sale of these clothes at the end of one year following the purchase is forecast at $149,700. Determine the internal rate of return of this project.

The internal rate of return is the discount rate which will make the project's net present value equal 0. To calculate it, we use the following steps:

(A) Set up the net present value calculation using the internal rate of return as the discount rate.
(B) Set the net present value equal to 0.
(C) Solve for the internal rate of return.

Step A:

$$NPV = -\$142,514 + \frac{\$149,700}{(1 + IRR)}$$

Step B:

$$0 = -\$142,514 + \frac{\$149,700}{(1 + IRR)}$$

Step C:

$$0 = -\$142,514 + \frac{\$149,700}{(1 + IRR)}$$

$$\$142,514 = \frac{\$149,700}{(1 + IRR)}$$

$$\$142,514 \times (1 + IRR) = \$149,700$$

$$1 + IRR = \frac{\$149,700}{\$142,514}$$

$$IRR = 1.0504 - 1 = 0.0504$$

It was simple to solve for the internal rate of return here because the project had a single cash flow occurring in the first year. You can also estimate the internal rate of return using the present value tables in Appendix 13B as follows: Calculate the present value factor $1/(1+IRR)$, and use the present value table in Appendix 13B–3 to determine the rate of return it represents. The present value factor is,

$$PV\ factor = \frac{1}{(1 + IRR)} = \frac{\$142,514}{\$149,700} = 0.952\ (rounded)$$

Use the 1-period line in the table in Exhibit 13B–3 because the cash flow occurs in period 1. Locate 0.952 (or the number closest to it). In our example, 0.952 occurs in the 1-period line under the 5% column. Therefore, we can conclude that the internal rate of return is approximately 5%.

The above was a very simple example to illustrate the principle underlying the calculation of the internal rate of return. The table method will provide a rough estimate, within 1%, of the internal rate of return and will only work for single cash flows or for annuities.[5] In practice, a project can last for several years, and have nonconstant cash flows. This makes the *mathematics* (step C) of the calculation complex, but steps A and B will stay the same. Practitioners use computer programs or spreadsheets to complete step C. To illustrate this, consider the next example.

---

[5]If the single cash flow occurs in year n, the present value factor is written as $1/(1+IRR)^n$. Locate the present value factor in the n-period line of Exhibit 13B–3 to find the rate of return. When cash flows are an annuity, calculate the annuity factor as follows:

Annuity factor = investment required ÷ net annual cash inflow

Then you would consult Exhibit 13B–4. If the number of periods is 5, you would look in the 5-period line for the annuity factor you calculated to see what rate of return it represents.

✓ **EXAMPLE F**

Rivers Company is considering a project for upgrading its wharves. The project cost is estimated at $2.1 million. The annual savings in maintenance costs and revenue from increased barge traffic is projected as follows:

| Year | 1 | 2 | 3 | 4 | 5 |
|---|---|---|---|---|---|
| Cash Flow | $490,000 | $445,000 | $476,000 | $510,000 | $435,000 |

The wharves will require further upgrading after five years, therefore management is interested in determining if the projected cash flows during the upcoming five-year period are sufficient to warrant proceeding with the proposed upgrade. Determine the internal rate of return of the project.

Step A:

$$NPV = -\$2,100,000 + \frac{\$490,000}{(1+IRR)} + \frac{\$445,000}{(1+IRR)^2} + \frac{\$476,000}{(1+IRR)^3} + \frac{\$510,000}{(1+IRR)^4} + \frac{\$435,000}{(1+IRR)^5}$$

Step B:

$$0 = -\$2,100,000 + \frac{\$490,000}{(1+IRR)} + \frac{\$445,000}{(1+IRR)^2} + \frac{\$476,000}{(1+IRR)^3} + \frac{\$510,000}{(1+IRR)^4} + \frac{\$435,000}{(1+IRR)^5}$$

Step C:
Use a spreadsheet program, such as Microsoft Excel. The screenshot below shows the answer.

| | A | B | C | D | E | F | G |
|---|---|---|---|---|---|---|---|
| 1 | | | | Rivers Company | | | |
| 2 | | | IRR Calculation for the Wharf Upgrading Project | | | | |
| 3 | | | | | | | |
| 4 | Year | 0 | 1 | 2 | 3 | 4 | 5 |
| 5 | Cash flow | -2,100,000 | $490,000 | $445,000 | $476,000 | $510,000 | $435,000 |
| 6 | | | | | | | |
| 7 | IRR | 3.9869% | | | | | |
| 8 | | | | | | | |

We used the formula = IRR(B5:G5, 0) in cell B7 to compute the internal rate of return. The syntax of the formula is

= IRR (*cell range for the cash flows, initial guess value for IRR*)

We used a value of 0 for the initial guess. The default is 0.1. The internal rate of return is 3.9869%.

## Interpretation and Use of the Internal Rate of Return

The project's internal rate of return is the rate of return "promised" by the cash flows of the project. If the wharf project at Rivers Company provides the cash flows that have been forecast for each year *and*, if each cash flow is immediately reinvested at the rate of 3.9869% per year, then the net present value of the project at a discount rate of 3.9869% will be equal to 0.

The above does not tell you how the internal rate of return can be used to decide if a project is worthwhile. For example, should Rivers Company go ahead with the wharf upgrade? To use the internal rate of return to decide whether to accept or reject a project, the internal rate of return must be compared with the company's cost of capital. The cost of capital will play the role of a *hurdle rate*. The logic behind this is that if the project cannot yield at least the cost of the funds tied up in it, it will not be profitable. The decision rule using the internal rate of return can be stated as follows: "If the internal rate of return is *equal* to or *greater* than the cost of capital, the project should be accepted. If the internal rate of return is *less* than the cost of capital, the project should be rejected."

Suppose the cost of the capital for the wharf project is 5%. Since the internal rate of return of 3.9869% is *less* than the hurdle rate of 5%, Rivers Company will reject the project.

The idea that a project should earn a rate of return greater than the cost of capital to be acceptable is very appealing. This is the basic principle of the internal rate of return method. But the complexity behind the calculation of the internal rate of return can make it appear mysterious. Note that the cost of capital in the internal rate of return method is the hurdle rate. In the net present value method, the cost of capital is the *discount rate*.

## Comparison of the Internal Rate of Return and the Net Present Value Methods

There are two issues to consider when comparing the internal rate of return and the net present value methods. The internal rate of return method assumes that the cash flows of the project are reinvested, when received, *at a rate equal to the internal rate of return*. This is a difficult assumption to satisfy, in practice, especially when the internal rate of return is large. The reason is that when cash flows are received, it is unlikely that the firm has other investment opportunities that can provide a rate of return as high as the internal rate of return. It is more reasonable to expect that the firm will have access to projects that will provide a rate of return equalling the opportunity cost of capital. For example, the cash flows can be used to pay off creditors or redeem shares. Such a move will yield a return equal to the opportunity cost of capital. In the net present value method, this is precisely the assumption made, namely, that the cash flows are reinvested at the firm's cost of capital. This makes the net present value method more attractive.

The second issue has to do with the question that many managers ask about the two methods: "Will the two methods provide an identical signal about whether projects should be accepted or rejected?" The answer here is that the net present value will always provide the correct signal regarding acceptance or rejection of project. The internal rate of return method *can in certain situations* provide the wrong signal. A complete explanation of this point cannot be given here, but the bottom line can be stated simply as, "you can always trust the signal provided by the project's net present value." For this reason, if you are going to use only one method, it is better to stick to the net present value method.

# Other Approaches to Capital Budgeting Decisions

The net present value and internal rate of return methods have gained widespread acceptance as decision-making tools. Other methods of making capital budgeting decisions are also used, however, and are preferred by some managers. In this section, we discuss two such methods known as *payback* and *simple rate of return*. Both methods have been in use for many years but have been declining in popularity as primary tools for project evaluation.

## The Payback Method

**Learning Objective 5**
Compute the payback period for an investment.

The payback method focuses on the *payback period*. The **payback period** is the length of time that it takes for a project to recoup its initial cost out of the cash receipts that it generates. This period is sometimes referred to as "the time that it takes for an investment to pay for itself." The basic premise of the payback method is that the more quickly the cost of an investment can be recovered, the more desirable is the investment.

The payback period is expressed in years. *When the net annual cash inflow is the same every year*, the following formula can be used to compute the payback period:

$$\text{Payback period} = \frac{\text{Investment required}}{\text{Net annual cash inflow*}} \tag{2}$$

*If new equipment is replacing old equipment, this becomes incremental net annual cash inflow.

To illustrate the payback method, assume the following data:

EXAMPLE G

York Company needs a new milling machine. The company is considering two machines: machine A and machine B. Machine A costs $15,000 and will reduce operating costs by $5,000 per year. Machine B costs only $12,000 but will also reduce operating costs by $5,000 per year.

*Required:*
Which machine should be purchased according to the payback method?

$$\text{Machine A payback period} = \frac{\$15,000}{\$5,000} = 3.0 \text{ years}$$

$$\text{Machine B payback period} = \frac{\$12,000}{\$5,000} = 2.4 \text{ years}$$

According to the payback calculations, York Company should purchase machine B, since it has a shorter payback period than machine A.

## Payback and Uneven Cash Flows

When the cash flows associated with an investment project change from year to year, the simple payback formula that we just outlined is no longer usable, and the computations involved in deriving the payback period can be fairly complex. Consider the following data:

| Year | Investment | Cash Inflow |
|------|-----------|-------------|
| 1 | $4,000 | $1,000 |
| 2 | | –0– |
| 3 | | 2,000 |
| 4 | 2,000 | 1,000 |
| 5 | | 500 |
| 6 | | 3,000 |
| 7 | | 2,000 |
| 8 | | 2,000 |

What is the payback period on this investment? The answer is 5.5 years, but to obtain this figure, it is necessary to track the unrecovered investment year by year. The steps involved in this process are shown in Exhibit 13–7. By the middle of the sixth year, sufficient cash inflows will have been realized to recover the entire investment of $6,000 ($4,000 + $2,000).

| Year | (1)<br>Beginning<br>Unrecovered<br>Investment | (2)<br>Investment | (3)<br>Cash<br>Inflow | (4)<br>Ending<br>Unrecovered<br>Investment<br>(1) + (2) − (3) |
|------|------|------|------|------|
| 1 | $ 0 | $4,000 | $1,000 | $3,000 |
| 2 | 3,000 | | –0– | 3,000 |
| 3 | 3,000 | | 2,000 | 1,000 |
| 4 | 1,000 | 2,000 | 1,000 | 2,000 |
| 5 | 2,000 | | 500 | 1,500 |
| 6 | 1,500 | | 3,000 | –0– |
| 7 | –0– | | 2,000 | –0– |
| 8 | –0– | | 2,000 | –0– |

**Exhibit 13–7**
Payback and Uneven
Cash Flows

## An Extended Example of Payback

As shown by formula (2) given earlier, the payback period is computed by dividing the investment in a project by the net annual cash inflows that the project will generate. If new equipment is replacing old equipment, then any salvage to be received on disposal of the old equipment should be deducted from the cost of the new equipment, and only the *incremental* investment should be used in the payback computation. In addition, any depreciation deducted in arriving at the project's net income must be added back to obtain the project's expected net annual cash inflow. To illustrate, assume the following data:

**EXAMPLE H**

Goodtime Fun Centres Inc. operates many outlets in the eastern provinces. Some of the vending machines in one of its outlets provide very little revenue, and so the company is considering removing the machines and installing equipment to dispense soft ice cream. The equipment would cost $80,000 and have an eight-year useful life. Incremental annual revenues and costs associated with the sale of ice cream would be as follows:

| | |
|---|---:|
| Sales | $150,000 |
| Less cost of ingredients | 90,000 |
| Contribution margin | 60,000 |
| Less fixed expenses: | |
|    Salaries | 27,000 |
|    Maintenance | 3,000 |
|    Depreciation | 10,000 |
| Total fixed expenses | 40,000 |
| Net income | $ 20,000 |

The vending machines can be sold for a $5,000 scrap value. What is the payback period of the proposed project?

An analysis of the payback period of the proposed equipment is given in Exhibit 13–8. Several things should be noted from the data in this exhibit. First, note that depreciation is added back to net income to obtain the net annual cash inflow from the new equipment. As stated earlier in the chapter, depreciation is not a cash outlay; thus, it must be added back to net income to adjust net income to a cash basis. Second, note in the payback

**Exhibit 13–8**

Computation of the Payback Period

Step 1:　*Compute the net annual cash inflow.* Since the net annual cash inflow is not given, it must be computed before the payback period can be determined:

| | |
|---|---:|
| Net income (given above) | $20,000 |
| Add: Noncash deduction for depreciation | 10,000 |
| Net annual cash flow | $30,000 |

Step 2:　*Compute the payback period.* Using the net annual cash inflow figure from above, the payback period can be determined as follows:

| | |
|---|---:|
| Cost of the new equipment | $80,000 |
| Less salvage value of old equipment | 5,000 |
| Investment required | $75,000 |

$$\text{Payback period} = \frac{\text{Investment required}}{\text{Net annual cash inflow}}$$

$$= \frac{\$75,000}{\$30,000} = 2.5 \text{ years}$$

computation that the salvage value from the old machines has been deducted from the cost of the new equipment and that only the incremental investment has been used in computing the payback period.

The proposed equipment has a payback period of 2.5 years.

## Evaluation of the Payback Method

The payback period only tells a manager how long it will take for a project to recover its investment. It *does not say anything about a project's profitability*. It is possible for a project to have a shorter payback in comparison with another project *and* not be as profitable. There are three reasons for payback to potentially mislead a manager.

DIFFERENT USEFUL LIVES    Consider Example G on page 499. Machine B has a shorter payback period than machine A. This suggests that machine B is preferable. But the example did not provide any data on the useful lives of the machines. Suppose that machine A has a 10 year useful life, whereas machine B has a useful life of five years. Note that when the useful lives of alternative projects are different, simple comparisons of their net present value or payback period should not be made. Why? It will take two purchases of machine B to provide the same service as machine A. If a manager is going to only use a machine for five years, then the analysis should include the disposal value of machine A. On the other hand, if the manager intends to operate the machine for 10 years, then the analysis of machine B should include the cash flow from the second purchase of machine B in year 5. Clearly, an analysis which relies only on the payback period will miss these points.

TIME VALUE OF MONEY    The payback period weighs all cash flows equally, irrespective of the when the cash flows occur. But we know that cash flows received in an earlier time period are more valuable than those received in a later time period. This flaw in the payback period method can cause a manager to make a wrong decision. Consider the following simple example. Two alternative projects cost $8,000 each. The cash flows from these projects are shown below.

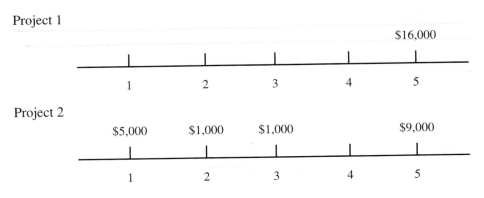

Both projects have a payback period of five years, but project 2 will return most of its cash flows earlier and is, thus, more desirable, a point that will be missed if one relies only on the payback period.

**CASH FLOWS BEYOND THE PAYBACK CUTOFF DATE**   Sometimes, managers specify that projects must meet a *cutoff* date criterion for the payback period for the project to be acceptable. Such a policy will throw out any project that fails to return its cost by the cutoff date. This can be dangerous, since the cash flows that occur beyond the cutoff date are never considered. Consider the following data:

Project 1

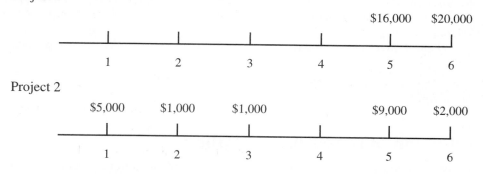

Project 2

Now, suppose that project 1 and 2 both have a cost of $7,000 and that management wants a payback period of four years or less. Project 2 which has a payback of three years will pass this test, but project 1 will fail the test and will be rejected. But a net present value analysis will take into consideration all of the cash flows of both projects. Such an analysis will show that project 1 is more profitable than project 2.

In a rapidly changing marketplace, it is not uncommon for managers to demand that projects have small payback periods because if the cash flows do not materialize in the first two years, they are highly unlikely to surface later. Textbook publishing is a good illustration of this idea. Publishers often tell authors that if a textbook is not adopted for use in its first two years after publishing, it is unlikely to find a market thereafter. This also explains why books undergo revision once every three or four years. Be careful. These instances do *not* justify the unquestioning use of the payback method. Note that when rapid payback is suggested, an assumption is made that cash flows beyond the cutoff date are unlikely to be obtained. Therefore, we hope that it is clear to you that the payback method will not always provide the proper signal for project acceptance or rejection and must be used very carefully.

# The Simple Rate of Return Method

**Learning Objective 6**
Compute the simple rate of return for an investment.

The **simple rate of return** method is another capital budgeting technique that does not involve discounted cash flows. The method is also known as the accounting rate of return, the unadjusted rate of return, and the financial statement method.

Unlike the other capital budgeting methods that we have discussed, the simple rate of return method does not focus on cash flows. Rather, it focuses on accounting net income. The approach is to estimate the revenues that will be generated by a proposed investment and then to deduct from these revenues all of the projected operating expenses associated with the project. This net income figure is then related to the initial investment in the project, as shown in the following formula:

$$\text{Simple rate of return} = \frac{\overset{\text{Incremental}}{\text{revenues}} - \overset{\text{Incremental expenses,}}{\text{including depreciation}}}{\text{Initial investment*}} = \overset{\text{Incremental}}{\text{net income}} \qquad (3)$$

*The investment should be reduced by any salvage from the sale of old equipment.

Or, if a cost reduction project is involved, formula (3) becomes:

$$\frac{\text{Simple rate}}{\text{of return}} = \frac{\begin{array}{c}\text{Cost} \\ \text{savings}\end{array} - \begin{array}{c}\text{Depreciation on} \\ \text{new equipment}\end{array}}{\text{Initial investment*}} \qquad (4)$$

*The investment should be reduced by any salvage
from the sale of old equipment.

### EXAMPLE I

Brigham Tea Inc. is a processor of a low-acid tea. The company is contemplating purchasing equipment for an additional processing line. The additional processing line would increase revenues by $90,000 per year. Incremental cash operating expenses would be $40,000 per year. The equipment would cost $180,000 and have a nine-year life. No salvage value is projected.

*Required:*
Compute the simple rate of return.

*SOLUTION:*
By applying the formula for the simple rate of return found in equation (3), we can compute the simple rate of return:

$$\frac{\text{Simple}}{\begin{array}{c}\text{rate of} \\ \text{return}\end{array}} = \frac{\left[\begin{array}{c}\$90,000 \\ \text{Incremental} \\ \text{revenues}\end{array}\right] - \left[\begin{array}{c}\$40,000 \text{ Cash operating expenses} \\ + \$20,000 \text{ Depreciation}\end{array}\right]}{\$180,000 \text{ Initial investment}}$$

$$= \frac{\$30,000}{\$180,000}$$

$$= 16.7\%$$

### EXAMPLE J

Midwest farms Inc. hires people on a part-time basis to sort eggs. The cost of this hand-sorting process is $30,000 per year. The company is investigating the purchase of an egg-sorting machine that would cost $90,000 and have a 15-year useful life. The machine would have negligible salvage value, and it would cost $10,000 per year to operate and maintain. The egg-sorting equipment currently being used could be sold now for a scrap value of $2,500.

*Required:*
Compute the simple rate of return on the new egg-sorting machine.

*SOLUTION:*
A cost reduction project is involved in this situation. By applying the formula for the simple rate of return found in equation (4), we can compute the simple rate of return as follows:

$$\frac{\text{Simple rate}}{\text{of return}} = \frac{\begin{array}{c}\$20,000^* \text{ Cost} \\ \text{savings}\end{array} - \begin{array}{c}\$6,000\dagger \text{ Depreciation} \\ \text{on new equipment}\end{array}}{\$90,000 - \$2,500}$$

$$= 16.0\%$$

*$30,000 − $10,000 = $20,000 cost savings.
†$90,000 ÷ 15 years = $6,000 depreciation.

## Criticisms of the Simple Rate of Return

The most damaging criticism of the simple rate of return method is that it does not consider the time value of money. A dollar received 10 years from now is viewed as being just as valuable as a dollar received today. Thus, the manager can be misled if the alternatives being considered have different cash flow patterns.

Additionally, many projects do not have uniform cash flows and incremental revenues and expenses over their useful lives. As a result, the simple rate of return will fluctuate from year to year, with the possibility that a project may appear to be desirable in some years and undesirable in other years. In contrast, the net present value method provides a single figure that summarizes all of the cash flows over the entire useful life of the project.

---

*in business today*  **Social Responsibility Issues in Ecuador**

The stagnant economy of Ecuador has provided an opportunity for Calgary-based oil company EnCana Corp. to dip into the abundant oil reserves of the South American country. Although the company insisted that a win-win situation would be realized for the Ecuadorian stakeholders, citizens have had to live in disarray due to a 500-kilometre Oleoducto de Crudos Pesados (OCP) (Spanish for "heavy crude oil pipeline.") The pipeline currently pumps approximately 50,000 barrels of oil per day. When the pipeline is complete, EnCana anticipates shipping as much as 90,000 barrels per day. This had led many people to protest against the "corporate greed and environmental irresponsibility" which has forced them to live in less than desirable conditions despite the fact the Ecuadorian government, concerned with carrying heavy international debt, has declared OCP a national priority. In mid-2001, the initial investment of US$900 million for OCP was financed by a range of international banks in the face of skepticism expressed by many observers. EnCana, aware of the criticisms of engaging in Third World projects, defended itself by referring to the opportunity provided by the project to boost the Ecuadorian industry. The company believes that whether it operates in Ecuador or Canada, "the objective should be to create wealth for society, including our shareholders, while leaving a legacy which absolutely minimizes negative impacts" (quoted in *World Energy Magazine* in March 2000). Delays, mounting costs, protests, and other uncertainties surrounding the project have led Moody's Investors Service to downgrade OCP's debt rating to almost junk status. EnCana, however, has not wavered in its commitment to the project. With the pipeline at the 85% completion stage, EnCana aims to stick with the project.

Source: McClearn, Matthew, "Down the Tube," *Canadian Business*, March 17, 2003, pp. 33–40. Reprinted with permission from *Canadian Business*.

---

# Postaudit of Investment Projects

A **postaudit** of an investment project involves a follow-up after the project has been approved to see whether or not expected results are actually realized. This is a key part of the capital budgeting process that provides an opportunity to see if realistic data are being submitted to support capital budgeting proposals. It also provides an opportunity to reinforce successful projects as needed, to strengthen or perhaps salvage projects that are encountering difficulty, to terminate unsuccessful projects before losses become too great, and to improve the overall quality of future investment proposals.

In performing a postaudit, the same technique should be used as was used in the original approval process. That is, if a project was approved on the basis of a net present value analysis, then the same procedure should be used in performing the postaudit. However, the data used in the postaudit analysis should be *actual observed data*, rather than estimated data. This affords management with an opportunity to make a side-by-side comparison to see how well the project has worked out. It also helps assure that estimated data received on future proposals will be carefully prepared, since the persons submitting the data will know that their estimates will be given careful scrutiny in the postaudit process. Actual results that are far out of line with original estimates should be carefully reviewed by management. Those managers responsible for the original estimates should be required to provide a full explanation of any major differences between estimated and actual results.[6]

---

[6]For further discussion, see Lawrence A. Gordon and Mary D. Myers, "Postauditing Capital Projects," *Management Accounting* 72, no. 7 (January 1991), pp. 39–42. This study of 282 large U.S. companies states that "an increasing number of firms are recognizing the importance of the postaudit stage" (p. 41).

# Investor

*you decide*

Each of the following situations is independent. Work out your own solution to each situation, and then check it against the solution provided.

1. John has just reached age 58. In 12 years, he plans to retire. Upon retiring, he would like to take an extended vacation, which he expects will cost at least $4,000. What lump-sum amount must he invest now to have the needed $4,000 at the end of 12 years if the rate of return is:
   a. Eight percent?
   b. Twelve percent?

2. The Morgans would like to send their daughter to an expensive music camp at the end of each of the next five years. The camp costs $1,000 a year. What lump-sum amount would have to be invested now to have the $1,000 at the end of each year if the rate of return is:
   a. Eight percent?
   b. Twelve percent?

3. You have just received an inheritance from a relative. You can invest the money and either receive a $20,000 lump-sum amount at the end of 10 years or receive $1,400 at the end of each year for the next 10 years. If your minimum desired rate of return is 12%, which alternative should you select?

# Summary

**LO1  Determine the acceptability of an investment project using the net present value method.**

Investment decisions should take into account the time value of money, since a dollar today is more valuable than a dollar received in the future. In the net present value method, future cash flows are discounted to their present value so that they can be compared on a valid basis with current cash outlays. The difference between the present value of the cash inflows and the present value of the cash outflows is called the project's net present value. If the net present value of the project is negative, the project is rejected. The company's cost of capital is often used as the discount rate in the net present value method.

**LO2  Prepare a net present value analysis of two competing investment projects using either the incremental-cost approach or the total-cost approach.**

When comparing two projects, the project with the highest net present value is the most desirable. The project with the highest net present value can be determined either by taking the net present value of the cash flows for each project or by taking the net present value of the differences in the cash flows between the two projects.

**LO3  Rank investment projects in order of preference using the profitability index.**

After screening out projects whose net present values are negative, the company may still have more projects than can be supported with available funds. The remaining projects can be ranked using the profitability index, which is computed by dividing the present value of the project's future net cash inflows by the required initial investment.

**LO4  Compute the internal rate of return of a project and determine its acceptability using the internal rate of return method.**

The internal rate of return of a project is the discount rate that makes the net present value of a project equal zero. If the internal rate of return is less than the discount rate, the project is rejected.

**LO5   Determine the payback period for an investment.**

The payback period is the number of periods that are required to recover the investment in a project from the project's cash inflows. The payback period is most useful for projects whose useful lives are short and uncertain. It is not, however, a generally reliable method for evaluating investment opportunities, since it ignores the time value of money and all cash flows that occur after the investment has been recovered.

**LO6   Compute the simple rate of return for an investment.**

The simple rate of return is determined by dividing a project's accounting net income by the initial investment in the project. The simple rate of return is not a reliable guide for evaluating potential projects, since it ignores the time value of money and its value may fluctuate from year to year.

# Guidance Answers to Decision Maker and You Decide

**NEGOTIATOR FOR THE RED SOX** (p. 489)

Apparently, the mayor is suggesting that 100% is the appropriate rate of return for discounting the cash flows that would be received by the city to their net present value. You might respond by pointing out that an organization's cost of capital is usually regarded as the minimum required rate of return. Because the City of Boston does not have shareholders, its cost of capital might be considered the average rate of return that must be paid to its long-term creditors. It is highly unlikely that the city pays interest of 100% on its long-term debt.

Note that it is very possible that the term return on investment is being misused either by the mayor, the media, or both in this situation. The mayor's goal might actually be a 100% recovery of the city's investment from the Red Sox. Rather than expecting a 100% return *on* investment, the mayor may simply want a 100% return *of* investment. Taking the time to clarify the mayor's intent might change the course of negotiations.

**INVESTOR** (p. 505)

The solutions to the three questions are presented below. If you did not know how to approach these problems or did not arrive at the correct answers, you should study Appendix 13A, The Concept of Present Value, at the end of the chapter.

1.  a.  The amount that must be invested now would be the present value of the $4,000, using a discount rate of 8%. From Table 13B–3 in Appendix 13B, the factor for a discount rate of 8% for 12 periods is 0.397. Multiplying this discount factor by the $4,000 needed in 12 years will give the amount of the present investment required: $4,000 × 0.397 = $1,588.

    b.  We will proceed as we did in (a) above, but this time we will use a discount rate of 12%. From Table 13B–3 in Appendix 13B, the factor for a discount rate of 12% for 12 periods is 0.257. Multiplying this discount factor by the $4,000 needed in 12 years will give the amount of the present investment required: $4,000 × 0.257 = $1,028.

    Note that as the discount rate (desired rate of return) increases, the present value decreases.

2.  This part differs from (1) above in that we are now dealing with an annuity, rather than with a single future sum. The amount that must be invested now will be the present value of the $1,000 needed at the end of each year for five years. Since we are dealing with an annuity, or a series of annual cash flows, we must refer to Table 13B–4 in Appendix 13B for the appropriate discount factor.

    a.  From Table 13B–4 in Appendix 13B, the discount factor for 8% for five periods is 3.993. Therefore, the amount that must be invested now to have $1,000 available at the end of each year for five years is $1,000 × 3.993 = $3,993.

    b.  From Table 13B–4 in Appendix 13B, the discount factor for 12% for five periods is 3.605. Therefore, the amount that must be invested now to have $1,000 available at the end of each year for five years is $1,000 × 3.605 = $3,605.

    Again, note that as the discount rate (desired rate of return) increases, the present value decreases. At a higher rate of return, we can invest less than would have been needed if a lower rate of return were being earned.

3.  For this part, we will need to refer to both Tables 13B–3 and 13B–4 in Appendix 13B. From Table 13B–3, we will need to find the discount factor for 12% for 10 periods, then apply it to the $20,000 lump sum to be received in 10 years. From Table 13B–4, we will need to find the discount factor for 12% for 10 periods, then apply it to the series of $1,400 payments to be received over the 10-year period. Whichever alternative has the higher present value is the one that should be selected.

$$\$20,000 \times 0.322 = \$6,440$$
$$\$1,400 \times 5.650 = \$7,910$$

Thus, you would prefer to receive the $1,400 per year for 10 years, rather than the $20,000 lump sum.

# Review Problem: Comparison of Capital Budgeting Methods

Lamar Company is studying a project that would have an eight-year life and require a $1,600,000 investment in equipment. At the end of eight years, the project would terminate and the equipment would have no salvage value. The project would provide net income each year as follows:

| | | |
|---|---|---|
| Sales ................................. | | $3,000,000 |
| Less variable expenses ................ | | 1,800,000 |
| Contribution margin ................... | | 1,200,000 |
| Less fixed expenses: | | |
| Advertising, salaries, and other | | |
| fixed out-of-pocket costs ........... | $700,000 | |
| Depreciation .................... | 200,000 | |
| Total fixed expenses ................. | | 900,000 |
| Net income ....................... | | $ 300,000 |

The company's discount rate is 18%.

**Required:**
1. Compute the net annual cash inflow from the project.
2. Compute the project's net present value. Is the project acceptable?
3. Compute the project's payback period. If the company requires a maximum payback of three years, is the project acceptable?
4. Compute the project's simple rate of return.

## SOLUTION TO REVIEW PROBLEM

1. The net annual cash inflow can be computed by deducting the cash expenses from sales:

| | |
|---|---|
| Sales ........................................... | $3,000,000 |
| Less variable expenses ......................... | 1,800,000 |
| Contribution margin ............................ | 1,200,000 |
| Less advertising, salaries, and other fixed | |
| out-of-pocket costs ......................... | 700,000 |
| Net annual cash inflow ......................... | $ 500,000 |

Or it can be computed by adding depreciation back to net income:

| | |
|---|---|
| Net income ..................................... | $300,000 |
| Add: Noncash deduction for depreciation ........ | 200,000 |
| Net annual cash inflow ......................... | $500,000 ✓ |

2. The net present value can be computed as follows:

| Item | Year(s) | Amount of Cash Flows | 18% Factor | Present Value of Cash Flows |
|---|---|---|---|---|
| Cost of new equipment ..... | Now | $(1,600,000) | 1.000 | $(1,600,000) |
| Net annual cash inflow ..... | 1–8 | 500,000 | 4.078 | 2,039,000 |
| Net present value ......... | | | | $ 439,000 ✓ |

Yes, the project is acceptable, since it has a positive net present value.

3. The formula for the payback period is:

$$\text{Payback period} = \frac{\text{Investment required}}{\text{Net annual cash inflow}}$$

$$= \frac{\$1,600,000}{\$500,000}$$

$$= 3.2 \text{ years}$$

No, the project is not acceptable when measured by the payback method. The 3.2 years payback period is greater than the maximum three years set by the company.

4. The formula for the simple rate of return is:

$$\text{Simple rate of return} = \frac{\overset{\text{Incremental}}{\text{revenues}} - \overset{\text{Incremental expenses,}}{\text{including depreciation}} = \overset{\text{Net}}{\text{income}}}{\text{Initial investment}}$$

$$= \frac{\$300,000}{\$1,600,000}$$

$$= 18.75\%$$

# Glossary

**Capital budgeting** The process of planning significant outlays on projects that have long-term implications, such as the purchase of new equipment or the introduction of a new product. (p. 484)

**Cost of capital** The average rate of return the company must pay to its long-term creditors and to shareholders for the use of their funds. (p. 489)

**Internal rate of return** The discount rate at which the net present value of an investment project is zero; thus, the internal rate of return represents the return promised by a project over its useful life. (p. 495)

**Net present value** The difference between the present value of the cash inflows and the present value of the cash outflows of an investment project. (p. 485)

**Out-of-pocket costs** Actual cash outlays for salaries, advertising, repairs, and similar costs. (p. 490)

**Payback period** The length of time that it takes for a project to recover its initial cost out of the cash receipts that it generates. (p. 598)

**Postaudit** The follow-up after a project has been approved and implemented to determine whether expected results are actually realized. (p. 504)

**Preference decision** A decision as to which of several competing acceptable investment proposals is best. (p. 485)

**Profitability index** The ratio of the present value of a project's cash inflows to the investment required. (p. 594)

**Screening decision** A decision as to whether a proposed investment meets some preset standard of acceptance. (p. 485)

**Simple rate of return** The rate of return computed by dividing a project's annual accounting net income by the initial investment required. (p. 502)

**Working capital** The excess of current assets over current liabilities. (p. 487)

# Appendix 13A | *The Concept of Present Value*

A dollar received today is more valuable than a dollar received a year from now for the simple reason that if you have a dollar today, you can put it in the bank and have more than a dollar a year from now. Since dollars today are worth more than dollars in the future, we need some means of weighting cash flows that are received at different times so that they can be compared. The theory of interest provides us with the means of making such comparisons. With a few simple calculations, we can adjust the value of a dollar received any number of years from now so that it can be compared with the value of a dollar in hand today.

**Learning Objective 7**

Explain the concept of present value and make present value computations.

## The Theory of Interest

If a bank pays 5% interest, then a deposit of $100 today will be worth $105 one year from now. This can be expressed in mathematical terms by means of the following equation:

$$F_1 = P(1 + r) \tag{5}$$

where $F_1$ = the amount to be received in one period, $P$ = the amount invested now, and $r$ = the rate of interest per period.

If the investment made now is $100 deposited in a bank savings account that is to earn interest at 5%, then $P$ = $100 and $r$ = 0.05. Under these conditions, $F_1$ = $105, the amount to be received in one year.

The $100 present outlay is called the **present value** of the $105 amount to be received in one year. It is also known as the *discounted value* of the future $105 receipt. The $100 figure represents the value in present terms of $105 to be received a year from now when the interest rate is 5%.

COMPOUND INTEREST   What if the $105 is left in the bank for a second year? In that case, by the end of the second year the original $100 deposit will have grown to $110.25:

| | |
|---|---:|
| Original deposit . . . . . . . . . . . . . . . . . . . . . . . . . . . . . . . . . . . . . . . . . | $100.00 |
| Interest for the first year: $100 × 0.05 . . . . . . . . . . . . . . . . . . | 5.00 |
| Amount at the end of the first year . . . . . . . . . . . . . . . . . . . . . | 105.00 |
| Interest for the second year: $105 × 0.05 . . . . . . . . . . . . . . . . | 5.25 |
| Amount at the end of the second year . . . . . . . . . . . . . . . . . . . | $110.25 |

Note that the interest for the second year is $5.25, as compared with only $5 for the first year. The reason for the greater interest earned during the second year is that during the second year, interest is being paid *on interest*. That is, the $5 interest earned during the first year has been left in the account and has been added to the original $100 deposit when computing interest for the second year. This is known as **compound interest.** The compounding we have done is annual compounding. Interest can be compounded on a

**Exhibit 13A–1**

The Relationship between
Present Value and Future Value

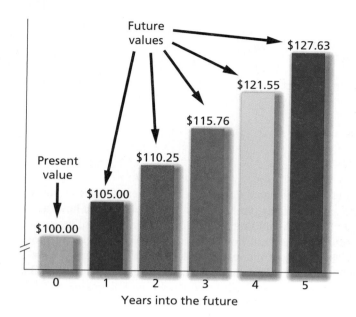

semiannual, quarterly, or even more frequent basis. The more frequently compounding is done, the more rapidly the balance will grow.

We can determine the balance in an account after $n$ periods using the following equation:

$$F_n = P(1 + r)^n \qquad (6)$$

where $n$ = the number of periods.

If $n = 2$ years and the interest rate is 5% per year, then our computation of the value of $F$ in two years will be as follows:

$$F_2 = \$100(1 + 0.05)^2$$

$$F_2 = \$110.25$$

**PRESENT VALUE AND FUTURE VALUE**   Exhibit 13A–1 shows the relationship between present value and future value as expressed in the theory of interest equations. As shown in the exhibit, if $100 is deposited in a bank at 5% interest, it will grow to $127.63 by the end of five years if interest is compounded annually.

## Computation of Present Value

An investment can be viewed in two ways. It can be viewed either in terms of its future value or in terms of its present value. We have seen from our computations above that if we know the present value of a sum (such as our $100 deposit), it is a relatively simple task to compute the sum's future value in $n$ years by using equation (6). But what if the tables are reversed and we know the *future* value of some amount but not its present value?

For example, assume that you are to receive $200 two years from now. You know that the future value of this sum is $200, since this is the amount that you will be receiving in two years. But what is the sum's present value—what is it worth *right now?* The present value of any sum to be received in the future can be computed by turning equation (6) around and solving for $P$:

$$P = \frac{F_n}{(1 + r)^n} \qquad (7)$$

In our example, $F = \$200$ (the amount to be received in the future), $r = 0.05$ (the rate of interest), and $n = 2$ (the number of years in the future that the amount is to be received).

$$P = \frac{\$200}{(1 + 0.05)^2}$$

$$P = \frac{\$200}{1.1025}$$

$$P = \$181.40$$

As shown by the computation above, the present value of a $200 amount to be received two years from now is $181.40 if the interest rate is 5%. In effect, $181.40 received *right now* is equivalent to $200 received two years from now if the rate of return is 5%. The $181.40 and the $200 are just two ways of looking at the same thing.

The process of finding the present value of a future cash flow, which we have just completed, is called **discounting.** We have *discounted* the $200 to its present value of $181.40. The 5% interest figure that we have used to find this present value is called the **discount rate.** Discounting future sums to their present value is a common practice in business, particularly in capital budgeting decisions.

If you have a power key ($y^x$) on your calculator, the above calculations are fairly easy. However, some of the present value formulas we will be using are more complex and difficult to use. Fortunately, tables are available in which many of the calculations have already been done for you. For example, Table 13B–3 in Appendix 13B shows the discounted present value of $1 to be received at various periods in the future at various interest rates. The table indicates that the present value of $1 to be received two periods from now at 5% is 0.907. Since in our example we want to know the present value of $200, rather than just $1, we need to multiply the factor in the table by $200:

$$\$200 \times 0.907 = \$181.40$$

This answer is the same as we obtained earlier using the formula in equation (7).

## Present Value of a Series of Cash Flows

Although some investments involve a single sum to be received (or paid) at a single point in the future, other investments involve a *series* of cash flows. A series (or stream) of identical cash flows is known as an **annuity.** To provide an example, assume that a firm has just purchased some government bonds in order to temporarily invest funds that are being held for future plant expansion. The bonds will yield interest of $15,000 each year and will be held for five years. What is the present value of the stream of interest receipts from the bonds? As shown in Exhibit 13A–2, the present value of this stream is $54,075 if we assume a discount rate of 12% compounded annually. The discount factors used in this exhibit were taken from Table 13B–3 in Appendix 13B.

Two points are important in connection with Exhibit 13A–2. First, note that the farther we go forward in time, the smaller is the present value of the $15,000 interest receipt. The present value of $15,000 received a year from now is $13,395, as compared with only $8,505 for the $15,000 interest payment to be received five years from now. This point simply underscores the fact that money has a time value.

**Exhibit 13A–2**
Present Value of a Series of Cash Receipts

| Year | Factor at 12% (Table 13B–3) | Interest Received | Present Value |
|------|------|------|------|
| 1 | 0.893 | $15,000 | $13,395 |
| 2 | 0.797 | 15,000 | 11,955 |
| 3 | 0.712 | 15,000 | 10,680 |
| 4 | 0.636 | 15,000 | 9,540 |
| 5 | 0.567 | 15,000 | 8,505 |
| | | | $54,075 |

The second point is that the computations in Exhibit 13A–2 involved unnecessary work. The same present value of $54,075 could have been obtained more easily by referring to Table 13B–4 in Appendix 13B. Table 13B–4 contains the present value of $1 to be received each year over a *series* of years at various interest rates. Table 13B–4 has been derived by simply adding together the factors from Table 13B–3. To illustrate, we used the factors below from Table 13B–3 in the computations in Exhibit 13A–2:

| Year | Table 13B–3 Factors at 12% |
|------|------|
| 1 . . . . . . . . . . . . . | 0.893 |
| 2 . . . . . . . . . . . . . | 0.797 |
| 3 . . . . . . . . . . . . . | 0.712 |
| 4 . . . . . . . . . . . . . | 0.636 |
| 5 . . . . . . . . . . . . . | 0.567 |
|  | 3.605 |

The sum of the five factors above is 3.605. Note from Table 13B–4 that the factor for $1 to be received each year for five years at 12% is also 3.605. If we use this factor and multiply it by the $15,000 annual cash inflow, then we get the same $54,075 present value that we obtained earlier in Exhibit 13A–2.

$$\$15,000 \times 3.605 = \$54,075$$

Therefore, when computing the present value of a series (or stream) of equal cash flows, Table 13B–4 should be used.

To summarize, the present value tables in Appendix 13B should be used as follows:

Table 13B–3: This table should be used to find the present value of a single cash flow (such as a single payment or receipt) occurring in the future.

Table 13B–4: This table should be used to find the present value of a series (or stream) of identical cash flows beginning at the end of the current year and continuing into the future.

The use of both of these tables is illustrated in various exhibits in the main body of the chapter. *When a present value factor appears in an exhibit, you should take the time to trace it back into either Table 13B–3 or Table 13B–4 to get acquainted with the tables and how they work.*

# Glossary for Appendix 13A

**Annuity** A series, or stream, of identical cash flows. (p. 511)
**Compound interest** The process of paying interest on interest in an investment. (p. 509)
**Discount rate** The rate of return that is used to find the present value of a future cash flow. (p. 511)
**Discounting** The process of finding the present value of a future cash flow. (p. 511)
**Present value** The value now of an amount that will be received in some future period. (p. 509)

# Appendix 13B | *Future Value and Present Value Tables*

**Exhibit 13B–1**
Future Value of $1;
$F_n = P(1 + r)^n$

| Periods | 4% | 6% | 8% | 10% | 12% | 14% | 20% |
|---|---|---|---|---|---|---|---|
| 1 | 1.040 | 1.060 | 1.080 | 1.100 | 1.120 | 1.140 | 1.200 |
| 2 | 1.082 | 1.124 | 1.166 | 1.210 | 1.254 | 1.300 | 1.440 |
| 3 | 1.125 | 1.191 | 1.260 | 1.331 | 1.405 | 1.482 | 1.728 |
| 4 | 1.170 | 1.263 | 1.361 | 1.464 | 1.574 | 1.689 | 2.074 |
| 5 | 1.217 | 1.338 | 1.469 | 1.611 | 1.762 | 1.925 | 2.488 |
| 6 | 1.265 | 1.419 | 1.587 | 1.772 | 1.974 | 2.195 | 2.986 |
| 7 | 1.316 | 1.504 | 1.714 | 1.949 | 2.211 | 2.502 | 3.583 |
| 8 | 1.369 | 1.594 | 1.851 | 2.144 | 2.476 | 2.853 | 4.300 |
| 9 | 1.423 | 1.690 | 1.999 | 2.359 | 2.773 | 3.252 | 5.160 |
| 10 | 1.480 | 1.791 | 2.159 | 2.594 | 3.106 | 3.707 | 6.192 |
| 11 | 1.540 | 1.898 | 2.332 | 2.853 | 3.479 | 4.226 | 7.430 |
| 12 | 1.601 | 2.012 | 2.518 | 3.139 | 3.896 | 4.818 | 8.916 |
| 13 | 1.665 | 2.133 | 2.720 | 3.452 | 4.364 | 5.492 | 10.699 |
| 14 | 1.732 | 2.261 | 2.937 | 3.798 | 4.887 | 6.261 | 12.839 |
| 15 | 1.801 | 2.397 | 3.172 | 4.177 | 5.474 | 7.138 | 15.407 |
| 20 | 2.191 | 3.207 | 4.661 | 6.728 | 9.646 | 13.743 | 38.338 |
| 30 | 3.243 | 5.744 | 10.063 | 17.450 | 29.960 | 50.950 | 237.376 |
| 40 | 4.801 | 10.286 | 21.725 | 45.260 | 93.051 | 188.884 | 1469.772 |

**Exhibit 13B–2**
Future Value of an Annuity of $1
in Arrears;
$F_n = \dfrac{(1 + r)^n - 1}{r}$

| Periods | 4% | 6% | 8% | 10% | 12% | 14% | 20% |
|---|---|---|---|---|---|---|---|
| 1 | 1.000 | 1.000 | 1.000 | 1.000 | 1.000 | 1.000 | 1.000 |
| 2 | 2.040 | 2.060 | 2.080 | 2.100 | 2.120 | 2.140 | 2.200 |
| 3 | 3.122 | 3.184 | 3.246 | 3.310 | 3.374 | 3.440 | 3.640 |
| 4 | 4.247 | 4.375 | 4.506 | 4.641 | 4.779 | 4.921 | 5.368 |
| 5 | 5.416 | 5.637 | 5.867 | 6.105 | 6.353 | 6.610 | 7.442 |
| 6 | 6.633 | 6.975 | 7.336 | 7.716 | 8.115 | 8.536 | 9.930 |
| 7 | 7.898 | 8.394 | 8.923 | 9.487 | 10.089 | 10.730 | 12.916 |
| 8 | 9.214 | 9.898 | 10.637 | 11.436 | 12.300 | 13.233 | 16.499 |
| 9 | 10.583 | 11.491 | 12.488 | 13.580 | 14.776 | 16.085 | 20.799 |
| 10 | 12.006 | 13.181 | 14.487 | 15.938 | 17.549 | 19.337 | 25.959 |
| 11 | 13.486 | 14.972 | 16.646 | 18.531 | 20.655 | 23.045 | 32.150 |
| 12 | 15.026 | 16.870 | 18.977 | 21.385 | 24.133 | 27.271 | 39.580 |
| 13 | 16.627 | 18.882 | 21.495 | 24.523 | 28.029 | 32.089 | 48.497 |
| 14 | 18.292 | 21.015 | 24.215 | 27.976 | 32.393 | 37.581 | 59.196 |
| 15 | 20.024 | 23.276 | 27.152 | 31.773 | 37.280 | 43.842 | 72.035 |
| 20 | 29.778 | 36.786 | 45.762 | 57.276 | 75.052 | 91.025 | 186.688 |
| 30 | 56.085 | 79.058 | 113.283 | 164.496 | 241.333 | 356.787 | 1181.882 |
| 40 | 95.026 | 154.762 | 259.057 | 442.593 | 767.090 | 1342.025 | 7343.858 |

## Exhibit 13B–3

Present Value of $1; $P = \dfrac{F_n}{(1 + r)^n}$

| Period | 4% | 5% | 6% | 8% | 10% | 12% | 14% | 16% | 18% | 20% | 22% | 24% | 26% | 28% | 30% | 40% |
|---|---|---|---|---|---|---|---|---|---|---|---|---|---|---|---|---|
| 1 | 0.962 | 0.952 | 0.943 | 0.926 | 0.909 | 0.893 | 0.877 | 0.862 | 0.847 | 0.833 | 0.820 | 0.806 | 0.794 | 0.781 | 0.769 | 0.714 |
| 2 | 0.925 | 0.907 | 0.890 | 0.857 | 0.826 | 0.797 | 0.769 | 0.743 | 0.718 | 0.694 | 0.672 | 0.650 | 0.630 | 0.610 | 0.592 | 0.510 |
| 3 | 0.889 | 0.864 | 0.840 | 0.794 | 0.751 | 0.712 | 0.675 | 0.641 | 0.609 | 0.579 | 0.551 | 0.524 | 0.500 | 0.477 | 0.455 | 0.364 |
| 4 | 0.855 | 0.823 | 0.792 | 0.735 | 0.683 | 0.636 | 0.592 | 0.552 | 0.516 | 0.482 | 0.451 | 0.423 | 0.397 | 0.373 | 0.350 | 0.260 |
| 5 | 0.822 | 0.784 | 0.747 | 0.681 | 0.621 | 0.567 | 0.519 | 0.476 | 0.437 | 0.402 | 0.370 | 0.341 | 0.315 | 0.291 | 0.269 | 0.186 |
| 6 | 0.790 | 0.746 | 0.705 | 0.630 | 0.564 | 0.507 | 0.456 | 0.410 | 0.370 | 0.335 | 0.303 | 0.275 | 0.250 | 0.227 | 0.207 | 0.133 |
| 7 | 0.760 | 0.711 | 0.665 | 0.583 | 0.513 | 0.452 | 0.400 | 0.354 | 0.314 | 0.279 | 0.249 | 0.222 | 0.198 | 0.178 | 0.159 | 0.095 |
| 8 | 0.731 | 0.677 | 0.627 | 0.540 | 0.467 | 0.404 | 0.351 | 0.305 | 0.266 | 0.233 | 0.204 | 0.179 | 0.157 | 0.139 | 0.123 | 0.068 |
| 9 | 0.703 | 0.645 | 0.592 | 0.500 | 0.424 | 0.361 | 0.308 | 0.263 | 0.225 | 0.194 | 0.167 | 0.144 | 0.125 | 0.108 | 0.094 | 0.048 |
| 10 | 0.676 | 0.614 | 0.558 | 0.463 | 0.386 | 0.322 | 0.270 | 0.227 | 0.191 | 0.162 | 0.137 | 0.116 | 0.099 | 0.085 | 0.073 | 0.035 |
| 11 | 0.650 | 0.585 | 0.527 | 0.429 | 0.350 | 0.287 | 0.237 | 0.195 | 0.162 | 0.135 | 0.112 | 0.094 | 0.079 | 0.066 | 0.056 | 0.025 |
| 12 | 0.625 | 0.557 | 0.497 | 0.397 | 0.319 | 0.257 | 0.208 | 0.168 | 0.137 | 0.112 | 0.092 | 0.076 | 0.062 | 0.052 | 0.043 | 0.018 |
| 13 | 0.601 | 0.530 | 0.469 | 0.368 | 0.290 | 0.229 | 0.182 | 0.145 | 0.116 | 0.093 | 0.075 | 0.061 | 0.050 | 0.040 | 0.033 | 0.013 |
| 14 | 0.577 | 0.505 | 0.442 | 0.340 | 0.263 | 0.205 | 0.160 | 0.125 | 0.099 | 0.078 | 0.062 | 0.049 | 0.039 | 0.032 | 0.025 | 0.009 |
| 15 | 0.555 | 0.481 | 0.417 | 0.315 | 0.239 | 0.183 | 0.140 | 0.108 | 0.084 | 0.065 | 0.051 | 0.040 | 0.031 | 0.025 | 0.020 | 0.006 |
| 16 | 0.534 | 0.458 | 0.394 | 0.292 | 0.218 | 0.163 | 0.123 | 0.093 | 0.071 | 0.054 | 0.042 | 0.032 | 0.025 | 0.019 | 0.015 | 0.005 |
| 17 | 0.513 | 0.436 | 0.371 | 0.270 | 0.198 | 0.146 | 0.108 | 0.080 | 0.060 | 0.045 | 0.034 | 0.026 | 0.020 | 0.015 | 0.012 | 0.003 |
| 18 | 0.494 | 0.416 | 0.350 | 0.250 | 0.180 | 0.130 | 0.095 | 0.069 | 0.051 | 0.038 | 0.028 | 0.021 | 0.016 | 0.012 | 0.009 | 0.002 |
| 19 | 0.475 | 0.396 | 0.331 | 0.232 | 0.164 | 0.116 | 0.083 | 0.060 | 0.043 | 0.031 | 0.023 | 0.017 | 0.012 | 0.009 | 0.007 | 0.002 |
| 20 | 0.456 | 0.377 | 0.312 | 0.215 | 0.149 | 0.104 | 0.073 | 0.051 | 0.037 | 0.026 | 0.019 | 0.014 | 0.010 | 0.007 | 0.005 | 0.001 |
| 21 | 0.439 | 0.359 | 0.294 | 0.199 | 0.135 | 0.093 | 0.064 | 0.044 | 0.031 | 0.022 | 0.015 | 0.011 | 0.008 | 0.006 | 0.004 | 0.001 |
| 22 | 0.422 | 0.342 | 0.278 | 0.184 | 0.123 | 0.083 | 0.056 | 0.038 | 0.026 | 0.018 | 0.013 | 0.009 | 0.006 | 0.004 | 0.003 | 0.001 |
| 23 | 0.406 | 0.326 | 0.262 | 0.170 | 0.112 | 0.074 | 0.049 | 0.033 | 0.022 | 0.015 | 0.010 | 0.007 | 0.005 | 0.003 | 0.002 | |
| 24 | 0.390 | 0.310 | 0.247 | 0.158 | 0.102 | 0.066 | 0.043 | 0.028 | 0.019 | 0.013 | 0.008 | 0.006 | 0.004 | 0.003 | 0.002 | |
| 25 | 0.375 | 0.295 | 0.233 | 0.146 | 0.092 | 0.059 | 0.038 | 0.024 | 0.016 | 0.010 | 0.007 | 0.005 | 0.003 | 0.002 | 0.001 | |
| 26 | 0.361 | 0.281 | 0.220 | 0.135 | 0.084 | 0.053 | 0.033 | 0.021 | 0.014 | 0.009 | 0.006 | 0.004 | 0.002 | 0.002 | 0.001 | |
| 27 | 0.347 | 0.268 | 0.207 | 0.125 | 0.076 | 0.047 | 0.029 | 0.018 | 0.011 | 0.007 | 0.005 | 0.003 | 0.002 | 0.001 | 0.001 | |
| 28 | 0.333 | 0.255 | 0.196 | 0.116 | 0.069 | 0.042 | 0.026 | 0.016 | 0.010 | 0.006 | 0.004 | 0.002 | 0.002 | 0.001 | 0.001 | |
| 29 | 0.321 | 0.243 | 0.185 | 0.107 | 0.063 | 0.037 | 0.022 | 0.014 | 0.008 | 0.005 | 0.003 | 0.002 | 0.001 | 0.001 | | |
| 30 | 0.308 | 0.231 | 0.174 | 0.099 | 0.057 | 0.033 | 0.020 | 0.012 | 0.007 | 0.004 | 0.003 | 0.002 | 0.001 | 0.001 | | |
| 40 | 0.208 | 0.142 | 0.097 | 0.046 | 0.022 | 0.011 | 0.005 | 0.003 | 0.001 | 0.001 | | | | | | |

# Exhibit 13B–4

Present Value of an Annuity of $1 in Arrears; $P_n = \dfrac{1}{r}\left[1 - \dfrac{1}{(1+r)^n}\right]$

| Period | 4% | 5% | 6% | 8% | 10% | 12% | 14% | 16% | 18% | 20% | 22% | 24% | 26% | 28% | 30% | 40% |
|---|---|---|---|---|---|---|---|---|---|---|---|---|---|---|---|---|
| 1 | 0.962 | 0.952 | 0.943 | 0.926 | 0.909 | 0.893 | 0.877 | 0.862 | 0.847 | 0.833 | 0.820 | 0.806 | 0.794 | 0.781 | 0.769 | 0.714 |
| 2 | 1.886 | 1.859 | 1.833 | 1.783 | 1.736 | 1.690 | 1.647 | 1.605 | 1.566 | 1.528 | 1.492 | 1.457 | 1.424 | 1.392 | 1.361 | 1.224 |
| 3 | 2.775 | 2.723 | 2.673 | 2.577 | 2.487 | 2.402 | 2.322 | 2.246 | 2.174 | 2.106 | 2.042 | 1.981 | 1.923 | 1.868 | 1.816 | 1.589 |
| 4 | 3.630 | 3.546 | 3.465 | 3.312 | 3.170 | 3.037 | 2.914 | 2.798 | 2.690 | 2.589 | 2.494 | 2.404 | 2.320 | 2.241 | 2.166 | 1.879 |
| 5 | 4.452 | 4.330 | 4.212 | 3.993 | 3.791 | 3.605 | 3.433 | 3.274 | 3.127 | 2.991 | 2.864 | 2.745 | 2.635 | 2.532 | 2.436 | 2.035 |
| 6 | 5.242 | 5.076 | 4.917 | 4.623 | 4.355 | 4.111 | 3.889 | 3.685 | 3.498 | 3.326 | 3.167 | 3.020 | 2.885 | 2.759 | 2.643 | 2.168 |
| 7 | 6.002 | 5.786 | 5.582 | 5.206 | 4.868 | 4.564 | 4.288 | 4.039 | 3.812 | 3.605 | 3.416 | 3.242 | 3.083 | 2.937 | 2.802 | 2.263 |
| 8 | 6.733 | 6.463 | 6.210 | 5.747 | 5.335 | 4.968 | 4.639 | 4.344 | 4.078 | 3.837 | 3.619 | 3.421 | 3.241 | 3.076 | 2.925 | 2.331 |
| 9 | 7.435 | 7.108 | 6.802 | 6.247 | 5.759 | 5.328 | 4.946 | 4.607 | 4.303 | 4.031 | 3.786 | 3.566 | 3.366 | 3.184 | 3.019 | 2.379 |
| 10 | 8.111 | 7.722 | 7.360 | 6.710 | 6.145 | 5.650 | 5.216 | 4.833 | 4.494 | 4.192 | 3.923 | 3.662 | 3.465 | 3.269 | 3.092 | 2.414 |
| 11 | 8.760 | 8.306 | 7.887 | 7.139 | 6.495 | 5.938 | 5.453 | 5.029 | 4.656 | 4.327 | 4.035 | 3.776 | 3.544 | 3.335 | 3.147 | 2.438 |
| 12 | 9.385 | 8.863 | 8.384 | 7.536 | 6.814 | 6.194 | 5.660 | 5.197 | 4.793 | 4.439 | 4.127 | 3.851 | 3.606 | 3.387 | 3.190 | 2.456 |
| 13 | 9.986 | 9.394 | 8.853 | 7.904 | 7.103 | 6.424 | 5.842 | 5.342 | 4.910 | 4.533 | 4.203 | 3.912 | 3.656 | 3.427 | 3.223 | 2.468 |
| 14 | 10.563 | 9.899 | 9.295 | 8.244 | 7.367 | 6.628 | 6.002 | 5.468 | 5.008 | 4.611 | 4.265 | 3.962 | 3.695 | 3.459 | 3.249 | 2.477 |
| 15 | 11.118 | 10.380 | 9.712 | 8.559 | 7.606 | 6.811 | 6.142 | 5.575 | 5.092 | 4.675 | 4.315 | 4.001 | 3.726 | 3.483 | 3.268 | 2.484 |
| 16 | 11.652 | 10.838 | 10.106 | 8.851 | 7.824 | 6.974 | 6.265 | 5.669 | 5.162 | 4.730 | 4.357 | 4.033 | 3.751 | 3.503 | 3.283 | 2.489 |
| 17 | 12.166 | 11.274 | 10.477 | 9.122 | 8.022 | 7.120 | 6.373 | 5.749 | 5.222 | 4.775 | 4.391 | 4.059 | 3.771 | 3.518 | 3.295 | 2.492 |
| 18 | 12.659 | 11.690 | 10.828 | 9.372 | 8.201 | 7.250 | 6.467 | 5.818 | 5.273 | 4.812 | 4.419 | 4.080 | 3.786 | 3.529 | 3.304 | 2.494 |
| 19 | 13.134 | 12.085 | 11.158 | 9.604 | 8.365 | 7.366 | 6.550 | 5.877 | 5.316 | 4.844 | 4.442 | 4.097 | 3.799 | 3.539 | 3.311 | 2.496 |
| 20 | 13.590 | 12.462 | 11.470 | 9.818 | 8.514 | 7.469 | 6.623 | 5.929 | 5.353 | 4.870 | 4.460 | 4.110 | 3.808 | 3.546 | 3.316 | 2.497 |
| 21 | 14.029 | 12.821 | 11.764 | 10.017 | 8.649 | 7.562 | 6.687 | 5.973 | 5.384 | 4.891 | 4.476 | 4.121 | 3.816 | 3.551 | 3.320 | 2.498 |
| 22 | 14.451 | 13.163 | 12.042 | 10.201 | 8.772 | 7.645 | 6.743 | 6.011 | 5.410 | 4.909 | 4.488 | 4.130 | 3.822 | 3.556 | 3.323 | 2.498 |
| 23 | 14.857 | 13.489 | 12.303 | 10.371 | 8.883 | 7.718 | 6.792 | 6.044 | 5.432 | 4.925 | 4.499 | 4.137 | 3.827 | 3.559 | 3.325 | 2.499 |
| 24 | 15.247 | 13.799 | 12.550 | 10.529 | 8.985 | 7.784 | 6.835 | 6.073 | 5.451 | 4.937 | 4.507 | 4.143 | 3.831 | 3.562 | 3.327 | 2.499 |
| 25 | 15.622 | 14.094 | 12.783 | 10.675 | 9.077 | 7.843 | 6.873 | 6.097 | 5.467 | 4.948 | 4.514 | 4.147 | 3.834 | 3.564 | 3.329 | 2.499 |
| 26 | 15.983 | 14.375 | 13.003 | 10.810 | 9.161 | 7.896 | 6.906 | 6.118 | 5.480 | 4.956 | 4.520 | 4.151 | 3.837 | 3.566 | 3.330 | 2.500 |
| 27 | 16.330 | 14.643 | 13.211 | 10.935 | 9.237 | 7.943 | 6.935 | 6.136 | 5.492 | 4.964 | 4.525 | 4.154 | 3.839 | 3.567 | 3.331 | 2.500 |
| 28 | 16.663 | 14.898 | 13.406 | 11.051 | 9.307 | 7.984 | 6.961 | 6.152 | 5.502 | 4.970 | 4.528 | 4.157 | 3.840 | 3.568 | 3.331 | 2.500 |
| 29 | 16.984 | 15.141 | 13.591 | 11.158 | 9.370 | 8.022 | 6.983 | 6.166 | 5.510 | 4.975 | 4.531 | 4.159 | 3.841 | 3.569 | 3.332 | 2.500 |
| 30 | 17.292 | 15.373 | 13.765 | 11.258 | 9.427 | 8.055 | 7.003 | 6.177 | 5.517 | 4.979 | 4.534 | 4.160 | 3.842 | 3.569 | 3.332 | 2.500 |
| 40 | 19.793 | 17.159 | 15.046 | 11.925 | 9.779 | 8.244 | 7.105 | 6.234 | 5.548 | 4.997 | 4.544 | 4.166 | 3.846 | 3.571 | 3.333 | 2.500 |

# Appendix 13C | Inflation and Capital Budgeting

Inflation is the term commonly used to refer to increases in the price level of an economy as time passes. Capital budgeting analysis should reflect inflation, if it exists, to enable managers to make appropriate decisions. In this Appendix, we will explain how inflation impacts capital budgeting analysis.

Throughout our discussion of capital budgeting in this chapter, we made the unrealistic assumption that there will be no inflation over the life of the project. This means that the price of a good is constant from year to year and is equal to today's price. In other words, the *purchasing power* of the dollar is the same as it is currently, regardless of when in the future that dollar is received. The current year is referred to as the *base year*. And all the future cash flows are said to be *real* cash flows. **Real cash flows** are cash flows whose purchasing power is equal to the purchasing power of money in the base year. Now let us bring inflation in.

## MANAGEMENT ACCOUNTING IN ACTION

Trichy Company is a textiles company, with its head office in Montreal, Quebec, and manufacturing operations based in South India. The company's products are primarily for markets in Canada, Oceania, and the Caribbean. The company is considering a project requiring an outlay this year of $310 million. The project involves manufacturing and marketing a unique piece of unisex clothing called *lungi*. The lungi is worn wrapped around the waist (like a towel) and extends down to cover the ankles. In extremely hot climates, it keeps the wearer cool and comfortable. Lungis can be made using a variety of fabrics. Trichy Company is planning to use a special proprietary blend of cotton and silk. The project leader is Arun Swamy. Arun proposed the project and obtained approval based on his projection of a net cash flow of $150 million each year for three years. The company president is Meena Iyer. Meena and Arun are meeting to discuss the lungi project.

*Meena:* I like the project, Arun. We must come up with more of these in the future. With clothing fads coming and going, we can't afford to get into figuring out how long fashion trends are going to last.

*Arun:* You are right. I am confident about my cash flow projections. I think the market is there and will be there for the three years we are looking to. The lungi's fashion relevance is sure to last that long!

*Meena:* I am concerned with the news from last week that the Bank of Canada is expecting inflation to be around the 2% rate for the next three years. I don't recall if your cash flow projections considered inflation.

*Arun:* You are right. My cash flow estimates had been made on the assumption that inflation was not going to be a factor. However, I have reworked the numbers assuming an inflation rate of 2%. Let me show you what I have.

Arun Swamy's original cash flow projections had been made before he realized that inflation was going to be at 2%. Those cash flows reflect the purchasing power of money in 2004 and therefore are real cash flows. This is shown below.

| | Now (2004) | 2005 | 2006 | 2007 |
|---|---|---|---|---|
| Cash flow in year 2004 dollars | -$310 | $150 | $150 | $150 |

The impact of inflation is that it increases the price level in future years. Since inflation of 2% is expected, the price level next year (2005) will be 2% higher. That is:

$$\text{Year 2005 price} = \text{Year 2004 price} + 2\% \times \text{Year 2004 price}$$
$$= \text{Year 2004 price} \times (1.02)$$

The price level in Year 2006 will be 2% higher than in 2005. Therefore,

$$\text{Year 2006 price} = \text{Year 2005 price} + 2\% \times \text{Year 2005 price}$$
$$= \text{Year 2005 price} \times (1.02)$$
$$= \text{Year 2004 price} \times (1.02) \times (1.02)$$
$$= \text{Year 2004 price} \times (1.02)^2$$
$$= \text{Year 2004 price} \times (1.040)$$

We could go on in this way to calculate the price levels for the remaining years, but there is a formula to make it easier. The numbers 1.02 and 1.040 are referred to as *price-index* numbers. They tell you how to determine the price level in a future year given the base year's price level and the rate of inflation. A price index number is calculated using the following formula. Assuming the base year is year 0, we have

$$\text{Price index number for year } n = (1 + \text{inflation rate})^n$$

Applying this formula we can determine the price index numbers for the years 2005, 2006, and 2007, as shown below.

|  | Now (2004) | 2005 | 2006 | 2007 |
|---|---|---|---|---|
| Price index (annual inflation rate = 2%) | 1.000 | 1.020 | 1.040 | 1.061 |

The *price* in year *n* is then calculated as:

$$\text{Year } n \text{ price} = \text{Base year price} \times \text{price index number for year } n$$
$$= \text{Base year price} \times (1 + \text{inflation rate})^n$$

This last step is important because it tells you the price you must pay for a product *in year n*, assuming there is inflation expected between the base year and year *n*.

The implication of an increasing price level in future years is that it reduces the purchasing power of money. To understand this, suppose someone promised to pay you $150 in 2006 and you agreed to it *before* you knew there was going to be inflation. This means you are expecting to be able to buy for $150 in year 2006 whatever $150 can get you in year 2004. But now you are expecting inflation at 2%. This means that goods that cost $150 in 2004 will cost $150 × price index for 2006 = $150 × 1.040 = $156.06. You are going to have to get more than $150 in 2006 to be able to buy then what you can buy today for $150.

By multiplying a real cash flow by the corresponding price index number, the original real cash flow can be expressed in terms of the purchasing power of money in the year the cash flow is received. Such cash flows are called **nominal cash flows.** A nominal cash flow is said to be price adjusted because it will reflect the price level expected to exist in the year the cash flow will occur. The amount of $156.06 is therefore a nominal cash flow. It reflects the price level expected to exist in 2006, the year the cash flow occurs.

Arun Swamy's original cash flow estimates which were real cash flows can be converted to nominal cash flows using the price index numbers as shown below.

| Item | Now (2004) | 2005 | 2006 | 2007 |
|---|---|---|---|---|
| Cash flow in year 2004 dollars | -$310 | $150 | $150 | $150 |
| Price index (annual inflation rate = 2%) | 1.000 | 1.020 | 1.040 | 1.061 |
| Nominal cash flow | -$310 | $153 | $156.06 | $159.181 |

## Implications for Capital Budgeting

When Arun discovered that there was going to be inflation of 2% during the life of the project, he knew that he had to demonstrate that the project will have a positive net present value after taking inflation into account. His first step in "reworking the numbers," was to convert the real cash flows to nominal cash flows as shown on the previous page.

The second step involves determining the cost of capital. Arun Swamy had used a cost of capital of 20% in his original analysis. This cost of capital figure does not reflect expected inflation. It is called the *real cost of capital (or rate of return)*. A real rate of return compensates investors only for the risk associated with the project's operations. It does not compensate them for the decline in purchasing power of money due to inflation that can occur during the life of the project. When investors expect inflation, they will demand a premium for inflation in addition to the risk-premium contained in the real rate of return. When the cost of capital also includes an inflation premium, it is called the **nominal rate of return.** Nominal rates are also referred to as market-based returns because the market rates always reflect expected inflation.

Arun's second step was to calculate the nominal cost of capital. The nominal cost of capital is calculated as follows:

> Real cost of capital
> + Inflation rate
> <u>+ Real cost of capital × Inflation rate [this is called the combined effect]</u>
> Nominal cost of capital

Arun's final step was to calculate the project's net present value by applying the *nominal* cost of capital to the *nominal* cash flows. The calculations are shown in Exhibit 13C–1.

## Exhibit 13C–1
Capital Budgeting and Inflation

| | |
|---|---|
| Real cost of capital .......................... | 0.20 |
| Inflation factor ............................. | 0.02 |
| Combined effect (20% × 2%) .............. | <u>0.004</u> |
| Nominal cost of capital .................... | <u><u>0.224</u></u> (or 22.4%) |

### Project NPV: Inflation considered

| | Now (2004) | 2005 | 2006 | 2007 |
|---|---|---|---|---|
| Nominal cash flow ....................................... | -$310 | $153 | $156.06 | $159.181 |
| PV factor at nominal cost of capital (22.4%)* ................ | 1.000 | 0.817 | 0.667 | 0.545 |
| Present value of yearly nominal cash flow .................. | -$310 | $125 | $104.16 | $86.80 |
| Net present value ....................................... $5.972 | | | | |

### Project NPV: Inflation not considered

| | Now (2004) | 2005 | 2006 | 2007 |
|---|---|---|---|---|
| Real cash flows (Year 2004 dollars) ...................... | -$310 | $150 | $150 | $150 |
| PV factor at real cost of capital (20%)** .................... | 1.000 | 0.833 | 0.694 | 0.579 |
| Present value of yearly real cash flow ..................... | -$310 | $125 | $104.16 | $86.80 |
| Net present value ....................................... $5.972 | | | | |

*PV factors are calculated from the formula $1/(1+r)^n$ where $r$ is the relevant rate of return and $n$ is the number of years. The calculations are: $1/(1.224) = 0.817$ for 2005 i.e., Year 1; $1/(1.224)^2 = 0.667$ for 2006 and $1/(1.224)^3 = 0.545$ for 2006.
**PV factors are: $1/1.2 = 0.833$ for 2005; $1/(1.2)^2 = 0.694$ for 2006 and $1/(1.2)^3 = 0.579$ for 2007.

*Meena:* I can see what you have done. You converted your original cash flows to reflect the effect of 2% expected inflation, and you also converted your original cost of capital to reflect the expected inflation rate. Naturally, whether you discount the original cash flows by the original cost of capital or the inflation-adjusted cash flows by the inflation-adjusted cost of capital, the project's net present value remains the same.

*Arun:* You got it. The key is to keep like things together. We must be careful to apply the inflation-adjusted cost of capital only to inflation-adjusted cash flows. If the cash flows do not reflect the impact of inflation we must use a cost of capital that also does not include inflation.

*Meena:* Very well, but let me ask you, how confident are you with your cash flow projections that reflect inflation? Are you confident, for example, that the project will generate the projected cash inflow of $156.06 million in 2006? You originally called for a cash inflow of $150 million in 2006 before you expected inflation. What if we still get only $150 million?

*Arun:* That is an excellent question. Regardless of whether cash flows reflect inflation or not, we must be confident about our projections. So, you are right in asking if I have thought through the analysis that led me to forecast annual cash flows of $150 million and considered if inflation is going to affect some factors differently. Clearly, if we actually end up with only $150 million in 2006 instead of $156.06, the project's bottom line will take a hit. I am confident my team has done a thorough job of looking into the projections. We went back and looked again at the factors affecting the project's operations. We believe that the only effect inflation will have is to increase all cash flows annually by 2%; so I think we are going to be fine.

*Meena:* All right, let's get going!

## Glossary for Appendix 13C

**Nominal cash flow** A cash flow expressed in terms of the price level of the period in which the cash flow occurs. (p. 517)

**Nominal rate of return** An interest which includes a premium for inflation. (p. 518)

**Real cash flow** A cash flow expressed in terms of the purchasing power of money in a base year. A real cash flow does not reflect the loss of purchasing power of money from inflation. (p. 516)

# *Appendix 13D* | *Income Taxes in Capital Budgeting Decisions*

In this Appendix, we will incorporate income taxes into capital budgeting analysis. Tax rules are complex. Because capital budgeting involves so many different concepts, such as discounting, cash flow analysis, relevant costs, and so on, we did not include taxes in the analysis described in the chapter. To keep the analysis within reasonable bounds, we make the following simplifying assumptions:

- Taxable income equals net income as computed for financial reports.
- The tax rate is a flat percentage of taxable income.
- Net income is always positive, and therefore we will not consider tax losses.

These assumptions will allow us to consider the most important implications of income taxes for capital budgeting without getting overwhelmed by the complexities of the actual tax regulations.

## Taxes and Income

Income tax is a cash outflow for the company. In situations where corporations pay taxes, what is important for capital budgeting analysis is that we consider *after-tax cash flows*. After-tax cash flow is calculated as:

$$\text{After-tax cash flow} = \text{Pre-tax cash flow} \times (1 - \text{tax rate})$$

Consider Example A. We assume that revenues and expenses are cash flows.

### EXAMPLE A

|  | 2005 |
|---|---|
| Revenues | $150,000.00 |
| Tax-deductible operating expenses | 120,000.00 |
| Taxable income | $30,000.00 |
| Tax (40%) | 12,000.00 |
| After-tax income | $ 18,000.00 |

You can see from this example that:

$$\begin{aligned} \text{After-tax income} &= \text{Taxable income} \times (1 - \text{tax rate}) \\ &= \$30,000 \times 0.60 \\ &= \$18,000 \end{aligned}$$

We should emphasize the importance of the assumption that all revenues and all expenses were cash flows. In this case, after-tax net income and after-tax net cash flow are equal. If there is a tax deductible expense that is not a cash flow, then net income after tax will not be the same as net cash flow after-tax. For capital budgeting, only net after-tax cash flow is relevant. The most important noncash tax deductible expense is depreciation. The impact of depreciation and taxes on capital budgeting analysis is the next topic.

# Capital Cost Allowance for Depreciation

The allowance for depreciation permitted by the Canada Revenue Agency (CRA) is called the Capital Cost Allowance or CCA. The method of calculating CCA is the *declining balance method*. In this method, the amount to be depreciated is multiplied by the depreciation rate to obtain the capital cost allowance. For income tax purposes, the CRA allows a company to deduct only CCA. Depreciation calculated by any other method, even if permitted under generally accepted accounting principles (GAAP) is not allowed as a deduction. The depreciation rate is specified by the CRA. A different rate exists for various types of assets. The CCA calculated in the *first year* of asset ownership is based on a depreciation rate that is one-half of the rate applicable to subsequent years. The calculation of CCA is illustrated in Example B.

**EXAMPLE B**

A machine is purchased for $300,000. The CRA depreciation rate is 30%. Determine the annual CCA for the first five years.

The calculation of CCA is shown below.

| (1) Year | (2) Undepreciated Capital Cost | (3) CCA rate | (4) CCA |
|---|---|---|---|
| 1 | $300,000.00 | 15% | $45,000.00 |
| 2 | 255,000.00 | 30% | 76,500.00 |
| 3 | 178,500.00 | 30% | 53,550.00 |
| 4 | 124,950.00 | 30% | 37,485.00 |
| 5 | 87,465.00 | 30% | 26,239.50 |

The amount to be depreciated is called the Undepreciated Capital Cost (UCC). The UCC of an asset for the first year will be its acquisition cost (including transport cost and installation cost), which we will denote as C. Note that the CCA for year 1 is based on a 15% rate, which is one-half of the normal rate of 30%. This is the 50% or half-year rule. The reason for this rule is to prevent a company from buying an asset on the last day of its tax year and claim CCA for the entire year. Clearly, the company cannot claim it has *used* the equipment for the period for which it is claiming the CCA.

From a capital budgeting point of view, CCA provides a *tax shield* for the company claiming CCA. The tax shield each year is simply the tax rate multiplied by the CCA amount. This is the amount by which a company's tax is reduced because depreciation is claimed as a deduction from income, even though it is not a cash expense. Assuming a 40% tax rate and a cost of capital of 10% the schedule below shows the annual CCA tax shield for the first five years.

> **Learning Objective 9**
> Understand the impact of the tax deductibility of depreciation expense on the cash flows of a project.

| (1) Year | (2) Undepreciated Capital Cost | (3) CCA rate | (4) CCA | (5) CCA Tax Shield (4) × 40% | (6) PV Factor (10%) | (7) PV of Tax Shields (6) × (7) |
|---|---|---|---|---|---|---|
| 1 | $300,000.00 | 15% | $45,000.00 | $18,000.00 | 0.909 | $16,363.64 |
| 2 | 255,000.00 | 30% | 76,500.00 | 30,600.00 | 0.826 | 25,289.26 |
| 3 | 178,500.00 | 30% | 53,550.00 | 21,420.00 | 0.751 | 16,093.16 |
| 4 | 124,950.00 | 30% | 37,485.00 | 14,994.00 | 0.683 | 10,241.10 |
| 5 | 87,465.00 | 30% | 26,239.50 | 10,495.80 | 0.621 | 6,517.07 |

The declining balance method is unique in that if the company never disposes the asset, the UCC of the asset will get smaller and smaller each year, but *it will never become zero*. The implication of this is that the asset can continue to generate CCA tax shields forever, if it is never disposed. How realistic is it to assume that assets are kept forever? We admit, not very. Assets will likely be disposed at the end of a project and can be expected to have some salvage value. How can we determine the present value of the CCA tax shields in such cases*? To fully answer this question we must learn about the CCA asset class system.

## Asset Class System

Our previous example showed you how to calculate CCA for a single asset. Normally, when we think of depreciation, we think of depreciating individual assets. The total depreciation is the sum of the depreciation calculated for each asset. In Canada, CCA is not calculated on an asset-by-asset basis. Instead, assets are pooled into asset classes. And the declining balance method is used to determine the CCA *of the asset class*. The total CCA for a year is the sum of the CCA calculated for each class or pool of assets. In special situations, a company is permitted to place an asset *by itself* in a pool. In this case, the pool will have only that asset, and calculating CCA for the class is like calculating CCA individually for the asset. It is very important to know if you are dealing with an asset class with several assets in it or if the asset class only has a single asset. We will not be dealing with the single asset class situation.

## Present Value of CCA Tax Shields for Finite Period of Ownership

We are interested in CCA only because CCA provides a tax shield. If an asset is owned and used for a period of $n$ years, we want to know the present value of the CCA tax shields for the $n$ years the asset was owned. The formula is:

$$PV = \frac{Cdt}{d+k} \times \frac{1+0.5k}{1+k} - \frac{Sdt}{d+k}(1+k)^{-n}$$

where,

     $C$ = Acquisiton cost of the asset (purchase price plus installation and shipping)
     $d$ = CCA rate
     $t$  = tax rate
     $k$ = cost of capital
     $S$ = the proceeds from salvage.

**EXAMPLE C**

An asset is purchased for $300,000. It is placed in an asset class with plenty of other assets. The CCA rate for the asset class is 30%. The tax rate is 40%. The asset is disposed in year 5 for $87,500. The cost of capital is 10%. Determine the present value of the CCA tax shields from owning the asset for five years.

Applying the formula to the problem data gives:

$$PV = \frac{\$300,000 \times 0.30 \times 0.40}{0.30 + 0.10} \times \frac{1 + 0.5 \times 0.1}{1 + 0.1} - \frac{\$87,500 \times 0.3 \times 0.4}{0.3 + 0.1} \times (1.1)^{-5}$$

$$= \$85,909.09 - \$16,299.18$$

$$= \$69,609.90$$

---

*Simply adding up the present value of the tax shields year by year, like those in the schedule, will not always give the correct answer. The reasons for this will take us too deep into tax regulations.

# A Comprehensive Example of Taxes and Capital Budgeting

Laurentian Manufacturing and Fabrication Company (LMF) owns the mineral rights to nickel ore on a tract of land. LMF is considering a project that involves opening a mine on the property to extract the nickel. The project involves setting up operations in La Ronge, Saskatchewan. The following data pertain to this project:

| | |
|---|---|
| Purchase of equipment | $250,000 |
| Working capital needed | $75,000 |
| Estimated annual cash receipts | $415,000 |
| Estimated annual cash expenses for Salaries, utilities, etc. | $240,000 |
| Cost of road repairs in 6 years | $40,000 |
| Salvage value of equipment in 10 years | $60,000 |

> **Learning Objective 10**
> Compute the capital cost allowance of depreciable assets used for a project and incorporate the computations into a net present value analysis of the project.

LMF believes that after 10 years the mine will have played out and plans to shut down the project at that time. The equipment is going to be placed in a CCA class with a CCA rate of 10%. The company's tax rate is 40%. The cost of capital is 12%, which is the rate expected by the market for projects of similar risk as this one. All dollar amounts are in nominal terms, meaning that they reflect the purchasing power of money in the year of the cash flow. The company expects that the required investment in working capital at the start of the project will be recovered, in full, when the project ends.

Should LMF proceed with the project? The solution is given in Exhibit 13D–1. Study the solution carefully, and note the following points. Keep in mind that there can be minor differences due to rounding if you are following the calculations step by step in your calculator.

**INITIAL INVESTMENT**   The initial cost of equipment is included in full, with no reduction for taxes. This represents an *investment*, not an expense, and so no tax adjustment is made.

## Exhibit 13D–1

Comprehensive Example of Income Taxes and Capital Budgeting

| | A | B | C | D | E | F | G | H | I | J |
|---|---|---|---|---|---|---|---|---|---|---|
| 17 | | | | | | | | **Per Year** | | |
| 18 | | | | | | | | | | |
| 19 | | | | | | Cash receipts | | $415,000 | | |
| 20 | | | | | | Cash expenses | | 140,000 | | |
| 21 | | | | | | Net operating cash flow before tax | | $275,000 | | |
| 22 | | | | | | | | | **PV factor at 12%** | **Present value of after-tax cash flows** |
| 23 | **Items and computations** | | | | **Year(s)** | **Amount** | **Tax effect** | **After-tax cash flow** | | |
| 24 | Cost of Equipment | | | | Now | ($250,000) | nil | ($250,000) | 1 | ($250,000.00) |
| 25 | Investment in working capital | | | | Now | (75,000) | nil | (75,000) | 1 | (75,000.00) |
| 26 | Net operating cash flow after tax | | | | 1-10 | 275,000 | 0.6 | 165,000 | 5.65 | 932,286.80 |
| 27 | Road repairs | | | | 6 | (40,000) | 0.6 | (24,000) | 0.507 | (2,159.15) |
| 28 | Release of working capital (100% of investment) | | | | 10 | 75,000 | nil | 75,000 | 0.322 | 24,147.99 |
| 29 | Present value of CCA tax shields from equipment | | | | Now | 39,507.05 | nil | 39,507.05 | 1 | 39,507.05 |
| 30 | Salvage proceeds, Equipment | | | | 10 | 60,000.00 | nil | 60,000.00 | 0.322 | 19,318.39 |
| 31 | Net present value | | | | | | | | | $678,101.08 |
| 32 | | | | | | | | | | |
| 33 | | | | | | | | | | |
| 34 | **Supporting Calculations:** | | | | | | | | | |
| 35 | CCA tax shields Calculations | | | | | | | | | |
| 36 | Equipment | | | | | | | | | |
| 37 | Present value of CCA tax shields assuming asset is kept forever | | | | Now | $43,019.48 | nil | $43,019.48 | 1.00 | $43,019.48 |
| 38 | less the present value of CCA tax shields lost on disposal | | | | 10 | $10,909.09 | nil | $10,909.09 | 0.32 | 3,512.44 |
| 39 | Present value of CCA tax shields for 10 years | | | | | | | | | $39,507.05 |
| 40 | | | | | | | | | | |

**WORKING CAPITAL**   Note that the working capital required for the project is included in full at the start of the project. There is no reduction for taxes. Working capital is considered an investment and not an expense.

**NET ANNUAL OPERATING CASH FLOW AFTER TAXES**   The annual cash receipt from sales is adjusted at the top of the exhibit by subtracting the annual cash expenses to obtain the net annual operating cash flow before taxes. This was done to simplify the calculations. The net cash flow before tax, $275,000, is adjusted for taxes by multiplying it by $1 -$ tax rate to obtain the annual net cash flow after taxes of $165,000. The present value of this 10-year annuity is obtained by multiplying by the *10-year annuity factor* of 5.65.

**ROAD REPAIRS**   This *tax deductible expense* occurs in year 6. The after-tax expense is obtained by multiplying the pre-tax amount by $1 -$ tax rate. Since the cash flow occurs in year 6, the present value is obtained by multiplying by the present value factor of 0.507.

**RELEASE OF WORKING CAPITAL**   The full amount of the investment is recovered in year 10. There is no tax on the recovery, which is simply the return of invested funds to the company. The present value of the amount recovered is determined by multiplying by the 10-year present value factor of 0.322.

**CCA TAX SHIELDS**

$$PV = \frac{Cdt}{d+k} \times \frac{1+0.5k}{1+k} - \frac{Sdt}{d+k} \times (1+k)^{-n}$$

$$PV = \frac{\$250,000 \times 0.1 \times 0.4}{0.1+0.12} \times \frac{1+0.5 \times 0.12}{1.12} - \frac{\$60,000 \times 0.1 \times 0.4}{0.1+0.12} \times (1.12)^{-10}$$

$$PV = \$43,019.48 - \$10,909.09 \times 0.322$$

$$PV = \$39,507.05$$

**SALVAGE PROCEEDS**   Salvage value of the equipment is not subject to tax. This is recovery of investment. Since the cash flow occurs in year 10, it must be discounted to *now* by multiplying by the 10-year present value factor of 0.322 $(1/(1.12)^{10})$.

Since the net present value is positive ($678,101), the company should proceed with the project. This recommendation is based on the assumption that management has confidence in the cash flow projections and other data including its estimate of the cost of capital.

# Questions

**13–1**   What is the difference between capital budgeting screening decisions and capital budgeting preference decisions?
**13–2**   What is meant by the term *time value of money?*
**13–3**   What is meant by the term *discounting?*
**13–4**   Why is the net present value method of making capital budgeting decisions superior to other methods, such as the payback and simple rate of return methods?
**13–5**   What is net present value? Can it ever be negative? Explain.
**13–6**   If a firm has to pay interest of 14% on long-term debt, then its cost of capital is 14%. Do you agree? Explain.
**13–7**   What is meant by an investment project's internal rate of return? How is the internal rate of return computed?
**13–8**   Explain how the cost of capital serves as a screening tool when dealing with the net present value method.

**13–9**  As the discount rate increases, the present value of a given future cash flow also increases. Do you agree? Explain.

**13–10**  Refer to Exhibit 13–2. Is the return on this investment proposal exactly 20%, slightly more than 20%, or slightly less than 20%? Explain.

**13–11**  Why are preference decisions sometimes called *rationing* decisions?

**13–12**  How is the profitability index computed, and what does it measure?

**13–13**  What is the preference rule for ranking investment projects under the net present value method?

**13–14**  Can an investment with a profitability index of less than 1.00 be an acceptable investment? Explain.

**13–15**  What is meant by the term *payback period?* How is the payback period determined?

**13–16**  How can the payback method be useful to the manager?

**13–17**  What is the major criticism of the payback and simple rate of return methods of making capital budgeting decisions?

# Brief Exercises

## BRIEF EXERCISE 13–1   Net Present Value Method (LO1)

The management of Kunkel Company is considering the purchase of a machine that would reduce operating costs. The machine will cost $40,000, and it will last for eight years. At the end of the eight-year period, the machine will have zero scrap value. Use of the machine will reduce operating costs by $7,000 per year. The company requires a minimum return of 12% before taxes on all investment projects.

*Required:*
1. Determine the net present value of the investment in the machine.
2. What is the difference between the total, undiscounted cash inflows and cash outflows over the entire life of the machine?

## BRIEF EXERCISE 13–2   Net Present Value Analysis of Competing Projects (LO2)

Labeau Products Ltd., of Perth, Australia, has $35,000 to invest. The company is trying to decide between two alternative uses for the funds. The alternatives are:

|  | Invest in Project X | Invest in Project Y |
|---|---|---|
| Investment required . . . . . . . . . . . . . . . . . . . . . . . | $35,000 | $ 35,000 |
| Annual cash inflows . . . . . . . . . . . . . . . . . . . . . . . | 9,000 | — |
| Single cash inflow at the end of 10 years . . . . . . . . | — | 150,000 |
| Life of the project . . . . . . . . . . . . . . . . . . . . . . . . | 10 years | 10 years |

The company's discount rate is 18%.

*Required:*
Which alternative would you recommend that the company accept? Show all computations using the net present value approach. Prepare a separate computation for each project.

## BRIEF EXERCISE 13–3   Profitability Index (LO3)

Information on four investment proposals is given below:

|  | Investment Proposal | | | |
|---|---|---|---|---|
|  | A | B | C | D |
| Investment required . . . . . . . . . | $(90,000) | $(100,000) | $(70,000) | $(120,000) |
| Present value of cash inflows  . . | 126,000 | 90,000 | 105,000 | 160,000 |
| Net present value . . . . . . . . . . . | $ 36,000 | $ (10,000) | $ 35,000 | $ 40,000 |
| Life of the project  . . . . . . . . . . | 5 years | 7 years | 6 years | 6 years |

*Required:*
1. Compute the profitability index for each investment proposal.
2. Rank the proposals in terms of preference.

**BRIEF EXERCISE 13–4    Payback Method (LO4)**
The management of Unter Corporation is considering an investment with the following characteristics:

| Year | Investment | Cash Inflow |
|------|-----------|-------------|
| 1 ............. | $15,000 | $1,000 |
| 2 ............. | 8,000 | 2,000 |
| 3 ............. | — | 2,500 |
| 4 ............. | — | 4,000 |
| 5 ............. | — | 5,000 |
| 6 ............. | — | 6,000 |
| 7 ............. | — | 5,000 |
| 8 ............. | — | 4,000 |
| 9 ............. | — | 3,000 |
| 10 ............. | — | 2,000 |

*Required:*
1. Determine the payback period of the investment.
2. Would the payback period be affected if the cash inflow in the last year were several times as large?

**BRIEF EXERCISE 13–5    Simple Rate of Return Method (LO6)**
The management of Ballard MicroBrew is considering the purchase of an automated bottling machine for $120,000. The machine would replace an old piece of equipment that costs $30,000 per year to operate. The new machine would have a useful life of 10 years with no salvage value. The new machine would cost $12,000 per year to operate. The old machine currently in use could be sold now for a scrap value of $40,000.

*Required:*
Compute the simple rate of return on the new automated bottling machine.

**BRIEF EXERCISE 13–6    (Appendix 13A) Present Value Concepts (LO7)**
Each of the following parts is independent.
1. The Atlantic Medical Clinic can purchase a new computer system that will save $7,000 annually in billing costs. The computer system will last for eight years and have no salvage value. What is the maximum purchase price that the Atlantic Medical Clinic should be willing to pay for the new computer system if the clinic's required rate of return is:
   a. Sixteen percent?
   b. Twenty percent?
2. The Caldwell *Herald* newspaper reported the following story:

   > Frank Ormsby of Caldwell is the state's newest millionaire. By choosing the six winning numbers on last week's state lottery, Mr. Ormsby has won the week's grand prize totalling $1.6 million. The State Lottery Commission has indicated that Mr. Ormsby will receive his prize in 20 annual installments of $80,000 each.

   a. If Mr. Ormsby can invest money at a 12% rate of return, what is the present value of his winnings?
   b. Is it correct to say that Mr. Ormsby is the "state's newest millionaire"? Explain your answer.
3. Fraser Company will need a new warehouse in five years. The warehouse will cost $500,000 to build. What lump-sum amount should the company invest now to have the $500,000 available at the end of the five-year period? Assume that the company can invest money at:
   a. Ten percent.
   b. Fourteen percent.

# Exercises

**EXERCISE 13–1    Net Present Value Analysis (LO1)**
Windhoek Mines Ltd., of Namibia, is contemplating the purchase of equipment to exploit a mineral deposit that is located on land to which the company has mineral rights. An engineering and cost analysis has been

made, and it is expected that the following cash flows would be associated with opening and operating a mine in the area:

| | |
|---|---:|
| Cost of new equipment and timbers ........................ | R275,000 |
| Working capital required ................................. | 100,000 |
| Net annual cash receipts .................................. | 120,000* |
| Cost to construct new roads in three years .................. | 40,000 |
| Salvage value of equipment in four years ................... | 65,000 |

*Receipts from sales of ore, less out-of-pocket costs for salaries, utilities, insurance, and so forth.

The currency in Namibia is the rand, here denoted by R.

It is estimated that the mineral deposit would be exhausted after four years of mining. At that point, the working capital would be released for reinvestment elsewhere. The company's discount rate is 20%.

**Required:**
Determine the net present value of the proposed mining project. Should the project be accepted? Explain.

**EXERCISE 13–2    Net Present Value Analysis of Competing Projects (LO2)**
Perrot Industries has $100,000 to invest. The company is trying to decide between two alternative uses of the funds. The alternatives are:

| | Project | |
|---|---|---|
| | **A** | **B** |
| Cost of equipment required ................ | $100,000 | — |
| Working capital investment required ........ | — | $100,000 |
| Annual cash inflows ..................... | 21,000 | 16,000 |
| Salvage value of equipment in six years ...... | 8,000 | — |
| Life of the project ...................... | 6 years | 6 years |

The working capital needed for project B will be released at the end of six years for investment elsewhere. Perrot Industries' discount rate is 14%.

**Required:**
Which investment alternative (if either) would you recommend that the company accept? Show all computations using the net present value format. Prepare a separate computation for each project.

**EXERCISE 13–3    Profitability Index (LO3)**
The management of Revco Products is exploring five different investment opportunities. Information on the five projects under study is given below:

| | Project Number | | | | |
|---|---|---|---|---|---|
| | **1** | **2** | **3** | **4** | **5** |
| Investment required ....... | $(270,000) | $(450,000) | $(400,000) | $(360,000) | $(480,000) |
| Present value of cash inflows at a 10% discount rate .......... | 336,140 | 522,970 | 379,760 | 433,400 | 567,270 |
| Net present value ......... | $ 66,140 | $ 72,970 | $ (20,240) | $ 73,400 | $ 87,270 |
| Life of the project ......... | 6 years | 3 years | 5 years | 12 years | 6 years |

The company's required rate of return is 10%; thus, a 10% discount rate has been used in the present value computations above. Limited funds are available for investment, and so the company cannot accept all of the available projects.

***Required:***

1. Compute the profitability index for each investment project.
2. Rank the five projects according to preference, in terms of:
   a. Net present value.
   b. Profitability index.
3. Which ranking do you prefer? Why?

### EXERCISE 13–4    Payback and Simple Rate of Return Methods (LO5, LO6)

A piece of laboursaving equipment has just come onto the market that Mitsui Electronics Ltd. could use to reduce costs in one of its plants in Japan. Relevant data relating to the equipment follow (currency is in thousands of yen, denoted by ¥):

| | |
|---|---:|
| Purchase cost of the equipment ............................. | ¥432,000 |
| Annual cost savings that will be provided by the equipment ...... | ¥90,000 |
| Life of the equipment .................................... | 12 years |

***Required:***

1. Compute the payback period for the equipment. If the company requires a payback period of four years or less, would the equipment be purchased?
2. Compute the simple rate of return on the equipment. Use straight-line depreciation based on the equipment's useful life. Would the equipment be purchased if the company requires a rate of return of at least 14%?

### EXERCISE 13–5    Basic Present Value Concepts (LO2)

Kathy Myers frequently purchases shares and bonds, but she is uncertain how to determine the rate of return that she is earning. For example, three years ago she paid $13,000 for 200 common shares of Malti Company. She received a $420 cash dividend on the shares at the end of each year for three years. At the end of three years, she sold the shares for $16,000. Kathy would like to earn a return of at least 14% on all of her investments. She is not sure whether the Malti Company shares provided a 14% return and would like some help with the necessary computations.

***Required:***

Using the net present value method, determine whether or not the Malti Company shares provided a 14% return. Round all computations to the nearest whole dollar.

### EXERCISE 13–6    (Appendix 13D) After-Tax Costs (LO9)

1. Stoffer Company has hired a management consulting firm to review and make recommendations concerning Stoffer's organizational structure. The consulting firm's fee will be $100,000. What will be the after-tax cost of the consulting firm's fee if Stoffer's tax rate is 30%?
2. The Green Hills Riding Club has redirected its advertising toward a different sector of the market. As a result of this change in advertising, the club's annual revenues have increased by $40,000. If the club's tax rate is 30%, what is the after-tax benefit from the increased revenues?
3. The Golden Eagles Basketball Team has just installed an electronic scoreboard in its playing arena at a cost of $210,000. For tax purposes, the entire original cost of the electronic scoreboard will be written off over 15 years. Determine the first three years' tax savings from the CCA tax shield. Assume that the income tax rate is 30% and the cost of capital is 10%.

### EXERCISE 13–7    (Appendix 13D) After-Tax Cash Flows in Net Present Value Analysis (LO2, LO9, LO10)

Kramer Corporation is considering two investment projects, each of which would require $50,000. Cost and cash flow data concerning the two projects follow:

| | Project A | Project B |
|---|---|---|
| Investment in high-speed photocopier ........... | $50,000 | |
| Investment in working capital.................. | | $50,000 |
| Net annual cash inflows ...................... | 9,000 | 9,000 |
| Life of the project .......................... | 8 years | 8 years |

The high-speed photocopier will have a salvage value of $5,000 in eight years. For tax purposes, the company computes CCA deductions assuming a 20% rate. The photocopier would be depreciated over eight years. At the end of eight years, the investment in working capital would be released for use elsewhere. The company requires an after-tax return of 10% on all investments. The tax rate is 30%.

**Required:**
Compute the net present value of each investment project. (Round all dollar amounts to the nearest whole dollar.)

### EXERCISE 13–8  Basic Net Present Value and Internal Rate of Return Analysis (LO2, LO4)
(Ignore income taxes.) Consider each case below independently:
1. Minden Company requires a minimum return of 15% on all investments. The company can purchase a new machine at a cost of $40,350. The new machine would generate cash inflows of $15,000 per year and have a four-year life with no salvage value. Compute the machine's net present value. (Use the format shown in Exhibit 13–1.) Is the machine an acceptable investment? Explain.
2. Leven Products, Inc. is investigating the purchase of a new grinding machine that has a projected life of 15 years. It is estimated that the machine will save $20,000 per year in cash operating costs. What is the machine's internal rate of return if it costs $111,500 new?
3. Sunset Press has just purchased a new trimming machine that cost $14,125. The machine is expected to save $2,500 per year in cash operating costs and to have a 10-year life. Compute the machine's internal rate of return. If the company's cost of capital is 16%, did it make a wise investment? Explain.

### EXERCISE 13–9  Internal Rate of Return and Net Present Value  (LO2, LO4)
Scalia's Cleaning Service is investigating the purchase of an ultrasound machine for cleaning window blinds. The machine would cost $136,700, including invoice cost, freight, and training of employees to operate it. Scalia's has estimated that the new machine would increase the company's cash flows, net of expenses, by $25,000 per year. The machine would have a 14-year useful life with no expected salvage value.

**Required:**
(Ignore income taxes.)
1. Compute the machine's internal rate of return to the nearest whole percent.
2. Compute the machine's net present value. Use a discount rate of 16%, and use the format shown in Exhibit 13–5. Why do you have a zero net present value?
3. Suppose that the new machine would increase the company's annual cash flows, net of expenses, by only $20,000 per year. Under these conditions, compute the internal rate of return to the nearest whole percent.

### EXERCISE 13–10   (Appendix 13D) Net Present Value Analysis including Income Taxes (LO10)
Vyasa Publishing Company hires students from the local university to collate pages on various printing jobs. This collating is all done by hand, at a cost of $60,000 per year. A collating machine has just come onto the market that could be used in place of the student help. The machine would cost $170,000 and have a 15-year useful life. It would require an operator at an annual cost of $18,000 and have annual maintenance costs of $7,000. New roller pads would be needed on the machine in eight years at a total cost of $20,000. The salvage value of the machine in 15 years would be $40,000.

For tax purposes, the company computes CCA deductions at 30%. Management requires a 14% after-tax return on all equipment purchases. The company's tax rate is 40%.

**Required:**
1. Determine the before-tax net annual cost savings that the new collating machine will provide.
2. Using the data from (1) above and other data from the exercise, compute the collating machine's net present value. (Round all dollar amounts to the nearest whole dollar.) Would you recommend that the machine be purchased?

# Problems

### PROBLEM 13–1   Basic Net Present Value Analysis (LO1)
The Sweetwater Candy Company would like to buy a new machine that would automatically "dip" chocolates. The dipping operation is currently done largely by hand. The machine the company is considering costs $120,000. The manufacturer estimates that the machine would be usable for 12 years but would require the replacement of several key parts at the end of the sixth year. These parts would cost $9,000, including installation. After 12 years, the machine could be sold for about $7,500.

The company estimates that the cost to operate the machine will be only $7,000 per year. The present method of dipping chocolates costs $30,000 per year. In addition to reducing costs, the new machine will increase production by 6,000 boxes of chocolates per year. The company realizes a contribution margin of $1.50 per box. A 20% rate of return is required on all investments.

CHECK FIGURE
(1) Annual cash flows:
$32,000

*Required:*
1. What are the net annual cash inflows that will be provided by the new dipping machine?
2. Compute the new machine's net present value. Use the incremental cost approach and round all dollar amounts to the nearest whole dollar.

CHECK FIGURE
(1) Annual cash receipts: $31,650

**PROBLEM 13–2    Net Present Value Analysis** (LO1)

In eight years, Kent Duncan will retire. He has $150,000 to invest, and he is exploring the possibility of opening a self-service auto wash. The auto wash could be managed in the free time he has available from his regular occupation, and it could be closed easily when he retires. After careful study, Mr. Duncan has determined the following:

a. A building in which an auto wash could be installed is available under an eight-year lease at a cost of $1,700 per month.
b. Purchase and installation costs of equipment would total $150,000. In eight years the equipment could be sold for about 10% of its original cost.
c. An investment of an additional $2,000 would be required to cover working capital needs for cleaning supplies, change funds, and so forth. After eight years, this working capital would be released for investment elsewhere.
d. Both an auto wash and a vacuum service would be offered with a wash costing $1.50 and the vacuum costing 25 cents per use.
e. The only variable costs associated with the operation would be 23 cents per wash for water and 10 cents per use of the vacuum for electricity.
f. In addition to rent, monthly costs of operation would be: cleaning, $450; insurance, $75; and maintenance, $500.
g. Gross receipts from the auto wash would be about $1,350 per week. According to the experience of other auto washes, 70% of the customers using the wash would also use the vacuum.

Mr. Duncan will not open the auto wash unless it provides at least a 10% return, since this is the amount that could be earned by simply placing the $150,000 in high-grade securities.

*Required:*
1. Assuming that the auto wash will be open 52 weeks a year, compute the expected net annual cash receipts (gross cash receipts less cash disbursements) from its operation. (Do not include the cost of the equipment, the working capital, or the salvage value in these computations.)
2. Would you advise Mr. Duncan to open the car wash? Show computations using the net present value method of investment analysis. Round all dollar figures to the nearest whole dollar.

CHECK FIGURE
(1) NPV: $2,119 in favour of new truck

**PROBLEM 13–3    Total-Cost and Incremental-Cost Approaches** (LO2)

Bilboa Freightlines, S.A., of Panama, has a small truck that it uses for intracity deliveries. The truck is in bad repair and must be either overhauled or replaced with a new truck. The company has assembled the following information. (Panama uses the U.S. dollar as its currency):

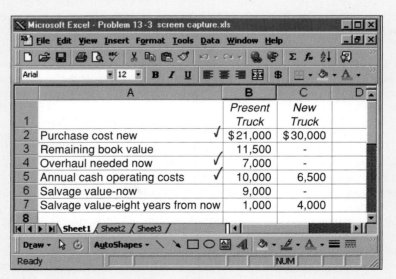

| | Present Truck | New Truck | |
|---|---|---|---|
| Purchase cost new | $21,000 | $30,000 | |
| Remaining book value | 11,500 | - | |
| Overhaul needed now | 7,000 | - | |
| Annual cash operating costs | 10,000 | 6,500 | |
| Salvage value-now | 9,000 | - | |
| Salvage value-eight years from now | 1,000 | 4,000 | |

If the company keeps and overhauls its present delivery truck, then the truck will be usable for eight more years. If a new truck is purchased, it will be used for eight years, after which it will be traded in on another truck. The new truck would be diesel-operated, resulting in a substantial reduction in annual operating costs, as shown above.

The company computes depreciation on a straight-line basis. All investment projects are evaluated using a 16% discount rate.

*Required:*
1. Should Bilboa Freightlines keep the old truck or purchase the new one? Use the total-cost approach to net present value in making your decision. Round to the nearest whole dollar.
2. Redo (1) above, this time using the incremental-cost approach.

### PROBLEM 13–4   Keep or Sell Property (LO2)
Raul Martinas, professor of languages at Eastern University, owns a small office building adjacent to the university campus. He acquired the property 10 years ago at a total cost of $530,000—$50,000 for the land and $480,000 for the building. He has just received an offer from a realty company that wants to purchase the property; however, the property has been a good source of income over the years, and so Professor Martinas is unsure whether he should keep it or sell it. His alternatives are:

*Keep the property.* Professor Martinas' accountant has kept careful records of the income realized from the property over the past 10 years. These records indicate the following annual revenues and expenses:

| | | |
|---|---:|---:|
| Rental receipts ................... | | $140,000 |
| Less building expenses: | | |
| Utilities ...................... | $25,000 | |
| Depreciation of building .......... | 16,000 | |
| Property taxes and insurance ....... | 18,000 | |
| Repairs and maintenance .......... | 9,000 | |
| Custodial help and supplies ........ | 40,000 | 108,000 |
| Net operating income .............. | | $ 32,000 |

Professor Martinas makes a $12,000 mortgage payment each year on the property. The mortgage will be paid off in eight more years. He has been depreciating the building by the straight-line method, assuming a salvage value of $80,000 for the building which he still thinks is an appropriate figure. He feels sure that the building can be rented for another 15 years. He also feels sure that 15 years from now the land will be worth three times what he paid for it.

*Sell the property.* A realty company has offered to purchase the property by paying $175,000 immediately and $26,500 per year for the next 15 years. Control of the property would go to the realty company immediately. To sell the property, Professor Martinas would need to pay the mortgage off, which could be done by making a lump-sum payment of $90,000.

*Required:*
Assume that Professor Martinas requires a 12% rate of return. Would you recommend he keep or sell the property? Show computations using the total-cost approach to net present value.

### PROBLEM 13–5   Ranking of Projects (LO3)
Oxford Company has limited funds available for investment and must ration the funds among five competing projects. Selected information on the five projects follows:

| Project | Investment Required | Net Present Value | Life of the Project (years) |
|---|---:|---:|:---:|
| A ........... | $160,000 | $44,323 | 7 |
| B .......... | 135,000 | 42,000 | 12 |
| C .......... | 100,000 | 35,035 | 7 |
| D ........... | 175,000 | 38,136 | 3 |
| E .......... | 150,000 | (8,696) | 6 |

The net present values above have been computed using a 10% discount rate. The company wants your assistance in determining which project to accept first, which to accept second, and so on.

**Required:**
1. Compute the profitability index for each project.
2. In order of preference, rank the five projects in terms of:
   a. Net present value.
   b. Profitability index.
3. Which ranking do you prefer? Why?

**PROBLEM 13–6   Simple Rate of Return and Payback Methods** (LO5, LO6)

Sharkey's Fun Centre contains a number of electronic games as well as a miniature golf course and various rides located outside the building. Paul Sharkey, the owner, would like to construct a water slide on one portion of his property. Mr. Sharkey has gathered the following information about the slide:

a. Water slide equipment could be purchased and installed at a cost of $330,000. According to the manufacturer, the slide would be usable for 12 years after which it would have no salvage value.
b. Mr. Sharkey would use straight-line depreciation on the slide equipment.
c. To make room for the water slide, several rides would be dismantled and sold. These rides are fully depreciated, but they could be sold for $60,000 to an amusement park in a nearby city.
d. Mr. Sharkey has concluded that about 50,000 more people would use the water slide each year than have been using the rides. The admission price would be $3.60 per person (the same price that the Fun Centre has been charging for the rides).
e. On the basis of experience at other water slides, Mr. Sharkey estimates that incremental operating expenses each year for the slide would be: salaries, $85,000; insurance, $4,200; utilities, $13,000; and maintenance, $9,800.

**Required:**
1. Prepare an income statement showing the expected incremental net income each year from the water slide.
2. Compute the simple rate of return expected from the water slide. On the basis of this computation, would the water slide be constructed if Mr. Sharkey requires a simple rate of return of at least 14% on all investments?
3. Compute the payback period for the water slide. If Mr. Sharkey requires a payback period of five years or less, would the water slide be constructed?

**PROBLEM 13–7   Simple Rate of Return and Payback Analyses of Two Machines** (LO5, LO6)

Westwood Furniture Company is considering the purchase of two different items of equipment, as described below:

*Machine A.* A compacting machine has just come onto the market that would permit Westwood Furniture Company to compress sawdust into various shelving products. At present the sawdust is disposed of as a waste product. The following information is available on the machine:

a. The machine would cost $420,000 and would have a 10% salvage value at the end of its 13-year useful life. The company uses straight-line depreciation and considers salvage value in computing depreciation deductions.
b. The shelving products manufactured from use of the machine would generate revenues of $300,000 per year. Variable manufacturing costs would be 20% of sales.
c. Fixed expenses associated with the new shelving products would be (per year): advertising, $40,000: salaries, $110,000; utilities, $5,200; and insurance, $800.

*Machine B.* A second machine has come onto the market that would allow Westwood Furniture Company to automate a sanding process that is now done largely by hand. The following information is available:

a. The new sanding machine would cost $234,000 and would have no salvage value at the end of its 13-year useful life. The company would use straight-line depreciation on the new machine.
b. Several old pieces of sanding equipment that are fully depreciated would be disposed of at a scrap value of $9,000.
c. The new sanding machine would provide substantial annual savings in cash operating costs. It would require an operator at an annual salary of $16,350 and $5,400 in annual maintenance costs. The current, hand-operated sanding procedure costs the company $78,000 per year in total.

Westwood Furniture Company requires a simple rate of return of 15% on all equipment purchases. Also, the company will not purchase equipment unless the equipment has a payback period of four years or less.

*Required:*
1. For machine A:
   a. Prepare an income statement showing the expected net income each year from the new shelving products. Use the contribution format.
   b. Compute the simple rate of return.
   c. Compute the payback period.
2. For machine B:
   a. Compute the simple rate of return.
   b. Compute the payback period.
3. According to the company's criteria, which machine, if either, should the company purchase?

**PROBLEM 13–8   Net Present Value Analysis of Securities (LO2)**
Linda Clark received $175,000 from her mother's estate. She placed the funds into the hands of a broker, who purchased the following securities on Linda's behalf:

a. Common shares were purchased at a cost of $95,000. The shares paid no dividends, but they were sold for $160,000 at the end of three years.
b. Preferred shares were purchased at their par value of $30,000. The shares paid a 6% dividend (based on par value) each year for three years. At the end of three years, the shares were sold for $27,000.
c. Bonds were purchased at a cost of $50,000. The bonds paid $3,000 in interest every six months. After three years, the bonds were sold for $52,700. (Note: In discounting a cash flow that occurs semiannually, the procedure is to halve the discount rate and double the number of periods. Use the same procedure in discounting the proceeds from the sale.)

The securities were all sold at the end of three years so that Linda would have funds available to open a new business venture. The broker stated that the investments had earned more than a 16% return, and he gave Linda the following computation to support his statement:

| | |
|---|---:|
| Common shares: | |
| Gain on sale ($160,000 − $95,000) | $65,000 |
| Preferred shares: | |
| Dividends paid (6% × $30,000 × 3 years) | 5,400 |
| Loss on sale ($27,000 − $30,000) | (3,000) |
| Bonds: | |
| Interest paid ($3,000 × 6 periods) | 18,000 |
| Gain on sale ($52,700 − $50,000) | 2,700 |
| Net gain on all investments | $88,100 |

$$\frac{\$88,100 \div 3 \text{ years}}{\$175,000} = 16.8\%$$

*Required:*
1. Using a 16% discount rate, compute the net present value of *each* of the three investments. On which investment(s) did Linda earn a 16% rate of return? (Round computations to the nearest whole dollar.)
2. Considering all three investments together, did Linda earn a 16% rate of return? Explain.
3. Linda wants to use the $239,700 proceeds ($160,000 + $27,000 + $52,700 = $239,700) from sale of the securities to open a retail store under a 12-year franchise contract. What net annual cash inflow must the store generate for Linda to earn a 14% return over the 12-year period? Round computations to the nearest whole dollar.

**PROBLEM 13–9   (Appendix 13D) Basic Net Present Value Analysis including Income Taxes (LO10)**
Rapid Parcel Service has been offered an eight-year contract to deliver mail and small parcels between army installations. To accept the contract, the company would have to purchase several new delivery trucks at a total cost of $450,000. Other data relating to the contract follow:

| | |
|---|---:|
| Net annual cash receipts (before taxes) from the contract. | $108,000 |
| Cost of overhauling the motors in the trucks in five years | 45,000 |
| Salvage value of the trucks at termination of the contract | 20,000 |

If the contract was accepted, several old, fully depreciated trucks would be sold at a total price of $30,000. These funds would be used to help purchase the new trucks. For tax purposes, the company computes CCA deductions at 30%. The trucks would be depreciated over eight years for accounting purposes. The company requires a 12% after-tax return on all equipment purchases. The tax rate is 30%.

*Required:*

Compute the net present value of this investment opportunity. Round all dollar amounts to the nearest whole dollar. Would you recommend that the contract be accepted?

**PROBLEM 13–10    Internal Rate of Return; Sensitivity Analysis  (LO4)**

Dr. Heidi Floss is the managing partner of the Crestwood Dental Clinic. Floss is trying to determine whether or not the clinic should move patient files and other items out of a spare room in the clinic and use the room for dental work. She has determined that it would require an investment of $142,950 for equipment and related costs of getting the room ready for use. On the basis of receipts being generated from other rooms in the clinic, Black estimates that the new room would generate a net cash inflow of $37,500 per year. The equipment purchased for the room would have a seven-year estimated useful life.

*Required:*

(Ignore income taxes.)

1. Compute the internal rate of return on the equipment for the new room to the nearest whole percent. Verify your answer by computing the net present value of the equipment using the internal rate of return you have computed as the discount rate.
2. Although seven years is the average life for dental equipment, Floss knows that due to changing technology, this life can vary substantially. Compute the internal rate of return to the nearest whole percent if the life of the equipment was (*a*) five years and (*b*) nine years, rather than seven years. Is there any information provided by these computations that you would be particularly anxious to show Floss?
3. Refer to the original data. Assume that the equipment is purchased and that the room is opened for dental use. However, due to an increasing number of dentists in the area, the clinic is able to generate only $30,000 per year in net cash receipts from the new room. At the end of five years, the clinic closes the room and sells the equipment to a newly licensed dentist for a cash price of $61,375. Compute the internal rate of return (to the nearest whole percent) that the clinic earned on its investment over the five-year period. Round all dollar amounts to the nearest whole dollar. (Hint: A useful way to proceed is to find the discount rate that will cause the net present value of the investment to be equal to, or near, zero).

**PROBLEM 13–11    Simple Rate of Return; Payback; Internal Rate of Return (LO4, LO6)**

Château Beaune is a family-owned winery located in the Burgundy region of France, headed by Gerard Despinoy. The harvesting season in early fall is the busiest part of the year for the winery, and many part-time workers are hired to help pick and process grapes. Despinoy is investigating the purchase of a harvesting machine that would significantly reduce the amount of labour required in the picking process. The harvesting machine is built to straddle grapevines, which are laid out in low-lying rows. Two workers are carried on the machine just above ground level, one on each side of the vine. As the machine slowly crawls through the vineyard, the workers cut bunches of grapes from the vines, and the grapes fall into a hopper. The machine separates the grapes from the stems and other woody debris. The debris is then pulverized and spread behind the machine as a rich ground mulch. Despinoy has gathered the following information relating to the decision of whether to purchase the machine (the French currency is the euro, which is denoted by the symbol €):

a. The winery would save €190,000 per year in labour costs with the new harvesting machine. In addition, the company would no longer have to purchase and spread ground mulch—at an annual savings of €10,000.
b. The harvesting machine would cost €480,000. It would have an estimated 12-year useful life and zero salvage value. The winery uses straight-line depreciation.
c. Annual out-of-pocket costs associated with the harvesting machine would be insurance, €1,000; fuel, €9,000; and a maintenance contract, €12,000. In addition, two operators would be hired and trained for the machine, and they would be paid a total of €70,000 per year, including all benefits.
d. Despinoy feels that the investment in the harvesting machine should earn at least a 16% rate of return.

*Required:*

(Ignore income taxes.)

1. Determine the annual net savings in cash operating costs that would be realized if the harvesting machine was purchased.

2. Compute the simple rate of return expected from the harvesting machine. (Hint: This is a cost-reduction project.)

3. Compute the payback period on the harvesting machine. Despinoy will not purchase equipment unless it has a payback period of five years or less. Under this criterion, should the harvesting machine be purchased?

4. Compute (to the nearest whole percent) the internal rate of return promised by the harvesting machine. On the basis of this computation, does it appear that the simple rate of return is an accurate guide in investment decisions?

**PROBLEM 13–12  (Appendix 13D) Net Present Value Analysis including Income Taxes** (LO10)

The Crescent Drilling Company owns the drilling rights to several tracts of land on which natural gas has been found. The amount of gas on some of the tracts is somewhat marginal, and the company is unsure whether it would be profitable to extract and sell the gas that these tracts contain. One such tract is Tract 410, on which the following information has been gathered:

| | |
|---|---|
| Investment in equipment needed for extraction work . . . . . . . . . . . . . . . . . . . . . | $600,000 |
| Working capital investment needed . . . . . . . . . . . | 85,000 |
| Annual cash receipts from sale of gas, net of related cash operating expenses (before taxes). . . . . . . . . . . . . . . . . . | 110,000 |
| Cost of restoring land at completion of extraction work. . . . . . . . . . . . . . . . . . . . . | 70,000 |

The natural gas in Tract 410 would be exhausted after 10 years of extraction work. The equipment would have a useful life of 15 years, but it could be sold for only 15% of its original cost when extraction was completed. For tax purposes, the company would depreciate the equipment using a CCA rate of 20%. The tax rate is 30%, and the company's after-tax discount rate is 10%. The working capital would be released for use elsewhere at the completion of the project.

*Required:*

1. Compute the net present value of Tract 410. Round all dollar amounts to the nearest whole dollar.
2. Would you recommend that the investment project be undertaken?

**PROBLEM 13–13   Bill Lee is Considering How to Invest $195,000** (LO10)

A small discount perfume shop is available for sale at a nearby factory outlet centre. The business can be purchased from its current owner for $195,000. The following information relates to this purchase:

a. Of the purchase price, $85,000 would be for fixtures and other depreciable items. The remainder would be for the company's working capital (inventory, accounts receivable, and cash). The fixtures and other depreciable items would have a remaining useful life of at least 12 years but would be depreciated for tax reporting purposes using a CCA rate of 20%. At the end of 12 years, these depreciable items would have a negligible salvage value; however, the working capital would be released for reinvestment elsewhere.

b. Store records indicate that sales have averaged $400,000 per year, and out-of-pocket costs have averaged $370,000 per year (*not* including income taxes). These out-of-pocket costs include rent on the building, cost of goods sold, utilities, and wages and salaries for the sales staff and the store manager. Lee plans to entrust the day-to-day operations of the store to the manager.

c. Lee's tax rate is 35%.

d. Lee wants an after-tax return on her investment of at least 8%.

*Required:*

Advise Lee as to whether the shop should be purchased. (Round all dollar amounts to the nearest whole dollar.)

# Building Your Skills

**ANALYTICAL THINKING**   (LO2)

Top-Quality Stores Inc. owns a nationwide chain of supermarkets. The company is going to open another store soon, and a suitable building site has been located in an attractive and rapidly growing area. In discussing how the company can acquire the desired building and other facilities needed to open the new store, Sam Watkins, the company's vice-president in charge of sales, stated, "I know most of our competitors are

**CHECK FIGURE**
(1) NPV: $78,001 in favour of leasing

starting to lease facilities, rather than buy, but I just can't see the economics of it. Our development people tell me that we can buy the building site, put a building on it, and get all the store fixtures we need for just $850,000. They also say that property taxes, insurance, and repairs would run $20,000 a year. When you figure that we plan to keep a site for 18 years, that's a total cost of $1,210,000. But then when you realize that the property will be worth at least a half million in 18 years, that's a net cost to us of only $710,000. What would it cost to lease the property?"

"I understand that Beneficial Insurance Company is willing to purchase the building site, construct a building and install fixtures to our specifications, and then lease the facility to us for 18 years at an annual lease payment of $120,000," replied Lisa Coleman, the company's executive vice-president.

"That's just my point," said Sam. "At $120,000 a year, it would cost us a cool $2,160,000 over the 18 years. That's three times what it would cost to buy, and what would we have left at the end? Nothing! The building would belong to the insurance company!"

"You're overlooking a few things," replied Lisa. "For one thing, the treasurer's office says that we could only afford to put $350,000 down if we buy the property, and then we would have to pay the other $500,000 off over four years at $175,000 a year. So, there would be some interest involved on the purchase side that you haven't figured in."

"But that little bit of interest is nothing compared with over 2 million bucks for leasing," said Sam. "Also, if we lease, I understand we would have to put up an $8,000 security deposit that we wouldn't get back until the end. And besides that, we would still have to pay all the yearly repairs and maintenance costs just like we owned the property. No wonder those insurance companies are so rich if they can swing deals like this."

"Well, I'll admit that I don't have all the figures sorted out yet," replied Lisa. "But I do have the operating cost breakdown for the building, which includes $7,500 annually for property taxes, $8,000 for insurance, and $4,500 for repairs and maintenance. If we lease, Beneficial will handle its own insurance costs and, of course, the owner will have to pay the property taxes. I'll put all this together and see if leasing makes any sense with our required rate of return of 16%. The president wants a presentation and recommendation in the executive committee meeting tomorrow. Let's see, development said the first lease payment would be due now and the remaining ones due in years 1–17. Development also said that this store should generate a net cash inflow that's well above the average for our stores."

*Required:*
1. Using the net present value approach, determine whether Top-Quality Stores Inc. should lease or buy the new facility. Assume that you will be making your presentation before the company's executive committee, and remember that the president detests sloppy, disorganized reports.
2. What reply will you make in the meeting if Sam Watkins brings up the issue of the building's future sales value?

## COMMUNICATING IN PRACTICE   (LO1, LO5, LO6)

Use an online yellow pages directory, such as www.comfind.com, or www.athand.com, to find a manufacturer in your area that has a website. Make an appointment with the controller or chief financial officer of the company. Before your meeting, find out as much as you can about the organization's operations from its website.

*Required:*
After asking the following questions about a capital budgeting decision that was made by the management of the company, write a brief memorandum to your instructor that summarizes the information obtained from the company's website and addresses what you found out during your interview.
1. What was the nature of the capital project?
2. What was the total cost of the capital project?
3. Did the project costs stay within budget (or estimate)?
4. What financial criteria were used to evaluate the project?

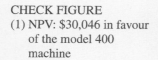

CHECK FIGURE
(1) NPV: $30,046 in favour of the model 400 machine

## TEAMWORK IN ACTION   (LO1, LO2, LO3)

Kingsley Products Ltd. is using a model 400 shaping machine to make one of its products. The company is expecting to have a large increase in demand for the product and is anxious to expand its productive capacity. Two possibilities are under consideration:

*Alternative 1.* Purchase another model 400 shaping machine to operate along with the currently owned model 400 machine.

*Alternative 2.* Purchase a model 800 shaping machine and use the currently owned model 400 machine as standby equipment. The model 800 machine is a high-speed unit with double the capacity of the model 400 machine.

The following additional information is available on the two alternatives:

a. Both the model 400 machine and the model 800 machine have a 10-year life from the time they are first used in production. The scrap value of both machines is negligible and can be ignored. Straight-line depreciation is used.

b. The cost of a new model 800 machine is $300,000.

c. The model 400 machine now in use cost $160,000 three years ago. Its present book value is $112,000, and its present market value is $90,000.

d. A new model 400 machine costs $170,000 now. If the company decides not to buy the model 800 machine, then the currently owned model 400 machine will have to be replaced in seven years at a cost of $200,000. The replacement machine will be sold at the end of the tenth year for $140,000.

e. Production over the next 10 years is expected to be:

| Year | Production in Units |
| --- | --- |
| 1 | 40,000 |
| 2 | 60,000 |
| 3 | 80,000 |
| 4–10 | 90,000 |

f. The two models of machines are not equally efficient. Comparative variable costs per unit are:

| | Model | |
| --- | --- | --- |
| | 400 | 800 |
| Materials per unit | $0.25 | $0.40 |
| Direct labour per unit | 0.49 | 0.16 |
| Supplies and lubricants per unit | 0.06 | 0.04 |
| Total variable cost per unit | $0.80 | $0.60 |

g. The model 400 machine is less costly to maintain than the model 800 machine. Annual repairs and maintenance costs on a model 400 machine are $2,500.

h. Repairs and maintenance costs on a model 800 machine, with a model 400 machine used as standby, would total $3,800 per year.

i. No other factory costs will change as a result of the decision between the two machines.

j. Kingsley Products requires a 20% rate of return on all investments.

*Required:*
The team should discuss and then respond to the following. All team members should agree with and understand the answers (including the calculations supporting the answers) and be prepared to report the information developed in class. (Each teammate can assume responsibility for a different part of the presentation.)

1. Which alternative should the company choose? Use the net present value approach.

2. Suppose that the cost of labour increases by 10%. Would this make the model 800 machine more or less desirable? Explain. No computations are needed.

3. Suppose that the cost of materials doubles. Would this make the model 800 machine more or less desirable? Explain. No computations are needed.

Do not forget to check out Taking It to the Net and other quizzes and resources at the Online Learning Centre at www.mcgrawhill.ca/college/garrison.

# Chapter Fourteen

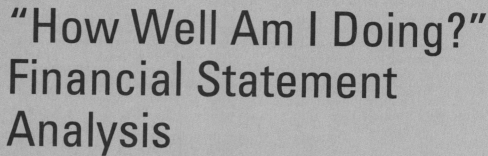

# "How Well Am I Doing?" Financial Statement Analysis

## A Look Back

Decisions relating to capital budgeting involve significant outlays on long-term projects. Various techniques used for capital budgeting decisions were discussed and illustrated in chapter 13.

## A Look at This Chapter

In Chapter 14, we focus on the analysis of financial statements to help forecast the financial health of a company. We discuss the use of trend data, comparisons with other organizations, and the analysis of fundamental financial ratios.

## A Look Ahead (See Book Website)

The cash flow statement is covered in Chapter 15 available online on the books' website www.mcgrawhill.ca/college/garrison. How to classify various types of cash inflows and outflows is addressed along with the interpretation of information reported on that financial statement.

## Chapter Outline

**Limitations of Financial Statement Analysis**
- Comparison of Financial Data
- The Need to Look beyond Ratios

**Statements in Comparative and Common-Size Forms**
- Dollar and Percentage Changes on Statements
- Common-Size Statements

**Ratio Analysis—The Common Shareholder**
- Earnings per Share
- Price-Earnings Ratio
- Dividend Payout and Yield Ratios
- Return on Total Assets
- Return on Common Shareholders' Equity

- Financial Leverage
- Book Value per Share

**Ratio Analysis—The Short-Term Creditor**
- Working Capital
- Current Ratio
- Acid-Test (Quick) Ratio
- Accounts Receivable Turnover
- Inventory Turnover

**Ratio Analysis—The Long-Term Creditor**
- Times Interest Earned Ratio
- Debt-to-Equity Ratio

**Summary of Ratios and Sources of Comparative Ratio Data**

## DECISION FEATURE The Future of Biotechnology

With the biotechnology industry, worldwide, showing promising signs of success, Canada can claim to be one of the contributors to that success. Canada is a prime location for biotechnology research. Given its abundant natural resources and its focus on health, agriculture, and environment, Canada is home to over 400 biotech firms generating nearly $5 billion in annual revenue.

BioSyntech Inc., a creator of specialized drug delivery products, has reaped the success of its BST-Gel technology market which could be worth several billion dollars. According to Amine Selmani, the company's CEO, BioSyntech is in a position to accelerate the clinical development of its BST-InPod and BST-Fill products to the European market in 2003. It secured a $1.2-million line of credit along with a $2.5-million equity loan and a $1-million reserve to support the company's operations well after 2003.

It is not easy to commercialize biotech research projects. In Canada, the average lead time is about 10 years from discovering genes to obtaining regulatory approval. Specifically, it takes about 800 days to jump over regulatory hurdles and can cost at least $20 million. According to Janet Lambert, president of BiotecCanada, the majority of her members exhaust their financial resources within 12 months. Furthermore, commercialization requires the ability to mass-produce. But current methods of production are not easily scalable due to engineering complexity. This has meant that developing and installing mass-production facilities is costly—requiring upward of US$250 million. There is a definite lack of cash, since funding for many promising projects tend to go dry. Lambert also attests that if funding continues to deplete, there is a higher risk that Canadian biotech companies will be bought out by their American counterparts or be forced to divest their intellectual capital.

Increasingly, biotech firms have to look to the financial markets for much needed financial capital. For companies like BioSyntech and others, the challenge will be to portray their past financial performance and future financial expectations in a manner consistent with established guidelines for financial reporting and to ensure that their message about their future potential financial performance gets across with clarity and precision to the financial marketplace.

This challenge has been brought into sharp relief by recent widely publicized accounting scandals involving Enron, World Com, and Nortel, where these companies failed spectacularly

### Learning Objectives

*After studying Chapter 14, you should be able to:*

**LO1** Prepare and interpret financial statements in comparative and common-size forms.

**LO2** Compute and interpret the financial ratios used to measure the well being of the common shareholder.

**LO3** Compute and interpret the financial ratios used to measure the well being of the short-term creditor.

**LO4** Compute and interpret the financial ratios used to measure the well being of the long-term creditor.

to meet the challenge. Investors, suppliers of capital, and others are going to be looking at company financial reports and other data with greater caution when deciding whether to chip in to acquire a financial stake in these companies.

Sources: Holloway, Andy, "Welcome to the Bioeconomy," *Canadian Business*, September 2, 2002, pp. 28–35; Watson, Thomas, "Sea Treasures," *Canadian Business*, September 2, 2002, pp. 38–40; Watson, Thomas, "The Pig as Factory," *Canadian Business*, September 2, 2002, pp. 52–54. Reprinted with permission from *Canadian Business*.

**A**ll financial statements are essentially historical documents. They tell what *has happened* during a particular period of time. However, most users of financial statements are concerned about what *will happen* in the future. Shareholders are concerned with future earnings and dividends. Creditors are concerned with the company's future ability to repay its debts. Managers are concerned with the company's ability to finance future expansion. Despite the fact that financial statements are historical documents, they can still provide valuable information bearing on all of these concerns.

Financial statement analysis involves careful selection of data from financial statements for the primary purpose of forecasting the financial health of the company. This is accomplished by examining trends in key financial data, comparing financial data across companies, and analyzing key financial ratios. In this chapter, we consider some of the more important ratios and other analytical tools that financial analysts use.

Managers are also vitally concerned with the financial ratios discussed in this chapter. First, the ratios provide indicators of how well the company and its business units are performing. Some of these ratios would ordinarily be used in a balanced scorecard approach as discussed in Chapter 9. The specific ratios selected depend on the company's strategy. For example, a company that wants to emphasize responsiveness to customers may closely monitor the inventory turnover ratio discussed later in this chapter. Second, since managers must report to shareholders and may wish to raise funds from external sources, managers must pay attention to the financial ratios used by external investors to evaluate the company's investment potential and creditworthiness.

*in business today*  **Those AOL Disks You Received**

During the late 1990s, investors seemed to eagerly embrace any dot-com company that was losing money. However, there was a time when investors were more cautious, and startup companies were under a lot of pressure to report positive earnings. This was the case in the mid-1990s as America Online was building its base of online customers.

AOL recorded the costs that it incurred to advertise its online services and mail disks to millions of potential subscribers as assets. Accounting professors and stock analysts were critical of the practice; these costs did not meet the asset criteria. Finally, in 1996, the company agreed that the costs should instead be expensed as incurred and wrote off $385 million of assets that were on its balance sheet.

AOL would have reported losses, rather than earnings, during six separate quarters in 1994, 1995, and 1996 if the company had expensed the costs as they were incurred. Some wonder whether the millions of online customers who subscribed to AOL would have flocked to the company if it had been reporting losses at that time. They also wonder if AOL would have been able to pull off its $160 billion deal to acquire Time-Warner in June if it had not been so successful in signing up online customers during the mid-1990s.

The SEC ultimately charged that the company should have been expensing the costs as incurred. During May 2000, the agency levied a fine of $3.5 million against AOL. Even though the SEC's investigation took years to complete, analysts agree that it sends a message to Internet-based businesses. Stock analysts will be taking a closer look at accounting policies, and they can react more quickly than the SEC can.

Source: David Henry, "AOL Pays $3.5M to Settle SEC Case," *USA Today*, May 16, 2000, p. 3B. Copyright 2000, *USA Today*. Reprinted with permission.

# Limitations of Financial Statement Analysis

Although financial statement analysis is a highly useful tool, it has two limitations that we must mention before proceeding any further. These two limitations involve the comparability of financial data between companies and the need to look beyond ratios.

## Comparison of Financial Data

Comparisons of one company with another can provide valuable clues about the financial health of an organization. Unfortunately, differences in accounting methods between companies sometimes make it difficult to compare the companies' financial data. For example, if one firm values its inventories by the LIFO method and another firm by the average cost method, then direct comparisons of financial data, such as inventory valuations and cost of goods sold, between the two firms may be misleading. Sometimes, enough data are presented in footnotes to the financial statements to restate data to a comparable basis. Otherwise, the analyst should keep in mind the lack of comparability of the data before drawing any definite conclusions. Nevertheless, even with this limitation in mind, comparisons of key ratios with other companies and with industry averages often suggest avenues for further investigation.

## The Need to Look beyond Ratios

An inexperienced analyst may assume that ratios are sufficient in themselves as a basis for judgments about the future. Nothing could be farther from the truth. Conclusions based on ratio analysis must be regarded as tentative. Ratios should not be viewed as an end but, rather, as a *starting point*, as indicators of what to pursue in greater depth. They raise many questions, but they rarely answer any questions by themselves.

In addition to ratios, other sources of data should be analyzed in order to make judgments about the future of an organization. The analyst should look, for example, at industry trends, technological changes, changes in consumer tastes, changes in broad economic factors, and changes within the firm itself. A recent change in a key management position, for example, might provide a basis for optimism about the future, even though the past performance of the firm (as shown by its ratios) may have been mediocre.

*you* *decide*   **Credit Analyst**

You work for a company that sells industrial products to businesses. Your company routinely sells products to customers on credit—expecting to be repaid within a specified period. A potential customer has asked for an extension of the payment terms on a very large sale to a later date than your company usually allows. You have been asked to determine the creditworthiness of this customer. You have been provided with a copy of the company's financial statements and accompanying footnotes that were included in the company's most recent annual report. What other information should you obtain before you begin your analysis?

# Statements in Comparative and Common-Size Forms

**Learning Objective 1**
Prepare and interpret financial statements in comparative and common-size forms.

Concept 14–1

Few figures appearing on financial statements have much significance standing by themselves. It is the relationship of one figure to another and the amount and direction of change over time that are important in financial statement analysis. How does the analyst key in on significant relationships? How does the analyst dig out the important trends and changes in a company? Three analytical techniques are widely used:

1. Dollar and percentage changes on statements.
2. Common-size statements.
3. Ratios.

The first and second techniques are discussed in this section; the third technique is discussed in the remainder of the chapter. To illustrate these analytical techniques, we analyze the financial statements of Brickey Electronics, a producer of computer components.

## Dollar and Percentage Changes on Statements

A good place to begin in financial statement analysis is to put statements in comparative form. This consists of little more than putting two or more years' data side by side. Statements cast in comparative form underscore movements and trends and may give the analyst valuable clues as to what to expect.

Examples of financial statements placed in comparative form are given in Exhibits 14–1 and 14–2. These statements of Brickey Electronics reveal the firm has been experiencing substantial growth. The data on these statements are used as a basis for discussion throughout the remainder of the chapter.

**Exhibit 14–1**

**BRICKEY ELECTRONICS**
**Comparative Balance Sheet**
**December 31, 2004, and 2003**
**(dollars in thousands)**

| | 2004 | 2003 | Increase (Decrease) Amount | Increase (Decrease) Percent |
|---|---|---|---|---|
| **Assets** | | | | |
| Current assets: | | | | |
| Cash ...................... | $ 1,200 | $ 2,350 | $(1,150) | (48.9)%* |
| Accounts receivable, net ...... | 6,000 | 4,000 | 2,000 | 50.0% |
| Inventory .................. | 8,000 | 10,000 | (2,000) | (20.0)% |
| Prepaid expenses ............ | 300 | 120 | 180 | 150.0% |
| Total current assets ............ | 15,500 | 16,470 | (970) | (5.9)% |
| Property and equipment: | | | | |
| Land ...................... | 4,000 | 4,000 | –0– | –0–% |
| Buildings and equipment, net .. | 12,000 | 8,500 | 3,500 | 41.2% |
| Total property and equipment .... | 16,000 | 12,500 | 3,500 | 28.0% |
| Total assets .................. | $31,500 | $28,970 | $ 2,530 | 8.7% |
| **Liabilities and Shareholders' Equity** | | | | |
| Current liabilities: | | | | |
| Accounts payable ............ | $ 5,800 | $ 4,000 | $ 1,800 | 45.0% |
| Accrued payables ............ | 900 | 400 | 500 | 125.0% |
| Notes payable, short term ..... | 300 | 600 | (300) | (50.0)% |
| Total current liabilities .......... | 7,000 | 5,000 | 2,000 | 40.0% |
| Long-term liabilities: | | | | |
| Bonds payable, 8% .......... | 7,500 | 8,000 | (500) | (6.3)% |
| Total liabilities ................ | 14,500 | 13,000 | 1,500 | 11.5% |
| Shareholders' equity: | | | | |
| Preferred shares, $100 par, 6%, $100 liquidation value ...... | 2,000 | 2,000 | –0– | –0–% |
| Common shares, $12 par ...... | 6,000 | 6,000 | –0– | –0–% |
| Additional paid-in capital ..... | 1,000 | 1,000 | –0– | –0–% |
| Total paid-in capital ............ | 9,000 | 9,000 | –0– | –0–% |
| Retained earnings ........... | 8,000 | 6,970 | 1,030 | 14.8% |
| Total shareholders' equity ....... | 17,000 | 15,970 | 1,030 | 6.4% |
| Total liabilities and shareholders' equity .......... | $31,500 | $28,970 | $ 2,530 | 8.7% |

*Since we are measuring the amount of change between 2003 and 2004, the dollar amounts for 2003 become the base figures for expressing these changes in percentage form. For example, Cash decreased by $1,150 between 2003 and 2004. This decrease expressed in percentage form is computed as follows: $1,150 ÷ $2,350 = 48.9%. Other percentage figures in this exhibit and Exhibit 14–2 are computed in the same way.

**HORIZONTAL ANALYSIS** Comparison of two or more years' financial data is known as **horizontal analysis** or **trend analysis.** Horizontal analysis is facilitated by showing changes between years in both dollar *and* percentage forms, as has been done in Exhibits 14–1 and 14–2. Showing changes in dollar form helps the analyst focus on key factors that have affected profitability or financial position. For example, observe in Exhibit 14–2

**Exhibit 14–2**

| | | | Increase (Decrease) | |
|---|---|---|---|---|
| | 2004 | 2003 | Amount | Percent |

**BRICKEY ELECTRONICS**
**Comparative Income Statement and Reconciliation**
**of Retained Earnings**
**For the Years Ended December 31, 2004, and 2003**
**(dollars in thousands)**

| | 2004 | 2003 | Amount | Percent |
|---|---|---|---|---|
| Sales . . . . . . . . . . . . . . . . . . . . . . | $52,000 | $48,000 | $4,000 | 8.3% |
| Cost of goods sold . . . . . . . . . . . . | 36,000 | 31,500 | 4,500 | 14.3% |
| Gross margin . . . . . . . . . . . . . . . . | 16,000 | 16,500 | (500) | (3.0)% |
| Operating expenses: | | | | |
|   Selling expenses . . . . . . . . . . . . | 7,000 | 6,500 | 500 | 7.7% |
|   Administrative expenses . . . . . . | 5,860 | 6,100 | (240) | (3.9)% |
| Total operating expenses . . . . . . . . | 12,860 | 12,600 | 260 | 2.1% |
| Net operating income . . . . . . . . . . . | 3,140 | 3,900 | (760) | (19.5)% |
| Interest expense . . . . . . . . . . . . . . . | 640 | 700 | (60) | (8.6)% |
| Net income before taxes . . . . . . . . | 2,500 | 3,200 | (700) | (21.9)% |
| Less income taxes (30%) . . . . . . . . | 750 | 960 | (210) | (21.9)% |
| Net income . . . . . . . . . . . . . . . . . . | 1,750 | 2,240 | $ (490) | (21.9)% |
| Dividends to preferred shareholders, $6 per share (see Exhibit 14–1) . . . . . . . . . . | 120 | 120 | | |
| Net income remaining for common shareholders . . . . . . . . | 1,630 | 2,120 | | |
| Dividends to common shareholders, $1.20 per share . . | 600 | 600 | | |
| Net income added to retained earnings . . . . . . . . . . . . | 1,030 | 1,520 | | |
| Retained earnings, beginning of year . . . . . . . . . . . . . . . . . . . | 6,970 | 5,450 | | |
| Retained earnings, end of year . . . | $ 8,000 | $ 6,970 | | |

that sales for 2004 were up $4 million over 2003 but that this increase in sales was more than negated by a $4.5 million increase in cost of goods sold.

Showing changes between years in percentage form helps the analyst gain *perspective* and gain a feel for the *significance* of the changes that are taking place. A $1 million increase in sales is much more significant if the prior year's sales were $2 million than if the prior year's sales were $20 million. In the first situation, the increase would be 50%—undoubtedly a significant increase for any firm. In the second situation, the increase would be only 5%—perhaps just a reflection of normal growth.

**TREND PERCENTAGES**  Horizontal analysis of financial statements can also be carried out by computing *trend percentages*. **Trend percentages** state several years' financial data in terms of a base year. The base year equals 100%, with all other years stated as some percentage of this base. To illustrate, consider McDonald's Corporation, the largest global foodservice retailer, with more than 26,000 restaurants worldwide. McDonald's enjoyed tremendous growth during the 1990s, as evidenced by the following data:

| | 1999 | 1998 | 1997 | 1996 | 1995 | 1994 | 1993 | 1992 | 1991 | 1990 | 1989 |
|---|---|---|---|---|---|---|---|---|---|---|---|
| Sales (millions) . . . . | $13,259 | $12,421 | $11,409 | $10,687 | $9,795 | $8,321 | $7,408 | $7,133 | $6,695 | $6,640 | $6,066 |
| Net income (millions) . . . . . . . | $ 1,948 | $ 1,550 | $ 1,642 | $ 1,573 | $1,427 | $1,224 | $1,083 | $ 959 | $ 860 | $ 802 | $ 727 |

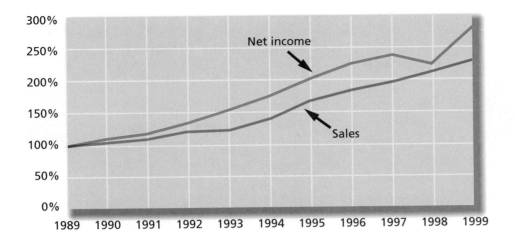

**Exhibit 14–3**
McDonald's Corporation
Trend Analysis of Sales and
Net Income

By simply looking at these data, one can see that sales increased in every year. But how rapidly have sales been increasing, and have the increases in net income kept pace with the increases in sales? It is difficult to answer these questions by looking at the raw data alone. The increases in sales and the increases in net income can be put into better perspective by stating them in terms of trend percentages, with 1989 as the base year. These percentages (all rounded) are set forth below:

| | 1999 | 1998 | 1997 | 1996 | 1995 | 1994 | 1993 | 1992 | 1991 | 1990 | 1989 |
|---|---|---|---|---|---|---|---|---|---|---|---|
| Sales* ........... | 219% | 205% | 188% | 176% | 161% | 137% | 122% | 118% | 110% | 109% | 100% |
| Net income ....... | 268% | 213% | 226% | 216% | 196% | 168% | 149% | 132% | 118% | 110% | 100% |

*For 1990, $6,640 ÷ $6,066 = 109%; for 1991, $6,695 ÷ $6,066 = 110%, and so on.

The trend analysis is particularly striking when the data are plotted as in Exhibit 14–3. McDonald's sales growth was impressive throughout the entire 11-year period, but it was outpaced by even higher growth in the company's net income. A review of the company's income statement reveals that the dip in net income growth in 1998 was attributable, in part, to the $161.6 million that McDonald's spent to implement its "Made for You" program and a special charge of $160 million that related to a home office productivity initiative. Both amounts are separately disclosed on the company's income statement.

## Common-Size Statements

Key changes and trends can also be highlighted by the use of *common-size statements*. A **common-size statement** is one that shows the items appearing on it in percentage form as well as in dollar form. Each item is stated as a percentage of some total of which that item is a part. The preparation of common-size statements is known as **vertical analysis.**

Common-size statements are particularly useful when comparing data from different companies. For example, in one year, Wendy's net income was about $110 million, whereas McDonald's was $1,427 million. This comparison is somewhat misleading because of the dramatically different sizes of the two companies. To put this in better perspective, the net income figures can be expressed as a percentage of the sales revenues of each company. Since Wendy's sales revenues were $1,746 million and McDonald's were $9,794 million, Wendy's net income as a percentage of sales was about 6.3% and McDonald's was about 14.6%. While the comparison still favours McDonald's, the contrast between the two companies has been placed on a more comparable basis.

**THE BALANCE SHEET**   One application of the vertical analysis idea is to state the separate assets of a company as percentages of total assets. A common-size statement of this type is shown in Exhibit 14–4 for Brickey Electronics.

**Exhibit 14–4**

| BRICKEY ELECTRONICS<br>Common-Size Comparative Balance Sheet<br>December 31, 2004, and 2003<br>(dollars in thousands) | | | Common-Size<br>Percentages | |
|---|---|---|---|---|
| | **2004** | **2003** | **2004** | **2003** |
| **Assets** | | | | |
| Current assets: | | | | |
| Cash ..................... | $ 1,200 | $ 2,350 | 3.8%* | 8.1% |
| Accounts receivable, net ....... | 6,000 | 4,000 | 19.0% | 13.8% |
| Inventory ................... | 8,000 | 10,000 | 25.4% | 34.5% |
| Prepaid expenses ............. | 300 | 120 | 1.0% | 0.4% |
| Total current assets ............ | 15,500 | 16,470 | 49.2% | 56.9% |
| Property and equipment: | | | | |
| Land ..................... | 4,000 | 4,000 | 12.7% | 13.8% |
| Buildings and equipment, net ... | 12,000 | 8,500 | 38.1% | 29.3% |
| Total property and equipment ..... | 16,000 | 12,500 | 50.8% | 43.1% |
| Total assets ................... | $31,500 | $28,970 | 100.0% | 100.0% |
| **Liabilities and<br>Shareholders' Equity** | | | | |
| Current liabilities: | | | | |
| Accounts payable ............ | $ 5,800 | $ 4,000 | 18.4% | 13.8% |
| Accrued payables ............ | 900 | 400 | 2.8% | 1.4% |
| Notes payable, short term ...... | 300 | 600 | 1.0% | 2.1% |
| Total current liabilities .......... | 7,000 | 5,000 | 22.2% | 17.3% |
| Long-term liabilities: | | | | |
| Bonds payable, 8% ........... | 7,500 | 8,000 | 23.8% | 27.6% |
| Total liabilities ................ | 14,500 | 13,000 | 46.0% | 44.9% |
| Shareholders' equity: | | | | |
| Preferred shares, $100, 6%,<br>$100 liquidation value ...... | 2,000 | 2,000 | 6.4% | 6.9% |
| Common shares, $12 par ...... | 6,000 | 6,000 | 19.0% | 20.7% |
| Additional paid-in capital ...... | 1,000 | 1,000 | 3.2% | 3.5% |
| Total paid-in capital ............ | 9,000 | 9,000 | 28.6% | 31.1% |
| Retained earnings ............ | 8,000 | 6,970 | 25.4% | 24.0% |
| Total shareholders' equity ........ | 17,000 | 15,970 | 54.0% | 55.1% |
| Total liabilities and<br>shareholders' equity .......... | $31,500 | $28,970 | 100.0% | 100.0% |

*Each asset account on a common-size statement is expressed in terms of total assets, and each liability and equity account is expressed in terms of total liabilities and shareholders' equity. For example, the percentage figure above for Cash in 2004 is computed as follows: $1,200 ÷ $31,500 = 3.8%.

Note from Exhibit 14–4 that placing all assets in common-size form clearly shows the relative importance of the current assets as compared with the noncurrent assets. It also shows that significant changes have taken place in the *composition* of the current assets over the last year. Note, for example, that the receivables have increased in relative importance and that both cash and inventory have declined in relative importance. Judging from the sharp increase in receivables, the deterioration in the cash position may be a result of inability to collect from customers.

**Exhibit 14–5**

| | 2004 | 2003 | Common-Size Percentages 2004 | 2003 |
|---|---|---|---|---|
| **BRICKEY ELECTRONICS** Common-Size Comparative Income Statement For the Years Ended December 31, 2004, and 2003 (dollars in thousands) | | | | |
| Sales | $52,000 | $48,000 | 100.0% | 100.0% |
| Cost of goods sold | 36,000 | 31,500 | 69.2% | 65.6% |
| Gross margin | 16,000 | 16,500 | 30.8% | 34.4% |
| Operating expenses: | | | | |
| Selling expenses | 7,000 | 6,500 | 13.5% | 13.5% |
| Administrative expenses | 5,860 | 6,100 | 11.3% | 12.7% |
| Total operating expenses | 12,860 | 12,600 | 24.7% | 26.2% |
| Net operating income | 3,140 | 3,900 | 6.0% | 8.1% |
| Interest expense | 640 | 700 | 1.2% | 1.5% |
| Net income before taxes | 2,500 | 3,200 | 4.8% | 6.7% |
| Income taxes (30%) | 750 | 960 | 1.4% | 2.0% |
| Net income | $ 1,750 | $ 2,240 | 3.4% | 4.7% |

*The percentage figures for each year are expressed in terms of total sales for the year. For example, the percentage figure for cost of goods sold in 2004 is computed as follows: $36,000 ÷ $52,000 = 69.2%.

**THE INCOME STATEMENT** Another application of the vertical analysis idea is to place all items on the income statement in percentage form in terms of sales. A common-size statement of this type is shown in Exhibit 14–5.

By placing all items on the income statement in common size in terms of sales, it is possible to see at a glance how each dollar of sales is distributed among the various costs, expenses, and profits. And by placing successive years' statements side by side, it is easy to spot interesting trends. For example, as shown in Exhibit 14–5, the cost of goods sold as a percentage of sales increased from 65.6% in 2000 to 69.2% in 2004. Or looking at this from a different viewpoint, the *gross margin percentage* declined from 34.4% in 2003 to 30.8% in 2003. Managers and investment analysts often pay close attention to the gross margin percentage, since it is considered a broad gauge of profitability. The **gross margin percentage** is computed as follows:

$$\text{Gross margin percentage} = \frac{\text{Gross margin}}{\text{Sales}}$$

The gross margin percentage tends to be more stable for retailing companies than for other service companies and for manufacturers, since the cost of goods sold in retailing excludes fixed costs. When fixed costs are included in the cost of goods sold figure, the gross margin percentage tends to increase and decrease with sales volume. With increases in sales volume, the fixed costs are spread across more units and the gross margin percentage improves.

While a higher gross margin percentage is generally considered to be better than a lower gross margin percentage, there are exceptions. Some companies purposely choose a strategy emphasizing low prices (and hence low gross margins). An increasing gross margin in such a company might be a sign that the company's strategy is not being effectively implemented.

Common-size statements are also very helpful in pointing out efficiencies and inefficiencies that might otherwise go unnoticed. To illustrate, in 2004, Brickey Electronics' selling expenses increased by $500,000 over 2003. A glance at the common-size income statement shows, however, that on a relative basis, selling expenses were no higher in 2004 than in 2003. In each year they represented 13.5% of sales.

# Ratio Analysis—The Common Shareholder

**Learning Objective 2**
Compute and interpret the financial ratios used to measure the well being of the common shareholder.

Concept 14–2

A number of financial ratios are used to assess how well the company is doing from the standpoint of the shareholders. These ratios naturally focus on net income, dividends, and shareholders' equities.

## Earnings per Share

An investor buys a share in the hope of realizing a return in the form of either dividends or future increases in the value of the share. Since earnings form the basis for dividend payments, as well as the basis for future increases in the value of shares, investors are always interested in a company's reported *earnings per share*. Probably no single statistic is more widely quoted or relied on by investors than earnings per share, although it has some inherent limitations, as discussed below.

**Earnings per share** is computed by dividing net income available for common shareholders by the average number of common shares outstanding during the year. "Net income available for common shareholders" is net income less dividends paid to the owners of the company's preferred shares.[1]

$$\text{Earnings per share} = \frac{\text{Net income} - \text{Preferred dividends}}{\text{Average number of common shares outstanding}}$$

Using the data in Exhibits 14–1 and 14–2, we see that the earnings per share for Brickey Electronics for 2004 would be computed as follows:

$$\frac{\$1,750,000 - \$120,000}{(500,000 \text{ shares}^* + 500,000 \text{ shares})/2} = \$3.26$$

$$^*\$6,000,000 \div 12 = 500,000 \text{ shares.}$$

## Price-Earnings Ratio

The relationship between the market price of a share and its current earnings per share is often quoted in terms of a **price-earnings ratio.** If we assume that the current market price for Brickey Electronics' shares is $40 each, the company's price-earnings ratio would be computed as follows:

$$\text{Price-earnings ratio} = \frac{\text{Market price per share}}{\text{Earnings per share}}$$

$$\frac{\$40}{\$3.26} = 12.3$$

The price-earnings ratio is 12.3; that is, the shares are selling for about 12.3 times their current earnings per share.

---

[1]Another complication can arise when a company has issued securities, such as executive stock options or warrants, that can be converted into common shares. If these conversions were to take place, the same earnings would have to be distributed among a greater number of common shares. Therefore, a supplemental earnings per share figure, called diluted earnings per share, may have to be computed. Refer to a current intermediate financial accounting text for details.

The price-earnings ratio is widely used by investors as a general guideline in gauging share values. A high price-earnings ratio means that investors are willing to pay a premium for the company's shares—presumably because the company is expected to have higher than average future earnings growth. Conversely, if investors believe a company's future earnings growth prospects are limited, the company's price-earnings ratio will be relatively low. For example, not long ago, the share prices of some dot-com companies—particularly those with little or no earnings—were selling at levels that gave rise to unprecedented price-earnings ratios. However, these price-earnings ratios were unsustainable in the long run and the companies' share prices eventually fell.

## Dividend Payout and Yield Ratios

Investors hold shares in a company because they anticipate an attractive return. The return sought is not always dividends. Many investors prefer not to receive dividends. Instead, they prefer to have the company retain all earnings and reinvest them internally in order to support growth. The shares of companies that adopt this approach, loosely termed *growth shares*, may enjoy rapid upward movement in market price. Other investors prefer to have a dependable, current source of income through regular dividend payments. Such investors seek out shares with consistent dividend records and payout ratios.

**THE DIVIDEND PAYOUT RATIO**   The **dividend payout ratio** gauges the portion of current earnings being paid out in dividends. Investors who seek growth in market price would like this ratio to be small, whereas investors who seek dividends prefer it to be large. This ratio is computed by relating dividends per share to earnings per share for common shares:

$$\text{Dividend payout ratio} = \frac{\text{Dividends per share}}{\text{Earnings per share}}$$

For Brickey Electronics, the dividend payout ratio for 2004 is computed as follows:

$$\frac{\$1.20 \text{ (see Exhibit 14–2)}}{\$3.26} = 36.8\%$$

There is no such thing as a "right" payout ratio, even though it should be noted that the ratio tends to be similar for companies within a particular industry. Industries with ample opportunities for growth at high rates of return on assets tend to have low payout ratios, whereas payout ratios tend to be high in industries with limited reinvestment opportunities.

**THE DIVIDEND YIELD RATIO**   The **dividend yield ratio** is obtained by dividing the current dividends per share by the current market price per share:

$$\text{Dividend yield ratio} = \frac{\text{Dividends per share}}{\text{Market price per share}}$$

The market price for Brickey Electronics' shares is $40 each, and so the dividend yield is computed as follows:

$$\frac{\$1.20}{\$40} = 3.0\%$$

The dividend yield ratio measures the rate of return (in the form of cash dividends only) that would be earned by an investor who buys the common shares at the current market price. A low dividend yield ratio is neither bad nor good by itself. As discussed above, a company may pay out very little dividends because it has ample opportunities for reinvesting funds within the company at high rates of return.

## Return on Total Assets

Managers have both *financing* and *operating* responsibilities. Financing responsibilities relate to how one *obtains* the funds needed to provide for the assets in an organization. Operating responsibilities relate to how one *uses* the assets once they have been obtained. Both are vital to a well-managed firm. However, care must be taken not to confuse or mix the two when assessing the performance of a manager. That is, whether funds have been obtained from creditors or from shareholders should not be allowed to influence one's assessment of *how well* the assets have been employed since being received by the firm.

The **return on total assets** is a measure of operating performance that shows how well assets have been employed. It is defined as follows:

$$\text{Return on total assets} = \frac{\text{Net income} + [\text{Interest expense} \times (1 - \text{Tax rate})]}{\text{Average total assets}}$$

Adding interest expense back to net income results in an adjusted earnings figure that shows what earnings would have been if the assets had been acquired solely by selling shares. With this adjustment, the return on total assets can be compared for companies with differing amounts of debt or over time for a single company that has changed its mix of debt and equity. Thus, the measurement of how well the assets have been employed is not influenced by how the assets were financed. Note that the interest expense is placed on an after-tax basis by multiplying it by the factor $(1 - \text{Tax rate})$.

The return on total assets for Brickey Electronics for 2001 would be computed as follows (from Exhibits 14–1 and 14–2):

| | |
|---|---:|
| Net income ........................................... | $ 1,750,000 |
| Add back interest expense: $640,000 × (1 − 0.30) .......... | 448,000 |
| Total (a) ........................................... | $ 2,198,000 |
| Assets, beginning of year ............................. | $28,970,000 |
| Assets, end of year .................................. | 31,500,000 |
| Total .............................................. | $60,470,000 |
| Average total assets: $60,470,000 ÷ 2 (b) ............... | $30,235,000 |
| Return on total assets, (a) ÷ (b) ........................ | 7.3% |

Brickey Electronics earned a return of 7.3% on average assets employed over the last year.

## Return on Common Shareholders' Equity

One of the primary reasons for operating a corporation is to generate income for the benefit of the common shareholders. One measure of a company's success in this regard is the **return on common shareholders' equity,** which divides the net income remaining for common shareholders by the average common shareholders' equity for the year. The formula is as follows:

$$\frac{\text{Return on common}}{\text{shareholders' equity}} = \frac{\text{Net income} - \text{Preferred dividends}}{\text{Average common shareholders' equity}}$$

$$\text{where} \quad \frac{\text{Average common}}{\text{shareholders' equity}} = \frac{\text{Average total shareholders' equity}}{- \text{Average preferred shares}}$$

For Brickey Electronics, the return on common shareholders' equity is 11.3% for 2004 as shown below:

| | |
|---|---|
| Net income | $ 1,750,000 |
| Deduct preferred dividends | 120,000 |
| Net income remaining for common shareholders (a) | $ 1,630,000 |
| Average shareholders' equity | $16,485,000* |
| Deduct average preferred shares | 2,000,000† |
| Average common shareholders' equity (b) | $14,485,000 |
| Return on common shareholders' equity, (a) ÷ (b) | 11.3% |

\*$15,970,000 + $17,000,000 = $32,970,000; $32,970,000 ÷ 2 = $16,485,000.
†$2,000,000 + $2,000,000 = $4,000,000; $4,000,000 ÷ 2 = $2,000,000.

Compare the return on common shareholders' equity above (11.3%) with the return on total assets computed in the preceding section (7.3%). Why is the return on common shareholders' equity so much higher? The answer lies in the principle of *financial leverage*. Financial leverage is discussed in the following paragraphs.

## Financial Leverage

**Financial leverage** (often called *leverage* for short) involves acquiring assets with funds that have been obtained from creditors or from preferred shareholders at a fixed rate of return. If the assets in which the funds are invested are able to earn a rate of return *greater* than the fixed rate of return required by the funds' suppliers, then the company has **positive financial leverage** and the common shareholders benefit.

For example, suppose that CTV is able to earn an after-tax return of 12% on its broadcasting assets. If the company can borrow from creditors at a 10% interest rate to expand its assets, then the common shareholders can benefit from positive leverage. The borrowed funds invested in the business will earn an after-tax return of 12%, but the after-tax interest cost of the borrowed funds will be only 7% [10% interest rate × (1 − 0.30) = 7%]. The difference will go to the common shareholders.

We can see this concept in operation in the case of Brickey Electronics. Note from Exhibit 14–1 that the company's bonds payable bear a fixed interest rate of 8%. The after-tax interest cost of these bonds is only 5.6% [8% interest rate × (1 − 0.30) = 5.6%]. The company's assets are generating an after-tax return of 7.3%, as we computed earlier. Since this return on assets is greater than the after-tax interest cost of the bonds, leverage is positive, and the difference accrues to the benefit of the common shareholders. This explains, in part, why the return on common shareholders' equity (11.3%) is greater than the return on total assets (7.3%).

Unfortunately, leverage is a two-edged sword. If assets are unable to earn a high enough rate to cover the interest costs of debt and preferred dividends (**negative financial leverage**), *the common stockholder suffers.*

**THE IMPACT OF INCOME TAXES**   Debt and preferred shares are not equally efficient in generating positive leverage. The reason is that interest on debt is tax deductible, whereas preferred dividends are not. This usually makes debt a much more effective source of positive leverage than preferred shares.

To illustrate this point, suppose that the Nursing Home Corporation of Canada is considering three ways of financing a $100 million expansion of its chain of nursing homes:

1. $100 million from an issue of common shares.
2. $50 million from an issue of common shares, and $50 million from an issue of preferred shares bearing a dividend rate of 8%.
3. $50 million from an issue of common shares, and $50 million from an issue of bonds bearing an interest rate of 8%.

**Exhibit 14–6**

Leverage from Preferred Shares and Long-Term Debt

| | Alternatives: $100,000,000 Issue of Securities | | |
| --- | --- | --- | --- |
| | **Alternative 1:** $100,000,000 **Common Shares** | **Alternative 2:** $50,000,000 **Common Shares;** $50,000,000 **Preferred Shares** | **Alternative 3:** $50,000,000 **Common Shares;** $50,000,000 **Bonds** |
| Earnings before interest and taxes .................. | $ 15,000,000 | $15,000,000 | $15,000,000 |
| Deduct interest expense (8% × $50,000,000) ......... | — | — | 4,000,000 |
| Net income before taxes ......................... | 15,000,000 | 15,000,000 | 11,000,000 |
| Deduct income taxes (30%) ...................... | 4,500,000 | 4,500,000 | 3,300,000 |
| Net income ..................................... | 10,500,000 | 10,500,000 | 7,700,000 |
| Deduct preferred dividends (8% × $50,000,000) ...... | — | 4,000,000 | — |
| Net income remaining for common (a) ............. | $ 10,500,000 | $ 6,500,000 | $ 7,700,000 |
| Common shareholders' equity (b) ................. | $100,000,000 | $50,000,000 | $50,000,000 |
| Return on common shareholders' equity (a) ÷ (b) ..... | 10.5% | 13.0% | 15.4% |

Assuming that the Nursing Home Corporation of Canada can earn an additional $15 million each year before interest and taxes as a result of the expansion, the operating results under each of the three alternatives are shown in Exhibit 14–6.

If the entire $100 million is raised from an issue of common shares, then the return to the common shareholders will be only 10.5%, as shown under alternative 1 in the exhibit. If half of the funds are raised from an issue of preferred shares, then the return to the common shareholders increases to 13%, due to the positive effects of leverage. However, if half of the funds are raised from an issue of bonds, then the return to the common shareholders jumps to 15.4%, as shown under alternative 3. Thus, long-term debt is much more efficient in generating positive leverage than is preferred shares. The reason is that the interest expense on long-term debt is tax deductible, whereas the dividends on preferred shares are not.

**THE DESIRABILITY OF LEVERAGE**     Because of leverage, having some debt in the capital structure can substantially benefit the common shareholder. For this reason, most companies today try to maintain a level of debt that is considered to be normal within the industry. Many companies, such as commercial banks and other financial institutions, rely heavily on leverage to provide an attractive return on their common shares.

## Book Value per Share

Another statistic frequently used in attempting to assess the well being of the common shareholder is book value per share. The **book value per share** measures the amount that would be distributed to holders of each common share if all assets were sold at their balance sheet carrying amounts (i.e., book values) and if all creditors were paid off. Thus, book value per share is based entirely on historical costs. The formula for computing it is as follows:

$$\text{Book value per share} = \frac{\text{Common shareholders' equity (Total shareholders' equity } - \text{ Preferred shares)}}{\text{Number of common shares outstanding}}$$

| | |
| --- | --- |
| Total shareholders' equity (see Exhibit 14–1) .... | $17,000,000 |
| Deduct preferred shares (see Exhibit 14–1) ..... | 2,000,000 |
| Common shareholders' equity ............... | $15,000,000 |

"How Well Am I Doing?" Financial Statement Analysis

**553**

The book value per share of Brickey Electronics' common shares is computed as follows:

$$\frac{\$15,000,000}{500,000 \text{ shares}} = \$30 \text{ per share}$$

If this book value is compared with the $40 market value of Brickey Electronics shares, then the share appears to be somewhat overpriced. However, as we discussed earlier, market prices reflect expectations about future earnings and dividends, whereas book value largely reflects the results of events that occurred in the past. Ordinarily, the market value of a share exceeds its book value. For example, in a recent year, Microsoft's common shares often traded at over four times their book value, and Coca-Cola's market value was over 17 times its book value.

To illustrate the computation and interpretation of financial ratios that are used to assess the company's performance from the standpoint of its shareholders, consider McDonald's Corporation. The data set forth below relate to the year ended December 31, 2001. (Averages were computed by adding together the beginning- and end-of-year amounts reported on the balance sheet, and dividing the total by two.)

| | |
|---|---|
| Net income . . . . . . . . . . . . . . . . . . . . . . . . . . . . | $1,948 million |
| Interest expense . . . . . . . . . . . . . . . . . . . . . . | $396 million |
| Tax rate . . . . . . . . . . . . . . . . . . . . . . . . . . . . | 32.5% |
| Average total assets . . . . . . . . . . . . . . . . . . . | $20,384 million |
| Preferred share dividends . . . . . . . . . . . . . . . | $0 million |
| Average common shareholders' equity . . . . . | $9,552 million |
| Common shares dividends per share . . . . . . . | $0.20 |
| Earnings per share . . . . . . . . . . . . . . . . . . . . | $1.44 |
| Market price per share—end-of-year . . . . . . . | $40.3125 |
| Book value per share—end-of-year . . . . . . . . | $5.80 |

$$\text{Return on total assets} = \frac{\$1,948 + [\$396 \times (1 - 0.325)]}{\$20,384} = 10.9\%$$

$$\begin{array}{l}\text{Return on common}\\\text{shareholders' equity}\end{array} = \frac{\$1,948 - \$0}{\$9,552} = 20.4\%$$

$$\text{Dividend payout ratio} = \frac{\$0.20}{\$1.44} = 13.9\%$$

$$\text{Dividend yield ratio} = \frac{\$0.20}{\$40.3125} = 0.50\%$$

The return on common shareholders' equity of 20.4% is higher than the return on total assets of 10.9%, and therefore, the company has positive financial leverage. (About half of the company's financing is provided by creditors; the rest is provided by common and preferred shareholders.) According to the company's annual report, "Given McDonald's high returns on equity and assets and our global growth opportunities, management believes reinvesting a significant portion of earnings back into the business is prudent. Accordingly, our per share dividend is low. However, we have increased the per-share dividend amount 25 times since our first dividend was paid in 1976. Additional dividend increases will be considered in the future." Indeed, only 13.9% of earnings are paid out in dividends. In relation to the share price, this is a dividend yield of less than 1%. Finally, note that the market value per share is almost seven times as large as the book value per share. This premium over book value reflects the market's perception that McDonald's earnings will continue to grow in the future.

# Ratio Analysis—The Short-Term Creditor

Short-term creditors, such as suppliers, want to be repaid on time. Therefore, they focus on the company's cash flows and on its working capital, since these are the company's primary sources of cash in the short run.

## Working Capital

The excess of current assets over current liabilities is known as **working capital.** The working capital for Brickey Electronics is computed below:

$$\text{Working capital} = \text{Current assets} - \text{Current liabilities}$$

|                      | 2004 | 2003 |
|----------------------|------|------|
| Current assets ......... | $15,500,000 | $16,470,000 |
| Current liabilities ...... | 7,000,000 | 5,000,000 |
| Working capital ....... | $ 8,500,000 | $11,470,000 |

The amount of working capital available to a firm is of considerable interest to short-term creditors, *since it represents assets financed from long-term capital sources that do not require near-term repayment.* Therefore, the greater the working capital, the greater is the cushion of protection available to short-term creditors and the greater is the assurance that short-term debts will be paid when due.

Although it is always comforting to short-term creditors to see a large working capital balance, a large balance by itself is no assurance that debts will be paid when due. Rather than being a sign of strength, a large working capital balance may simply mean that obsolete inventory is being accumulated. Therefore, to put the working capital figure into proper perspective, it must be supplemented with other analytical work. The following four ratios (the current ratio, the acid-test ratio, the accounts receivable turnover, and the inventory turnover) should all be used in connection with an analysis of working capital.

## Current Ratio

The elements involved in the computation of working capital are frequently expressed in ratio form. A company's current assets divided by its current liabilities is known as the **current ratio:**

$$\text{Current ratio} = \frac{\text{Current assets}}{\text{Current liabilities}}$$

For Brickey Electronics, the current ratios for 2003 and 2004 would be computed as follows:

| 2004 | 2003 |
|------|------|
| $\dfrac{\$15,500,000}{\$7,000,000} = 2.21 \text{ to } 1$ | $\dfrac{\$16,470,00}{\$5,000,000} = 3.29 \text{ to } 1$ |

Although widely regarded as a measure of short-term debt-paying ability, the current ratio must be interpreted with great care. A *declining* ratio, as above, might be a sign of a deteriorating financial condition. On the other hand, it might be the result of eliminating obsolete inventories or other stagnant current assets. An *improving* ratio might be the result of an unwise stockpiling of inventory, or it might indicate an improving financial situation. In short, the current ratio is useful, but tricky to interpret. To avoid a blunder, the analyst must take a hard look at the individual assets and liabilities involved.

The general rule of thumb calls for a current ratio of 2 to 1. This rule is subject to many exceptions, depending on the industry and the firm involved. Some industries can operate quite successfully with a current ratio of slightly over 1 to 1. The adequacy of a current ratio depends heavily on the *composition* of the assets. For example, as we see in the table below, both Worthington Corporation and Greystone Inc. have current ratios of 2 to 1. However, they are not in comparable financial condition. Greystone is likely to have difficulty meeting its current financial obligations, since almost all of its current assets consist of inventory, rather than more liquid assets, such as cash and accounts receivable.

| | Worthington Corporation | Greystone, Inc. |
|---|---|---|
| Current assets: | | |
| Cash ................... | $ 25,000 | $ 2,000 |
| Accounts receivable, net .... | 60,000 | 8,000 |
| Inventory ............... | 85,000 | 160,000 |
| Prepaid expenses .......... | 5,000 | 5,000 |
| Total current assets (a) ....... | $175,000 | $175,000 |
| Current liabilities (b) ......... | $ 87,500 | $ 87,500 |
| Current ratio, (a) ÷ (b) ....... | 2 to 1 | 2 to 1 |

## Acid-Test (Quick) Ratio

The **acid-test (quick) ratio** is a much more rigorous test of a company's ability to meet its short-term debts. Inventories and prepaid expenses are excluded from total current assets, leaving only the more liquid (or "quick") assets to be divided by current liabilities.

$$\text{Acid-test ratio} = \frac{\text{Cash} + \text{Marketable securities} + \text{Current receivables*}}{\text{Current liabilities}}$$

*Current receivables include both accounts receivable and any short-term notes receivable.

The acid-test ratio is designed to measure how well a company can meet its obligations without having to liquidate or depend too heavily on its inventory. Since inventory may be difficult to sell in times of economic stress, it is generally felt that to be properly protected, each dollar of liabilities should be backed by at least $1 of quick assets. Thus, an acid-test ratio of 1 to 1 is usually viewed as adequate.

The acid-test ratios for Brickey Electronics for 2003 and 2004 are computed below:

| | 2004 | 2003 |
|---|---|---|
| Cash (see Exhibit 14–1) ..................... | $1,200,000 | $2,350,000 |
| Accounts receivable (see Exhibit 14–1) ......... | 6,000,000 | 4,000,000 |
| Total quick assets (a) ...................... | $7,200,000 | $6,350,000 |
| Current liabilities (see Exhibit 14–1) (b) ......... | $7,000,000 | $5,000,000 |
| Acid-test ratio, (a) ÷ (b) ..................... | 1.03 to 1 | 1.27 to 1 |

Although Brickey Electronics has an acid-test ratio for 2004 that is within the acceptable range, an analyst might be concerned about several disquieting trends revealed on the company's balance sheet. Note in Exhibit 14–1 that short-term debts are rising, while the cash position seems to be deteriorating. Perhaps the weakened cash position is a result of the greatly expanded volume of accounts receivable. One wonders why the accounts receivable have been allowed to increase so rapidly in so brief a time.

In short, as with the current ratio, the acid-test ratio should be interpreted with one eye on its basic components.

## Accounts Receivable Turnover

The **accounts receivable turnover** is a rough measure of how many times a company's accounts receivable have been turned into cash during the year. It is frequently used in conjunction with an analysis of working capital, since a smooth flow from accounts receivable into cash is an important indicator of the "quality" of a company's working capital and is critical to the company's ability to operate. The accounts receivable turnover is computed by dividing sales on account (i.e., credit sales) by the average accounts receivable balance for the year.

$$\text{Accounts receivable turnover} = \frac{\text{Sales on account}}{\text{Average accounts receivable balance}}$$

Assuming that all sales for the year were on account, the accounts receivable turnover for Brickey Electronics for 2004 would be computed as follows:

$$\frac{\text{Sales on account}}{\text{Average accounts receivable balance}} = \frac{\$52,000,000}{\$5,000,000^*} = 10.4 \text{ times}$$

$^*\$4,000,000 + \$6,000,000 = \$10,000,000; \$10,000,000 \div 2 = \$5,000,000 \text{ average.}$

The turnover figure can then be divided into 365 to determine the average number of days being taken to collect an account (known as the **average collection period**).

$$\text{Average collection period} = \frac{365 \text{ days}}{\text{Accounts receivable turnover}}$$

The average collection period for Brickey Electronics for 2004 is computed as follows:

$$\frac{365}{10.4 \text{ times}} = 35 \text{ days}$$

This simply means that on average, it takes 35 days to collect on a credit sale. Whether the average of 35 days taken to collect an account is good or bad depends on the credit terms Brickey Electronics is offering its customers. If the credit terms are 30 days, then a 35-day average collection period would usually be viewed as very good. Most customers will tend to withhold payment for as long as the credit terms will allow and may even go over a few days. This factor, added to ever-present problems with a few slow-paying customers, can cause the average collection period to exceed normal credit terms by a week or so and should not cause great alarm.

On the other hand, if the company's credit terms are 10 days, then a 35-day average collection period is worrisome. The long collection period may result from many old unpaid accounts of doubtful collectability, or it may be a result of poor day-to-day credit management. The firm may be making sales with inadequate credit checks on customers, or perhaps no follow-ups are being made on slow accounts.

## Inventory Turnover

The **inventory turnover ratio** measures how many times a company's inventory has been sold and replaced during the year. It is computed by dividing the cost of goods sold by the average level of inventory on hand:

$$\text{Inventory turnover} = \frac{\text{Cost of goods sold}}{\text{Average inventory balance}}$$

The average inventory figure is the average of the beginning and ending inventory figures. Since Brickey Electronics has a beginning inventory of $10,000,000 and an ending inventory of $8,000,000, its average inventory for the year would be $9,000,000. The company's inventory turnover for 2004 would be computed as follows:

$$\frac{\text{Cost of goods sold}}{\text{Average inventory balance}} = \frac{\$36,000,000}{\$9,000,000} = 4 \text{ times}$$

The number of days being taken to sell the entire inventory one time (called the **average sale period**) can be computed by dividing 365 by the inventory turnover figure:

$$\text{Average sale period} = \frac{365 \text{ days}}{\text{Inventory turnover}}$$

$$\frac{365}{4 \text{ times}} = 91\frac{1}{4} \text{ days}$$

The average sale period varies from industry to industry. Grocery stores tend to turn their inventory over very quickly, perhaps as often as every 12 to 15 days. On the other hand, jewellery stores tend to turn their inventory over very slowly, perhaps only a couple of times each year.

If a firm has a turnover that is much slower than the average for its industry, then it may have obsolete goods on hand, or its inventory stocks may be needlessly high. Excessive inventories tie up funds that could be used elsewhere in operations. Managers sometimes argue that they must buy in very large quantities to take advantage of the best discounts being offered. But these discounts must be carefully weighed against the added costs of insurance, taxes, financing, and risks of obsolescence and deterioration that result from carrying added inventories.

Inventory turnover has been increasing in recent years as companies have adopted just-in-time (JIT) methods. Under JIT, inventories are purposely kept low, and thus a company utilizing JIT methods may have a very high inventory turnover as compared with other companies. Indeed, one of the goals of JIT is to increase inventory turnover by systematically reducing the amount of inventory on hand.

## Vice-President of Sales

*decision* maker

Although its credit terms require payment within 30 days, your company's average collection period is 33 days. A major competitor has an average collection period of 27 days. You have been asked to explain why your company is not doing as well as the competitor. You have investigated your company's credit policies and procedures and have concluded that they are reasonable and adequate under the circumstances. What rationale would you consider to explain why (1) the average collection period of your company exceeds the credit terms, and (2) the average collection period of the company is higher than that of its competitor?

# Ratio Analysis—The Long-Term Creditor

The position of long-term creditors differs from that of short-term creditors in that they are concerned with both the near-term *and* the long-term ability of a firm to meet its commitments. They are concerned with the near term, since the interest they are entitled to is normally paid on a current basis. They are concerned with the long term, since they want to be fully repaid on schedule.

Since the long-term creditor is usually faced with greater risks than the short-term creditor, firms are often required to agree to various restrictive covenants, or rules, for the long-term creditor's protection. Examples of such restrictive covenants include the maintenance of minimum working capital levels and restrictions on payment of dividends to common shareholders. Although these restrictive covenants are in widespread use, they are a poor second to adequate future *earnings* from the point of view of assessing protection and safety. Creditors do not want to go to court to collect their claims; they would much prefer staking the safety of their claims for interest and eventual repayment of principal on an orderly and consistent flow of funds from operations.

**Learning Objective 4**
Compute and interpret the financial ratios used to measure the well being of the long-term creditor.

## Times Interest Earned Ratio

The most common measure of the ability of a firm's operations to provide protection to the long-term creditor is the **times interest earned ratio.** It is computed by dividing earnings *before* interest expense and income taxes (i.e., net operating income) by the yearly interest charges that must be met:

$$\text{Times interest earned} = \frac{\text{Earnings before interest expense and income taxes}}{\text{Interest expense}}$$

For Brickey Electronics, the times interest earned ratio for 2004 would be computed as follows:

$$\frac{\$3,140,000}{\$640,000} = 4.9 \text{ times}$$

Earnings before income taxes must be used in the computation, since interest expense deductions come *before* income taxes are computed. Creditors have first claim on earnings. Only those earnings remaining after all interest charges have been provided for are subject to income taxes.

Generally, earnings are viewed as adequate to protect long-term creditors if the times interest earned ratio is 2 or more. Before making a final judgment, however, it would be necessary to look at a firm's long-term *trend* of earnings and evaluate how vulnerable the firm is to cyclical changes in the economy.

## Debt-to-Equity Ratio

Long-term creditors are also concerned with keeping a reasonable balance between the portion of assets provided by creditors and the portion of assets provided by the shareholders of a firm. This balance is measured by the **debt-to-equity ratio:**

$$\text{Debt-to-equity ratio} = \frac{\text{Total liabilities}}{\text{Shareholders' equity}}$$

|  | 2004 | 2003 |
|---|---|---|
| Total liabilities (a) ..................... | $14,500,000 | $13,000,000 |
| Shareholders' equity (b) .................. | $17,000,000 | $15,970,000 |
| Debt-to-equity ratio, (a) ÷ (b) ............. | 0.85 to 1 | 0.81 to 1 |

The debt-to-equity ratio indicates the amount of assets being provided by creditors for each dollar of assets being provided by the owners of a company. In 2003, creditors of Brickey Electronics were providing 81 cents of assets for each $1 of assets being provided by shareholders; the figure increased only slightly to 85 cents by 2004.

Creditors would like the debt-to-equity ratio to be relatively low. The lower the ratio, the greater is the amount of assets being provided by the owners of a company and the greater is the buffer of protection to creditors. By contrast, common shareholders would like the ratio to be relatively high, since through leverage, common shareholders can benefit from the assets being provided by creditors.

In most industries, norms have developed over the years that serve as guides to firms in their decisions as to the "right" amount of debt to include in the capital structure. Different industries face different risks. For this reason, the level of debt that is appropriate for firms in one industry is not necessarily a guide to the level of debt that is appropriate for firms in a different industry.

## Summary of Ratios and Sources of Comparative Ratio Data

Exhibit 14–7 contains a summary of the ratios discussed in this chapter. The formula for each ratio and a summary comment on each ratio's significance are included in the exhibit.

Exhibit 14–8 contains a listing of published sources that provide comparative ratio data organized by industry. These sources are used extensively by managers, investors, and analysts in doing comparative analyses and in attempting to assess the well being of companies. The World Wide Web also contains a wealth of financial and other data. A search engine, such as Alta Vista, Yahoo, or Excite, can be used to track down information on individual companies. Many companies have their own websites on which they post their latest financial reports and news of interest to potential investors. The *SEDAR* database listed in Exhibit 14–8 is a particularly rich source of data. It can be used by public companies to electronically file securities documents and by individuals to access information about public companies. It has been in operation since 1997.

**Exhibit 14–7**

Summary of Ratios

| Ratio | Formula | Significance |
|---|---|---|
| Gross margin percentage | Gross margin ÷ Sales | A broad measure of profitability |
| Earnings per share (of common shares) | (Net income − Preferred dividends) ÷ Average number of common shares outstanding | Tends to have an effect on the market price per share, as reflected in the price-earnings ratio |
| Price-earnings ratio | Market price per share ÷ Earnings per share | An index of whether a share is relatively cheap or relatively expensive in relation to current earnings |
| Dividend payout ratio | Dividends per share ÷ Earnings per share | An index showing whether a company pays out most of its earnings in dividends or reinvests the earnings internally |
| Dividend yield ratio | Dividends per share ÷ Market price per share | Shows the return in terms of cash dividends being provided by a share |
| Return on total assets | {Net income + [Interest expense × (1 − Tax rate)]} ÷ Average total assets | Measure of how well assets have been employed by management |
| Return on common shareholders' equity | (Net income − Preferred dividends) ÷ Average common shareholders' equity (Average total shareholders' equity − Average preferred shares) | When compared with the return on total assets, measures the extent to which financial leverage is working for or against common shareholders |
| Book value per share | Common shareholders' equity (Total shareholders' equity − Preferred shares) ÷ Number of common shares outstanding | Measures the amount that would be distributed to holders of common shares if all assets were sold at their balance sheet carrying amounts and if all creditors were paid off |
| Working capital | Current assets − Current liabilities | Measures the company's ability to repay current liabilities using only current assets |
| Current ratio | Current assets ÷ Current liabilities | Test of short-term debt-paying ability |
| Acid-test (quick) ratio | (Cash + Marketable securities + Current receivables) ÷ Current liabilities | Test of short-term debt-paying ability without having to rely on inventory |
| Accounts receivable turnover | Sales on account ÷ Average accounts receivable balance | A rough measure of how many times a company's accounts receivable have been turned into cash during the year |
| Average collection period (age of receivables) | 365 days ÷ Accounts receivable turnover | Measure of the average number of days taken to collect an account receivable |
| Inventory turnover | Cost of goods sold ÷ Average inventory balance | Measure of how many times a company's inventory has been sold during the year |
| Average sale period (turnover in days) | 365 days ÷ Inventory turnover | Measure of the average number of days taken to sell the inventory one time |
| Times interest earned | Earnings before interest expense and income taxes ÷ Interest expense | Measure of the company's ability to make interest payments |
| Debt-to-equity ratio | Total liabilities ÷ Shareholders' equity | Measure of the amount of assets being provided by creditors for each dollar of assets being provided by the shareholders |

## Exhibit 14–8
Published Sources of Financial Ratios

| Source | Content |
|---|---|
| *Almanac of Business and Industrial Financial Ratios.* Prentice-Hall. Published annually. | An exhaustive source that contains common-size income statements and financial ratios by industry and by size of companies within each industry. |
| *Annual Statement Studies.* Robert Morris Associates. Published annually. See www.rmahq.org/Ann_Studies/assstudies.html for definitions and explanations of ratios and balance sheet and income statement data that are contained in the Annual Statement Studies. | A widely used publication that contains common-size statements and financial ratios on individual companies. The companies are arranged by industry. |
| *Business & Company ASAP.* Database that is updated continuously. | Exhaustive database of business articles in periodicals for both industry and company information. Many of the articles are available in full text. Directory listings for over 150,000 companies are also included in the database. |
| *EDGAR.* Securities and Exchange Commission. Website that is updated continuously. www.sec.gov | An exhaustive database accessible on the World Wide Web that contains reports filed by companies with the SEC. These reports can be downloaded. |
| *EBSCOhost (Business Source Elite index).* EBSCO Publishing. Database that is continuously updated. | Exhaustive database of business articles in periodicals useful for both industry and company information. Full text is included from nearly 970 journals; indexing and abstracts are offered for over 1,650 journals. |
| *FreeEdgar.* EDGAR Online, Inc. Website that is updated continuously. www.freeedgar.com | A site that allows you to search SEC filings. Financial information can be downloaded directly into Excel worksheets. |
| *Hoover's Online.* Hoovers, Inc. Website that is updated continuously. www.hoovers.com | A site that provides capsule profiles for 10,000 U.S. companies with links to company websites, annual reports, stock charts, news articles, and industry information. |
| *Key Business Ratios.* Dun & Bradstreet. Published annually. | Fourteen commonly used financial ratios are computed for over 800 major industry groupings. |
| *Moody's Industrial Manual and Moody's Bank and Finance Manual.* Dun & Bradstreet. Published annually. | An exhaustive source that contains financial ratios on all companies listed on the New York Stock Exchange, the American Stock Exchange, and regional American exchanges. |
| *SEDAR.* (www.sedar.com) | An exhaustive database on the World Wide Web that can be used to access public company information in the public domain. |
| *Standard & Poor's Industry Survey.* Standard & Poor's. Published annually. | Various statistics, including some financial ratios, are given by industry and for leading companies within each industry grouping. |

# Summary

**LO1    Prepare and interpret financial statements in comparative and common-size forms.**

It is difficult to interpret raw data from financial statements without standardizing the data in some way so that it can be compared over time and across companies. For example, all of the financial data for a company can be expressed as a percentage of the data in some base year. This makes it easier to spot trends over time. To make it easier to compare companies, common-size financial statements are often used in which income statement data are expressed as a percentage of sales and balance sheet data are expressed as a percentage of total assets.

**LO2** **Compute and interpret the financial ratios used to measure the well being of the common shareholder.**

Common shareholders are most concerned with the company's earnings per share, price-earnings ratio, dividend payout and yield ratios, return on total assets, book value per share, and return on common shareholders' equity. Generally speaking, the higher these ratios, the better it is for common shareholders.

**LO3** **Compute and interpret the financial ratios used to measure the well being of the short-term creditor.**

Short-term creditors are most concerned with the company's ability to repay its debt in the near future. Consequently, these investors focus on the relation between current assets and current liabilities and the company's ability to generate cash. Specifically, short-term creditors monitor working capital, the current ratio, the acid-test (quick) ratio, accounts receivable turnover, and inventory turnover.

**LO4** **Compute and interpret the financial ratios used to measure the well being of the long-term creditor.**

Long-term creditors have many of the same concerns as short-term creditors but also monitor the times interest earned ratio and the debt-to-equity ratio. These ratios indicate the company's ability to pay interest out of operations and how heavily the company is financially levered.

# Guidance Answers to You Decide and Decision Maker

**CREDIT ANALYST** (p. 542)

You should request a copy of the entire annual report. Often, two other sections of the annual report, the president's letter and management's discussion and analysis, contain important information about the data set forth in the company's financial statements. If the company's financial statements are more than three or four months old, you will want to obtain copies of any quarterly reports or other forms that have been filed with the OSC since the company's year-end. You might also visit the company's website and use a periodicals database (see Exhibit 14–8) to search for articles that contain pertinent information about the company. For a basis of comparison, you should also obtain industry information (again, see Exhibit 14–8) and information about close competitors.

**VICE-PRESIDENT OF SALES** (p. 557)

An average collection period of 33 days means that on average it takes 33 days to collect on a credit sale. Whether the average of 33 days is acceptable or not depends on the credit terms that your company is offering to its customers. In this case, an average collection period of 33 days is good because the credit terms offered by your company are net 30 days. Why might the average collection period exceed the credit terms? Some customers may misjudge the amount of time that it takes mail to reach the company's offices. Certain customers may experience temporary cash shortages and delay payment for short periods of time. Others might be in the process of returning goods and have not paid for the goods that will be returned because they realize that a credit will be posted to their account. Still others may be in the process of resolving disputes regarding the goods that were shipped.

Turning to the competitor's average collection period of 27 days, it is possible that the competitor's credit terms are 25 days, rather than 30 days. Or, the competitor might be offering sales discounts to its customers (e.g., 2/10, n/30) for paying early. You should recall from your financial accounting course that sales discounts are offered as an incentive to customers to motivate them to pay invoices well in advance of the due date. If enough customers take advantage of the sales discounts, the average collection period will drop below 30 days.

# Review Problem: Selected Ratios and Financial Leverage

Starbucks Coffee Company is the leading retailer and roaster of specialty coffee in North America with over 1,000 stores offering freshly brewed coffee, pastries, and coffee beans. Data from recent financial statements are given below:

### STARBUCKS COFFEE COMPANY
### Comparative Balance Sheet
### (dollars in thousands)

| | End of Year | Beginning of Year |
|---|---|---|
| **Assets** | | |
| Current assets: | | |
| Cash | $126,215 | $ 20,944 |
| Marketable securities | 103,221 | 41,507 |
| Accounts receivable | 17,621 | 9,852 |
| Inventories | 83,370 | 123,657 |
| Other current assets | 9,114 | 9,390 |
| Total current assets | 339,541 | 205,350 |
| Property and equipment, net | 369,477 | 244,728 |
| Other assets | 17,595 | 18,100 |
| Total assets | $726,613 | $468,178 |
| **Liabilities and Shareholders' Equity** | | |
| Current liabilities: | | |
| Accounts payable | $ 38,034 | $ 28,668 |
| Short-term bank loans | 16,241 | 13,138 |
| Accrued payables | 18,005 | 13,436 |
| Other current liabilities | 28,811 | 15,804 |
| Total current liabilities | 101,091 | 71,046 |
| Long-term liabilities: | | |
| Bonds payable | 165,020 | 80,398 |
| Other long-term liabilities | 8,842 | 4,503 |
| Total liabilities | 274,953 | 155,947 |
| Shareholders' equity: | | |
| Preferred shares | –0– | –0– |
| Common shares and additional paid-in capital | 361,309 | 265,679 |
| Retained earnings | 90,351 | 46,552 |
| Total shareholders' equity | 451,660 | 312,231 |
| Total liabilities and sharesholders' equity | $726,613 | $468,178 |

Note: The effective interest rate on the bonds payable was about 5%.

### STARBUCKS COFFEE COMPANY
### Comparative Income Statement
### (dollars in thousands)

| | Current Year | Prior Year |
|---|---|---|
| Revenue | $696,481 | $465,213 |
| Cost of goods sold | 335,800 | 211,279 |
| Gross margin | 360,681 | 253,934 |
| Operating expenses: | | |
| Store operating expenses | $210,693 | $148,757 |
| Other operating expenses | 19,787 | 13,932 |
| Depreciation and amortization | 35,950 | 22,486 |
| General and administrative expenses | 37,258 | 28,643 |
| Total operating expenses | 303,688 | 213,818 |
| Net operating income | 56,993 | 40,116 |
| Gain on sale of investment | 9,218 | –0– |
| Plus interest income | 11,029 | 6,792 |
| Less interest expense | 8,739 | 3,765 |
| Net income before taxes | 68,501 | 43,143 |
| Less income taxes (about 38.5%) | 26,373 | 17,041 |
| Net income | $ 42,128 | $ 26,102 |

*Required:*

For the current year:

1. Compute the return on total assets.
2. Compute the return on common shareholders' equity.
3. Is Starbucks' financial leverage positive or negative? Explain.
4. Compute the current ratio.
5. Compute the acid-test (quick) ratio.
6. Compute the inventory turnover.
7. Compute the average sale period.
8. Compute the debt-to-equity ratio.

## SOLUTION TO REVIEW PROBLEM

1. Return on total assets:

$$\text{Return on total assets} = \frac{\text{Net Income} + [\text{Interest expense} \times (1 - \text{Tax rate})]}{\text{Average total assets}}$$

$$\frac{\$42,128 + [\$8,739 \times (1 - 0.385)]}{(\$726,613 + \$468,178)/2} = 8.0\% \text{ (rounded)}$$

2. Return on common shareholders' equity:

$$\text{Return on common shareholder's equity} = \frac{\text{Net income} - \text{Preferred dividends}}{\text{Average common shareholders' equity}}$$

$$\frac{\$42,128 - \$0}{(\$451,660 + \$312,231)/2} = 11.0\% \text{ (rounded)}$$

3. The company has positive financial leverage, since the return on common shareholders' equity (11%) is greater than the return on total assets (8%). The positive financial leverage was obtained from current liabilities and the bonds payable. The interest rate on the bonds is substantially less than the return on total assets.

4. Current ratio:

$$\text{Current ratio} = \frac{\text{Current assets}}{\text{Current liabilities}}$$

$$\frac{\$339,541}{\$101,091} = 3.36 \text{ (rounded)}$$

5. Acid-test (quick) ratio:

$$\text{Acid-test ratio} = \frac{\text{Cash} + \text{Marketable securities} + \text{Current receivables}}{\text{Current liabilities}}$$

$$\frac{\$126,215 + \$103,221 + \$17,621}{\$101,091} = 2.44 \text{ (rounded)}$$

This acid-test ratio is quite high and provides Starbucks with the ability to fund rapid expansion.

6. Inventory turnover:

$$\text{Inventory turnover} = \frac{\text{Cost of goods sold}}{\text{Average inventory balance}}$$

$$\frac{\$335,800}{(\$83,370 + \$123,657)/2} = 3.24 \text{ (rounded)}$$

7. Average sale period:

$$\text{Average sale period} = \frac{365 \text{ days}}{\text{Inventory turnover}}$$

$$\frac{365 \text{ days}}{3.24} = 113 \text{ days (rounded)}$$

8. Debt-to-equity ratio:

$$\text{Debt-to-equity ratio} = \frac{\text{Total liabilities}}{\text{Shareholders' equity}}$$

$$\frac{\$274{,}953}{\$451{,}660} = 0.61 \text{ (rounded)}$$

# Glossary

(Note: Definitions and formulas for all financial ratios are shown in Exhibit 14–7. These definitions and formulas are not repeated here.)

**Common-size statements** A statement that shows the items appearing on it in percentage form as well as in dollar form. On the income statement, the percentages are based on total sales revenue; on the balance sheet, the percentages are based on total assets. (p. 545)

**Financial leverage** Acquiring assets with funds that have been obtained from creditors or from preferred shareholders at a fixed rate of return. (p. 551)

**Horizontal analysis** A side-by-side comparison of two or more years' financial statements. (p. 543)

**Negative financial leverage** A situation in which the fixed return to a company's creditors and preferred shareholders is greater than the return on total assets. In this situation, the return on common shareholders' equity will be *less* than the return on total assets. (p. 551)

**Positive financial leverage** A situation in which the fixed return to a company's creditors and preferred shareholders is less than the return on total assets. In this situation, the return on common shareholders' equity will be *greater* than the return on total assets. (p. 551)

**Trend analysis** See *horizontal analysis.* (p. 543)

**Trend percentages** The expression of several years' financial data in percentage form in terms of a base year. (p. 544)

**Vertical analysis** The presentation of a company's financial statements in common-size form. (p. 545)

# Questions

**14–1**   Distinguish between horizontal and vertical analyses of financial statement data.

**14–2**   What is the basic purpose for examining trends in a company's financial ratios and other data? What other kinds of comparisons might an analyst make?

**14–3**   Assume that two companies in the same industry have equal earnings. Why might these companies have different price-earnings ratios?

**14–4**   Armcor Inc. is in a rapidly growing technological industry. Would you expect the company to have a high or low dividend payout ratio?

**14–5**   Distinguish between a manager's *financing* and *operating* responsibilities. Which of these responsibilities is the return on total assets ratio designed to measure?

**14–6**   What is meant by the dividend yield on a common shares investment?

**14–7**   What is meant by the term *financial leverage?*

**14–8**   The president of a medium-size plastics company was recently quoted in a business journal as stating, "We haven't had a dollar of interest-paying debt in over 10 years. Not many companies can say that." As a shareholder in this firm, how would you feel about its policy of not taking on interest-paying debt?

**14–9**   Why is it more difficult to obtain positive financial leverage from preferred shares than from long-term debt?

**14–10**   If a share's market value exceeds its book value, then the share is overpriced. Do you agree? Explain.

**14–11**   Weaver Company experiences a great deal of seasonal variation in its business activities. The company's high point in business activity is in June; its low point is in January. During which month would you expect the current ratio to be highest?

**14–12**   A company seeking a line of credit at a bank was turned down. Among other things, the bank stated that the company's 2 to 1 current ratio was not adequate. Give reasons why a 2-to-1 current ratio might not be adequate.

# Brief Exercises

**BRIEF EXERCISE 14–1    Trend Percentages (LO1)**

Rotorua Products Ltd. of New Zealand markets agricultural products for the burgeoning Asian consumer market. The company's current assets, current liabilities, and sales have been reported as follows over the last five years (year 5 is the most recent year):

|  | Year 5 | Year 4 | Year 3 | Year 2 | Year 1 |
|---|---|---|---|---|---|
| Sales ................. | $NZ2,250,000 | $NZ2,160,000 | $NZ2,070,000 | $NZ1,980,000 | $NZ1,800,000 |
| Cash ................... | $NZ 30,000 | $NZ 40,000 | $NZ 48,000 | $NZ 65,000 | $NZ 50,000 |
| Accounts receivable, net ... | 570,000 | 510,000 | 405,000 | 345,000 | 300,000 |
| Inventory .............. | 750,000 | 720,000 | 690,000 | 660,000 | 600,000 |
| Total current assets ....... | $NZ1,350,000 | $NZ1,270,000 | $NZ1,143,000 | $NZ1,070,000 | $NZ 950,000 |
| Current liabilities ........ | $NZ 640,000 | $NZ 580,000 | $NZ 520,000 | $NZ 440,000 | $NZ 400,000 |

$NZ stands for New Zealand dollars.

*Required:*

1. Express all of the asset, liability, and sales data in trend percentages. (Show percentages for each item.) Use year 1 as the base year and carry computations to one decimal place.
2. Comment on the results of your analysis.

**BRIEF EXERCISE 14–2    Common-Size Income Statement (LO1)**

A comparative income statement is given below for McKenzie Sales Ltd. of Toronto:

**McKENZIE SALES LTD.**
**Comparative Income Statement**
**For the Years Ended June 30, 2004, and 2003**

|  | 2004 | 2003 |
|---|---|---|
| Sales ........................ | $8,000,000 | $6,000,000 |
| Less cost of goods sold .......... | 4,984,000 | 3,516,000 |
| Gross margin ................ | 3,016,000 | 2,484,000 |
| Less operating expenses: |  |  |
|    Selling expenses ............. | 1,480,000 | 1,092,000 |
|    Administrative expenses ....... | 712,000 | 618,000 |
| Total expenses ................. | 2,192,000 | 1,710,000 |
| Net operating income ........... | 824,000 | 774,000 |
| Less interest expense ........... | 96,000 | 84,000 |
| Net income before taxes ......... | $ 728,000 | $ 690,000 |

Members of the company's board of directors are surprised to see that net income increased by only $38,000 when sales increased by two million dollars.

"How Well Am I Doing?" Financial Statement Analysis

**567**

*Required:*
1. Express each year's income statement in common-size percentages. Carry computations to one decimal place.
2. Comment briefly on the changes between the two years.

**BRIEF EXERCISE 14–3    Financial Ratios for Common Shareholders** (LO2)

Comparative financial statements for Weller Corporation for the fiscal year ending December 31 appear below. The company did not issue any new common or preferred shares during the year. A total of 800,000 common shares were outstanding. The interest rate on the bond payable was 12.0%, the income tax rate was 40%, and the dividend per share of common shares was $0.25. The market value of the company's common shares at the end of the year was $18 each. All of the company's sales are on account.

| WELLER CORPORATION<br>Comparative Balance Sheet<br>(dollars in thousands) | | |
|---|---|---|
| | **2003** | **2002** |
| **Assets** | | |
| Current assets: | | |
| Cash | $ 1,280 | $ 1,560 |
| Accounts receivable, net | 12,300 | 9,100 |
| Inventory | 9,700 | 8,200 |
| Prepaid expenses | 1,800 | 2,100 |
| Total current assets | 25,080 | 20,960 |
| Property and equipment: | | |
| Land | 6,000 | 6,000 |
| Buildings and equipment, net | 19,200 | 19,000 |
| Total property and equipment | 25,200 | 25,000 |
| Total assets | $50,280 | $45,960 |
| **Liabilities and Shareholders' Equity** | | |
| Current liabilities: | | |
| Accounts payable | $ 9,500 | $ 8,300 |
| Accrued payables | 600 | 700 |
| Notes payable, short term | 300 | 300 |
| Total current liabilities | 10,400 | 9,300 |
| Long-term liabilities: | | |
| Bonds payable | 5,000 | 5,000 |
| Total liabilities | 15,400 | 14,300 |
| Shareholders' equity: | | |
| Preferred shares | 2,000 | 2,000 |
| Common shares | 800 | 800 |
| Additional paid-in capital | 2,200 | 2,200 |
| Total paid-in capital | 5,000 | 5,000 |
| Retained earnings | 29,880 | 26,660 |
| Total sharesholders' equity | 34,880 | 31,660 |
| Total liabilities and shareholders' equity | $50,280 | $45,960 |

| WELLER CORPORATION<br>Comparative Income Statement and Reconciliation<br>(dollars in thousands) | 2003 | 2002 |
|---|---|---|
| Sales | $79,000 | $74,000 |
| Cost of goods sold | 52,000 | 48,000 |
| Gross margin | 27,000 | 26,000 |
| Operating expenses: | | |
|    Selling expenses | 8,500 | 8,000 |
|    Administrative expenses | 12,000 | 11,000 |
| Total operating expenses | 20,500 | 19,000 |
| Net operating income | 6,500 | 7,000 |
| Interest expense | 600 | 600 |
| Net income before taxes | 5,900 | 6,400 |
| Less income taxes | 2,360 | 2,560 |
| Net income | 3,540 | 3,840 |
| Dividends to preferred shareholders | 120 | 400 |
| Net income remaining for common<br>   shareholders | 3,420 | 3,440 |
| Dividends to common shareholders | 200 | 200 |
| Net income added to retained earnings | 3,220 | 3,240 |
| Retained earnings, beginning of year | 26,660 | 23,420 |
| Retained earnings, end of year | $29,880 | $26,660 |

*Required:*
Compute the following financial ratios for common shareholders for the year 2003:
1. Gross margin percentage.
2. Earnings per share of common shares.
3. Price-earnings ratio.
4. Dividend payout ratio.
5. Dividend yield ratio.
6. Return on total assets.
7. Return on common shareholders' equity.
8. Book value per share.

**BRIEF EXERCISE 14–4    Financial Ratios for Short-Term Creditors (LO3)**
Refer to the data in Brief Exercise 14–3 for Weller Corporation.

*Required:*
Compute the following financial data for short-term creditors for the year 2003:
1. Working capital.
2. Current ratio.
3. Acid-test ratio.
4. Accounts receivable turnover. (Assume that all sales are on account.)
5. Average collection period.
6. Inventory turnover.
7. Average sale period.

**BRIEF EXERCISE 14–5    Financial Ratios for Long-Term Creditors (LO4)**
Refer to the data in Brief Exercise 14–3 for Weller Corporation.

*Required:*
Compute the following financial ratios for long-term creditors for the year 2003:
1. Times interest earned ratio.
2. Debt-to-equity ratio.

### EXERCISE 14–1  Selected Financial Ratios for Common Shareholders (LO2)

Selected financial data from the June 30 year-end statements of Safford Company are given below:

| | |
|---|---:|
| Total assets ........................... | $3,600,000 |
| Long-term debt (12% interest rate) ......... | 500,000 |
| Preferred shares, $100 par, 8% ............ | 900,000 |
| Total shareholders' equity ................ | 2,400,000 |
| Interest paid on long-term debt ........... | 60,000 |
| Net income ............................ | 280,000 |

Total assets at the beginning of the year were $3,000,000; total shareholders' equity was $2,200,000. There has been no change in the preferred shares during the year. The company's tax rate is 30%.

*Required:*
1. Compute the return on total assets.
2. Compute the return on common shareholders' equity.
3. Is financial leverage positive or negative? Explain.

### EXERCISE 14–2  Selected Financial Data for Short-Term Creditors (LO3)

Norsk Optronics, ALS, of Bergen, Norway, had a current ratio of 2.5 to 1 on June 30 of the current year. On that date, the company's assets were:

| | | |
|---|---:|---:|
| Cash ..................................... | | Kr 90,000 |
| Accounts receivable ..................... | Kr300,000 | |
| Less allowance for doubtful accounts ....... | 40,000 | 260,000 |
| Inventory ................................ | | 490,000 |
| Prepaid expenses ........................ | | 10,000 |
| Plant and equipment, net ................. | | 800,000 |
| Total assets ............................. | | Kr1,650,000 |

The Norwegian currency is the krone, denoted here by the symbol Kr.

*Required:*
1. What was the company's working capital on June 30?
2. What was the company's acid-test (quick) ratio on June 30?
3. The company paid an account payable of Kr40,000 immediately after June 30.
   a. What effect did this transaction have on working capital? Show computations.
   b. What effect did this transaction have on the current ratio? Show computations.

### EXERCISE 14–3  Selected Financial Ratios (LO2, LO3, LO4)

The financial statements for Castile Products Inc. are given below:

### CASTILE PRODUCTS INC.
### Balance Sheet
### December 31

**Assets**

| | |
|---|---:|
| Current assets: | |
| Cash .............................. | $ 6,500 |
| Accounts receivable, net .............. | 35,000 |
| Merchandise inventory ............... | 70,000 |
| Prepaid expenses ................... | 3,500 |
| Total current assets .................. | 115,000 |
| Property and equipment, net ........... | 185,000 |
| Total assets ........................ | $300,000 |

| **Liabilities and Shareholders' Equity** | | |
|---|---|---|
| Liabilities: | | |
|  Current liabilities .................... | | $ 50,000 |
|  Bonds payable, 10% ................. | | 80,000 |
| Total liabilities ........................ | | 130,000 |
| Shareholders' equity: | | |
|  Common shares, $5 per value ......... | $ 30,000 | |
|  Retained earnings ................... | 140,000 | |
| Total shareholders' equity .............. | | 170,000 |
| Total liabilities and equity .............. | | $300,000 |

**CASTILE PRODUCTS INC.**
**Income Statement**
**For the Year Ended December 31**

| | |
|---|---|
| Sales ........................................ | $420,000 |
| Less cost of goods sold ............................. | 292,500 |
| Gross margin ...................................... | 127,500 |
| Less operating expenses ............................. | 89,500 |
| Net operating income ............................... | 38,000 |
| Interest expense ................................... | 8,000 |
| Net income before taxes ............................ | 30,000 |
| Income taxes (30%) ............................... | 9,000 |
| Net income ....................................... | $ 21,000 |

Account balances at the beginning of the year were: accounts receivable, $25,000; and inventory, $60,000. All sales were on account.

*Required:*
Compute financial ratios as follows:
1. Gross margin percentage.
2. Current ratio.
3. Acid-test (quick) ratio.
4. Debt-to-equity ratio.
5. Accounts receivable turnover in days.
6. Inventory turnover in days.
7. Times interest earned.
8. Book value per share.

**EXERCISE 14–4 Selected Financial Ratios for Common Shareholders (LO2)**
Refer to the financial statements for Castile Products Inc. in Exercise 14–3. In addition to the data in these statements, assume that Castile Products Inc. paid dividends of $2.10 per share during the year. Also assume that the company's common shares had a market price of $42 each at the end of the year and there was no change in the number of outstanding common shares during the year.

*Required:*
Compute financial ratios as follows:
1. Earnings per share.
2. Dividend payout ratio.
3. Dividend yield ratio.
4. Price-earnings ratio.

**EXERCISE 14–5 Selected Financial Ratios for Common Shareholders (LO2)**
Refer to the financial statements for Castile Products Inc. in Exercise 14–3. Assets at the beginning of the year totalled $280,000, and the shareholders' equity totalled $161,600.

*Required:*

Compute the following:

1. Return on total assets.
2. Return on common shareholders' equity.
3. Was financial leverage positive or negative for the year? Explain.

**PROBLEM 14–1 Common-Size Statements and Financial Ratios for Creditors** (LO1, LO3, LO4)

Paul Sabin organized Sabin Electronics 10 years ago in order to produce and sell several electronic devices on which he had secured patents. Although the company has been fairly profitable, it is now experiencing a severe cash shortage. For this reason, it is requesting a $500,000 long-term loan from Gulfport State Bank, $100,000 of which will be used to bolster the Cash account and $400,000 of which will be used to modernize certain key items of equipment. The company's financial statements for the two most recent years follow:

CHECK FIGURE
(1e) Inventory turnover this year: 5.0 times
(1g) Times interest earned last year: 4.9 times

### SABIN ELECTRONICS
### Comparative Balance Sheet

| | This Year | Last Year |
|---|---|---|
| **Assets** | | |
| Current assets: | | |
| Cash | $ 70,000 | $ 150,000 |
| Marketable securities | — | 18,000 |
| Accounts receivable, net | 480,000 | 300,000 |
| Inventory | 950,000 | 600,000 |
| Prepaid expenses | 20,000 | 22,000 |
| Total current assets | 1,520,000 | 1,090,000 |
| Plant and equipment, net | 1,480,000 | 1,370,000 |
| Total assets | $3,000,000 | $2,460,000 |
| **Liabilities and Shareholders' Equity** | | |
| Liabilities: | | |
| Current liabilities | $ 800,000 | $ 430,000 |
| Bonds payable, 12% | 600,000 | 600,000 |
| Total liabilities | 1,400,000 | 1,030,000 |
| Shareholders' equity: | | |
| Preferred shares, $25 par, 8% | 250,000 | 250,000 |
| Common shares, $10 par | 500,000 | 500,000 |
| Retained earnings | 850,000 | 680,000 |
| Total shareholders' equity | 1,600,000 | 1,430,000 |
| Total liabilities and equity | $3,000,000 | $2,460,000 |

### SABIN ELECTRONICS
### Comparative Income Statement

| | This Year | Last Year |
|---|---|---|
| Sales | $5,000,000 | $4,350,000 |
| Less cost of goods sold | 3,875,000 | 3,450,000 |
| Gross margin | 1,125,000 | 900,000 |
| Less operating expenses | 653,000 | 548,000 |
| Net operating income | 472,000 | 352,000 |
| Less interest expense | 72,000 | 72,000 |
| Net income before taxes | 400,000 | 280,000 |
| Less income taxes (30%) | 120,000 | 84,000 |
| Net income | 280,000 | 196,000 |

| Dividends paid: | | |
|---|---|---|
| Preferred dividends ................... | 20,000 | 20,000 |
| Common dividends ................... | 90,000 | 75,000 |
| Total dividends paid ................... | 110,000 | 95,000 |
| Net income retained .................... | 170,000 | 101,000 |
| Retained earnings, beginning of year ........ | 680,000 | 579,000 |
| Retained earnings, end of year .............. | $ 850,000 | $ 680,000 |

During the past year, the company introduced several new product lines and raised the selling prices on a number of old product lines in order to improve its profit margin. The company also hired a new sales manager, who has expanded sales into several new territories. Sales terms are 2/10, n/30. All sales are on account. Assume that the following ratios are typical of firms in the electronics industry:

| | |
|---|---|
| Current ratio ....................... | 2.5 to 1 |
| Acid-test (quick) ratio ............... | 1.3 to 1 |
| Average age of receivables ............ | 18 days |
| Inventory turnover in days ............ | 60 days |
| Debt-to-equity ratio ................. | 0.90 to 1 |
| Times interest earned ................ | 6.0 times |
| Return on total assets ................ | 13% |
| Price-earnings ratio .................. | 12 |

*Required:*
1. To assist the Gulfport State Bank in making a decision about the loan, compute the following ratios for both this year and last year:
   a. The amount of working capital.
   b. The current ratio.
   c. The acid-test (quick) ratio.
   d. The average age of receivables. (The accounts receivable at the beginning of last year totalled $250,000.)
   e. The inventory turnover in days. (The inventory at the beginning of last year totalled $500,000.)
   f. The debt-to-equity ratio.
   g. The number of times interest was earned.
2. For both this year and last year:
   a. Present the balance sheet in common-size format.
   b. Present the income statement in common-size format down through net income.
3. Comment on the results of your analysis in (1) and (2) above and make a recommendation as to whether or not the loan should be approved.

CHECK FIGURE
(1a) EPS this year: $5.20
(1c) Dividend payout ratio last year: 42.6%

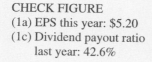

### PROBLEM 14–2  Financial Ratios for Common Shareholders (LO2)

Refer to the financial statements and other data in Problem 14–1. Assume that you are an account executive for a large brokerage house and that one of your clients has asked for a recommendation about the possible purchase of Sabin Electronics' shares. You are not acquainted with the shares and for this reason wish to do certain analytical work before making a recommendation.

*Required:*
1. You decide first to assess the well being of the common shareholders. For both this year and last year, compute:
   a. The earnings per share. There has been no change in preferred or common shares over the last two years.
   b. The dividend yield ratio for common. The company's shares are currently selling for $40 per share; last year it sold for $36 per share.
   c. The dividend payout ratio for common.
   d. The price-earnings ratio. How do investors regard Sabin Electronics as compared with other firms in the industry? Explain.
   e. The book value per share of common shares. Does the difference between market value and book value suggest that the shares are overpriced? Explain.

2. You decide next to assess the company's rate of return. Compute the following for both this year and last year:
   a. The return on total assets. (Total assets at the beginning of last year were $2,300,000.)
   b. The return on common equity. (Shareholders' equity at the beginning of last year was $1,329,000.)
   c. Is the company's financial leverage positive or negative? Explain.
3. Would you recommend that your client purchase Sabin Electronics' shares? Explain.

## PROBLEM 14–3  Effects of Financial Leverage (LO2)

CHECK FIGURE
(2) Return on common
equity method A:
11.9%

Several investors are in the process of organizing a new company. The investors believe that $1,000,000 will be needed to finance the new company's operations, and they are considering three methods of raising this amount of money.

*Method A:* All $1,000,000 can be obtained through issue of common shares.

*Method B:* $500,000 can be obtained through issue of common shares and the other $500,000 can be obtained through issue of $100 par value, 8% preferred shares.

*Method C:* $500,000 can be obtained through issue of common shares, and the other $500,000 can be obtained through issue of bonds carrying an interest rate of 8%.

The investors organizing the new company are confident that it can earn $170,000 each year before interest and taxes. The tax rate will be 30%.

### Required:

1. Assuming that the investors are correct in their earnings estimate, compute the net income that would go to the common shareholders under each of the three financing methods listed above.
2. Using the income data computed in (1) above, compute the return on common equity under each of the three methods.
3. Why do methods B and C provide a greater return on common equity than does method A? Why does method C provide a greater return on common equity than method B?

## PROBLEM 14–4  Effects of Transactions on Financial Ratios (LO3)

CHECK FIGURE
(1c) Acid-test ratio: 1.4 to 1

Denna Company's working capital accounts at the beginning of the year are given below:

| | A | B |
|---|---|---|
| 1 | Cash | $ 50,000 |
| 2 | Marketable Securities | 30,000 |
| 3 | Accounts Receivable, net | 200,000 |
| 4 | Inventory | 210,000 |
| 5 | Prepaid Expenses | 10,000 |
| 6 | Accounts Payable | 150,000 |
| 7 | Notes Due within One Year | 30,000 |
| 8 | Accrued Liabilities | 20,000 |

During the year, Denna Company completed the following transactions:

x. Paid a cash dividend previously declared, $12,000.
a. Issued additional capital shares for cash, $100,000.
b. Sold inventory costing $50,000 for $80,000, on account.
c. Wrote off uncollectible accounts in the amount of $10,000. The company uses the allowance method of accounting for bad debts.
d. Declared a cash dividend, $15,000.
e. Paid accounts payable, $50,000.
f. Borrowed cash on a short-term note with the bank, $35,000.
g. Sold inventory costing $15,000 for $10,000 cash.

h. Purchased inventory on account, $60,000.
i. Paid off all short-term notes due, $30,000.
j. Purchased equipment for cash, $15,000.
k. Sold marketable securities costing $18,000 for cash, $15,000.
l. Collected cash on accounts receivable, $80,000.

**Required:**
1. Compute the following amounts and ratios as of the beginning of the year:
   a. Working capital.
   b. Current ratio.
   c. Acid-test (quick) ratio.
2. Indicate the effect of each of the transactions given above on working capital, the current ratio, and the acid-test (quick) ratio. Give the effect in terms of increase, decrease, or none. Item (x) is given below as an example of the format to use:

| | The Effect on | | |
| Transaction | Working Capital | Current Ratio | Acid-Test Ratio |
|---|---|---|---|
| (x)   Paid a cash dividend previously declared .... | None | Increase | Increase |

**PROBLEM 14–5   Interpretation of Financial Ratios** (LO1, LO2, LO3)
Paul Ward is interested in the shares of Pecunious Products Inc. Before purchasing the shares, Mr. Ward would like to learn as much as possible about the company. However, all he has to go on is the current year's (Year 3) annual report, which contains no comparative data other than the summary of ratios given below:

| | Year 3 | Year 2 | Year 1 |
|---|---|---|---|
| Sales trend ..................... | 128.0 | 115.0 | 100.0 |
| Current ratio .................... | 2.5:1 | 2.3:1 | 2.2:1 |
| Acid-test (quick) ratio.............. | 0.8:1 | 0.9:1 | 1.1:1 |
| Accounts receivable turnover ........ | 9.4 times | 10.6 times | 12.5 times |
| Inventory turnover ............... | 6.5 times | 7.2 times | 8.0 times |
| Dividend yield ................... | 7.1% | 6.5% | 5.8% |
| Dividend payout ratio .............. | 40% | 50% | 60% |
| Return on total assets ............. | 12.5% | 11.0% | 9.5% |
| Return on common equity .......... | 14.0% | 10.0% | 7.8% |
| Dividends paid per share* .......... | $1.50 | $1.50 | $1.50 |

*There have been no changes in common shares outstanding over the three-year period.

Mr. Ward would like answers to a number of questions about the trend of events in Pecunious Products Inc. over the last three years. His questions are:

a. Is it becoming easier for the company to pay its bills as they come due?
b. Are customers paying their accounts at least as fast now as they were in year 1?
c. Is the total of the accounts receivable increasing, decreasing, or remaining constant?
d. Is the level of inventory increasing, decreasing, or remaining constant?
e. Is the market price of the company's shares going up or down?
f. Is the amount of the earnings per share increasing or decreasing?
g. Is the price-earnings ratio going up or down?
h. Is the company employing financial leverage to the advantage of the common shareholders?

**Required:**
Answer each of Mr. Ward's questions using the data given above. In each case, explain how you arrived at your answer.

## PROBLEM 14–6    Comprehensive Ratio Analysis (LO2, LO3, LO4)

You have just been hired as a loan officer at Slippery Rock State Bank. Your supervisor has given you a file containing a request from Lydex Company, a manufacturer of safety helmets, for a $3,000,000, five-year loan. Financial statement data on the company for the last two years follow:

CHECK FIGURE
(2a) EPS this year: $9.28
(2b) Dividend yield ratio
last year: 3.6%

### LYDEX COMPANY
### Comparative Balance Sheet

|  | This Year | Last Year |
|---|---|---|
| **Assets** | | |
| Current assets: | | |
| Cash | $ 960,000 | $ 1,260,000 |
| Marketable securities | –0– | 300,000 |
| Accounts receivable, net | 2,700,000 | 1,800,000 |
| Inventory | 3,900,000 | 2,400,000 |
| Prepaid expenses | 240,000 | 180,000 |
| Total current assets | 7,800,000 | 5,940,000 |
| Plant and equipment, net | 9,300,000 | 8,940,000 |
| Total assets | $17,100,000 | $14,880,000 |
| **Liabilities and Shareholders' Equity** | | |
| Liabilities: | | |
| Current liabilities | $ 3,900,000 | $ 2,760,000 |
| Note payable, 10% | 3,600,000 | 3,000,000 |
| Total liabilities | 7,500,000 | 5,760,000 |
| Shareholders' equity: | | |
| Preferred shares, 8%, $30 par value | 1,800,000 | 1,800,000 |
| Common shares, $80 par value | 6,000,000 | 6,000,000 |
| Retained earnings | 1,800,000 | 1,320,000 |
| Total shareholders' equity | 9,600,000 | 9,120,000 |
| Total liabilities and shareholders' equity | $17,100,000 | $14,880,000 |

### LYDEX COMPANY
### Comparative Income Statement

|  | This Year | Last Year |
|---|---|---|
| Sales (all on account) | $15,750,000 | $12,480,000 |
| Less cost of goods sold | 12,600,000 | 9,900,000 |
| Gross margin | 3,150,000 | 2,580,000 |
| Less operating expenses | 1,590,000 | 1,560,000 |
| Net operating income | 1,560,000 | 1,020,000 |
| Less interest expense | 360,000 | 300,000 |
| Net income before taxes | 1,200,000 | 720,000 |
| Less income taxes (30%) | 360,000 | 216,000 |
| Net income | 840,000 | 504,000 |
| Dividends paid: | | |
| Preferred dividends | 144,000 | 144,000 |
| Common dividends | 216,000 | 108,000 |
| Total dividends paid | 360,000 | 252,000 |
| Net income retained | 480,000 | 252,000 |
| Retained earnings, beginning of year | 1,320,000 | 1,068,000 |
| Retained earnings, end of year | $ 1,800,000 | $ 1,320,000 |

Helen McGuire, who just a year ago was appointed president of Lydex Company, argues that although the company has had a "spotty" record in the past, it has "turned the corner," as evidenced by a 25% jump in sales and by a greatly improved earnings picture between last year and this year. McGuire also points out that investors generally have recognized the improving situation at Lydex, as shown by the increase in market value of the company's common shares, which are currently selling for $72 per share (up from $40 per share last year). McGuire feels that with her leadership and with the modernized equipment that the $3,000,000 loan will permit the company to buy, profits will be even stronger in the future. McGuire has a reputation in the industry for being a good manager who runs a "tight" ship.

Not wanting to botch your first assignment, you decide to generate all the information that you can about the company. You determine that the following ratios are typical of firms in Lydex Company's industry:

| | |
|---|---|
| Current ratio | 2.3 to 1 |
| Acid-test (quick) ratio | 1.2 to 1 |
| Average age of receivables | 30 days |
| Inventory turnover | 60 days |
| Return on assets | 9.5% |
| Debt-to-equity ratio | 0.65 to 1 |
| Times interest earned | 5.7 |
| Price-earnings ratio | 10 |

*Required:*
1. You decide first to assess the rate of return that the company is generating. Compute the following for both this year and last year:
   a. The return on total assets. (Total assets at the beginning of last year were $12,960,000.)
   b. The return on common equity. (Shareholders' equity at the beginning of last year totalled $9,048,000. There has been no change in preferred or common shares over the last two years.)
   c. Is the company's financial leverage positive or negative? Explain.
2. You decide next to assess the well being of the common shareholders. For both this year and last year, compute:
   a. The earnings per share.
   b. The dividend yield ratio for common shares.
   c. The dividend payout ratio for common shares.
   d. The price-earnings ratio. How do investors regard Lydex Company as compared with other firms in the industry? Explain.
   e. The book value per share of common shares. Does the difference between market value per share and book value per share suggest that its current share price is a bargain? Explain.
   f. The gross margin percentage.
3. You decide, finally, to assess creditor ratios to determine both short-term and long-term debt-paying ability. For both this year and last year, compute:
   a. Working capital.
   b. The current ratio.
   c. The acid-test ratio.
   d. The average age of receivables. (The accounts receivable at the beginning of last year totalled $1,560,000.)
   e. The inventory turnover. (The inventory at the beginning of last year totalled $1,920,000.) Also compute the number of days required to turn the inventory one time (use a 365-day year).
   f. The debt-to-equity ratio.
   g. The number of times interest was earned.
4. Evaluate the data computed in (1) to (3) above, and using any additional data provided in the problem, make a recommendation to your supervisor as to whether the loan should be approved.

**PROBLEM 14–7   Common-Size Financial Statements (LO1)**
Refer to the financial statement data for Lydex Company given in Problem 14–6.
*Required:*
For both this year and last year:
1. Present the balance sheet in common-size format.
2. Present the income statement in common-size format down through net income.
3. Comment on the results of your analysis.

## PROBLEM 14–8   Effects of Transactions on Financial Ratios (LO2, LO3, LO4)

In the right-hand column below, certain financial ratios are listed. To the left of each ratio is a business transaction or event relating to the operating activities of Delta Company.

| Business Transaction or Event | Ratio |
|---|---|
| 1. The company declared a cash dividend. | Current ratio |
| 2. The company sold inventory on account at cost. | Acid-test (quick) ratio |
| 3. The company issued bonds with an interest rate of 8%. The company's return on assets is 10%. | Return on common shareholders' equity |
| 4. The company's net income decreased by 10% between last year and this year. Long-term debt remained unchanged. | Times interest earned |
| 5. A previously declared cash dividend was paid. | Current ratio |
| 6. The market price of the company's common shares dropped from 24½ to 20. The dividend paid per share remained unchanged. | Dividend payout ratio |
| 7. Obsolete inventory totalling $100,000 was written off as a loss. | Inventory turnover ratio |
| 8. The company sold inventory for cash at a profit. | Debt-to-equity ratio |
| 9. Changed customer credit terms from 2/10, n/30 to 2/15, n/30 to comply with a change in industry practice. | Accounts receivable turnover ratio |
| 10. Issued a common shares dividend on common shares. | Book value per share |
| 11. The market price of the company's common shares increased from 24½ to 30. | Book value per share |
| 12. The company paid $40,000 on accounts payable. | Working capital |
| 13. Issued a common shares tock dividend to common shareholders. | Earnings per share |
| 14. Paid accounts payable. | Debt-to-equity ratio |
| 15. Purchased inventory on open account. | Acid-test (quick) ratio |
| 16. Wrote off an uncollectible account against the Allowance for Bad Debts. | Current ratio |
| 17. The market price of the company's common shares increased from 24½ to 30. Earnings per share remained unchanged. | Price-earnings ratio |
| 18. The market price of the company's common shares increased from 24½ to 30. The dividend paid per share remained unchanged. | Dividend yield ratio |

***Required:***

Indicate the effect that each business transaction or event would have on the ratio listed opposite to it. State the effect in terms of increase, decrease, or no effect on the ratio involved, and give the reason for your choice of answer. In all cases, assume that the current assets exceed the current liabilities both before and after the event or transaction. Use the following format for your answers:

| Effect on Ratio | Reason for Increase, Decrease, or No Effect |
|---|---|
| 1. | |
| Etc. | |

## PROBLEM 14–9   Financial Ratios for Common Shareholders (LO2)

(Problems 14–10 and 14–11 delve more deeply into the data presented below. Each problem is independent.) Empire Labs Inc. was organized several years ago to produce and market several new "miracle drugs." The company is small but growing, and you are considering the purchase of some

CHECK FIGURE
(1a) EPS this year: $4.65
(2a) Return on total assets last year: 14.0%

of its common shares as an investment. The following data on the company are available for the past two years:

## EMPIRE LABS INC.
### Comparative Income Statement
### For the Years Ended December 31

|  | This Year | Last Year |
|---|---|---|
| Sales | $20,000,000 | $15,000,000 |
| Less cost of goods sold | 13,000,000 | 9,000,000 |
| Gross margin | 7,000,000 | 6,000,000 |
| Less operating expenses | 5,260,000 | 4,560,000 |
| Net operating income | 1,740,000 | 1,440,000 |
| Less interest expense | 240,000 | 240,000 |
| Net income before taxes | 1,500,000 | 1,200,000 |
| Less income taxes (30%) | 450,000 | 360,000 |
| Net income | $ 1,050,000 | $ 840,000 |

## EMPIRE LABS INC.
### Comparative Retained Earnings Statement
### For the Years Ended December 31

|  | This Year | Last Year |
|---|---|---|
| Retained earnings, January 1 | $2,400,000 | $1,960,000 |
| Add net income (above) | 1,050,000 | 840,000 |
| Total | 3,450,000 | 2,800,000 |
| Deduct cash dividends paid: |  |  |
| Preferred dividends | 120,000 | 120,000 |
| Common dividends | 360,000 | 280,000 |
| Total dividends paid | 480,000 | 400,000 |
| Retained earnings, December 31 | $2,970,000 | $2,400,000 |

## EMPIRE LABS INC.
### Comparative Balance Sheet
### December 31

|  | This Year | Last Year |
|---|---|---|
| **Assets** |  |  |
| Current assets: |  |  |
| Cash | $ 200,000 | $ 400,000 |
| Accounts receivable, net | 1,500,000 | 800,000 |
| Inventory | 3,000,000 | 1,200,000 |
| Prepaid expenses | 100,000 | 100,000 |
| Total current assets | 4,800,000 | 2,500,000 |
| Plant and equipment, net | 5,170,000 | 5,400,000 |
| Total assets | $9,970,000 | $7,900,000 |

| **Liabilities and Shareholders' Equity** | | |
|---|---|---|
| Liabilities: | | |
| Current liabilities . . . . . . . . . . . . . . . . . . . . . | $2,500,000 | $1,000,000 |
| Bonds payable, 12% . . . . . . . . . . . . . . . . . . | 2,000,000 | 2,000,000 |
| Total liabilities . . . . . . . . . . . . . . . . . . . . . . . . | 4,500,000 | 3,000,000 |
| Shareholders' equity: | | |
| Preferred shares, 8%, $10 par . . . . . . . . . . . | 1,500,000 | 1,500,000 |
| Common shares, $5 par . . . . . . . . . . . . . . . | 1,000,000 | 1,000,000 |
| Retained earnings . . . . . . . . . . . . . . . . . . . | 2,970,000 | 2,400,000 |
| Total shareholders' equity . . . . . . . . . . . . . . | 5,470,000 | 4,900,000 |
| Total liabilities and shareholders' equity . . . . . | $9,970,000 | $7,900,000 |

After some research, you have determined that the following ratios are typical of firms in the pharmaceutical industry:

| | |
|---|---|
| Dividend yield ratio . . . . . . . . . . . . . . . . . . . | 3% |
| Dividend payout ratio . . . . . . . . . . . . . . . . . . | 40% |
| Price-earnings ratio . . . . . . . . . . . . . . . . . . . . | 16 |
| Return on total assets . . . . . . . . . . . . . . . . . . | 13.5% |
| Return on common equity . . . . . . . . . . . . . . . | 20% |

The company's common shares are currently selling for $60 per share. Last year the shares sold for $45 per share.

There has been no change in the preferred or common shares outstanding over the last three years.

***Required:***

1. In analyzing the company, you decide first to compute the earnings per share and related ratios. For both last year and this year, compute:
   a. The earnings per share.
   b. The dividend yield ratio.
   c. The dividend payout ratio.
   d. The price-earnings ratio.
   e. The book value per common shares.
   f. The gross margin percentage.
2. You decide next to determine the rate of return that the company is generating. For both last year and this year, compute:
   a. The return on total assets. (Total assets were $6,500,000 at the beginning of last year.)
   b. The return on common shareholders' equity. (Common shareholders' equity was $2,900,000 at the beginning of last year.)
   c. Is financial leverage positive or negative? Explain.
3. On the basis of your work in (1) and (2) above, does the company's common shares seem to be an attractive investment? Explain.

**PROBLEM 14–10    Financial Ratios for Creditors** (LO3, LO4)

Refer to the data in Problem 14–9. Although Empire Labs Inc. has been very profitable since it was organized several years ago, the company is beginning to experience some difficulty in paying its bills as they come due. Management has approached Security National Bank requesting a two-year, $500,000 loan to bolster the cash account.

Security National Bank has assigned you to evaluate the loan request. You have gathered the following data relating to firms in the pharmaceutical industry:

| | |
|---|---|
| Current ratio . . . . . . . . . . . . . . . . . . . . . . . . | 2.4 to 1 |
| Acid-test (quick) ratio . . . . . . . . . . . . . . . . . | 1.2 to 1 |
| Average age of receivables . . . . . . . . . . . . | 16 days |
| Inventory turnover in days . . . . . . . . . . . . . | 40 days |
| Times interest earned . . . . . . . . . . . . . . . . . | 7 times |
| Debt-to-equity ratio . . . . . . . . . . . . . . . . . . | 0.70 to 1 |

CHECK FIGURE
(1b) Current ratio this year:
1.92 to 1
(1g) Debt-to-equity ratio
last year: 0.61 to 1

The following additional information is available on Empire Labs Inc.:

a. All sales are on account.
b. At the beginning of last year, the accounts receivable balance was $600,000 and the inventory balance was $1,000,000.

*Required:*

1. Compute the following amounts and ratios for both last year and this year:
   a. The working capital.
   b. The current ratio.
   c. The acid-test ratio.
   d. The accounts receivable turnover in days.
   e. The inventory turnover in days.
   f. The times interest earned.
   g. The debt-to-equity ratio.
2. Comment on the results of your analysis in (1) above.
3. Would you recommend that the loan be approved? Explain.

### PROBLEM 14–11   Common-Size Financial Statements (LO1)

Refer to the data in Problem 14–9. The president of Empire Labs Inc. is deeply concerned. Sales increased by $5 million from last year to this year, yet the company's net income increased by only a small amount. Also, the company's operating expenses went up this year, even though a major effort was launched during the year to cut costs.

*Required:*

1. For both last year and this year, prepare the income statement and the balance sheet in common-size format. Round computations to one decimal place.
2. From your work in (1) above, explain to the president why the increase in profits was so small this year. Were any benefits realized from the company's cost-cutting efforts? Explain.

# Building Your Skills

### ANALYTICAL THINKING   (LO2, LO3, LO4)

Incomplete financial statements for Pepper Industries follow:

| PEPPER INDUSTRIES Balance Sheet March 31 | |
|---|---|
| Current assets: | |
|   Cash | $       ? |
|   Accounts receivable, net | ? |
|   Inventory | ? |
| Total current assets | ? |
| Plant and equipment, net | ? |
| Total assets | $       ? |
| Liabilities: | |
|   Current liabilities | $  320,000 |
|   Bonds payable, 10% | ? |
| Total liabilities | ? |
| Shareholders' equity: | |
|   Common shares, $5 par value | ? |
|   Retained earnings | ? |
| Total shareholders' equity | ? |
| Total liabilities and shareholders' equity | $       ? |

## PEPPER INDUSTRIES
### Income Statement
### For the Year Ended March 31

| | |
|---|---|
| Sales | $4,200,000 |
| Less cost of goods sold | ? |
| Gross margin | ? |
| Less operating expenses | ? |
| Net operating income | ? |
| Less interest expense | 80,000 |
| Net income before taxes | ? |
| Less income taxes (30%) | ? |
| Net income | $  ? |

The following additional information is available about the company:

a. All sales during the year were on account.
b. There was no change in the number of common shares outstanding during the year.
c. The interest expense on the income statement relates to the bonds payable; the amount of bonds outstanding did not change during the year.
d. Selected balances at the *beginning* of the current fiscal year were:

| | |
|---|---|
| Accounts receivable | $  270,000 |
| Inventory | 360,000 |
| Total assets | 1,800,000 |

e. Selected financial ratios computed from the statements above for the current year are:

| | |
|---|---|
| Earnings per share | $2.30 |
| Debt-to-equity ratio | 0.875 to 1 |
| Accounts receivable turnover | 14.0 times |
| Current ratio | 2.75 to 1 |
| Return on total assets | 18.0% |
| Times interest earned | 6.75 times |
| Acid-test (quick) ratio | 1.25 to 1 |
| Inventory turnover | 6.5 times |

**Required:**
Compute the missing amounts on the company's financial statements. (Hint: What is the difference between the acid-test ratio and the current ratio?)

## COMMUNICATING IN PRACTICE   (LO1, LO2, LO3, LO4)

Typically, the market price of a company's shares takes a beating when the company announces that it has not met analysts' expectations. As a result, many companies are under a lot of pressure to meet analysts' revenue and earnings projections. Internet startups that have gone public fall into this category. To manage (that is, to inflate or smooth) earnings, managers sometimes record revenue that has not yet been earned by the company and/or delay the recognition of expenses that have been incurred.

Some recent examples illustrate how companies have attempted to manage their earnings. On March 20, 2000, MicroStrategy announced that it was forced to restate its 1999 earnings; revenue from multi-year contracts had been recorded in the first year instead of being spread over the lives of the related contracts as required by GAAP. On April 3, 2000, Legato Systems Inc. announced that it had restated its earnings; $7 million of revenue had been improperly recorded because customers had been promised that they could return the products purchased. As further discussed in this chapter, America Online overstated its net income during 1994, 1995, and 1996. In May 2000, upon completing its review of the company's accounting practices, the SEC levied a fine of $3.5 million against AOL. Just prior to the announcement of the fine levied on AOL, Helane Morrison, head of the SEC's San Francisco office, re-emphasized that the investigation of misleading financial statements is a top priority for the agency. [Sources: Jeff Shuttleworth, "Investors Beware: Dot.Coms Often Use Accounting Tricks," *Business Journal Serving San Jose & Silicon Valley*, April 14, 2000, p. 16; David Henry, "AOL Pays $3.5M to Settle SEC Case," *USA Today*, May 16, 2000, p. 3B.]

*Required:*

Write a memorandum to your instructor that answers the following questions. Use headings to organize the information presented in the memorandum. Include computations to support your answers, when appropriate.

1. Why would companies be tempted to manage earnings?
2. If the earnings that are reported by a company are misstated, how might this impact business decisions made about that company (such as the acquisition of the company by another business)?
3. What ethical issues, if any, arise when a company manages its earnings?
4. How would investors and financial analysts tend to view the financial statements of a company that has been known to manage its earnings in the past?

### ETHICS CHALLENGE (LO3, LO4)

Venice InLine Inc. was founded by Russ Perez to produce specialized in-line skates he had designed for doing aerial tricks. Up to this point, Russ has financed the company from his own savings and from retained profits. However, Russ now faces a cash crisis. In the year just ended, an acute shortage of high-impact roller bearings had developed just as the company was beginning production for the Christmas season. Russ had been assured by the suppliers that the roller bearings would be delivered in time to make Christmas shipments, but the suppliers had been unable to fully deliver on this promise. As a consequence, Venice In-Line had large stocks of unfinished skates at the end of the year and had been unable to fill all of the orders that had come in from retailers for the Christmas season. Consequently, sales were below expectations for the year, and Russ does not have enough cash to pay his creditors.

Well before the accounts payable were to become due, Russ visited a local bank and inquired about obtaining a loan. The loan officer at the bank assured Russ that there should not be any problem getting a loan to pay off his accounts payable—providing that on his most recent financial statements the current ratio was above 2.0, the acid-test ratio was above 1.0, and net operating income was at least four times the interest on the proposed loan. Russ promised to return later with a copy of his financial statements.

Russ would like to apply for a $80,000 six-month loan bearing an interest rate of 10% per year.

The unaudited financial reports of the company appear below:

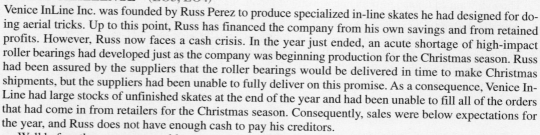

| VENICE INLINE INC.<br>Comparative Balance Sheet<br>As of December 31<br>(dollars in thousands) | | |
| --- | --- | --- |
| | **This Year** | **Last Year** |
| **Assets** | | |
| Current assets: | | |
| Cash ........................................ | $ 70 | $150 |
| Accounts receivable, net ...................... | 50 | 40 |
| Inventory .................................. | 160 | 100 |
| Prepaid expenses ........................... | 10 | 12 |
| Total current assets ......................... | 290 | 302 |
| Property and equipment ...................... | 270 | 180 |
| Total assets ................................ | $560 | $482 |

## Liabilities and Shareholders' Equity

|  |  |  |
|---|---|---|
| **Current liabilities:** |  |  |
| Accounts payable | $154 | $ 90 |
| Accrued payables | 10 | 10 |
| Total current liabilities | 164 | 100 |
| Long-term liabilities | — | — |
| Total liabilities | 164 | 100 |
| **Shareholders' equity:** |  |  |
| Common shares and additional paid-in capital | 100 | 100 |
| Retained earnings | 296 | 282 |
| Total shareholders' equity | 396 | 382 |
| Total liabilities and shareholders' equity | $560 | $482 |

### VENICE INLINE INC.
### Income Statement
### For the Year Ended December 31
### (dollars in thousands)

|  | **This Year** |
|---|---|
| Sales (all on accounts) | $420 |
| Cost of goods sold | 290 |
| Gross margin | 130 |
| **Operating expenses:** |  |
| Selling expenses | 42 |
| Administrative expenses | 68 |
| Total operating expenses | 110 |
| Net operating income | 20 |
| Interest expense | — |
| Net income before taxes | 20 |
| Less income taxes (30%) | 6 |
| Net income | $ 14 |

***Required:***
1. On the basis of the above unaudited financial statements and the statement made by the loan officer, would the company qualify for the loan?
2. Last year, Russ purchased and installed new, more efficient equipment to replace an older plastic injection moulding machine. Russ had originally planned to sell the old machine but found that it is still needed whenever the plastic injection moulding process is a bottleneck. When Russ discussed his cash flow problems with his brother-in-law, he suggested to Russ that the old machine be sold or at least reclassified as inventory on the balance sheet since it could be readily sold. At present, the machine is carried in the Property and Equipment account and could be sold for its net book value of $45,000. The bank does not require audited financial statements. What advice would you give to Russ concerning the machine?

**TEAMWORK IN ACTION**   (LO1, LO2, LO4)

Gauging the success of a company usually involves some assessment of the firm's earnings. When evaluating earnings, investors should consider the quality and sources of the company's earnings as well as their amount. In other words, the source of earnings is as important a consideration as the size of earnings.

Your team should discuss and then respond to the following questions. All team members should agree with and understand the answers (including the calculations supporting the answers) and be prepared to report in class. Each teammate can assume responsibility for a different part of the presentation.

*Required:*

1. Discuss the differences between operating profits and the bottom line—profits after all revenues and expenses.

2. Do you think a dollar of earnings coming from operations is any more or less valuable than a dollar of earnings generated from some other source below operating profits (e.g., one-time gains from selling assets or one-time write-offs for charges related to closing a plant)? Explain.

3. What is the concept of operating leverage? What is the relation between operating leverage and operating profits?

4. What is the concept of financial leverage? What is the relation between financial leverage and return on common shareholders' equity?

Do not forget to check out Taking It to the Net and other quizzes and resources at the Online Learning Centre at www.mcgrawhill.ca/college/garrison.

# Photo Credits

# Index

# List of Websites

1. http://www.coverall.ca/about_frame.html
   http://www.nqi.ca/english/CAE_recipients.htm
   http://www.cma-canada.org/ontario/00_index_60.asp
2. http://about.telus.com/investors/annualreport2002/english/downloads/annualreport2002.pdf
   http://about.telus.com/investors/operation/_efficiency.html
3. http://www.cme-mec.ca/national/documents/management_issues_survey_oct27_2002.pdf
4. http://www.bigrockbeer.com/pdfs/BRBIncomeTrust.pdf
5. http://www.maxustech.com
   http://www.businessfinancemag.com/archives.appfiles/Article.cfm?IssueID=95&ArticleID=4394&pg=2
   http://media.integratir.com/T.MOL.A/financials/2002CorpOverview_eng.pdf
6. www.investorfile.com
   www.globalrailway.com
7. www.canadianbusiness.com
   www.inthezonedelivery.com/articles.html
8. www.linkpath.com
9. http://www.ISO.ch/ISO/en/aboutISO/introduction/index.html
   http://www.scc.ca/nss/index_e.html
10. www.canadianbusiness.com
    www.comfind.com
    www.athand.com
11. www.focusmag.com/pages/royalbank.htm
12. http://www2.cdn-news.com/scripts/ccn-release.pl?/2002/07/30/0730005n.html
13. www.safeway.com
    www.midnightsuplantfood.com
    www.yukon.com/community/kluane/hj.html
    www.bearnorth.yukon.net
    www.comfind.com
    www.athand.com
14. (none)
15. http://www.sedar.com/csfsprod%2fdata28%2Ffilings%2F00410861%2F00000001%2FC:%5CWINDOWS%5C
    Desktop%5Cfilings%5filings%5Cturar.pdf
    www.comfind.com
    www.athand.com